THE NEVER WERES

FIONA SMYTH

annick press
toronto + new york + vancouver

Edited by David Wichman

Annick Press Ltd.

We acknowledge the support of the Canada Council for the Arts, the Ontario Arts Council, and the Government of Canada through the Canada Book Fund (CBF) for our publishing activities.

ONTARIO ARTS COUNCIL
CONSEIL DES ARTS DE L'ONTARIO

Cataloging in Publication

Smyth, Fiona
     The never weres / Fiona Smyth.

ISBN 978-1-55451-285-0 (bound).--ISBN 978-1-55451-284-3 (pbk.)

     I. Title.

PZ7.7.S69Nev 2011   j741.5'971   C2010-907478-5

Distributed in Canada by:
Firefly Books Ltd.
66 Leek Crescent
Richmond Hill, ON
L4B 1H1

Published in the U.S.A. by Annick Press (U.S.) Ltd.
Distributed in the U.S.A. by:
Firefly Books (U.S.) Inc.
P.O. Box 1338
Ellicott Station
Buffalo, NY 14205

© Mixed Sources
Product group from well-managed forests, controlled sources and recycled wood or fiber
www.fsc.org Cert no. SW-COC-001352
© 1996 Forest Stewardship Council
FSC

Printed in Canada

Visit us at: www.annickpress.com
Visit Fiona Smyth's blog at: theneverweres.blogspot.com

FOR MY
SISTERS:
SHEILA
AND
ALIX

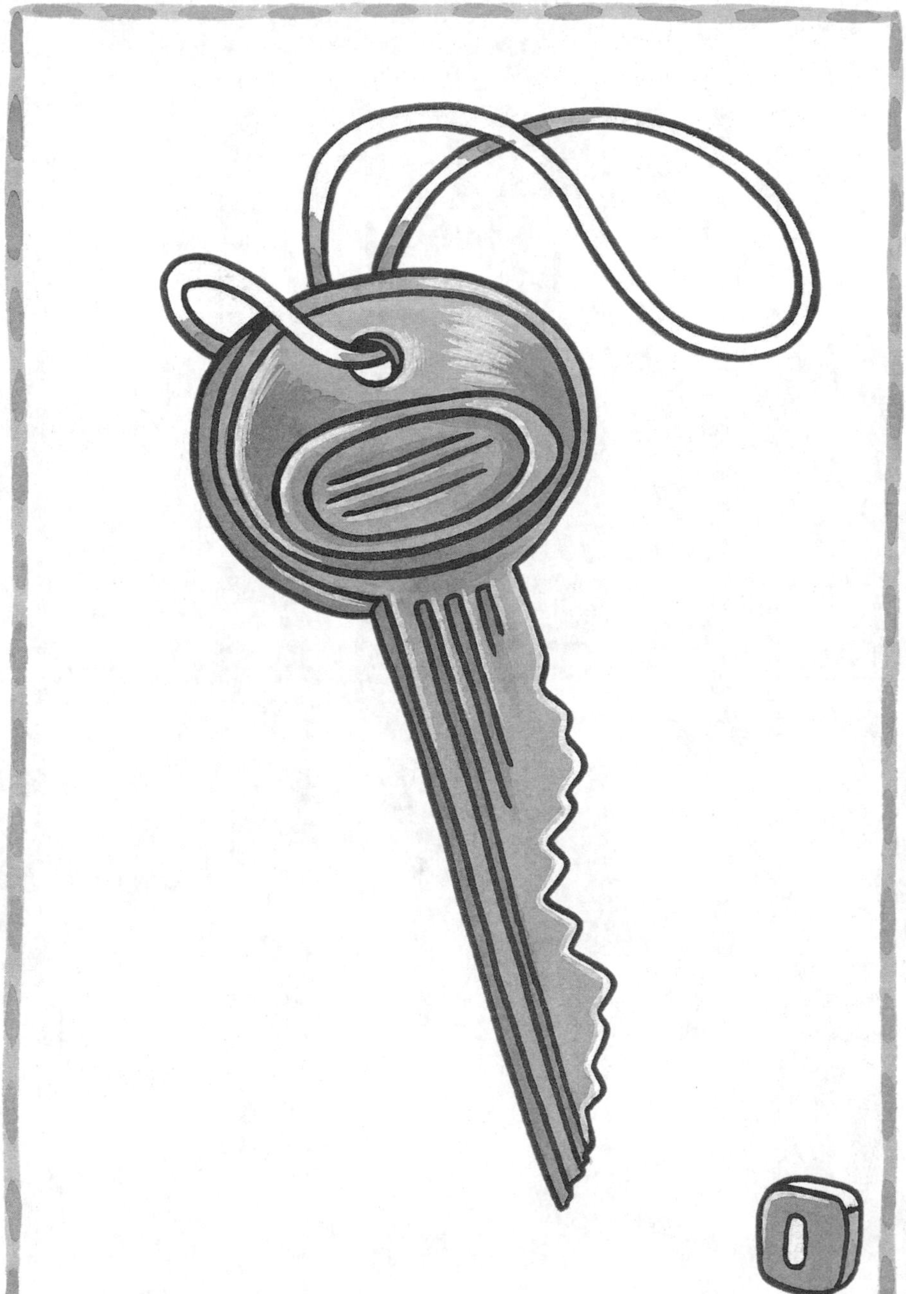
0

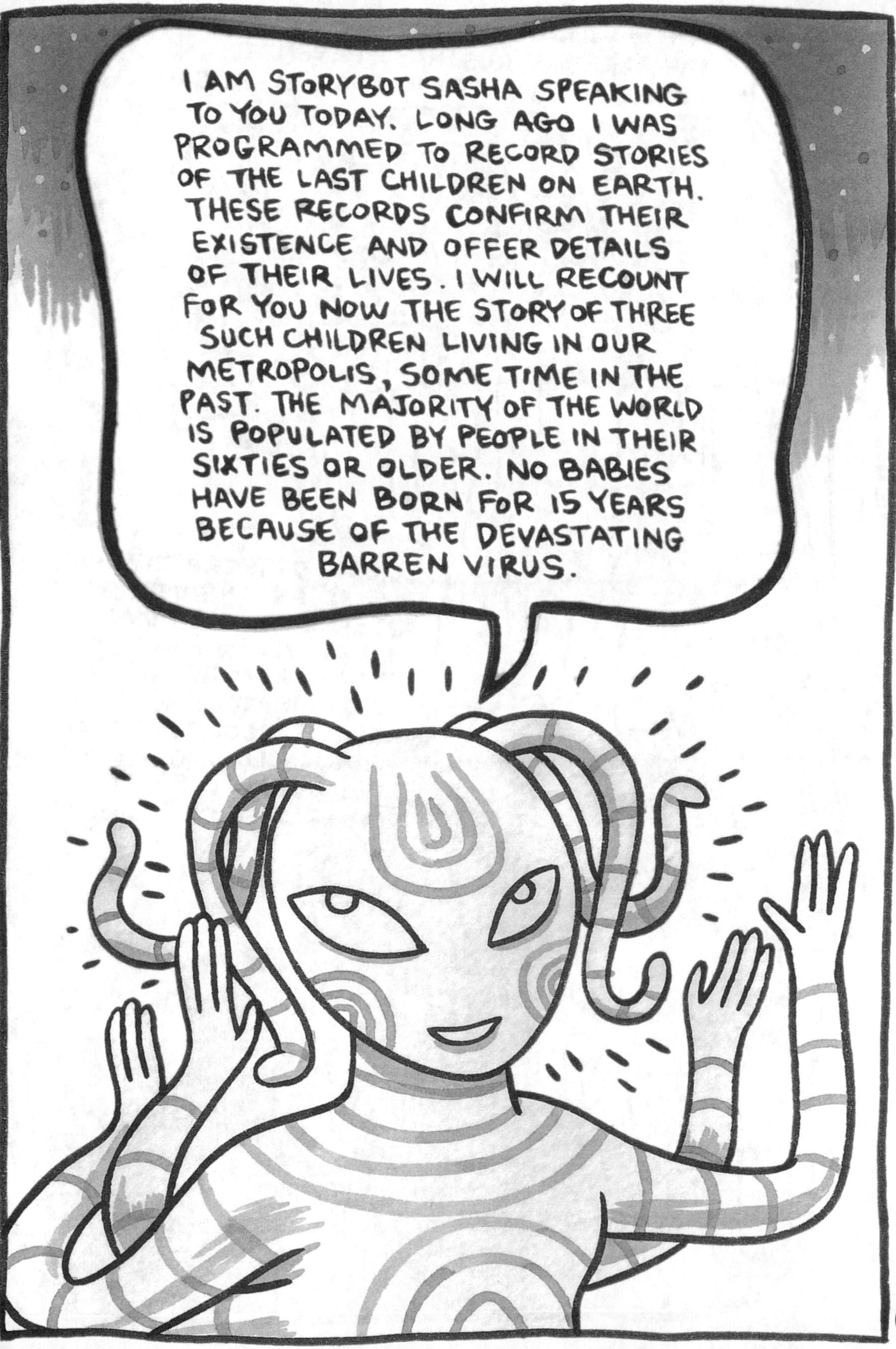
I AM STORYBOT SASHA SPEAKING TO YOU TODAY. LONG AGO I WAS PROGRAMMED TO RECORD STORIES OF THE LAST CHILDREN ON EARTH. THESE RECORDS CONFIRM THEIR EXISTENCE AND OFFER DETAILS OF THEIR LIVES. I WILL RECOUNT FOR YOU NOW THE STORY OF THREE SUCH CHILDREN LIVING IN OUR METROPOLIS, SOME TIME IN THE PAST. THE MAJORITY OF THE WORLD IS POPULATED BY PEOPLE IN THEIR SIXTIES OR OLDER. NO BABIES HAVE BEEN BORN FOR 15 YEARS BECAUSE OF THE DEVASTATING BARREN VIRUS.

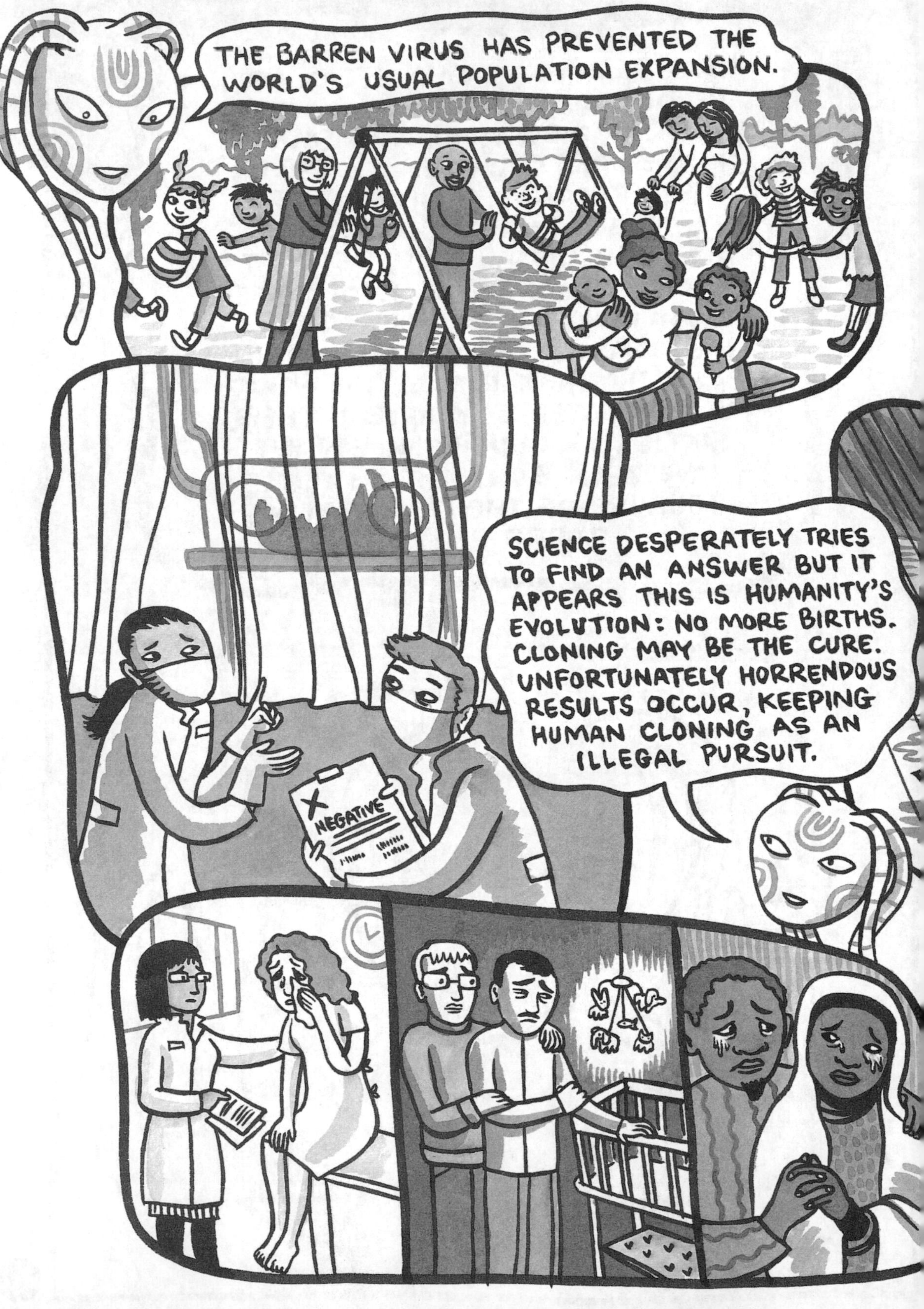
THE BARREN VIRUS HAS PREVENTED THE WORLD'S USUAL POPULATION EXPANSION.
SCIENCE DESPERATELY TRIES TO FIND AN ANSWER BUT IT APPEARS THIS IS HUMANITY'S EVOLUTION: NO MORE BIRTHS. CLONING MAY BE THE CURE. UNFORTUNATELY HORRENDOUS RESULTS OCCUR, KEEPING HUMAN CLONING AS AN ILLEGAL PURSUIT.
NEGATIVE

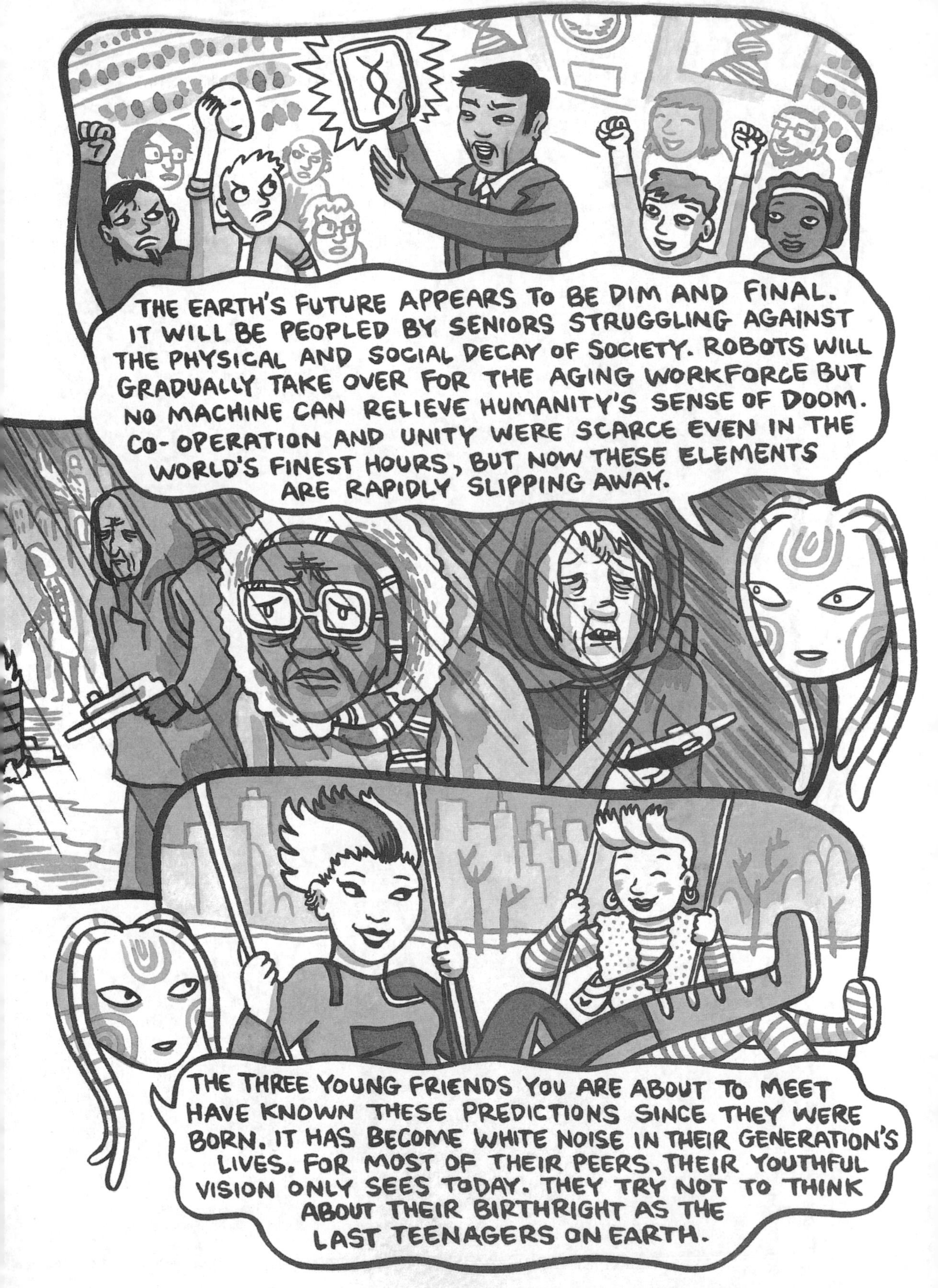
THE EARTH'S FUTURE APPEARS TO BE DIM AND FINAL. IT WILL BE PEOPLED BY SENIORS STRUGGLING AGAINST THE PHYSICAL AND SOCIAL DECAY OF SOCIETY. ROBOTS WILL GRADUALLY TAKE OVER FOR THE AGING WORKFORCE BUT NO MACHINE CAN RELIEVE HUMANITY'S SENSE OF DOOM. CO-OPERATION AND UNITY WERE SCARCE EVEN IN THE WORLD'S FINEST HOURS, BUT NOW THESE ELEMENTS ARE RAPIDLY SLIPPING AWAY.
THE THREE YOUNG FRIENDS YOU ARE ABOUT TO MEET HAVE KNOWN THESE PREDICTIONS SINCE THEY WERE BORN. IT HAS BECOME WHITE NOISE IN THEIR GENERATION'S LIVES. FOR MOST OF THEIR PEERS, THEIR YOUTHFUL VISION ONLY SEES TODAY. THEY TRY NOT TO THINK ABOUT THEIR BIRTHRIGHT AS THE LAST TEENAGERS ON EARTH.

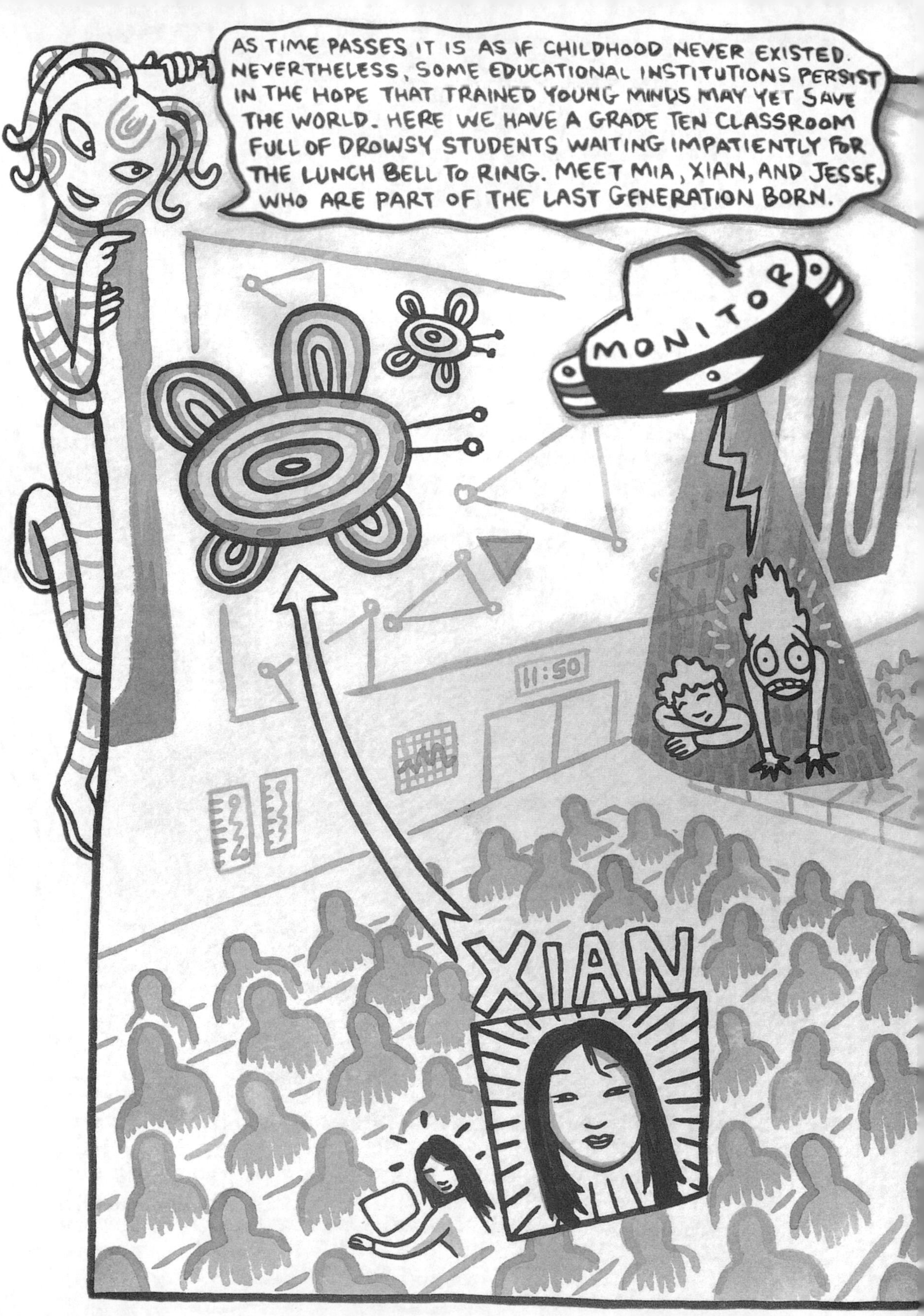
AS TIME PASSES IT IS AS IF CHILDHOOD NEVER EXISTED. NEVERTHELESS, SOME EDUCATIONAL INSTITUTIONS PERSIST IN THE HOPE THAT TRAINED YOUNG MINDS MAY YET SAVE THE WORLD. HERE WE HAVE A GRADE TEN CLASSROOM FULL OF DROWSY STUDENTS WAITING IMPATIENTLY FOR THE LUNCH BELL TO RING. MEET MIA, XIAN, AND JESSE, WHO ARE PART OF THE LAST GENERATION BORN.
MONITOR
11:50
XIAN

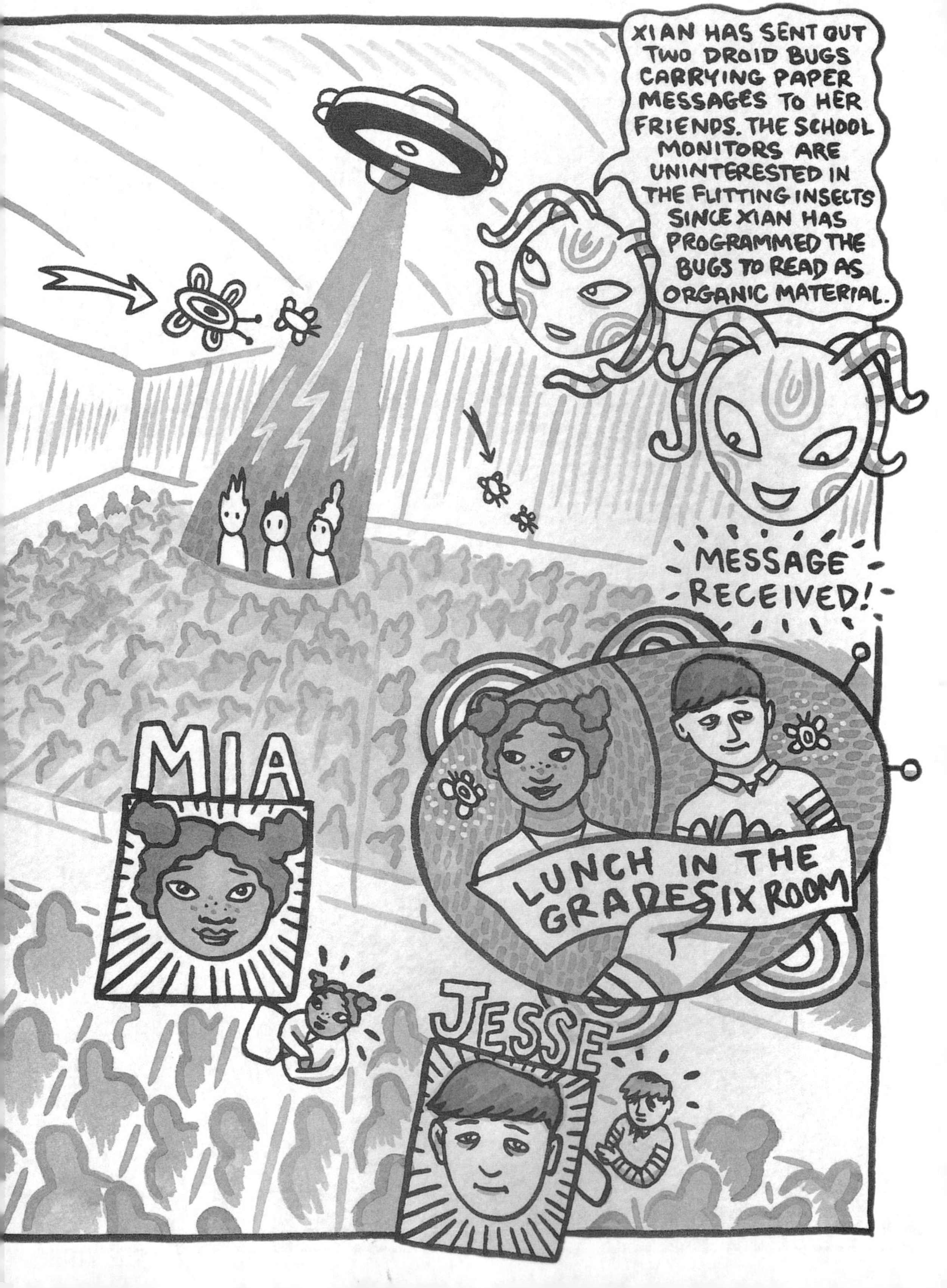
XIAN HAS SENT OUT TWO DROID BUGS CARRYING PAPER MESSAGES TO HER FRIENDS. THE SCHOOL MONITORS ARE UNINTERESTED IN THE FLITTING INSECTS SINCE XIAN HAS PROGRAMMED THE BUGS TO READ AS ORGANIC MATERIAL.
MESSAGE RECEIVED!
LUNCH IN THE GRADE SIX ROOM
MIA
JESSE

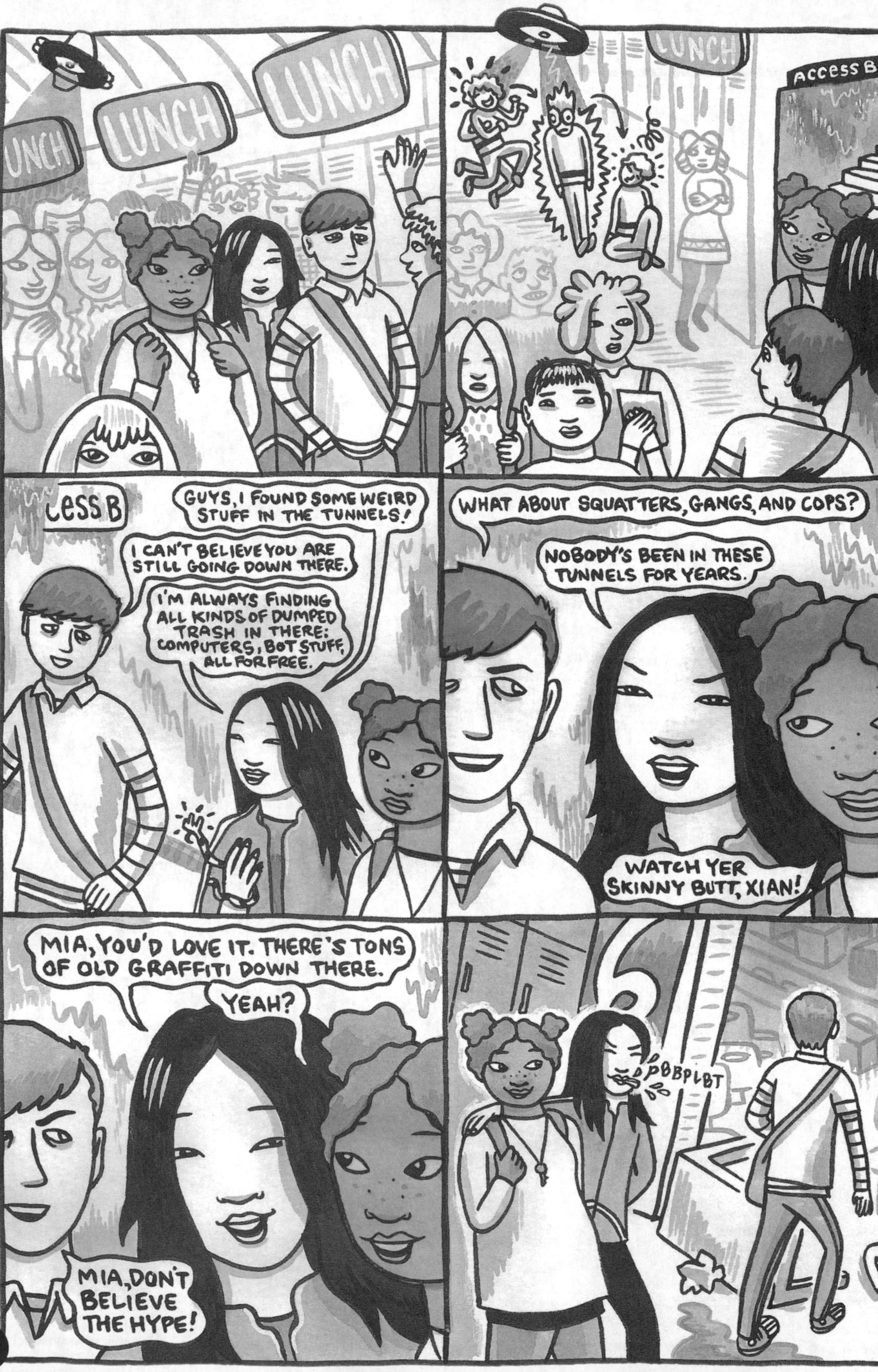
LUNCH
LUNCH
LUNCH
LUNCH
LUNCH
ACCESS B
CESS B
GUYS, I FOUND SOME WEIRD STUFF IN THE TUNNELS!
I CAN'T BELIEVE YOU ARE STILL GOING DOWN THERE.
I'M ALWAYS FINDING ALL KINDS OF DUMPED TRASH IN THERE: COMPUTERS, BOT STUFF, ALL FOR FREE.
WHAT ABOUT SQUATTERS, GANGS, AND COPS?
NOBODY'S BEEN IN THESE TUNNELS FOR YEARS.
WATCH YER SKINNY BUTT, XIAN!
MIA, YOU'D LOVE IT. THERE'S TONS OF OLD GRAFFITI DOWN THERE.
YEAH?
MIA, DON'T BELIEVE THE HYPE!
PBBPLBT

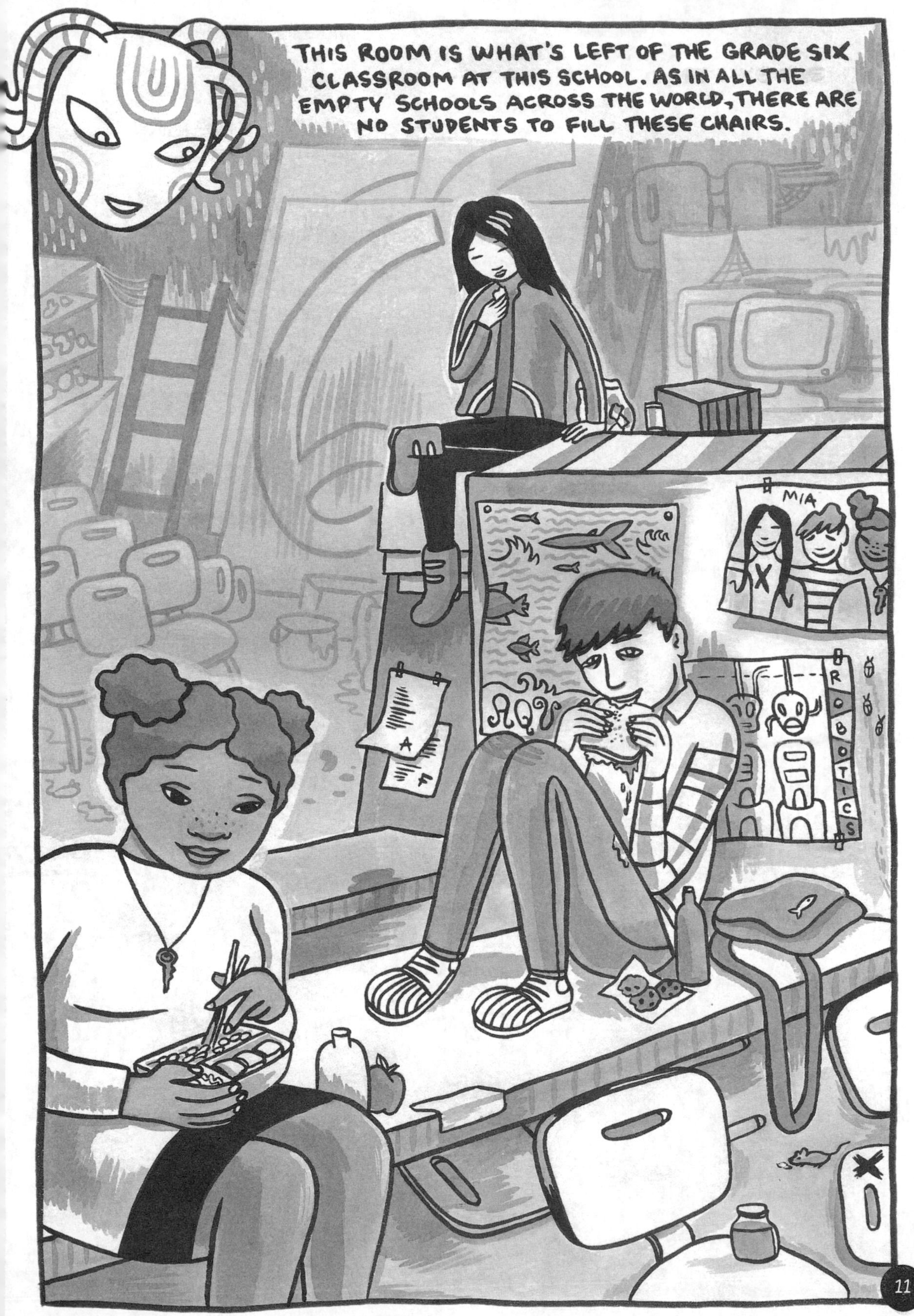
THIS ROOM IS WHAT'S LEFT OF THE GRADE SIX CLASSROOM AT THIS SCHOOL. AS IN ALL THE EMPTY SCHOOLS ACROSS THE WORLD, THERE ARE NO STUDENTS TO FILL THESE CHAIRS.
MIA
ROBOTICS

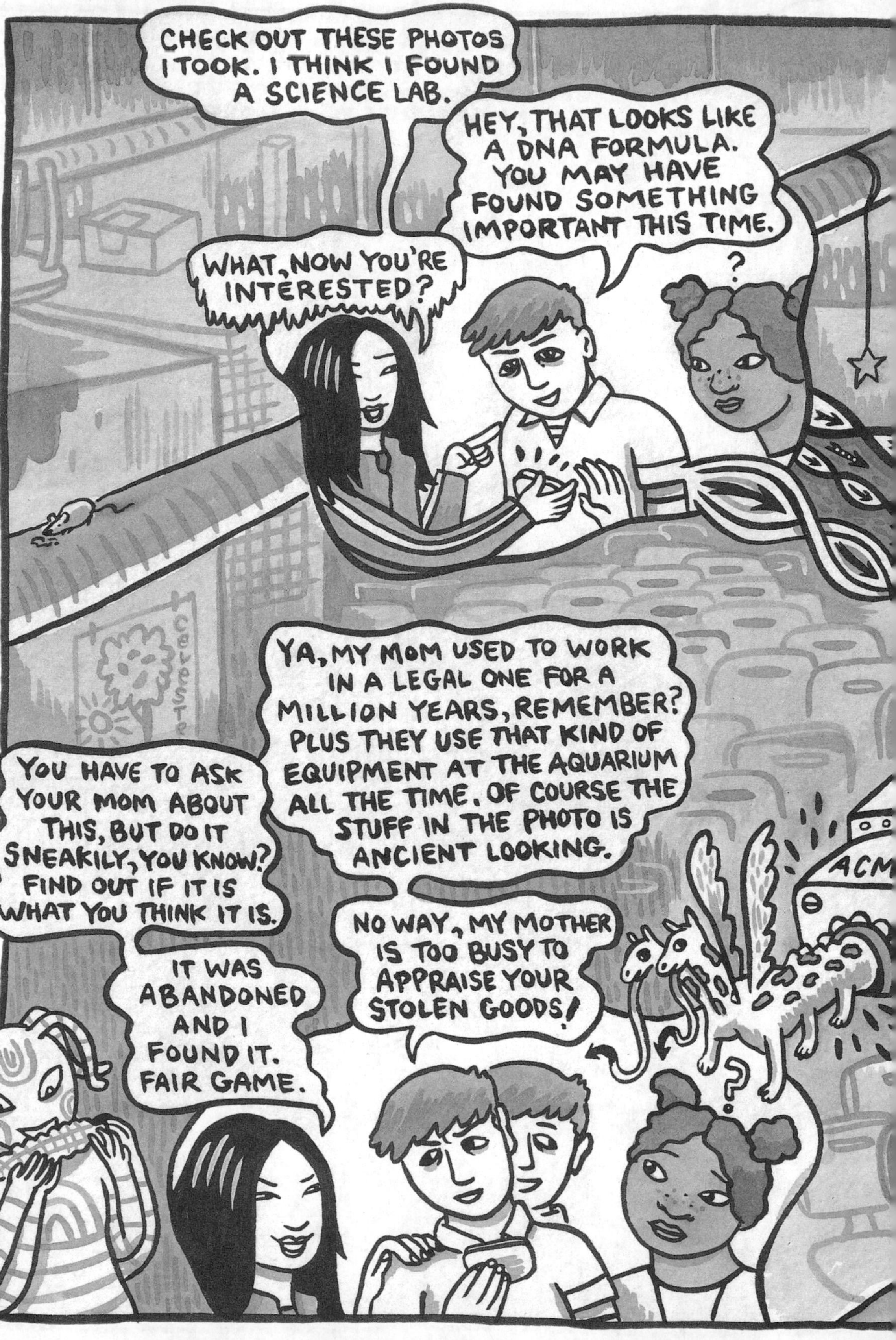
CHECK OUT THESE PHOTOS I TOOK. I THINK I FOUND A SCIENCE LAB.
HEY, THAT LOOKS LIKE A DNA FORMULA. YOU MAY HAVE FOUND SOMETHING IMPORTANT THIS TIME.
WHAT, NOW YOU'RE INTERESTED?
?
CELESTE
YA, MY MOM USED TO WORK IN A LEGAL ONE FOR A MILLION YEARS, REMEMBER? PLUS THEY USE THAT KIND OF EQUIPMENT AT THE AQUARIUM ALL THE TIME. OF COURSE THE STUFF IN THE PHOTO IS ANCIENT LOOKING.
YOU HAVE TO ASK YOUR MOM ABOUT THIS, BUT DO IT SNEAKILY, YOU KNOW? FIND OUT IF IT IS WHAT YOU THINK IT IS.
NO WAY, MY MOTHER IS TOO BUSY TO APPRAISE YOUR STOLEN GOODS!
IT WAS ABANDONED AND I FOUND IT. FAIR GAME.
?

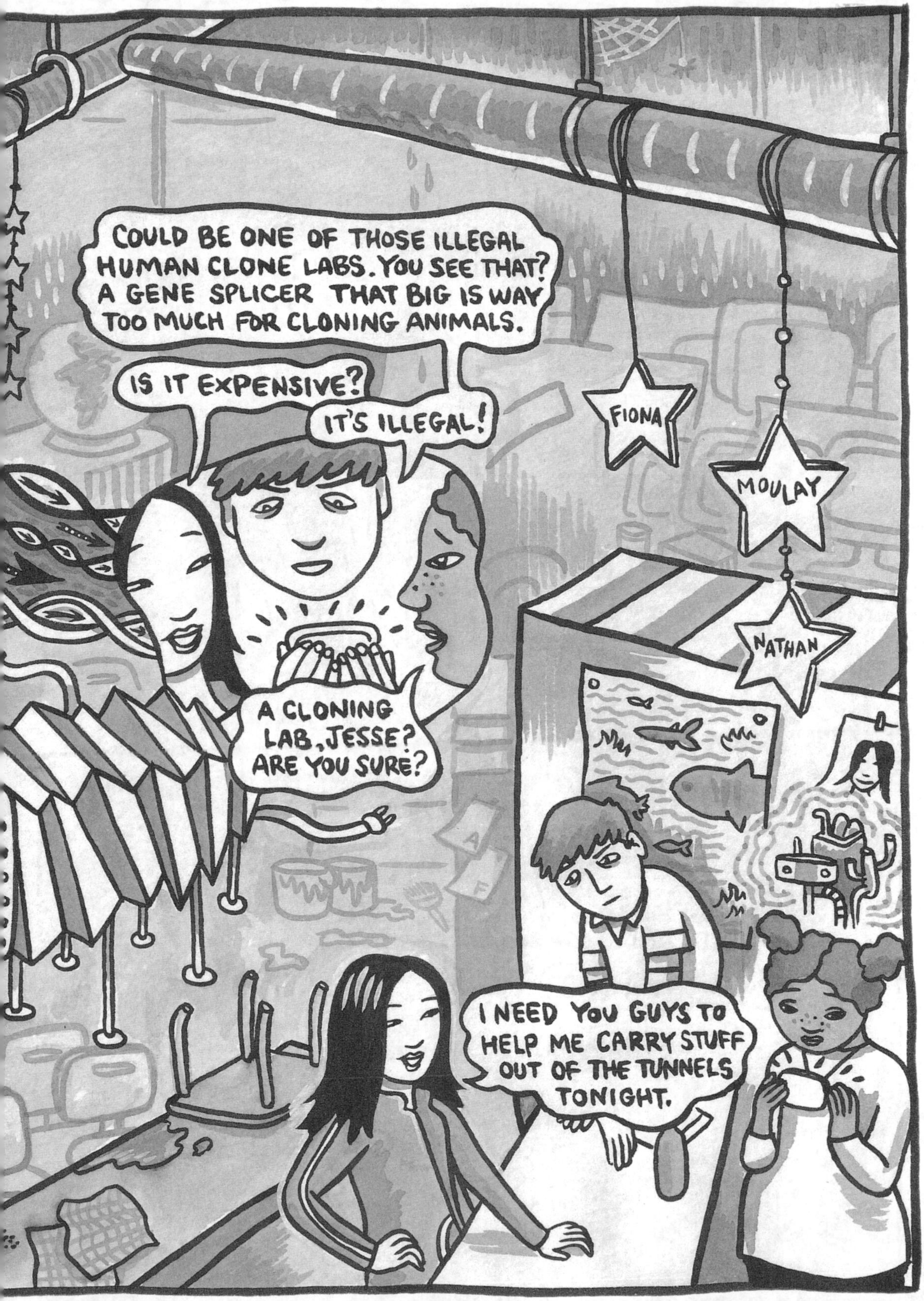
COULD BE ONE OF THOSE ILLEGAL HUMAN CLONE LABS. YOU SEE THAT? A GENE SPLICER THAT BIG IS WAY TOO MUCH FOR CLONING ANIMALS.
IS IT EXPENSIVE?
IT'S ILLEGAL!
FIONA
MOULAY
NATHAN
A CLONING LAB, JESSE? ARE YOU SURE?
I NEED YOU GUYS TO HELP ME CARRY STUFF OUT OF THE TUNNELS TONIGHT.

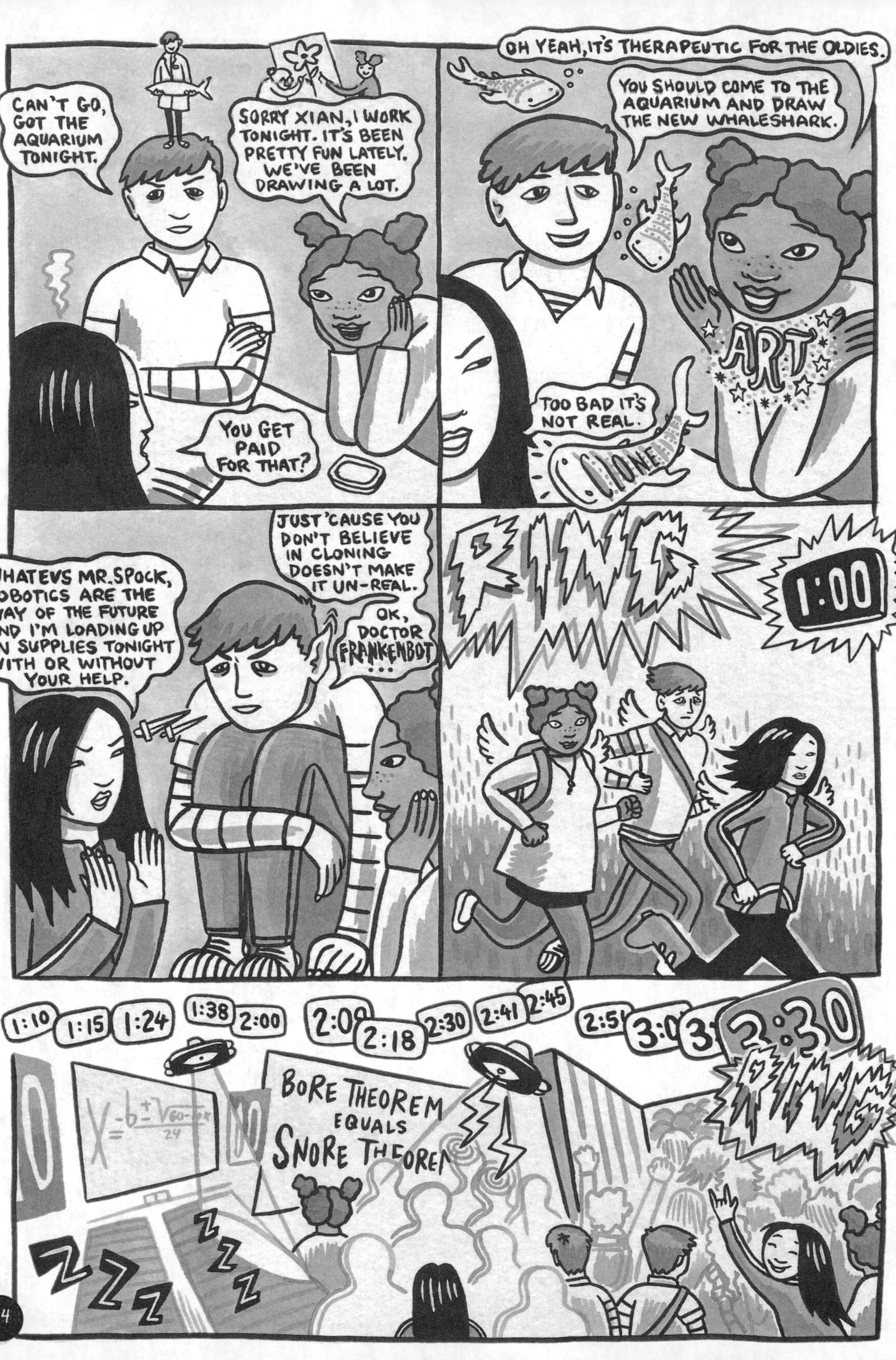
CAN'T GO, GOT THE AQUARIUM TONIGHT.
SORRY XIAN, I WORK TONIGHT. IT'S BEEN PRETTY FUN LATELY. WE'VE BEEN DRAWING A LOT.
YOU GET PAID FOR THAT?
OH YEAH, IT'S THERAPEUTIC FOR THE OLDIES.
YOU SHOULD COME TO THE AQUARIUM AND DRAW THE NEW WHALESHARK.
ART
TOO BAD IT'S NOT REAL.
CLONE
WHATEVS MR. SPOCK, ROBOTICS ARE THE WAY OF THE FUTURE AND I'M LOADING UP ON SUPPLIES TONIGHT WITH OR WITHOUT YOUR HELP.
JUST 'CAUSE YOU DON'T BELIEVE IN CLONING DOESN'T MAKE IT UN-REAL.
OK, DOCTOR FRANKENBOT ...
RING
1:00
1:10
1:15
1:24
1:38
2:00
2:18
2:30
2:41
2:45
2:30
BORE THEOREM EQUALS SNORE THEOREM
ZZZ
ZZZ
RING

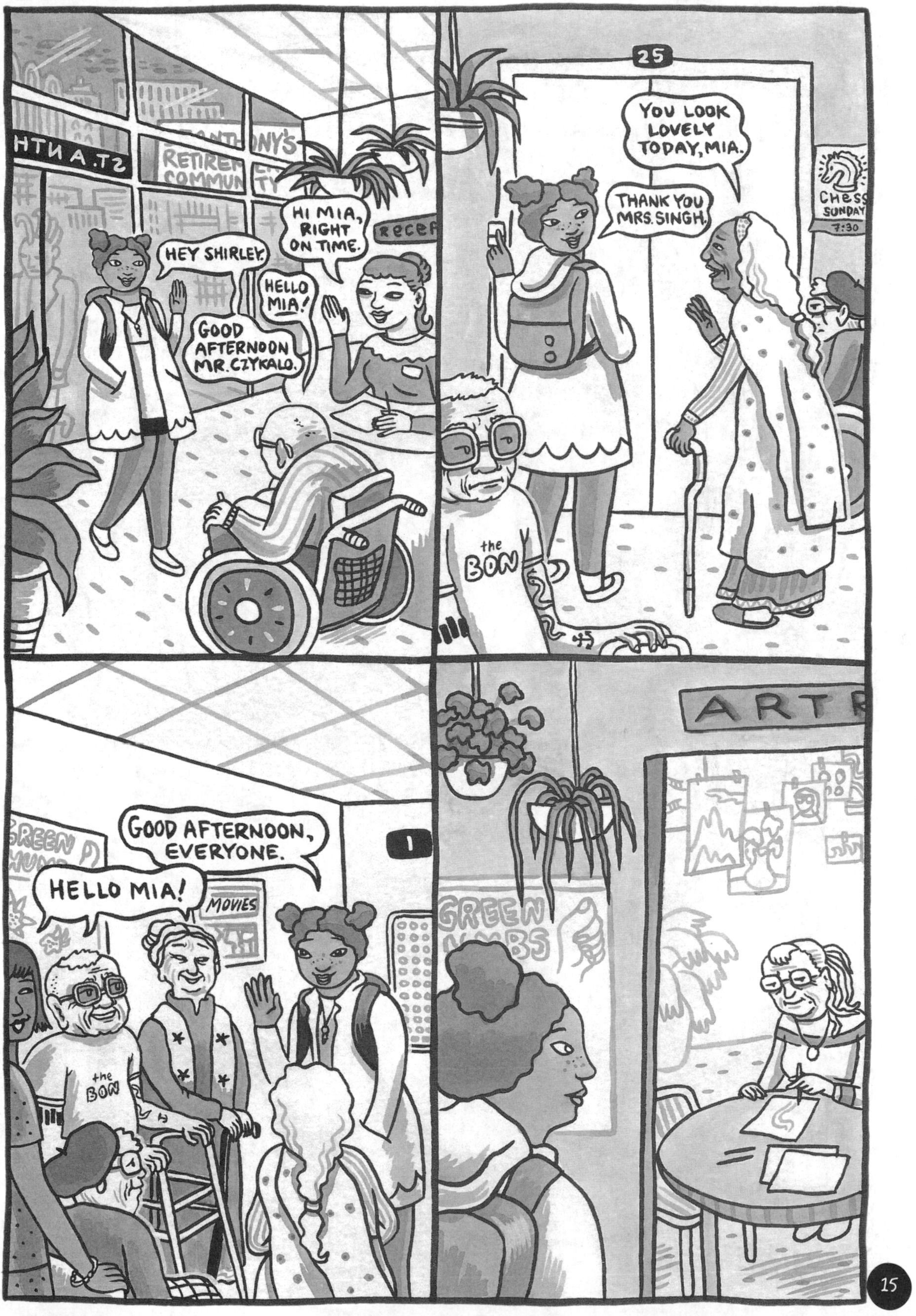
ST. A NTH
ST. ANTHONY'S RETIREMENT COMMUNITY
RECEP
HEY SHIRLEY.
HI MIA, RIGHT ON TIME.
HELLO MIA!
GOOD AFTERNOON MR. CZYKALO.
25
YOU LOOK LOVELY TODAY, MIA.
THANK YOU MRS. SINGH.
CHESS SUNDAY 7:30
the BON
GOOD AFTERNOON, EVERYONE.
HELLO MIA!
1
MOVIES
GREEN THUMBS
the BON
ART

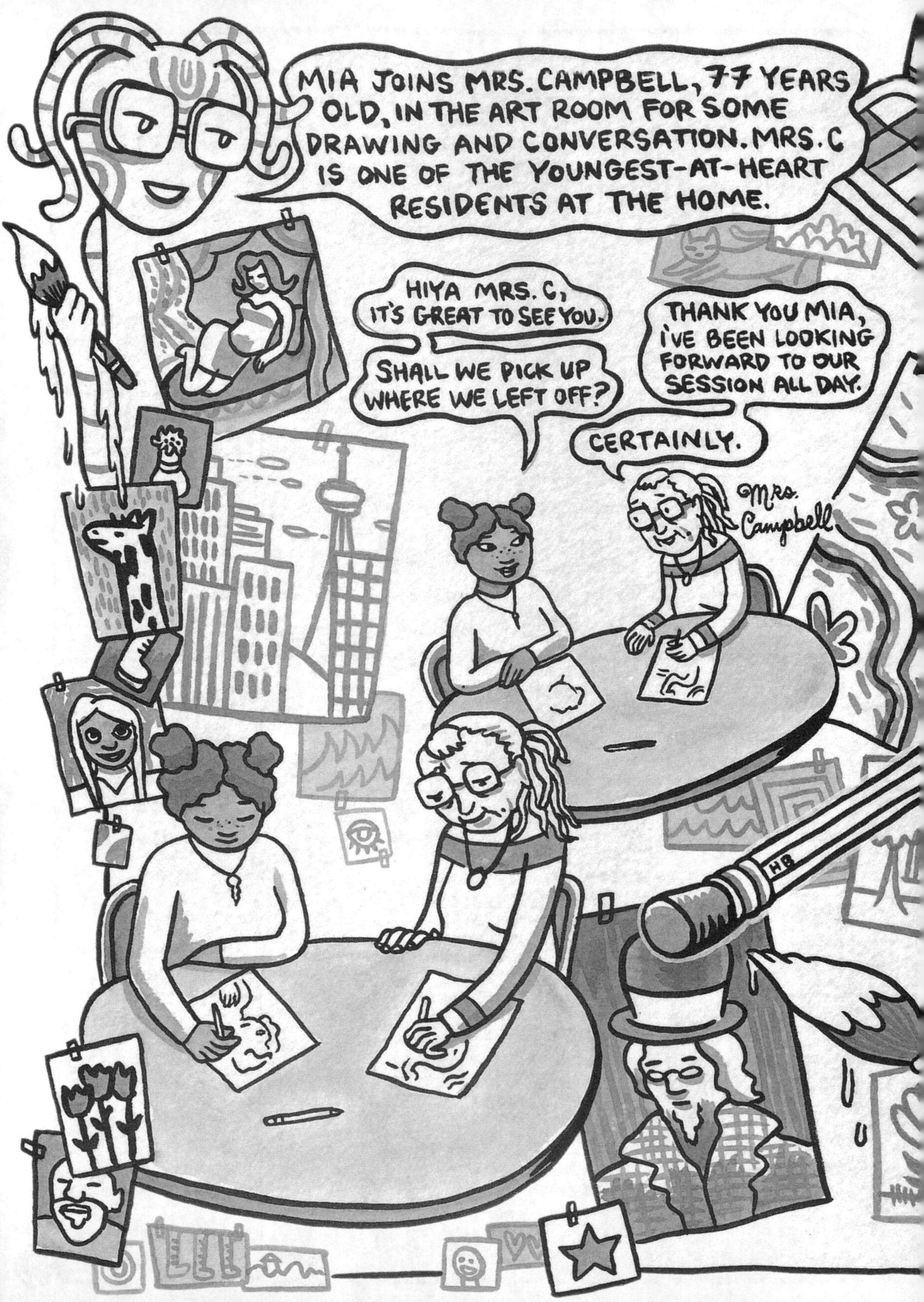
MIA JOINS MRS. CAMPBELL, 77 YEARS OLD, IN THE ART ROOM FOR SOME DRAWING AND CONVERSATION. MRS. C IS ONE OF THE YOUNGEST-AT-HEART RESIDENTS AT THE HOME.
HIYA MRS. C, IT'S GREAT TO SEE YOU.
THANK YOU MIA, I'VE BEEN LOOKING FORWARD TO OUR SESSION ALL DAY.
SHALL WE PICK UP WHERE WE LEFT OFF?
CERTAINLY.
Mrs. Campbell
HB

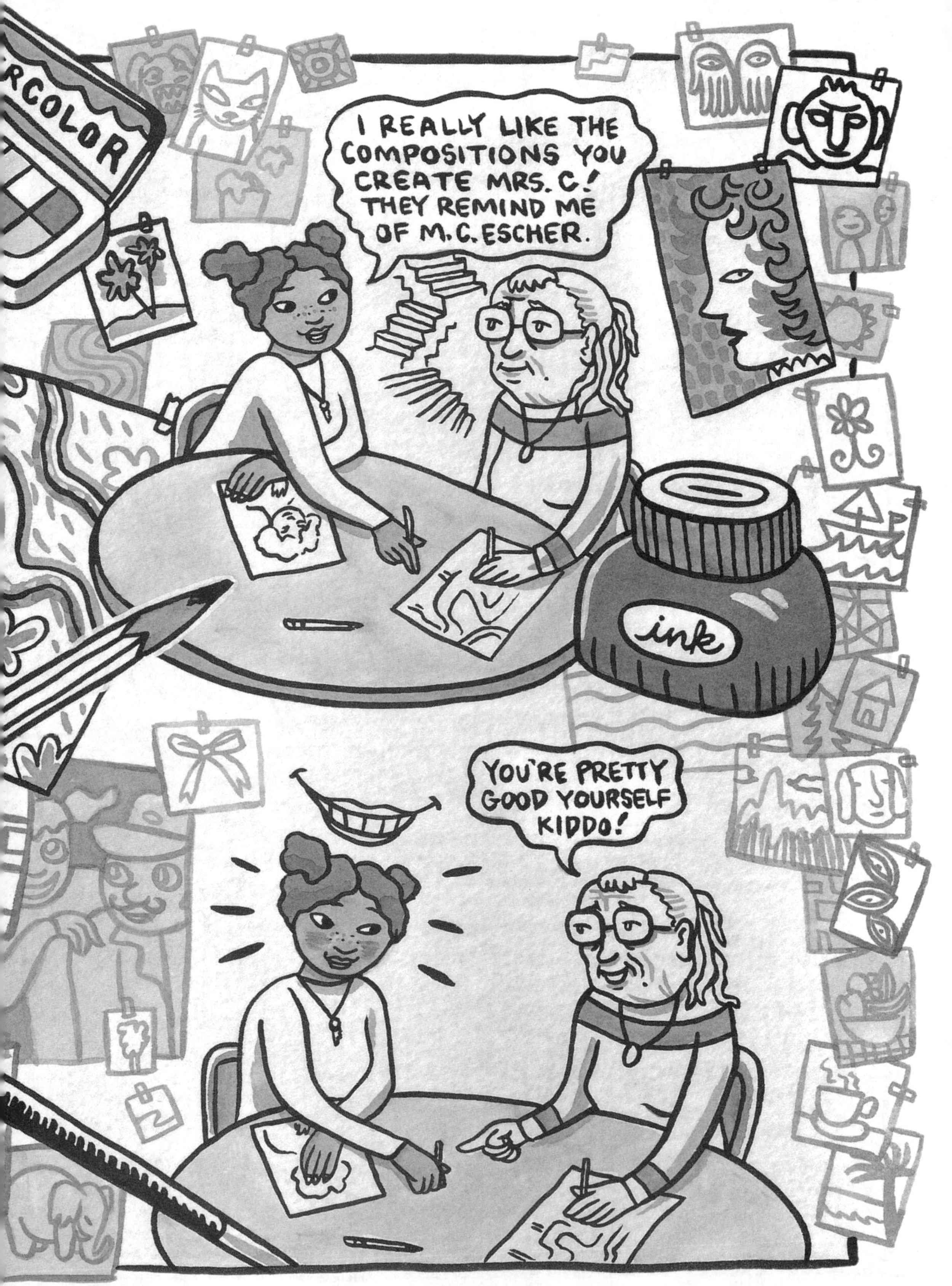
RCOLOR
I REALLY LIKE THE COMPOSITIONS YOU CREATE MRS. C! THEY REMIND ME OF M.C. ESCHER.
ink
YOU'RE PRETTY GOOD YOURSELF KIDDO!

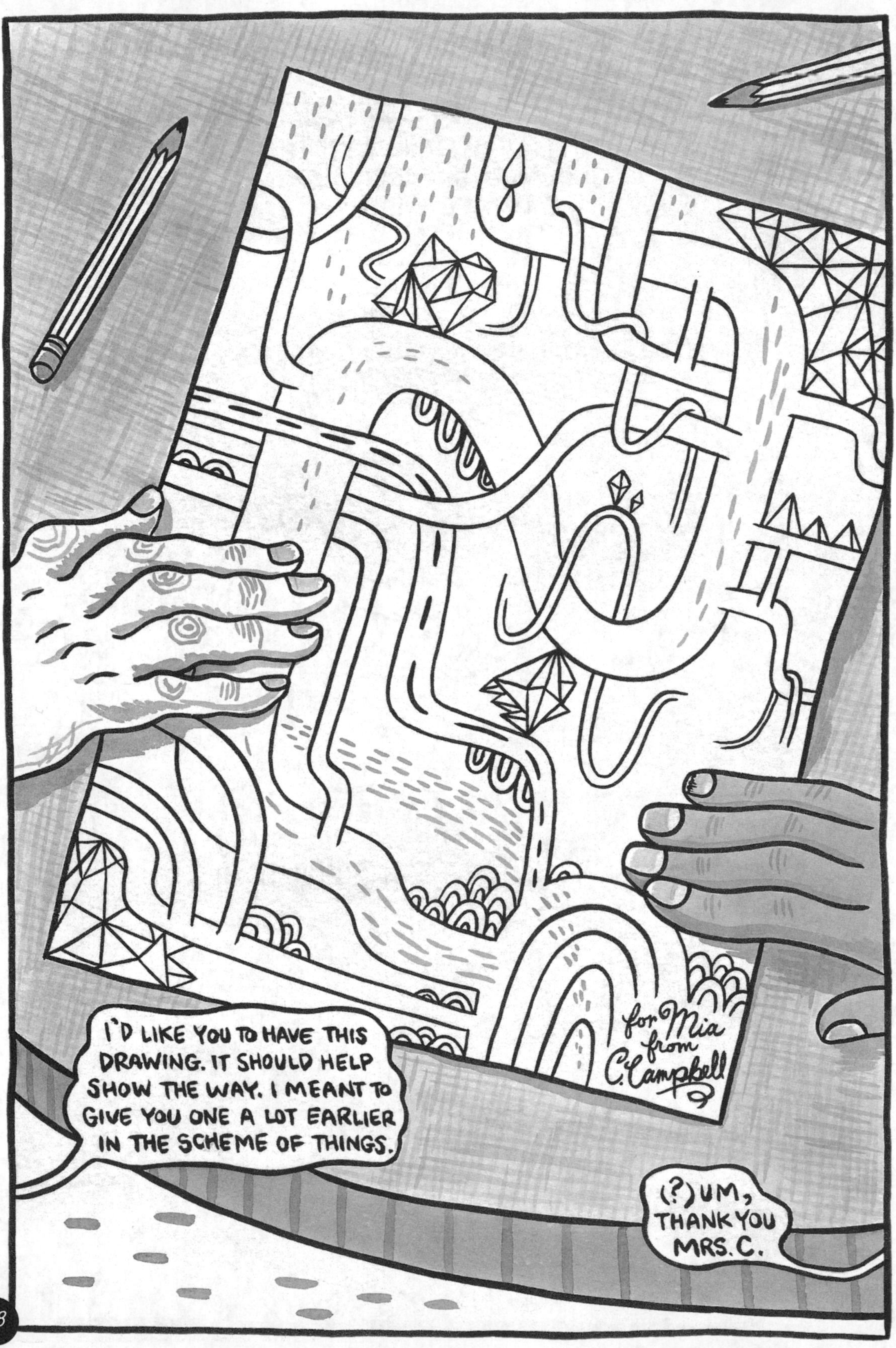
for Mia from C. Campbell
I'D LIKE YOU TO HAVE THIS DRAWING. IT SHOULD HELP SHOW THE WAY. I MEANT TO GIVE YOU ONE A LOT EARLIER IN THE SCHEME OF THINGS.
(?) UM, THANK YOU MRS. C.

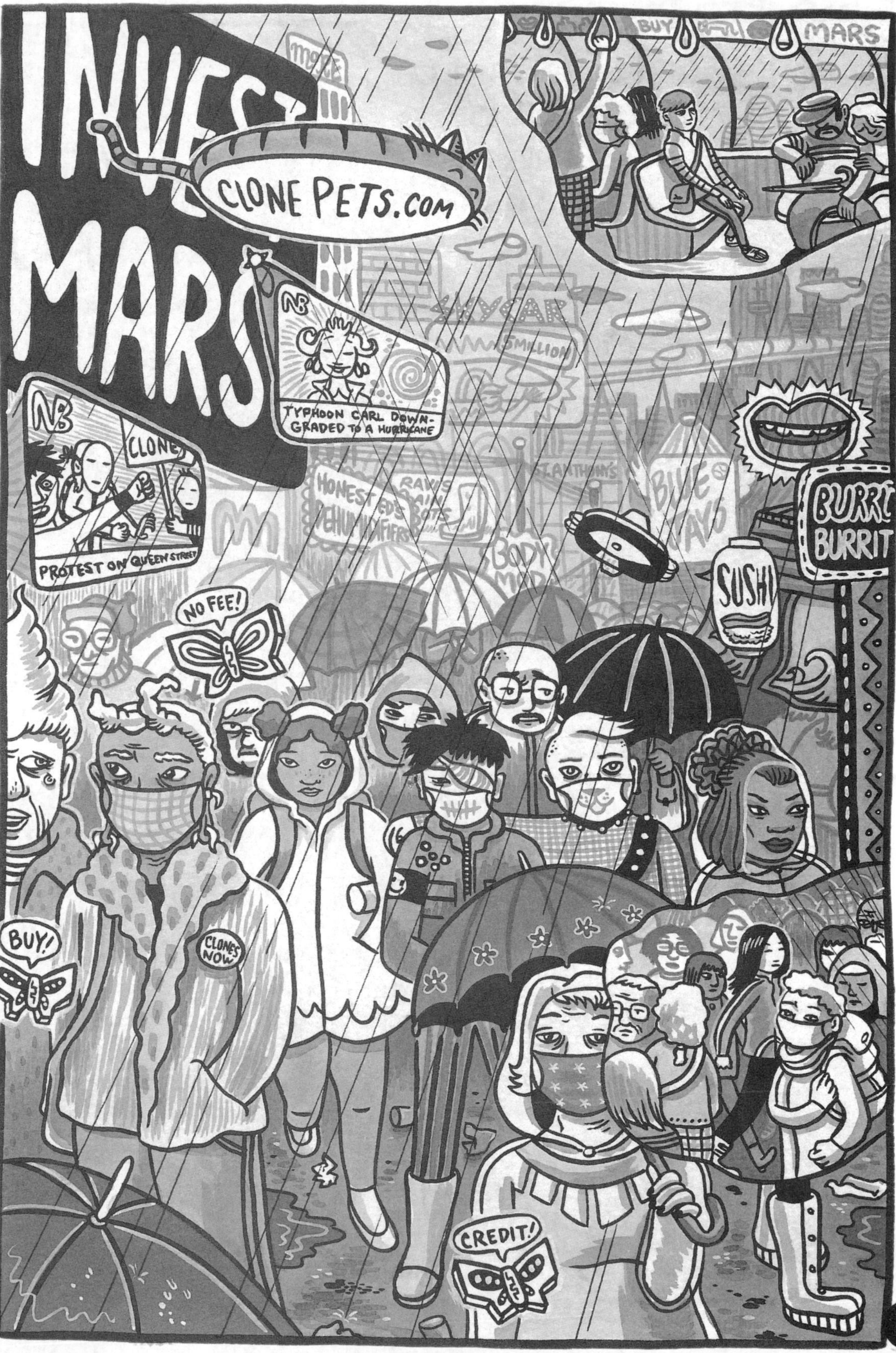
INVEST MARS
CLONEPETS.COM
BUY
MARS
TYPHOON CARL DOWN-GRADED TO A HURRICANE
CLONE
PROTEST ON QUEEN STREET
5MILLION
ST. ANTHONY'S
SUSHI
NO FEE!
BUY!
CLONES NOW
CREDIT!

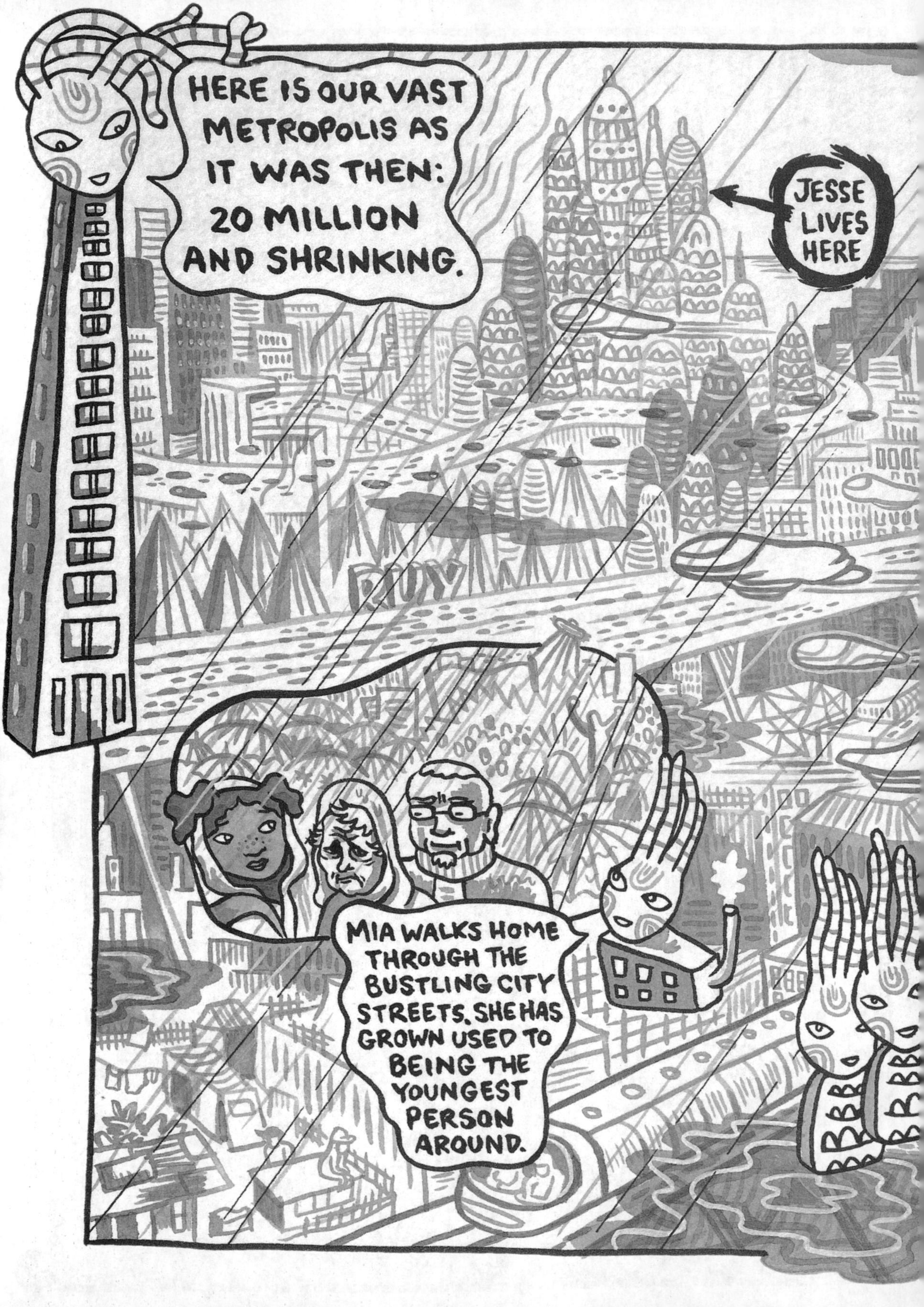
HERE IS OUR VAST METROPOLIS AS IT WAS THEN: 20 MILLION AND SHRINKING.
JESSE LIVES HERE
BUY
MIA WALKS HOME THROUGH THE BUSTLING CITY STREETS. SHE HAS GROWN USED TO BEING THE YOUNGEST PERSON AROUND.

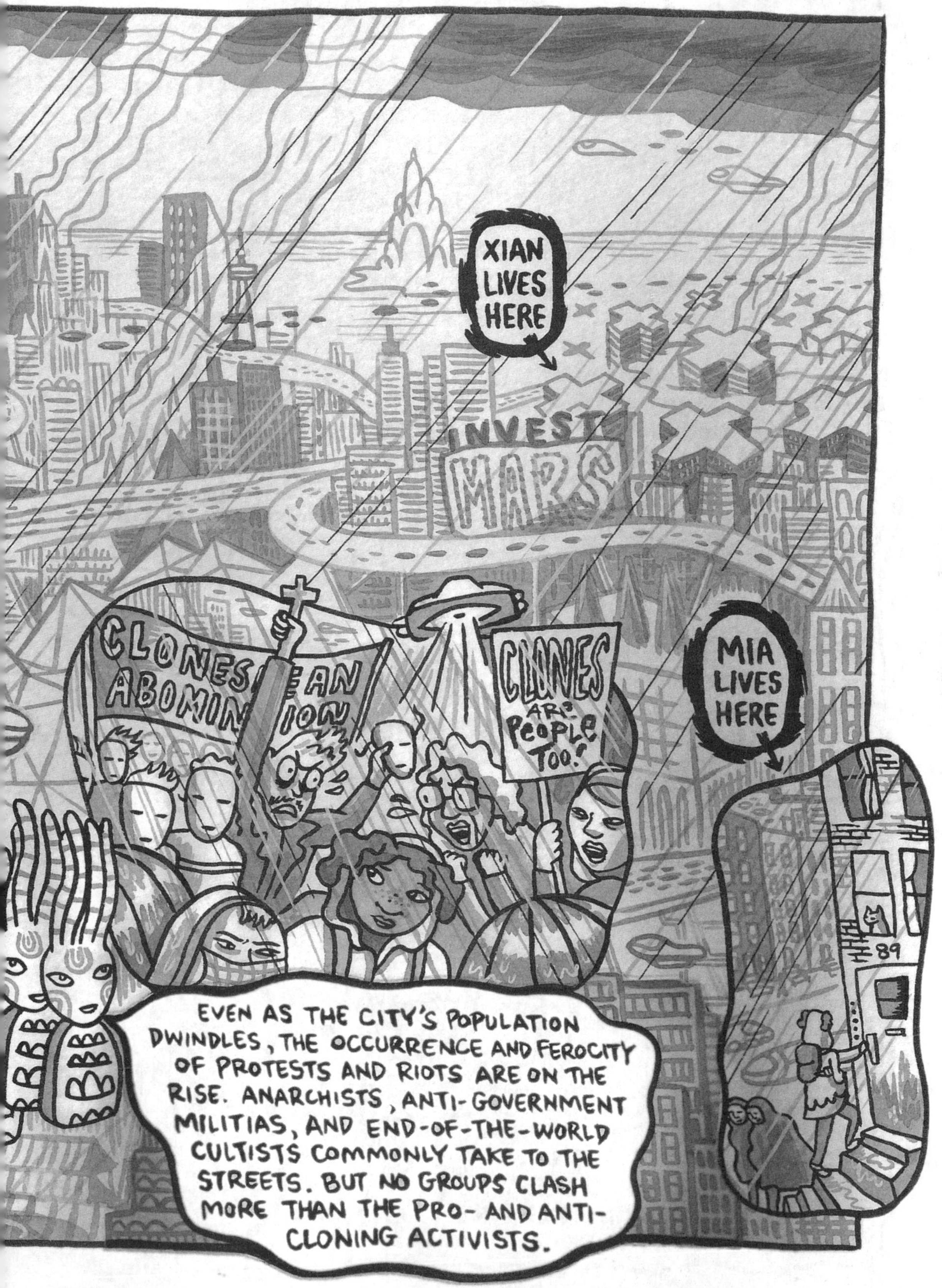
XIAN LIVES HERE
INVEST MARS
CLONES ARE AN ABOMINATION
CLONES ARE PEOPLE TOO!
MIA LIVES HERE
89
EVEN AS THE CITY'S POPULATION DWINDLES, THE OCCURRENCE AND FEROCITY OF PROTESTS AND RIOTS ARE ON THE RISE. ANARCHISTS, ANTI-GOVERNMENT MILITIAS, AND END-OF-THE-WORLD CULTISTS COMMONLY TAKE TO THE STREETS. BUT NO GROUPS CLASH MORE THAN THE PRO- AND ANTI-CLONING ACTIVISTS.

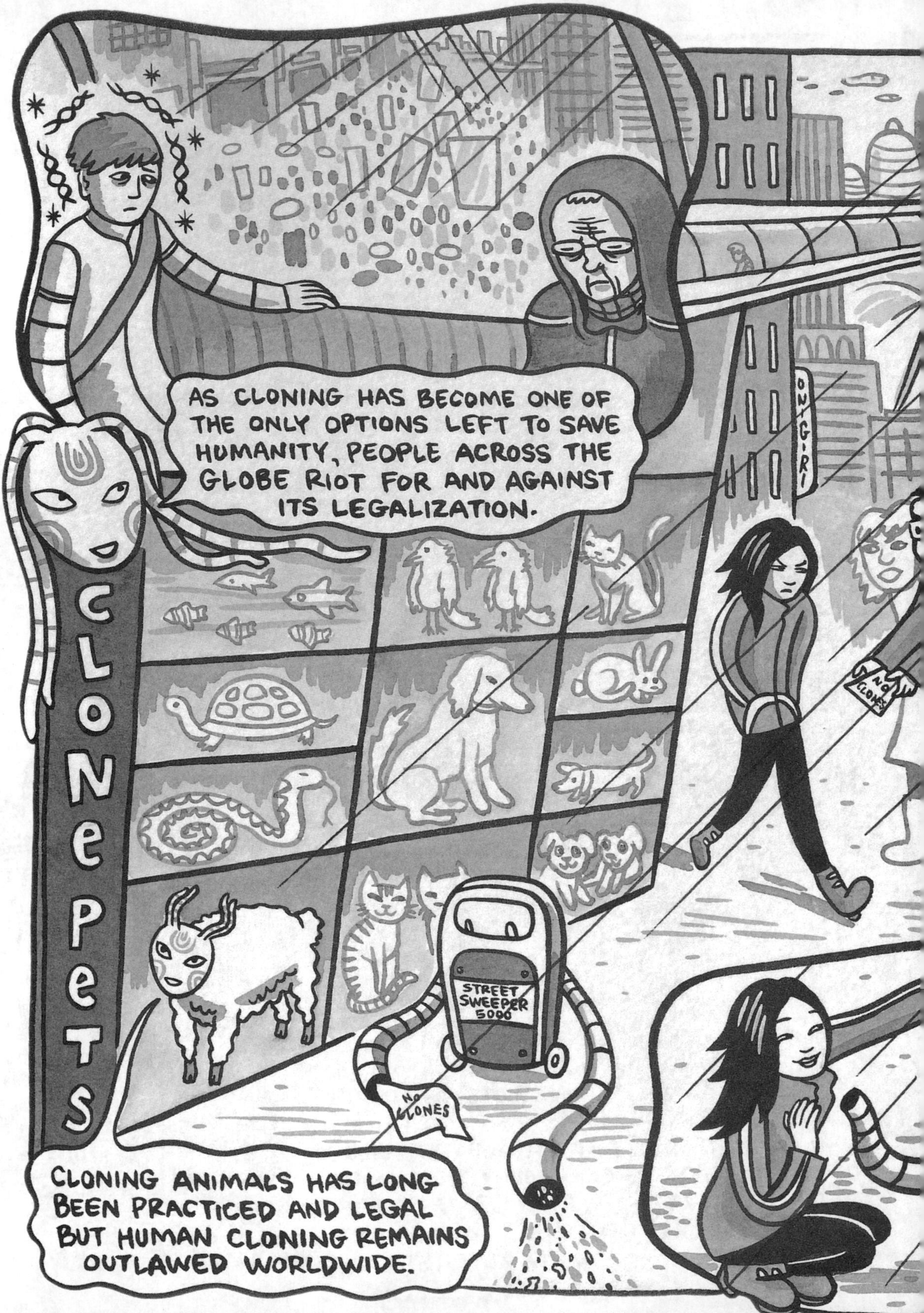
AS CLONING HAS BECOME ONE OF THE ONLY OPTIONS LEFT TO SAVE HUMANITY, PEOPLE ACROSS THE GLOBE RIOT FOR AND AGAINST ITS LEGALIZATION.
ONIGIRI
CLONE PETS
NO CLONES
STREET SWEEPER 5000
NO CLONES
CLONING ANIMALS HAS LONG BEEN PRACTICED AND LEGAL BUT HUMAN CLONING REMAINS OUTLAWED WORLDWIDE.

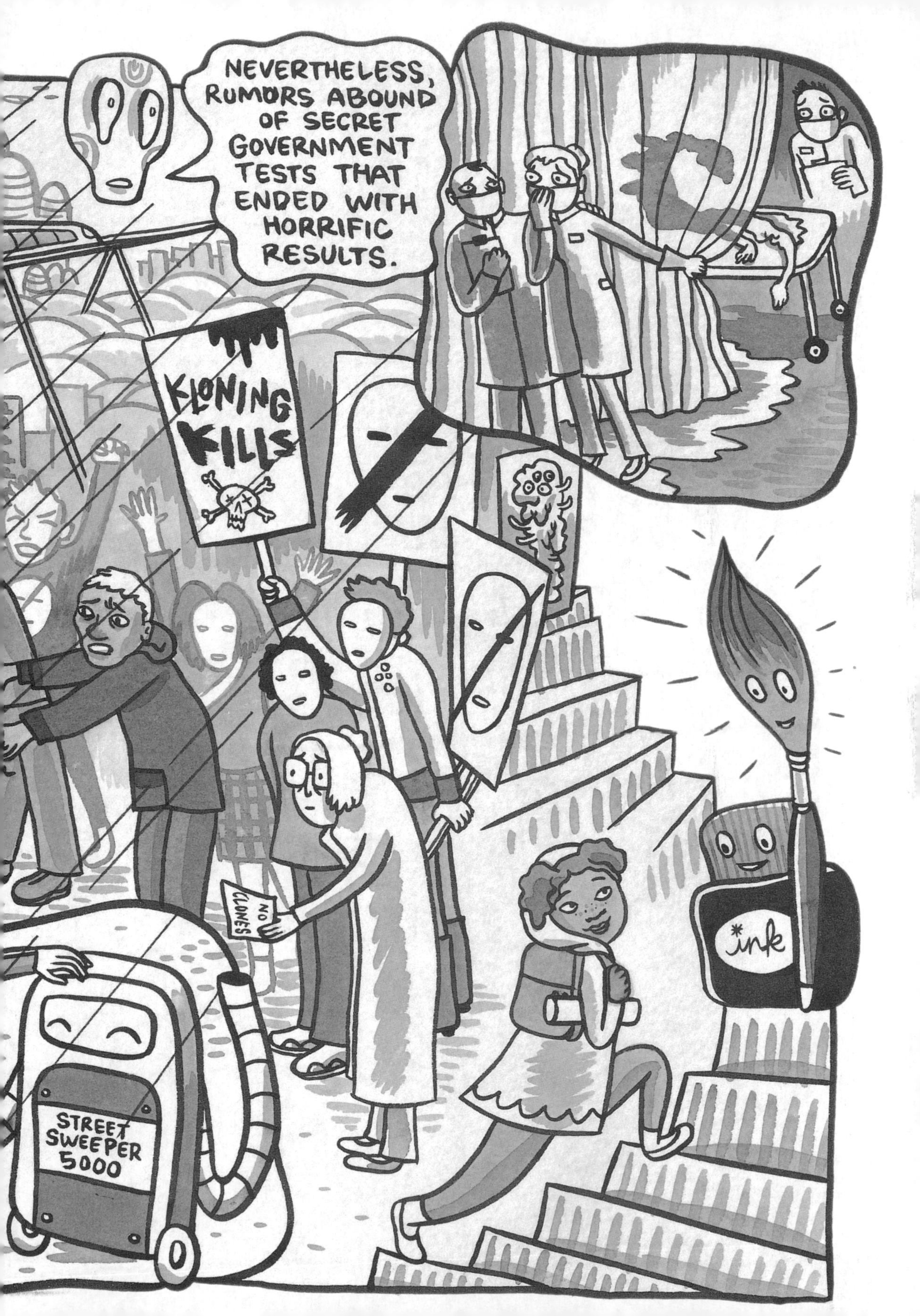
NEVERTHELESS, RUMORS ABOUND OF SECRET GOVERNMENT TESTS THAT ENDED WITH HORRIFIC RESULTS.
KLONING KILLS
NO CLONES
ink
STREET SWEEPER 5000

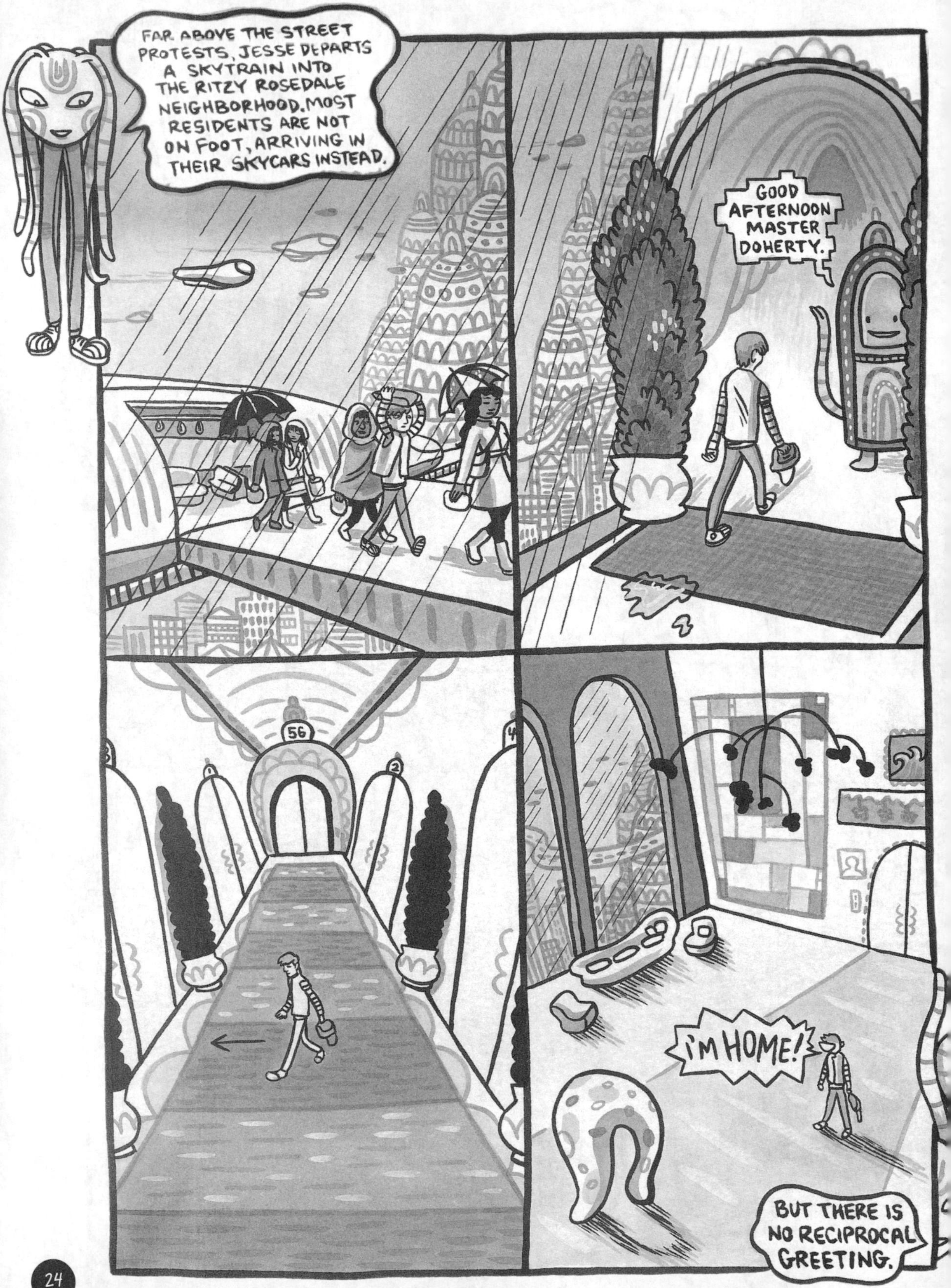
FAR ABOVE THE STREET PROTESTS, JESSE DEPARTS A SKYTRAIN INTO THE RITZY ROSEDALE NEIGHBORHOOD. MOST RESIDENTS ARE NOT ON FOOT, ARRIVING IN THEIR SKYCARS INSTEAD.
GOOD AFTERNOON MASTER DOHERTY.
56
I'M HOME!
BUT THERE IS NO RECIPROCAL GREETING.

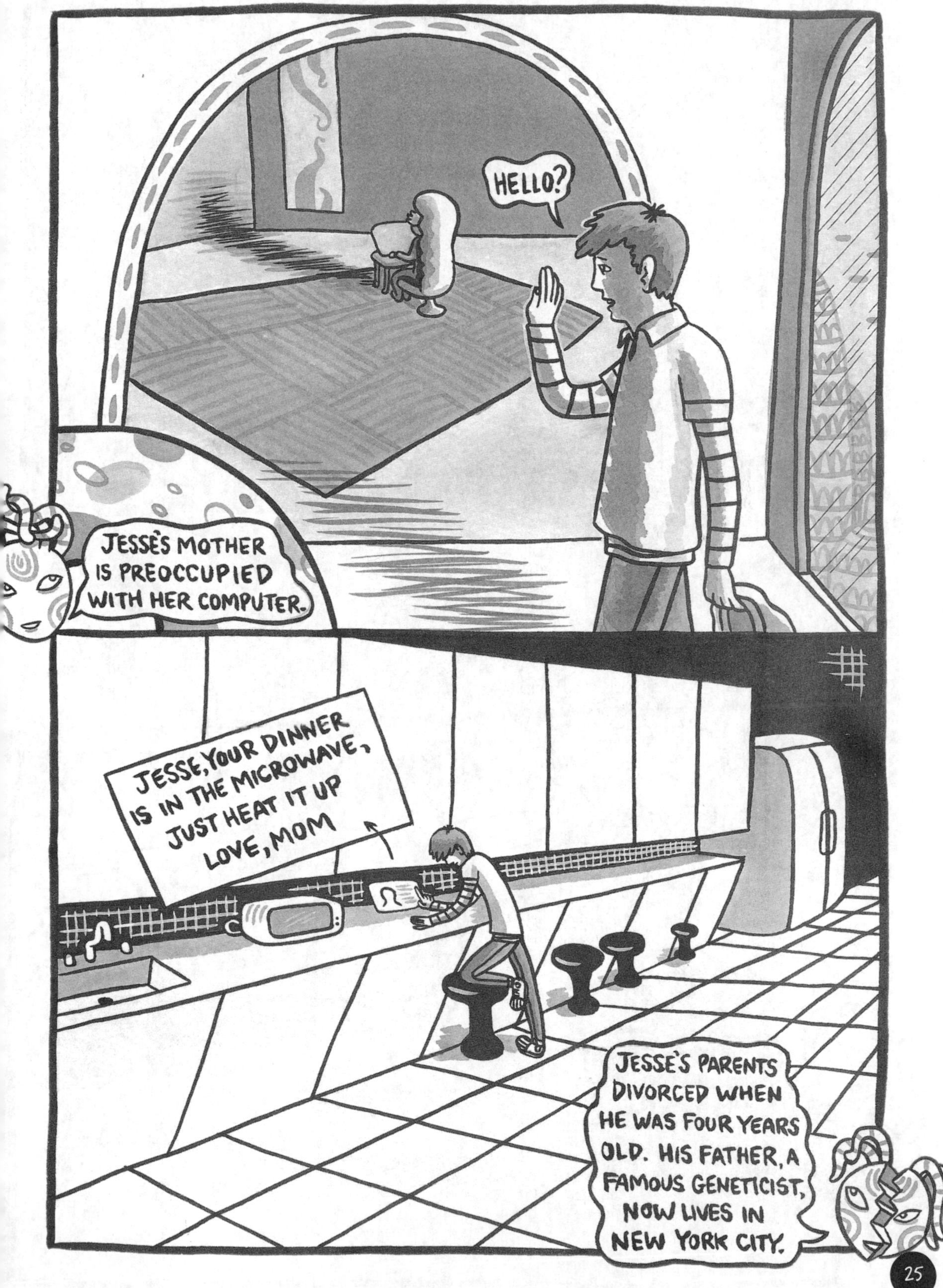
HELLO?
JESSE'S MOTHER IS PREOCCUPIED WITH HER COMPUTER.
JESSE, YOUR DINNER IS IN THE MICROWAVE, JUST HEAT IT UP LOVE, MOM
JESSE'S PARENTS DIVORCED WHEN HE WAS FOUR YEARS OLD. HIS FATHER, A FAMOUS GENETICIST, NOW LIVES IN NEW YORK CITY.

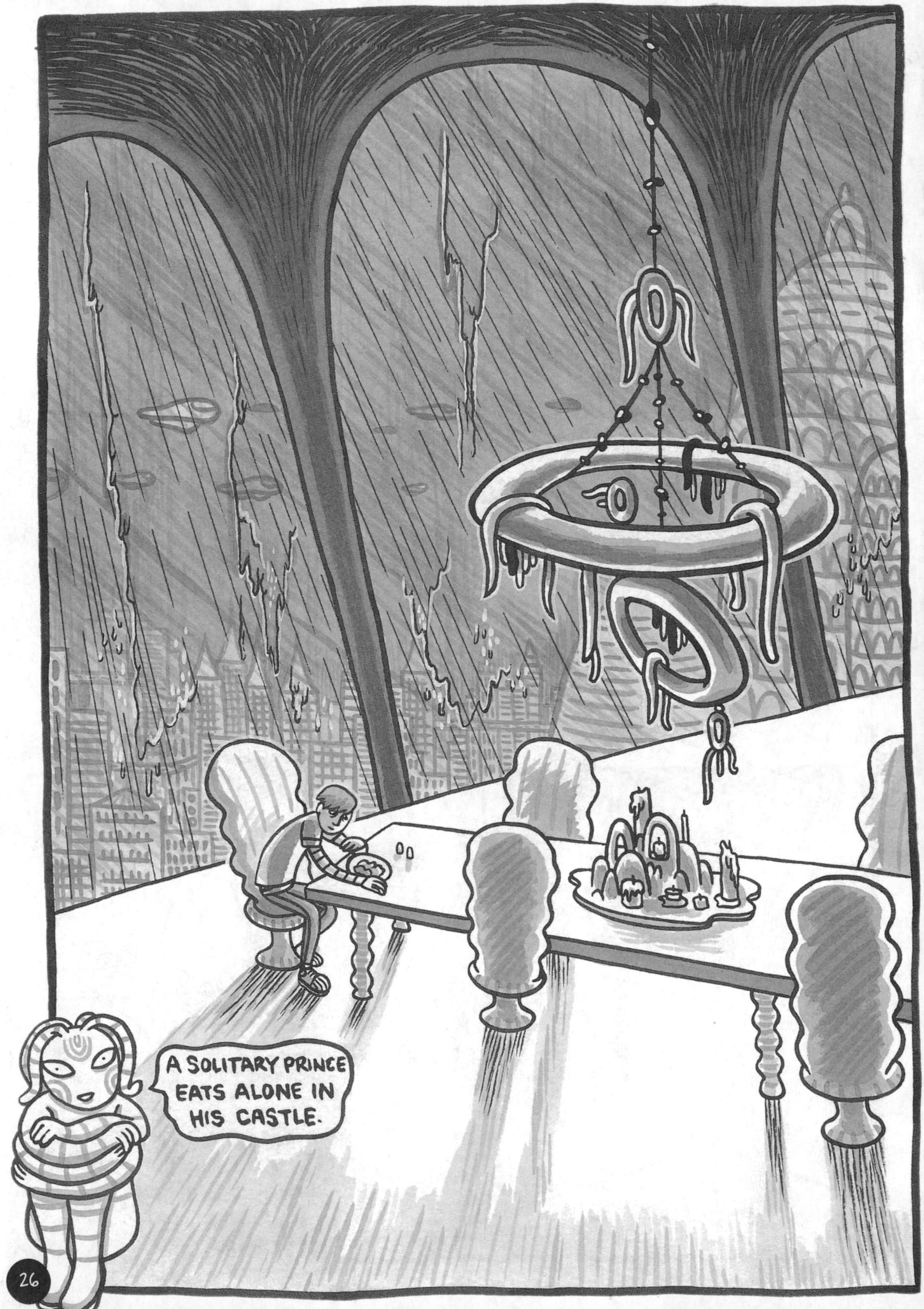
A SOLITARY PRINCE EATS ALONE IN HIS CASTLE.

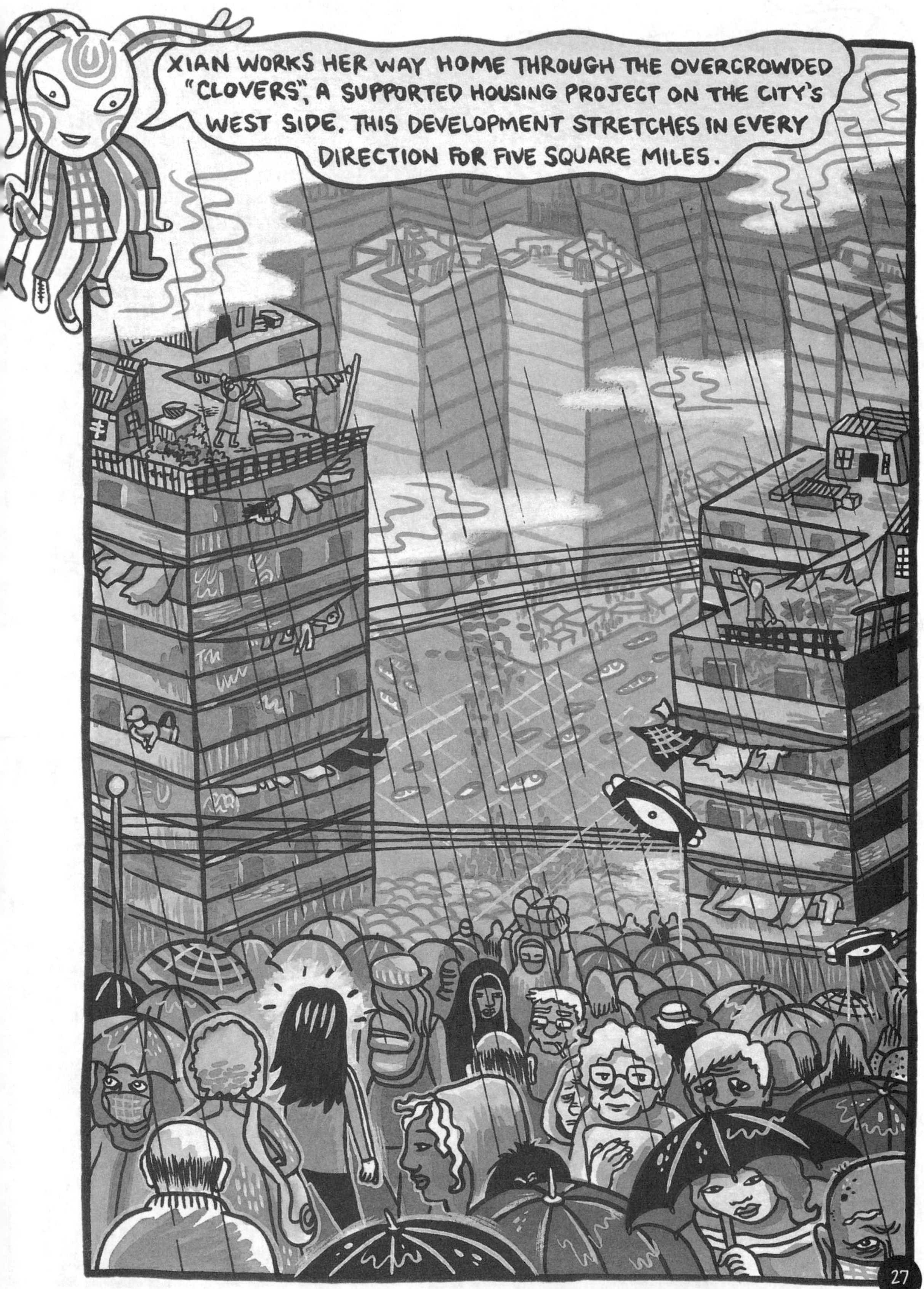
XIAN WORKS HER WAY HOME THROUGH THE OVERCROWDED "CLOVERS", A SUPPORTED HOUSING PROJECT ON THE CITY'S WEST SIDE. THIS DEVELOPMENT STRETCHES IN EVERY DIRECTION FOR FIVE SQUARE MILES.

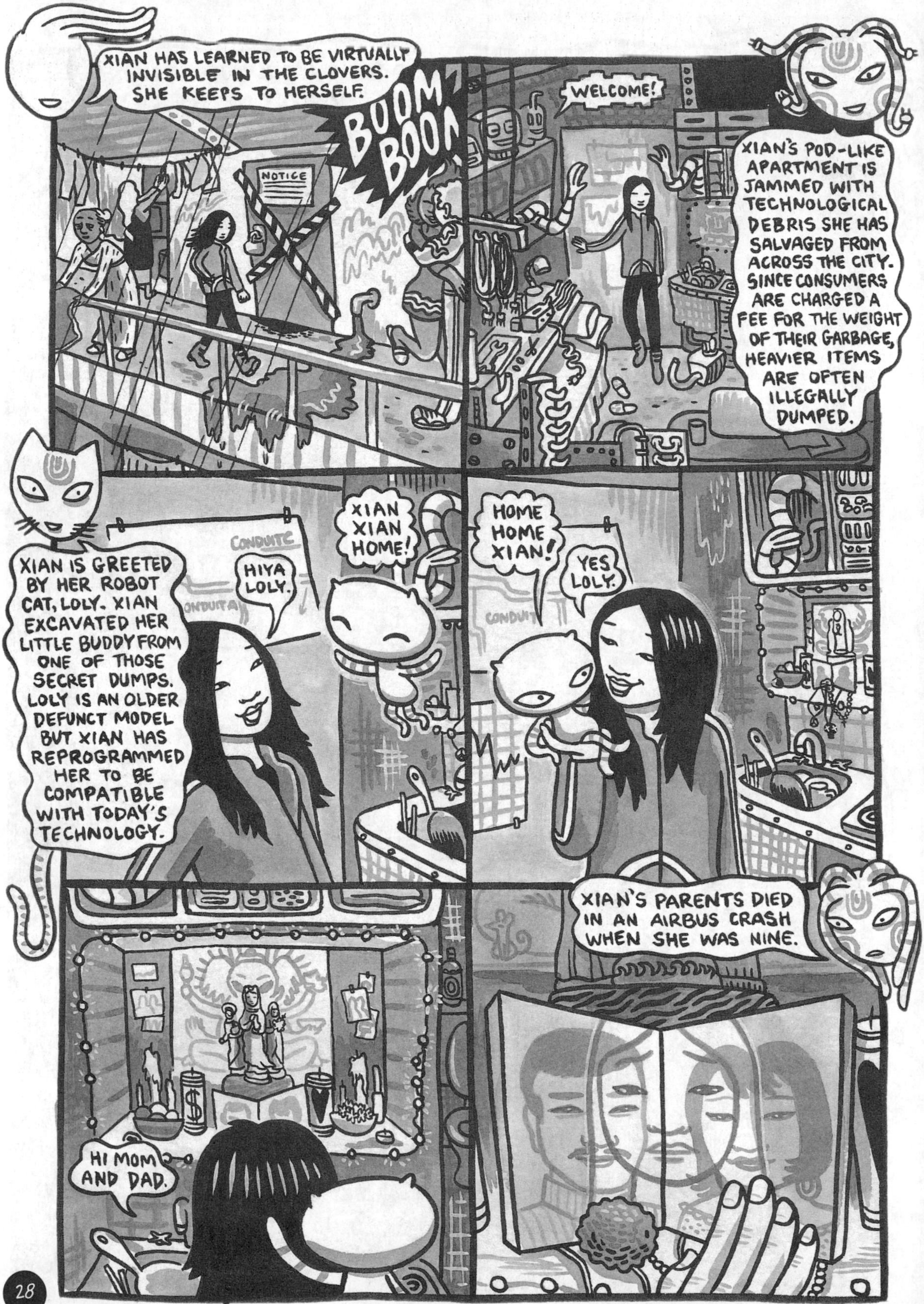

XIAN HAS LEARNED TO BE VIRTUALLY INVISIBLE IN THE CLOVERS. SHE KEEPS TO HERSELF.
NOTICE
BOOM BOOM
WELCOME!
XIAN'S POD-LIKE APARTMENT IS JAMMED WITH TECHNOLOGICAL DEBRIS SHE HAS SALVAGED FROM ACROSS THE CITY. SINCE CONSUMERS ARE CHARGED A FEE FOR THE WEIGHT OF THEIR GARBAGE, HEAVIER ITEMS ARE OFTEN ILLEGALLY DUMPED.
XIAN IS GREETED BY HER ROBOT CAT, LOLY. XIAN EXCAVATED HER LITTLE BUDDY FROM ONE OF THOSE SECRET DUMPS. LOLY IS AN OLDER DEFUNCT MODEL BUT XIAN HAS REPROGRAMMED HER TO BE COMPATIBLE WITH TODAY'S TECHNOLOGY.
CONDUITC
CONDUITA
XIAN XIAN HOME!
HIYA LOLY.
HOME HOME XIAN!
YES LOLY.
CONDUIT
HI MOM AND DAD.
XIAN'S PARENTS DIED IN AN AIRBUS CRASH WHEN SHE WAS NINE.

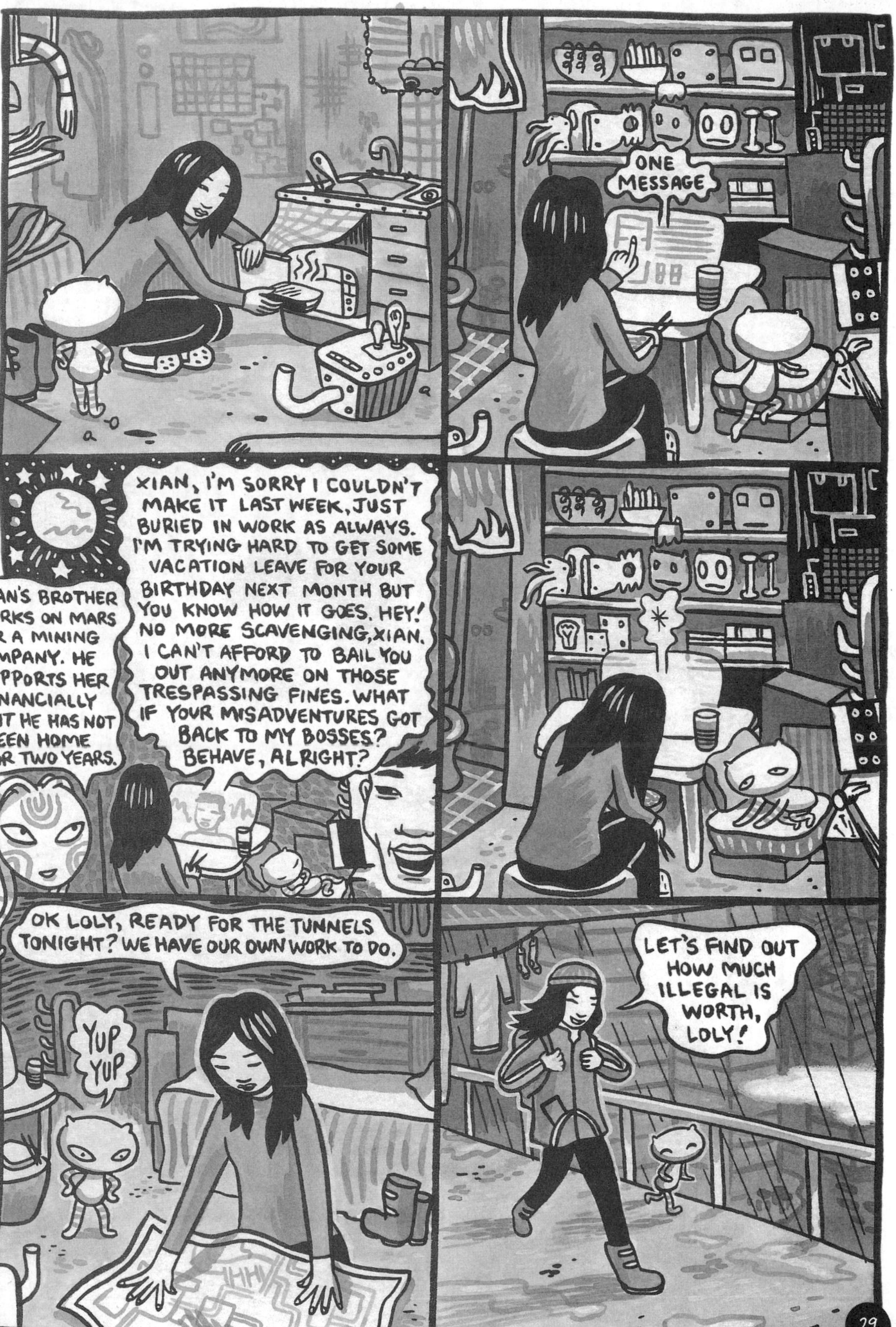
ONE MESSAGE
XIAN'S BROTHER WORKS ON MARS FOR A MINING COMPANY. HE SUPPORTS HER FINANCIALLY BUT HE HAS NOT BEEN HOME FOR TWO YEARS.
XIAN, I'M SORRY I COULDN'T MAKE IT LAST WEEK, JUST BURIED IN WORK AS ALWAYS. I'M TRYING HARD TO GET SOME VACATION LEAVE FOR YOUR BIRTHDAY NEXT MONTH BUT YOU KNOW HOW IT GOES. HEY! NO MORE SCAVENGING, XIAN. I CAN'T AFFORD TO BAIL YOU OUT ANYMORE ON THOSE TRESPASSING FINES. WHAT IF YOUR MISADVENTURES GOT BACK TO MY BOSSES? BEHAVE, ALRIGHT?
OK LOLY, READY FOR THE TUNNELS TONIGHT? WE HAVE OUR OWN WORK TO DO.
YUP YUP
LET'S FIND OUT HOW MUCH ILLEGAL IS WORTH, LOLY!

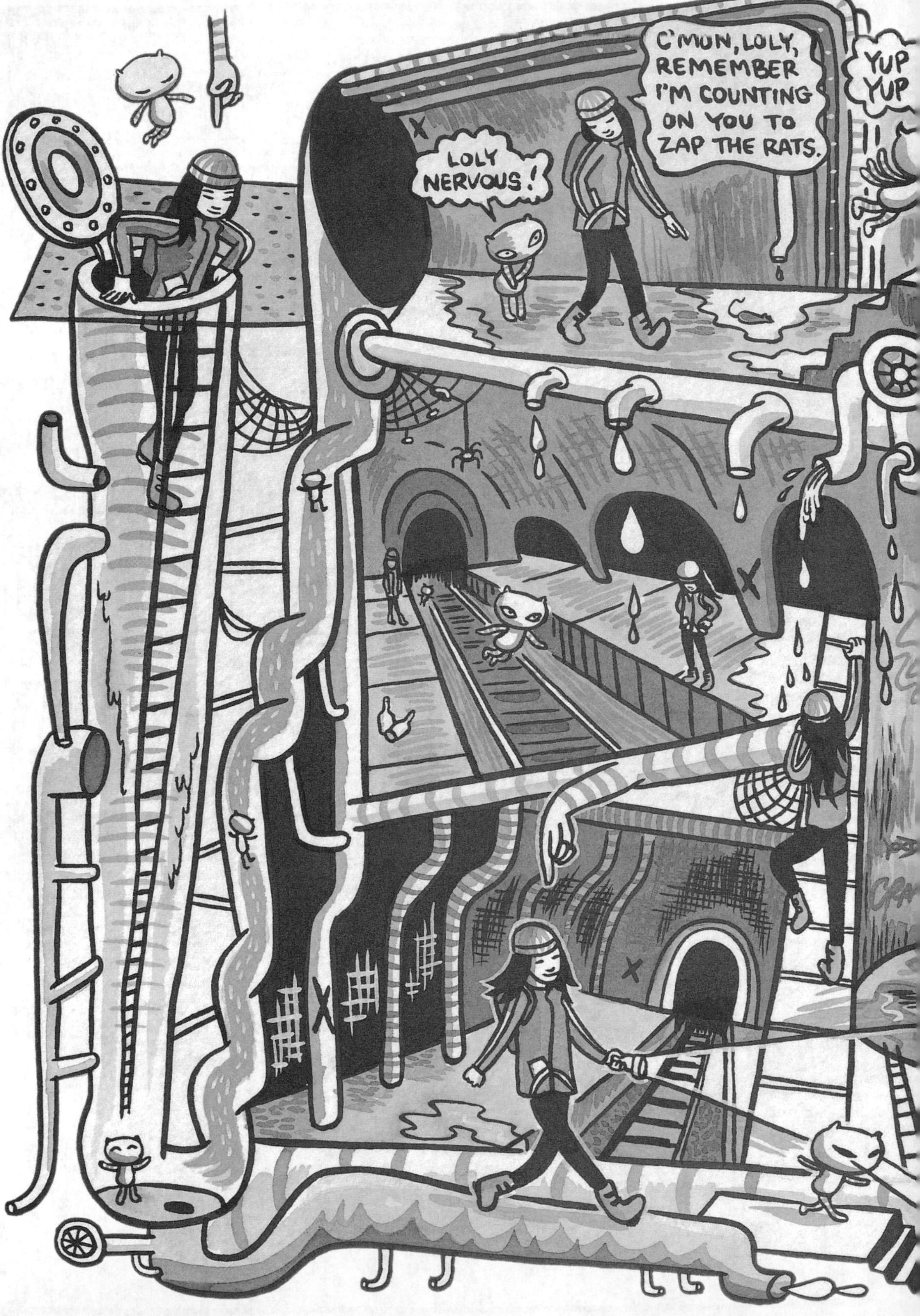
LOLY NERVOUS!
C'MON, LOLY, REMEMBER I'M COUNTING ON YOU TO ZAP THE RATS.
YUP YUP

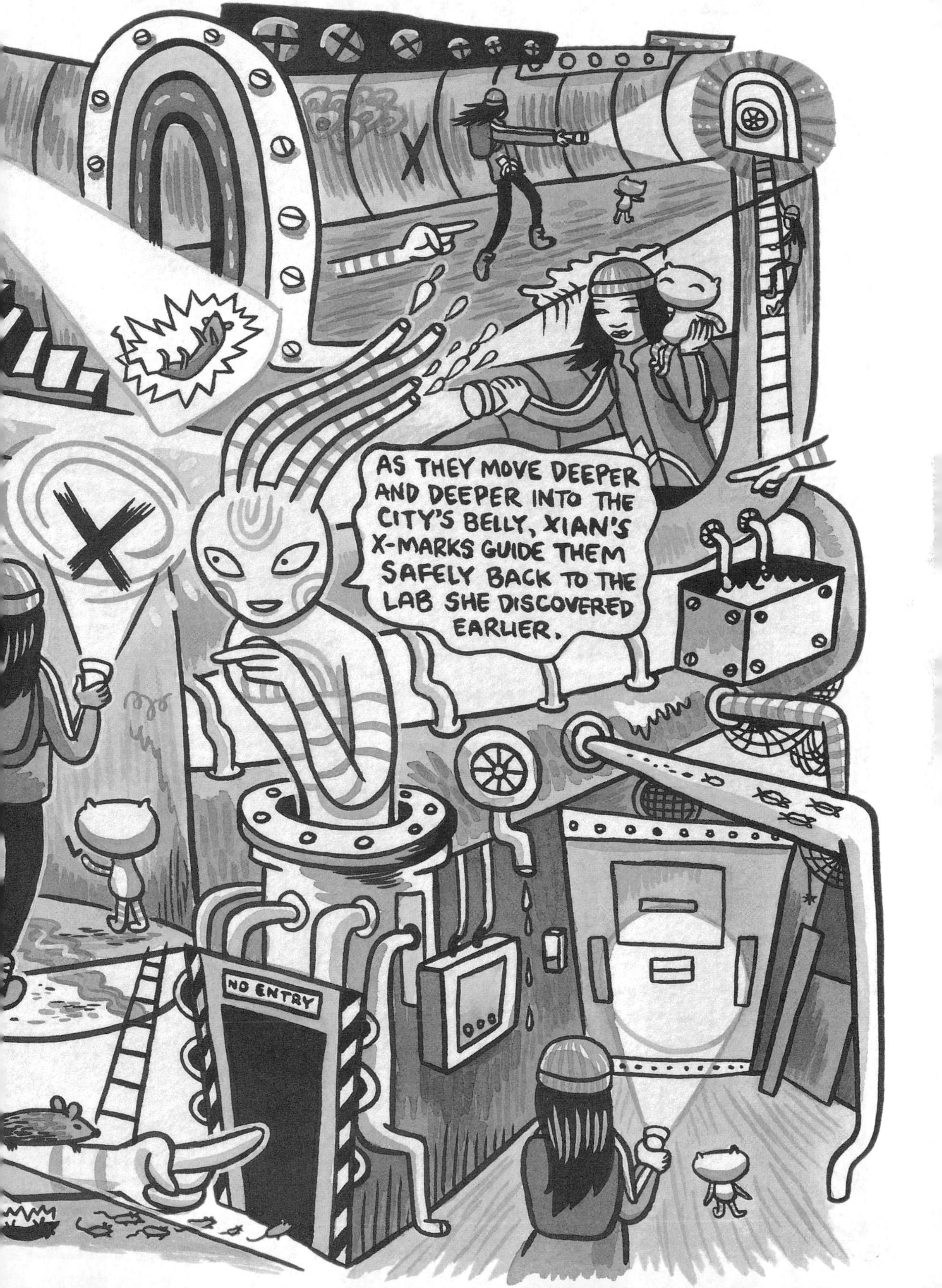
AS THEY MOVE DEEPER AND DEEPER INTO THE CITY'S BELLY, XIAN'S X-MARKS GUIDE THEM SAFELY BACK TO THE LAB SHE DISCOVERED EARLIER.
NO ENTRY

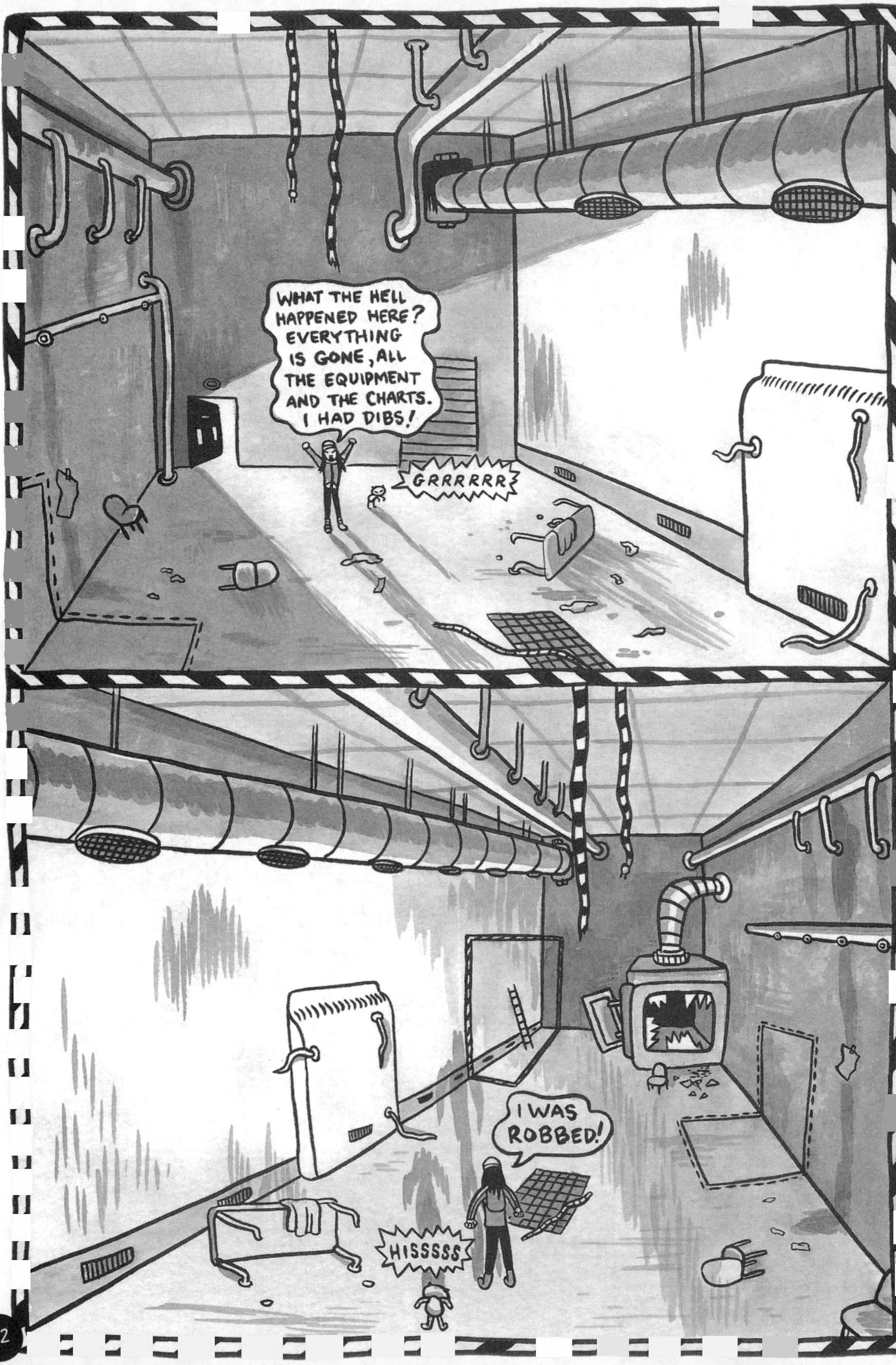
WHAT THE HELL HAPPENED HERE? EVERYTHING IS GONE, ALL THE EQUIPMENT AND THE CHARTS. I HAD DIBS!
GRRRRRR
I WAS ROBBED!
HISSSSS

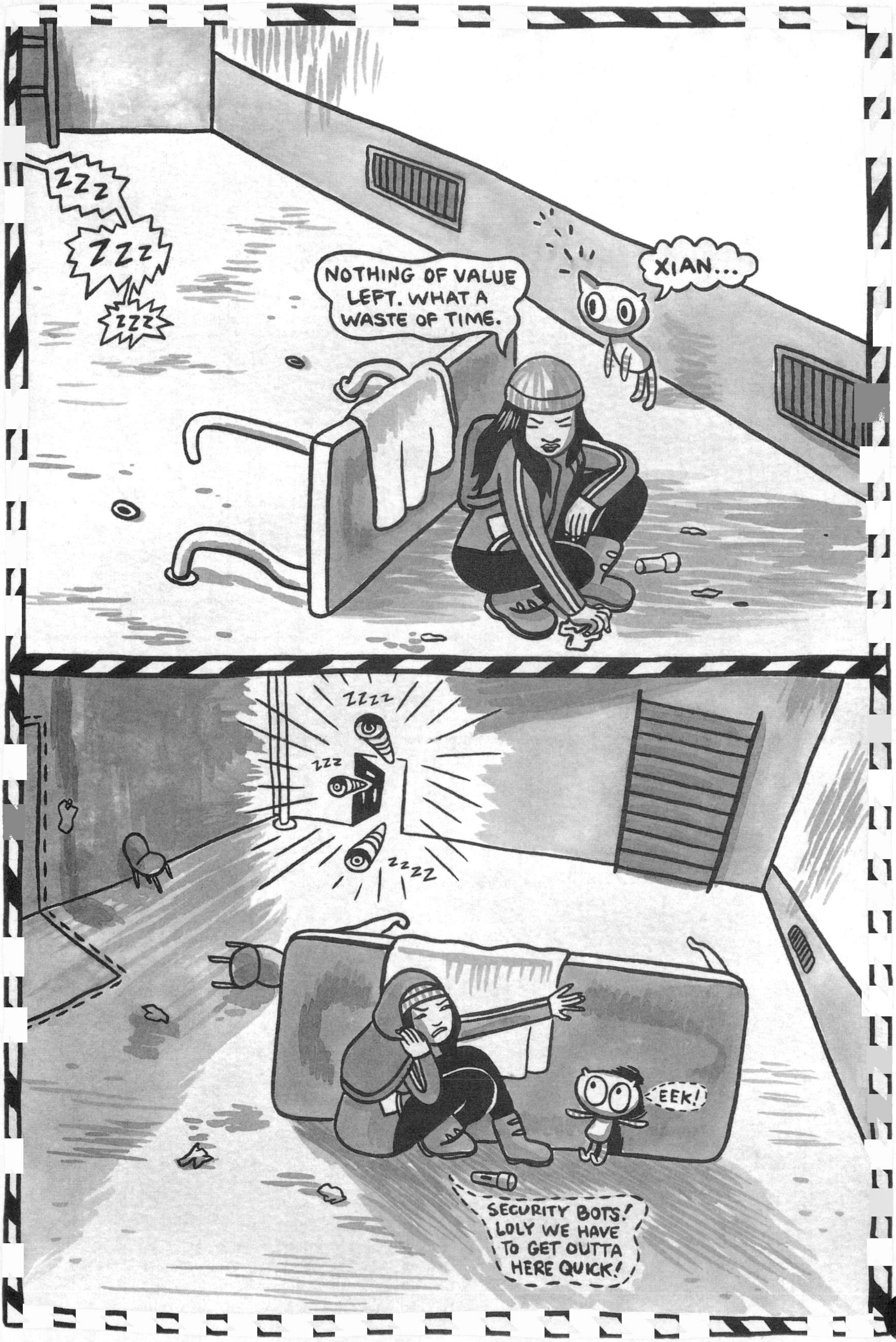
ZZZ
ZZZ
ZZZ
NOTHING OF VALUE LEFT. WHAT A WASTE OF TIME.
XIAN...
ZZZZ
ZZZ
ZZZZ
EEK!
SECURITY BOTS! LOLY WE HAVE TO GET OUTTA HERE QUICK!

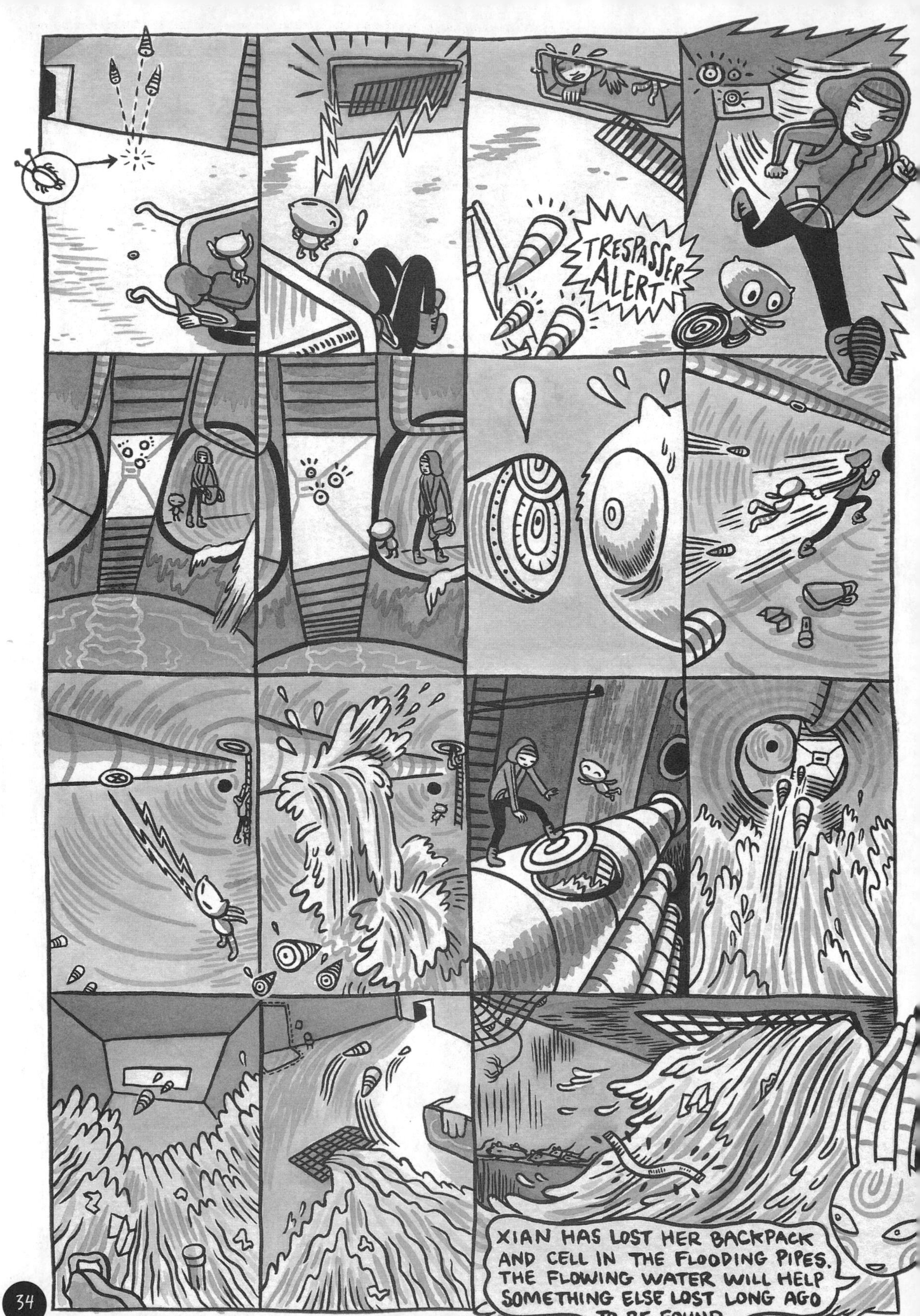
TRESPASSER ALERT
XIAN HAS LOST HER BACKPACK AND CELL IN THE FLOODING PIPES. THE FLOWING WATER WILL HELP SOMETHING ELSE LOST LONG AGO TO BE FOUND.

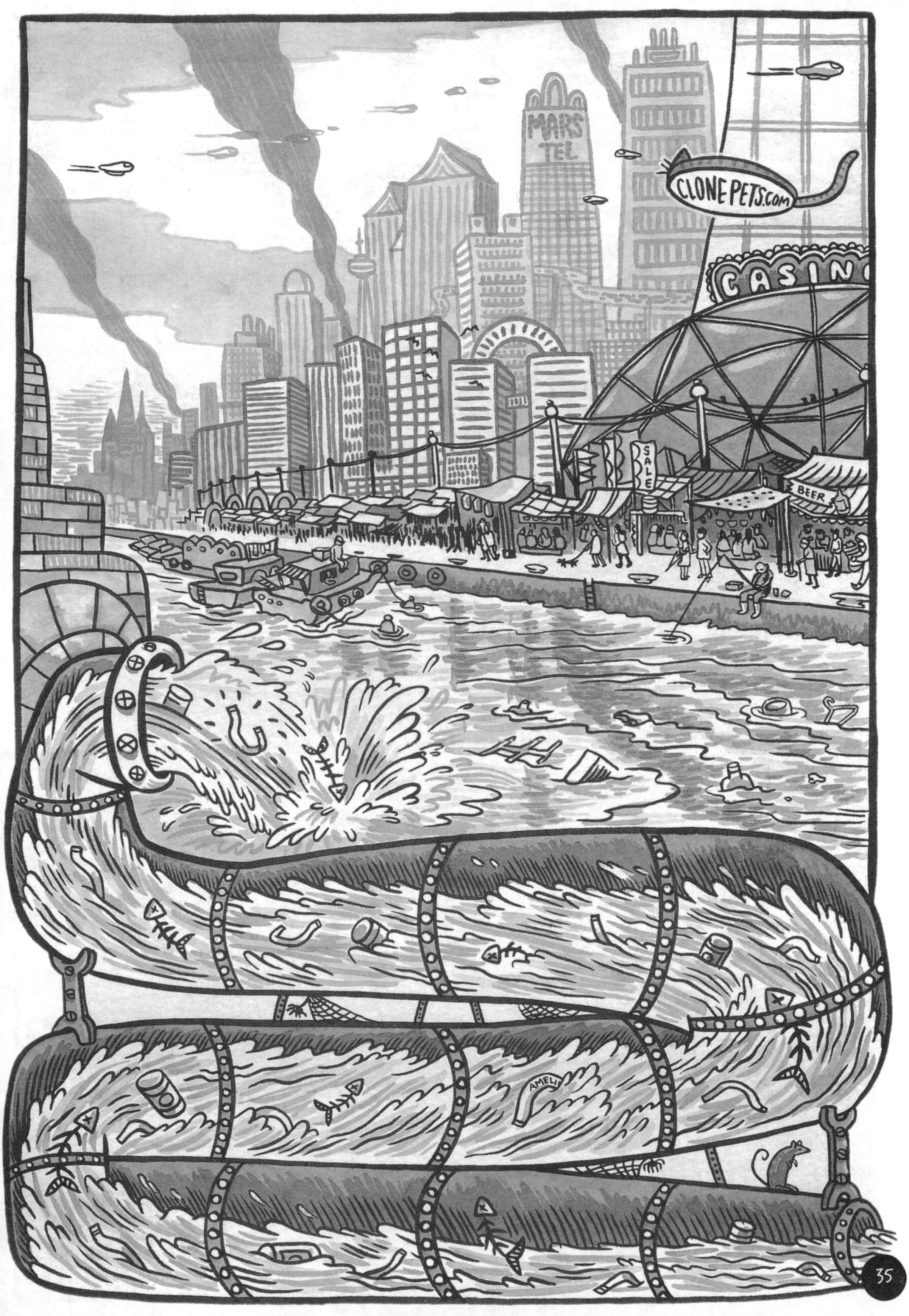
MARS TEL
CLONEPETS.com
CASINO
SALE
BEER
AMELI

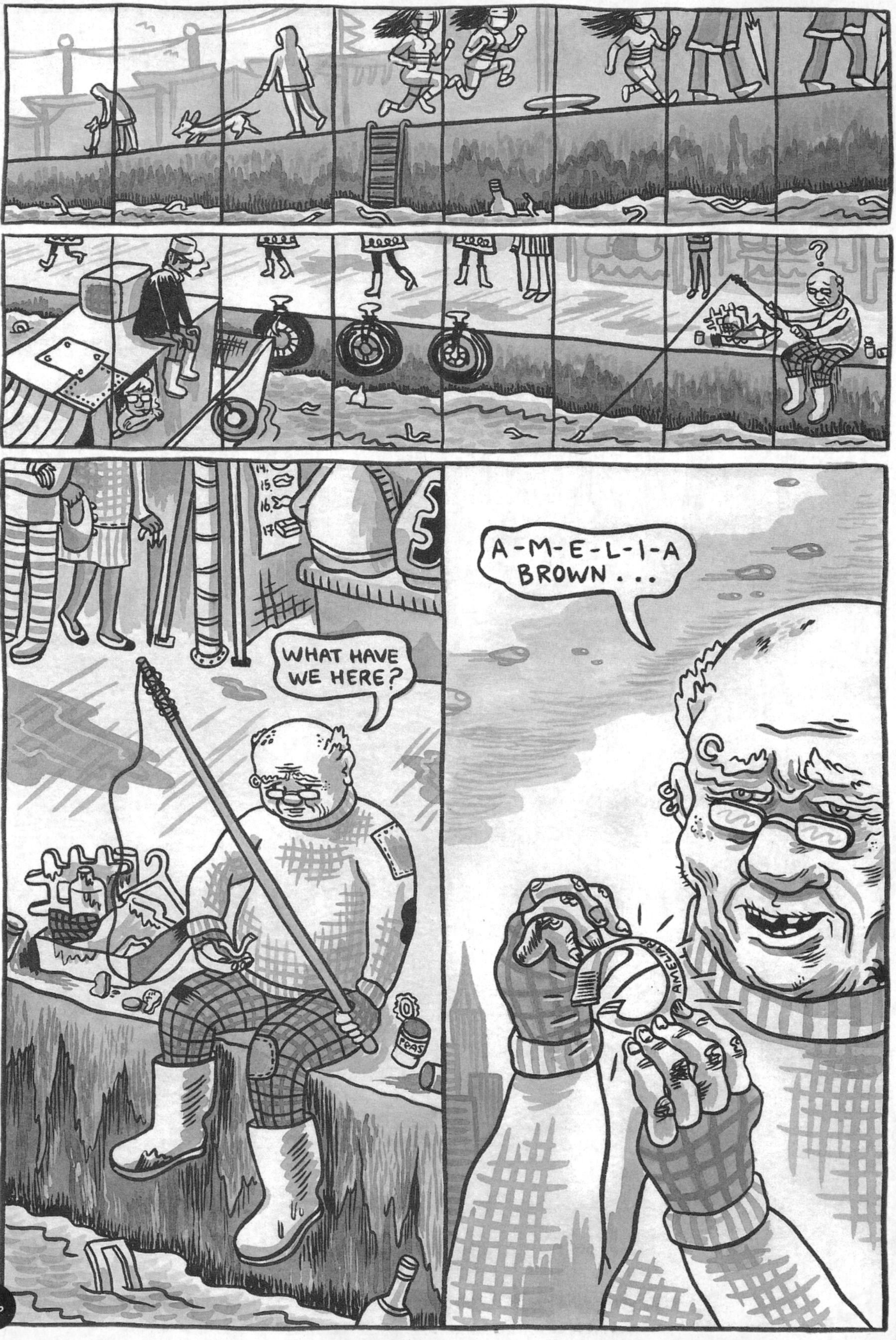
WHAT HAVE WE HERE?
A-M-E-L-I-A BROWN . . .

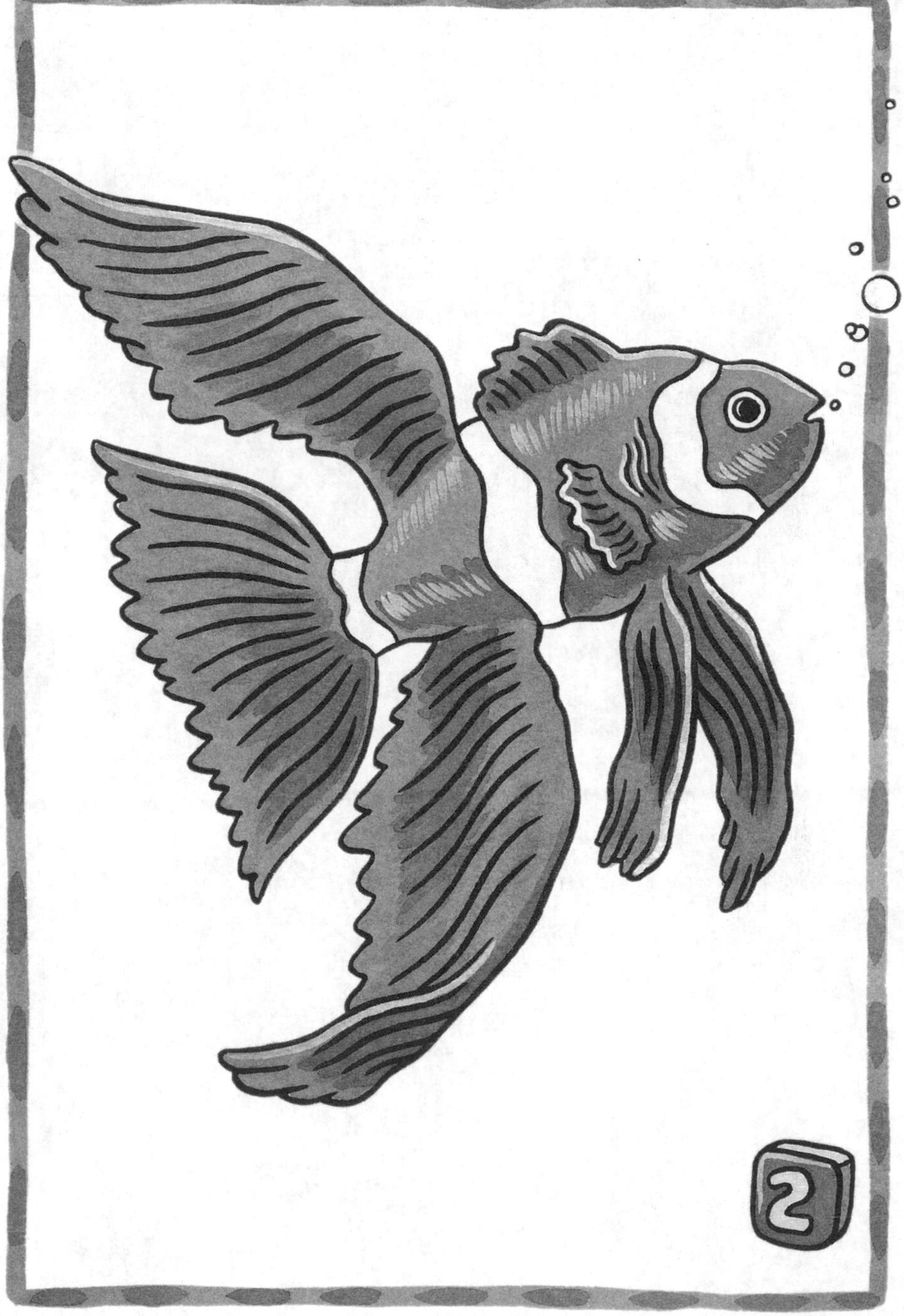
2

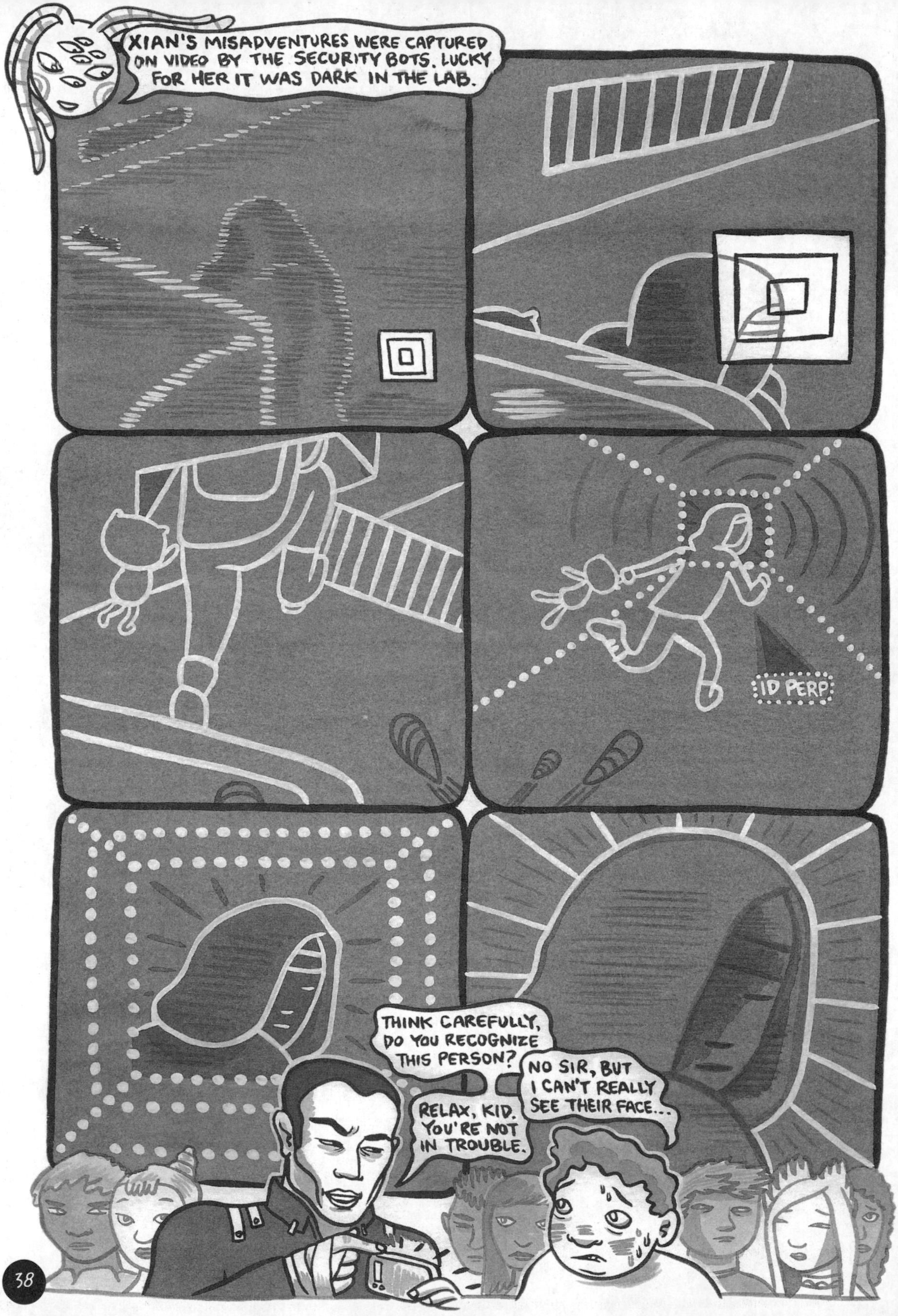
XIAN'S MISADVENTURES WERE CAPTURED ON VIDEO BY THE SECURITY BOTS. LUCKY FOR HER IT WAS DARK IN THE LAB.
ID PERP
THINK CAREFULLY, DO YOU RECOGNIZE THIS PERSON?
NO SIR, BUT I CAN'T REALLY SEE THEIR FACE...
RELAX, KID. YOU'RE NOT IN TROUBLE.

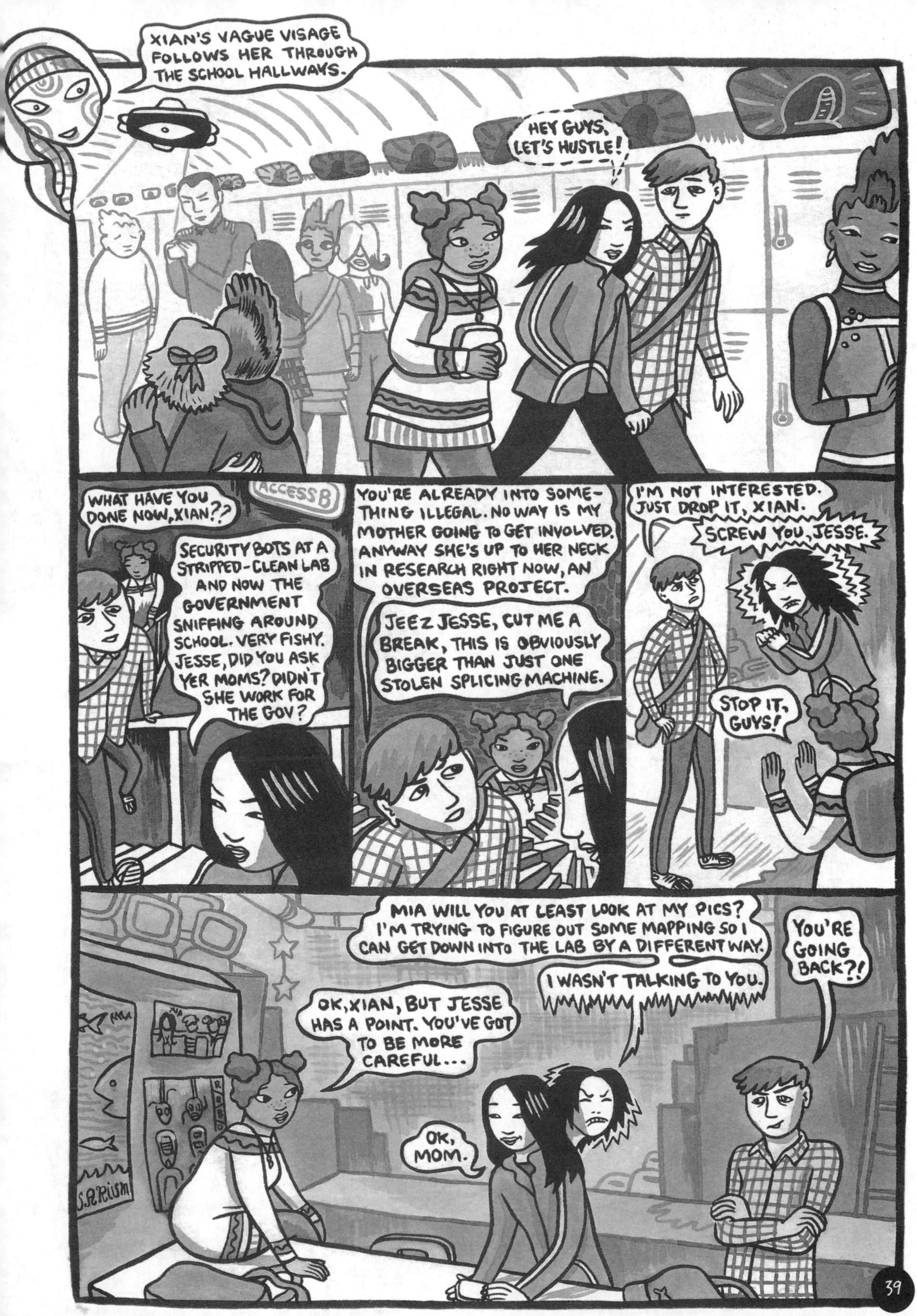
XIAN'S VAGUE VISAGE FOLLOWS HER THROUGH THE SCHOOL HALLWAYS.
HEY GUYS, LET'S HUSTLE!
ACCESS B
WHAT HAVE YOU DONE NOW, XIAN??
SECURITY BOTS AT A STRIPPED-CLEAN LAB AND NOW THE GOVERNMENT SNIFFING AROUND SCHOOL. VERY FISHY. JESSE, DID YOU ASK YER MOMS? DIDN'T SHE WORK FOR THE GOV?
YOU'RE ALREADY INTO SOMETHING ILLEGAL. NO WAY IS MY MOTHER GOING TO GET INVOLVED. ANYWAY SHE'S UP TO HER NECK IN RESEARCH RIGHT NOW, AN OVERSEAS PROJECT.
JEEZ JESSE, CUT ME A BREAK, THIS IS OBVIOUSLY BIGGER THAN JUST ONE STOLEN SPLICING MACHINE.
I'M NOT INTERESTED. JUST DROP IT, XIAN.
SCREW YOU, JESSE.
STOP IT, GUYS!
MIA WILL YOU AT LEAST LOOK AT MY PICS? I'M TRYING TO FIGURE OUT SOME MAPPING SO I CAN GET DOWN INTO THE LAB BY A DIFFERENT WAY.
YOU'RE GOING BACK?!
I WASN'T TALKING TO YOU.
OK, XIAN, BUT JESSE HAS A POINT. YOU'VE GOT TO BE MORE CAREFUL...
OK, MOM.
S.A.Rism

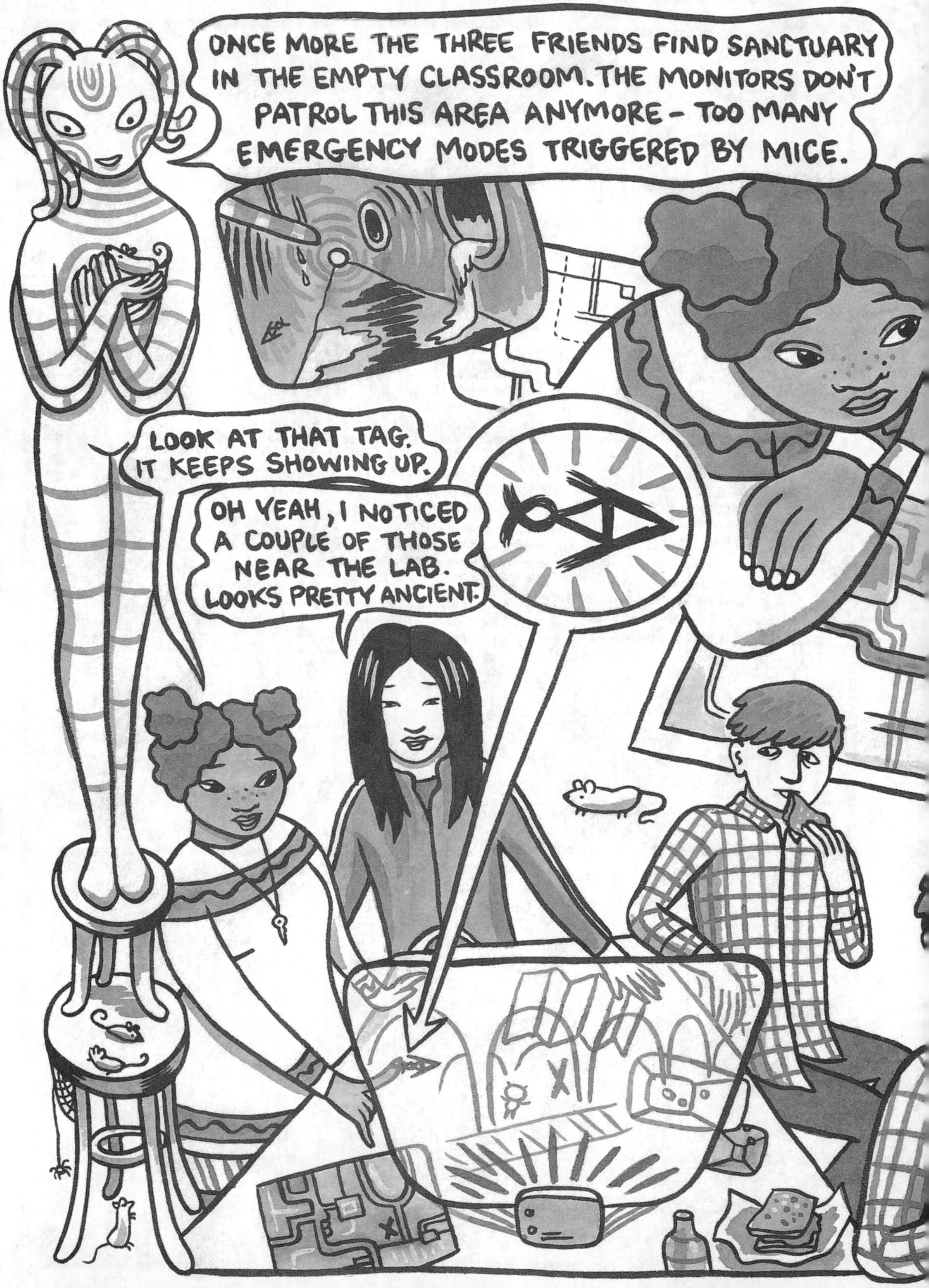
ONCE MORE THE THREE FRIENDS FIND SANCTUARY IN THE EMPTY CLASSROOM. THE MONITORS DON'T PATROL THIS AREA ANYMORE - TOO MANY EMERGENCY MODES TRIGGERED BY MICE.
LOOK AT THAT TAG. IT KEEPS SHOWING UP.
OH YEAH, I NOTICED A COUPLE OF THOSE NEAR THE LAB. LOOKS PRETTY ANCIENT.

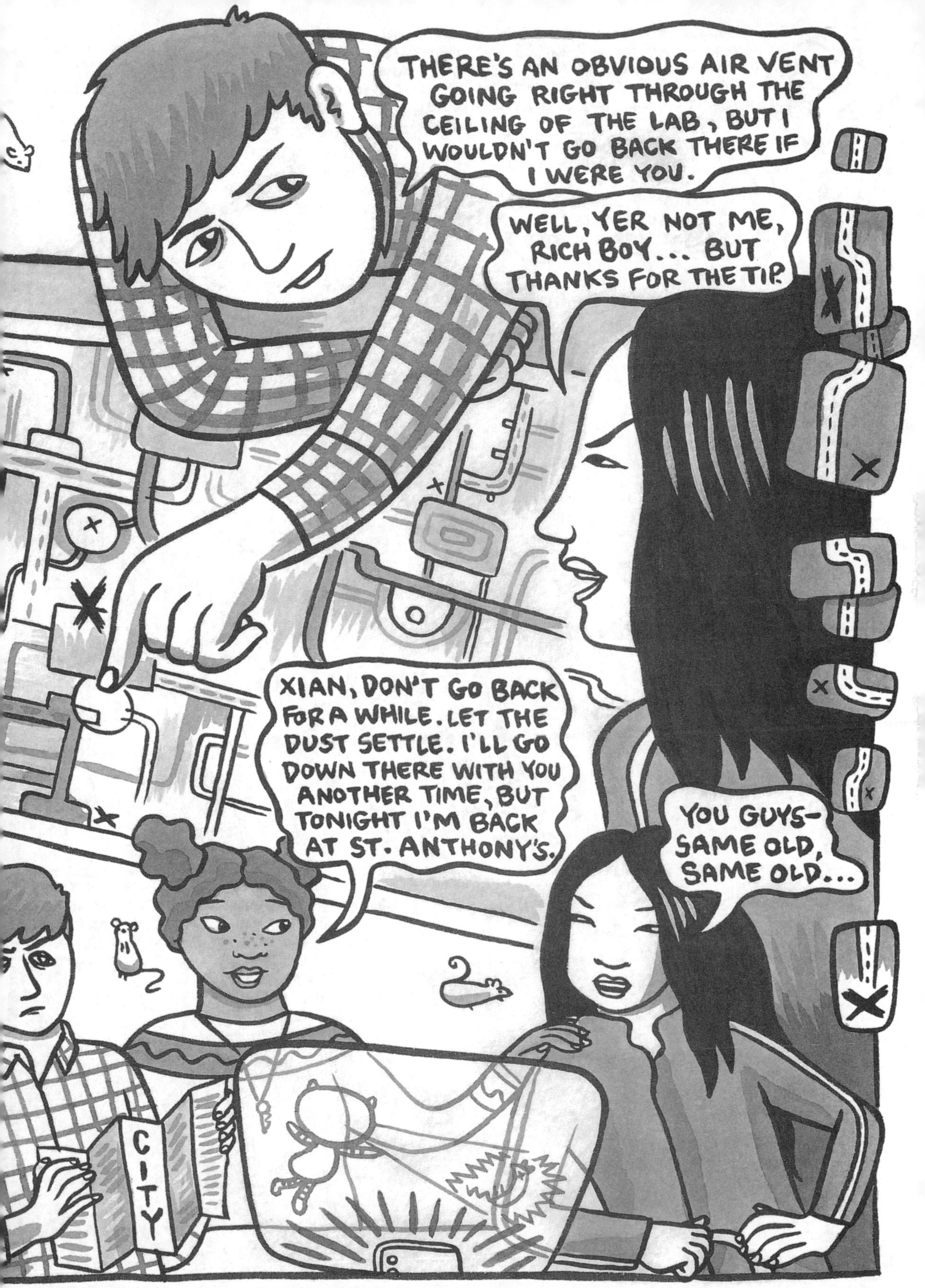
THERE'S AN OBVIOUS AIR VENT GOING RIGHT THROUGH THE CEILING OF THE LAB, BUT I WOULDN'T GO BACK THERE IF I WERE YOU.
WELL, YER NOT ME, RICH BOY... BUT THANKS FOR THE TIP.
XIAN, DON'T GO BACK FOR A WHILE. LET THE DUST SETTLE. I'LL GO DOWN THERE WITH YOU ANOTHER TIME, BUT TONIGHT I'M BACK AT ST. ANTHONY'S.
YOU GUYS-SAME OLD, SAME OLD...
CITY

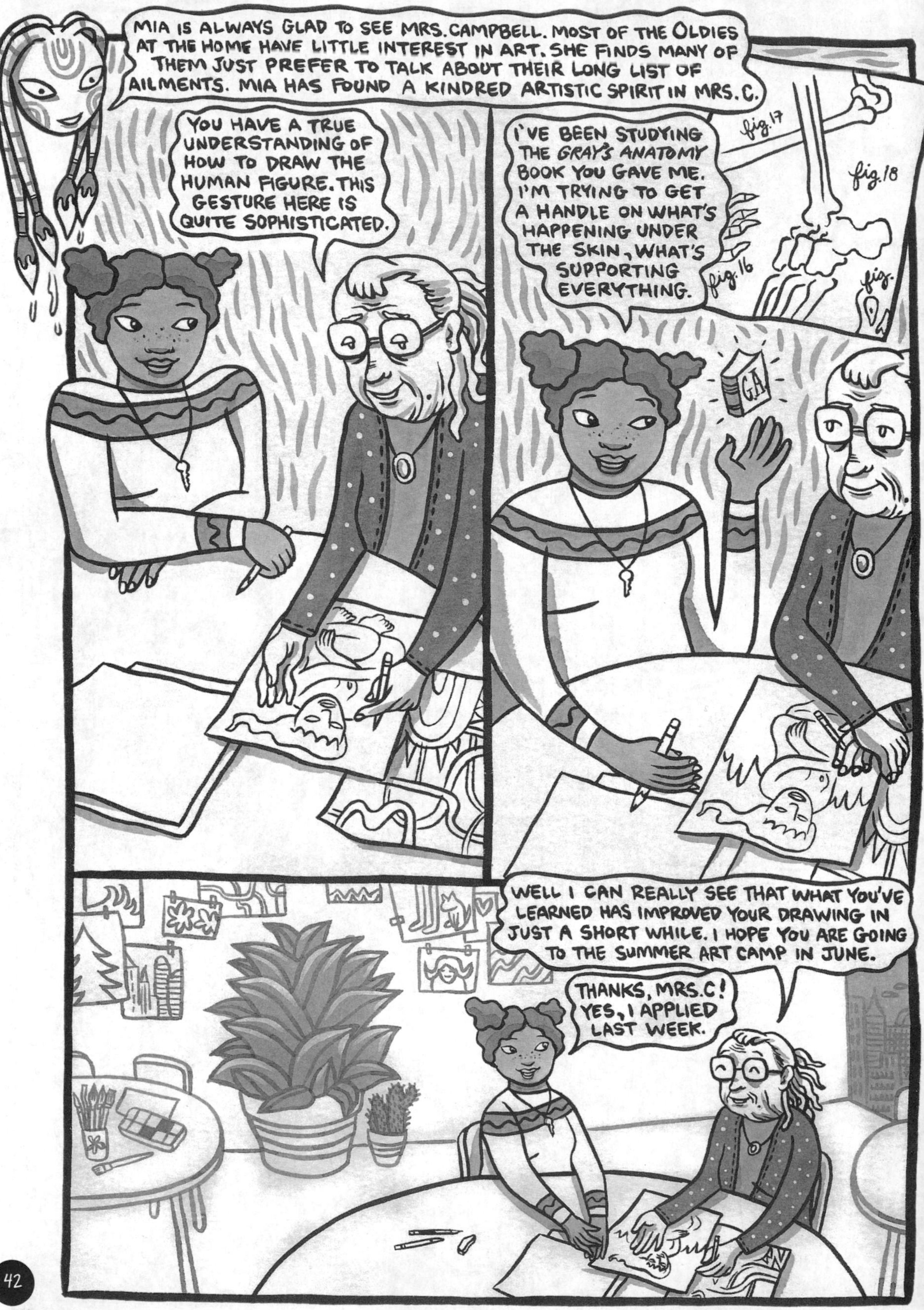
MIA IS ALWAYS GLAD TO SEE MRS. CAMPBELL. MOST OF THE OLDIES AT THE HOME HAVE LITTLE INTEREST IN ART. SHE FINDS MANY OF THEM JUST PREFER TO TALK ABOUT THEIR LONG LIST OF AILMENTS. MIA HAS FOUND A KINDRED ARTISTIC SPIRIT IN MRS. C.
YOU HAVE A TRUE UNDERSTANDING OF HOW TO DRAW THE HUMAN FIGURE. THIS GESTURE HERE IS QUITE SOPHISTICATED.
I'VE BEEN STUDYING THE *GRAY'S ANATOMY* BOOK YOU GAVE ME. I'M TRYING TO GET A HANDLE ON WHAT'S HAPPENING UNDER THE SKIN, WHAT'S SUPPORTING EVERYTHING.
fig. 17
fig. 18
fig. 16
fig.
G.A.
WELL I CAN REALLY SEE THAT WHAT YOU'VE LEARNED HAS IMPROVED YOUR DRAWING IN JUST A SHORT WHILE. I HOPE YOU ARE GOING TO THE SUMMER ART CAMP IN JUNE.
THANKS, MRS.C! YES, I APPLIED LAST WEEK.

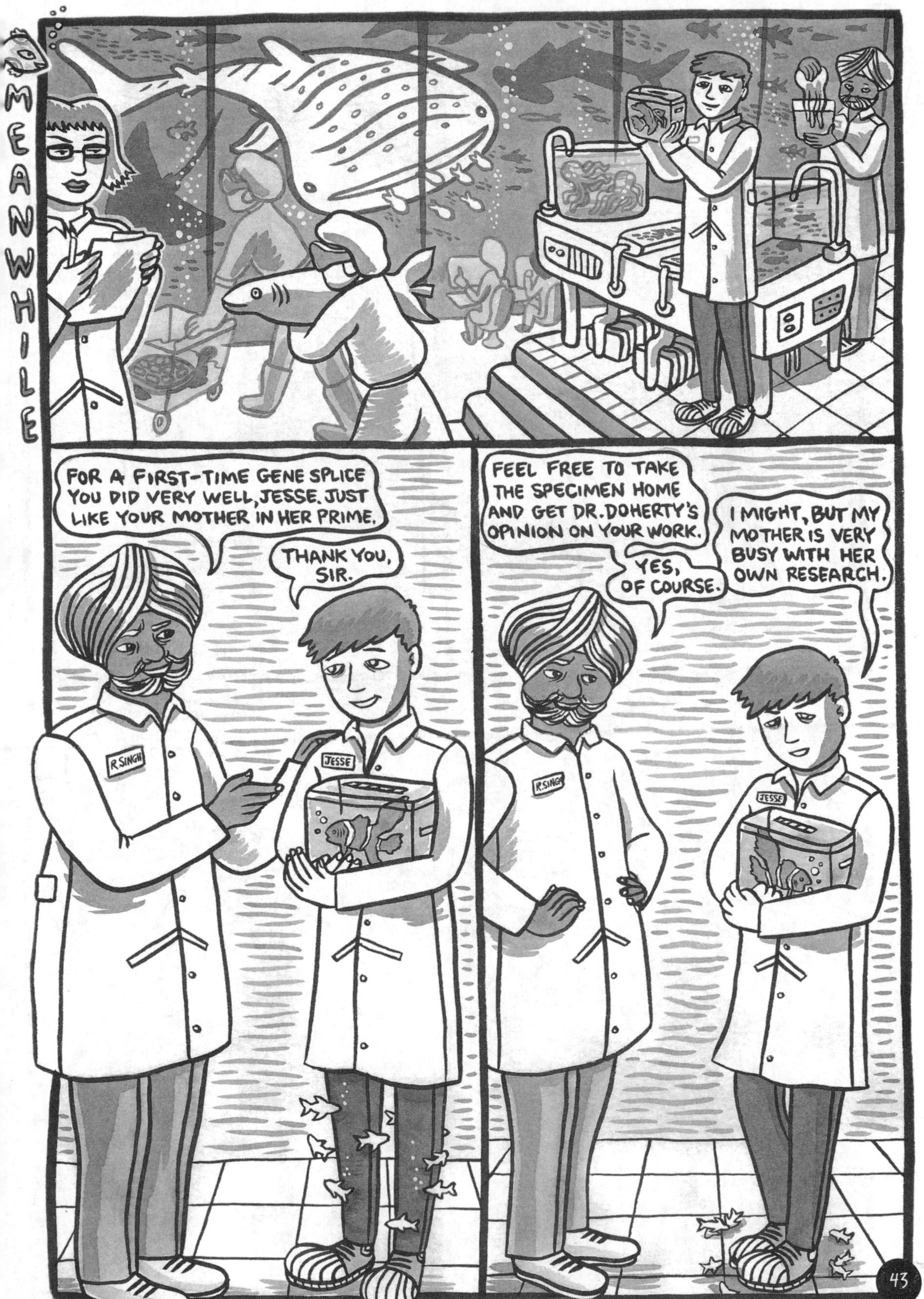
MEANWHILE
FOR A FIRST-TIME GENE SPLICE YOU DID VERY WELL, JESSE. JUST LIKE YOUR MOTHER IN HER PRIME.
THANK YOU, SIR.
R. SINGH
JESSE
FEEL FREE TO TAKE THE SPECIMEN HOME AND GET DR. DOHERTY'S OPINION ON YOUR WORK.
YES, OF COURSE.
I MIGHT, BUT MY MOTHER IS VERY BUSY WITH HER OWN RESEARCH.
R.SINGH
JESSE

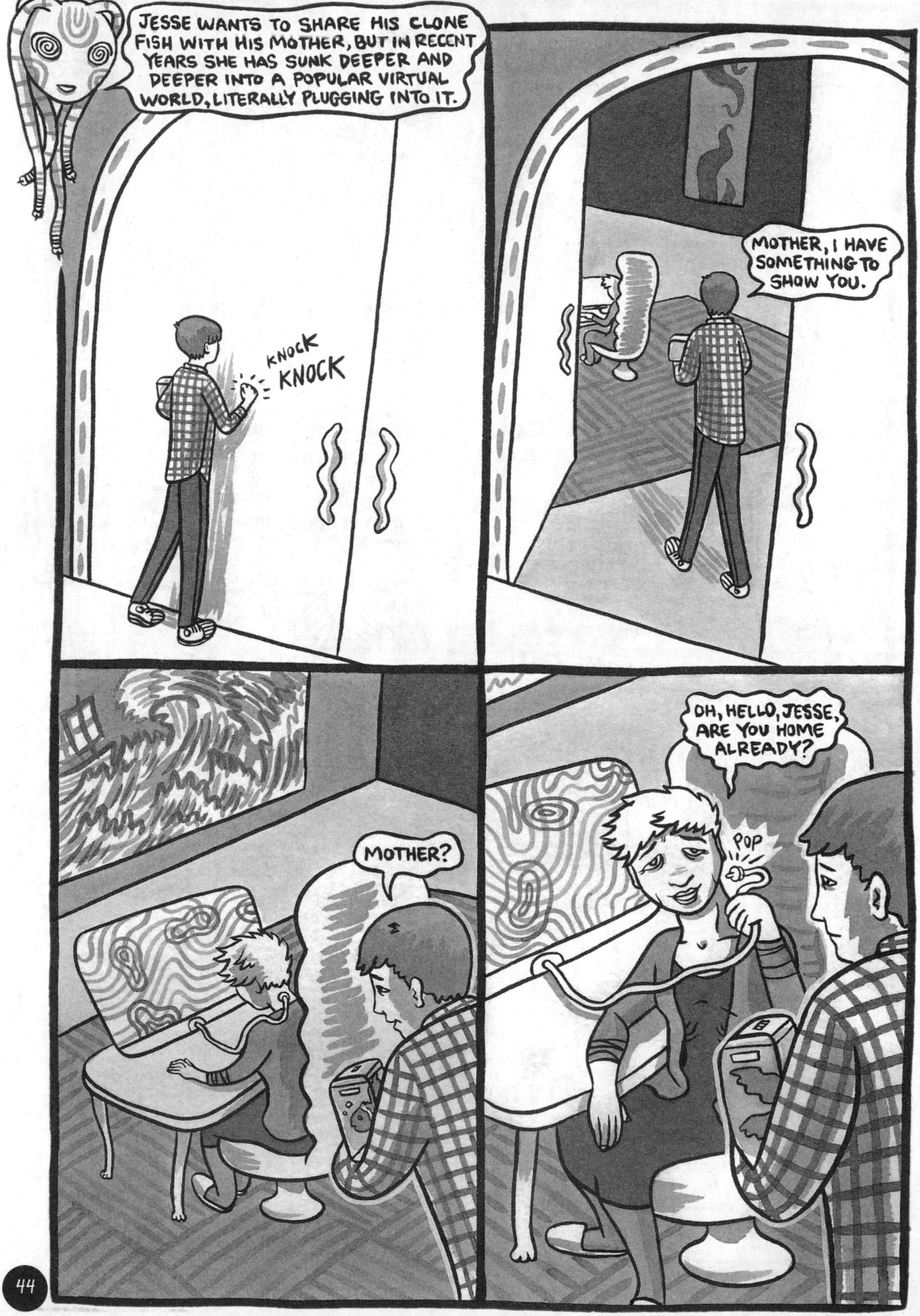
JESSE WANTS TO SHARE HIS CLONE FISH WITH HIS MOTHER, BUT IN RECENT YEARS SHE HAS SUNK DEEPER AND DEEPER INTO A POPULAR VIRTUAL WORLD, LITERALLY PLUGGING INTO IT.
KNOCK KNOCK
MOTHER, I HAVE SOMETHING TO SHOW YOU.
MOTHER?
POP
OH, HELLO, JESSE, ARE YOU HOME ALREADY?

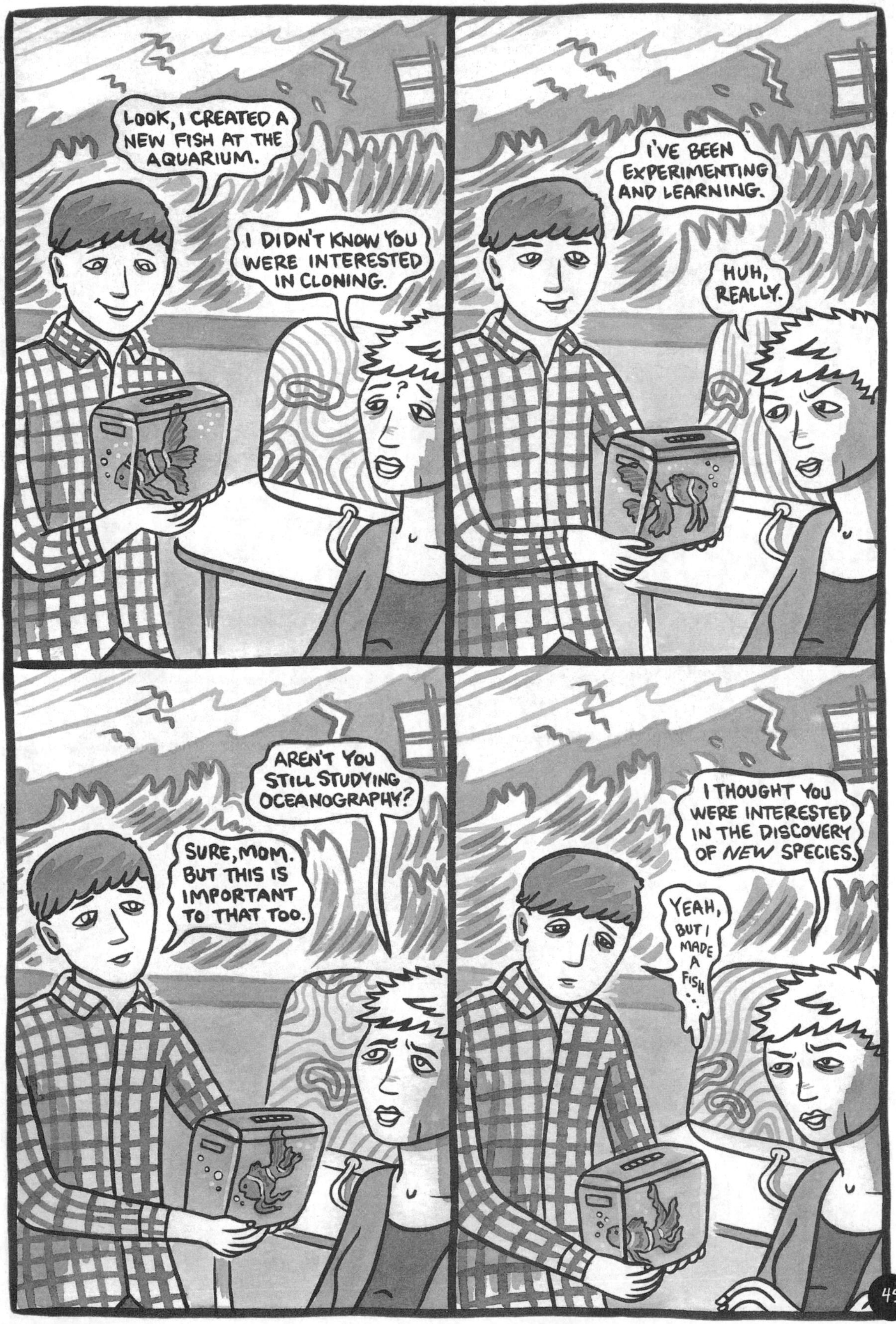
LOOK, I CREATED A NEW FISH AT THE AQUARIUM.
I DIDN'T KNOW YOU WERE INTERESTED IN CLONING.
I'VE BEEN EXPERIMENTING AND LEARNING.
HUH, REALLY.
AREN'T YOU STILL STUDYING OCEANOGRAPHY?
SURE, MOM. BUT THIS IS IMPORTANT TO THAT TOO.
I THOUGHT YOU WERE INTERESTED IN THE DISCOVERY OF *NEW* SPECIES.
YEAH, BUT I MADE A FISH...

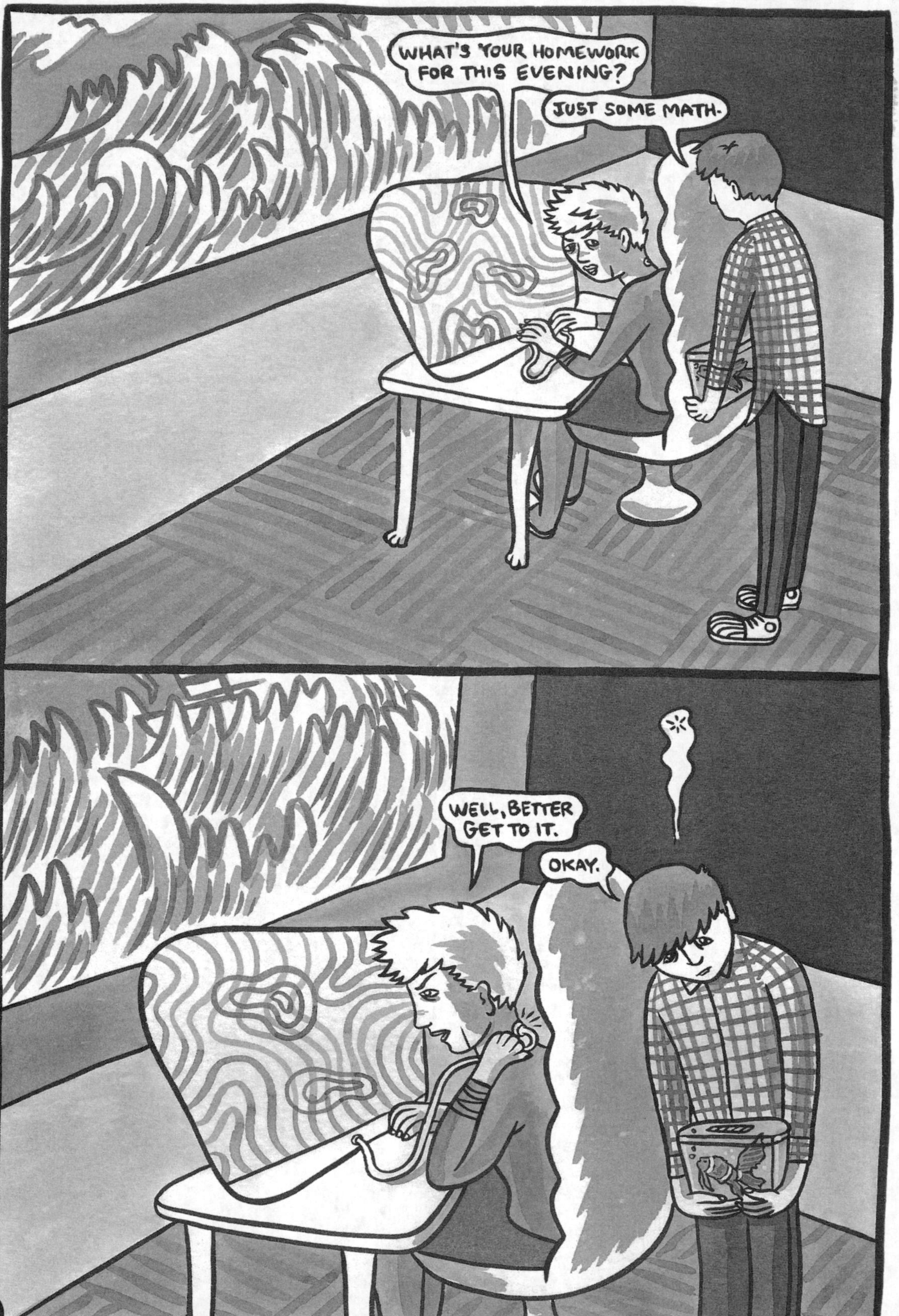
WHAT'S YOUR HOMEWORK FOR THIS EVENING?
JUST SOME MATH.
WELL, BETTER GET TO IT.
OKAY.

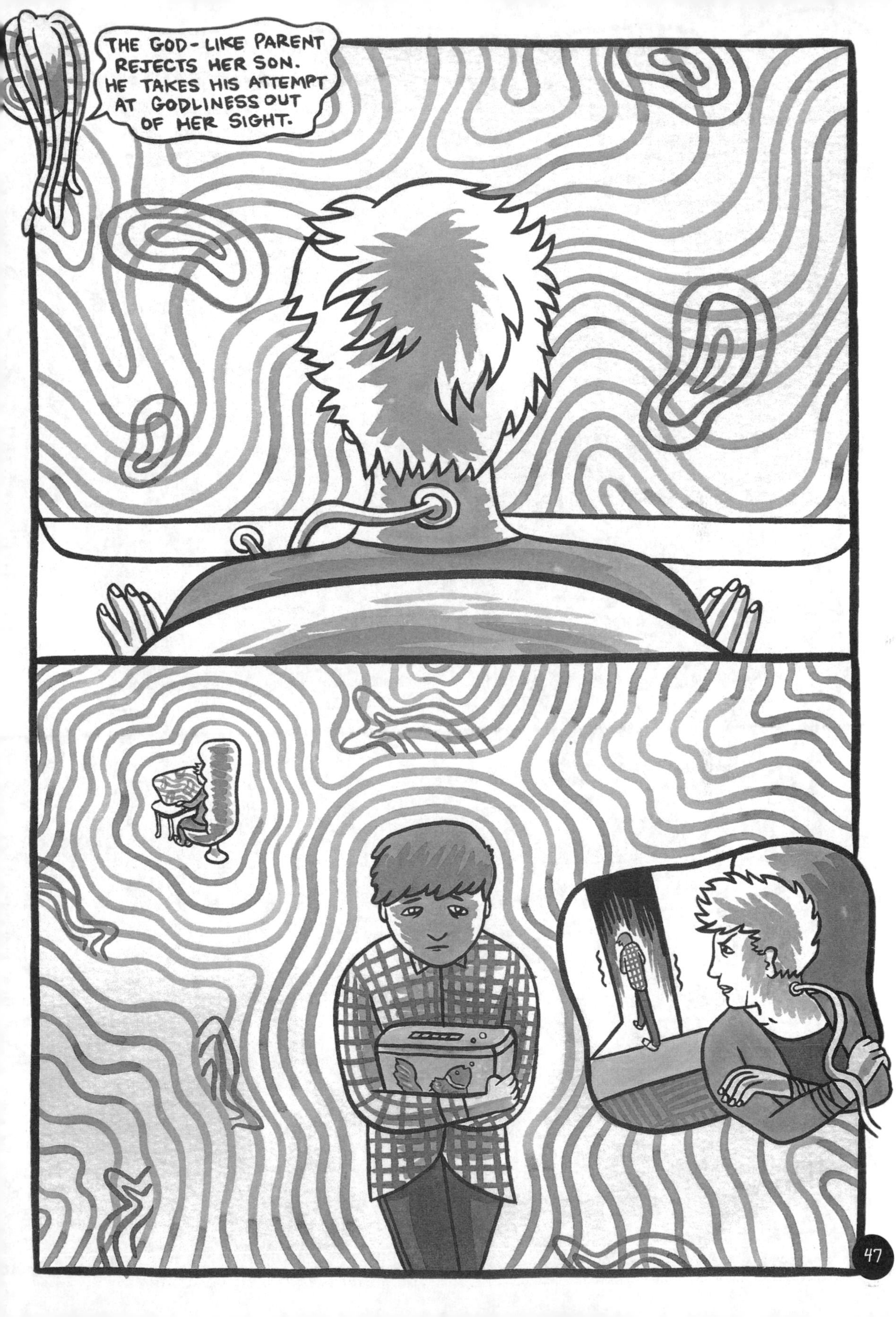
THE GOD-LIKE PARENT REJECTS HER SON. HE TAKES HIS ATTEMPT AT GODLINESS OUT OF HER SIGHT.

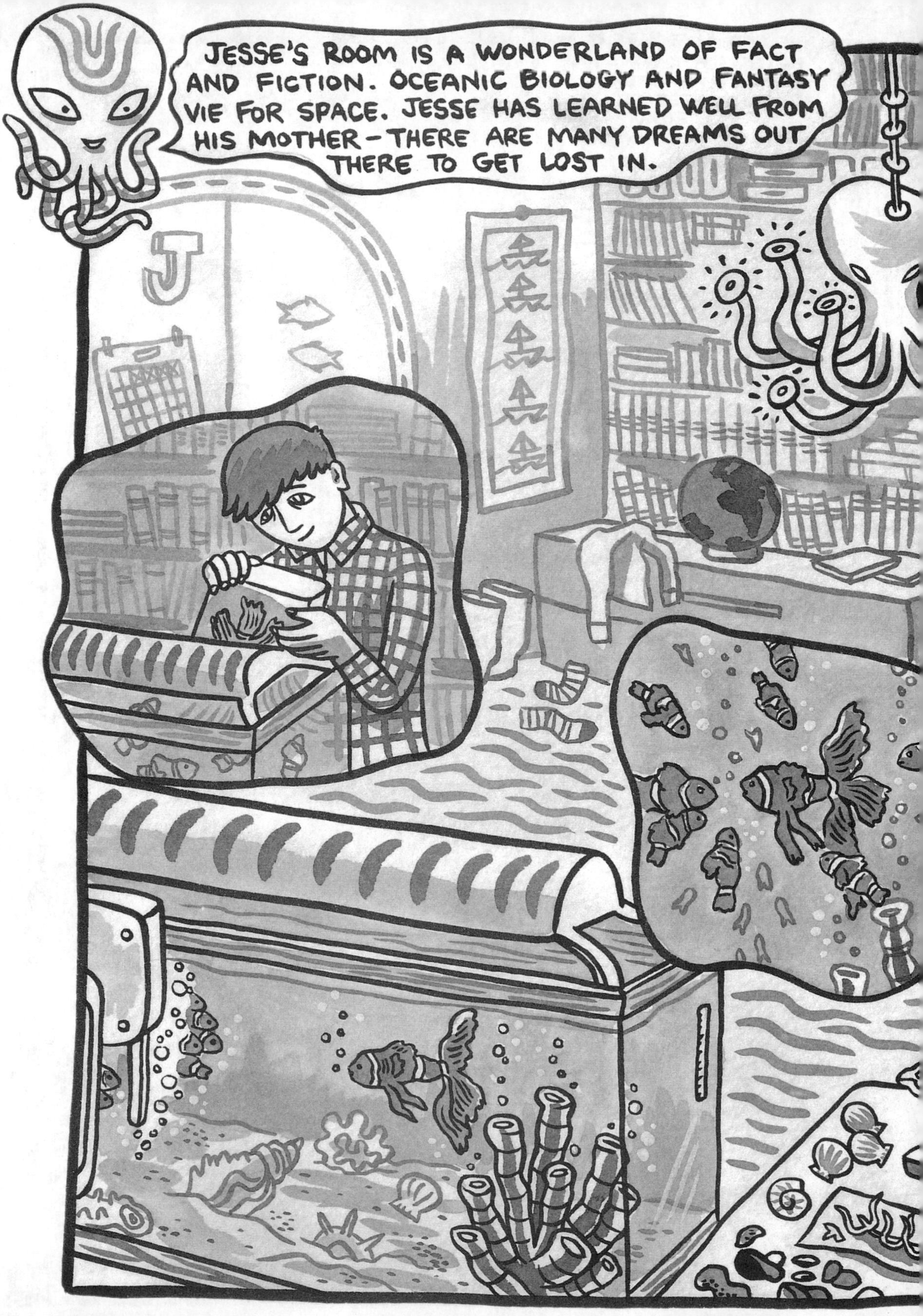
JESSE'S ROOM IS A WONDERLAND OF FACT AND FICTION. OCEANIC BIOLOGY AND FANTASY VIE FOR SPACE. JESSE HAS LEARNED WELL FROM HIS MOTHER – THERE ARE MANY DREAMS OUT THERE TO GET LOST IN.

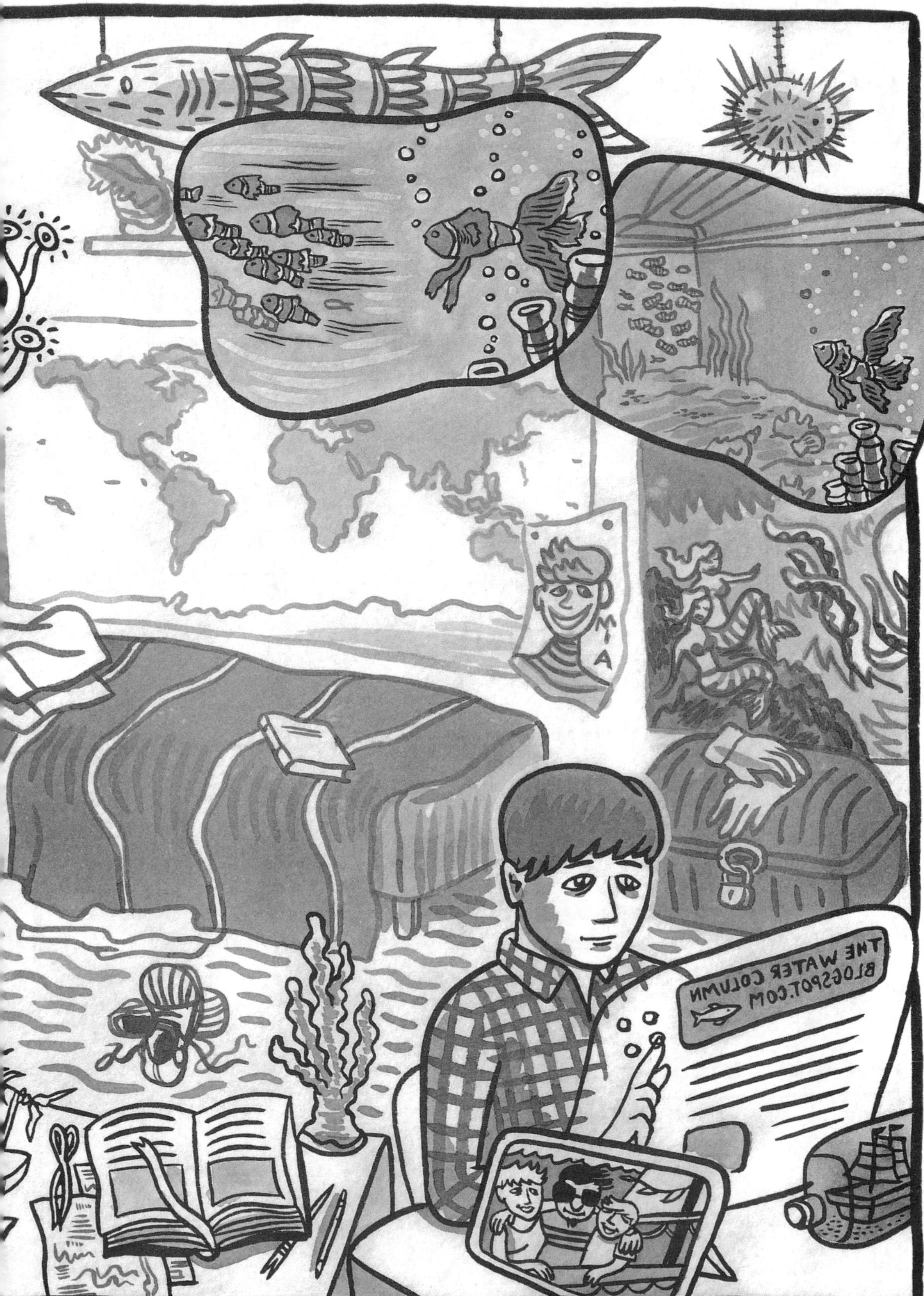
MIA
THE WATER COLUMN
BLOGSPOT.COM

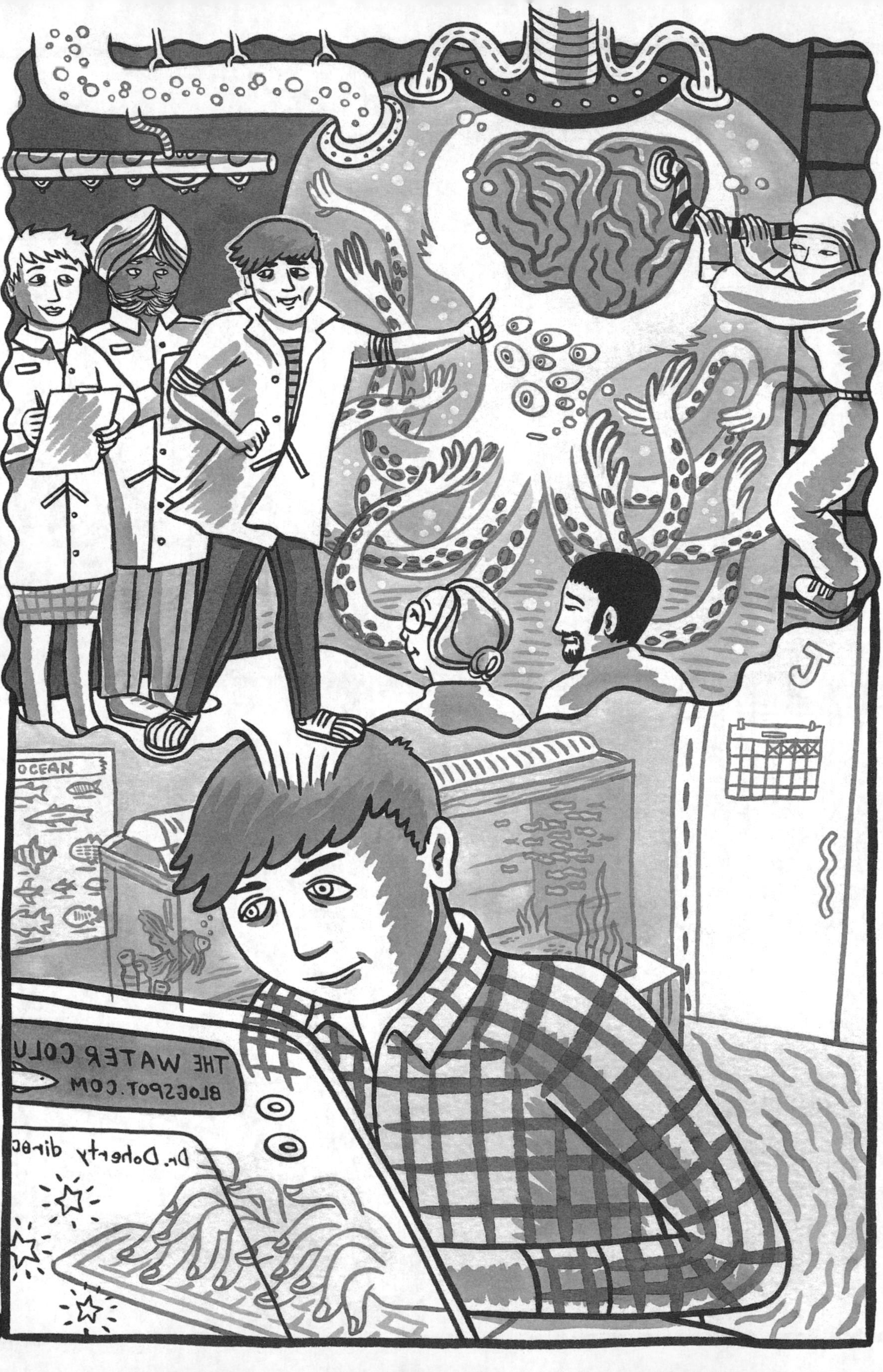
OCEAN
J
THE WATER COLU
BLOGSPOT.COM
Dr. Doherty direc

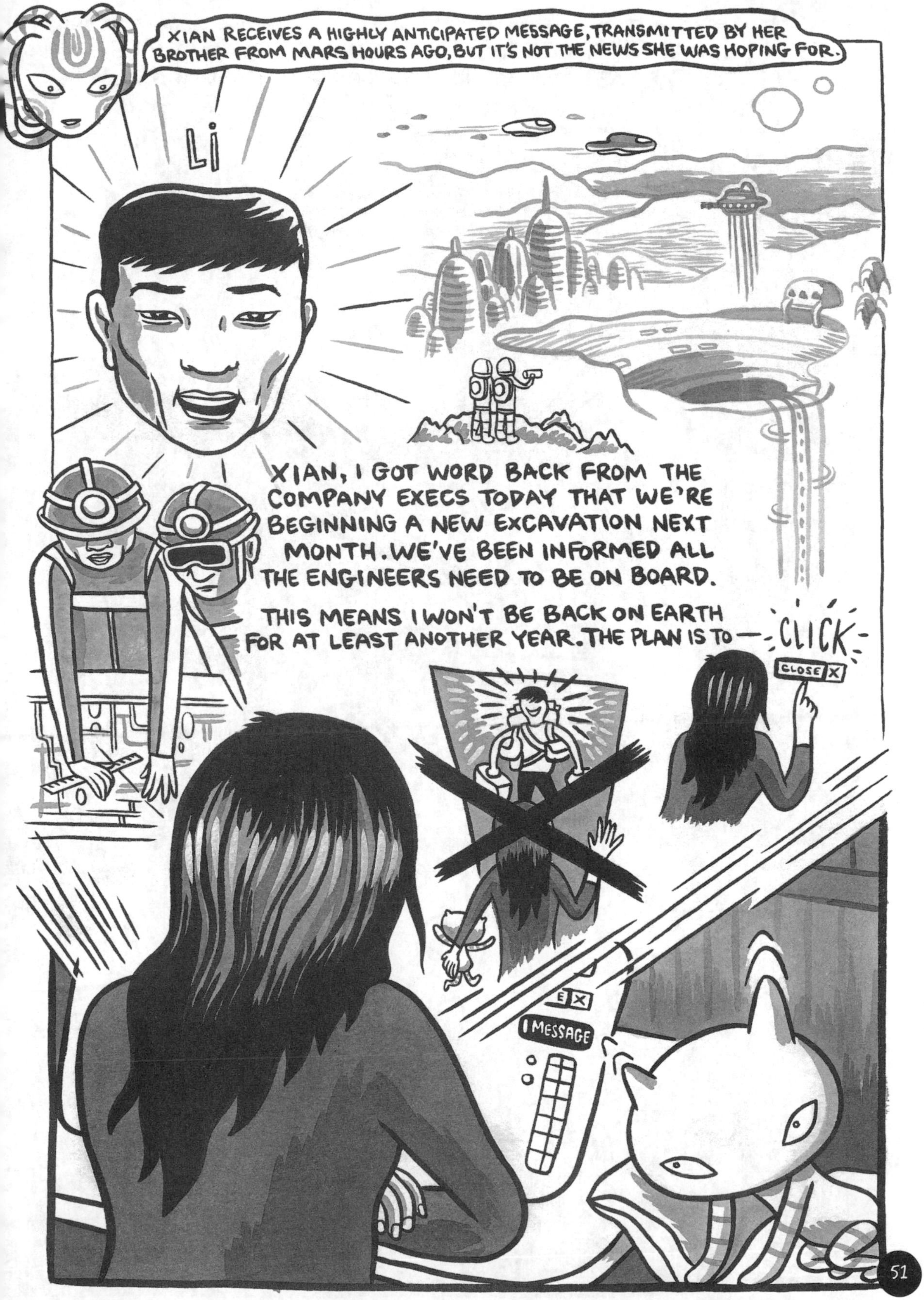
XIAN RECEIVES A HIGHLY ANTICIPATED MESSAGE, TRANSMITTED BY HER BROTHER FROM MARS HOURS AGO, BUT IT'S NOT THE NEWS SHE WAS HOPING FOR.
LI
XIAN, I GOT WORD BACK FROM THE COMPANY EXECS TODAY THAT WE'RE BEGINNING A NEW EXCAVATION NEXT MONTH. WE'VE BEEN INFORMED ALL THE ENGINEERS NEED TO BE ON BOARD.
THIS MEANS I WON'T BE BACK ON EARTH FOR AT LEAST ANOTHER YEAR. THE PLAN IS TO—
CLICK
CLOSE X
MESSAGE

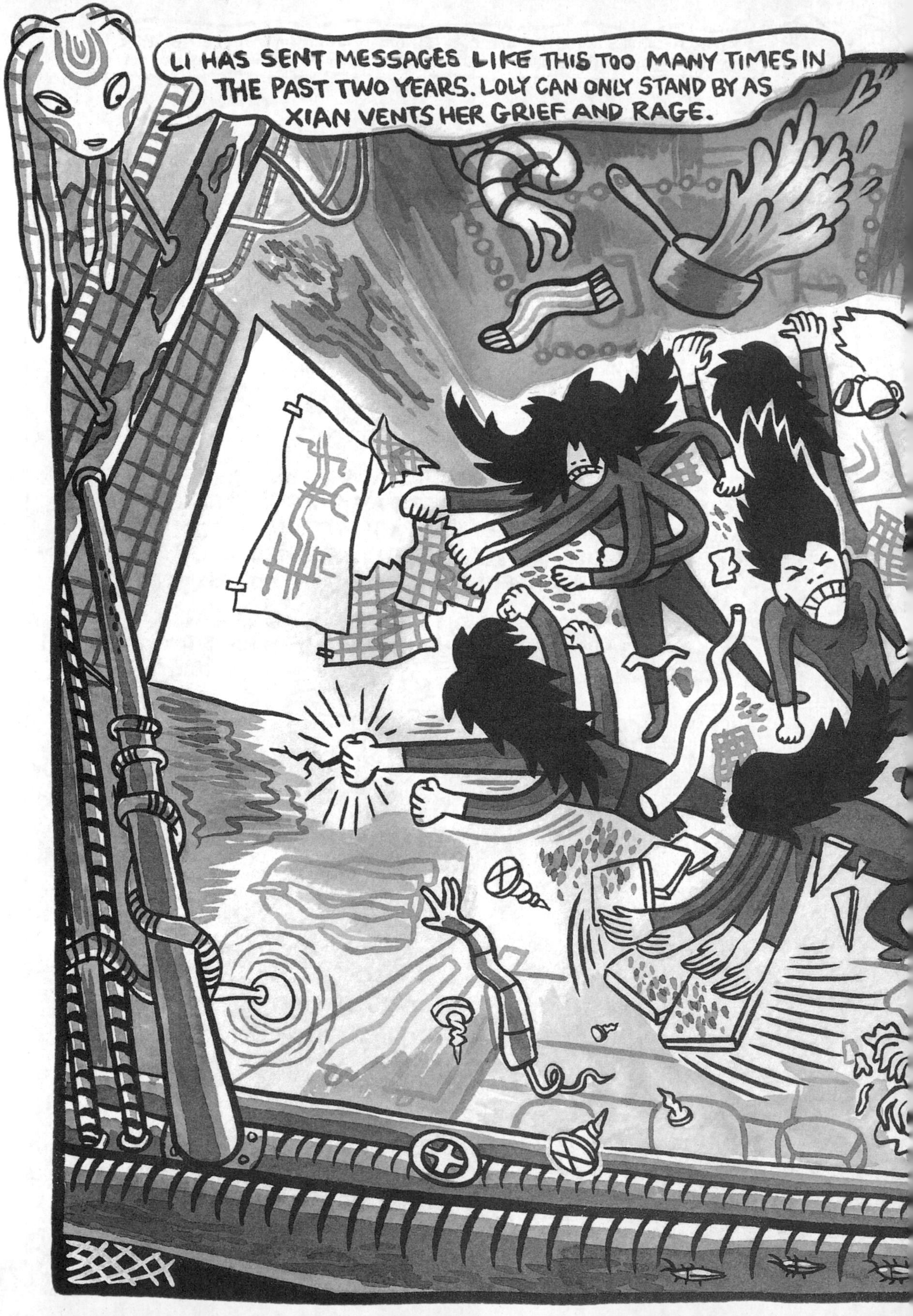
LI HAS SENT MESSAGES LIKE THIS TOO MANY TIMES IN THE PAST TWO YEARS. LOLY CAN ONLY STAND BY AS XIAN VENTS HER GRIEF AND RAGE.

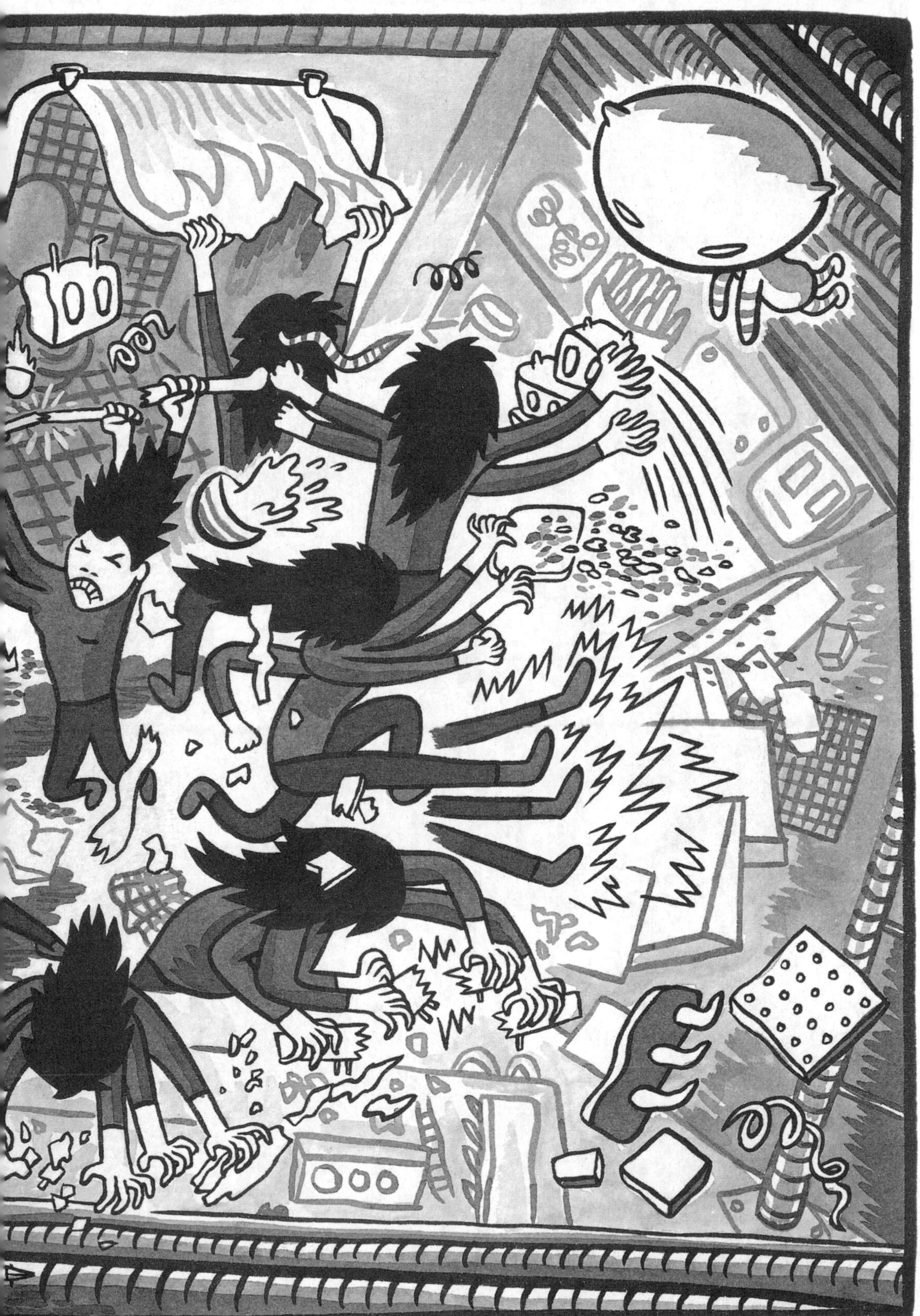

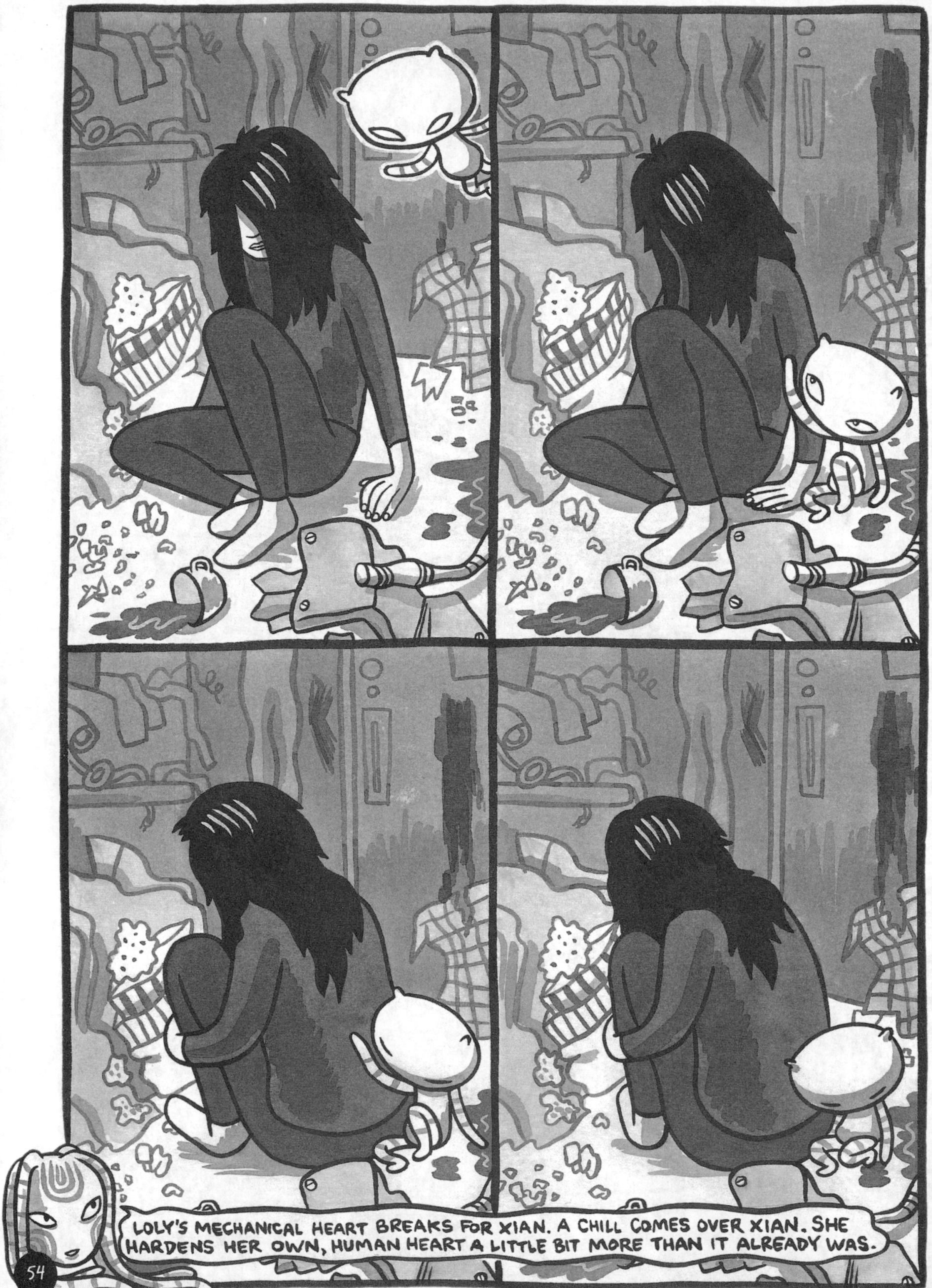
LOLY'S MECHANICAL HEART BREAKS FOR XIAN. A CHILL COMES OVER XIAN. SHE HARDENS HER OWN, HUMAN HEART A LITTLE BIT MORE THAN IT ALREADY WAS.

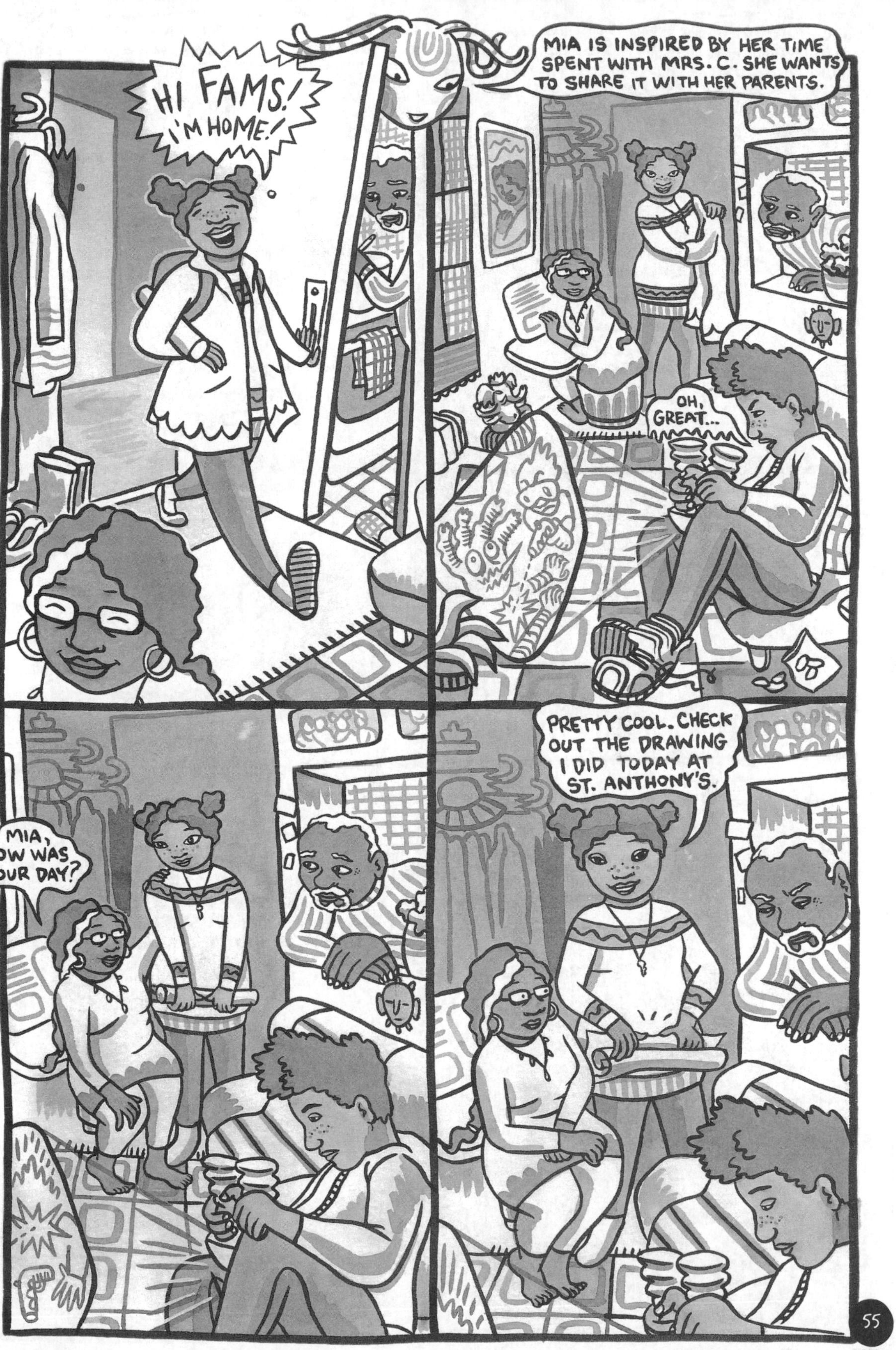
HI FAMS! I'M HOME!
MIA IS INSPIRED BY HER TIME SPENT WITH MRS. C. SHE WANTS TO SHARE IT WITH HER PARENTS.
OH, GREAT...
MIA, HOW WAS YOUR DAY?
PRETTY COOL. CHECK OUT THE DRAWING I DID TODAY AT ST. ANTHONY'S.

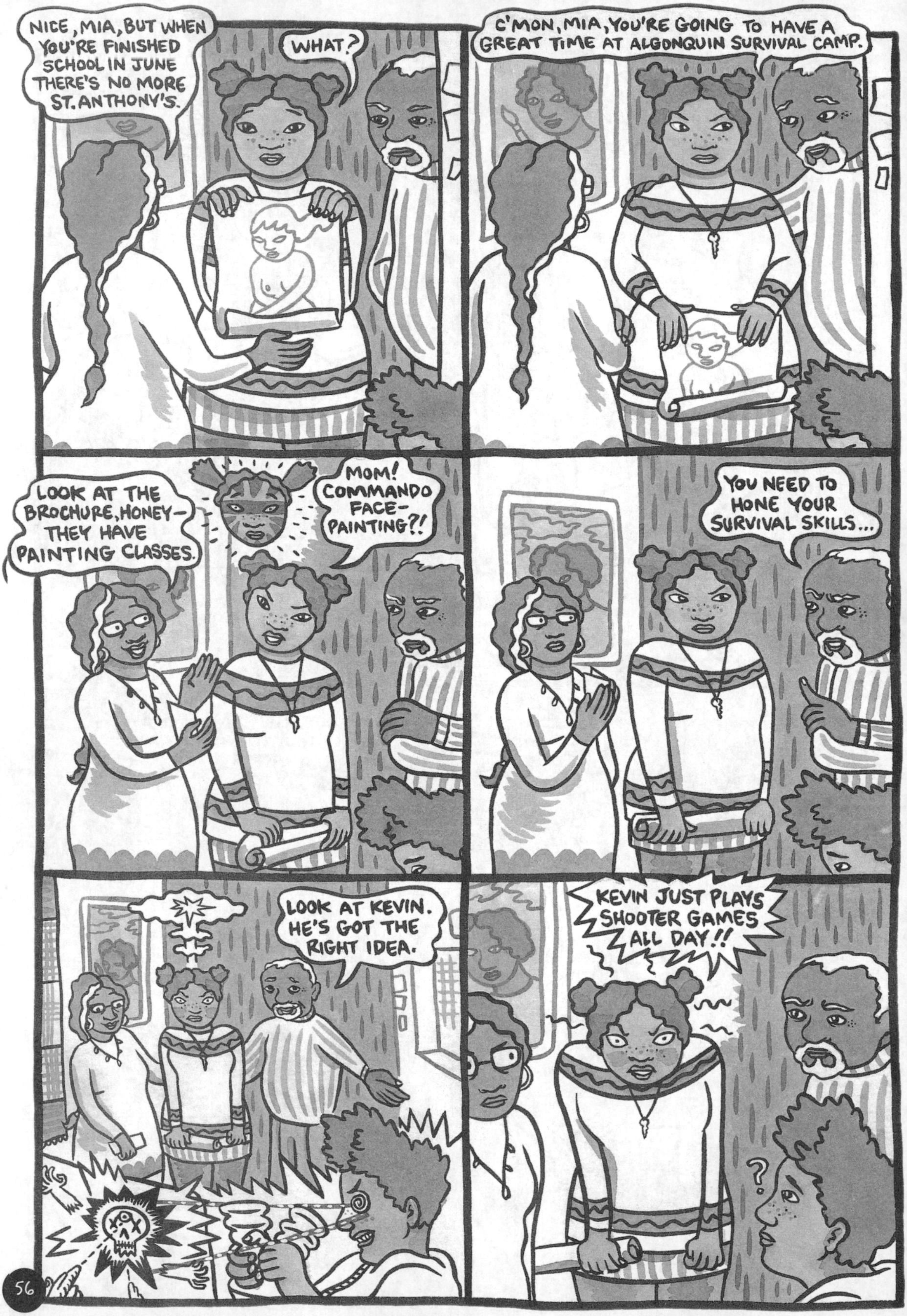
NICE, MIA, BUT WHEN YOU'RE FINISHED SCHOOL IN JUNE THERE'S NO MORE ST. ANTHONY'S.
WHAT?
C'MON, MIA, YOU'RE GOING TO HAVE A GREAT TIME AT ALGONQUIN SURVIVAL CAMP.
LOOK AT THE BROCHURE, HONEY— THEY HAVE PAINTING CLASSES.
MOM! COMMANDO FACE-PAINTING?!
YOU NEED TO HONE YOUR SURVIVAL SKILLS...
LOOK AT KEVIN. HE'S GOT THE RIGHT IDEA.
KEVIN JUST PLAYS SHOOTER GAMES ALL DAY!!

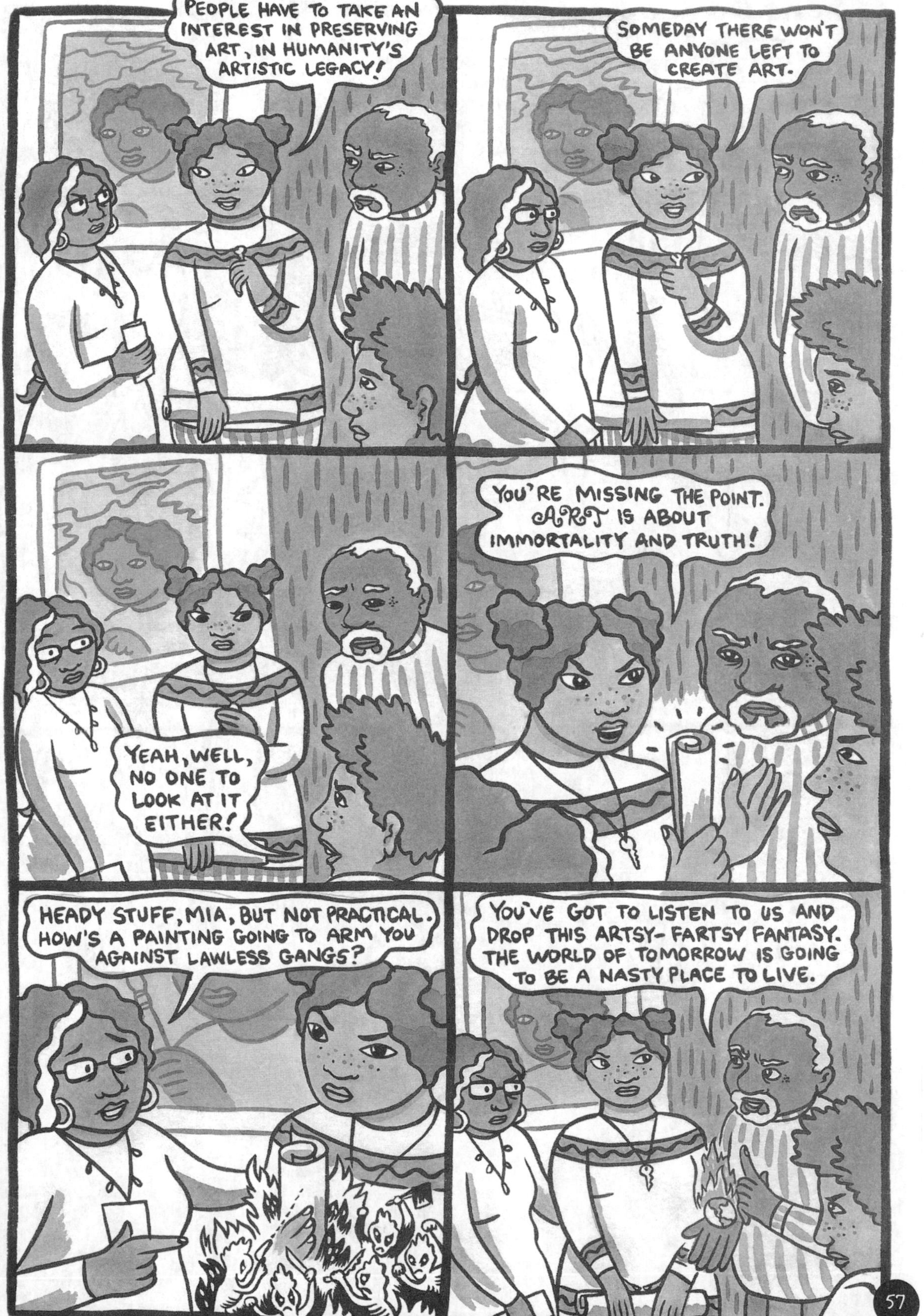
PEOPLE HAVE TO TAKE AN INTEREST IN PRESERVING ART, IN HUMANITY'S ARTISTIC LEGACY!
SOMEDAY THERE WON'T BE ANYONE LEFT TO CREATE ART.
YEAH, WELL, NO ONE TO LOOK AT IT EITHER!
YOU'RE MISSING THE POINT. ART IS ABOUT IMMORTALITY AND TRUTH!
HEADY STUFF, MIA, BUT NOT PRACTICAL. HOW'S A PAINTING GOING TO ARM YOU AGAINST LAWLESS GANGS?
YOU'VE GOT TO LISTEN TO US AND DROP THIS ARTSY-FARTSY FANTASY. THE WORLD OF TOMORROW IS GOING TO BE A NASTY PLACE TO LIVE.

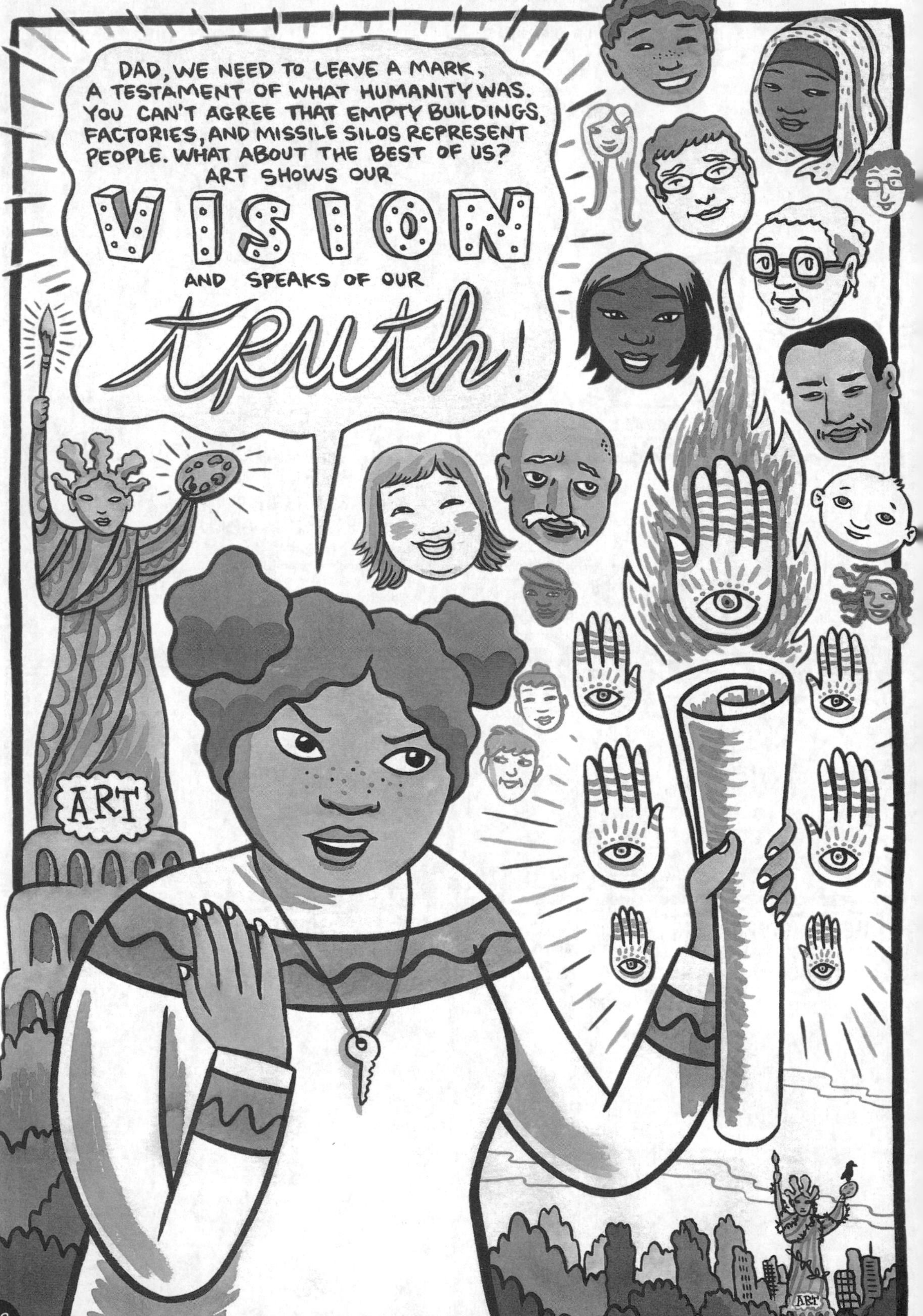
DAD, WE NEED TO LEAVE A MARK, A TESTAMENT OF WHAT HUMANITY WAS. YOU CAN'T AGREE THAT EMPTY BUILDINGS, FACTORIES, AND MISSILE SILOS REPRESENT PEOPLE. WHAT ABOUT THE BEST OF US? ART SHOWS OUR VISION AND SPEAKS OF OUR truth!
ART
ART

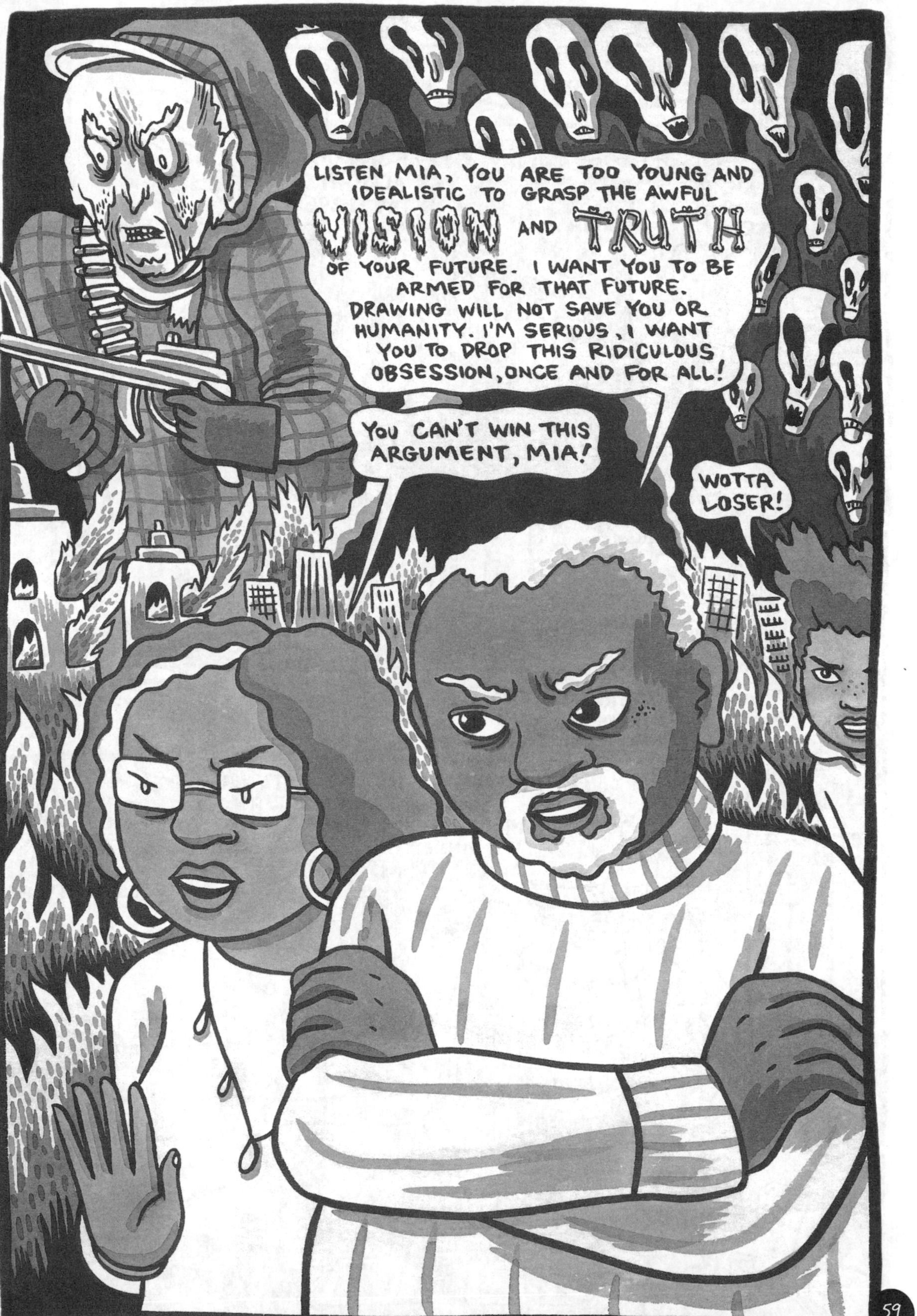
LISTEN MIA, YOU ARE TOO YOUNG AND IDEALISTIC TO GRASP THE AWFUL VISION AND TRUTH OF YOUR FUTURE. I WANT YOU TO BE ARMED FOR THAT FUTURE. DRAWING WILL NOT SAVE YOU OR HUMANITY. I'M SERIOUS, I WANT YOU TO DROP THIS RIDICULOUS OBSESSION, ONCE AND FOR ALL!
YOU CAN'T WIN THIS ARGUMENT, MIA!
WOTTA LOSER!

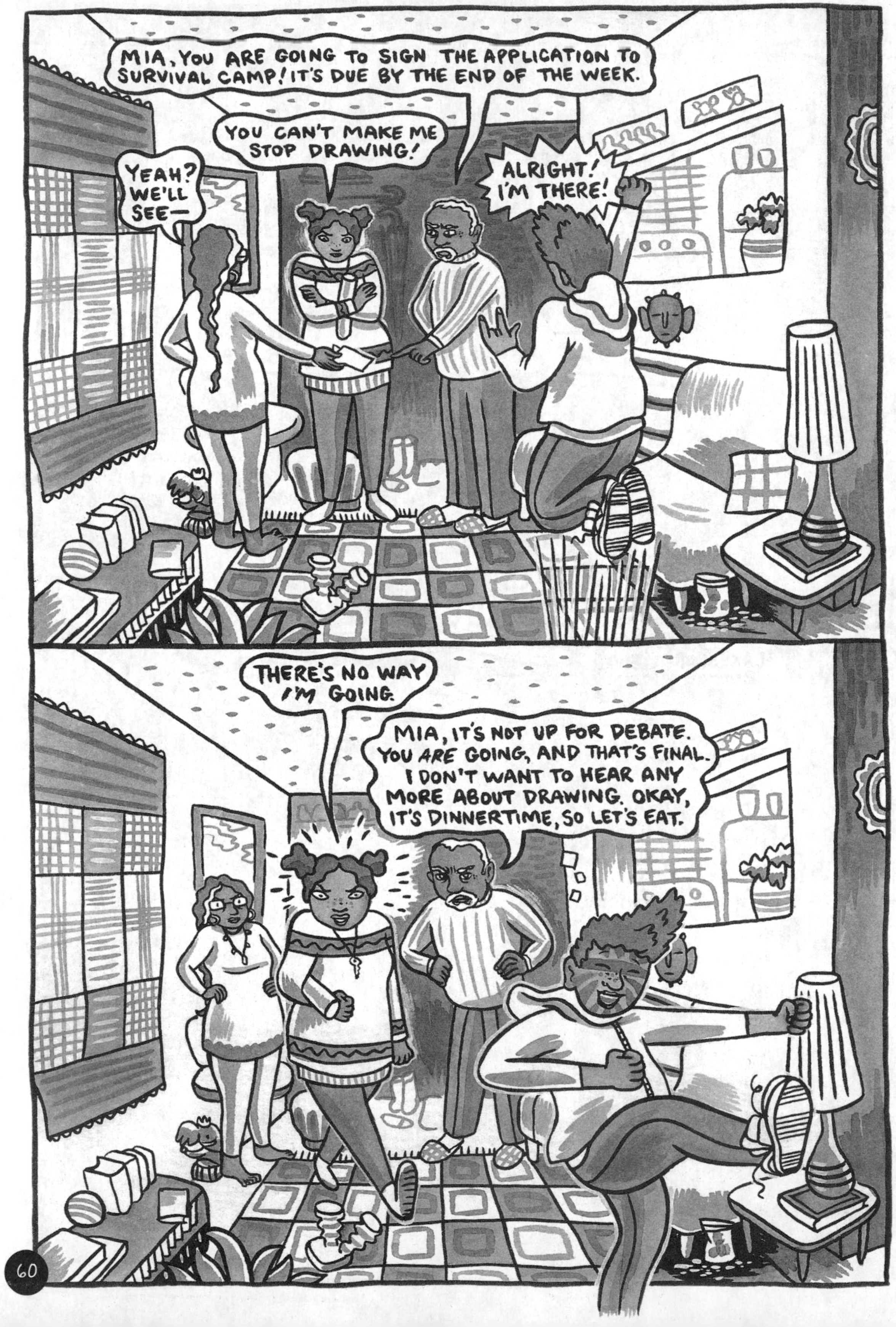
MIA, YOU ARE GOING TO SIGN THE APPLICATION TO SURVIVAL CAMP! IT'S DUE BY THE END OF THE WEEK.
YOU CAN'T MAKE ME STOP DRAWING!
YEAH? WE'LL SEE—
ALRIGHT! I'M THERE!
THERE'S NO WAY I'M GOING.
MIA, IT'S NOT UP FOR DEBATE. YOU ARE GOING, AND THAT'S FINAL. I DON'T WANT TO HEAR ANY MORE ABOUT DRAWING. OKAY, IT'S DINNERTIME, SO LET'S EAT.

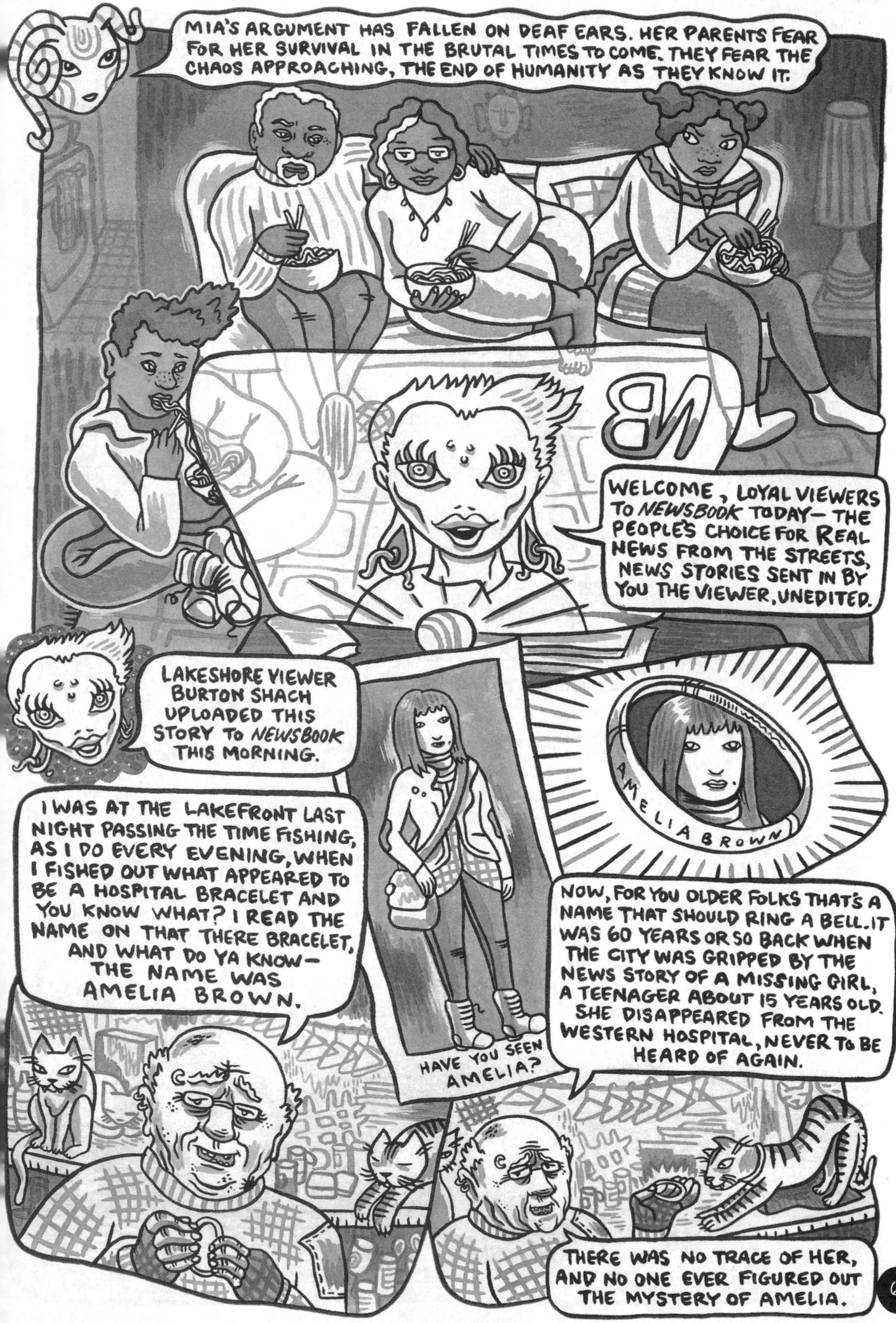
MIA'S ARGUMENT HAS FALLEN ON DEAF EARS. HER PARENTS FEAR FOR HER SURVIVAL IN THE BRUTAL TIMES TO COME. THEY FEAR THE CHAOS APPROACHING, THE END OF HUMANITY AS THEY KNOW IT.
NB
WELCOME, LOYAL VIEWERS TO NEWSBOOK TODAY— THE PEOPLE'S CHOICE FOR REAL NEWS FROM THE STREETS, NEWS STORIES SENT IN BY YOU THE VIEWER, UNEDITED.
LAKESHORE VIEWER BURTON SHACH UPLOADED THIS STORY TO NEWSBOOK THIS MORNING.
AMELIA BROWN
I WAS AT THE LAKEFRONT LAST NIGHT PASSING THE TIME FISHING, AS I DO EVERY EVENING, WHEN I FISHED OUT WHAT APPEARED TO BE A HOSPITAL BRACELET AND YOU KNOW WHAT? I READ THE NAME ON THAT THERE BRACELET, AND WHAT DO YA KNOW— THE NAME WAS AMELIA BROWN.
HAVE YOU SEEN AMELIA?
NOW, FOR YOU OLDER FOLKS THAT'S A NAME THAT SHOULD RING A BELL. IT WAS 60 YEARS OR SO BACK WHEN THE CITY WAS GRIPPED BY THE NEWS STORY OF A MISSING GIRL, A TEENAGER ABOUT 15 YEARS OLD. SHE DISAPPEARED FROM THE WESTERN HOSPITAL, NEVER TO BE HEARD OF AGAIN.
THERE WAS NO TRACE OF HER, AND NO ONE EVER FIGURED OUT THE MYSTERY OF AMELIA.

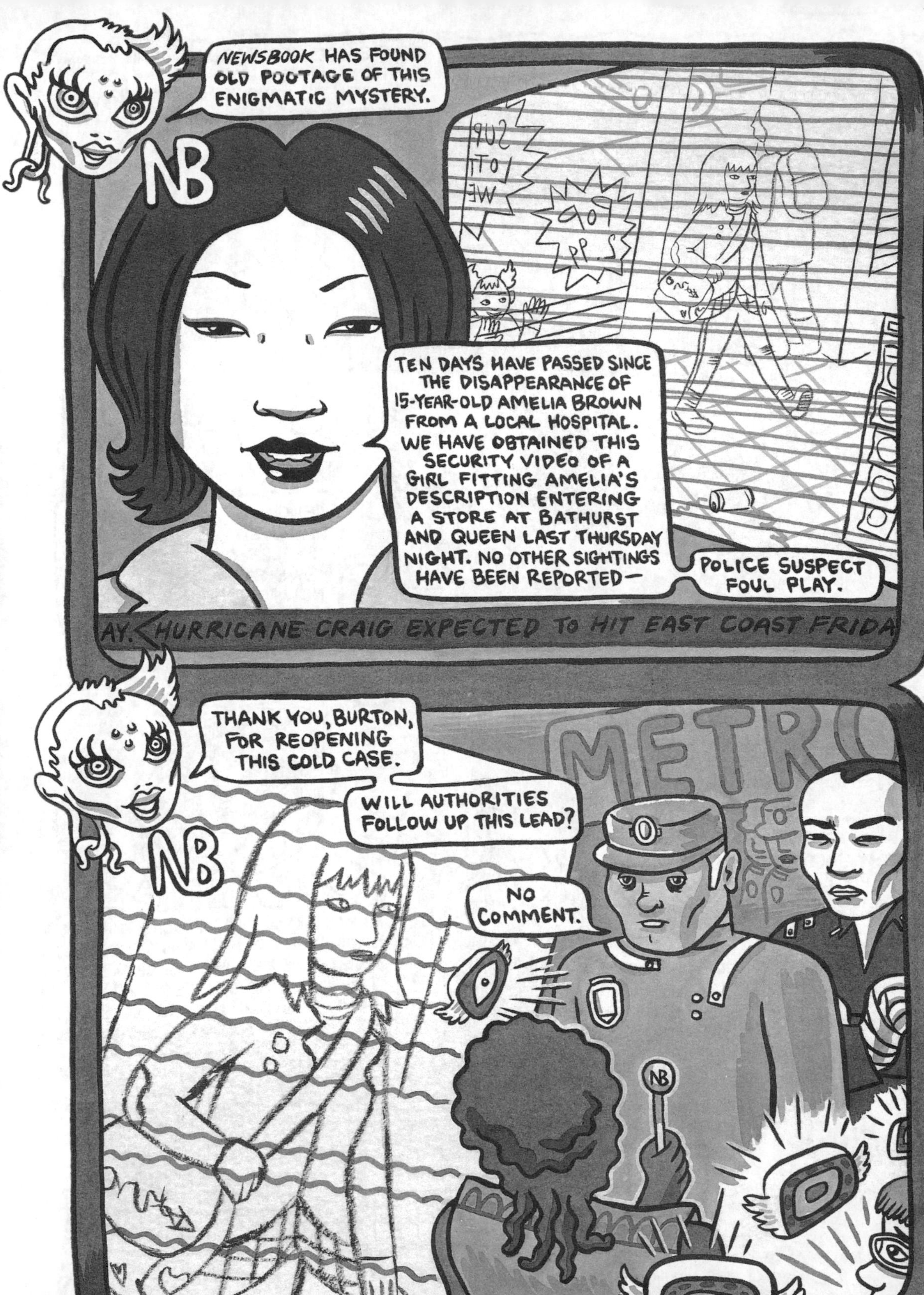
NB
NEWSBOOK HAS FOUND OLD FOOTAGE OF THIS ENIGMATIC MYSTERY.
TEN DAYS HAVE PASSED SINCE THE DISAPPEARANCE OF 15-YEAR-OLD AMELIA BROWN FROM A LOCAL HOSPITAL. WE HAVE OBTAINED THIS SECURITY VIDEO OF A GIRL FITTING AMELIA'S DESCRIPTION ENTERING A STORE AT BATHURST AND QUEEN LAST THURSDAY NIGHT. NO OTHER SIGHTINGS HAVE BEEN REPORTED—
POLICE SUSPECT FOUL PLAY.
AY. <HURRICANE CRAIG EXPECTED TO HIT EAST COAST FRIDA
NB
THANK YOU, BURTON, FOR REOPENING THIS COLD CASE.
WILL AUTHORITIES FOLLOW UP THIS LEAD?
METR
NO COMMENT.
NB

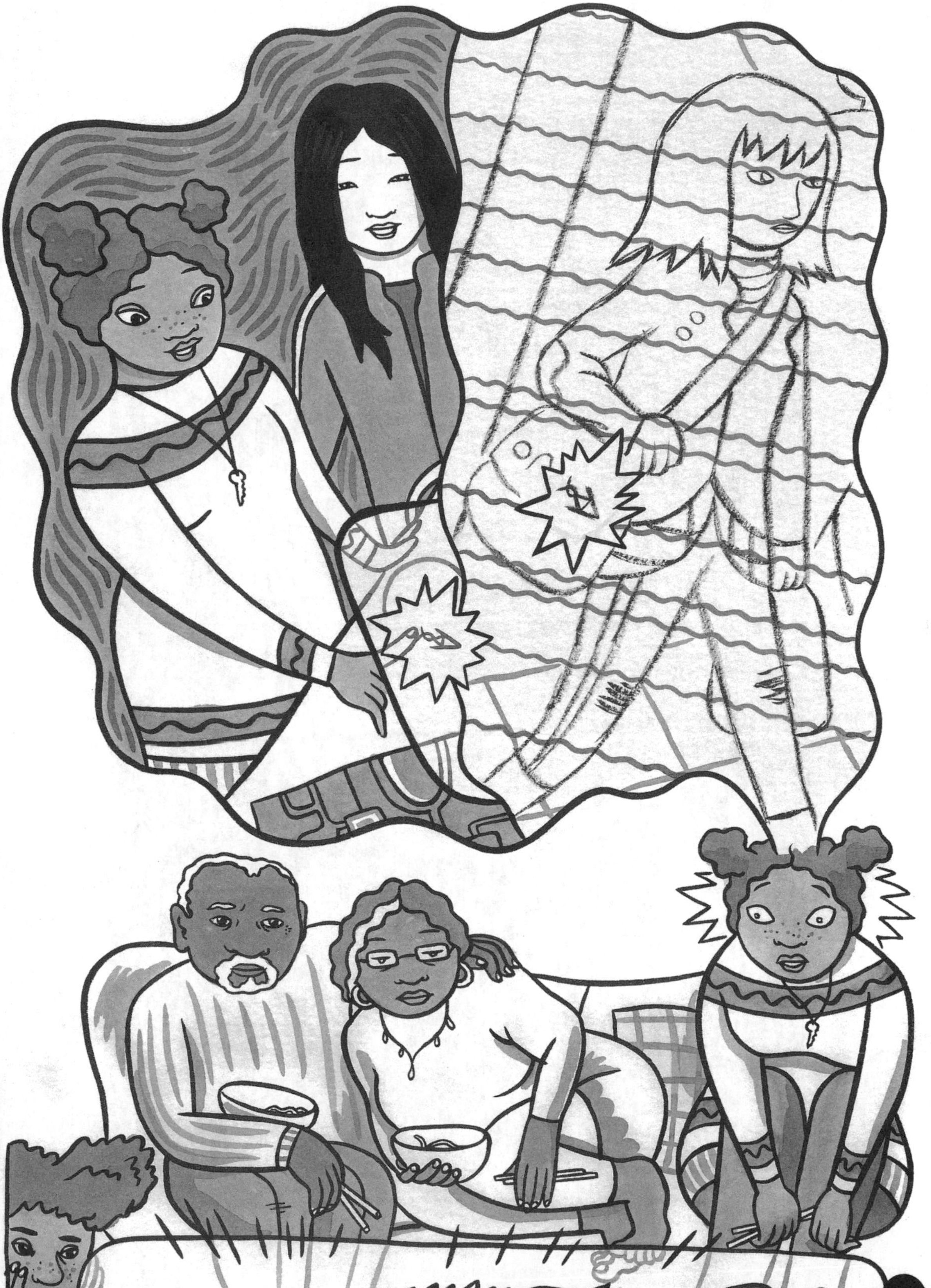

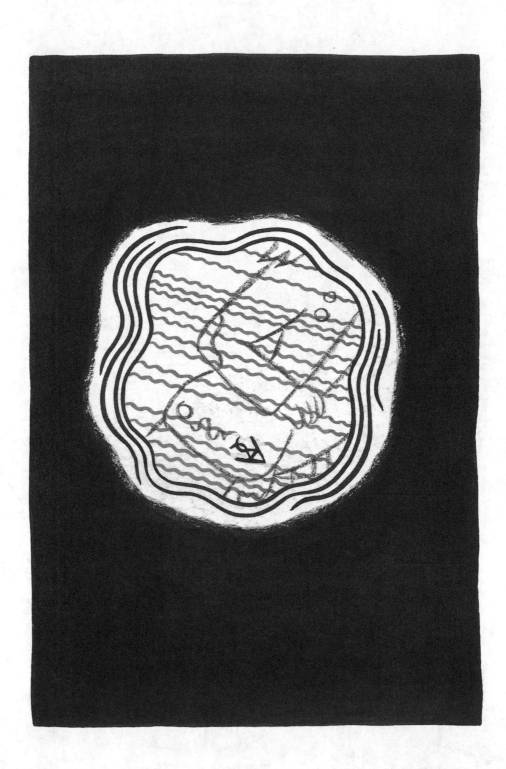

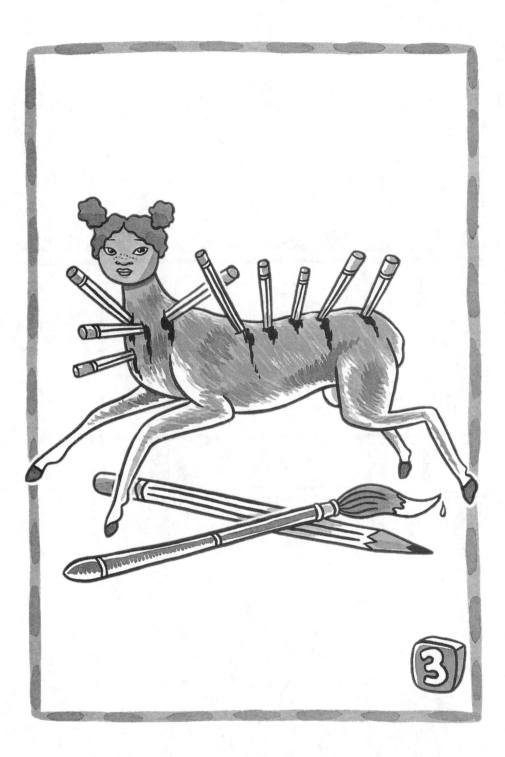

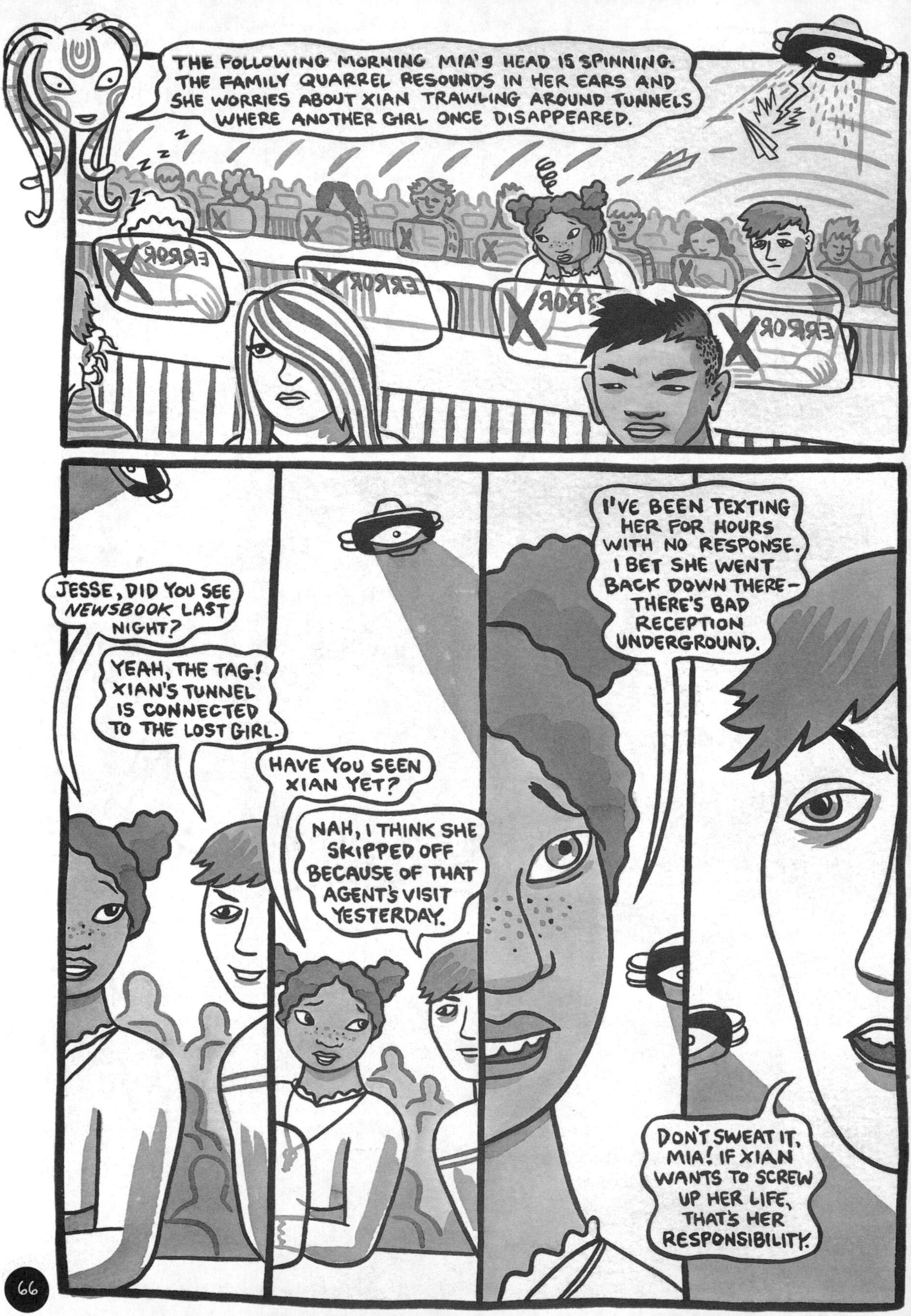
THE FOLLOWING MORNING MIA'S HEAD IS SPINNING. THE FAMILY QUARREL RESOUNDS IN HER EARS AND SHE WORRIES ABOUT XIAN TRAWLING AROUND TUNNELS WHERE ANOTHER GIRL ONCE DISAPPEARED.
JESSE, DID YOU SEE *NEWSBOOK* LAST NIGHT?
YEAH, THE TAG! XIAN'S TUNNEL IS CONNECTED TO THE LOST GIRL.
HAVE YOU SEEN XIAN YET?
NAH, I THINK SHE SKIPPED OFF BECAUSE OF THAT AGENT'S VISIT YESTERDAY.
I'VE BEEN TEXTING HER FOR HOURS WITH NO RESPONSE. I BET SHE WENT BACK DOWN THERE— THERE'S BAD RECEPTION UNDERGROUND.
DON'T SWEAT IT, MIA! IF XIAN WANTS TO SCREW UP HER LIFE, THAT'S HER RESPONSIBILITY.

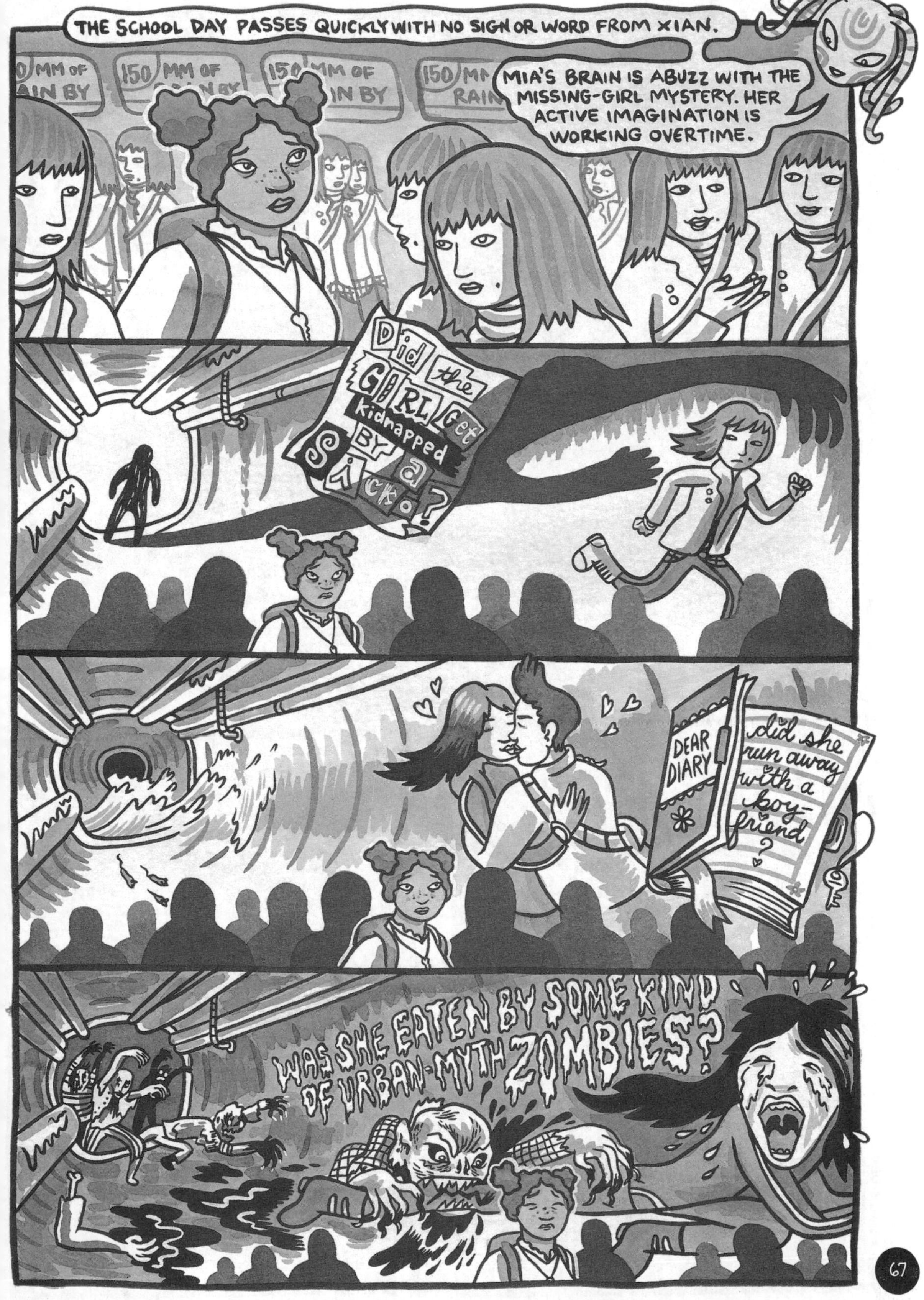
THE SCHOOL DAY PASSES QUICKLY WITH NO SIGN OR WORD FROM XIAN.
MIA'S BRAIN IS ABUZZ WITH THE MISSING-GIRL MYSTERY. HER ACTIVE IMAGINATION IS WORKING OVERTIME.
Did the GIRL Get kidnapped BY a Sicko?
DEAR DIARY
did she run away with a boyfriend?
WAS SHE EATEN BY SOME KIND OF URBAN-MYTH ZOMBIES?

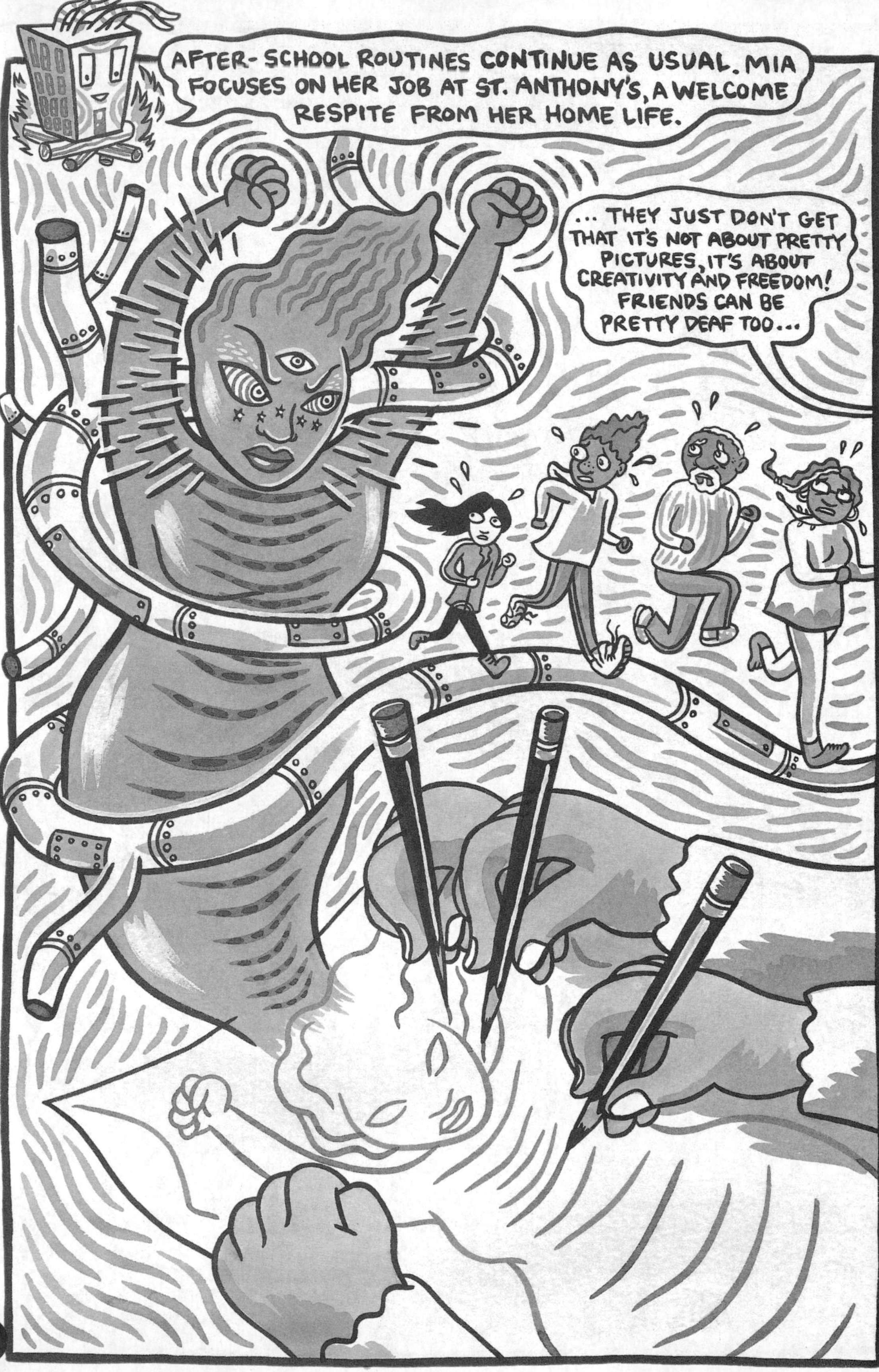
AFTER-SCHOOL ROUTINES CONTINUE AS USUAL. MIA FOCUSES ON HER JOB AT ST. ANTHONY'S, A WELCOME RESPITE FROM HER HOME LIFE.
... THEY JUST DON'T GET THAT IT'S NOT ABOUT PRETTY PICTURES, IT'S ABOUT CREATIVITY AND FREEDOM! FRIENDS CAN BE PRETTY DEAF TOO...

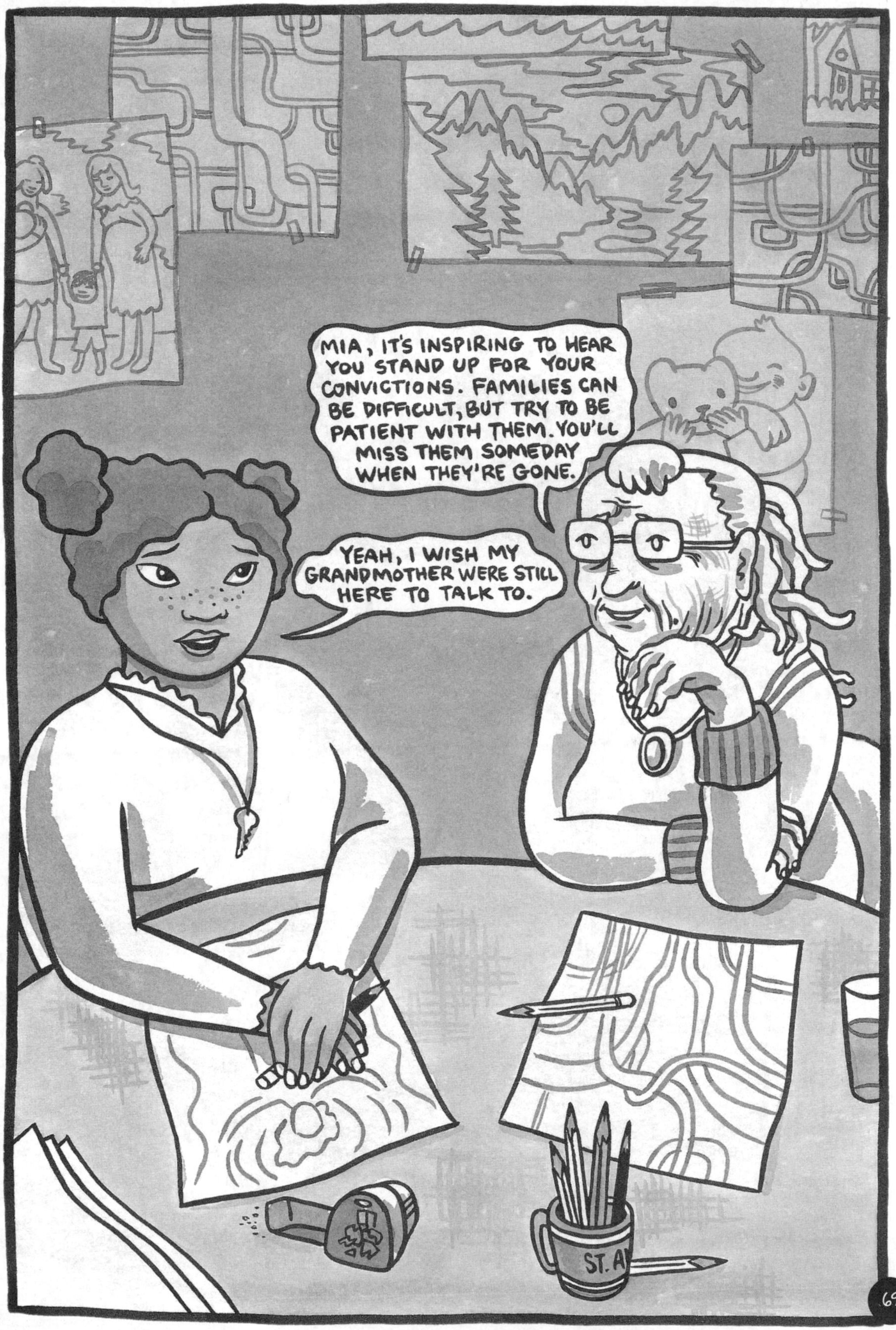
MIA, IT'S INSPIRING TO HEAR YOU STAND UP FOR YOUR CONVICTIONS. FAMILIES CAN BE DIFFICULT, BUT TRY TO BE PATIENT WITH THEM. YOU'LL MISS THEM SOMEDAY WHEN THEY'RE GONE.
YEAH, I WISH MY GRANDMOTHER WERE STILL HERE TO TALK TO.
ST. A

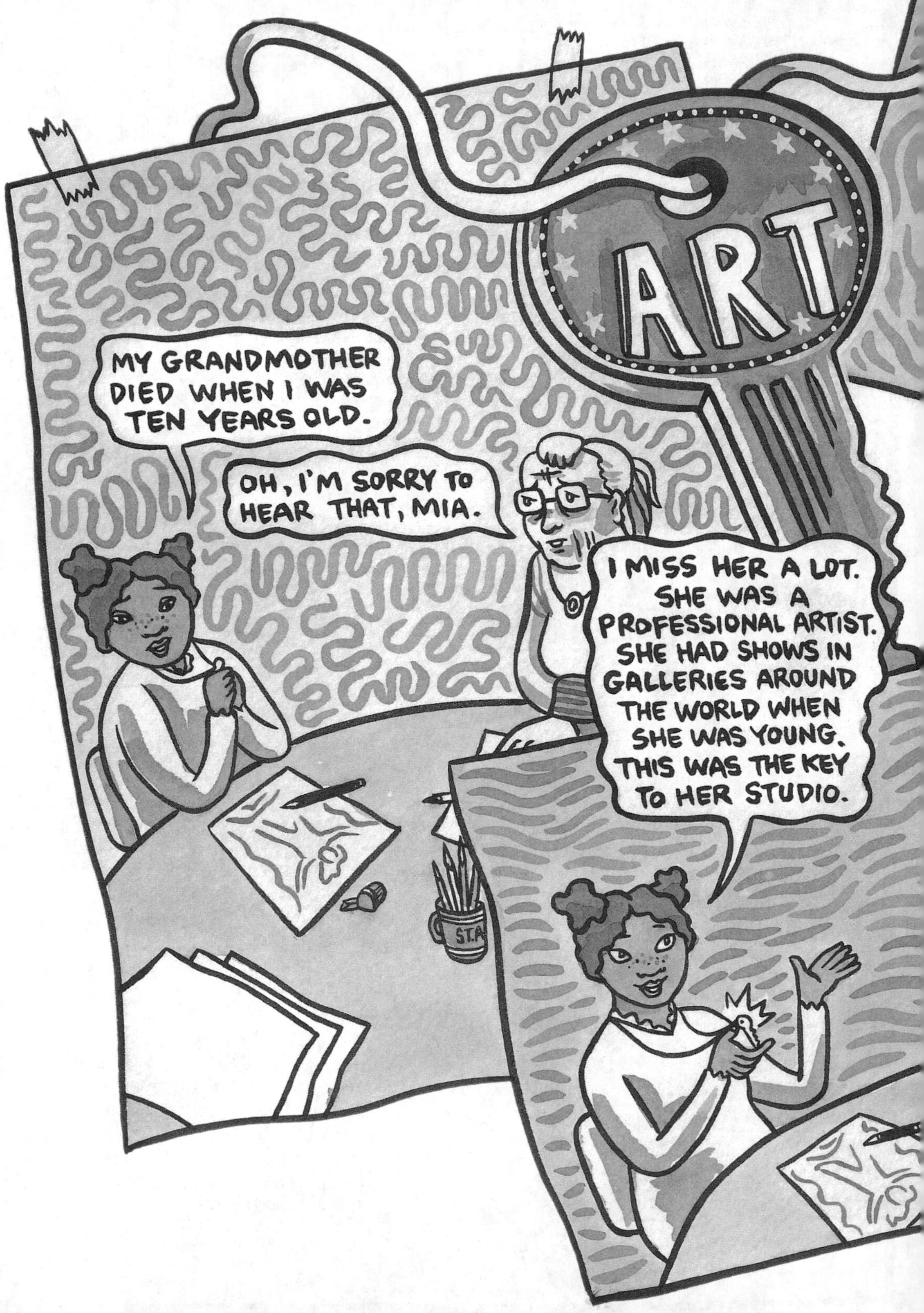
ART
MY GRANDMOTHER DIED WHEN I WAS TEN YEARS OLD.
OH, I'M SORRY TO HEAR THAT, MIA.
I MISS HER A LOT. SHE WAS A PROFESSIONAL ARTIST. SHE HAD SHOWS IN GALLERIES AROUND THE WORLD WHEN SHE WAS YOUNG. THIS WAS THE KEY TO HER STUDIO.

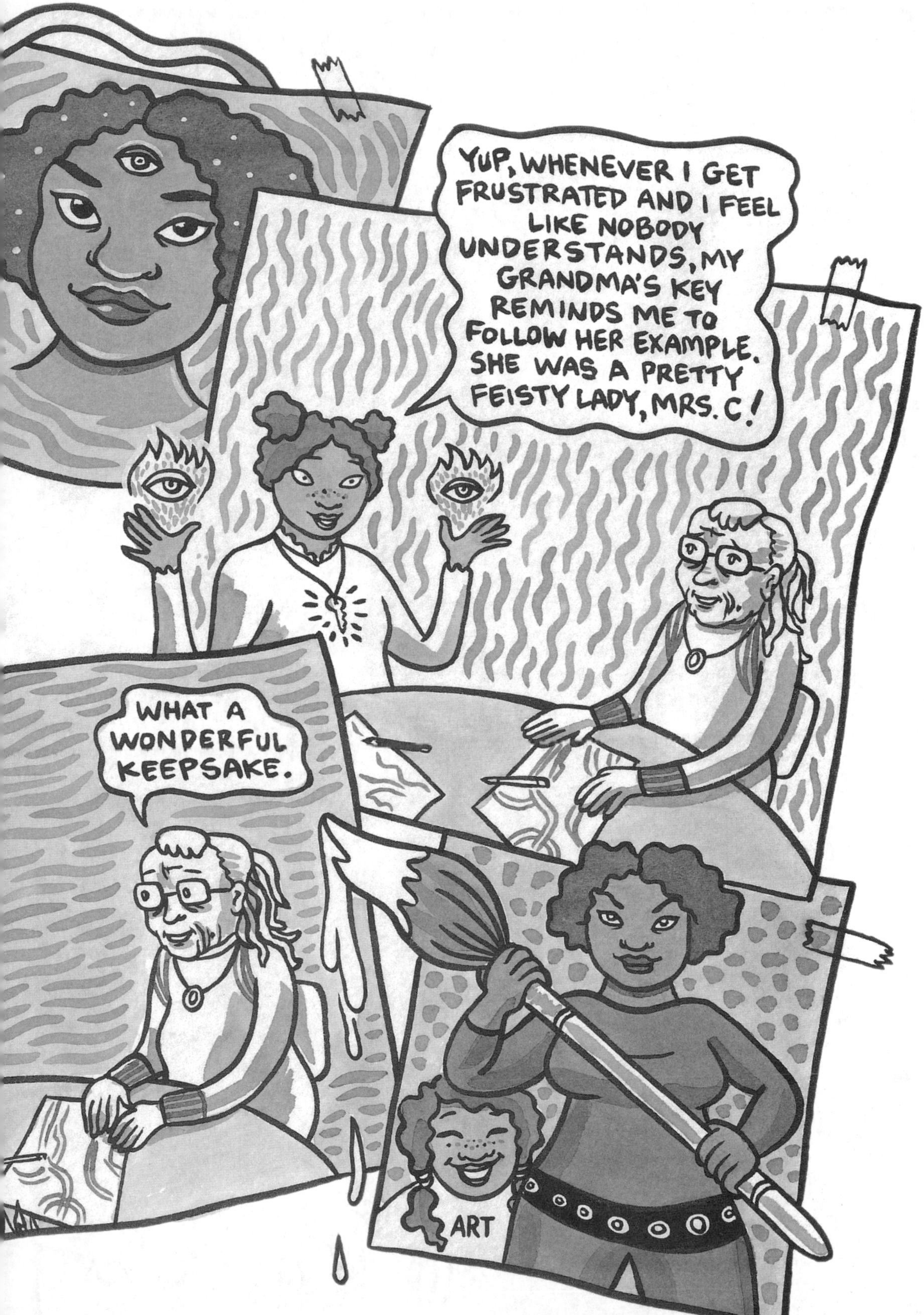
YUP, WHENEVER I GET FRUSTRATED AND I FEEL LIKE NOBODY UNDERSTANDS, MY GRANDMA'S KEY REMINDS ME TO FOLLOW HER EXAMPLE. SHE WAS A PRETTY FEISTY LADY, MRS. C!
WHAT A WONDERFUL KEEPSAKE.
ART

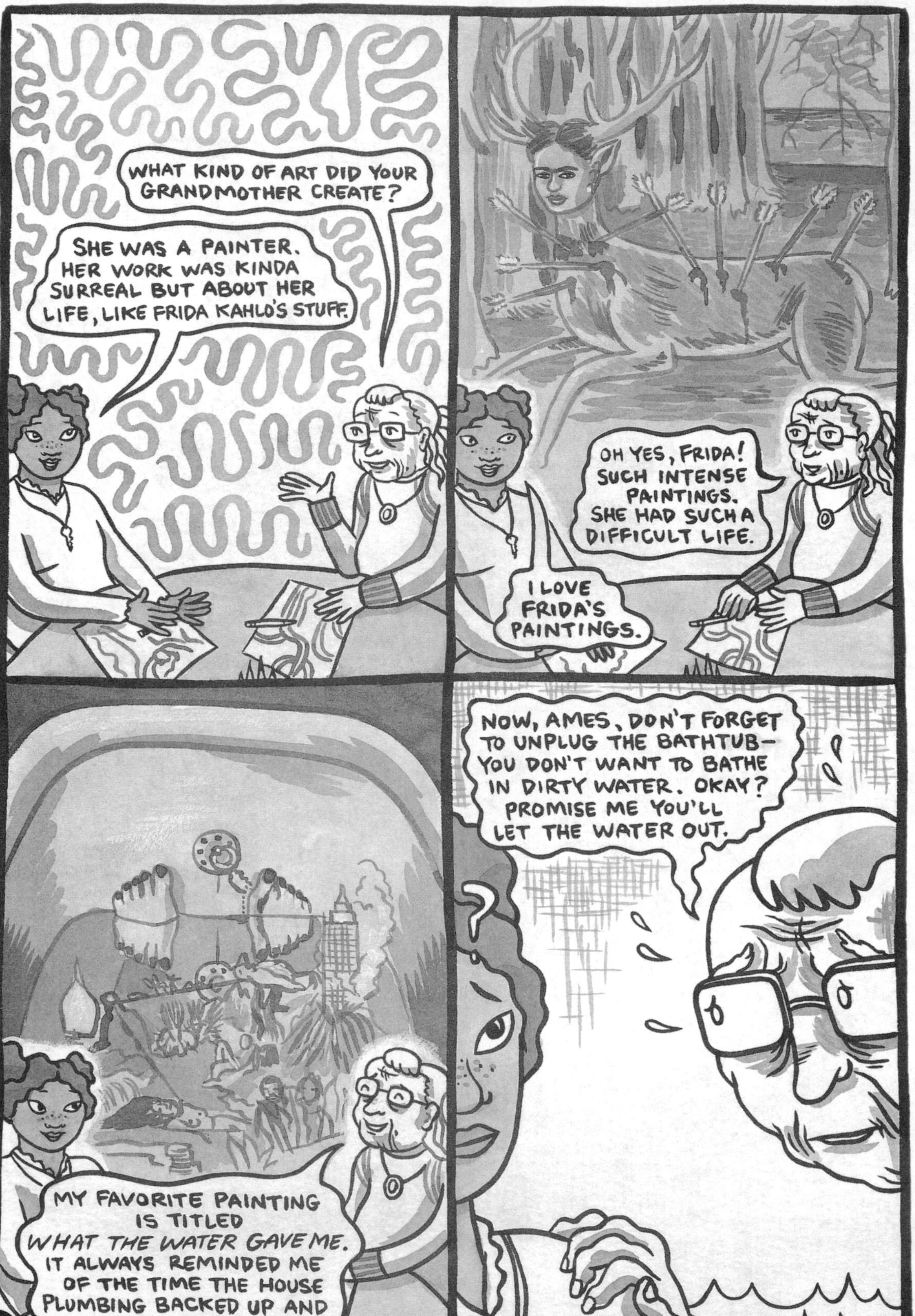
WHAT KIND OF ART DID YOUR GRANDMOTHER CREATE?
SHE WAS A PAINTER. HER WORK WAS KINDA SURREAL BUT ABOUT HER LIFE, LIKE FRIDA KAHLO'S STUFF.
OH YES, FRIDA! SUCH INTENSE PAINTINGS. SHE HAD SUCH A DIFFICULT LIFE.
I LOVE FRIDA'S PAINTINGS.
MY FAVORITE PAINTING IS TITLED *WHAT THE WATER GAVE ME.* IT ALWAYS REMINDED ME OF THE TIME THE HOUSE PLUMBING BACKED UP AND WE COULDN'T BATHE FOR A WEEK!
NOW, AMES, DON'T FORGET TO UNPLUG THE BATHTUB– YOU DON'T WANT TO BATHE IN DIRTY WATER. OKAY? PROMISE ME YOU'LL LET THE WATER OUT.

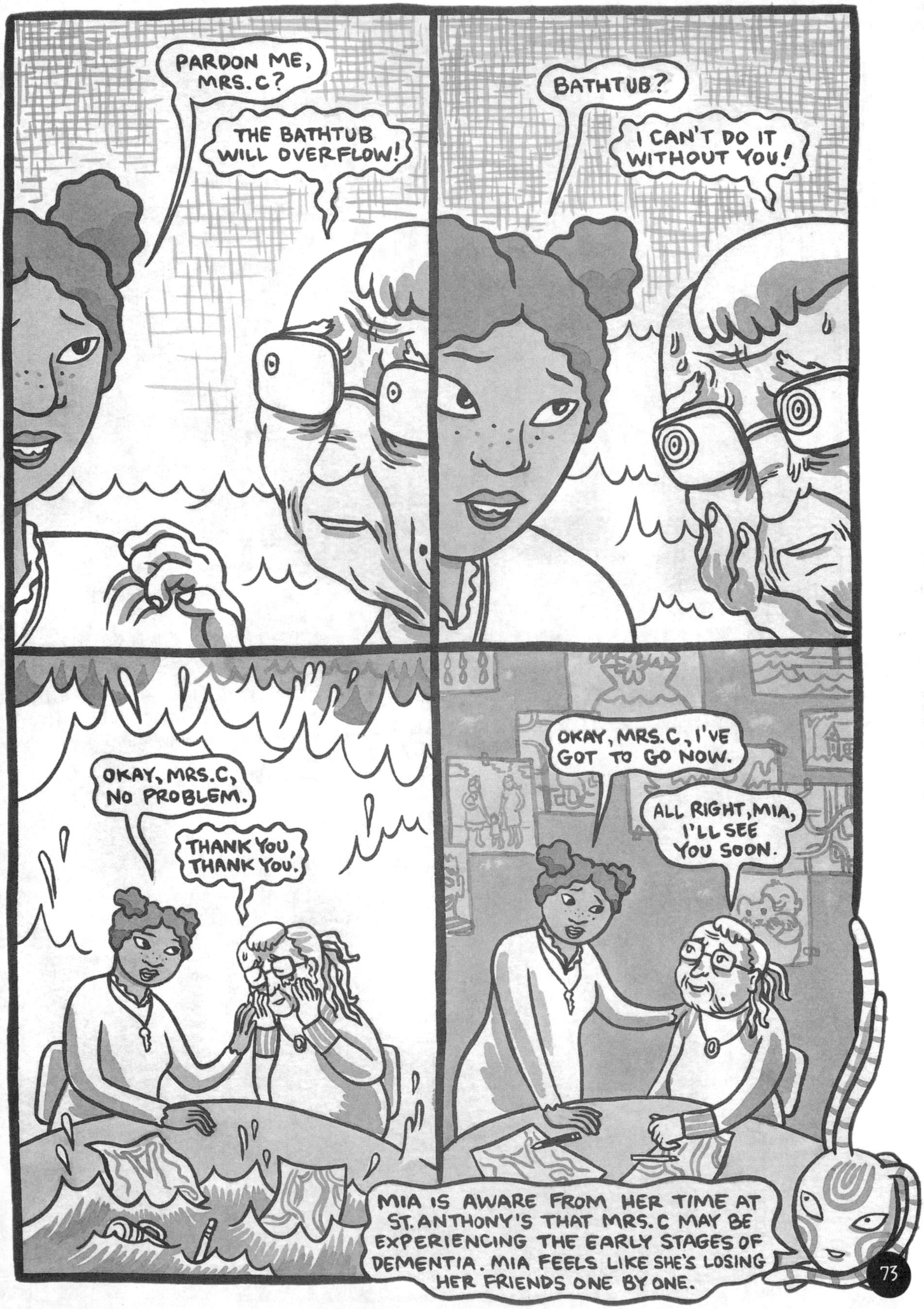
PARDON ME, MRS. C?
THE BATHTUB WILL OVERFLOW!
BATHTUB?
I CAN'T DO IT WITHOUT YOU!
OKAY, MRS. C, NO PROBLEM.
THANK YOU, THANK YOU.
OKAY, MRS. C, I'VE GOT TO GO NOW.
ALL RIGHT, MIA, I'LL SEE YOU SOON.
MIA IS AWARE FROM HER TIME AT ST. ANTHONY'S THAT MRS. C MAY BE EXPERIENCING THE EARLY STAGES OF DEMENTIA. MIA FEELS LIKE SHE'S LOSING HER FRIENDS ONE BY ONE.

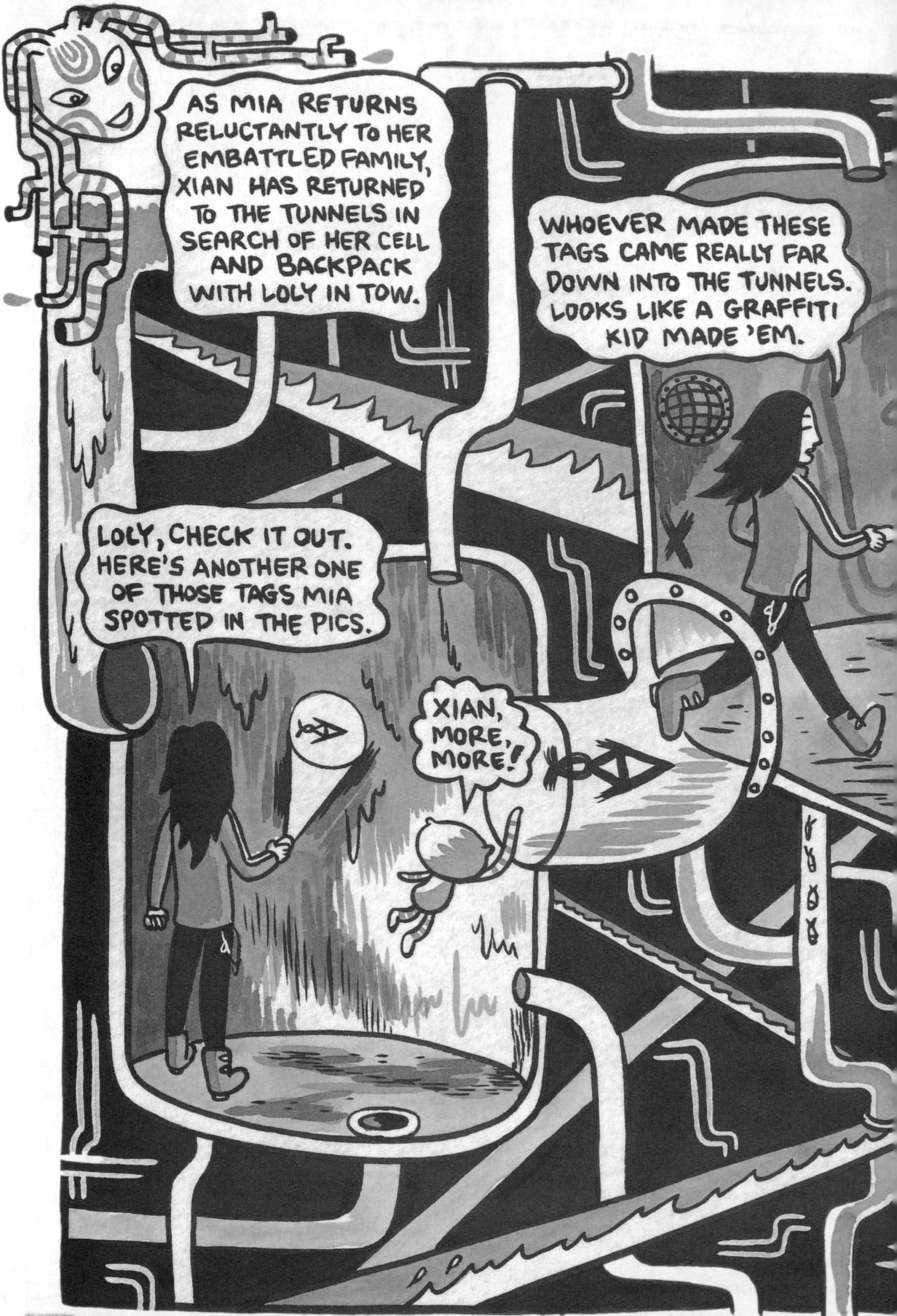
AS MIA RETURNS RELUCTANTLY TO HER EMBATTLED FAMILY, XIAN HAS RETURNED TO THE TUNNELS IN SEARCH OF HER CELL AND BACKPACK WITH LOLY IN TOW.
WHOEVER MADE THESE TAGS CAME REALLY FAR DOWN INTO THE TUNNELS. LOOKS LIKE A GRAFFITI KID MADE 'EM.
LOLY, CHECK IT OUT. HERE'S ANOTHER ONE OF THOSE TAGS MIA SPOTTED IN THE PICS.
XIAN, MORE, MORE!

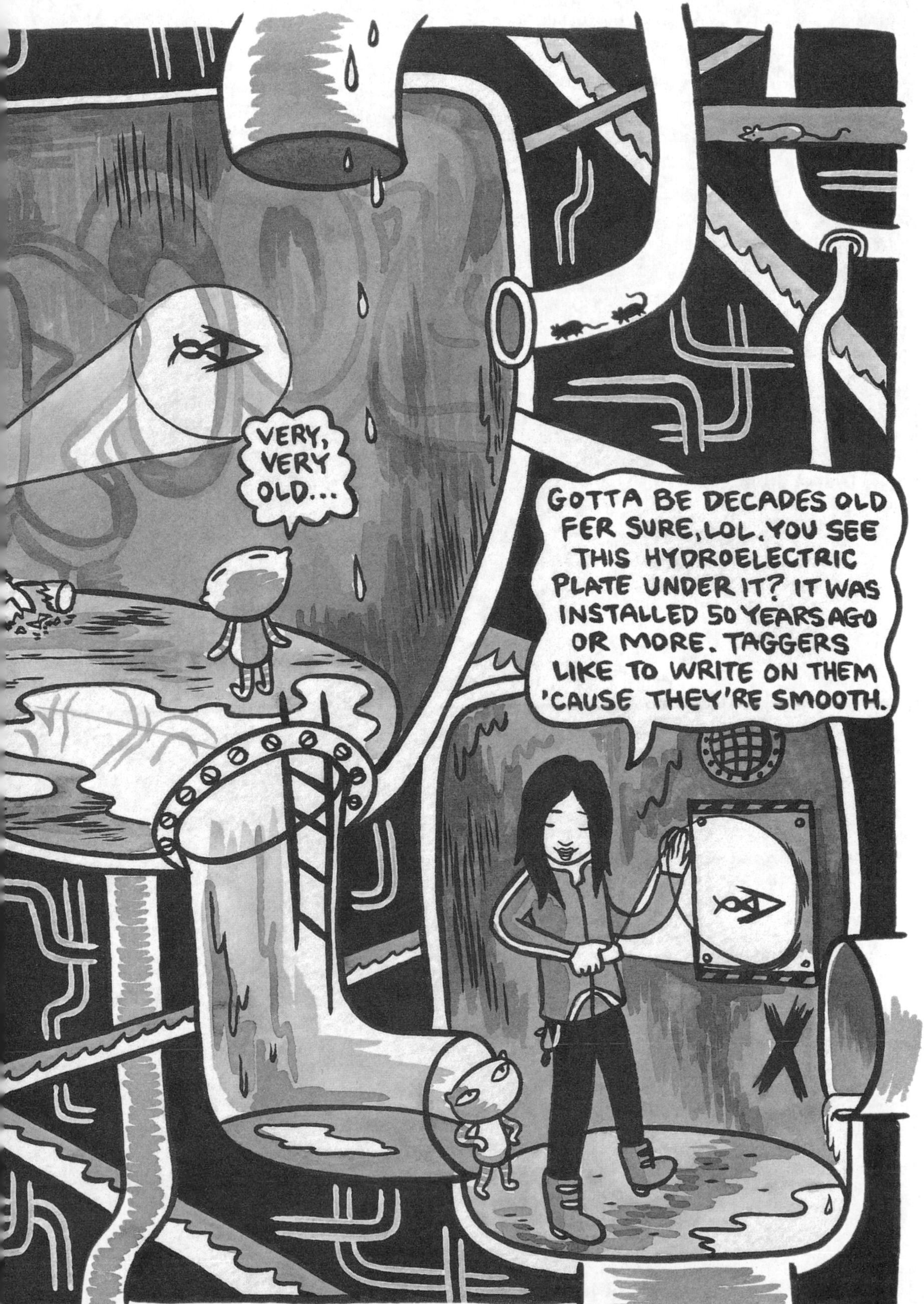
VERY, VERY OLD...
GOTTA BE DECADES OLD FER SURE, LOL. YOU SEE THIS HYDROELECTRIC PLATE UNDER IT? IT WAS INSTALLED 50 YEARS AGO OR MORE. TAGGERS LIKE TO WRITE ON THEM 'CAUSE THEY'RE SMOOTH.

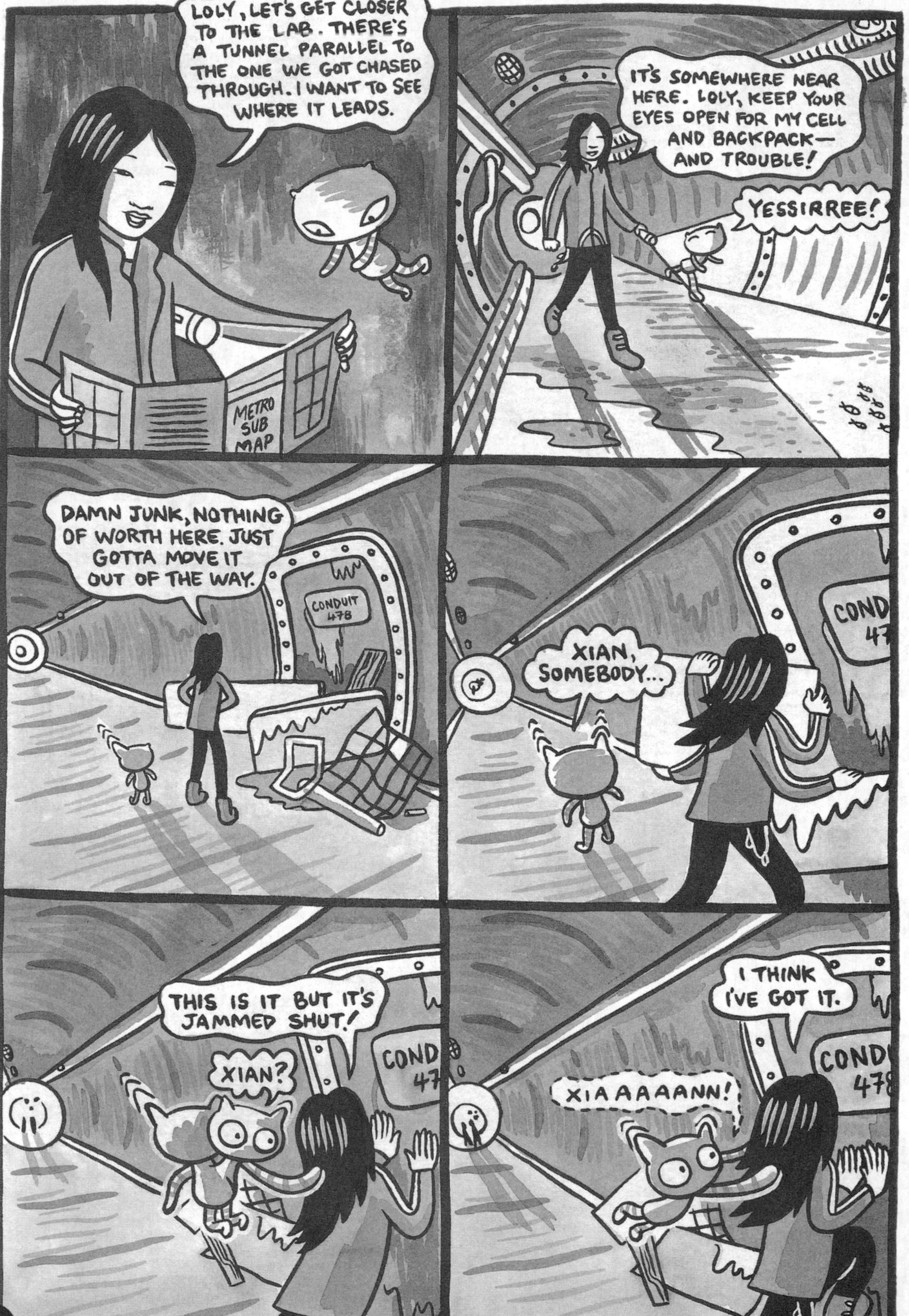
LOLY, LET'S GET CLOSER TO THE LAB. THERE'S A TUNNEL PARALLEL TO THE ONE WE GOT CHASED THROUGH. I WANT TO SEE WHERE IT LEADS.
METRO SUB MAP
IT'S SOMEWHERE NEAR HERE. LOLY, KEEP YOUR EYES OPEN FOR MY CELL AND BACKPACK— AND TROUBLE!
YESSIRREE!
DAMN JUNK, NOTHING OF WORTH HERE. JUST GOTTA MOVE IT OUT OF THE WAY.
CONDUIT 478
XIAN, SOMEBODY...
THIS IS IT BUT IT'S JAMMED SHUT!
XIAN?
I THINK I'VE GOT IT.
XIAAAAANN!

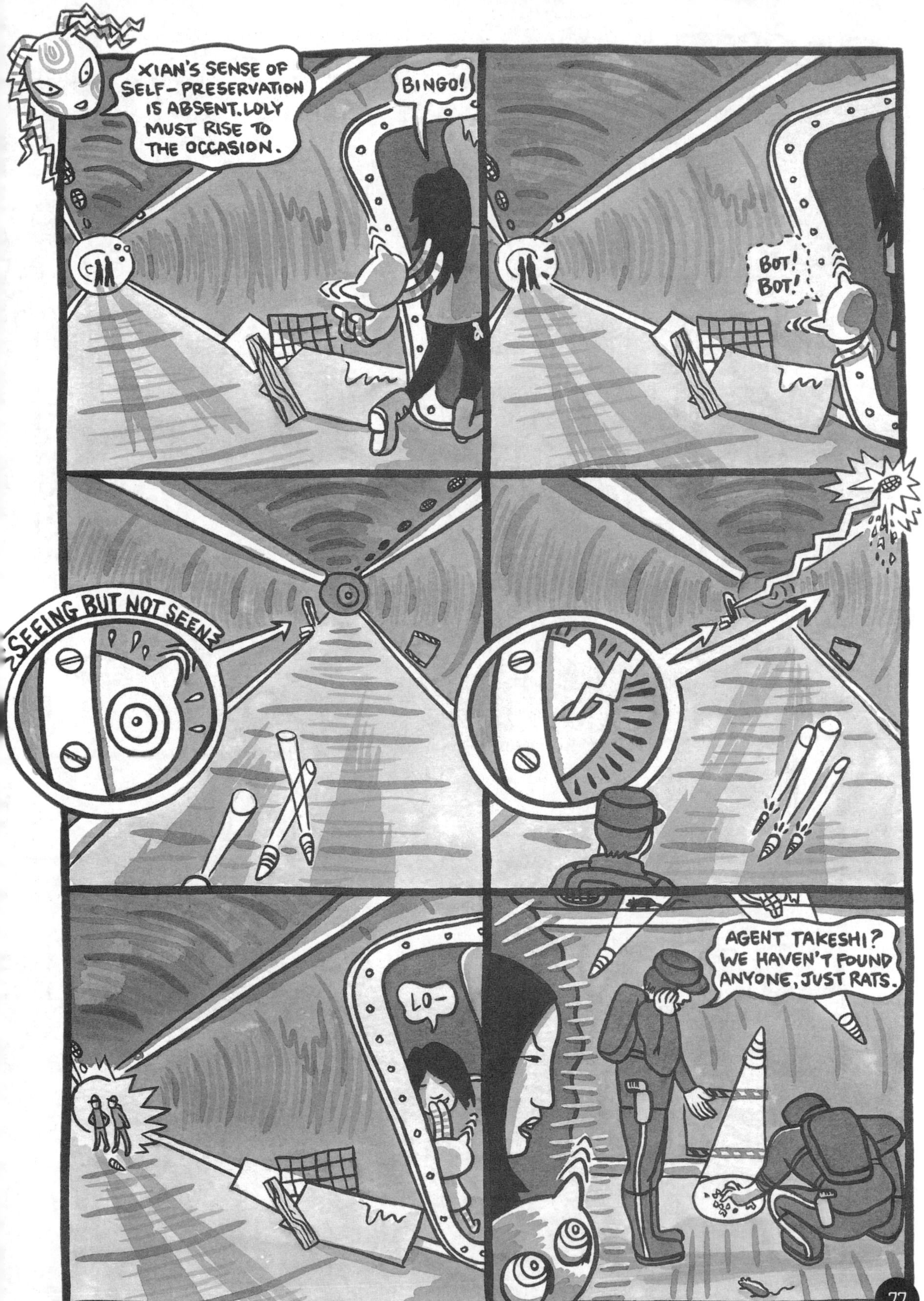
XIAN'S SENSE OF SELF-PRESERVATION IS ABSENT. LOLY MUST RISE TO THE OCCASION.
BINGO!
BOT! BOT!
SEEING BUT NOT SEEN
LO-
AGENT TAKESHI? WE HAVEN'T FOUND ANYONE, JUST RATS.

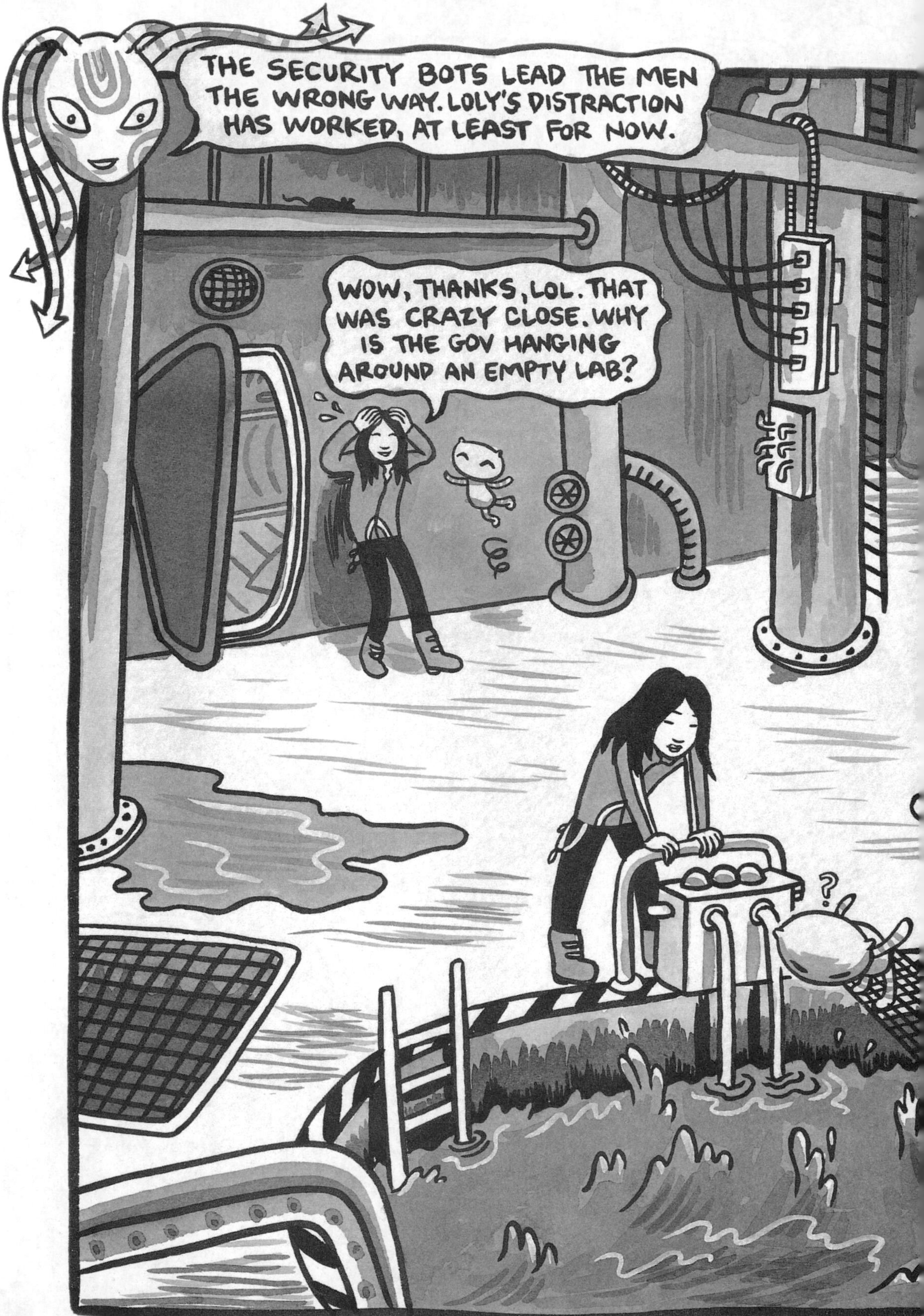
THE SECURITY BOTS LEAD THE MEN THE WRONG WAY. LOLY'S DISTRACTION HAS WORKED, AT LEAST FOR NOW.
WOW, THANKS, LOL. THAT WAS CRAZY CLOSE. WHY IS THE GOV HANGING AROUND AN EMPTY LAB?
?

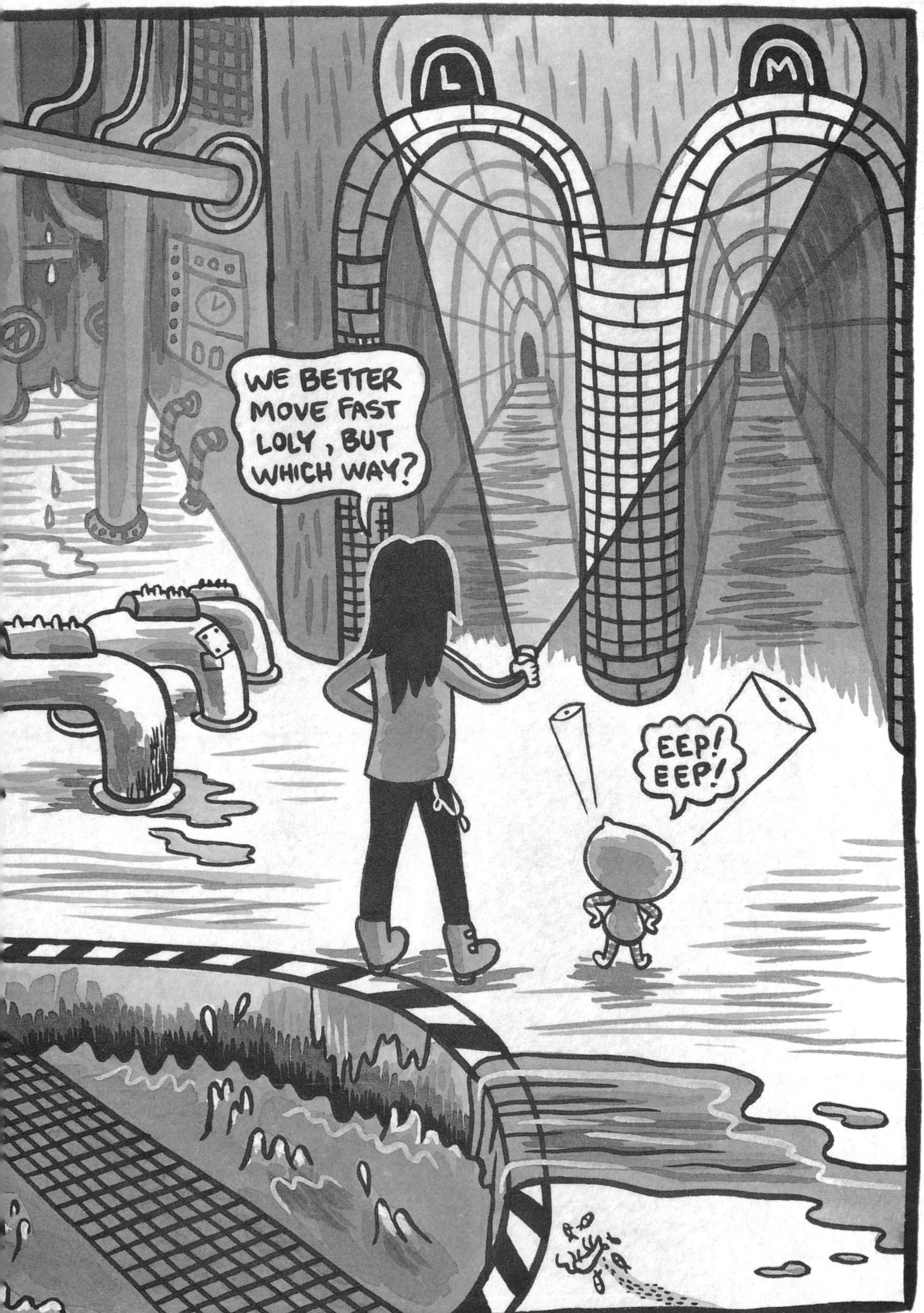
L
M
WE BETTER MOVE FAST LOLY, BUT WHICH WAY?
EEP! EEP!

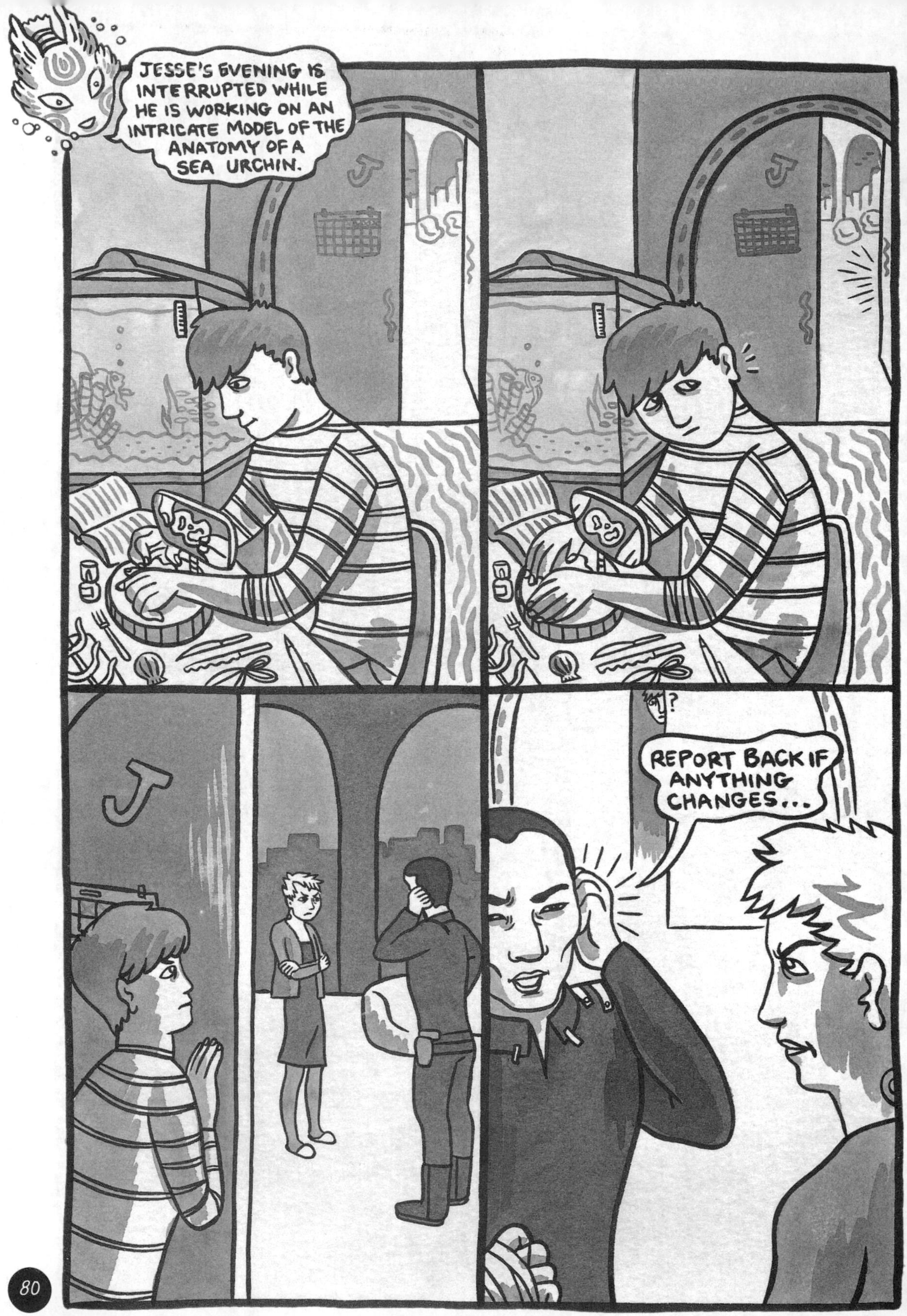

JESSE'S EVENING IS INTERRUPTED WHILE HE IS WORKING ON AN INTRICATE MODEL OF THE ANATOMY OF A SEA URCHIN.
?
REPORT BACK IF ANYTHING CHANGES...

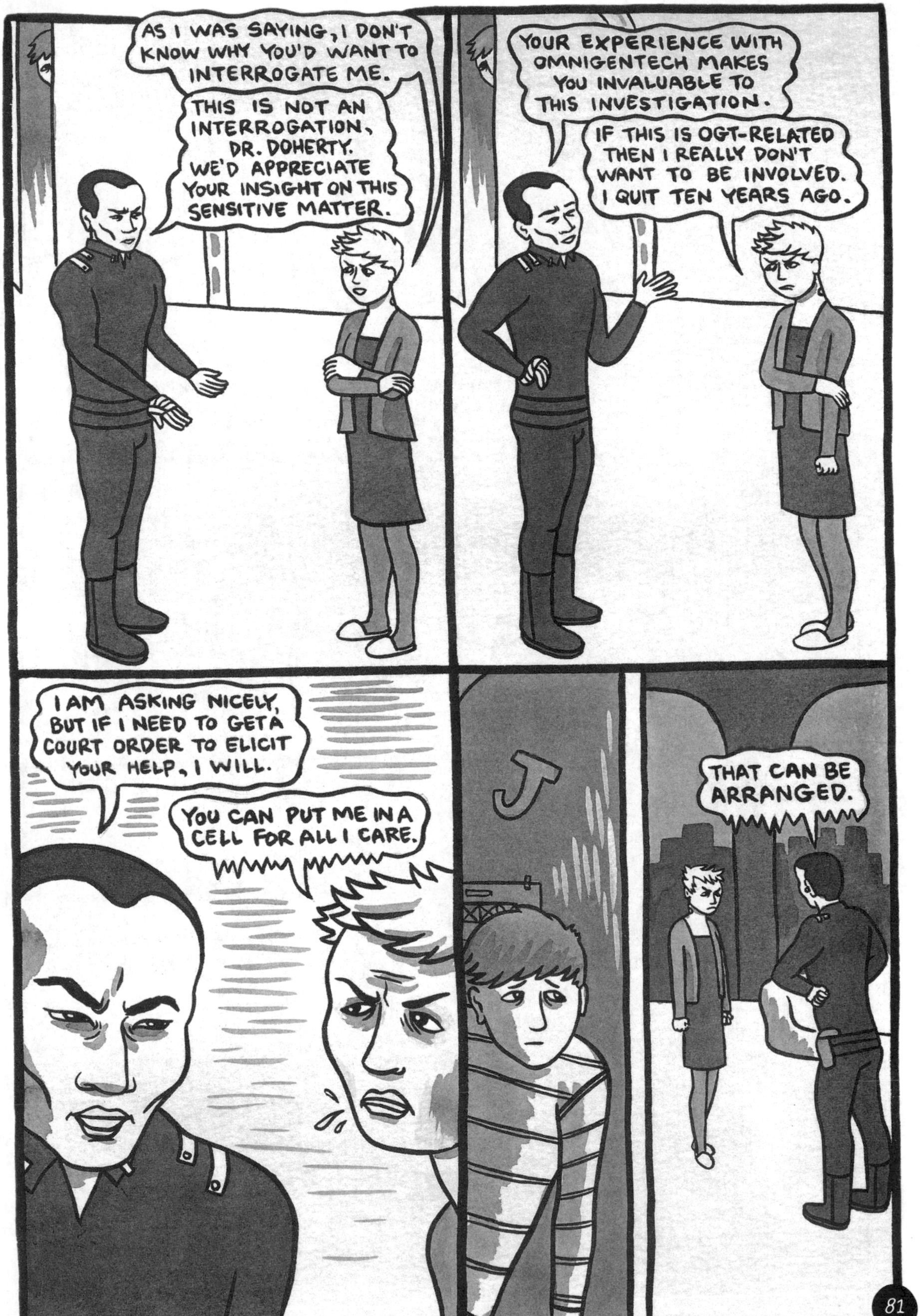
AS I WAS SAYING, I DON'T KNOW WHY YOU'D WANT TO INTERROGATE ME.
THIS IS NOT AN INTERROGATION, DR. DOHERTY. WE'D APPRECIATE YOUR INSIGHT ON THIS SENSITIVE MATTER.
YOUR EXPERIENCE WITH OMNIGENTECH MAKES YOU INVALUABLE TO THIS INVESTIGATION.
IF THIS IS OGT-RELATED THEN I REALLY DON'T WANT TO BE INVOLVED. I QUIT TEN YEARS AGO.
I AM ASKING NICELY, BUT IF I NEED TO GET A COURT ORDER TO ELICIT YOUR HELP, I WILL.
YOU CAN PUT ME IN A CELL FOR ALL I CARE.
J
THAT CAN BE ARRANGED.

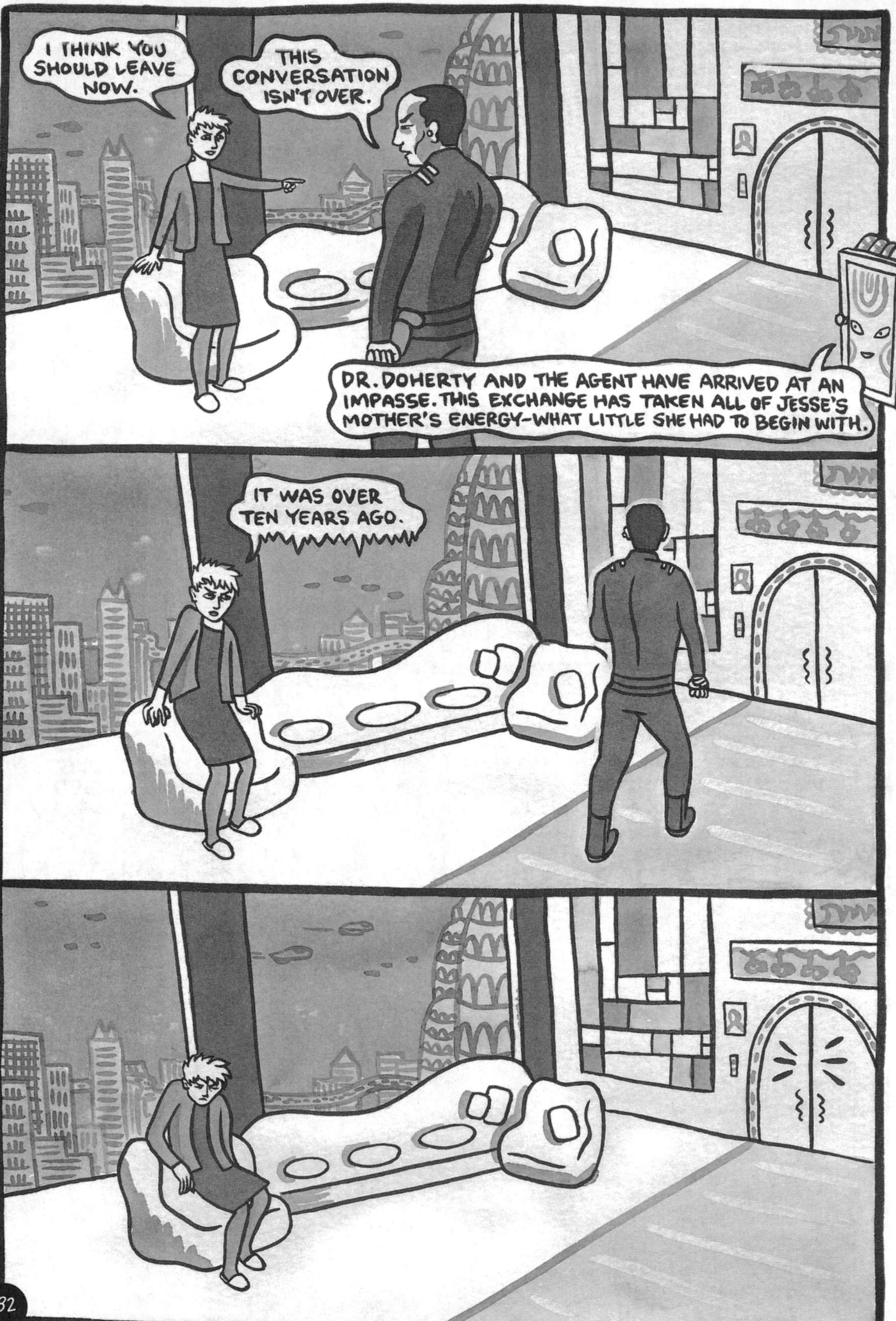
I THINK YOU SHOULD LEAVE NOW.
THIS CONVERSATION ISN'T OVER.
DR. DOHERTY AND THE AGENT HAVE ARRIVED AT AN IMPASSE. THIS EXCHANGE HAS TAKEN ALL OF JESSE'S MOTHER'S ENERGY—WHAT LITTLE SHE HAD TO BEGIN WITH.
IT WAS OVER TEN YEARS AGO.

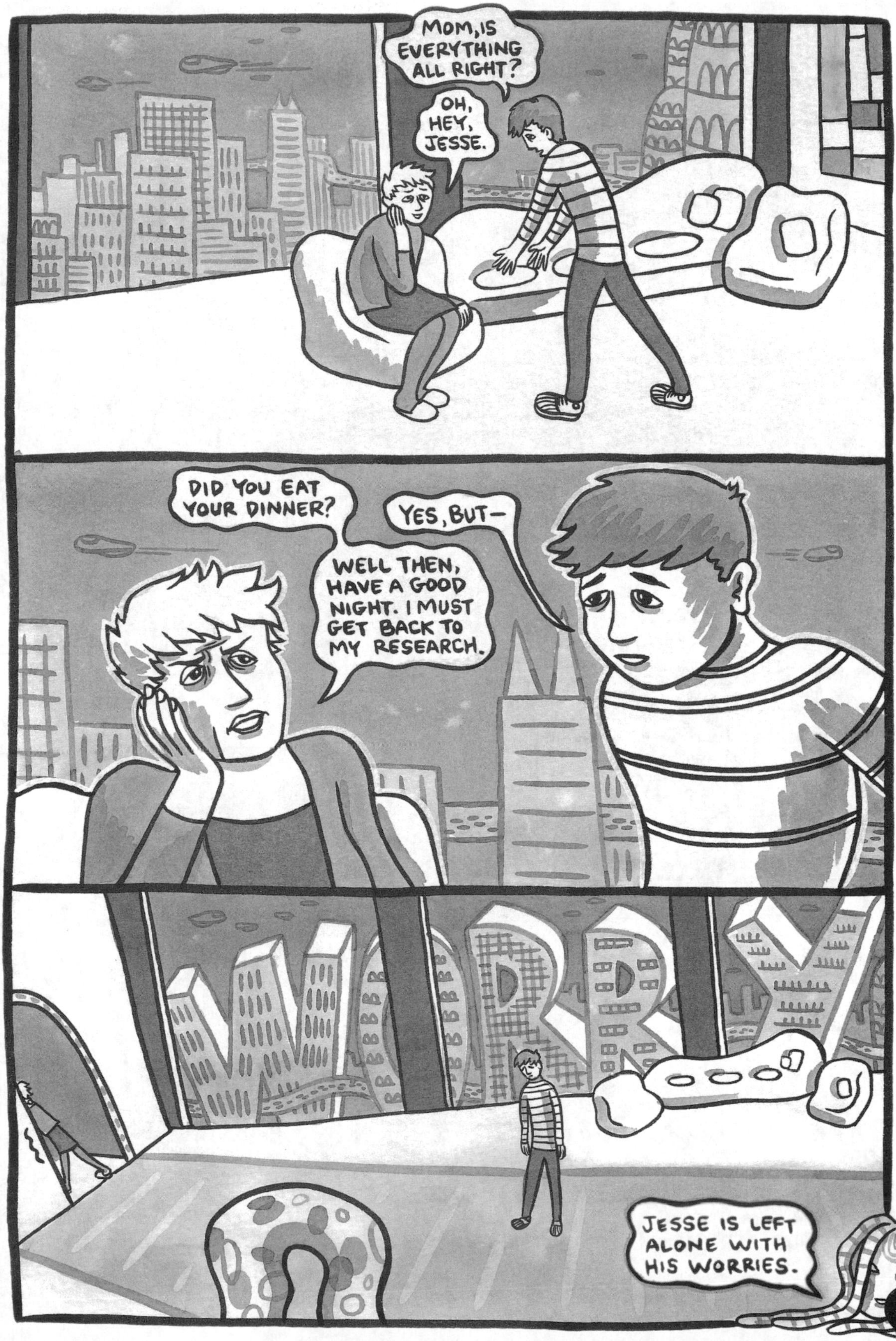
MOM, IS EVERYTHING ALL RIGHT?
OH, HEY, JESSE.
DID YOU EAT YOUR DINNER?
YES, BUT—
WELL THEN, HAVE A GOOD NIGHT. I MUST GET BACK TO MY RESEARCH.
WORRY
JESSE IS LEFT ALONE WITH HIS WORRIES.

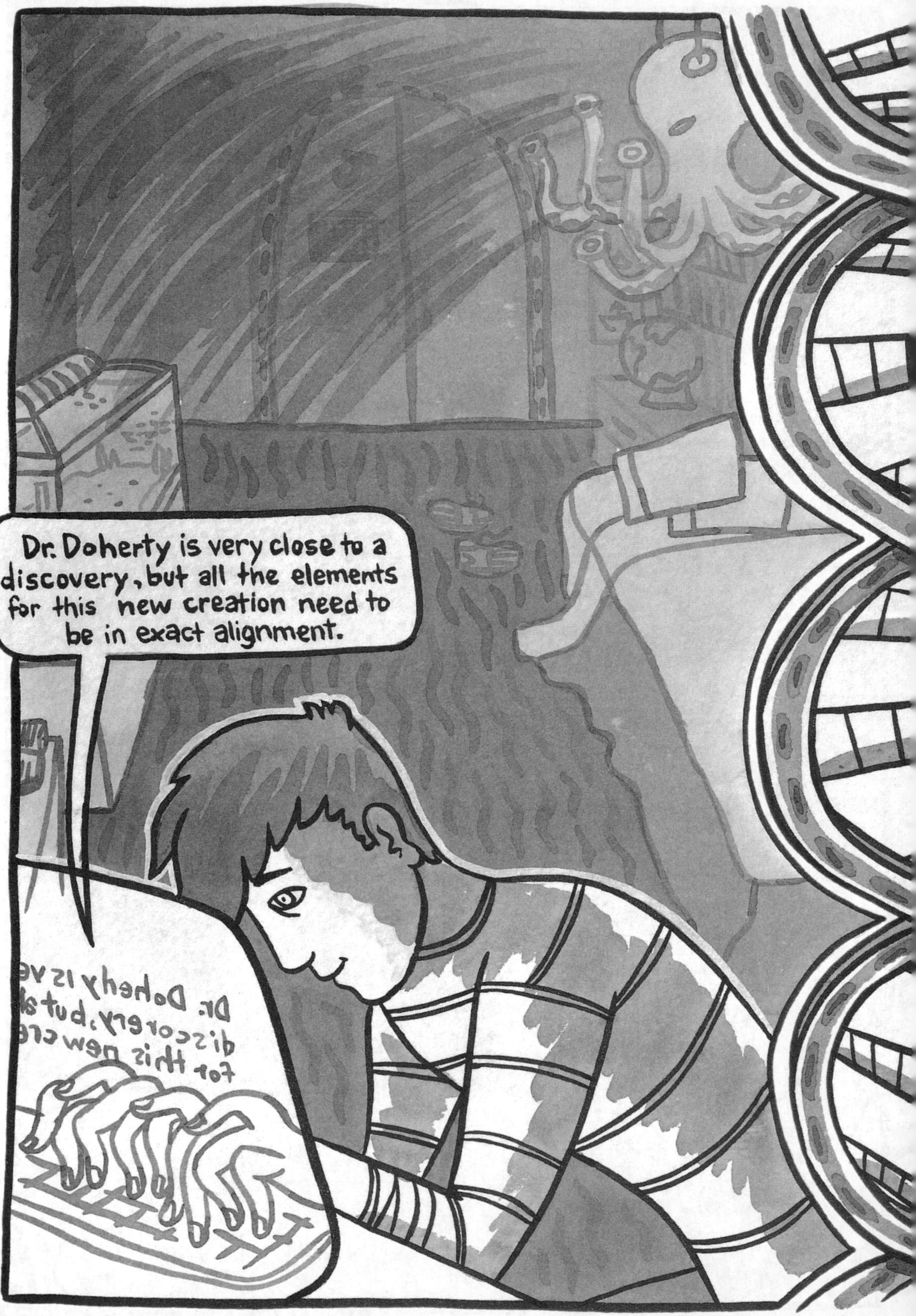
Dr. Doherty is very close to a discovery, but all the elements for this new creation need to be in exact alignment.

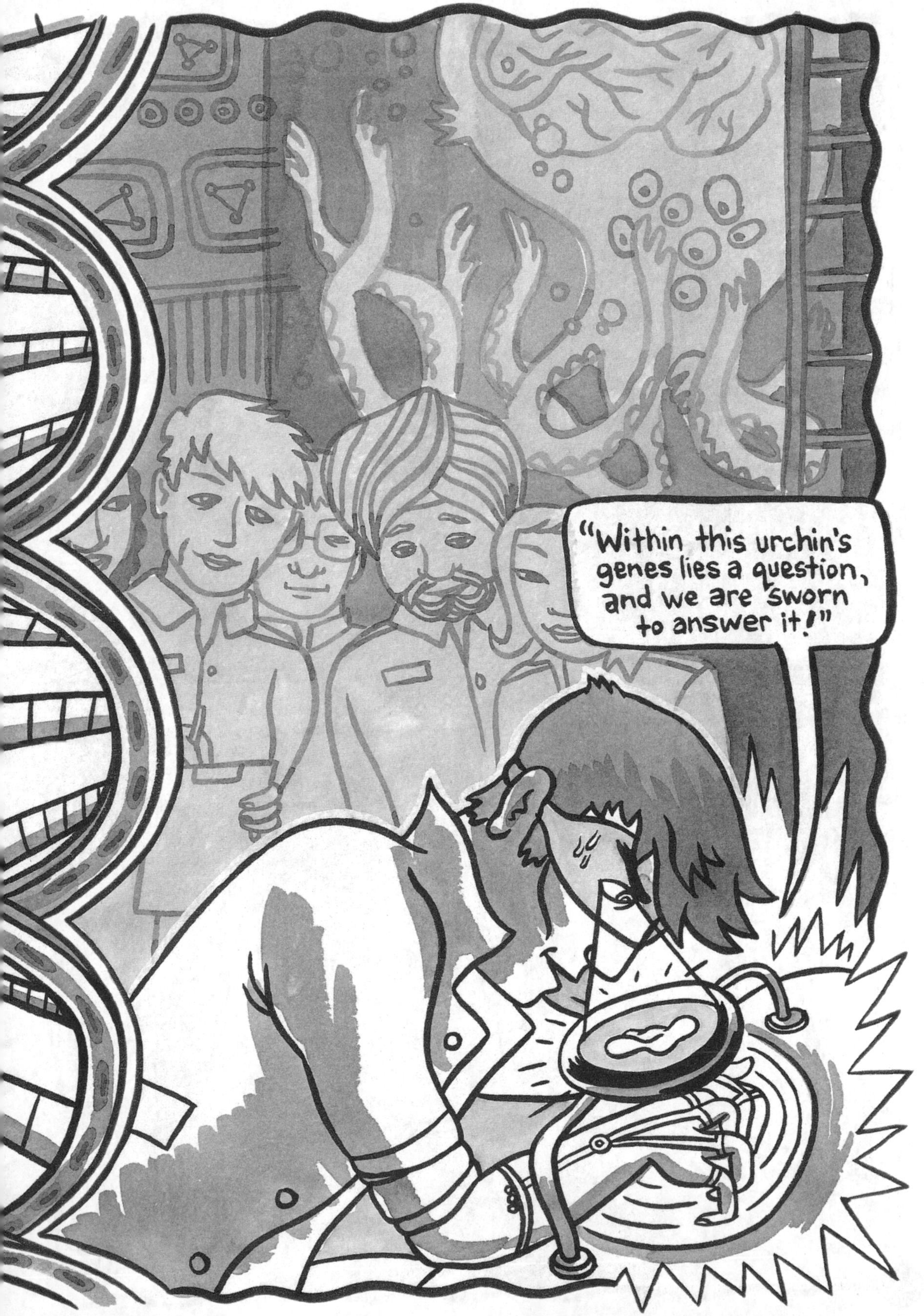
"Within this urchin's genes lies a question, and we are sworn to answer it!"

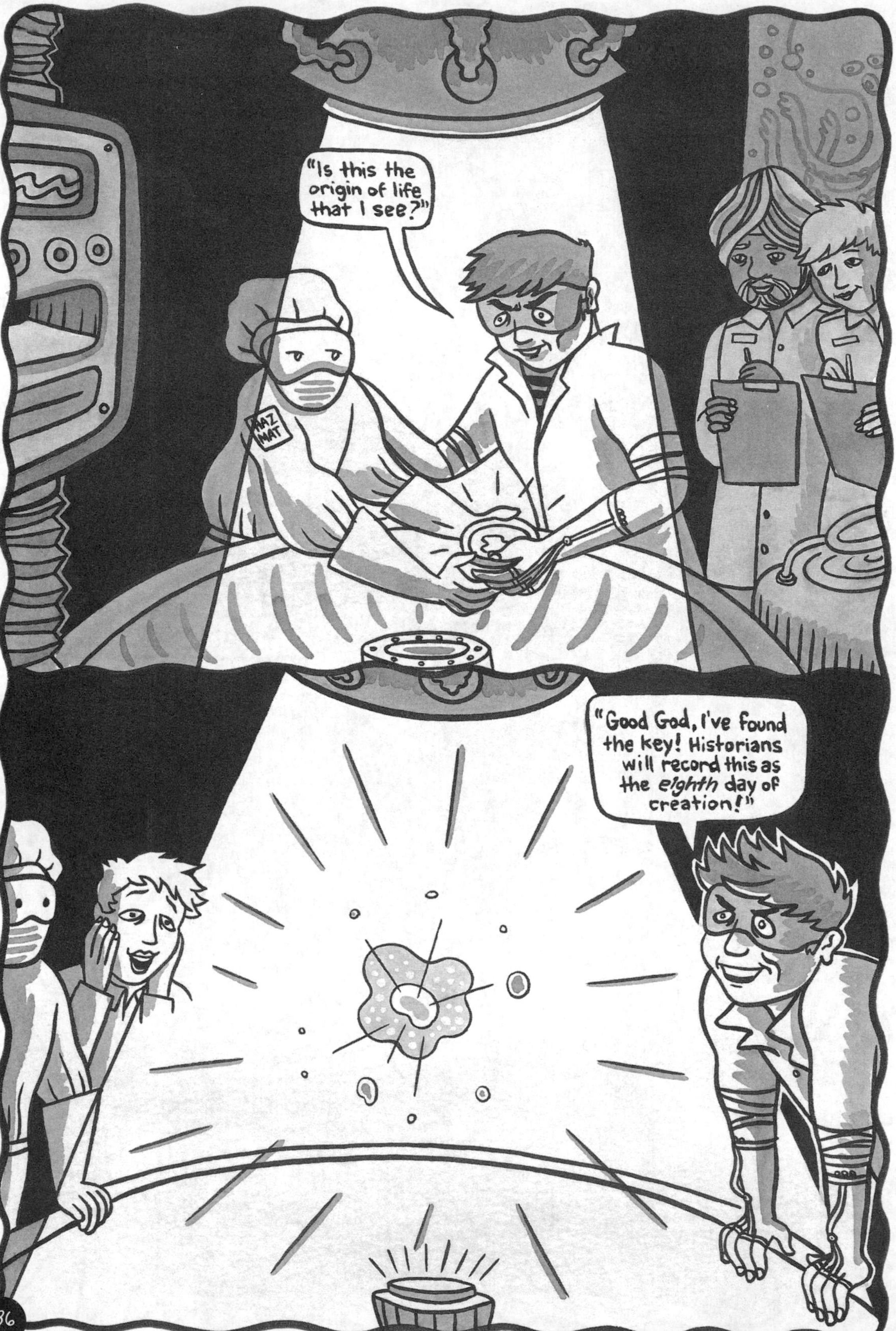
"Is this the origin of life that I see?"
"Good God, I've found the key! Historians will record this as the *eighth* day of creation!"

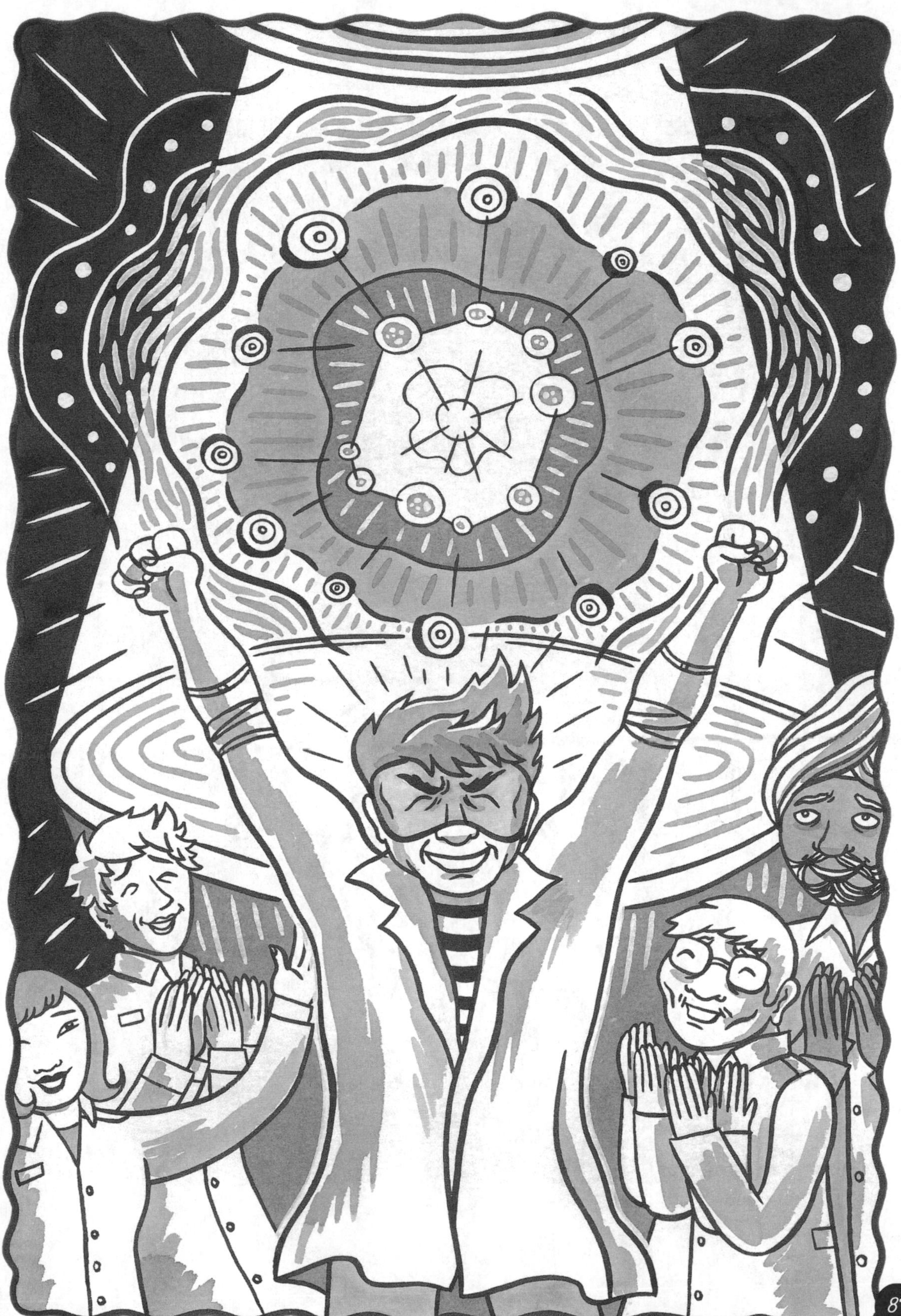

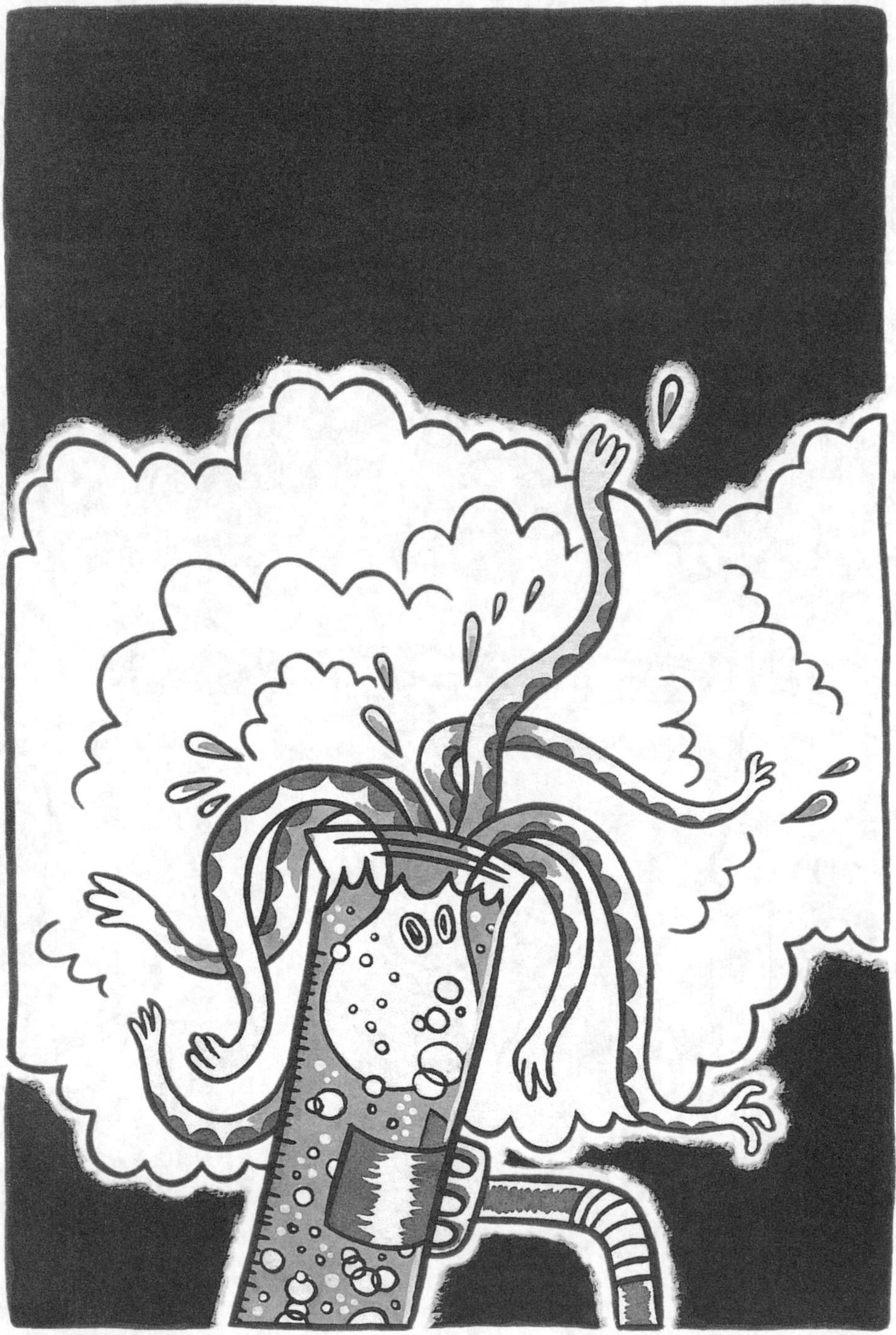

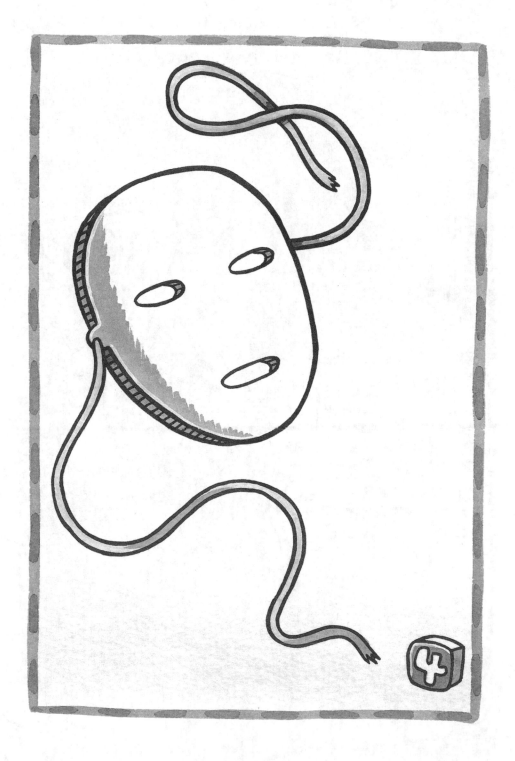

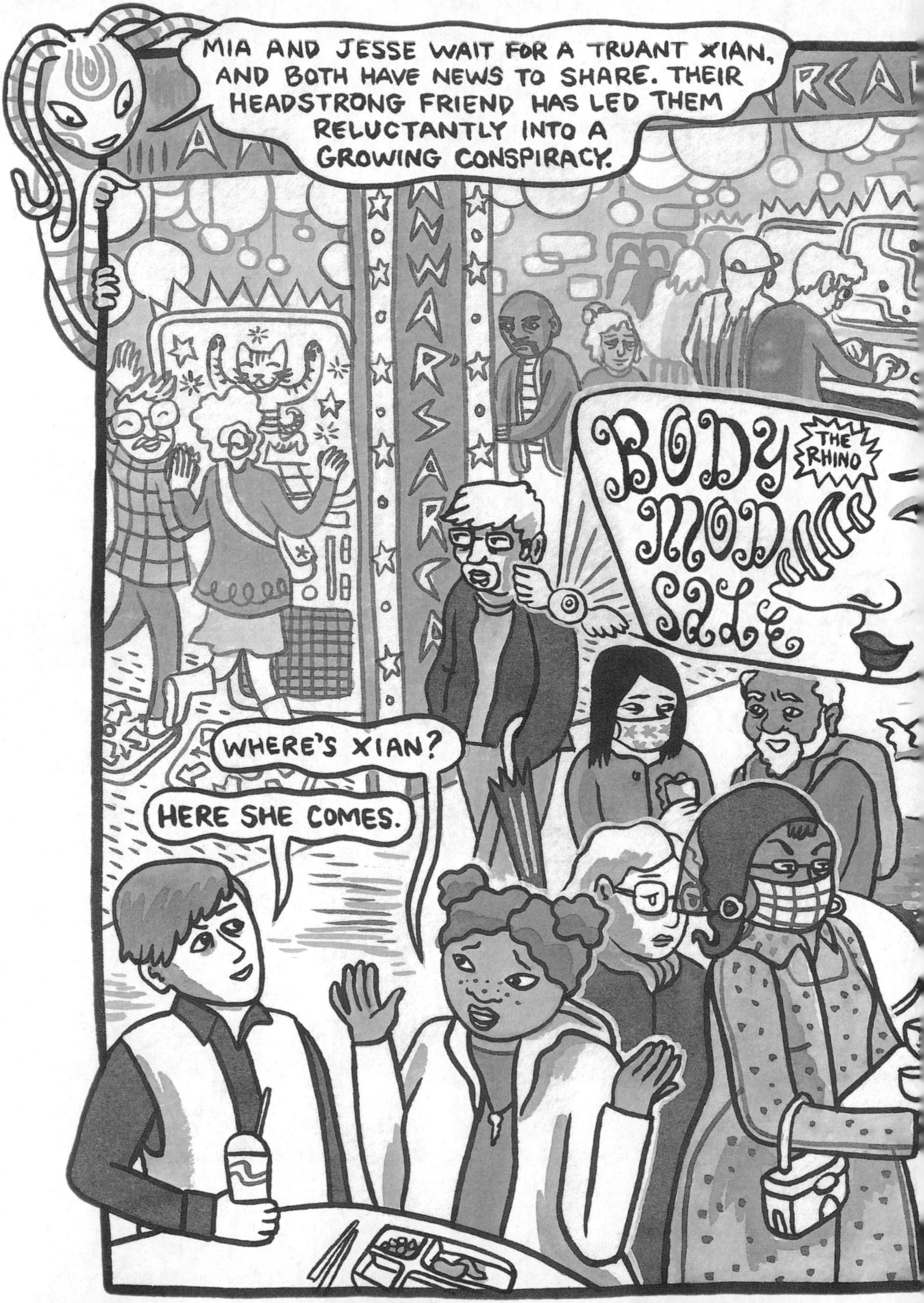
MIA AND JESSE WAIT FOR A TRUANT XIAN, AND BOTH HAVE NEWS TO SHARE. THEIR HEADSTRONG FRIEND HAS LED THEM RELUCTANTLY INTO A GROWING CONSPIRACY.
BODY MOD SALE
THE RHINO
WHERE'S XIAN?
HERE SHE COMES.

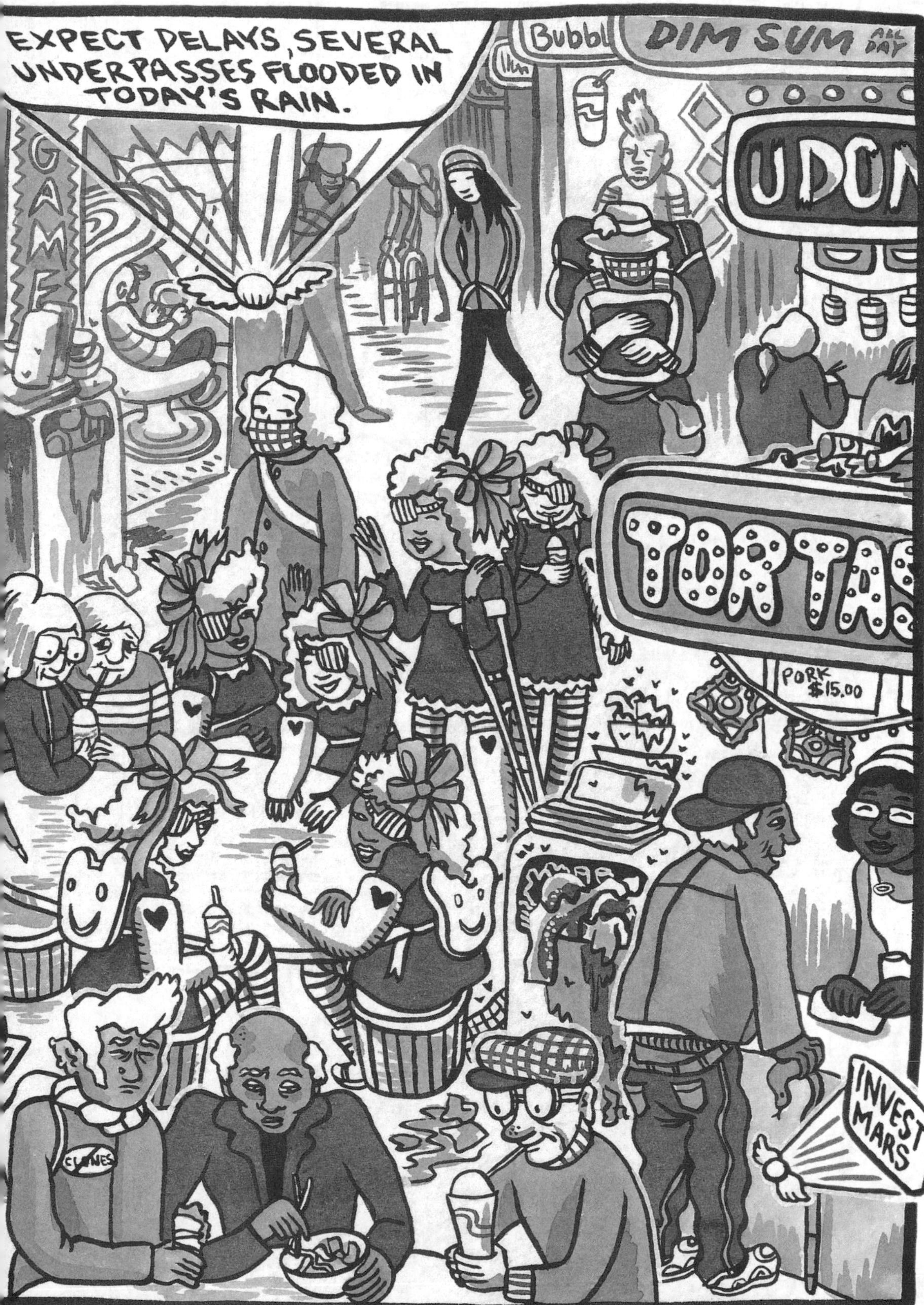

EXPECT DELAYS, SEVERAL UNDERPASSES FLOODED IN TODAY'S RAIN.
Bubbl
DIM SUM ALL DAY
UDON
GAME
TORTAS
PORK $15.00
CLONES
INVEST MARS

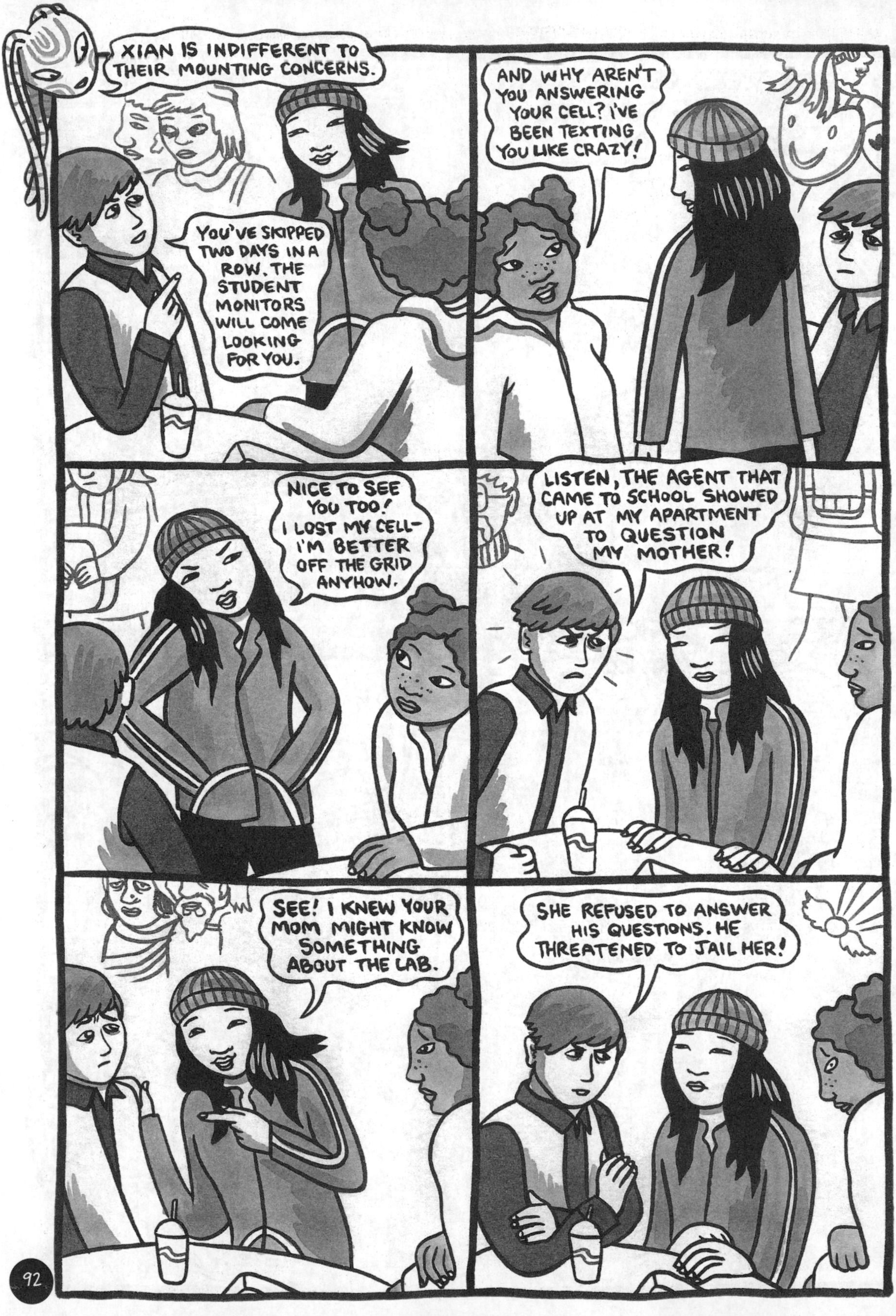
XIAN IS INDIFFERENT TO THEIR MOUNTING CONCERNS.
YOU'VE SKIPPED TWO DAYS IN A ROW. THE STUDENT MONITORS WILL COME LOOKING FOR YOU.
AND WHY AREN'T YOU ANSWERING YOUR CELL? I'VE BEEN TEXTING YOU LIKE CRAZY!
NICE TO SEE YOU TOO! I LOST MY CELL- I'M BETTER OFF THE GRID ANYHOW.
LISTEN, THE AGENT THAT CAME TO SCHOOL SHOWED UP AT MY APARTMENT TO QUESTION MY MOTHER!
SEE! I KNEW YOUR MOM MIGHT KNOW SOMETHING ABOUT THE LAB.
SHE REFUSED TO ANSWER HIS QUESTIONS. HE THREATENED TO JAIL HER!

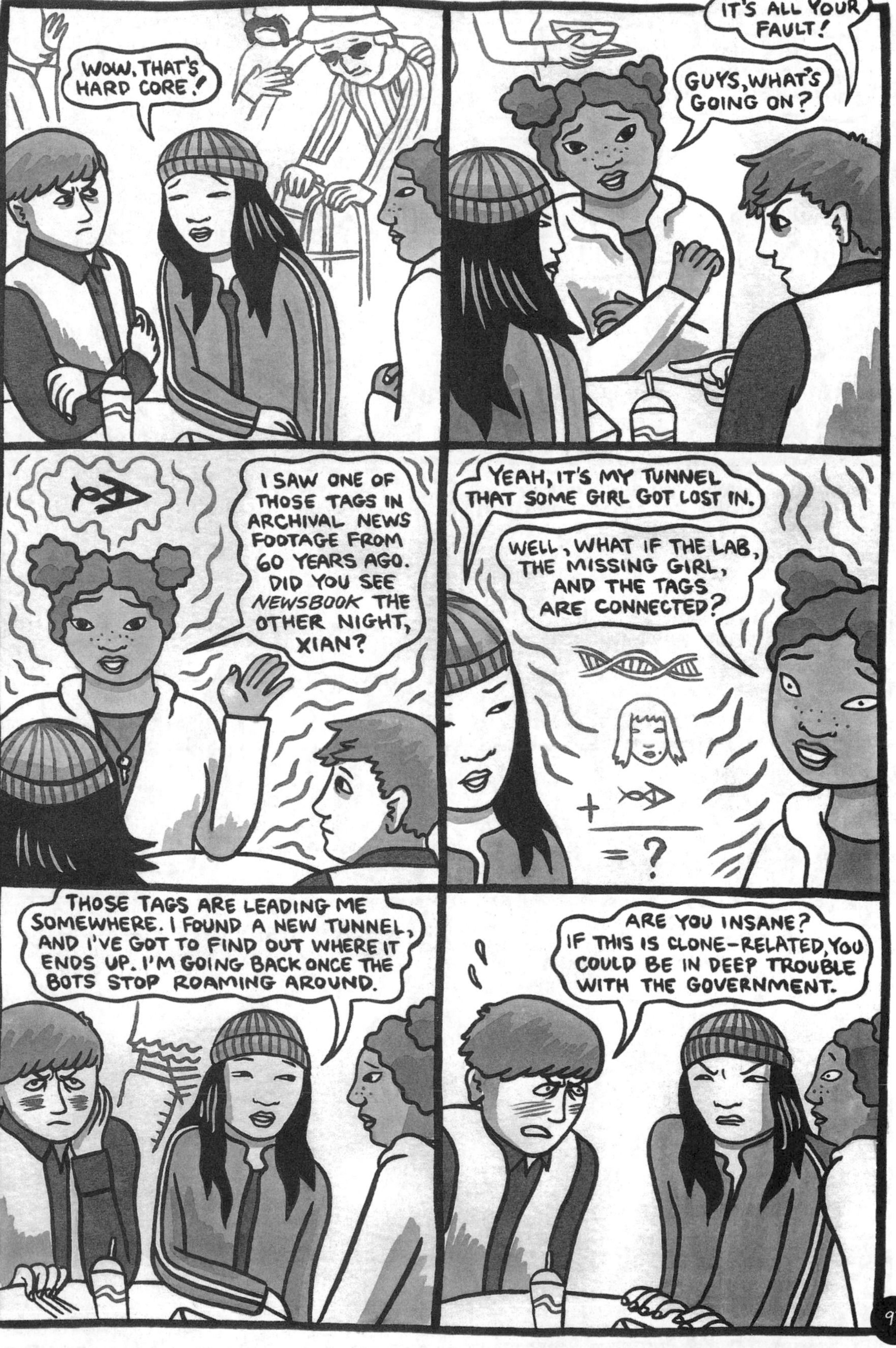
WOW, THAT'S HARD CORE!
IT'S ALL YOUR FAULT!
GUYS, WHAT'S GOING ON?
I SAW ONE OF THOSE TAGS IN ARCHIVAL NEWS FOOTAGE FROM 60 YEARS AGO. DID YOU SEE *NEWSBOOK* THE OTHER NIGHT, XIAN?
YEAH, IT'S MY TUNNEL THAT SOME GIRL GOT LOST IN.
WELL, WHAT IF THE LAB, THE MISSING GIRL, AND THE TAGS ARE CONNECTED?
+
= ?
THOSE TAGS ARE LEADING ME SOMEWHERE. I FOUND A NEW TUNNEL, AND I'VE GOT TO FIND OUT WHERE IT ENDS UP. I'M GOING BACK ONCE THE BOTS STOP ROAMING AROUND.
ARE YOU INSANE? IF THIS IS CLONE-RELATED, YOU COULD BE IN DEEP TROUBLE WITH THE GOVERNMENT.

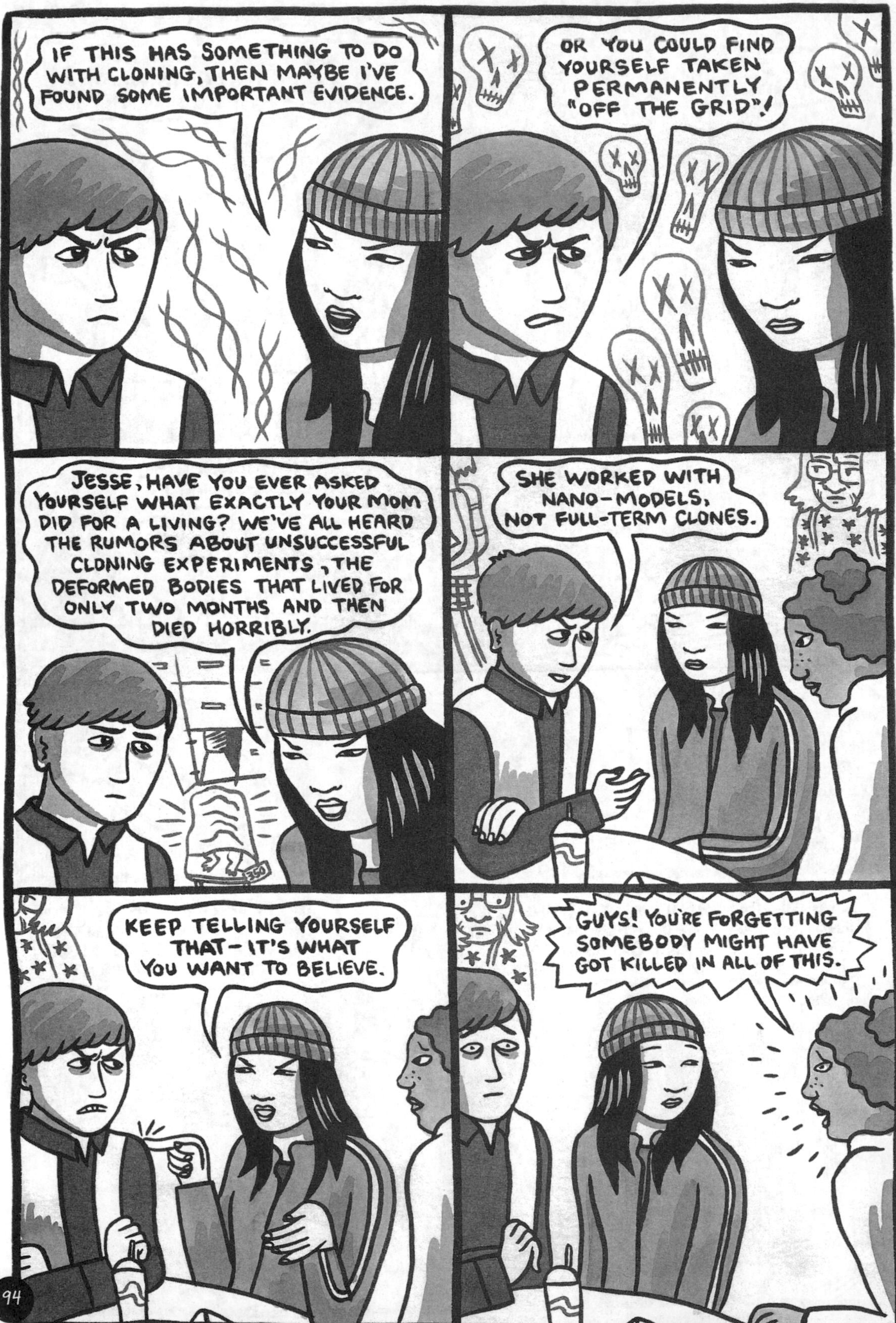
IF THIS HAS SOMETHING TO DO WITH CLONING, THEN MAYBE I'VE FOUND SOME IMPORTANT EVIDENCE.
OR YOU COULD FIND YOURSELF TAKEN PERMANENTLY "OFF THE GRID"!
JESSE, HAVE YOU EVER ASKED YOURSELF WHAT EXACTLY YOUR MOM DID FOR A LIVING? WE'VE ALL HEARD THE RUMORS ABOUT UNSUCCESSFUL CLONING EXPERIMENTS, THE DEFORMED BODIES THAT LIVED FOR ONLY TWO MONTHS AND THEN DIED HORRIBLY.
SHE WORKED WITH NANO-MODELS, NOT FULL-TERM CLONES.
KEEP TELLING YOURSELF THAT- IT'S WHAT YOU WANT TO BELIEVE.
GUYS! YOU'RE FORGETTING SOMEBODY MIGHT HAVE GOT KILLED IN ALL OF THIS.

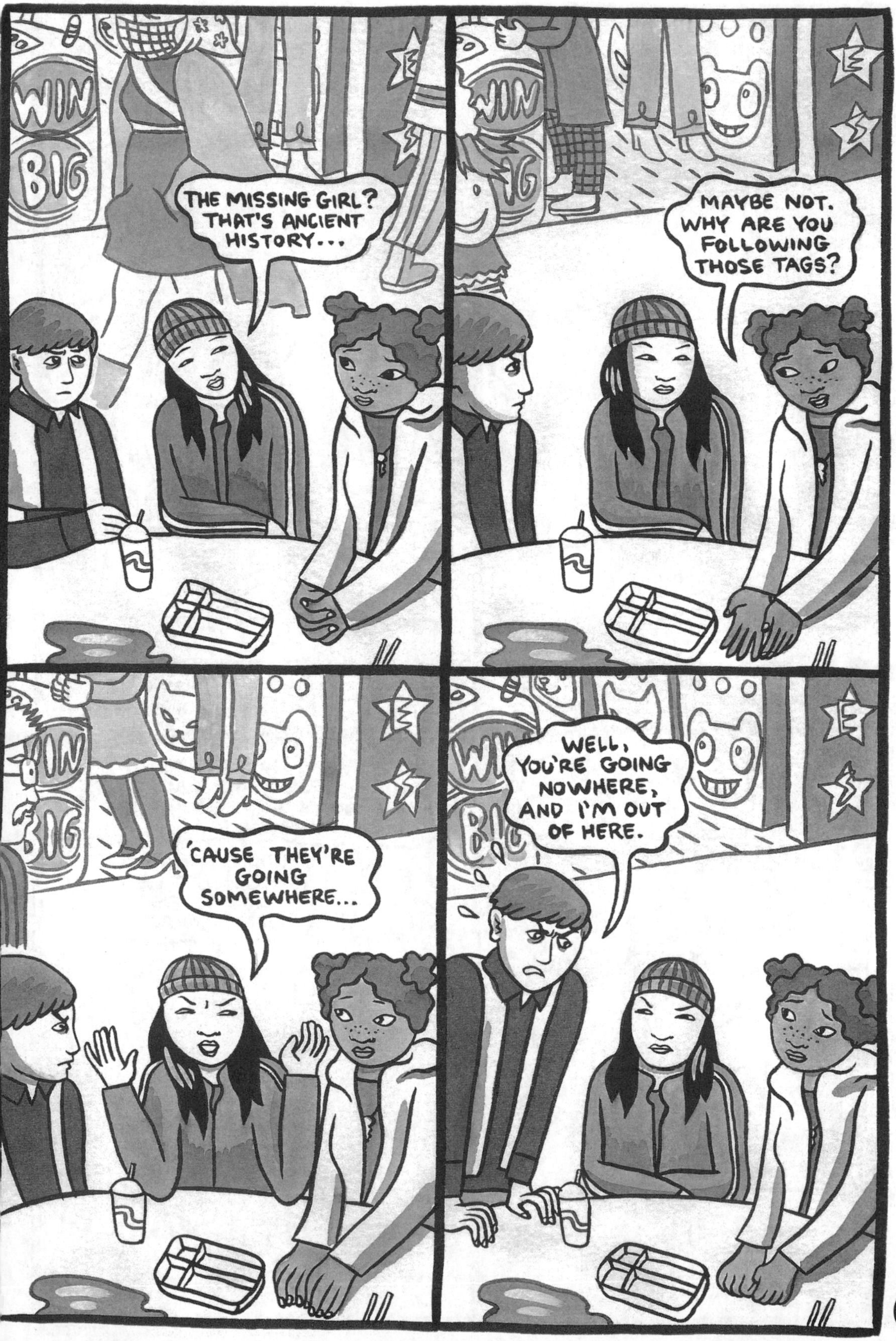
WIN BIG
THE MISSING GIRL? THAT'S ANCIENT HISTORY...
MAYBE NOT. WHY ARE YOU FOLLOWING THOSE TAGS?
'CAUSE THEY'RE GOING SOMEWHERE...
WELL, YOU'RE GOING NOWHERE, AND I'M OUT OF HERE.

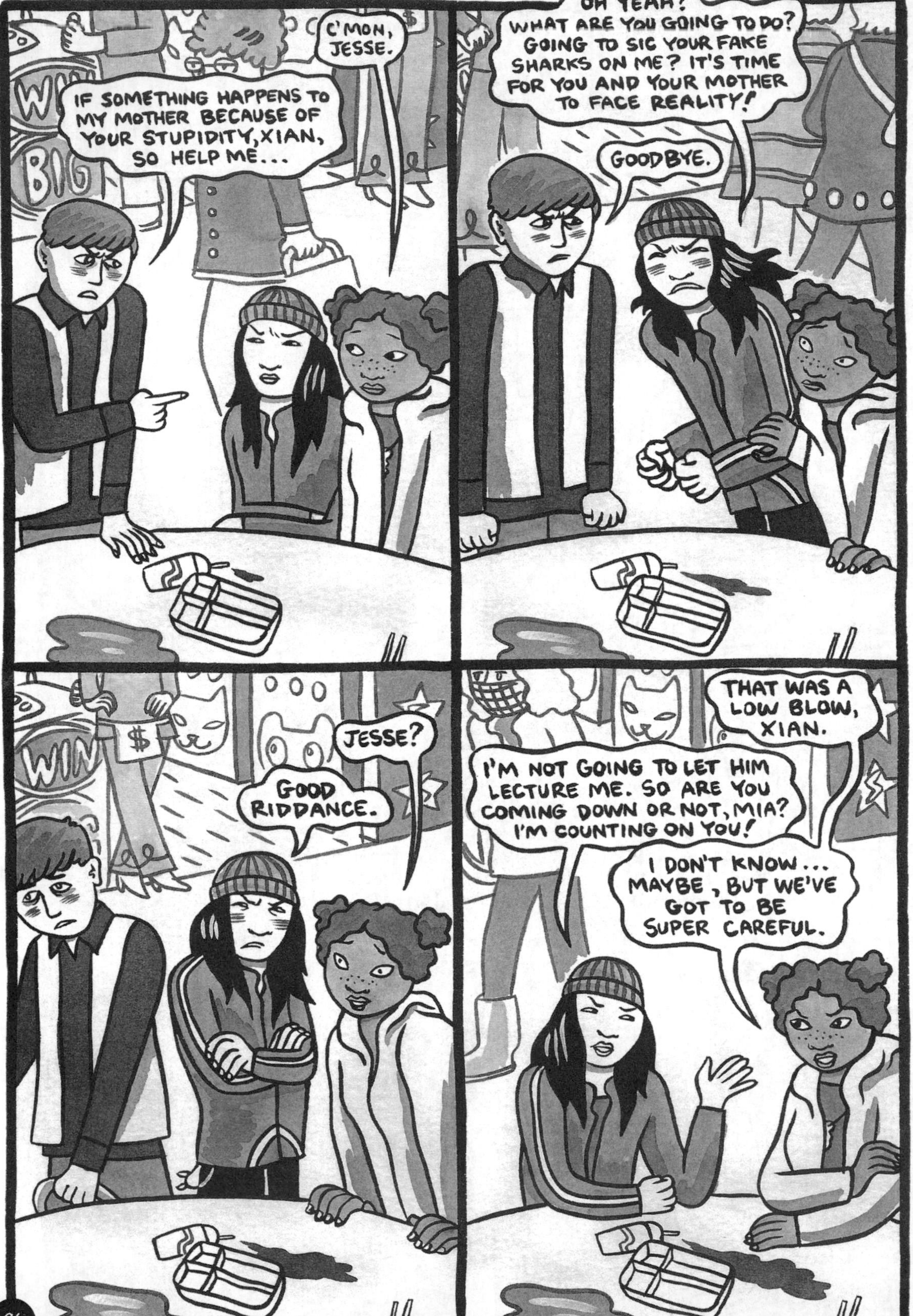
IF SOMETHING HAPPENS TO MY MOTHER BECAUSE OF YOUR STUPIDITY, XIAN, SO HELP ME...
C'MON, JESSE.
OH YEAH? WHAT ARE YOU GOING TO DO? GOING TO SIC YOUR FAKE SHARKS ON ME? IT'S TIME FOR YOU AND YOUR MOTHER TO FACE REALITY!
GOODBYE.
GOOD RIDDANCE.
JESSE?
THAT WAS A LOW BLOW, XIAN.
I'M NOT GOING TO LET HIM LECTURE ME. SO ARE YOU COMING DOWN OR NOT, MIA? I'M COUNTING ON YOU!
I DON'T KNOW... MAYBE, BUT WE'VE GOT TO BE SUPER CAREFUL.

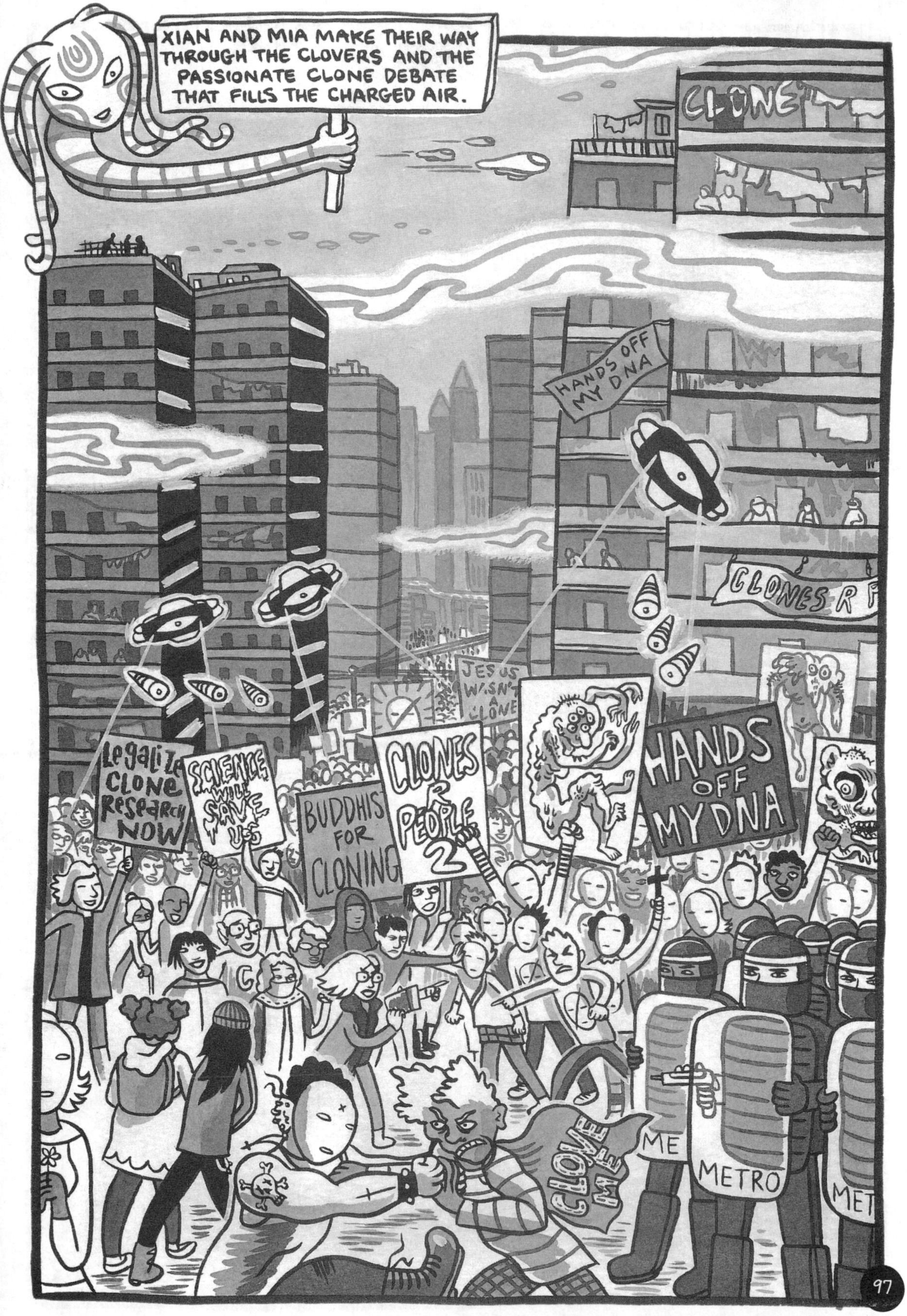
XIAN AND MIA MAKE THEIR WAY THROUGH THE CLOVERS AND THE PASSIONATE CLONE DEBATE THAT FILLS THE CHARGED AIR.
CLONE
HANDS OFF MY DNA
CLONES R
JESUS WASN'T A CLONE
LegaliZe CLONE ReSeaRCH NOW
SCIENCE WILL SAVE US
BUDDHISTS FOR CLONING
CLONES R PEOPLE 2
HANDS OFF MY DNA
CLONE ME
METRO

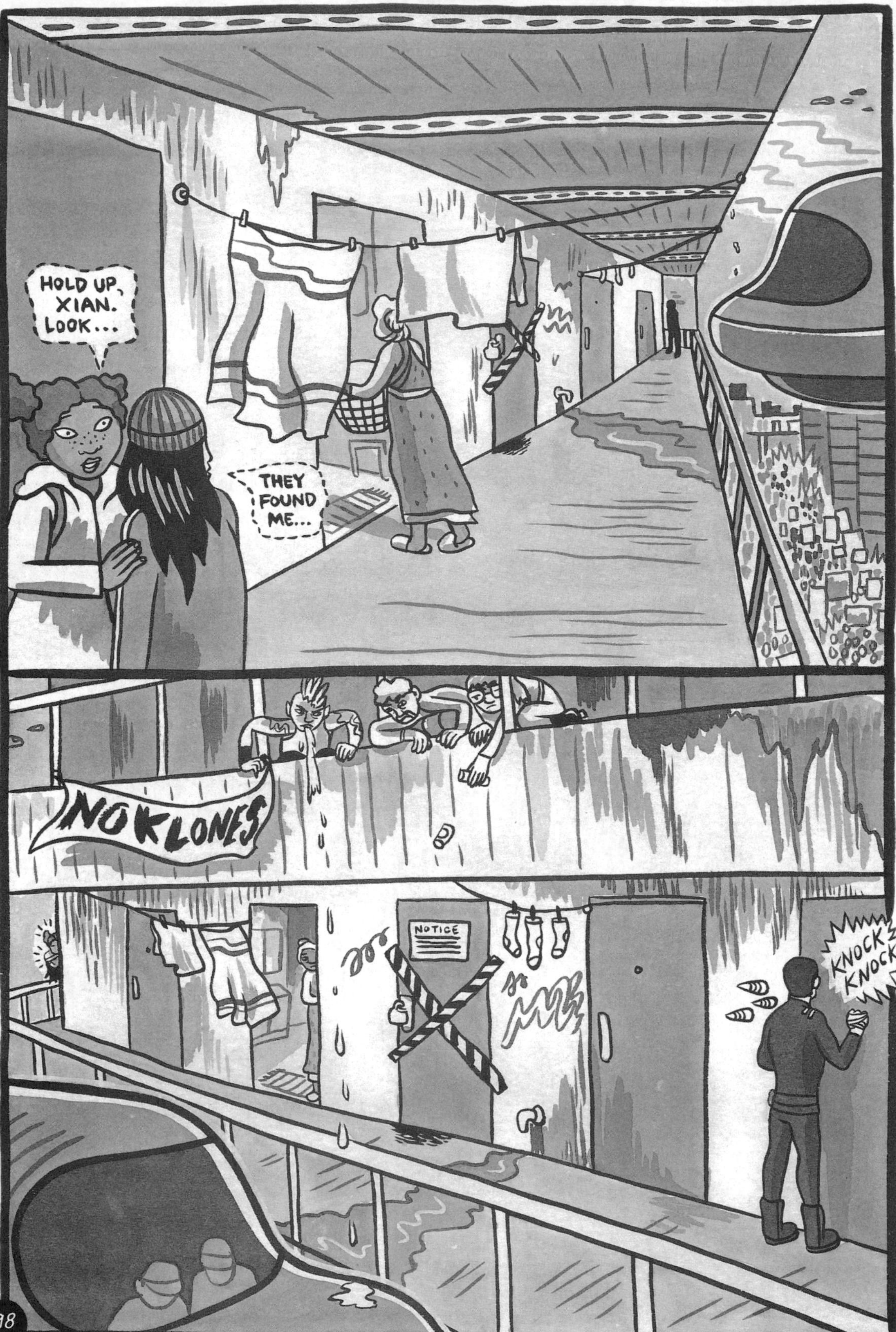
HOLD UP, XIAN. LOOK...
THEY FOUND ME...
NO KLONES
NOTICE
KNOCK KNOCK

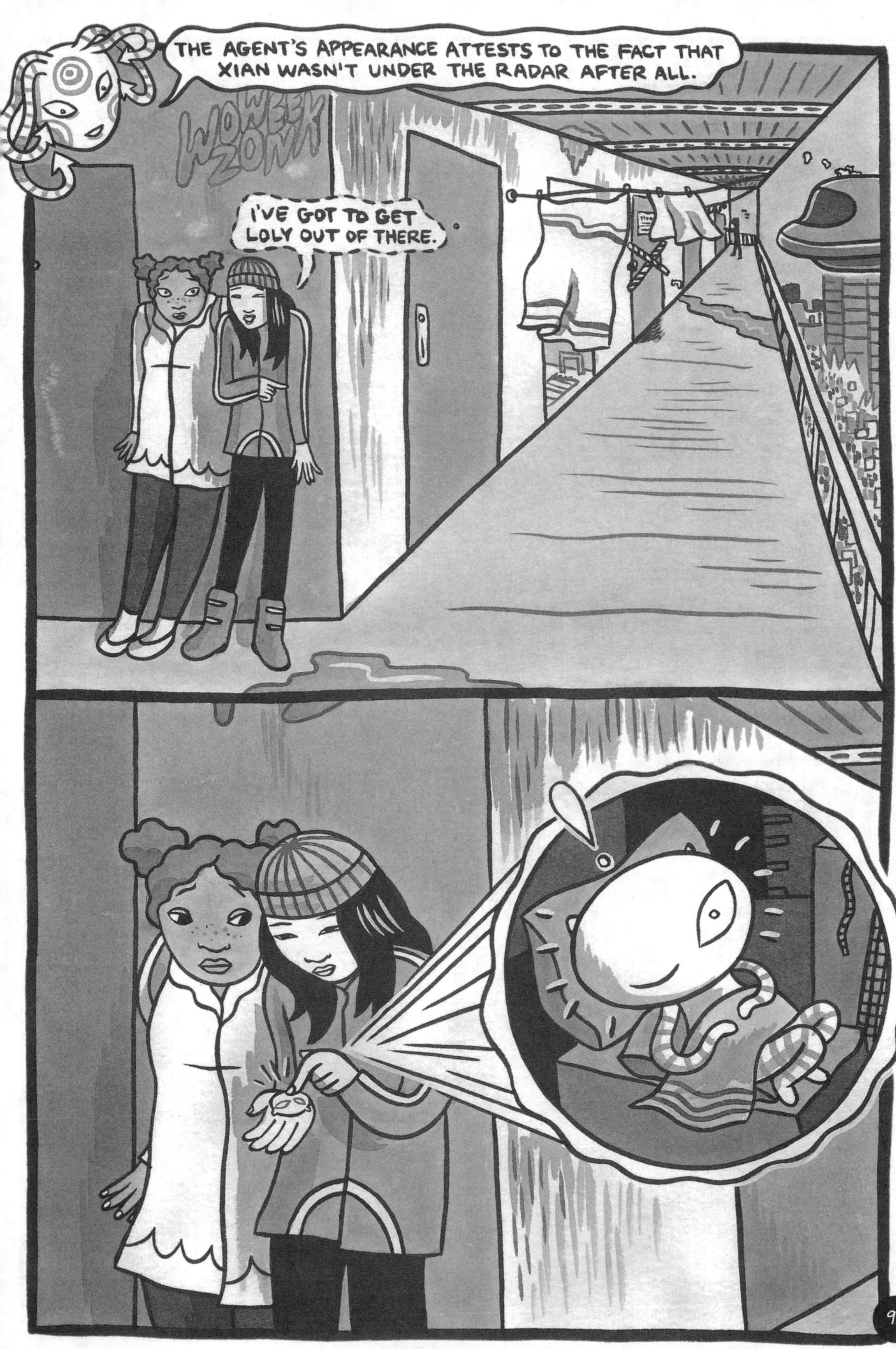
THE AGENT'S APPEARANCE ATTESTS TO THE FACT THAT XIAN WASN'T UNDER THE RADAR AFTER ALL.
I'VE GOT TO GET LOLY OUT OF THERE.

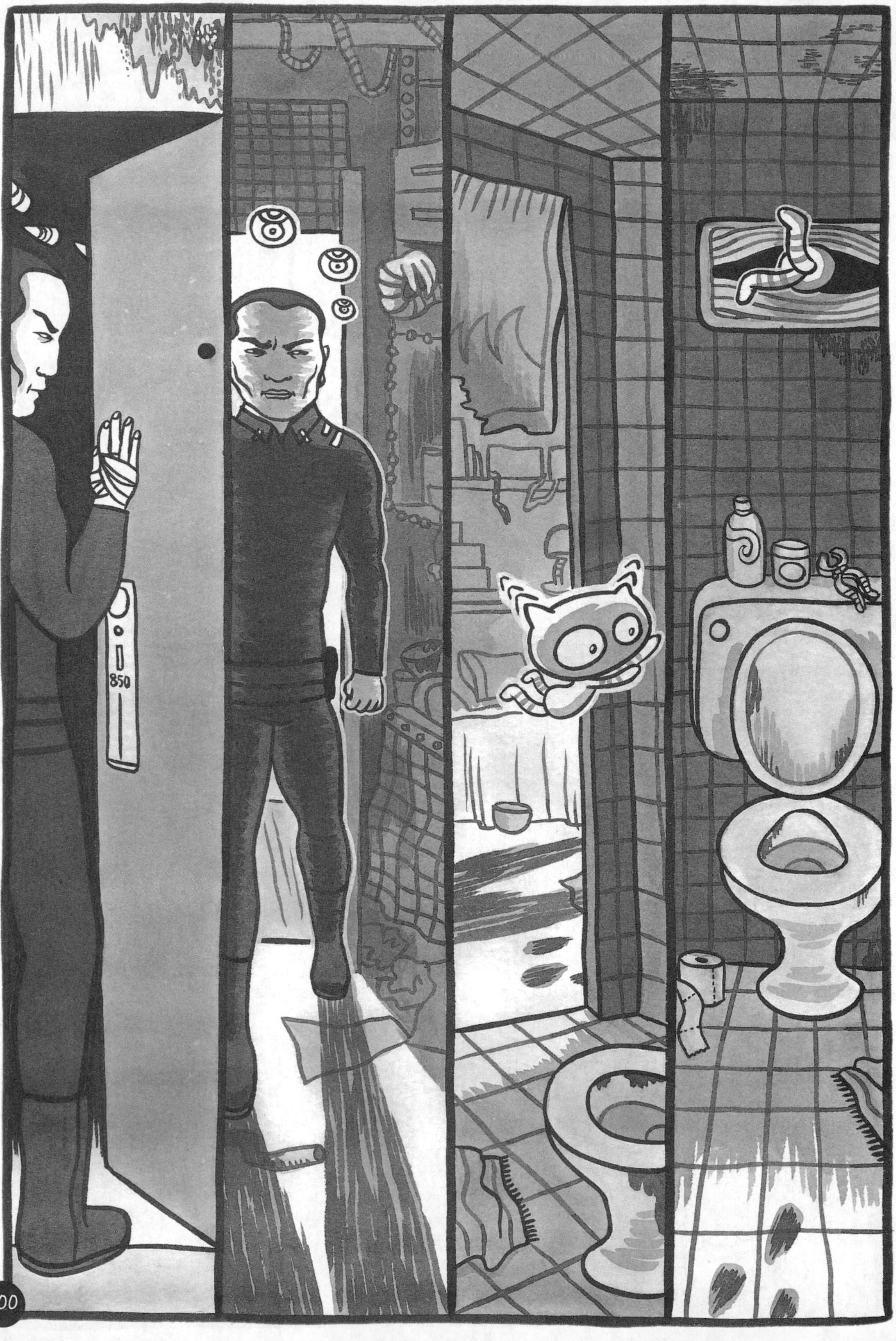
850

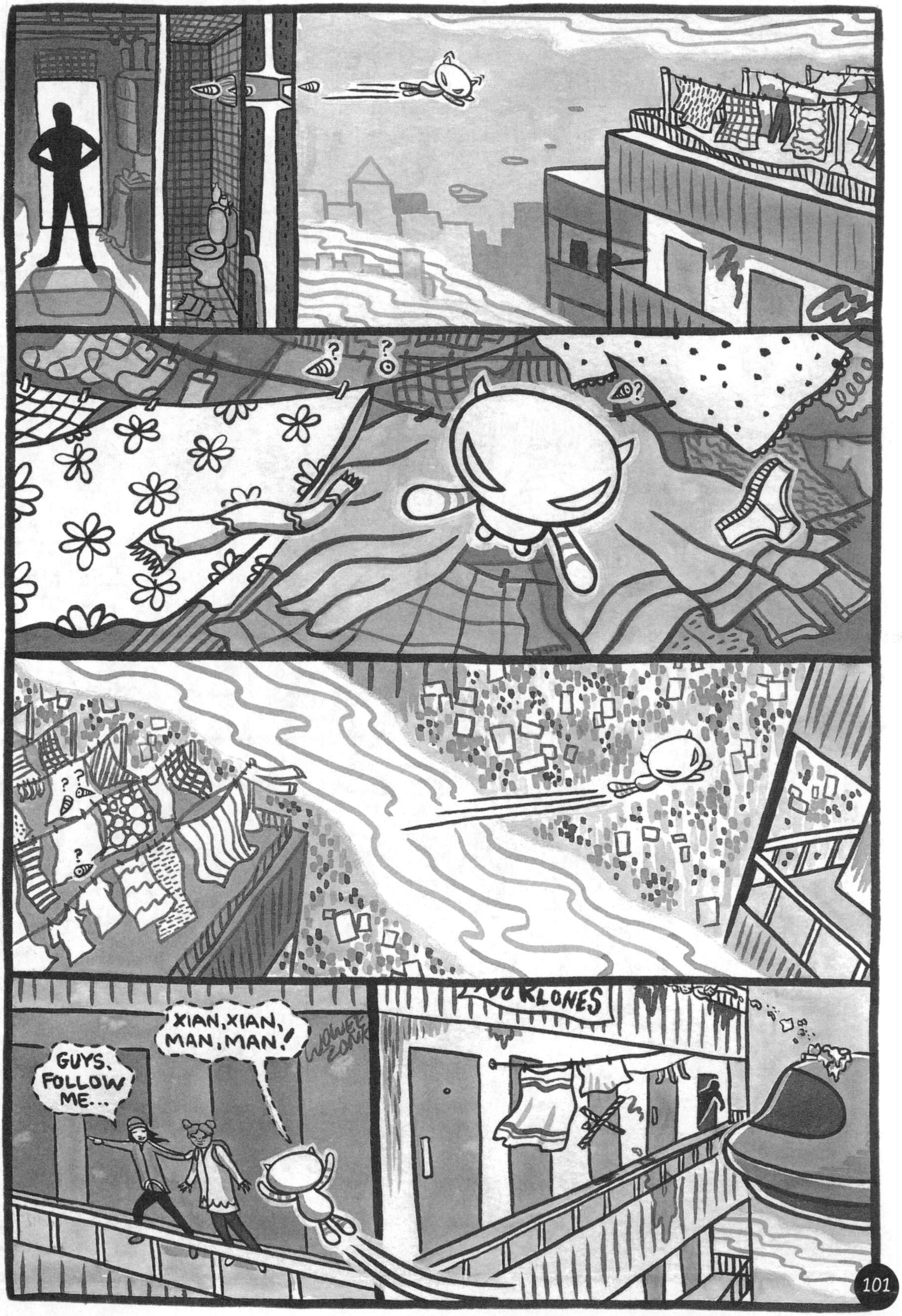
GUYS. FOLLOW ME...
XIAN, XIAN, MAN, MAN!

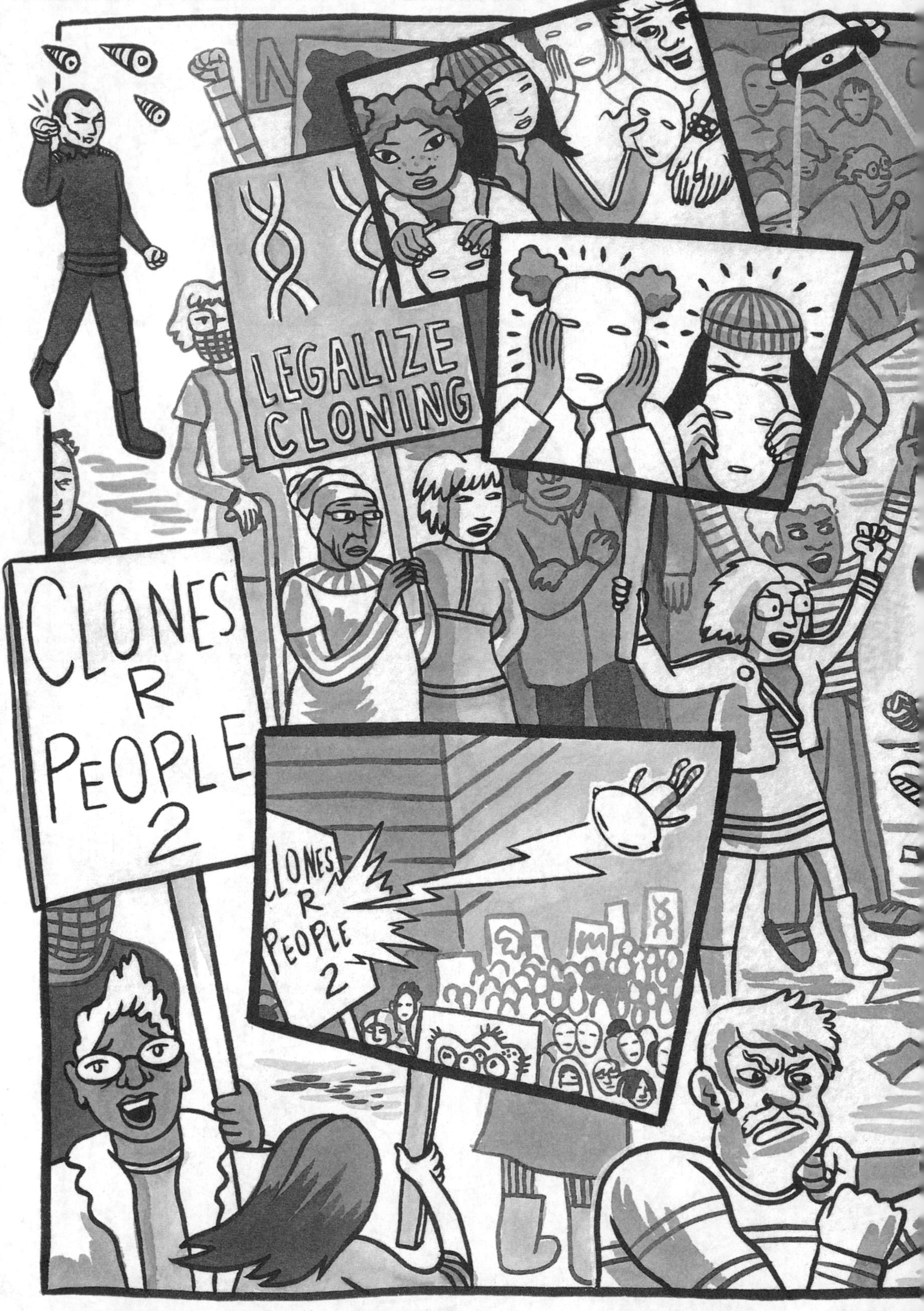
LEGALIZE CLONING
CLONES R PEOPLE 2
LONES R PEOPLE 2

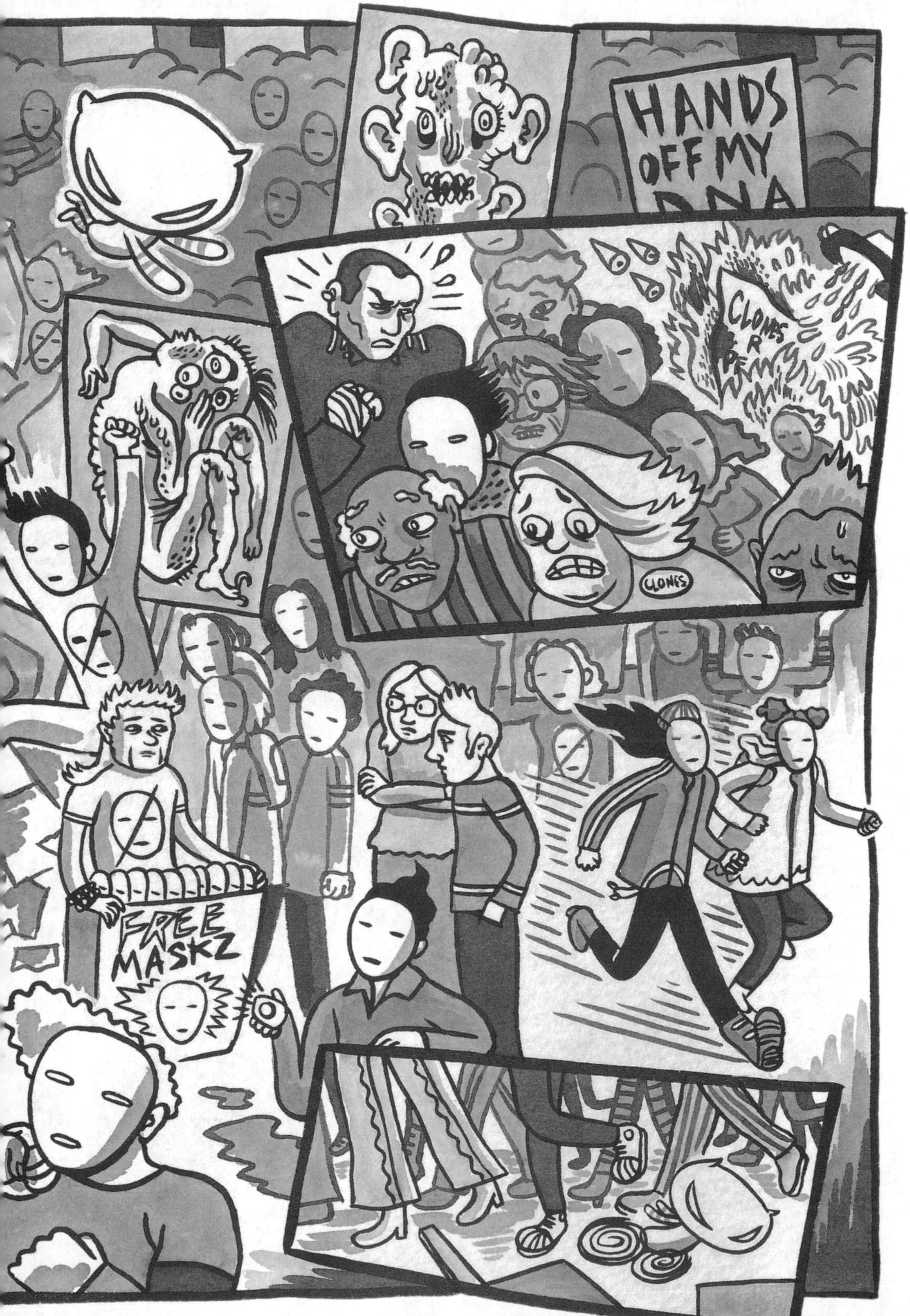
HANDS OFF MY
CLONES R
CLONES
FREE MASKZ

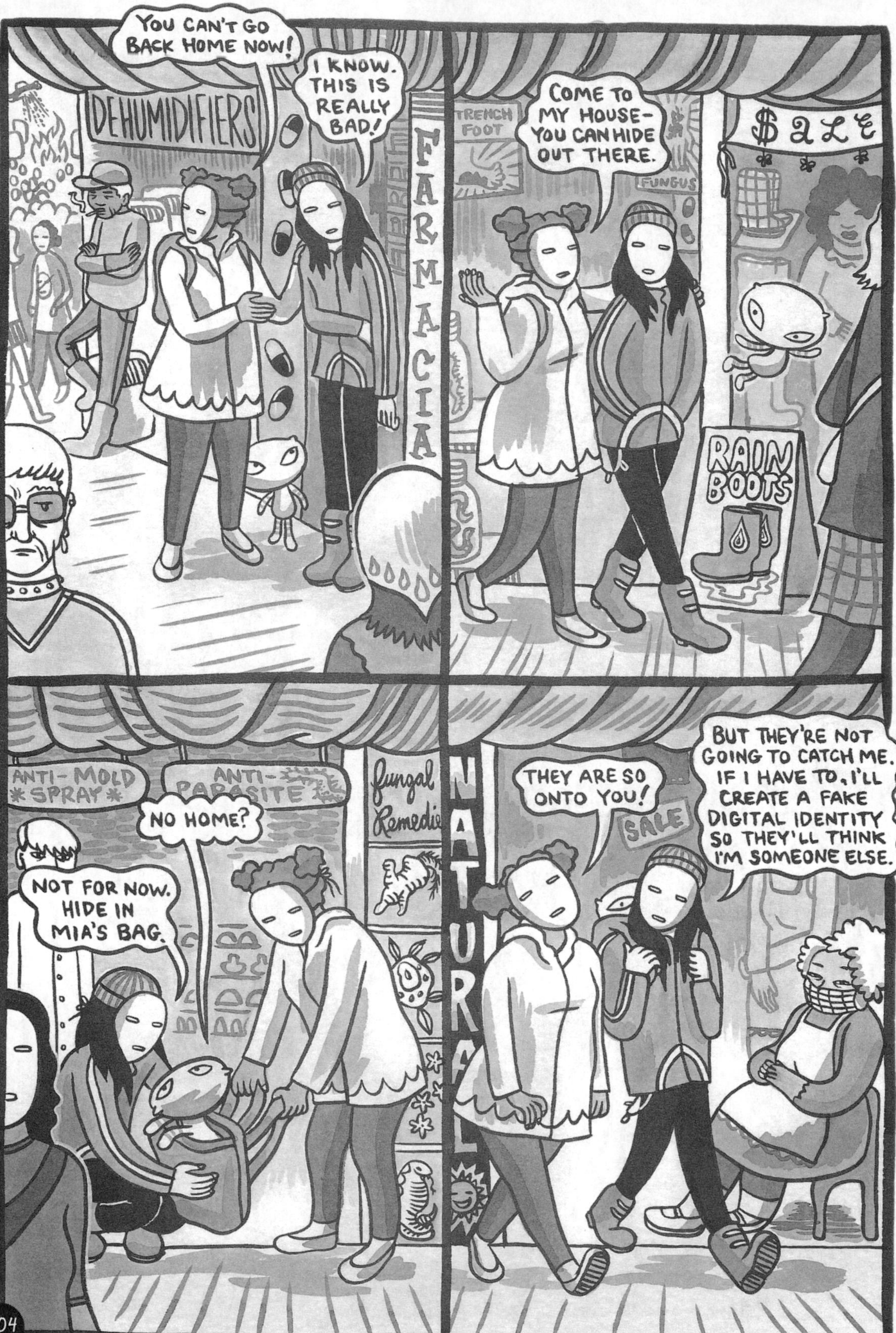
YOU CAN'T GO BACK HOME NOW!
I KNOW. THIS IS REALLY BAD!
DEHUMIDIFIERS
FARMACIA
COME TO MY HOUSE- YOU CAN HIDE OUT THERE.
TRENCH FOOT
FUNGUS
$ALE
RAIN BOOTS
ANTI-MOLD *SPRAY*
ANTI-PARASITE
fungal Remedie
NO HOME?
NOT FOR NOW. HIDE IN MIA'S BAG.
NATURAL
THEY ARE SO ONTO YOU!
SALE
BUT THEY'RE NOT GOING TO CATCH ME. IF I HAVE TO, I'LL CREATE A FAKE DIGITAL IDENTITY SO THEY'LL THINK I'M SOMEONE ELSE.

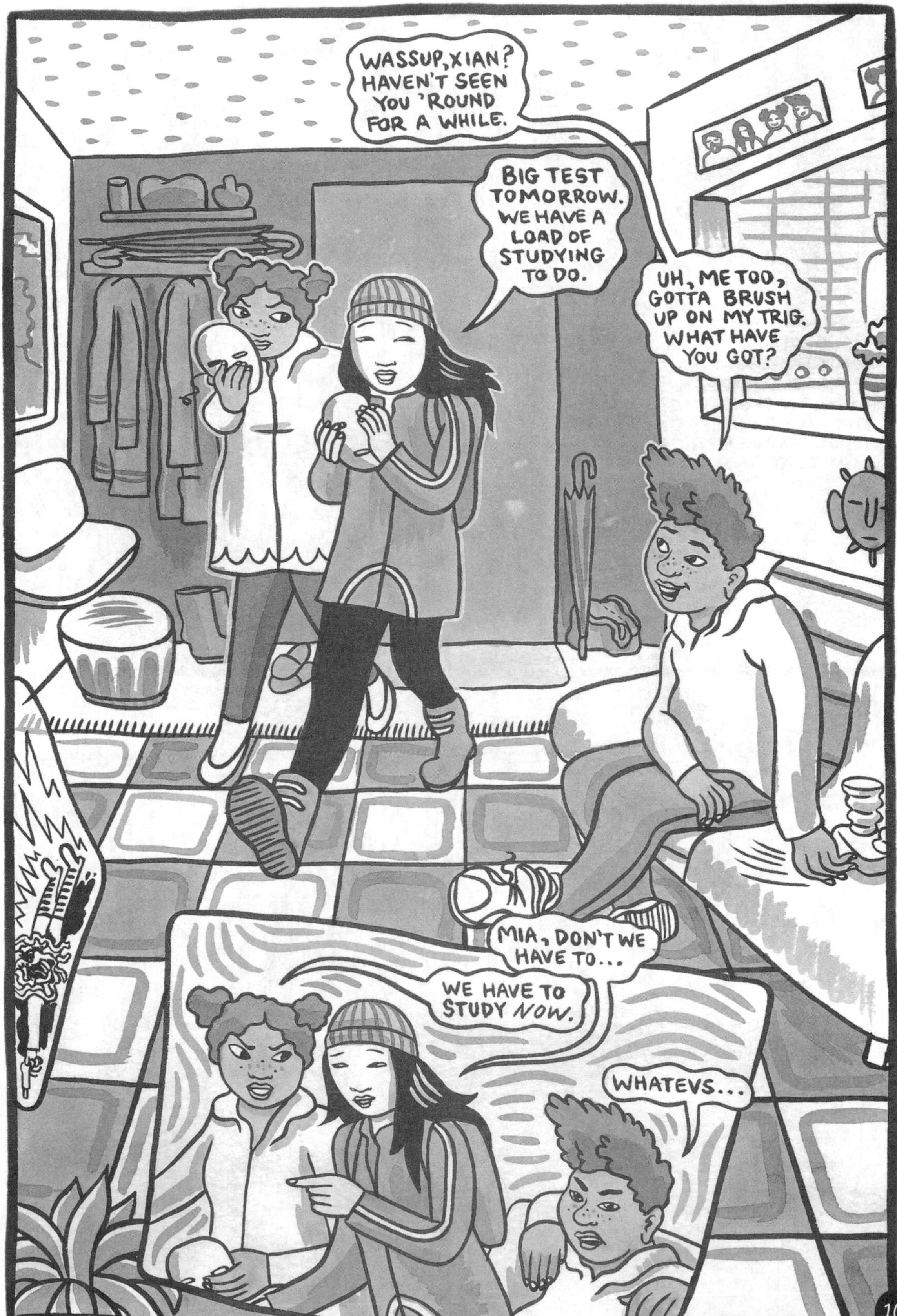
WASSUP, XIAN? HAVEN'T SEEN YOU 'ROUND FOR A WHILE.
BIG TEST TOMORROW. WE HAVE A LOAD OF STUDYING TO DO.
UH, ME TOO, GOTTA BRUSH UP ON MY TRIG. WHAT HAVE YOU GOT?
MIA, DON'T WE HAVE TO...
WE HAVE TO STUDY *NOW*.
WHATEVS...

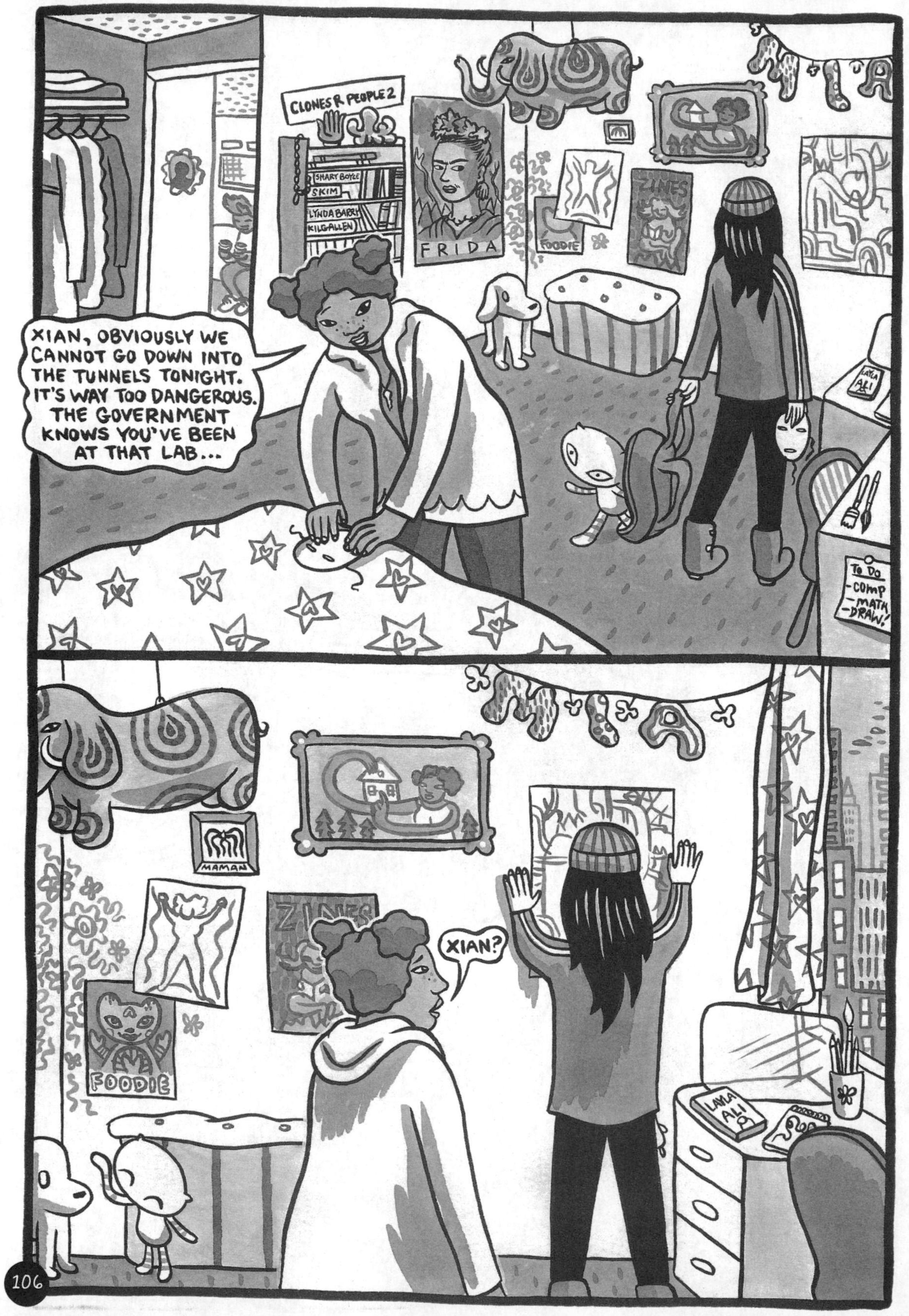
CLONES R PEOPLE 2
SHARY BOYLE
SKIM
LYNDA BARRY
KILGALLEN
FRIDA
ZINES
FOODIE
XIAN, OBVIOUSLY WE CANNOT GO DOWN INTO THE TUNNELS TONIGHT. IT'S WAY TOO DANGEROUS. THE GOVERNMENT KNOWS YOU'VE BEEN AT THAT LAB...
LAYLA ALI
To Do
-COMP
-MATH
-DRAW!
MAMAN
ZINES
FOODIE
XIAN?
LAYLA ALI

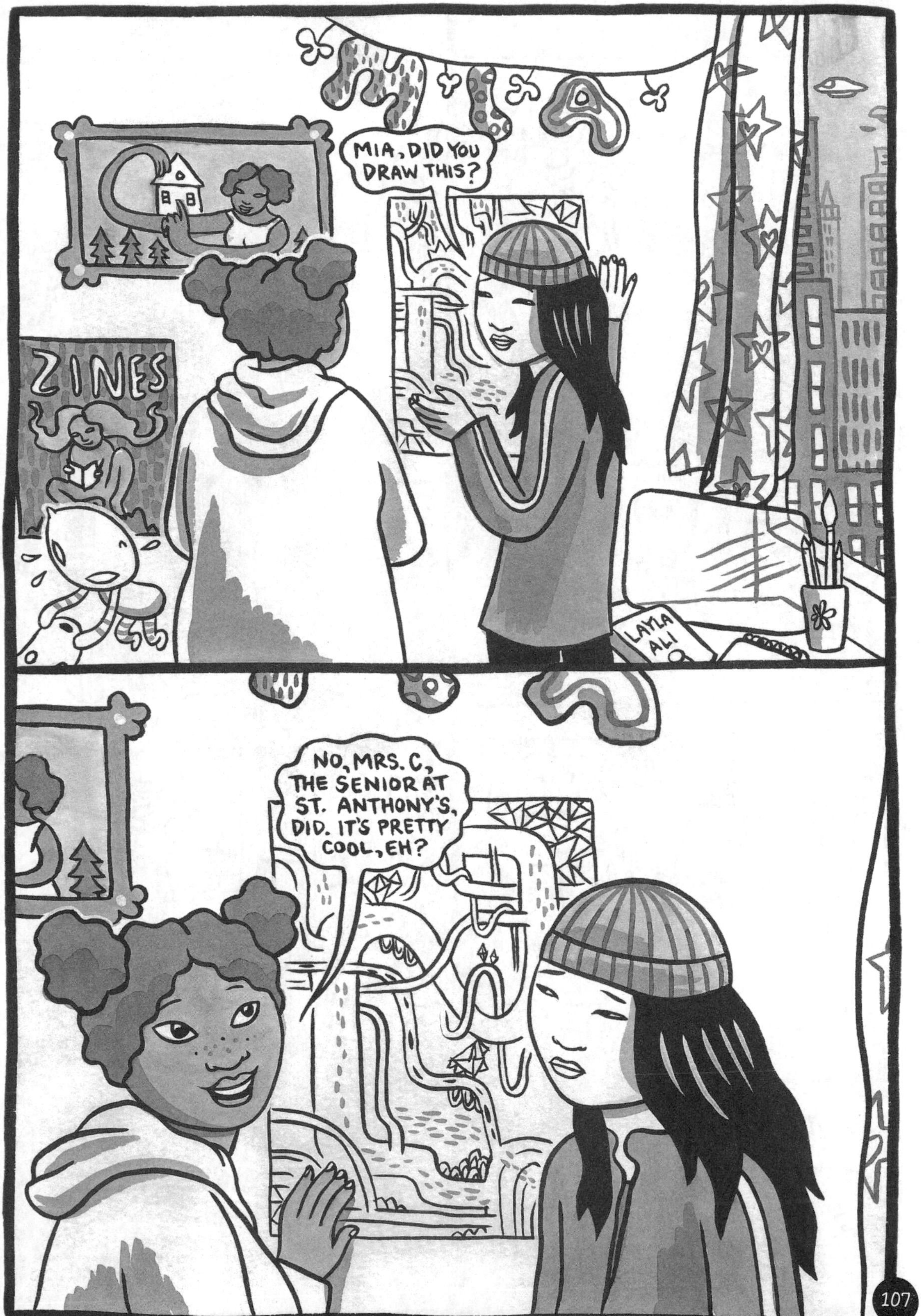

MIA
MIA, DID YOU DRAW THIS?
ZINES
LAYLA ALI
NO, MRS. C, THE SENIOR AT ST. ANTHONY'S, DID. IT'S PRETTY COOL, EH?

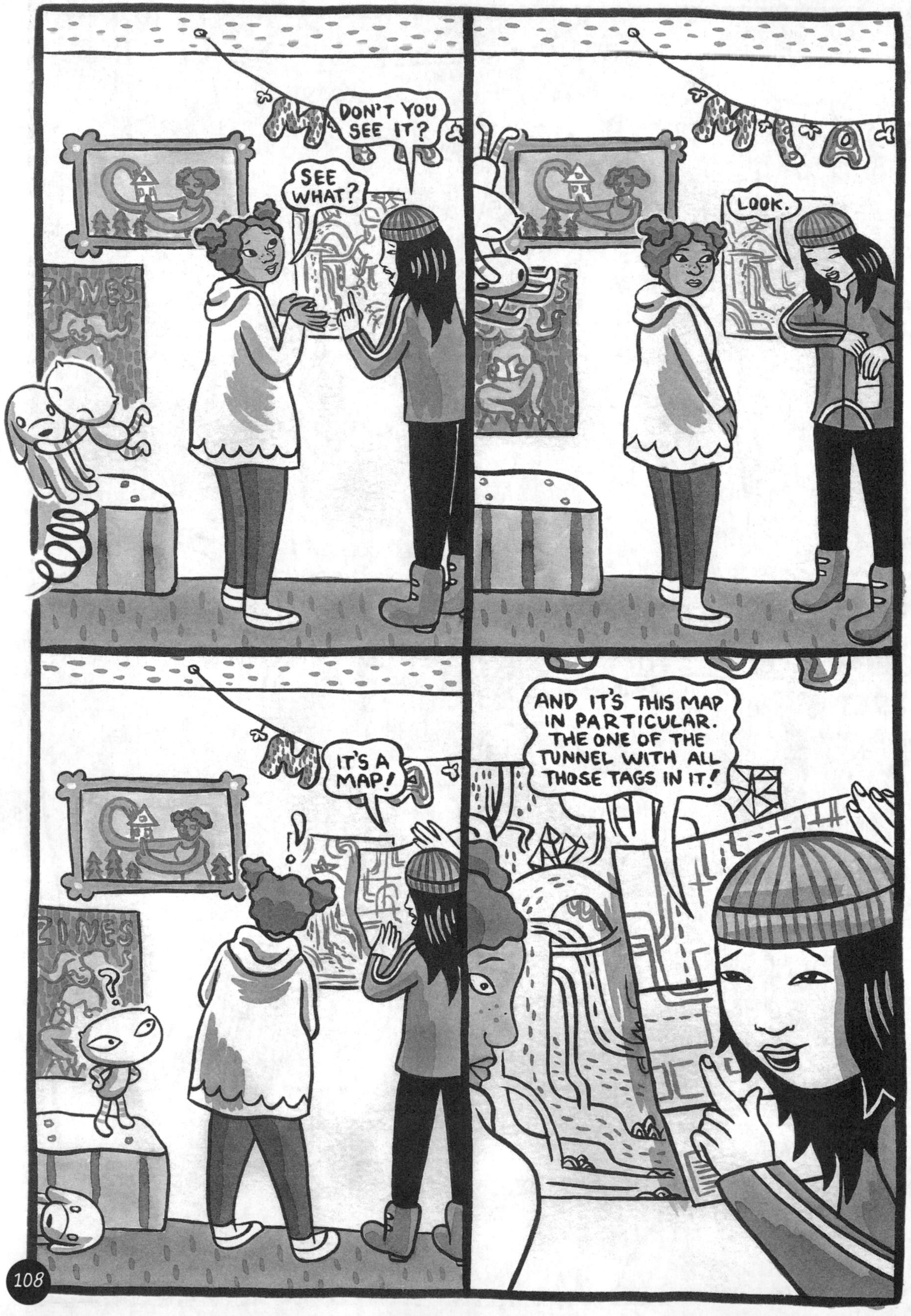
DON'T YOU SEE IT?
SEE WHAT?
LOOK.
IT'S A MAP!
AND IT'S THIS MAP IN PARTICULAR. THE ONE OF THE TUNNEL WITH ALL THOSE TAGS IN IT!

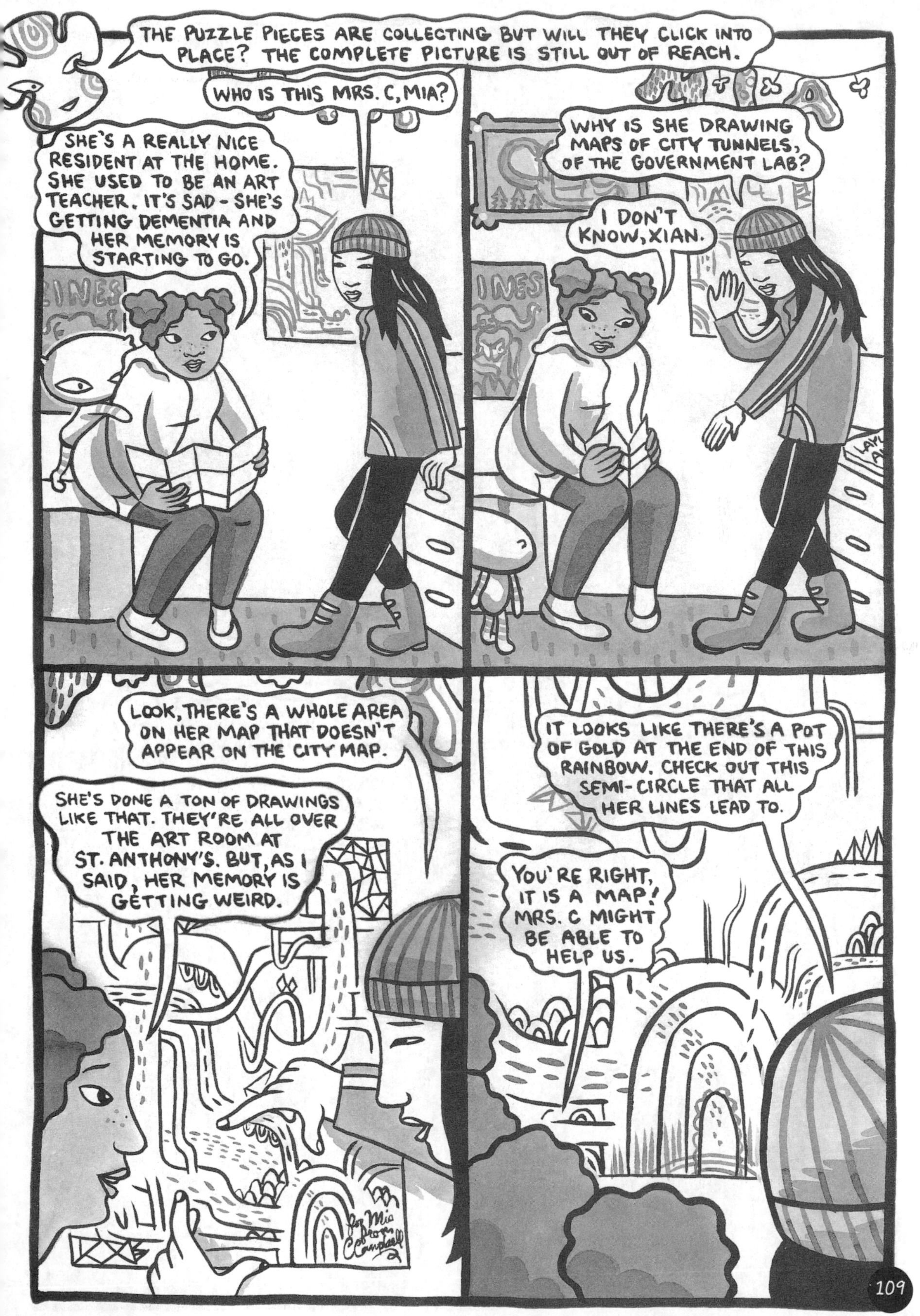
THE PUZZLE PIECES ARE COLLECTING BUT WILL THEY CLICK INTO PLACE? THE COMPLETE PICTURE IS STILL OUT OF REACH.
WHO IS THIS MRS. C, MIA?
SHE'S A REALLY NICE RESIDENT AT THE HOME. SHE USED TO BE AN ART TEACHER. IT'S SAD - SHE'S GETTING DEMENTIA AND HER MEMORY IS STARTING TO GO.
WHY IS SHE DRAWING MAPS OF CITY TUNNELS, OF THE GOVERNMENT LAB?
I DON'T KNOW, XIAN.
LOOK, THERE'S A WHOLE AREA ON HER MAP THAT DOESN'T APPEAR ON THE CITY MAP.
SHE'S DONE A TON OF DRAWINGS LIKE THAT. THEY'RE ALL OVER THE ART ROOM AT ST. ANTHONY'S. BUT, AS I SAID, HER MEMORY IS GETTING WEIRD.
IT LOOKS LIKE THERE'S A POT OF GOLD AT THE END OF THIS RAINBOW. CHECK OUT THIS SEMI-CIRCLE THAT ALL HER LINES LEAD TO.
YOU'RE RIGHT, IT IS A MAP! MRS. C MIGHT BE ABLE TO HELP US.

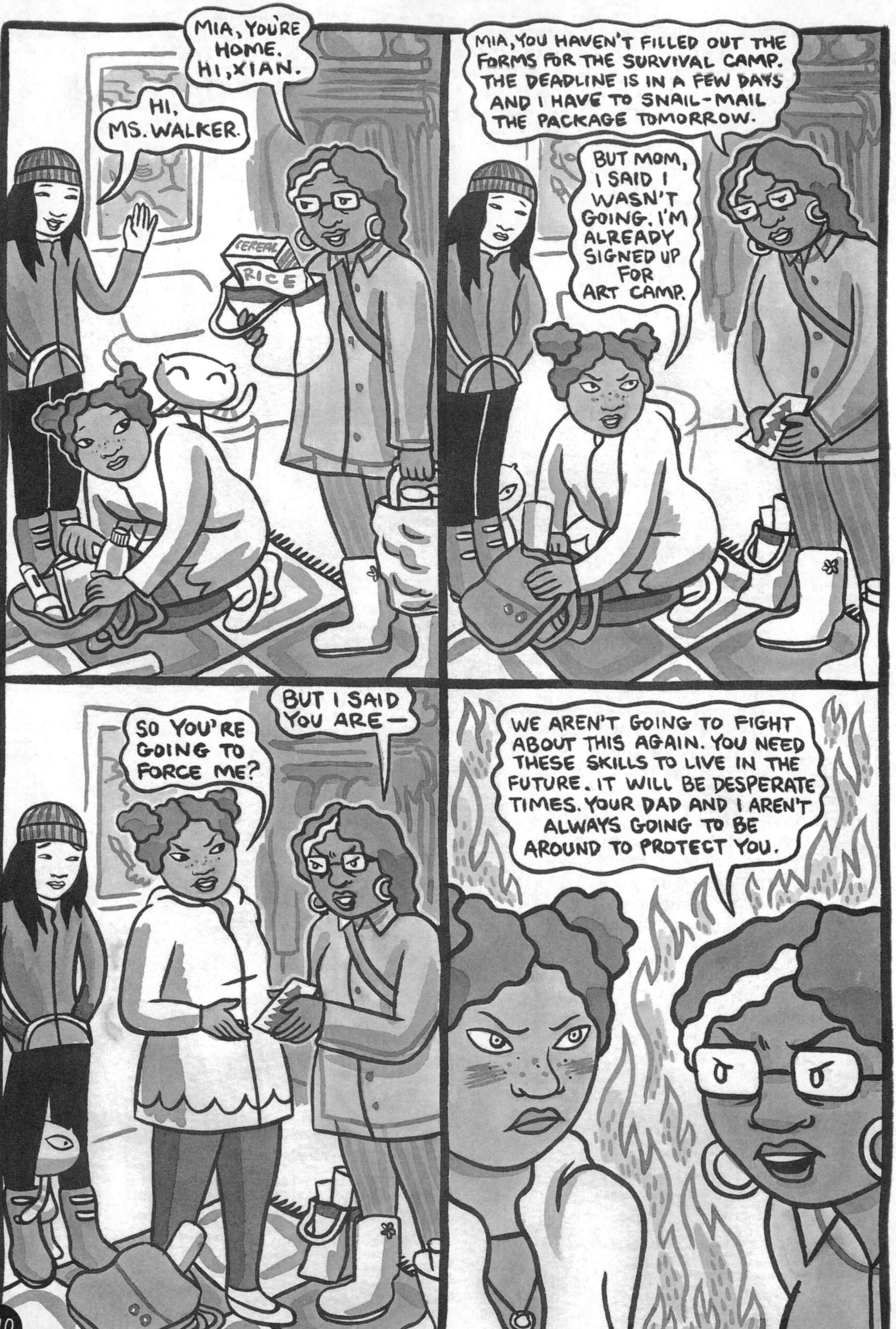
MIA, YOU'RE HOME. HI, XIAN.
HI, MS. WALKER.
CEREAL
RICE
MIA, YOU HAVEN'T FILLED OUT THE FORMS FOR THE SURVIVAL CAMP. THE DEADLINE IS IN A FEW DAYS AND I HAVE TO SNAIL-MAIL THE PACKAGE TOMORROW.
BUT MOM, I SAID I WASN'T GOING. I'M ALREADY SIGNED UP FOR ART CAMP.
SO YOU'RE GOING TO FORCE ME?
BUT I SAID YOU ARE—
WE AREN'T GOING TO FIGHT ABOUT THIS AGAIN. YOU NEED THESE SKILLS TO LIVE IN THE FUTURE. IT WILL BE DESPERATE TIMES. YOUR DAD AND I AREN'T ALWAYS GOING TO BE AROUND TO PROTECT YOU.

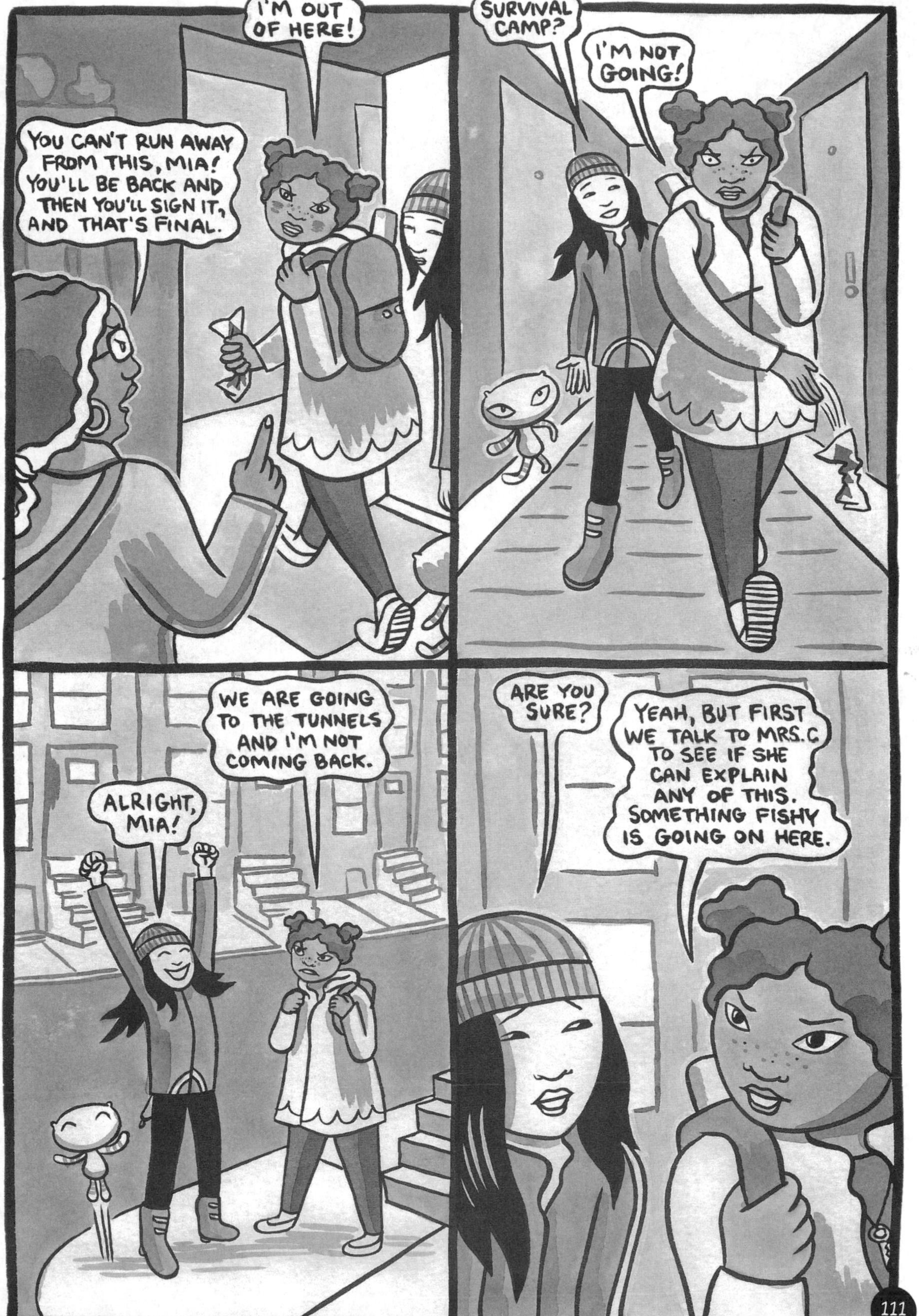
I'M OUT OF HERE!
YOU CAN'T RUN AWAY FROM THIS, MIA! YOU'LL BE BACK AND THEN YOU'LL SIGN IT, AND THAT'S FINAL.
SURVIVAL CAMP?
I'M NOT GOING!
WE ARE GOING TO THE TUNNELS AND I'M NOT COMING BACK.
ALRIGHT, MIA!
ARE YOU SURE?
YEAH, BUT FIRST WE TALK TO MRS. C TO SEE IF SHE CAN EXPLAIN ANY OF THIS. SOMETHING FISHY IS GOING ON HERE.

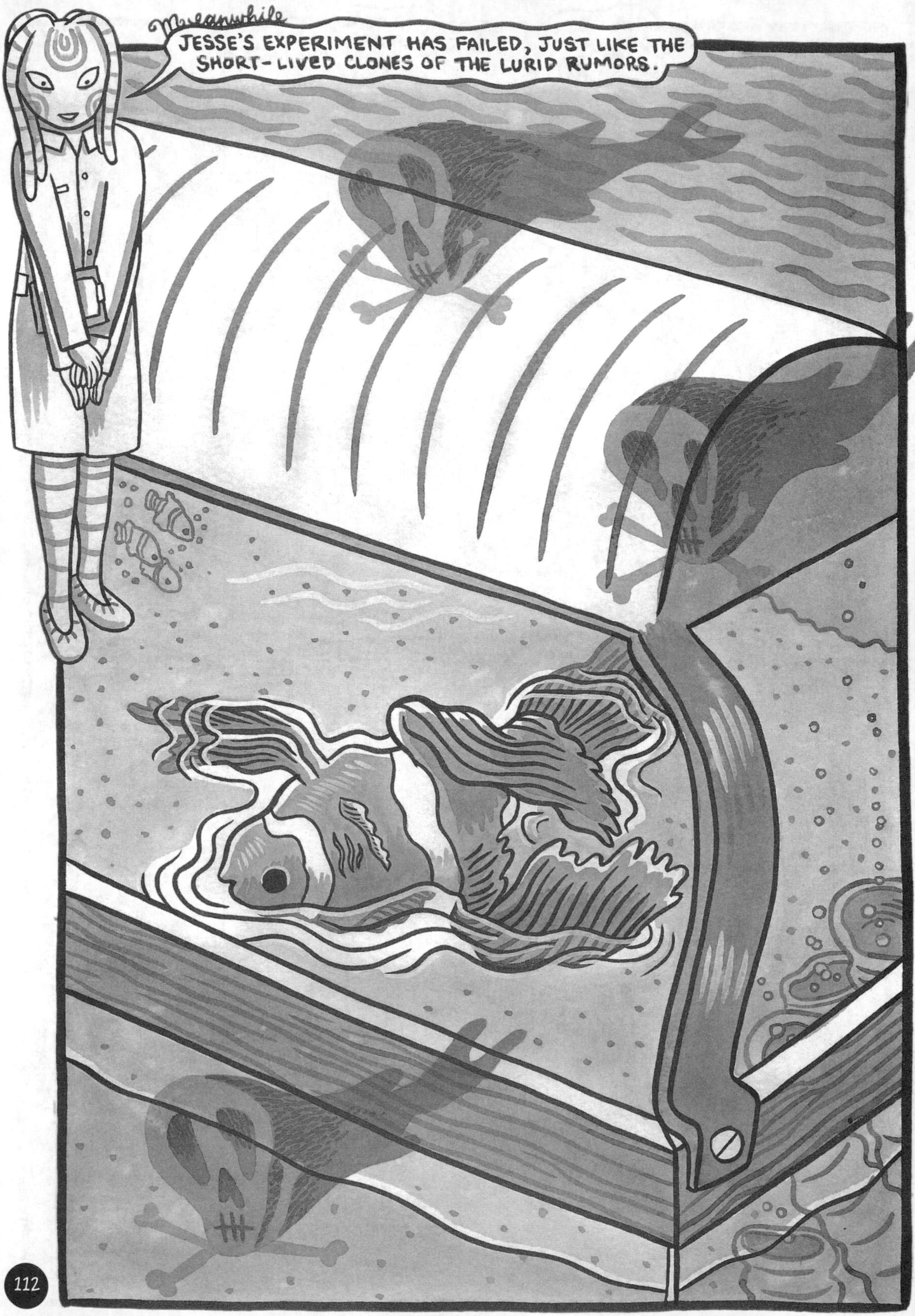
Meanwhile
JESSE'S EXPERIMENT HAS FAILED, JUST LIKE THE SHORT-LIVED CLONES OF THE LURID RUMORS.

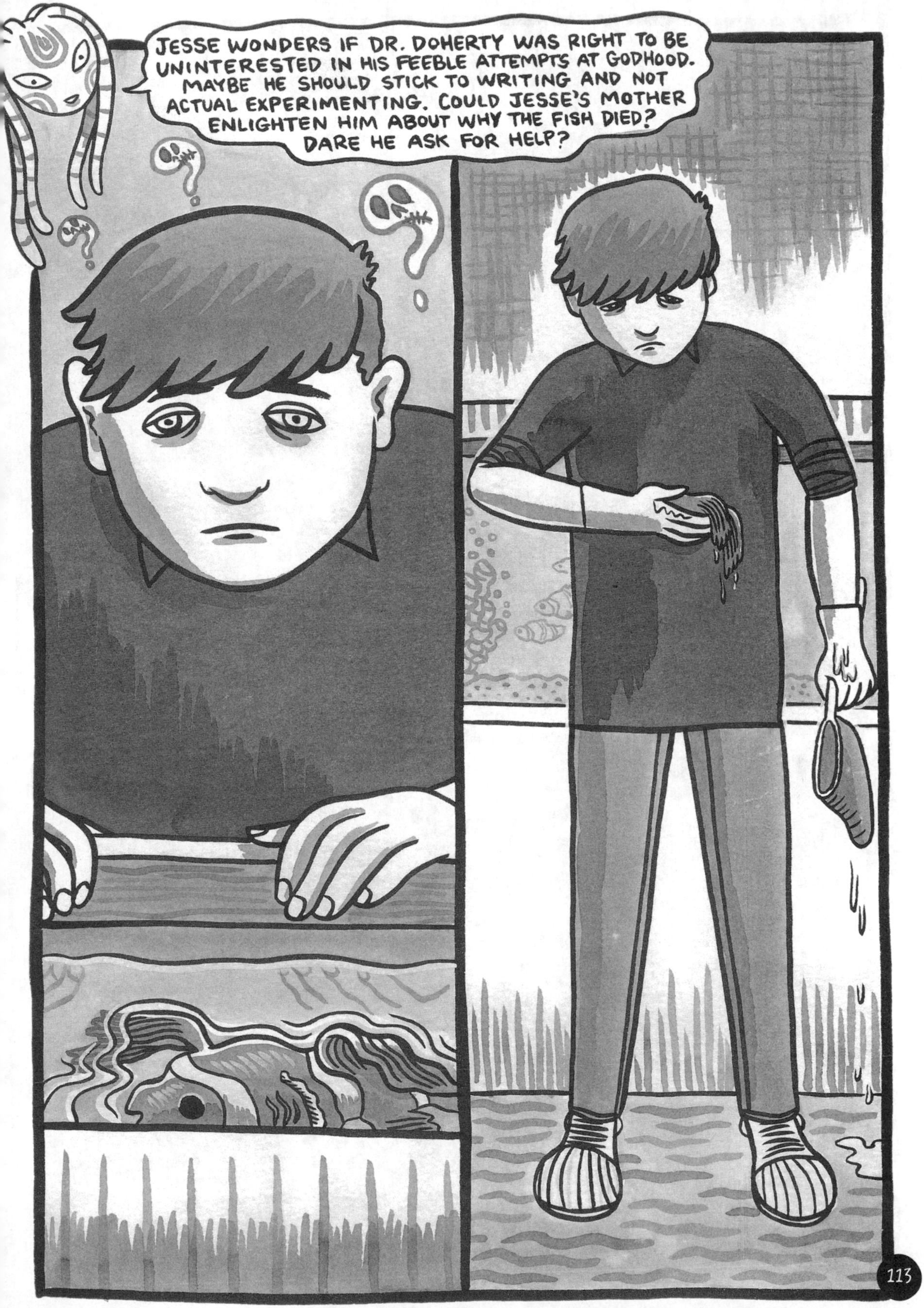
JESSE WONDERS IF DR. DOHERTY WAS RIGHT TO BE UNINTERESTED IN HIS FEEBLE ATTEMPTS AT GODHOOD. MAYBE HE SHOULD STICK TO WRITING AND NOT ACTUAL EXPERIMENTING. COULD JESSE'S MOTHER ENLIGHTEN HIM ABOUT WHY THE FISH DIED? DARE HE ASK FOR HELP?

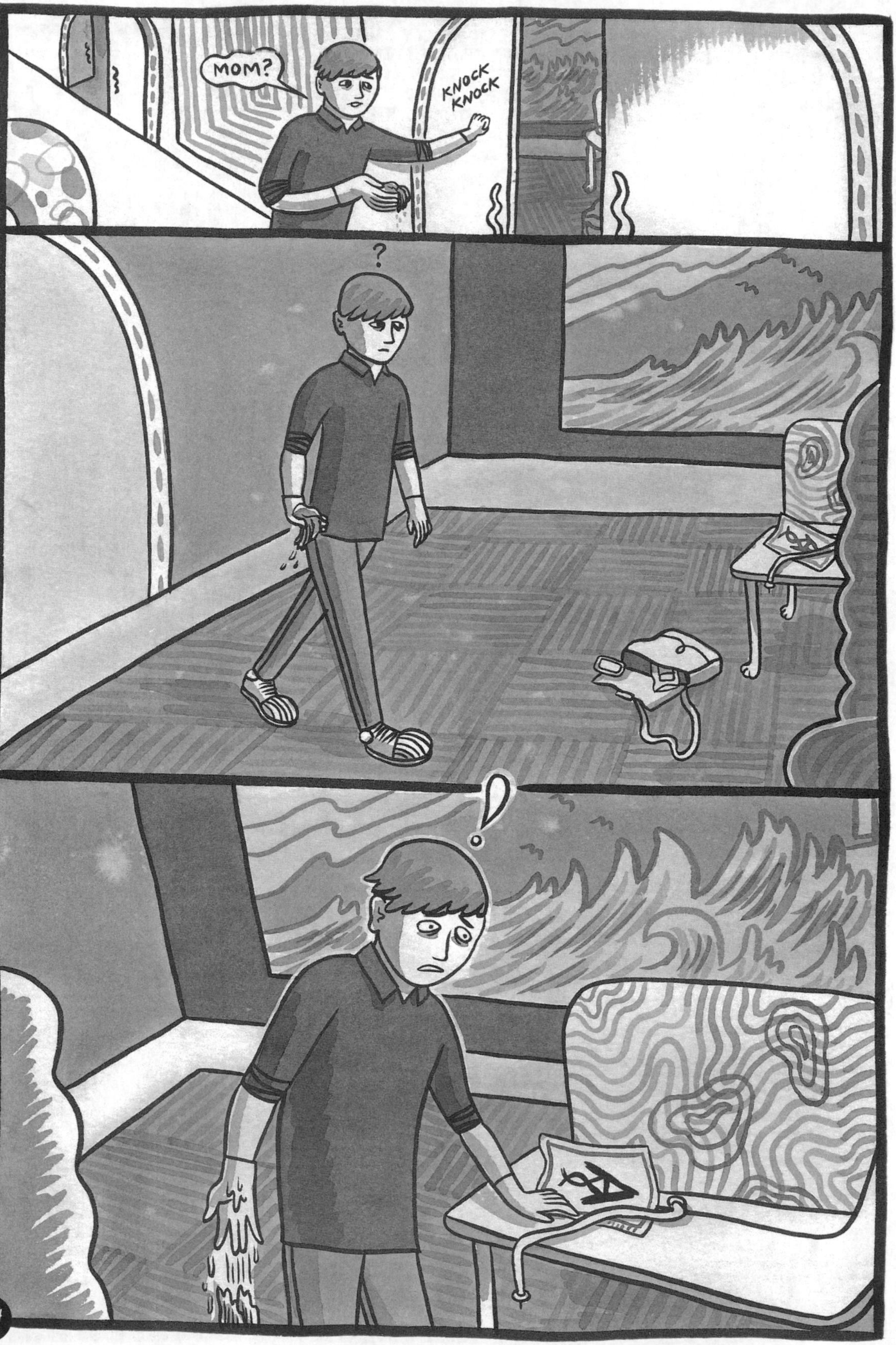
MOM?
KNOCK KNOCK
?
!

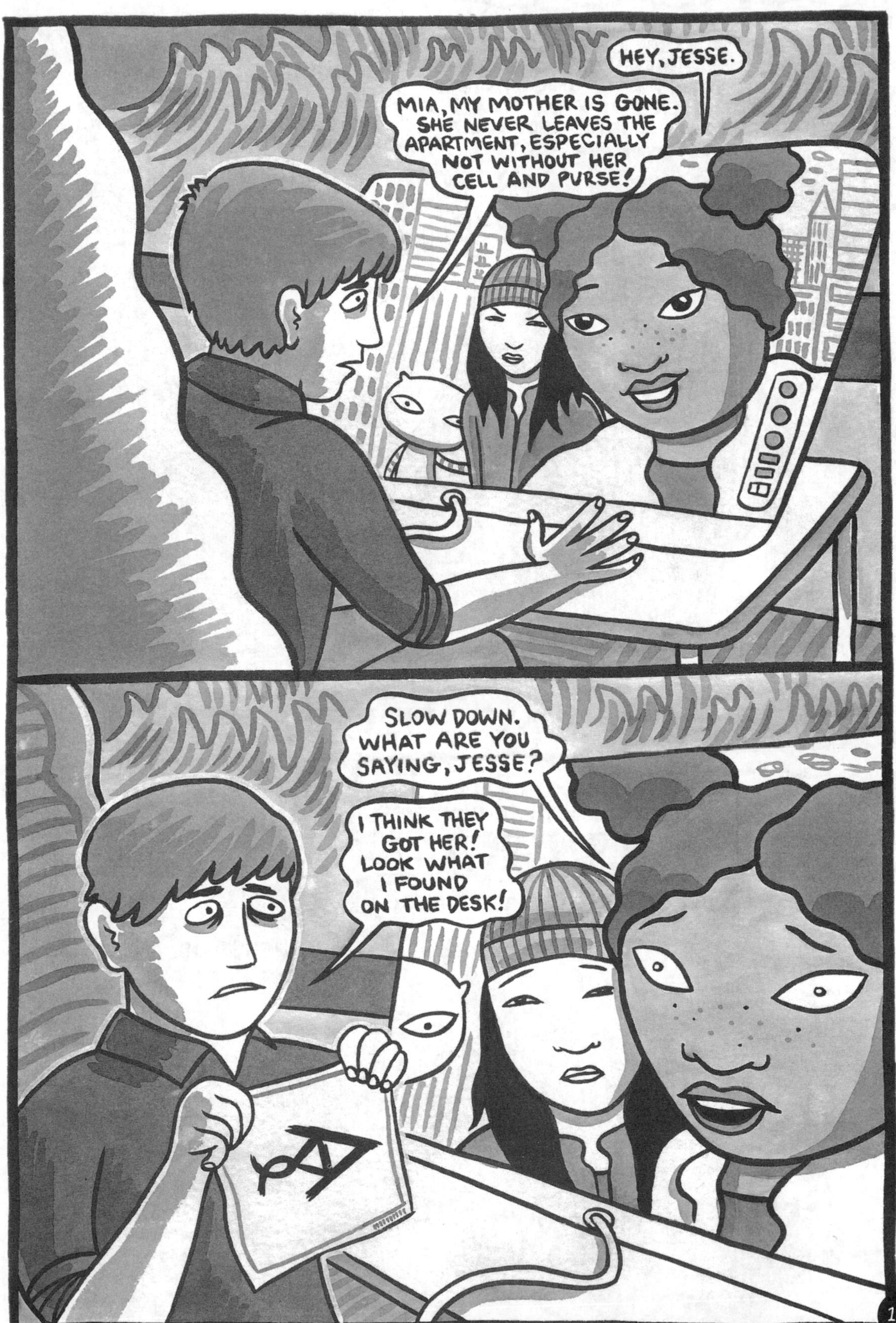
HEY, JESSE.
MIA, MY MOTHER IS GONE. SHE NEVER LEAVES THE APARTMENT, ESPECIALLY NOT WITHOUT HER CELL AND PURSE!
SLOW DOWN. WHAT ARE YOU SAYING, JESSE?
I THINK THEY GOT HER! LOOK WHAT I FOUND ON THE DESK!

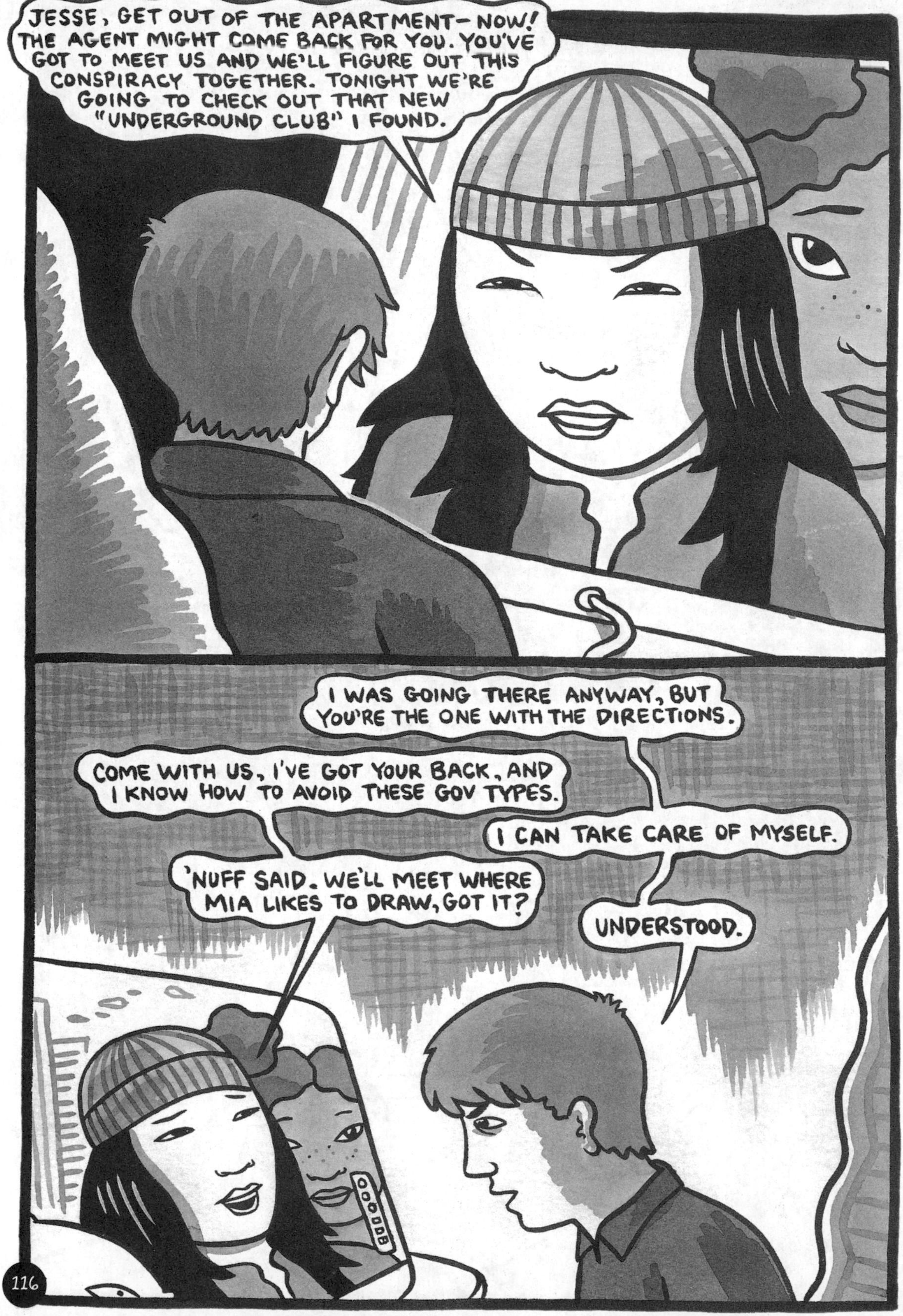
JESSE, GET OUT OF THE APARTMENT—NOW! THE AGENT MIGHT COME BACK FOR YOU. YOU'VE GOT TO MEET US AND WE'LL FIGURE OUT THIS CONSPIRACY TOGETHER. TONIGHT WE'RE GOING TO CHECK OUT THAT NEW "UNDERGROUND CLUB" I FOUND.
I WAS GOING THERE ANYWAY, BUT YOU'RE THE ONE WITH THE DIRECTIONS.
COME WITH US, I'VE GOT YOUR BACK, AND I KNOW HOW TO AVOID THESE GOV TYPES.
I CAN TAKE CARE OF MYSELF.
'NUFF SAID. WE'LL MEET WHERE MIA LIKES TO DRAW, GOT IT?
UNDERSTOOD.

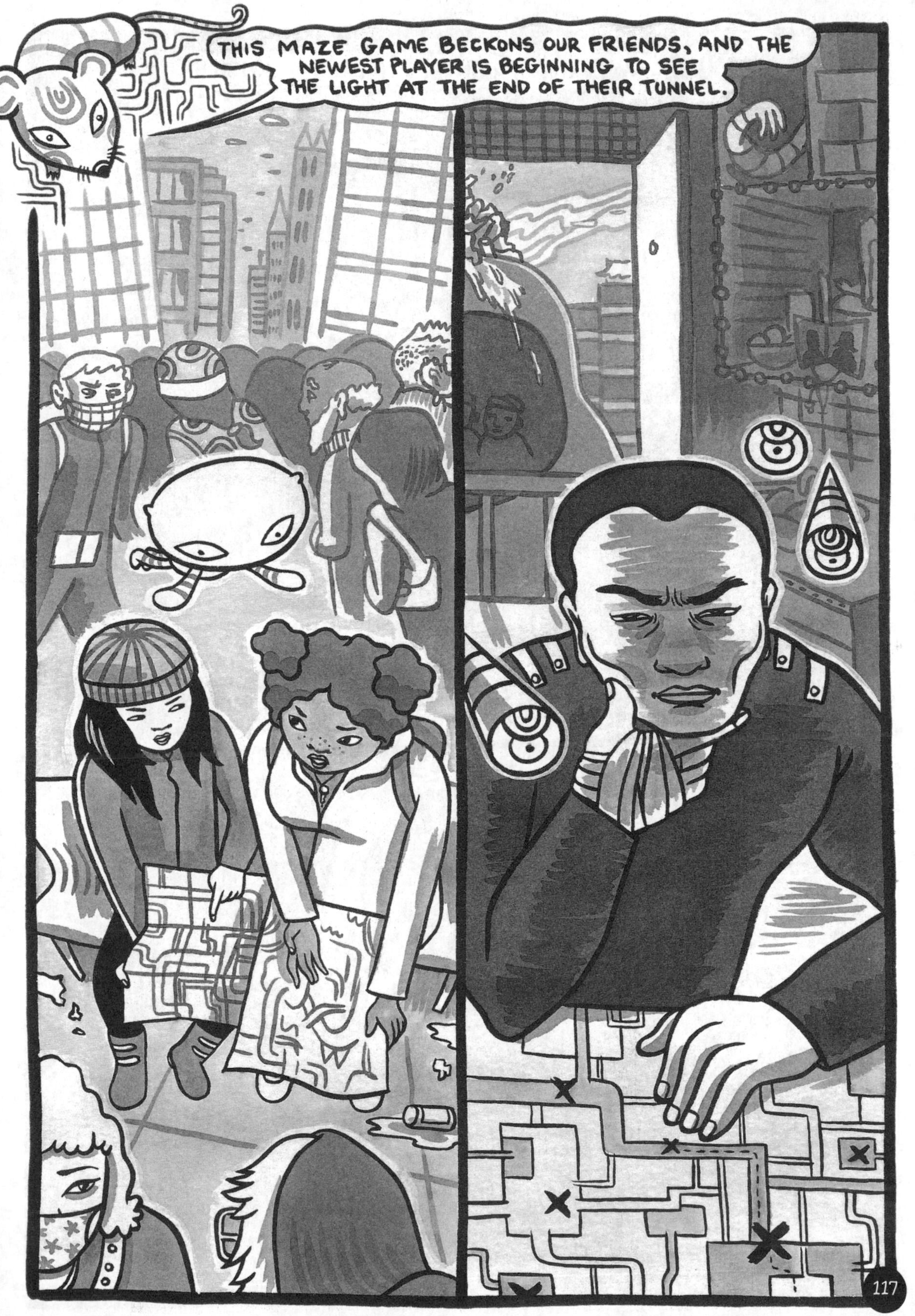
THIS MAZE GAME BECKONS OUR FRIENDS, AND THE NEWEST PLAYER IS BEGINNING TO SEE THE LIGHT AT THE END OF THEIR TUNNEL.

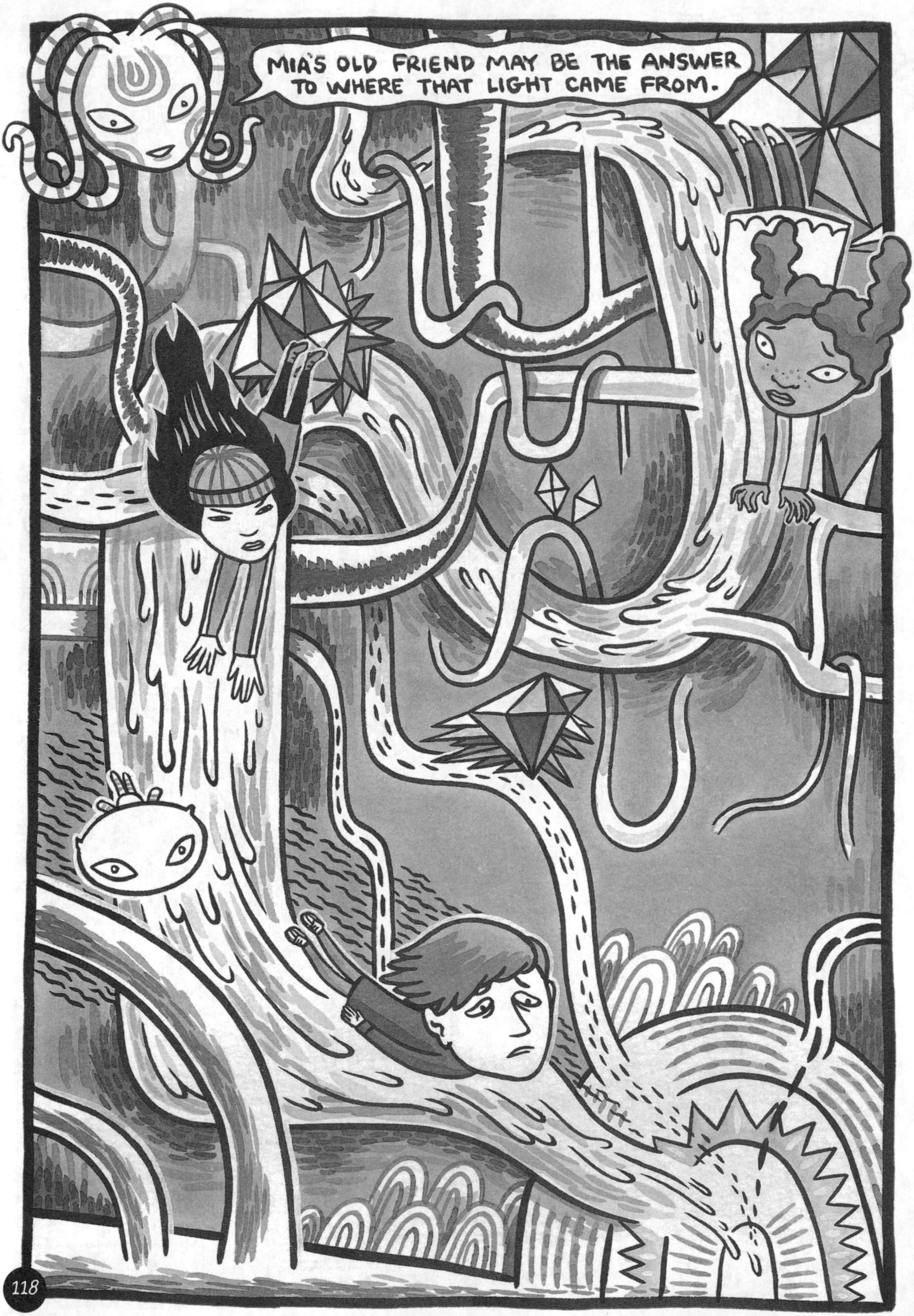
MIA'S OLD FRIEND MAY BE THE ANSWER TO WHERE THAT LIGHT CAME FROM.

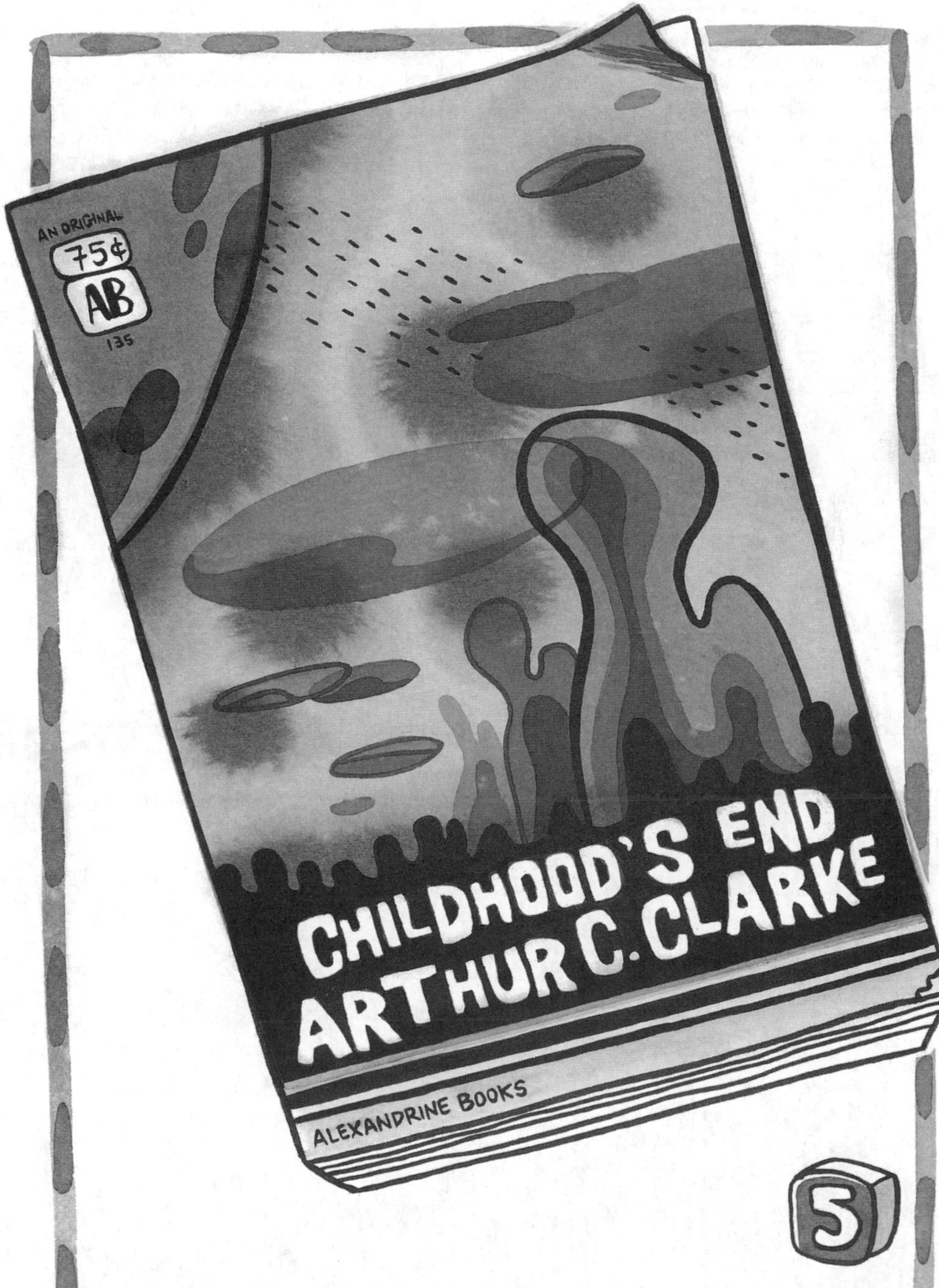
AN ORIGINAL
75¢
AB
135
CHILDHOOD'S END
ARTHUR C. CLARKE
ALEXANDRINE BOOKS
5

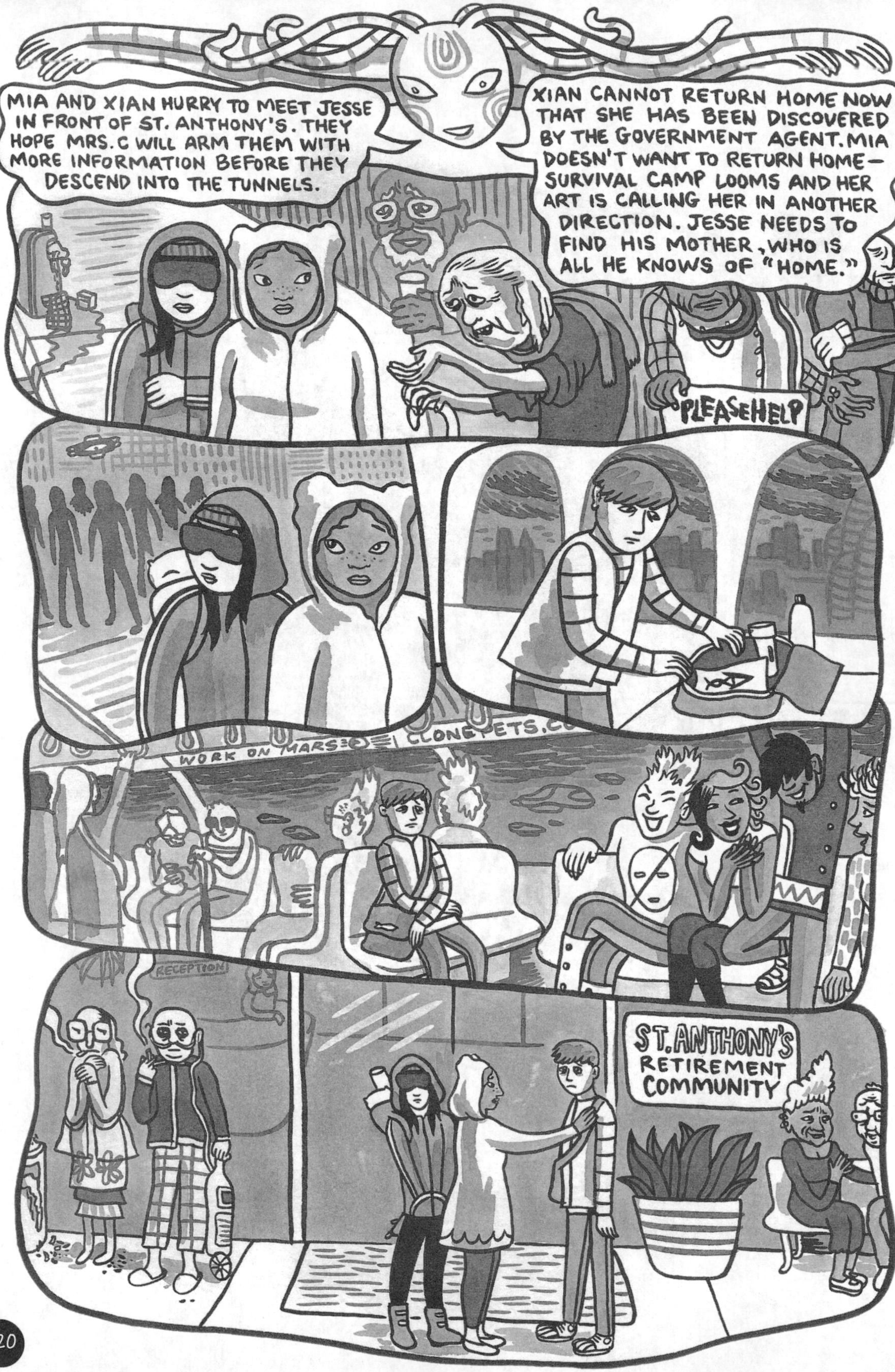
MIA AND XIAN HURRY TO MEET JESSE IN FRONT OF ST. ANTHONY'S. THEY HOPE MRS. C WILL ARM THEM WITH MORE INFORMATION BEFORE THEY DESCEND INTO THE TUNNELS.
XIAN CANNOT RETURN HOME NOW THAT SHE HAS BEEN DISCOVERED BY THE GOVERNMENT AGENT. MIA DOESN'T WANT TO RETURN HOME— SURVIVAL CAMP LOOMS AND HER ART IS CALLING HER IN ANOTHER DIRECTION. JESSE NEEDS TO FIND HIS MOTHER, WHO IS ALL HE KNOWS OF "HOME."
PLEASE HELP
WORK ON MARS
CLONEPETS.CO
RECEPTION
ST. ANTHONY'S RETIREMENT COMMUNITY

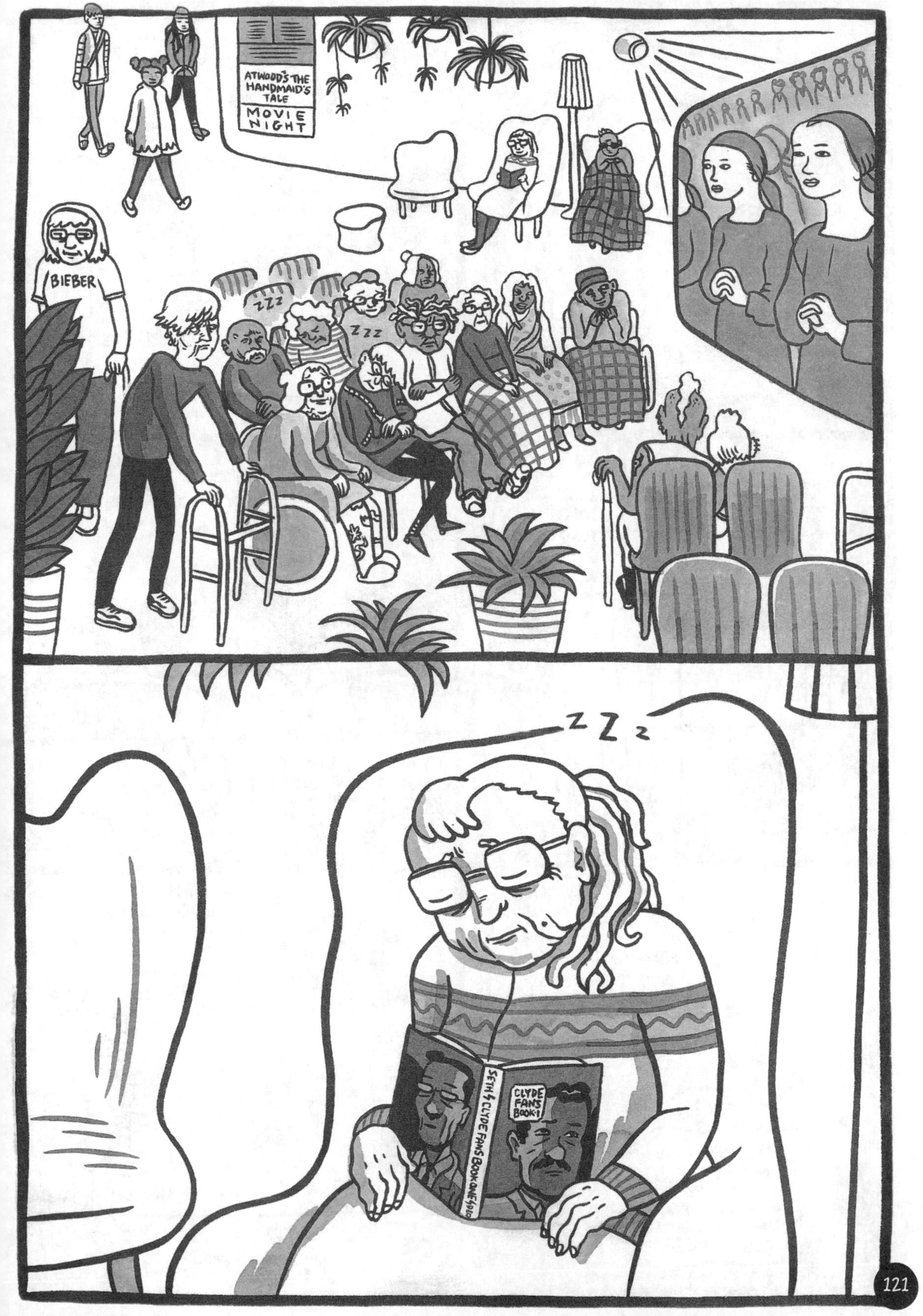
ATWOOD'S THE HANDMAID'S TALE
MOVIE NIGHT
BIEBER
ZZZ
ZZZ
ZZZ
CLYDE FANS BOOK 1
SETH'S CLYDE FANS BOOK ONE

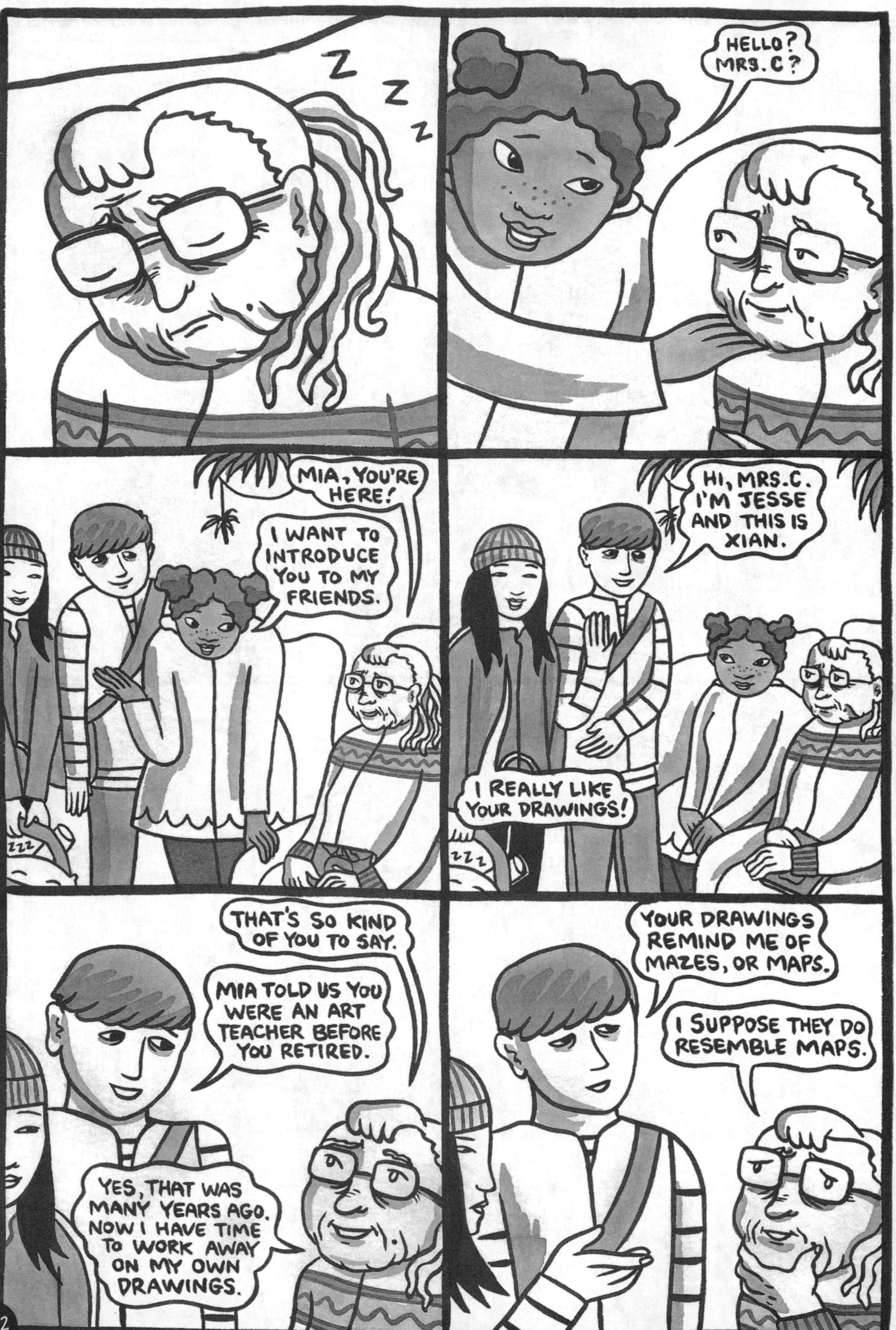
Z Z Z
HELLO? MRS. C?
MIA, YOU'RE HERE!
I WANT TO INTRODUCE YOU TO MY FRIENDS.
HI, MRS. C. I'M JESSE AND THIS IS XIAN.
I REALLY LIKE YOUR DRAWINGS!
THAT'S SO KIND OF YOU TO SAY.
MIA TOLD US YOU WERE AN ART TEACHER BEFORE YOU RETIRED.
YES, THAT WAS MANY YEARS AGO. NOW I HAVE TIME TO WORK AWAY ON MY OWN DRAWINGS.
YOUR DRAWINGS REMIND ME OF MAZES, OR MAPS.
I SUPPOSE THEY DO RESEMBLE MAPS.

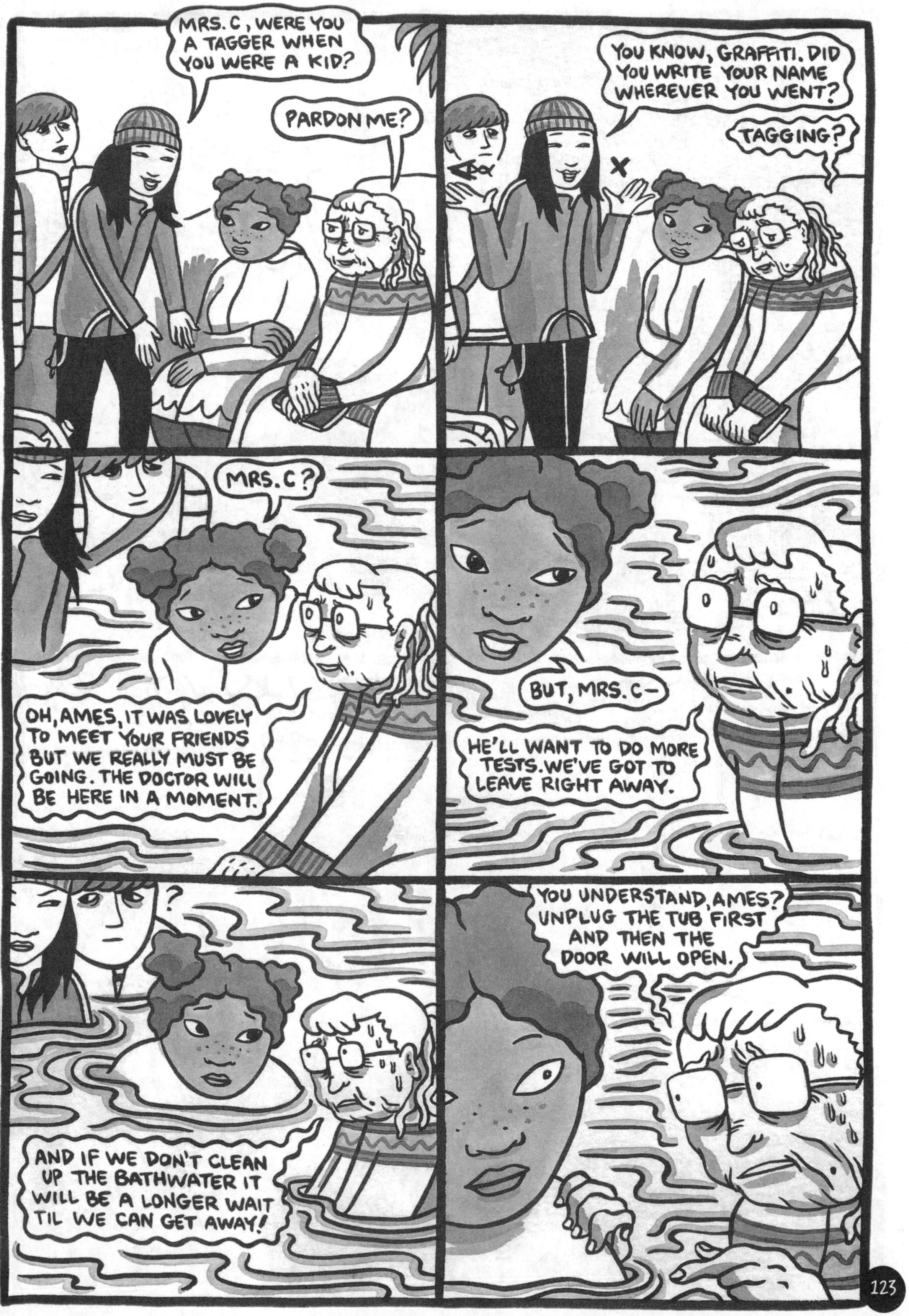
MRS. C, WERE YOU A TAGGER WHEN YOU WERE A KID?
PARDON ME?
YOU KNOW, GRAFFITI. DID YOU WRITE YOUR NAME WHEREVER YOU WENT?
TAGGING?
MRS. C?
OH, AMES, IT WAS LOVELY TO MEET YOUR FRIENDS BUT WE REALLY MUST BE GOING. THE DOCTOR WILL BE HERE IN A MOMENT.
BUT, MRS. C—
HE'LL WANT TO DO MORE TESTS. WE'VE GOT TO LEAVE RIGHT AWAY.
?
AND IF WE DON'T CLEAN UP THE BATHWATER IT WILL BE A LONGER WAIT TIL WE CAN GET AWAY!
YOU UNDERSTAND, AMES? UNPLUG THE TUB FIRST AND THEN THE DOOR WILL OPEN.

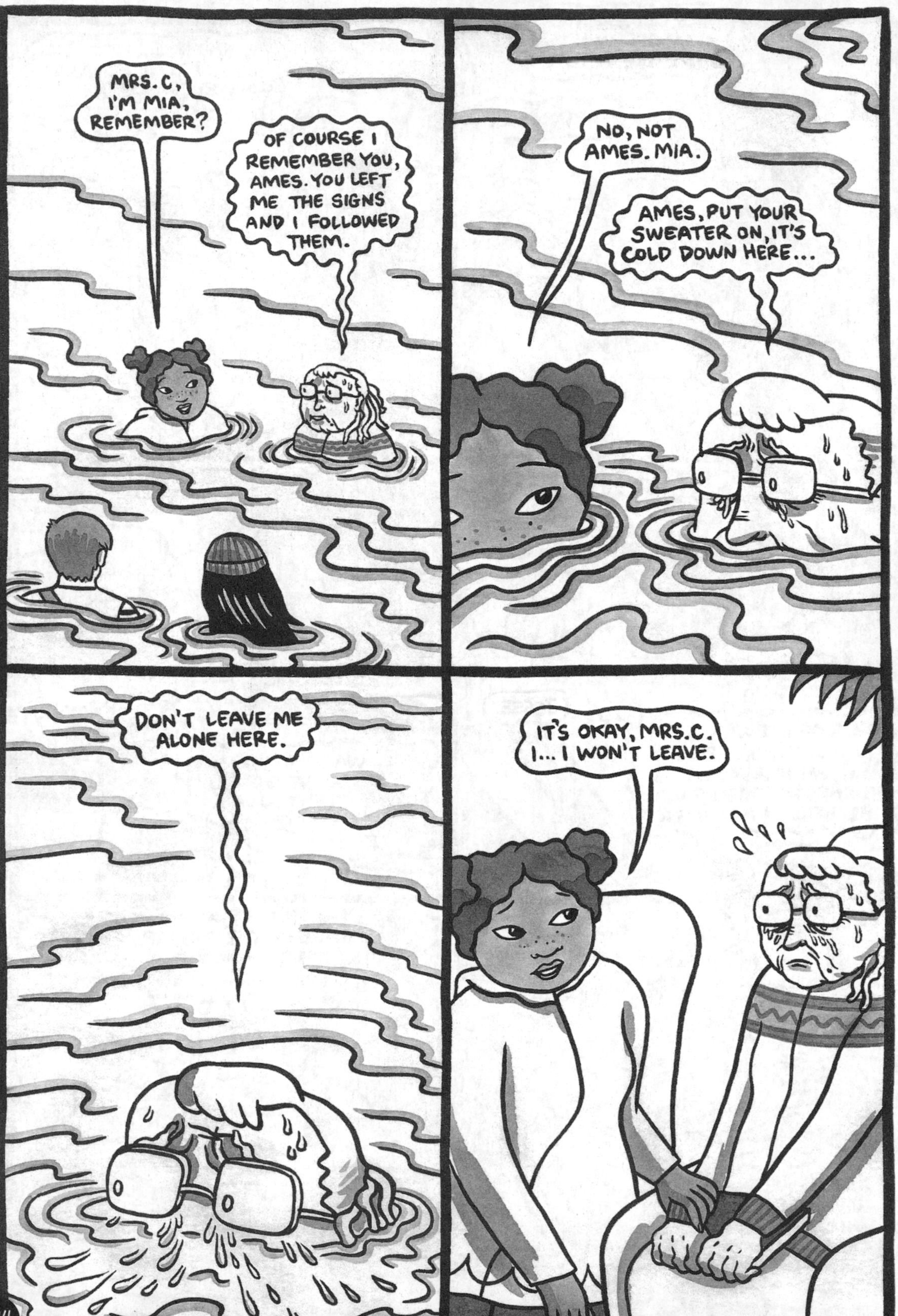
MRS. C, I'M MIA, REMEMBER?
OF COURSE I REMEMBER YOU, AMES. YOU LEFT ME THE SIGNS AND I FOLLOWED THEM.
NO, NOT AMES. MIA.
AMES, PUT YOUR SWEATER ON, IT'S COLD DOWN HERE...
DON'T LEAVE ME ALONE HERE.
IT'S OKAY, MRS. C. I... I WON'T LEAVE.

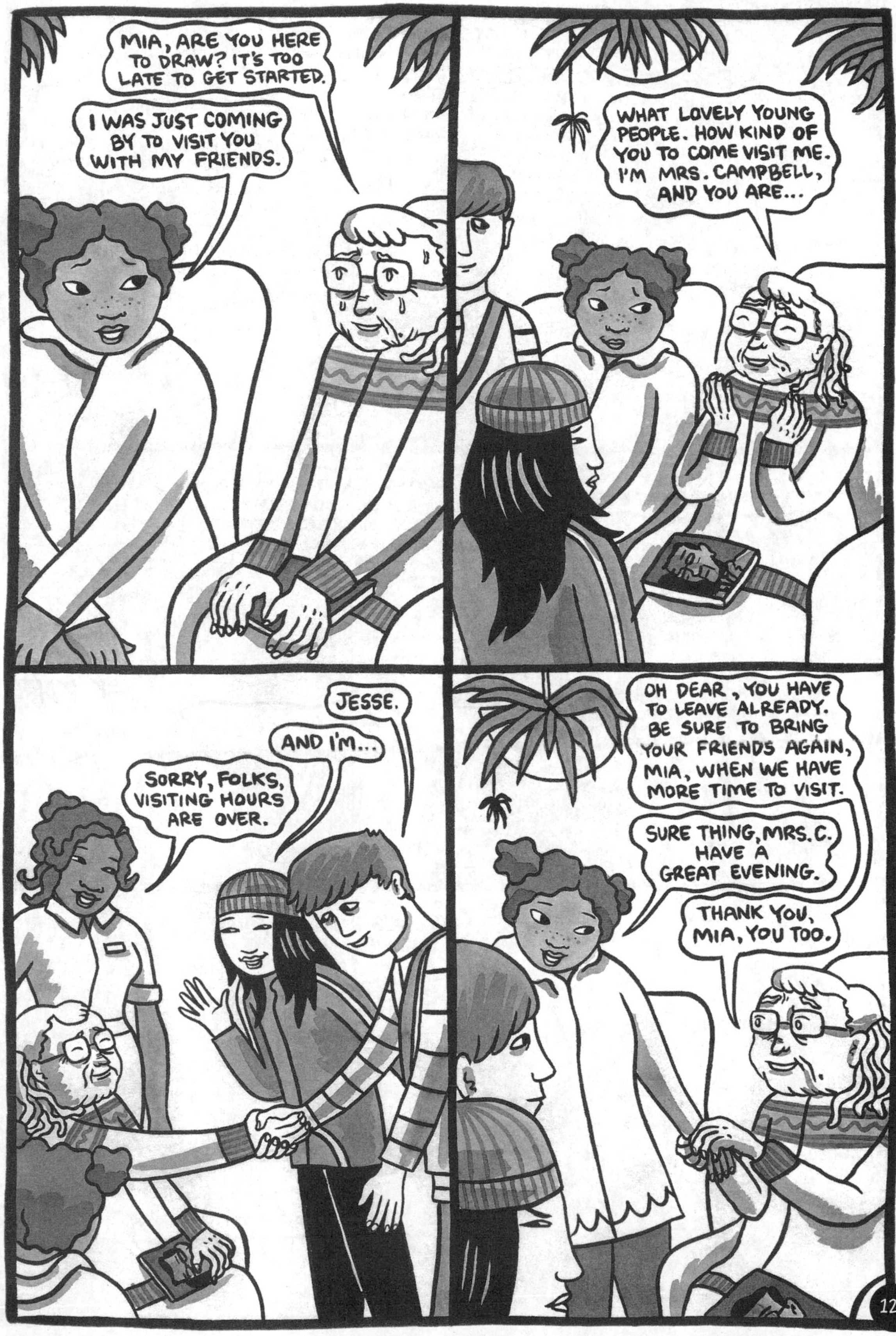

MIA, ARE YOU HERE TO DRAW? IT'S TOO LATE TO GET STARTED.
I WAS JUST COMING BY TO VISIT YOU WITH MY FRIENDS.
WHAT LOVELY YOUNG PEOPLE. HOW KIND OF YOU TO COME VISIT ME. I'M MRS. CAMPBELL, AND YOU ARE...
JESSE.
AND I'M...
SORRY, FOLKS, VISITING HOURS ARE OVER.
OH DEAR, YOU HAVE TO LEAVE ALREADY. BE SURE TO BRING YOUR FRIENDS AGAIN, MIA, WHEN WE HAVE MORE TIME TO VISIT.
SURE THING, MRS. C. HAVE A GREAT EVENING.
THANK YOU, MIA, YOU TOO.

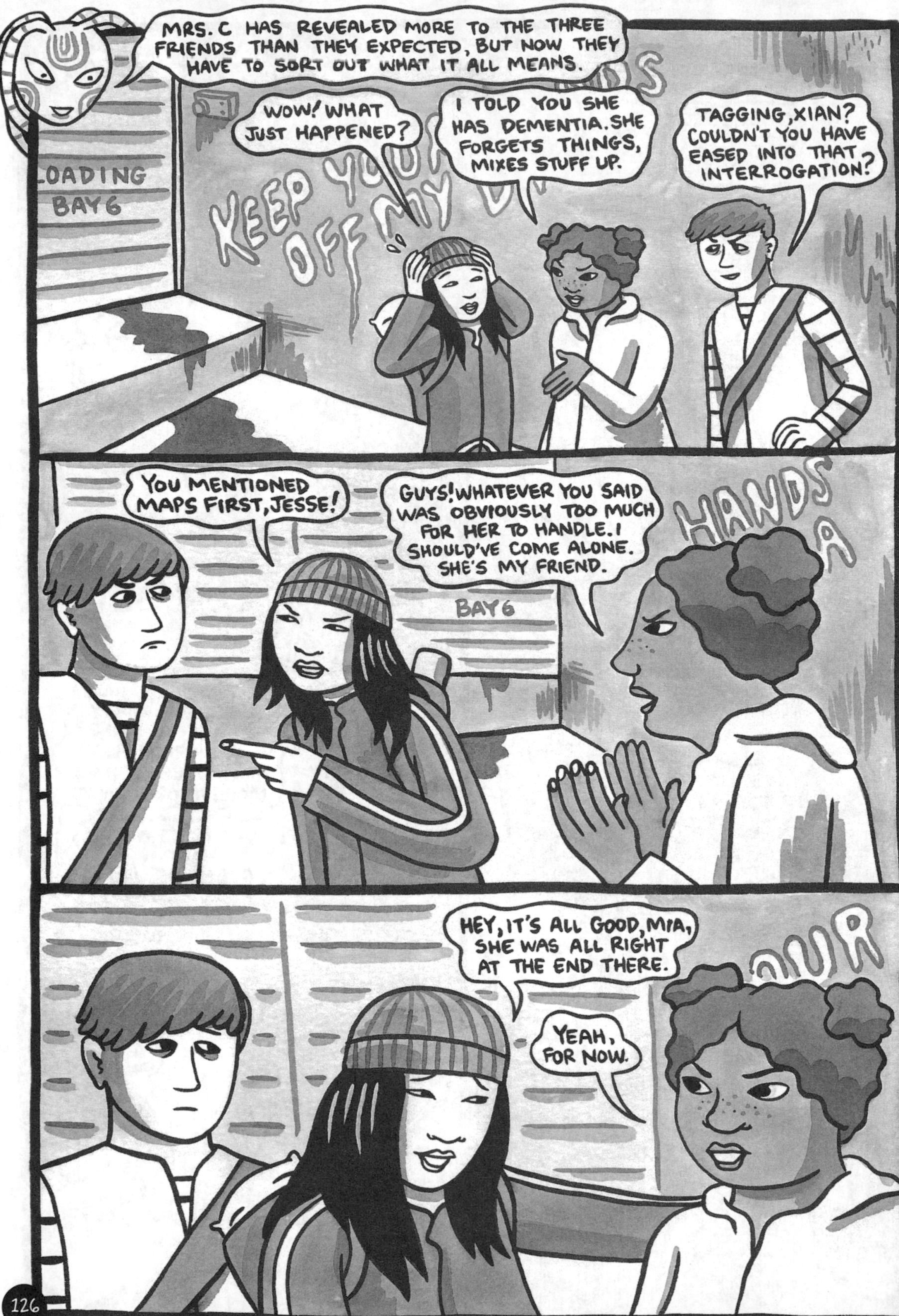

MRS. C HAS REVEALED MORE TO THE THREE FRIENDS THAN THEY EXPECTED, BUT NOW THEY HAVE TO SORT OUT WHAT IT ALL MEANS.
LOADING BAY 6
KEEP YOUR HANDS OFF MY
WOW! WHAT JUST HAPPENED?
I TOLD YOU SHE HAS DEMENTIA. SHE FORGETS THINGS, MIXES STUFF UP.
TAGGING, XIAN? COULDN'T YOU HAVE EASED INTO THAT INTERROGATION?
YOU MENTIONED MAPS FIRST, JESSE!
GUYS! WHATEVER YOU SAID WAS OBVIOUSLY TOO MUCH FOR HER TO HANDLE. I SHOULD'VE COME ALONE. SHE'S MY FRIEND.
BAY 6
HANDS
HEY, IT'S ALL GOOD, MIA, SHE WAS ALL RIGHT AT THE END THERE.
YEAH, FOR NOW.

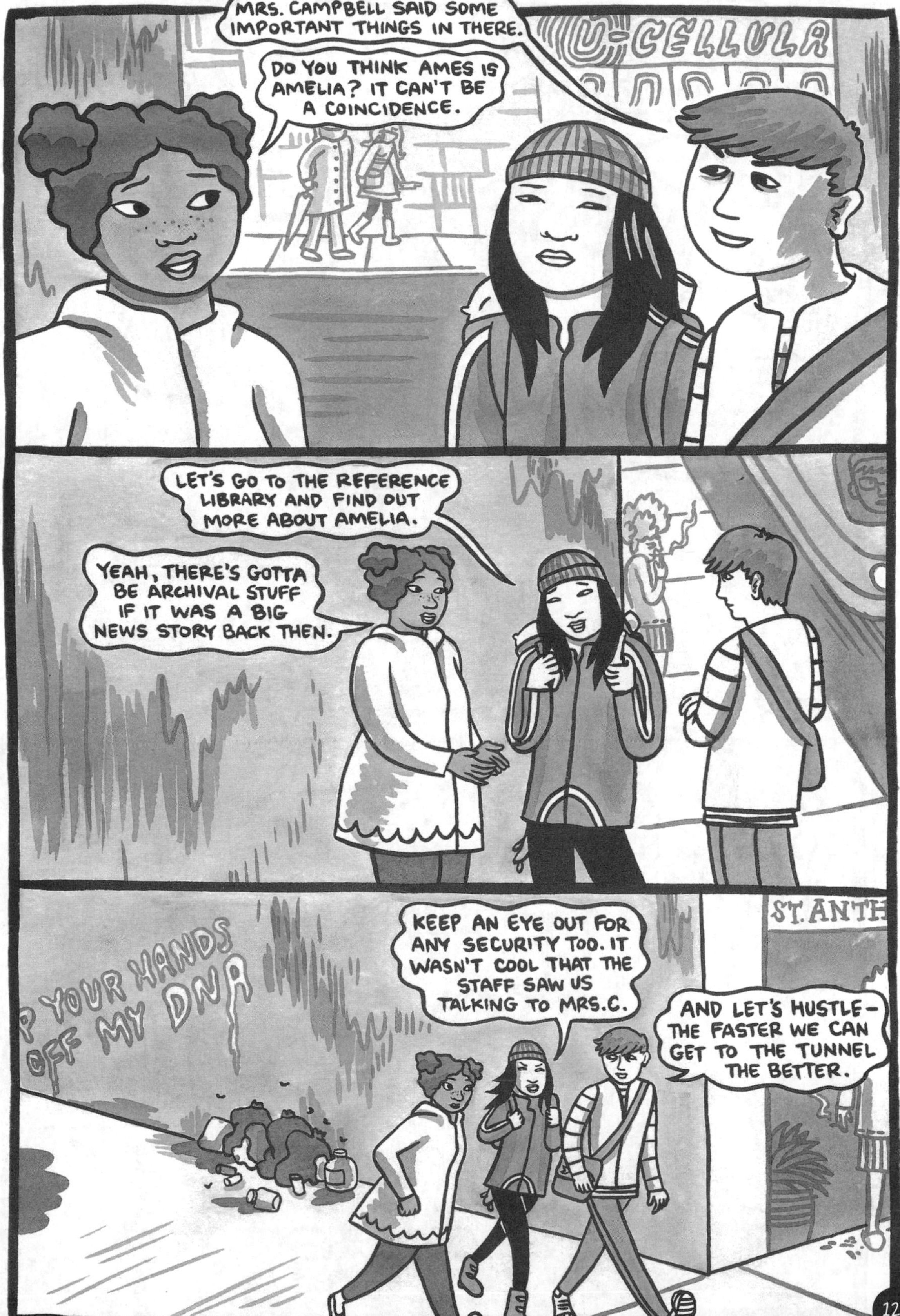
MRS. CAMPBELL SAID SOME IMPORTANT THINGS IN THERE.
DO YOU THINK AMES IS AMELIA? IT CAN'T BE A COINCIDENCE.
U-CELLULA
LET'S GO TO THE REFERENCE LIBRARY AND FIND OUT MORE ABOUT AMELIA.
YEAH, THERE'S GOTTA BE ARCHIVAL STUFF IF IT WAS A BIG NEWS STORY BACK THEN.
P YOUR HANDS OFF MY DNA
ST. ANTH
KEEP AN EYE OUT FOR ANY SECURITY TOO. IT WASN'T COOL THAT THE STAFF SAW US TALKING TO MRS. C.
AND LET'S HUSTLE—THE FASTER WE CAN GET TO THE TUNNEL THE BETTER.

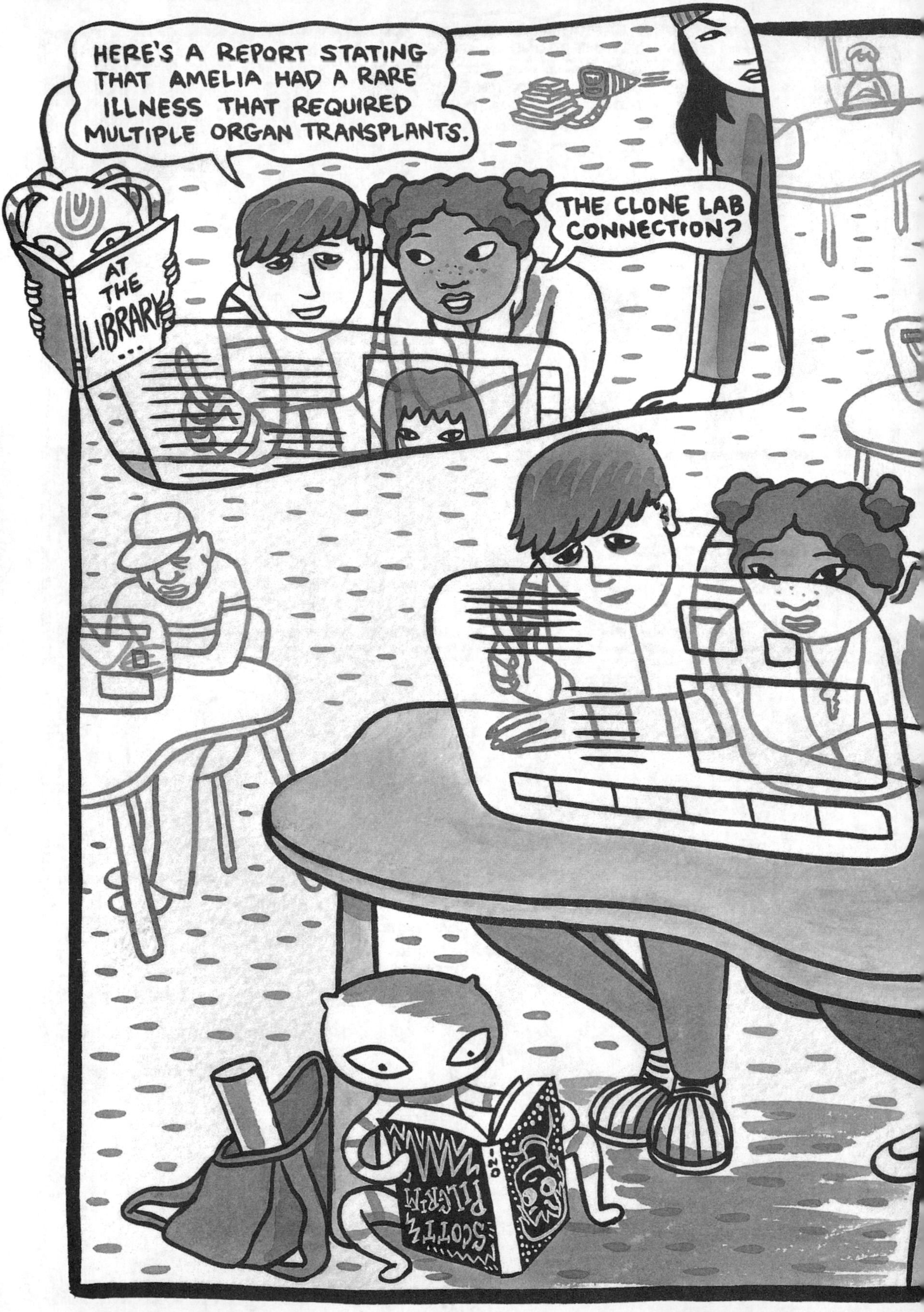
HERE'S A REPORT STATING THAT AMELIA HAD A RARE ILLNESS THAT REQUIRED MULTIPLE ORGAN TRANSPLANTS.
THE CLONE LAB CONNECTION?
AT THE LIBRARY...
SCOTT PILGRIM

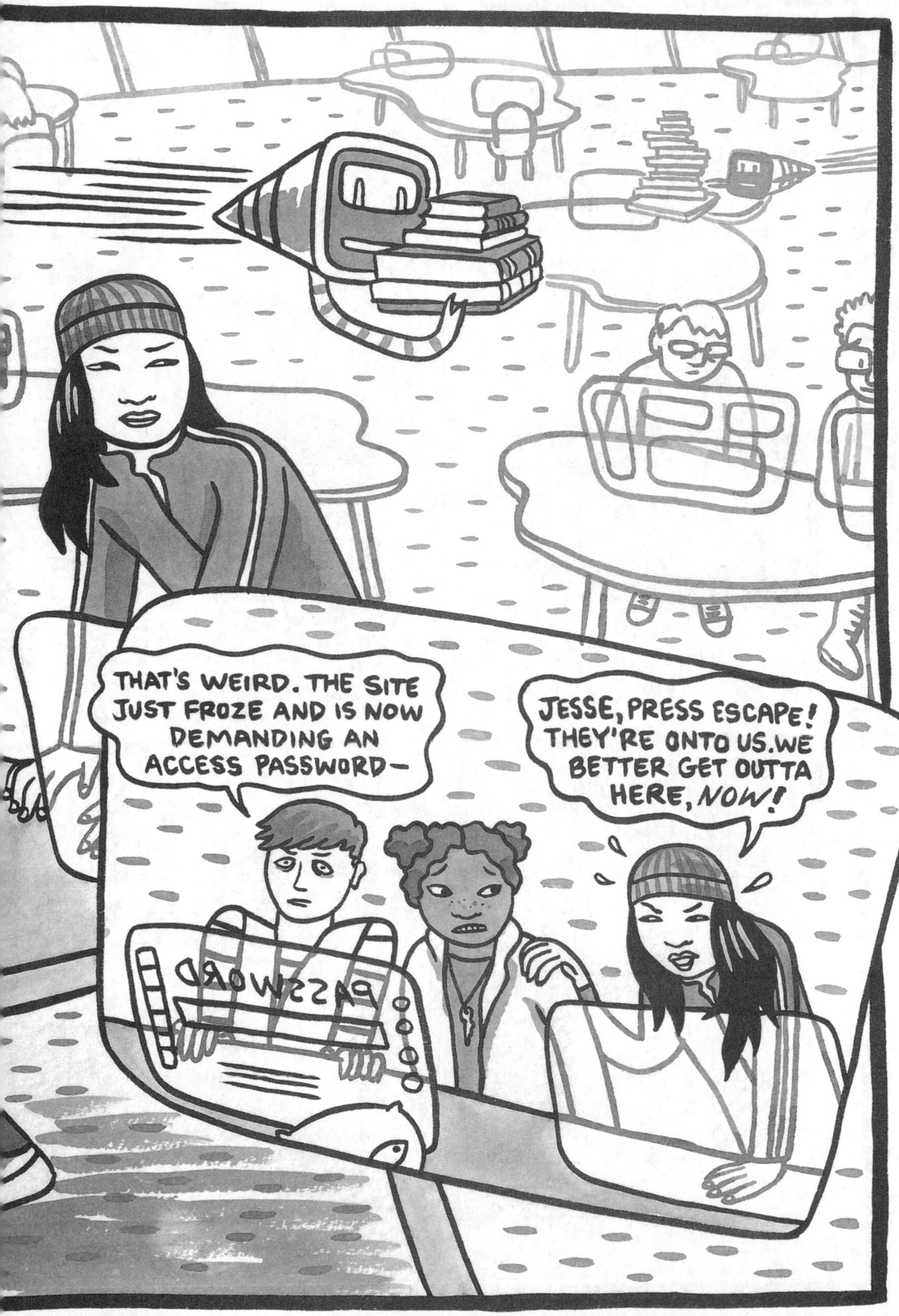
THAT'S WEIRD. THE SITE JUST FROZE AND IS NOW DEMANDING AN ACCESS PASSWORD—
JESSE, PRESS ESCAPE! THEY'RE ONTO US. WE BETTER GET OUTTA HERE, *NOW!*
PASSWORD

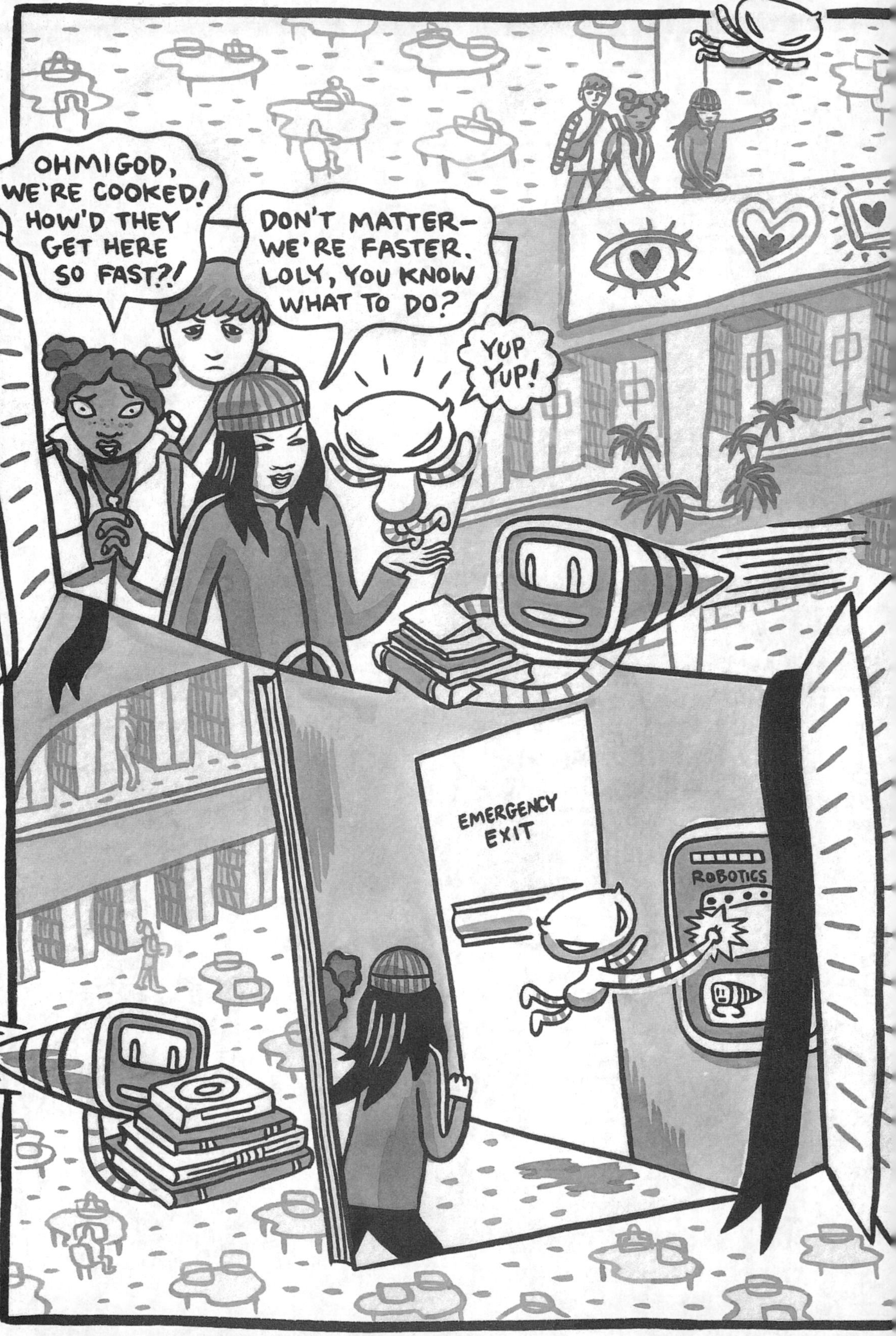
OHMIGOD, WE'RE COOKED! HOW'D THEY GET HERE SO FAST?!
DON'T MATTER- WE'RE FASTER. LOLY, YOU KNOW WHAT TO DO?
YUP YUP!
EMERGENCY EXIT
ROBOTICS

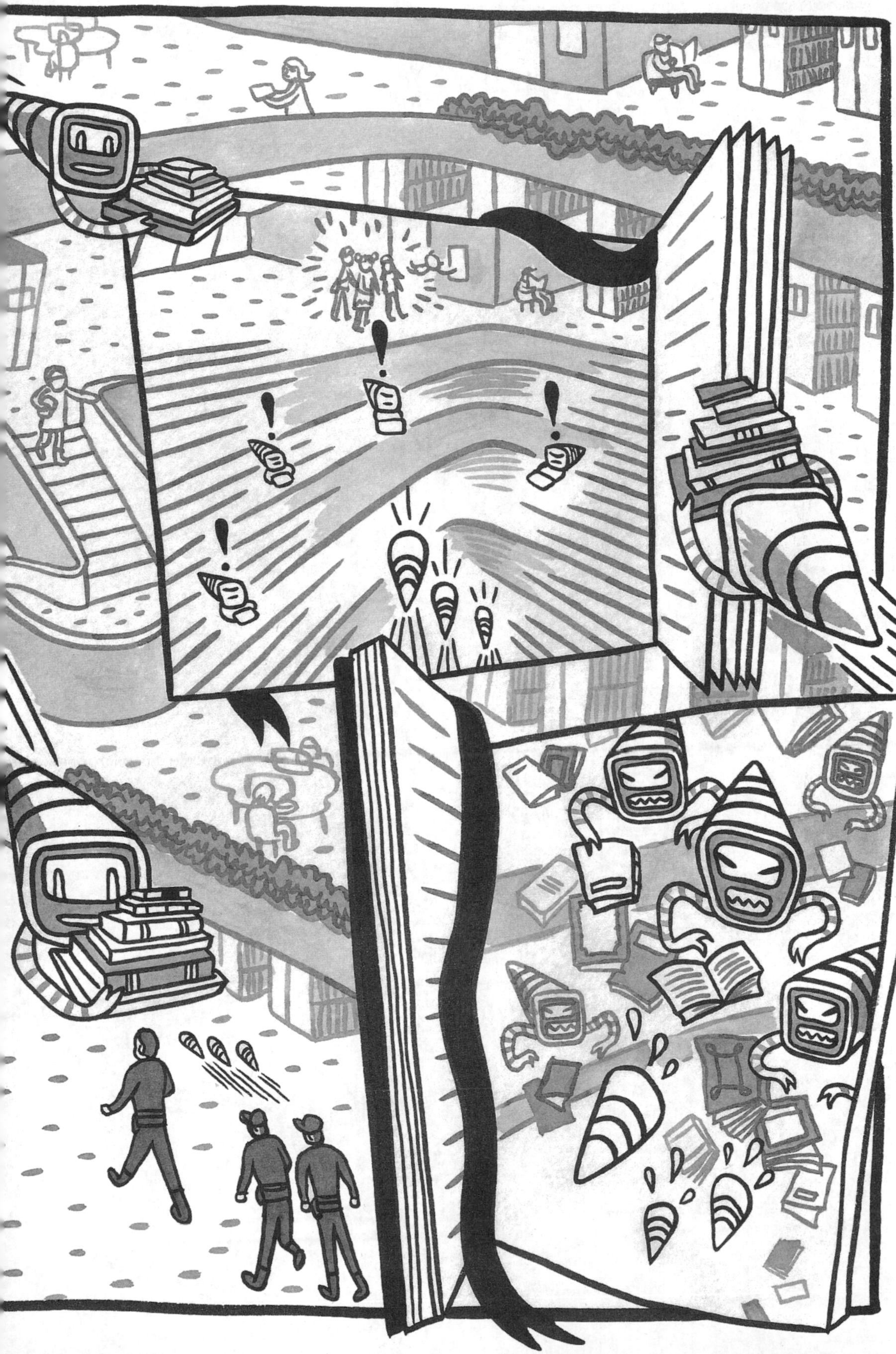

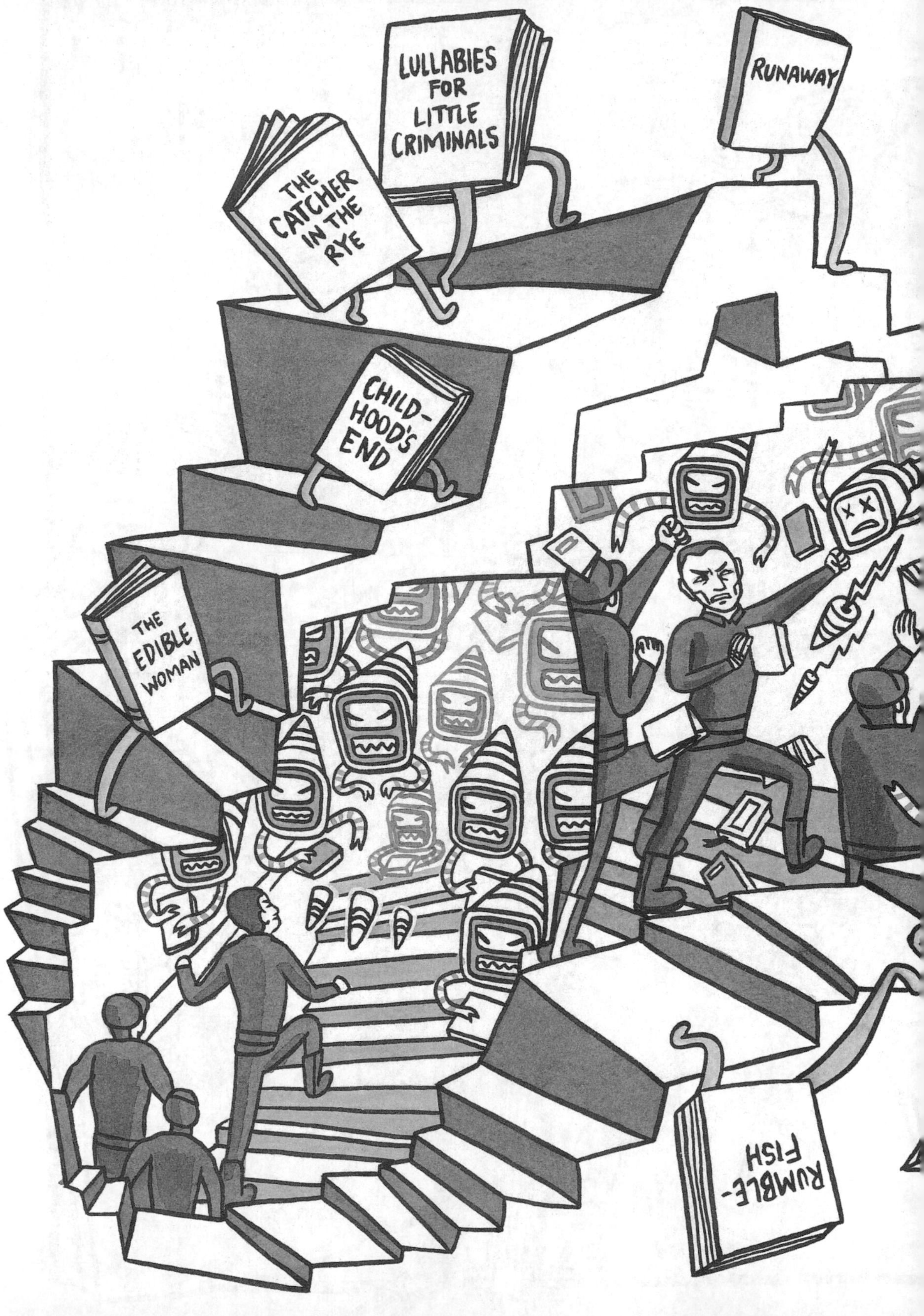
LULLABIES FOR LITTLE CRIMINALS
RUNAWAY
THE CATCHER IN THE RYE
CHILD-HOOD'S END
THE EDIBLE WOMAN
RUMBLE-FISH

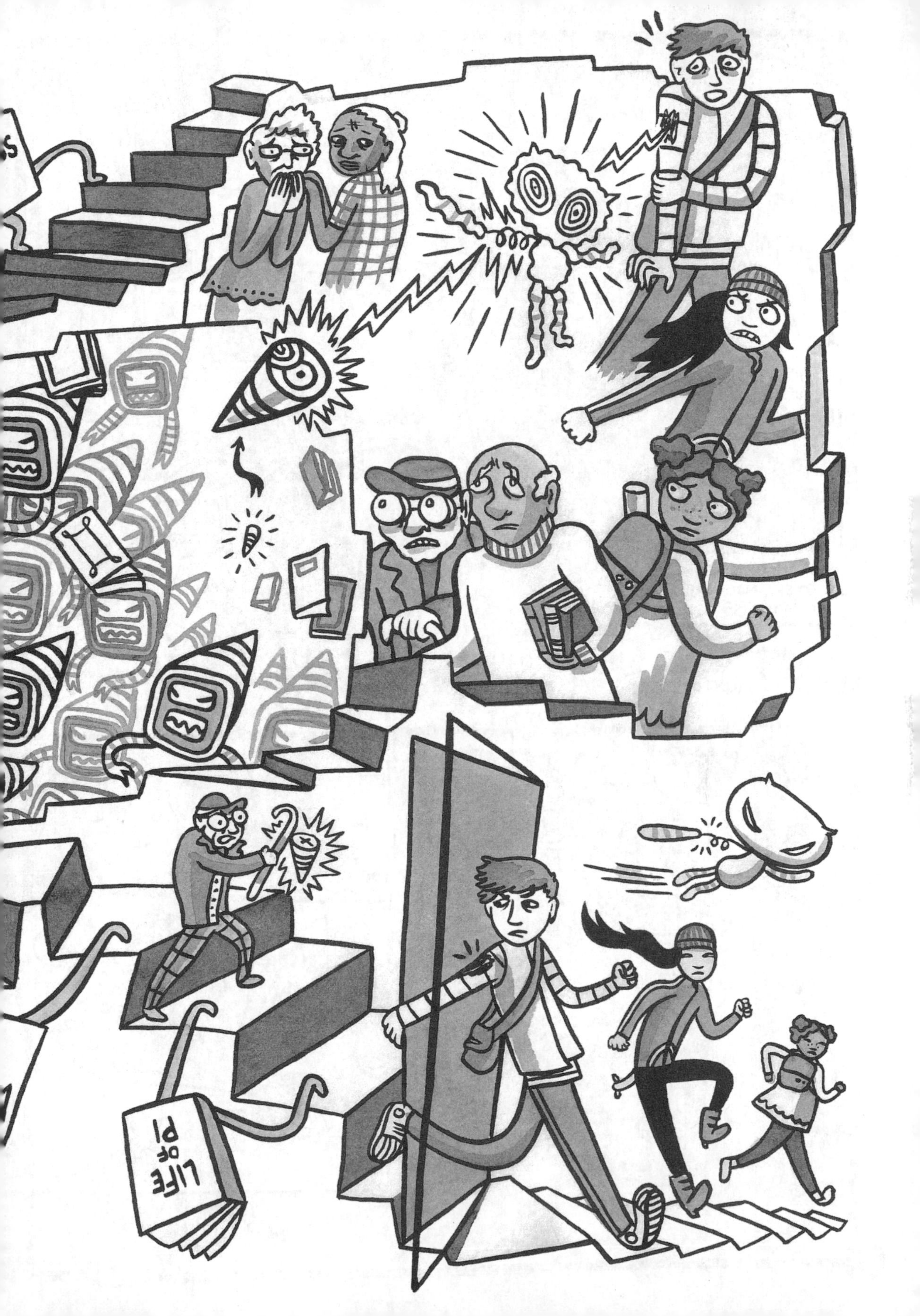
LIFE OF PI

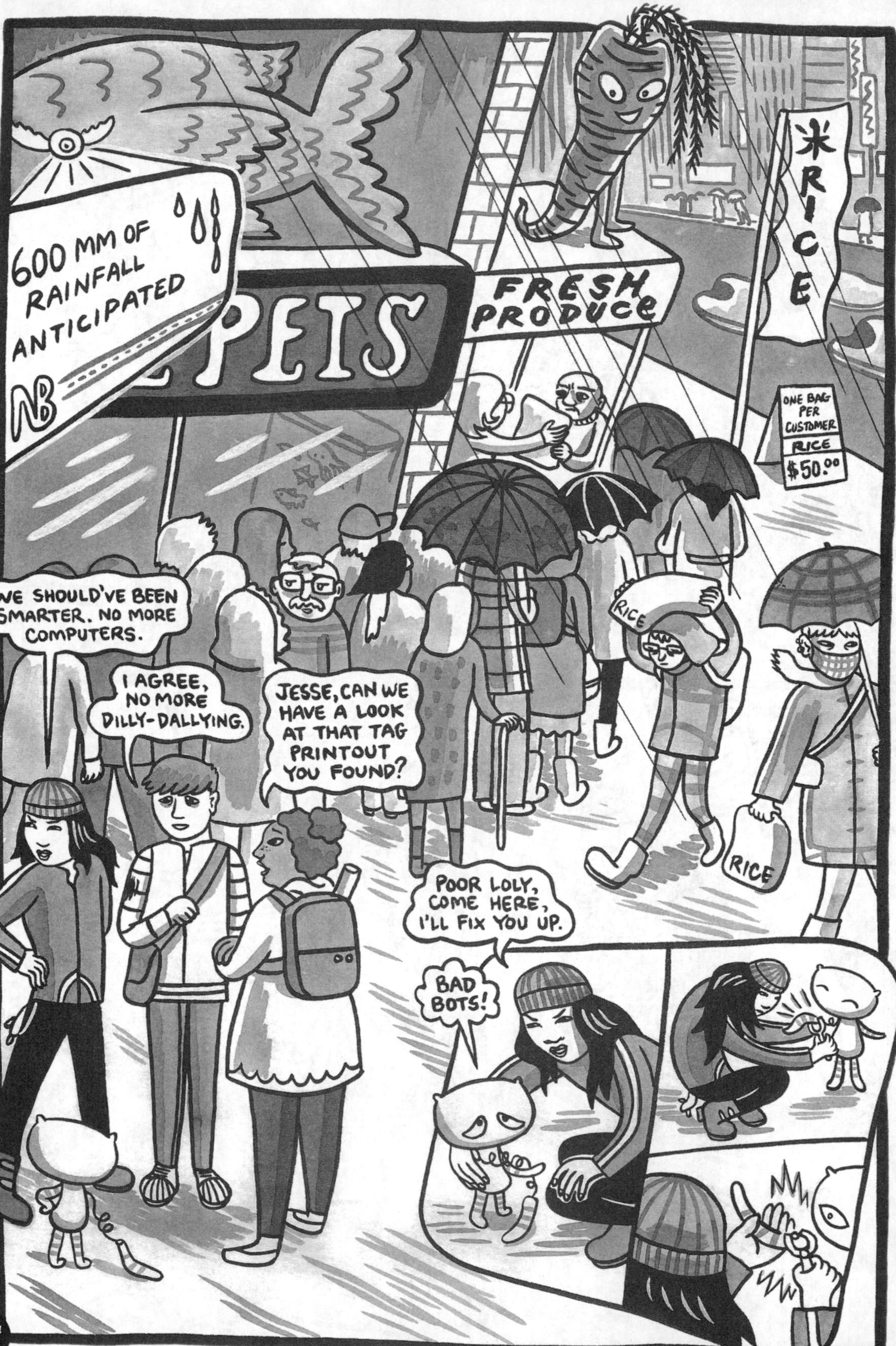
600 MM OF RAINFALL ANTICIPATED
NB
PETS
FRESH PRODUCE
米 RICE
ONE BAG PER CUSTOMER
RICE $50.00
WE SHOULD'VE BEEN SMARTER. NO MORE COMPUTERS.
I AGREE, NO MORE DILLY-DALLYING.
JESSE, CAN WE HAVE A LOOK AT THAT TAG PRINTOUT YOU FOUND?
RICE
RICE
POOR LOLY, COME HERE, I'LL FIX YOU UP.
BAD BOTS!

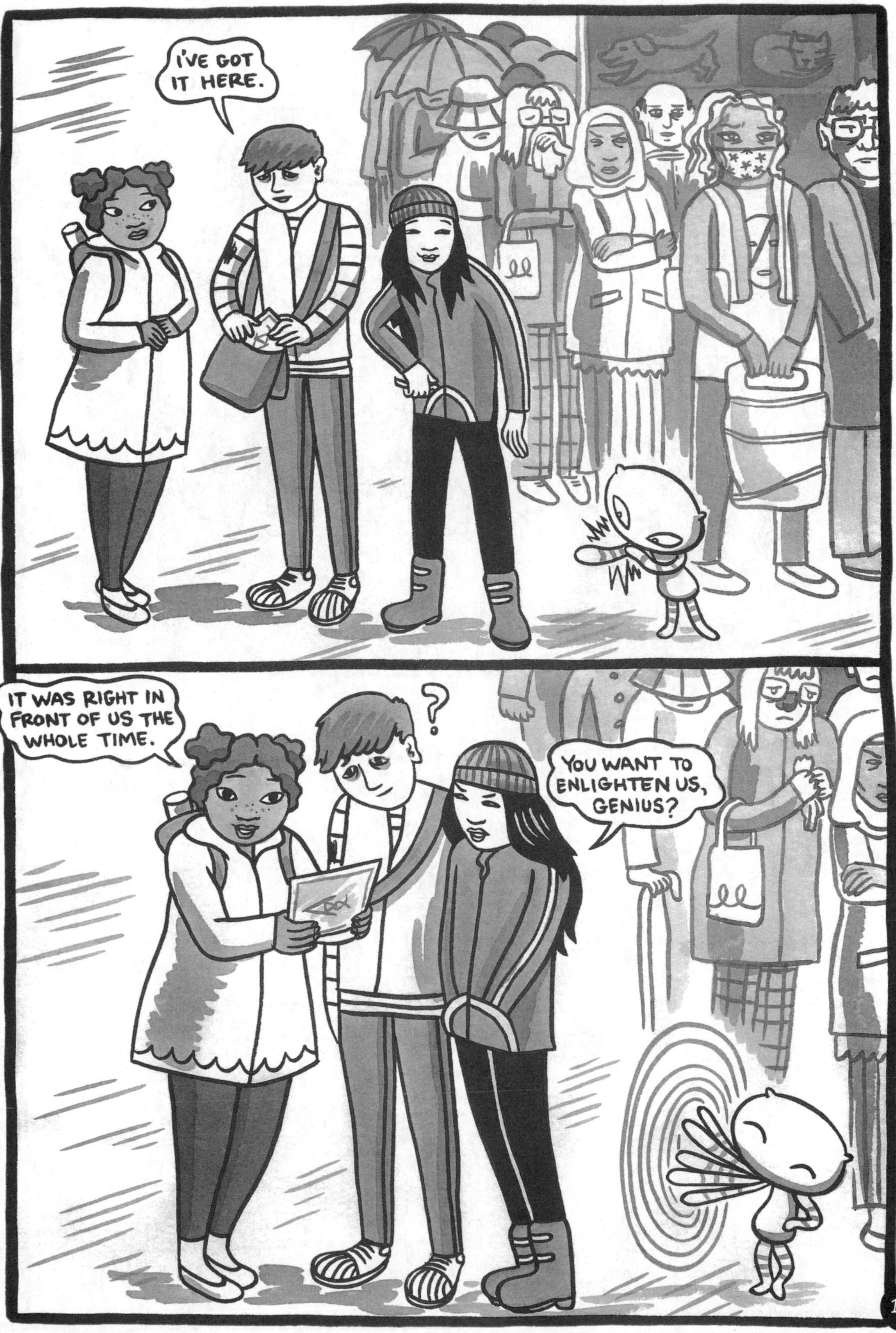
I'VE GOT IT HERE.
IT WAS RIGHT IN FRONT OF US THE WHOLE TIME.
?
YOU WANT TO ENLIGHTEN US, GENIUS?

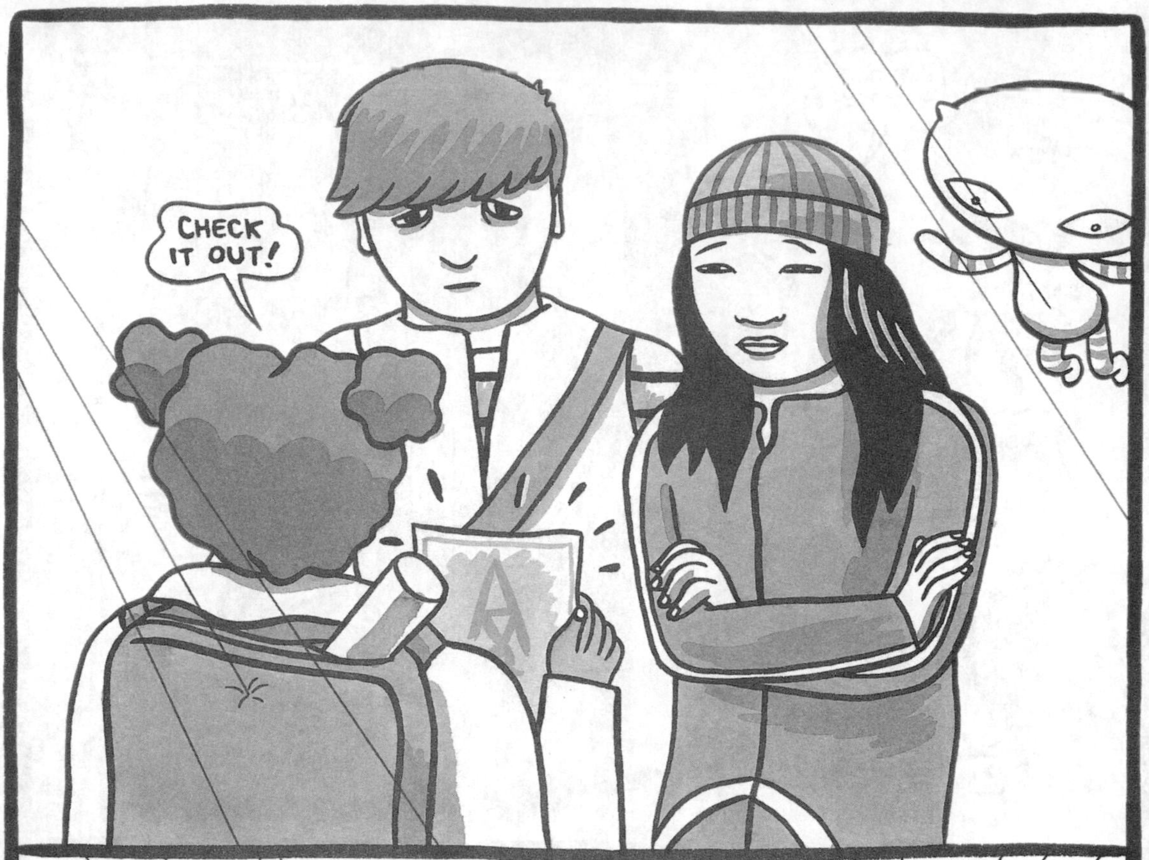
CHECK IT OUT!

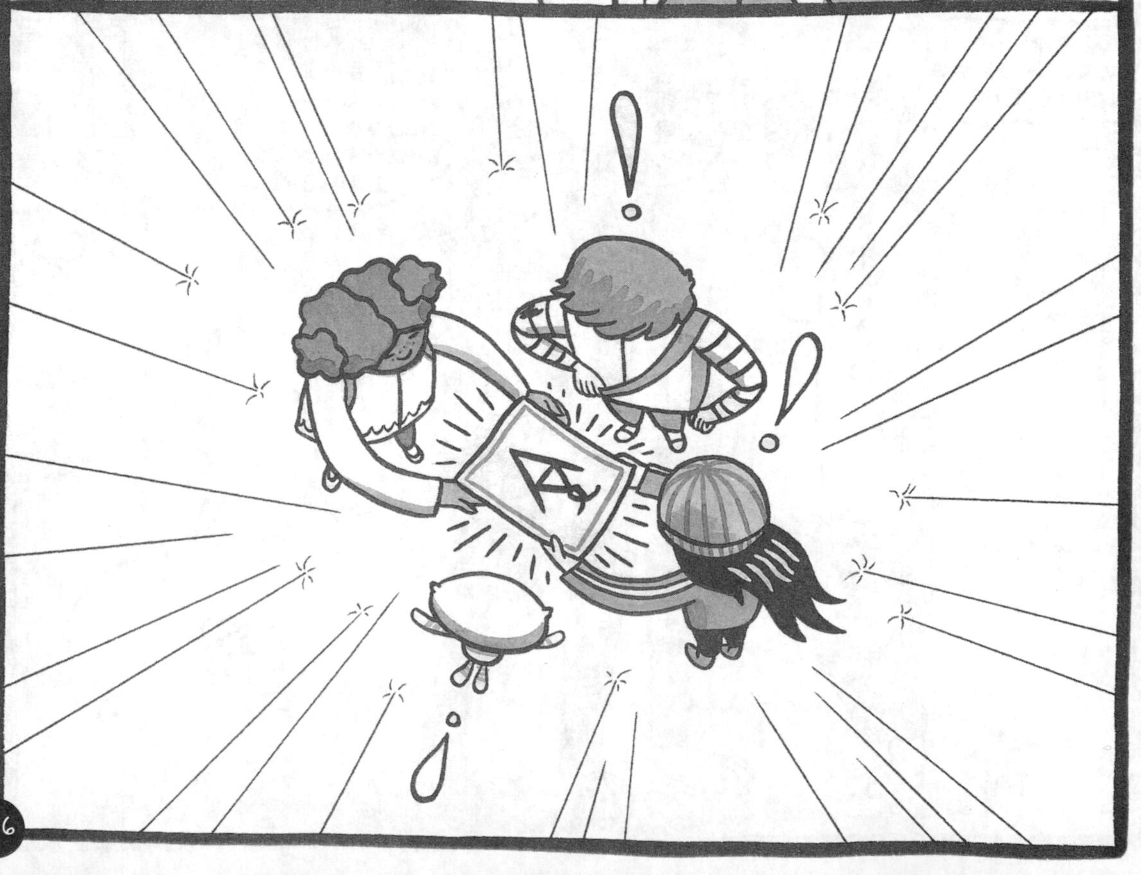
!
!
¡

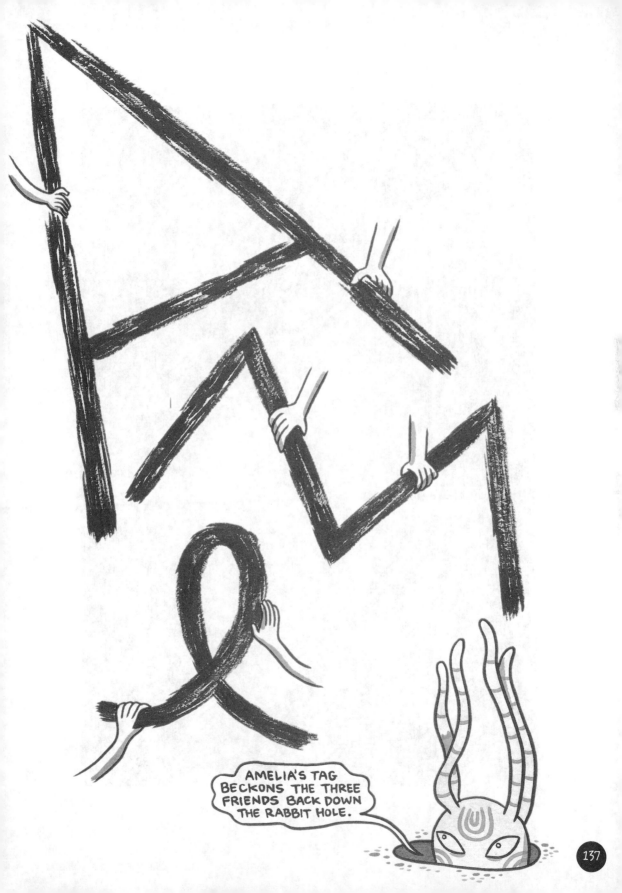

AMELIA'S TAG BECKONS THE THREE FRIENDS BACK DOWN THE RABBIT HOLE.

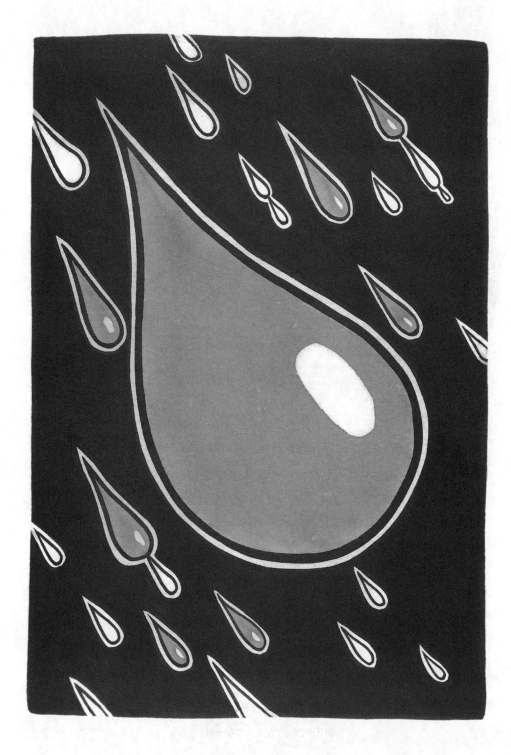

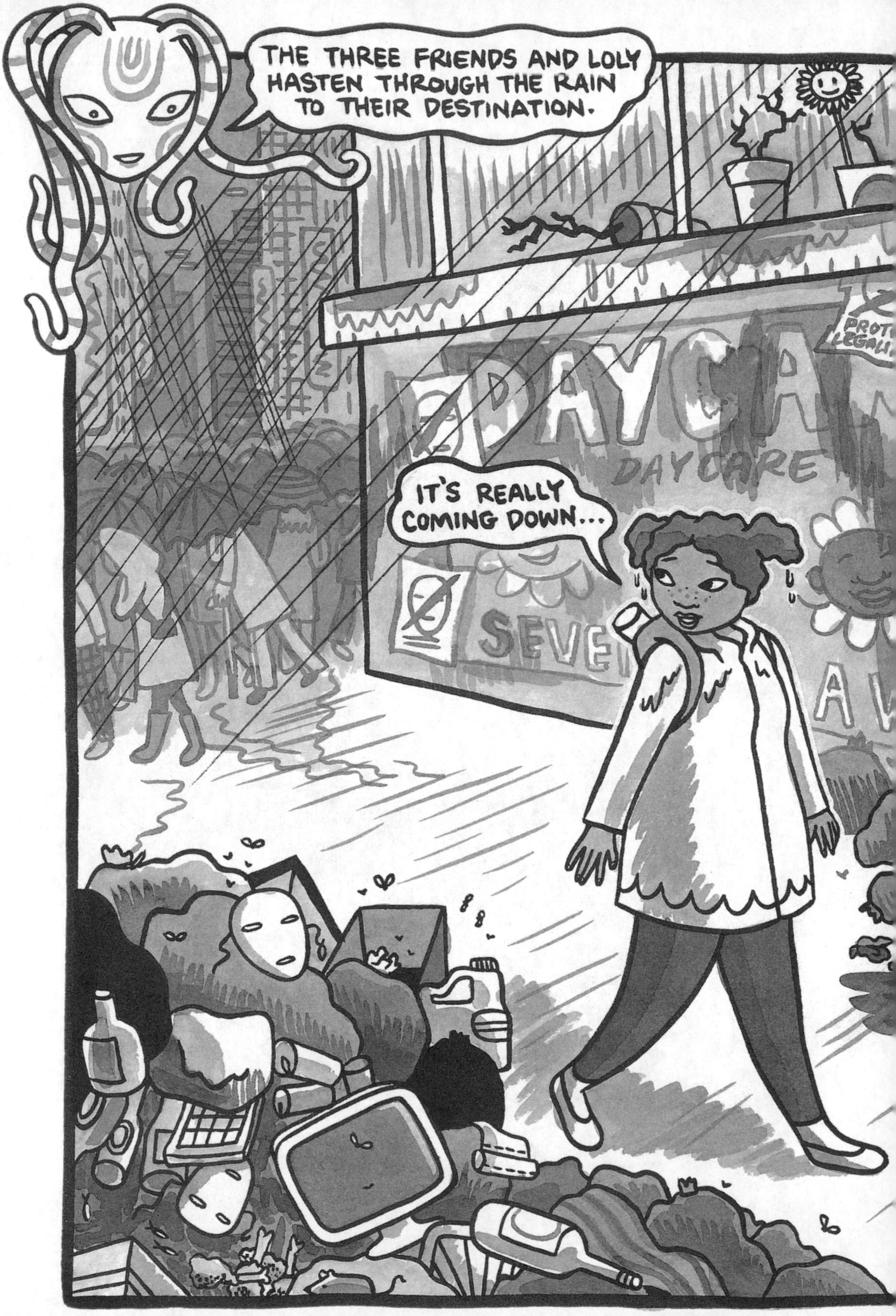
THE THREE FRIENDS AND LOLY HASTEN THROUGH THE RAIN TO THEIR DESTINATION.
DAYCARE
IT'S REALLY COMING DOWN...

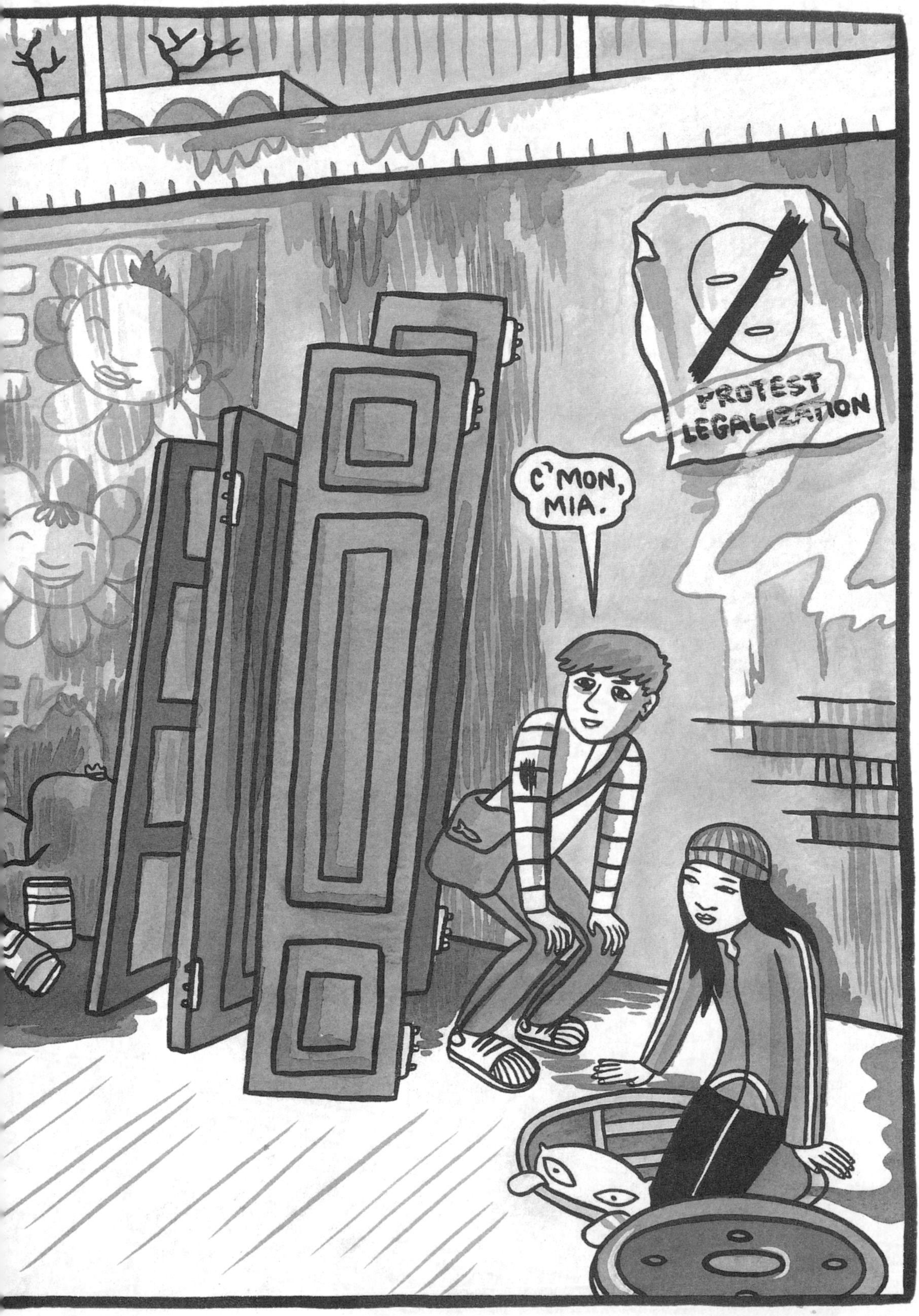
PROTEST LEGALIZATION
C'MON, MIA.

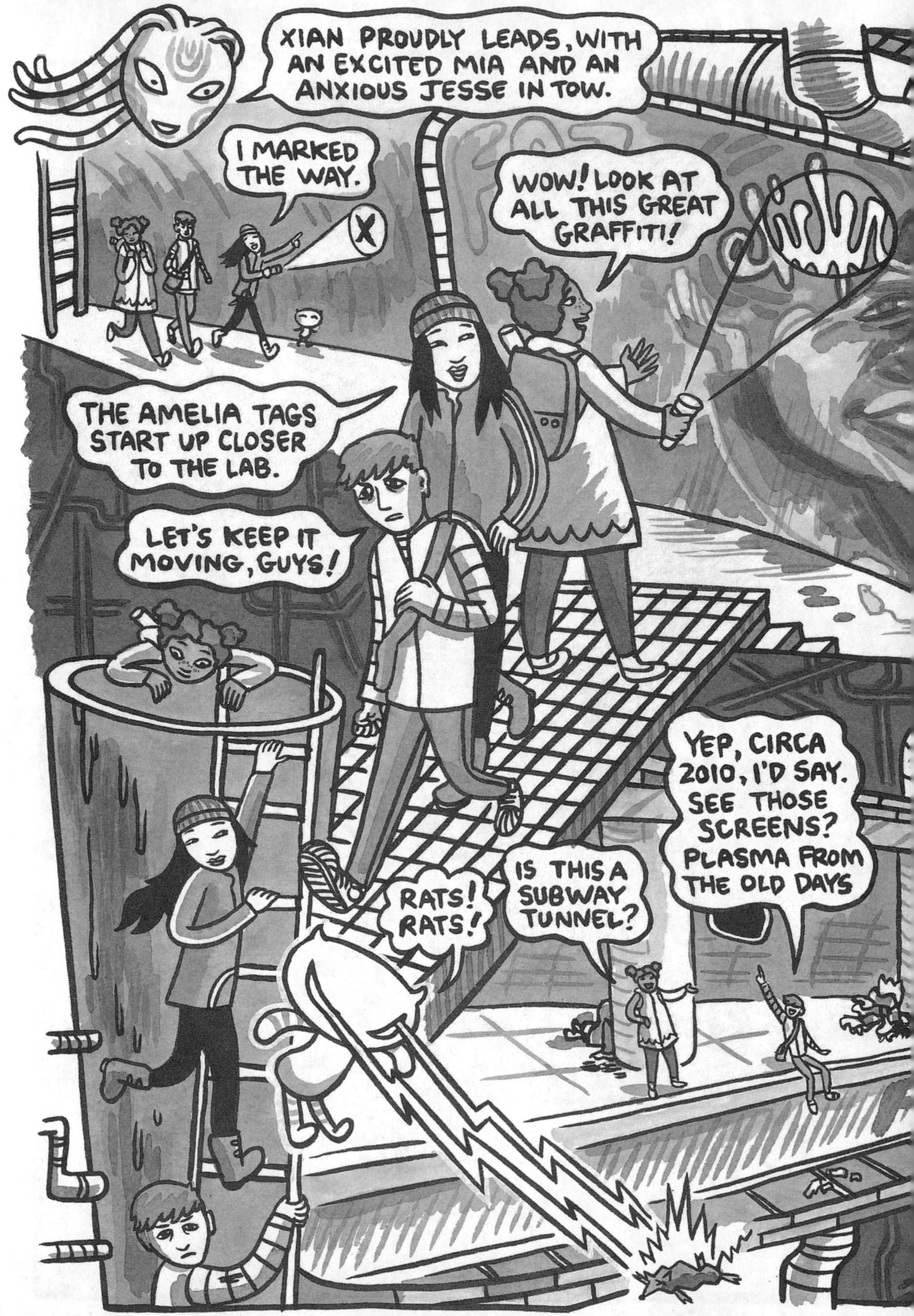
XIAN PROUDLY LEADS, WITH AN EXCITED MIA AND AN ANXIOUS JESSE IN TOW.
I MARKED THE WAY.
WOW! LOOK AT ALL THIS GREAT GRAFFITI!
THE AMELIA TAGS START UP CLOSER TO THE LAB.
LET'S KEEP IT MOVING, GUYS!
YEP, CIRCA 2010, I'D SAY. SEE THOSE SCREENS? PLASMA FROM THE OLD DAYS
IS THIS A SUBWAY TUNNEL?
RATS! RATS!

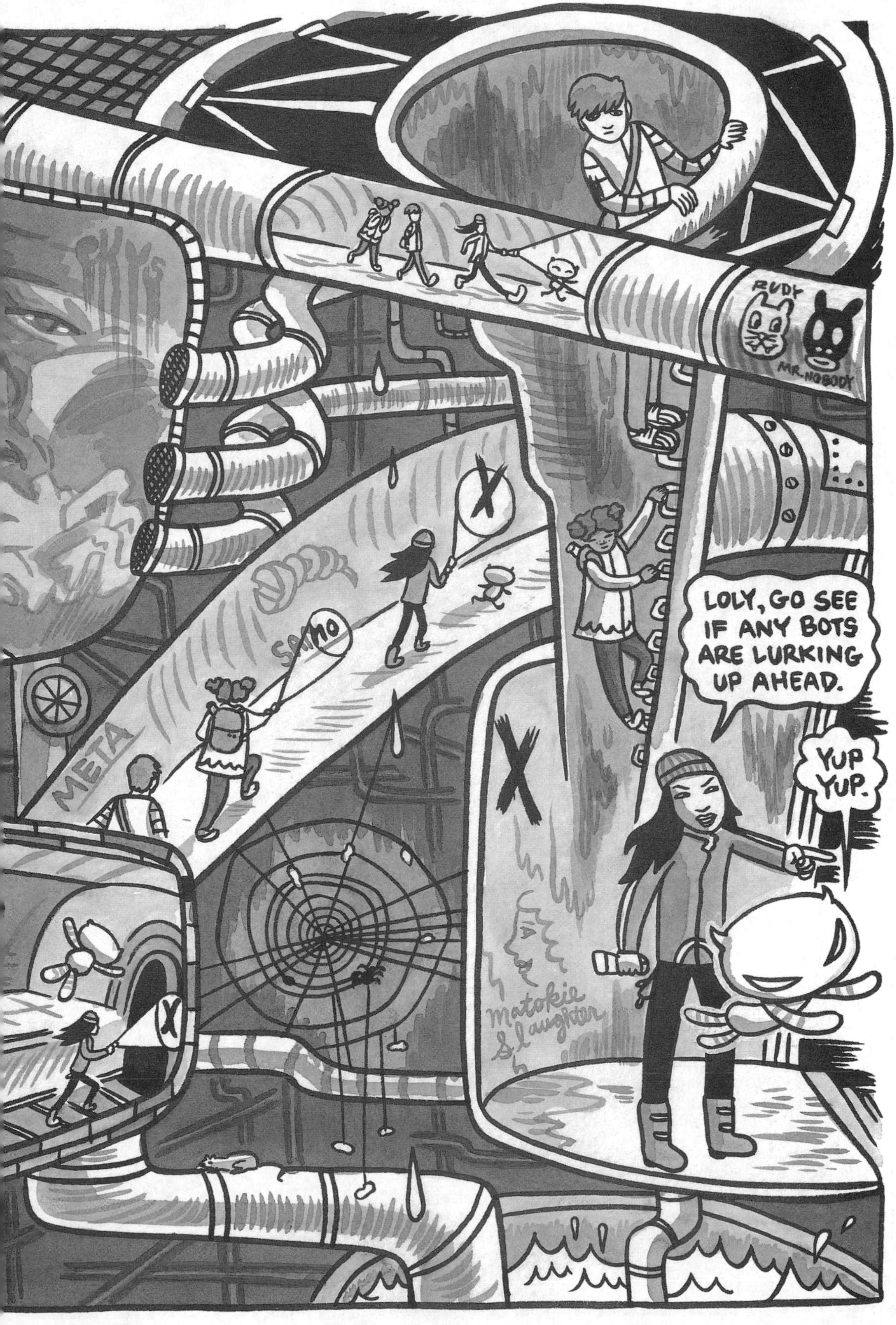
RUDY
MR. NOBODY
META
Matokie Slaughter
LOLY, GO SEE IF ANY BOTS ARE LURKING UP AHEAD.
YUP YUP.

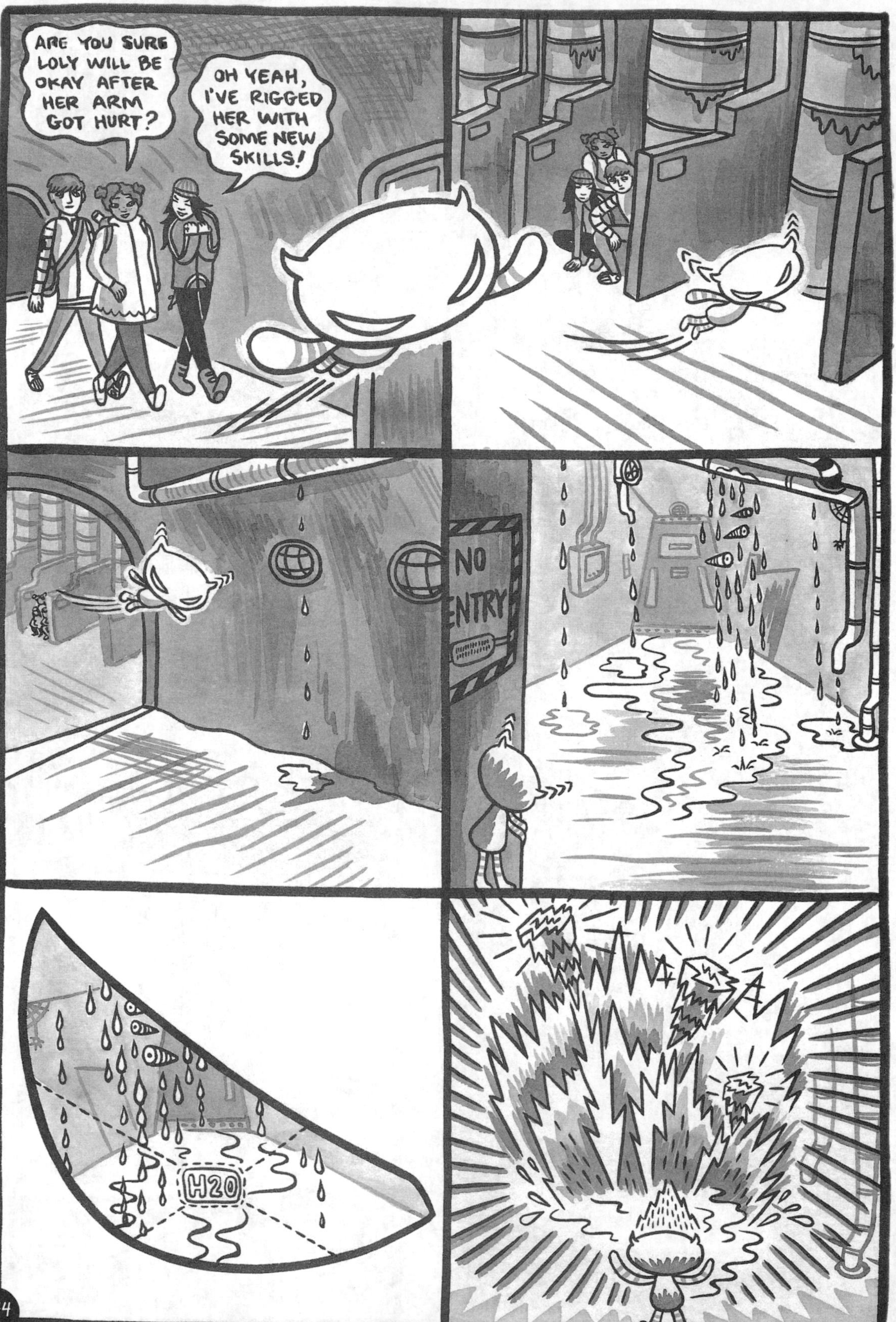
ARE YOU SURE LOLY WILL BE OKAY AFTER HER ARM GOT HURT?
OH YEAH, I'VE RIGGED HER WITH SOME NEW SKILLS!
NO ENTRY
H20

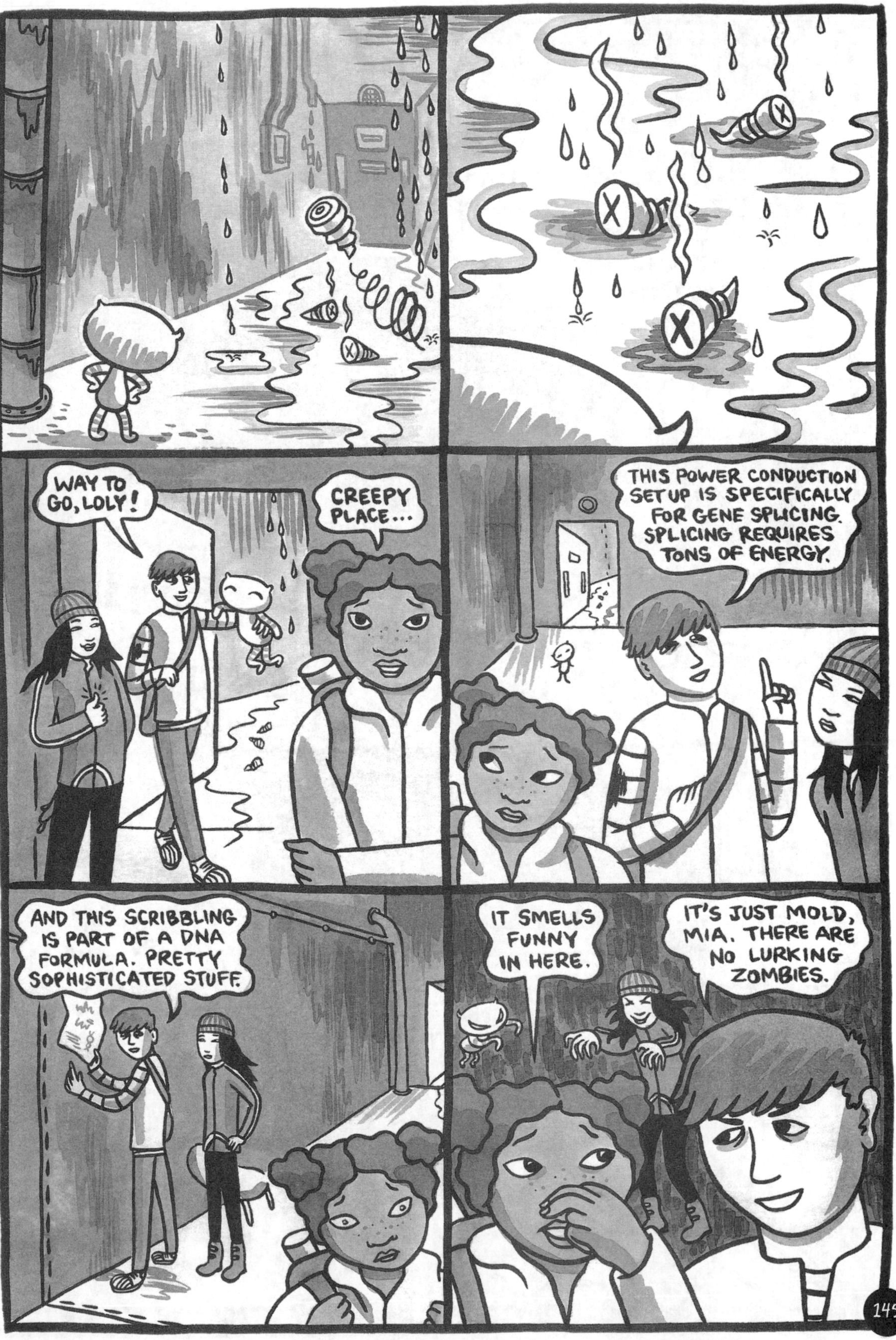
WAY TO GO, LOLY!
CREEPY PLACE...
THIS POWER CONDUCTION SETUP IS SPECIFICALLY FOR GENE SPLICING. SPLICING REQUIRES TONS OF ENERGY.
AND THIS SCRIBBLING IS PART OF A DNA FORMULA. PRETTY SOPHISTICATED STUFF.
IT SMELLS FUNNY IN HERE.
IT'S JUST MOLD, MIA. THERE ARE NO LURKING ZOMBIES.

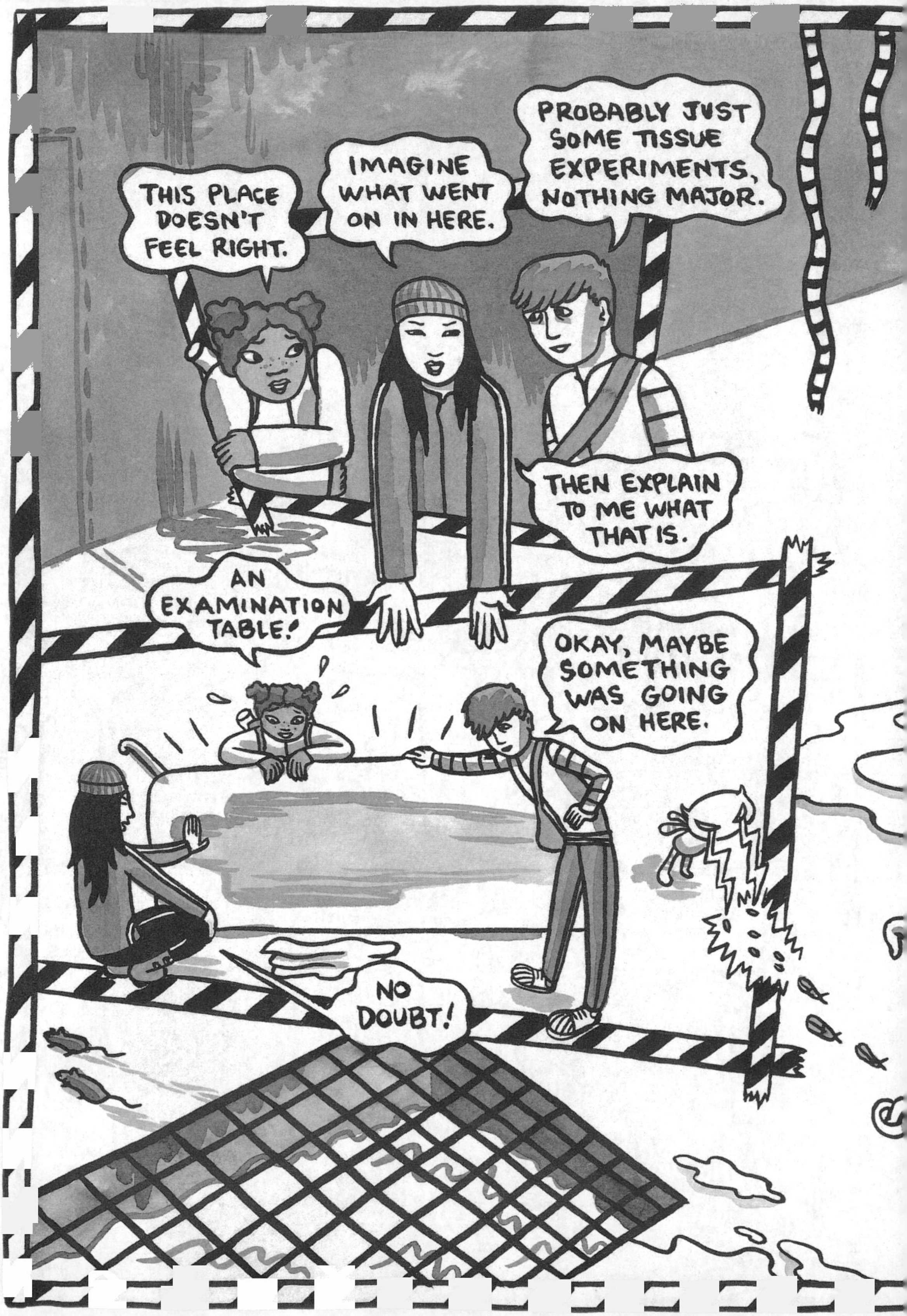
THIS PLACE DOESN'T FEEL RIGHT.
IMAGINE WHAT WENT ON IN HERE.
PROBABLY JUST SOME TISSUE EXPERIMENTS, NOTHING MAJOR.
THEN EXPLAIN TO ME WHAT THAT IS.
AN EXAMINATION TABLE!
OKAY, MAYBE SOMETHING WAS GOING ON HERE.
NO DOUBT!

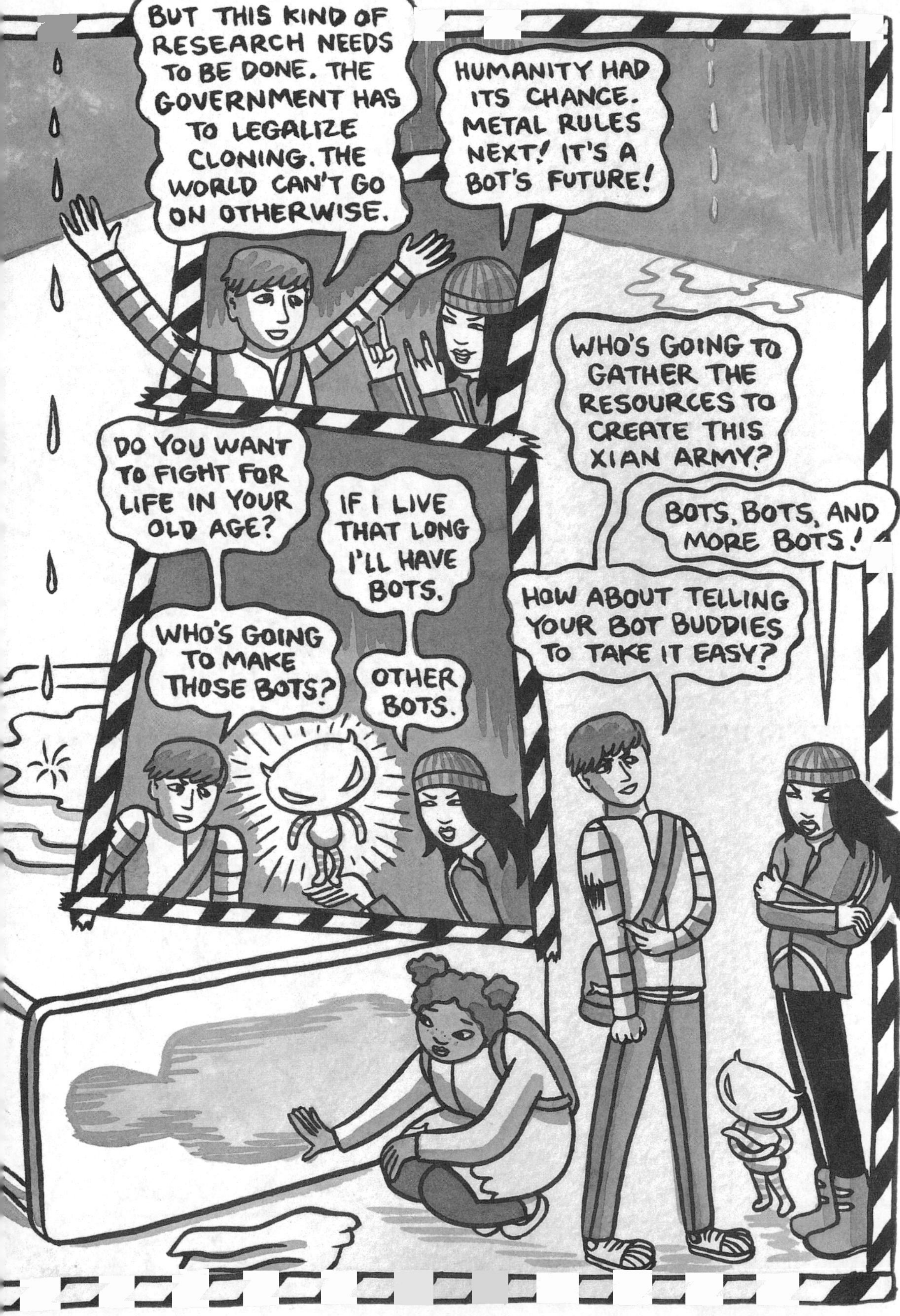

BUT THIS KIND OF RESEARCH NEEDS TO BE DONE. THE GOVERNMENT HAS TO LEGALIZE CLONING. THE WORLD CAN'T GO ON OTHERWISE.
HUMANITY HAD ITS CHANCE. METAL RULES NEXT! IT'S A BOT'S FUTURE!
DO YOU WANT TO FIGHT FOR LIFE IN YOUR OLD AGE?
IF I LIVE THAT LONG I'LL HAVE BOTS.
WHO'S GOING TO MAKE THOSE BOTS?
OTHER BOTS.
WHO'S GOING TO GATHER THE RESOURCES TO CREATE THIS XIAN ARMY?
BOTS, BOTS, AND MORE BOTS!
HOW ABOUT TELLING YOUR BOT BUDDIES TO TAKE IT EASY?

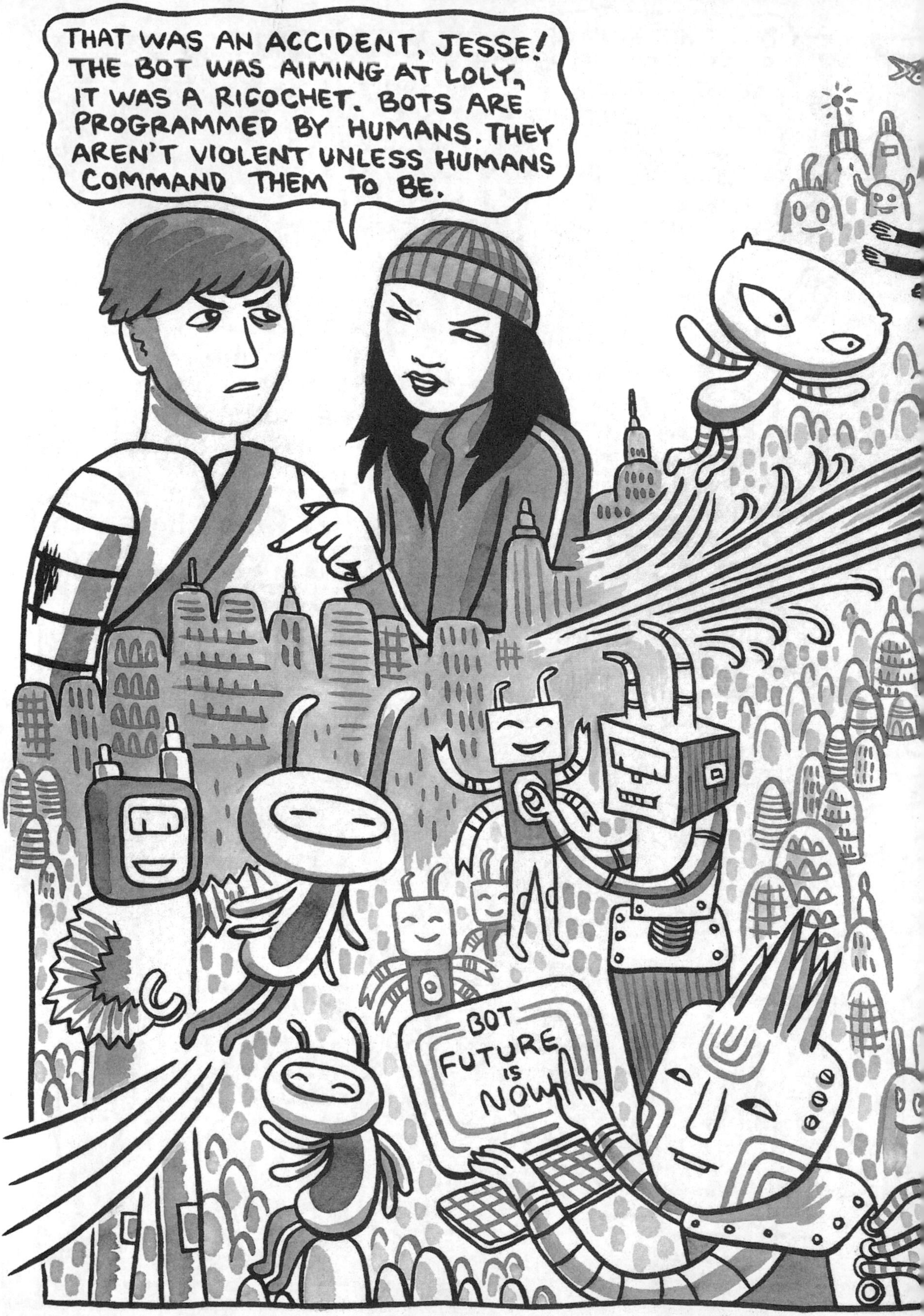
THAT WAS AN ACCIDENT, JESSE! THE BOT WAS AIMING AT LOLY, IT WAS A RICOCHET. BOTS ARE PROGRAMMED BY HUMANS. THEY AREN'T VIOLENT UNLESS HUMANS COMMAND THEM TO BE.
BOT FUTURE IS NOW

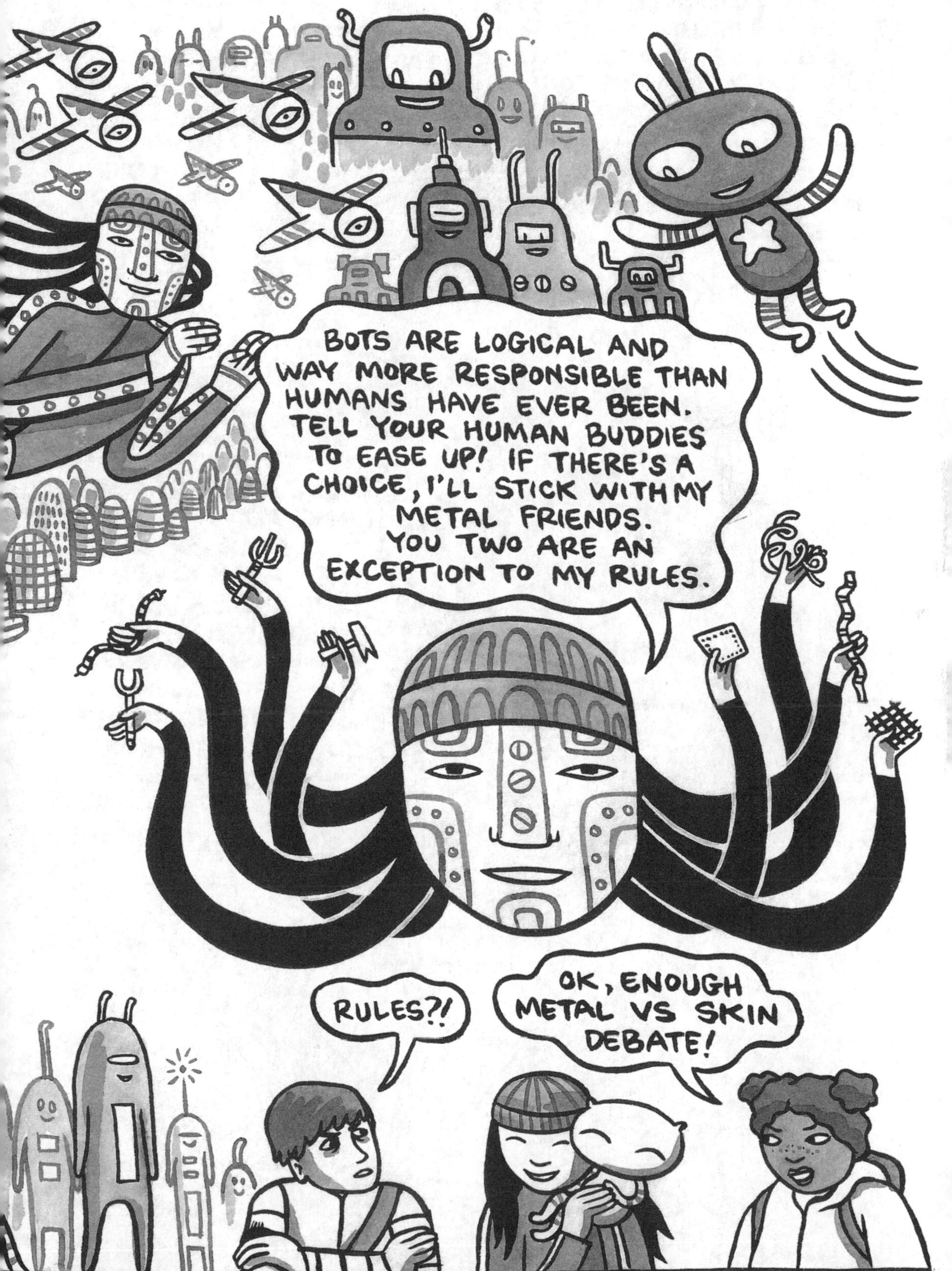
BOTS ARE LOGICAL AND WAY MORE RESPONSIBLE THAN HUMANS HAVE EVER BEEN. TELL YOUR HUMAN BUDDIES TO EASE UP! IF THERE'S A CHOICE, I'LL STICK WITH MY METAL FRIENDS. YOU TWO ARE AN EXCEPTION TO MY RULES.
RULES?!
OK, ENOUGH METAL VS SKIN DEBATE!

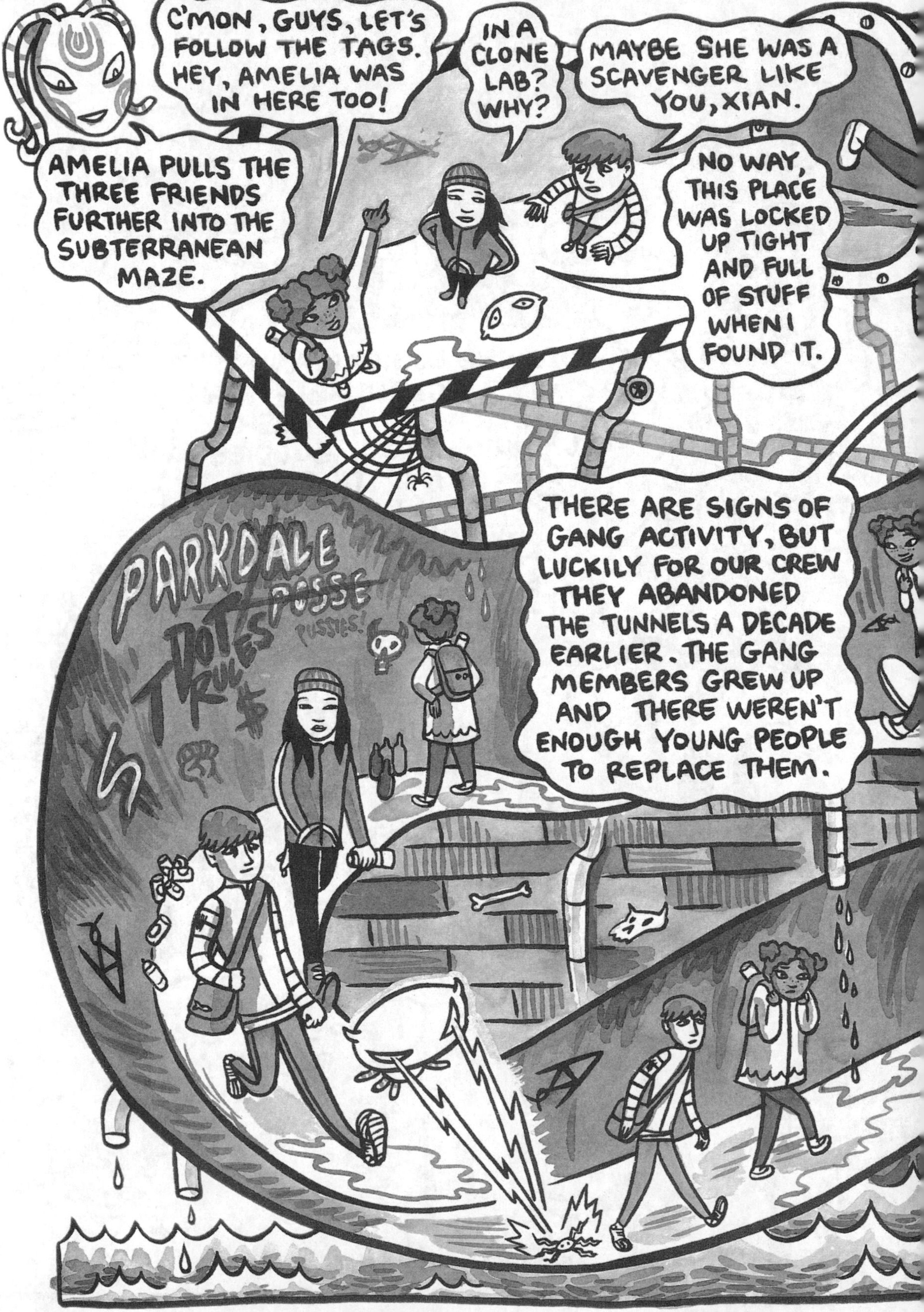
C'MON, GUYS, LET'S FOLLOW THE TAGS. HEY, AMELIA WAS IN HERE TOO!
IN A CLONE LAB? WHY?
MAYBE SHE WAS A SCAVENGER LIKE YOU, XIAN.
AMELIA PULLS THE THREE FRIENDS FURTHER INTO THE SUBTERRANEAN MAZE.
NO WAY, THIS PLACE WAS LOCKED UP TIGHT AND FULL OF STUFF WHEN I FOUND IT.
PARKDALE POSSE
T DOT RULES
PUSSIES!
THERE ARE SIGNS OF GANG ACTIVITY, BUT LUCKILY FOR OUR CREW THEY ABANDONED THE TUNNELS A DECADE EARLIER. THE GANG MEMBERS GREW UP AND THERE WEREN'T ENOUGH YOUNG PEOPLE TO REPLACE THEM.

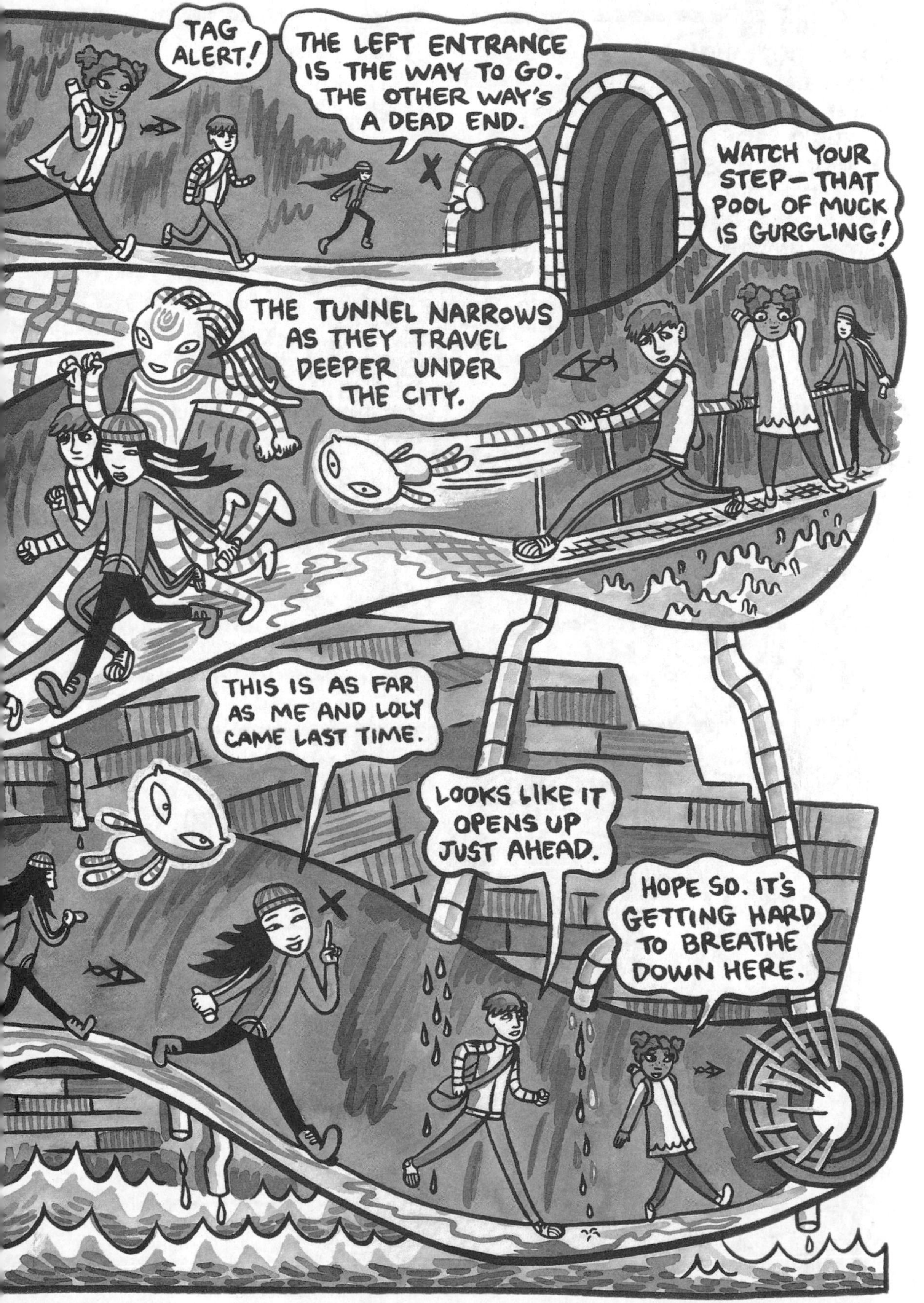
TAG ALERT!
THE LEFT ENTRANCE IS THE WAY TO GO. THE OTHER WAY'S A DEAD END.
WATCH YOUR STEP— THAT POOL OF MUCK IS GURGLING!
THE TUNNEL NARROWS AS THEY TRAVEL DEEPER UNDER THE CITY.
THIS IS AS FAR AS ME AND LOLY CAME LAST TIME.
LOOKS LIKE IT OPENS UP JUST AHEAD.
HOPE SO. IT'S GETTING HARD TO BREATHE DOWN HERE.

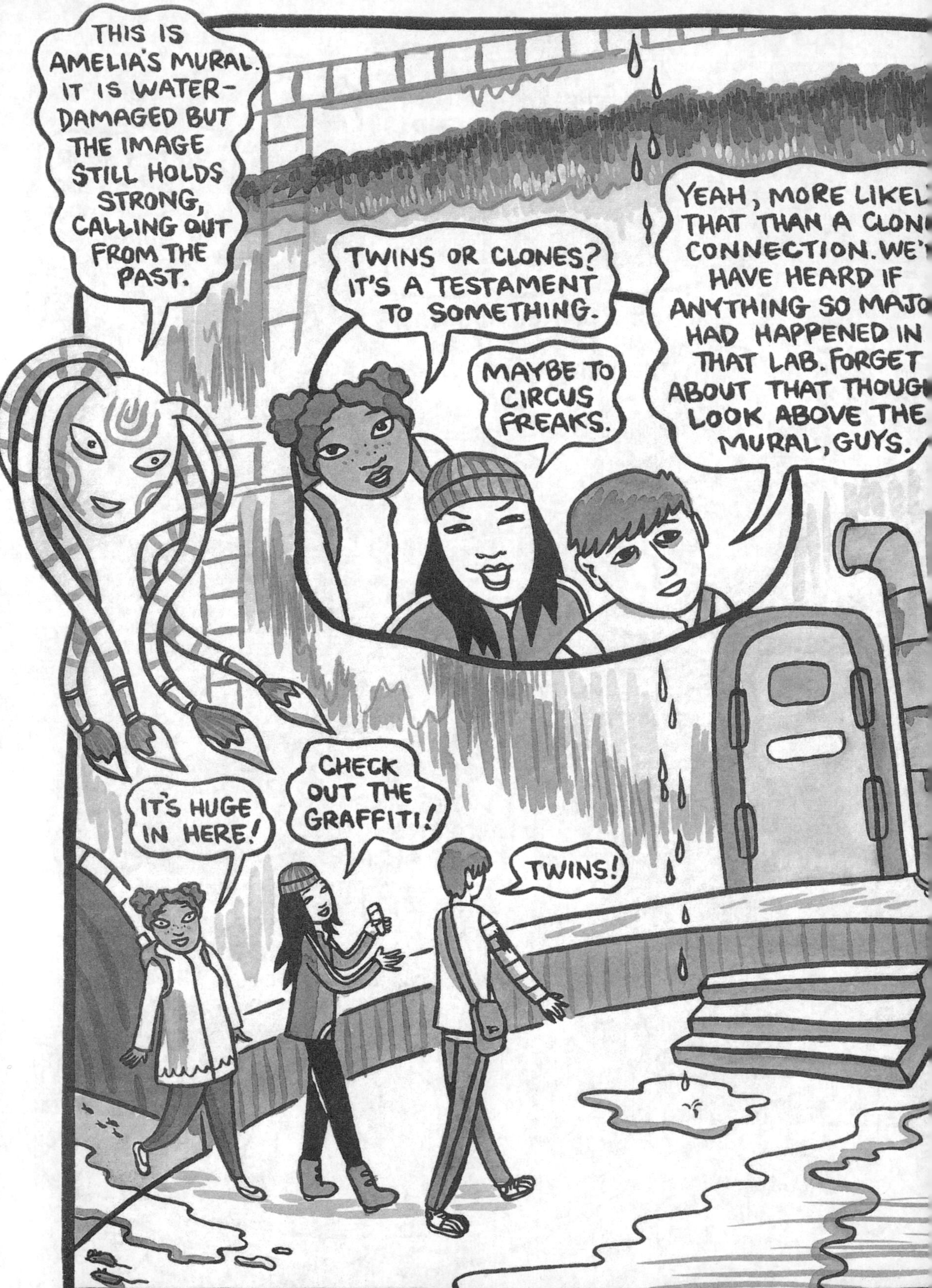
THIS IS AMELIA'S MURAL. IT IS WATER-DAMAGED BUT THE IMAGE STILL HOLDS STRONG, CALLING OUT FROM THE PAST.
TWINS OR CLONES? IT'S A TESTAMENT TO SOMETHING.
MAYBE TO CIRCUS FREAKS.
YEAH, MORE LIKEL THAT THAN A CLON CONNECTION. WE' HAVE HEARD IF ANYTHING SO MAJO HAD HAPPENED IN THAT LAB. FORGET ABOUT THAT THOUG LOOK ABOVE THE MURAL, GUYS.
IT'S HUGE IN HERE!
CHECK OUT THE GRAFFITI!
TWINS!

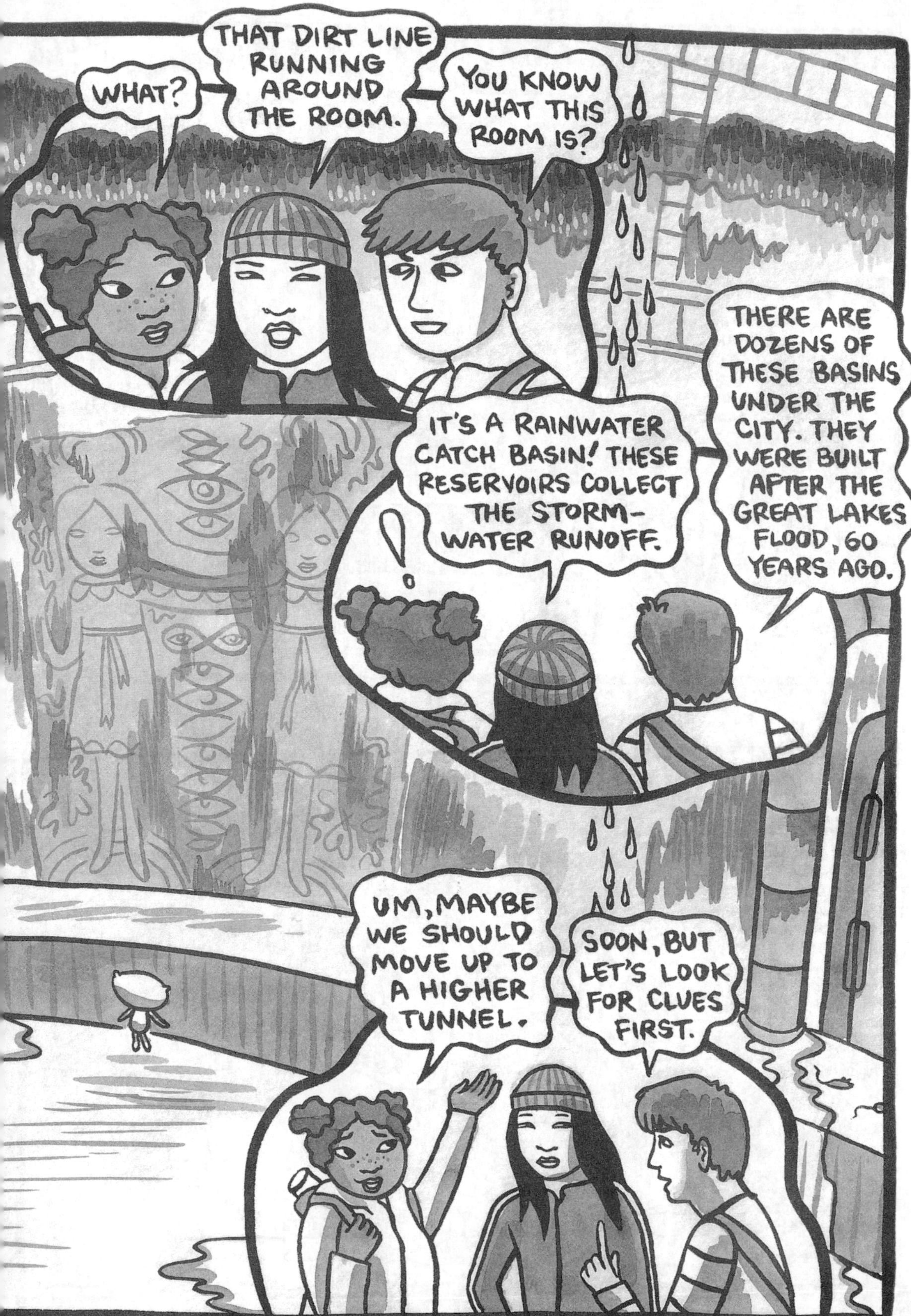
WHAT?
THAT DIRT LINE RUNNING AROUND THE ROOM.
YOU KNOW WHAT THIS ROOM IS?
IT'S A RAINWATER CATCH BASIN! THESE RESERVOIRS COLLECT THE STORM-WATER RUNOFF.
THERE ARE DOZENS OF THESE BASINS UNDER THE CITY. THEY WERE BUILT AFTER THE GREAT LAKES FLOOD, 60 YEARS AGO.
UM, MAYBE WE SHOULD MOVE UP TO A HIGHER TUNNEL.
SOON, BUT LET'S LOOK FOR CLUES FIRST.

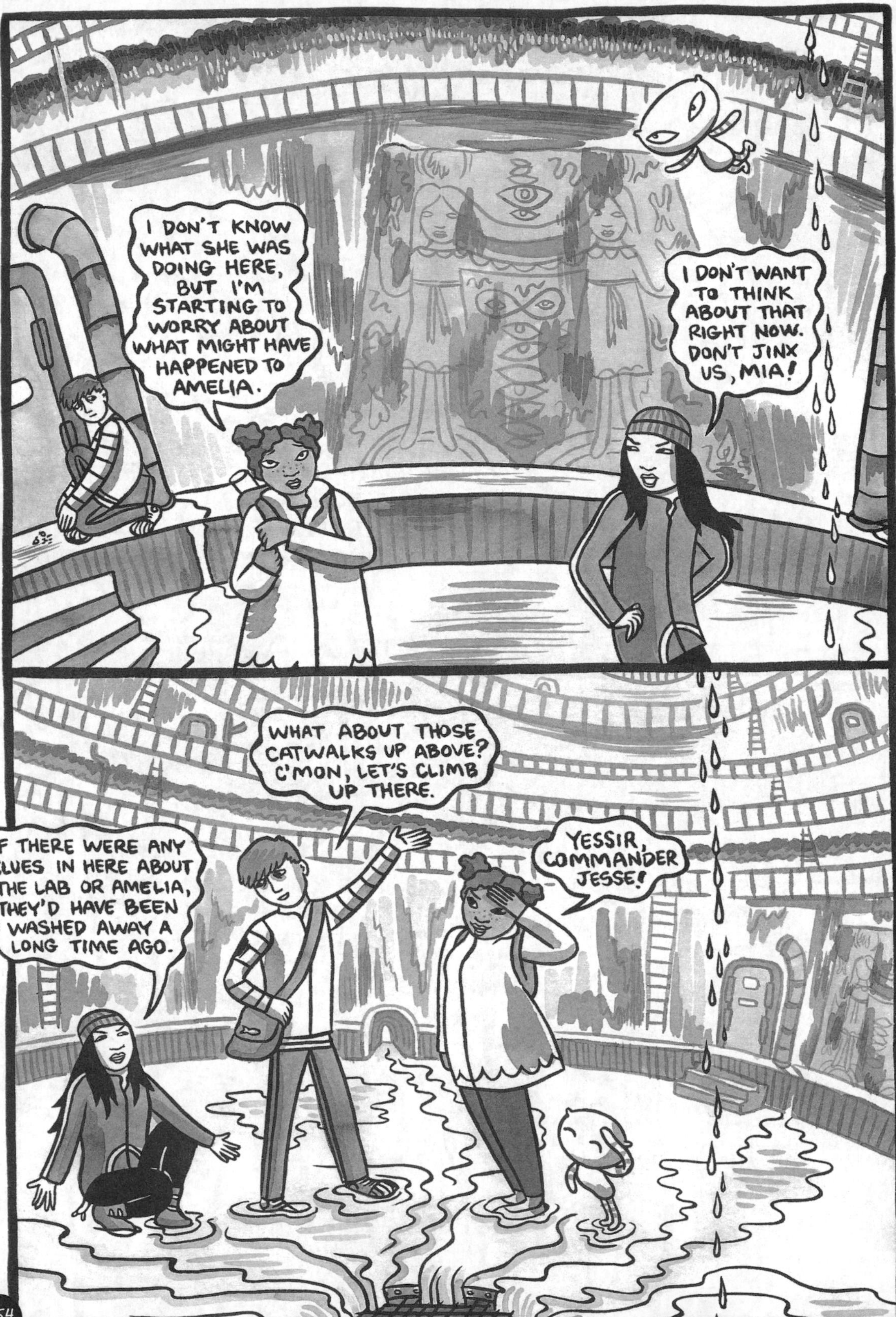
I DON'T KNOW WHAT SHE WAS DOING HERE, BUT I'M STARTING TO WORRY ABOUT WHAT MIGHT HAVE HAPPENED TO AMELIA.
I DON'T WANT TO THINK ABOUT THAT RIGHT NOW. DON'T JINX US, MIA!
IF THERE WERE ANY CLUES IN HERE ABOUT THE LAB OR AMELIA, THEY'D HAVE BEEN WASHED AWAY A LONG TIME AGO.
WHAT ABOUT THOSE CATWALKS UP ABOVE? C'MON, LET'S CLIMB UP THERE.
YESSIR, COMMANDER JESSE!

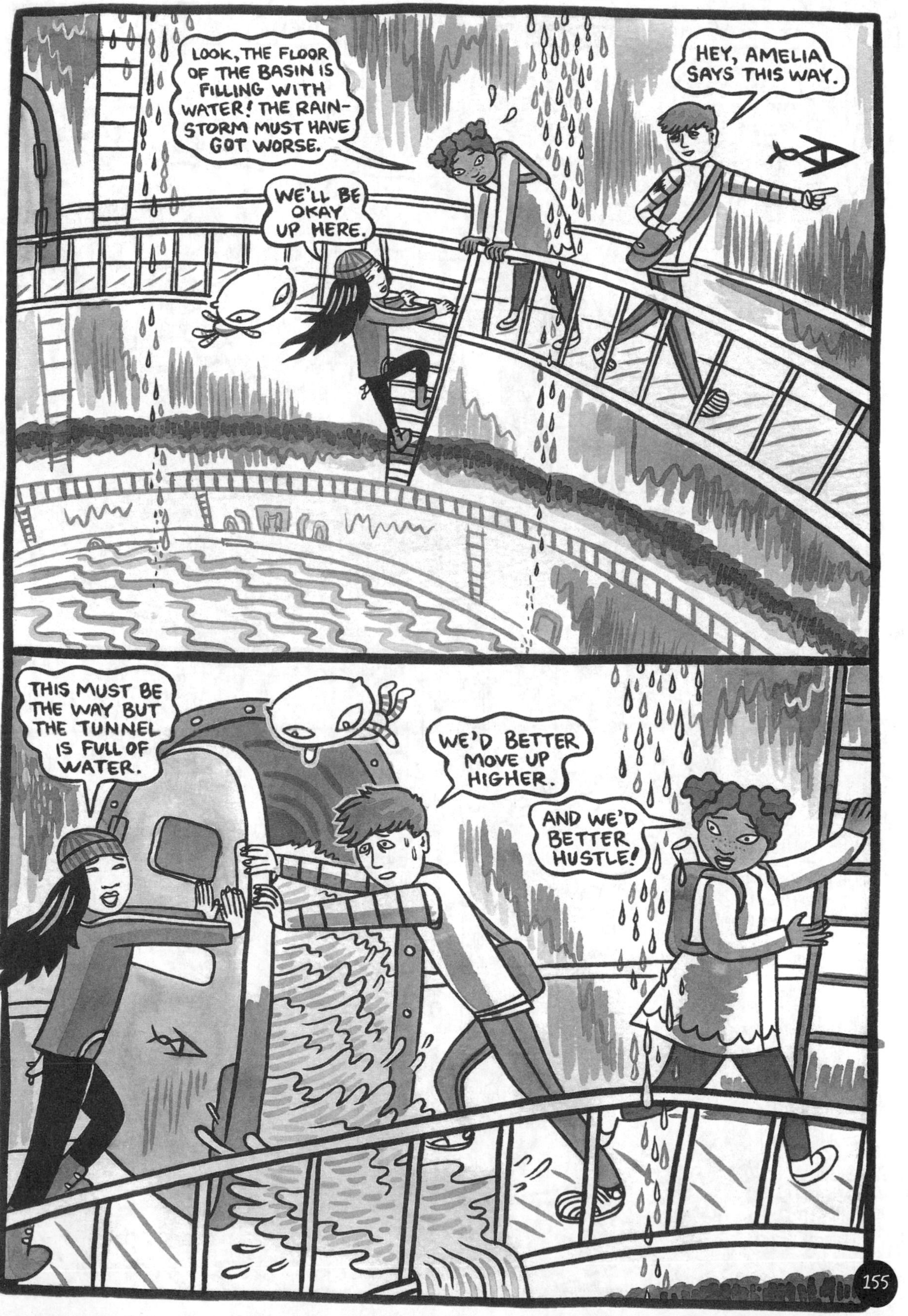
LOOK, THE FLOOR OF THE BASIN IS FILLING WITH WATER! THE RAIN-STORM MUST HAVE GOT WORSE.
HEY, AMELIA SAYS THIS WAY.
WE'LL BE OKAY UP HERE.
THIS MUST BE THE WAY BUT THE TUNNEL IS FULL OF WATER.
WE'D BETTER MOVE UP HIGHER.
AND WE'D BETTER HUSTLE!

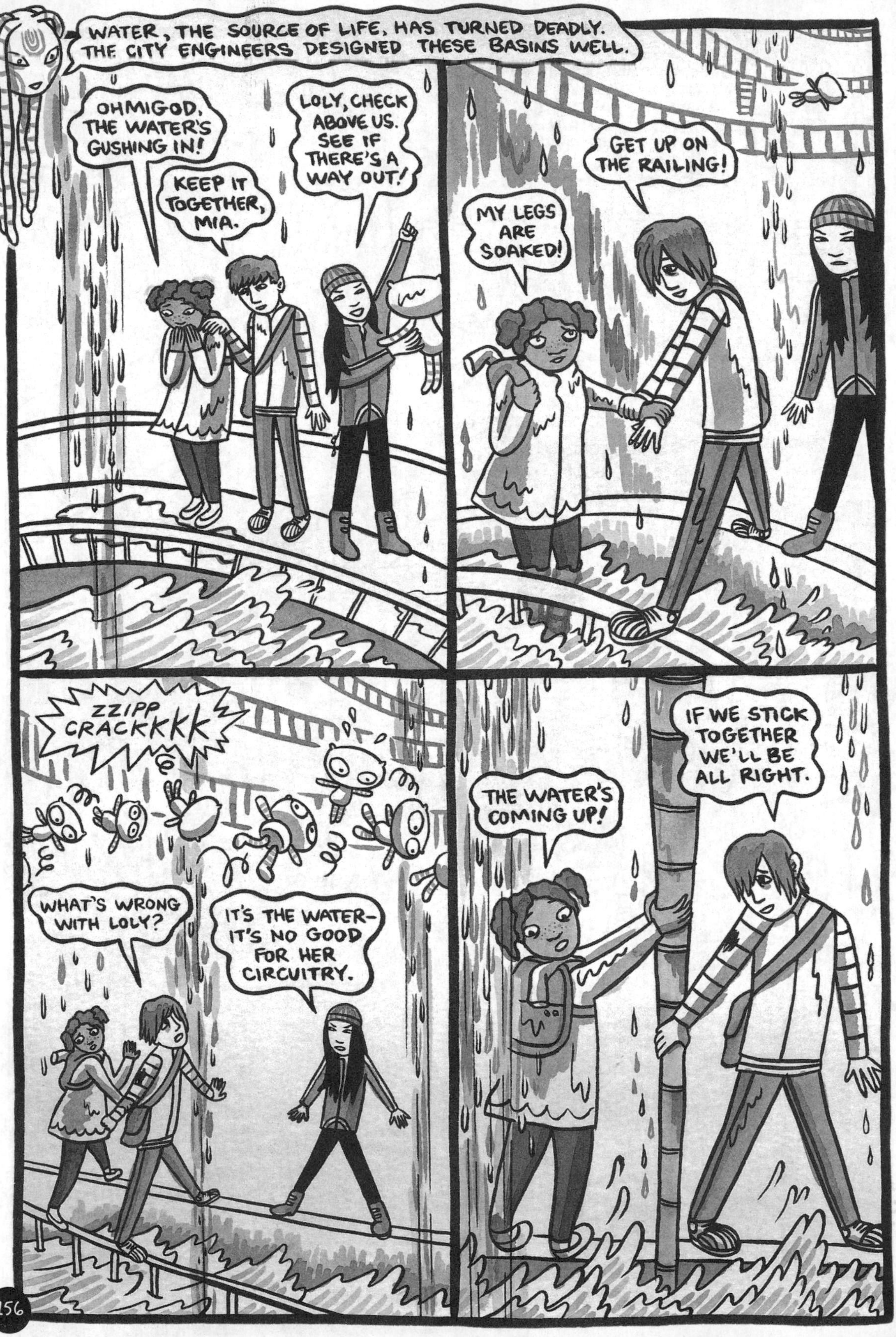

WATER, THE SOURCE OF LIFE, HAS TURNED DEADLY. THE CITY ENGINEERS DESIGNED THESE BASINS WELL.
OHMIGOD, THE WATER'S GUSHING IN!
KEEP IT TOGETHER, MIA.
LOLY, CHECK ABOVE US. SEE IF THERE'S A WAY OUT!
GET UP ON THE RAILING!
MY LEGS ARE SOAKED!
ZZIPP CRACKKKK
WHAT'S WRONG WITH LOLY?
IT'S THE WATER- IT'S NO GOOD FOR HER CIRCUITRY.
IF WE STICK TOGETHER WE'LL BE ALL RIGHT.
THE WATER'S COMING UP!

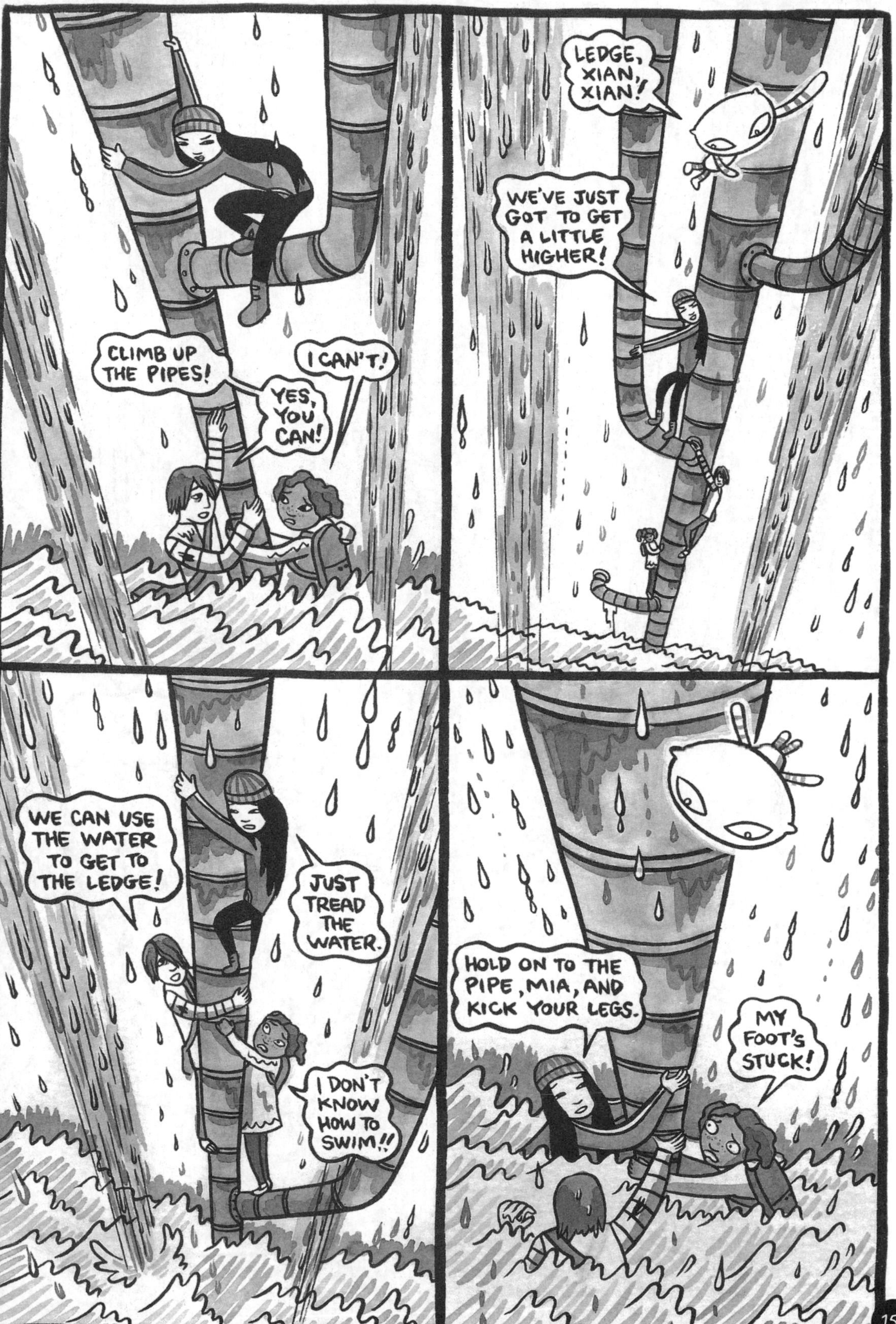
CLIMB UP THE PIPES!
YES, YOU CAN!
I CAN'T!
LEDGE, XIAN, XIAN!
WE'VE JUST GOT TO GET A LITTLE HIGHER!
WE CAN USE THE WATER TO GET TO THE LEDGE!
JUST TREAD THE WATER.
I DON'T KNOW HOW TO SWIM!!
HOLD ON TO THE PIPE, MIA, AND KICK YOUR LEGS.
MY FOOT'S STUCK!

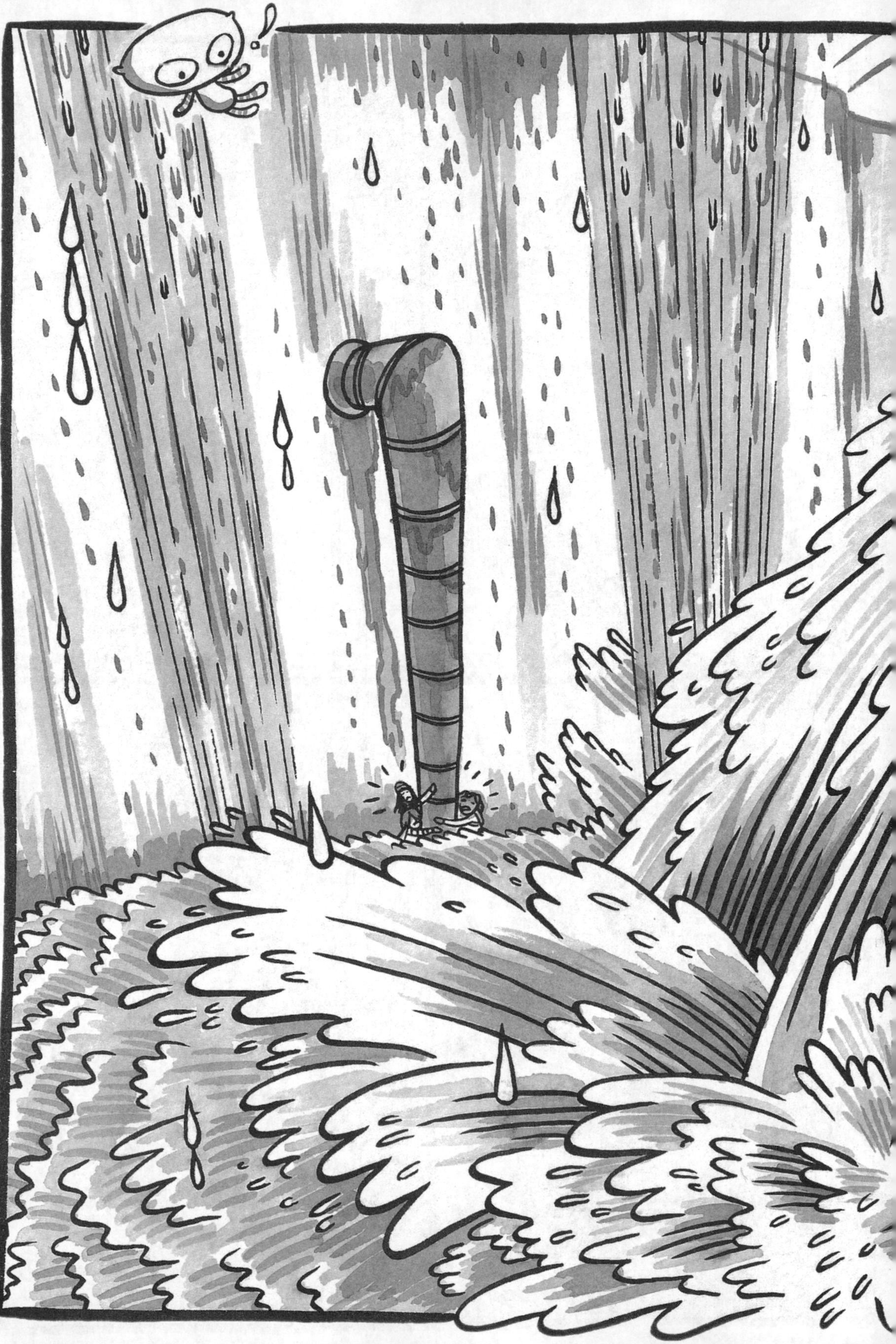
!

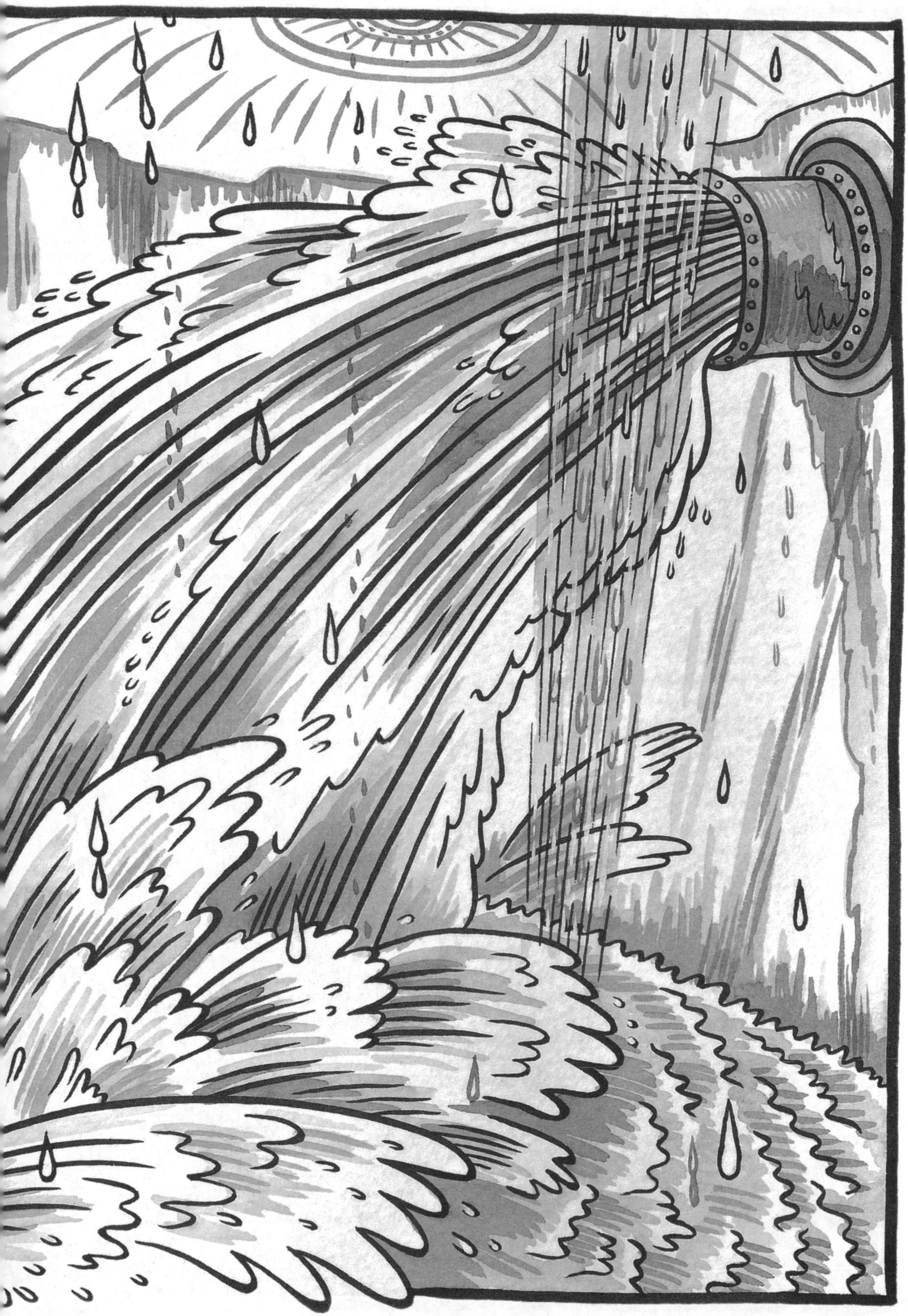

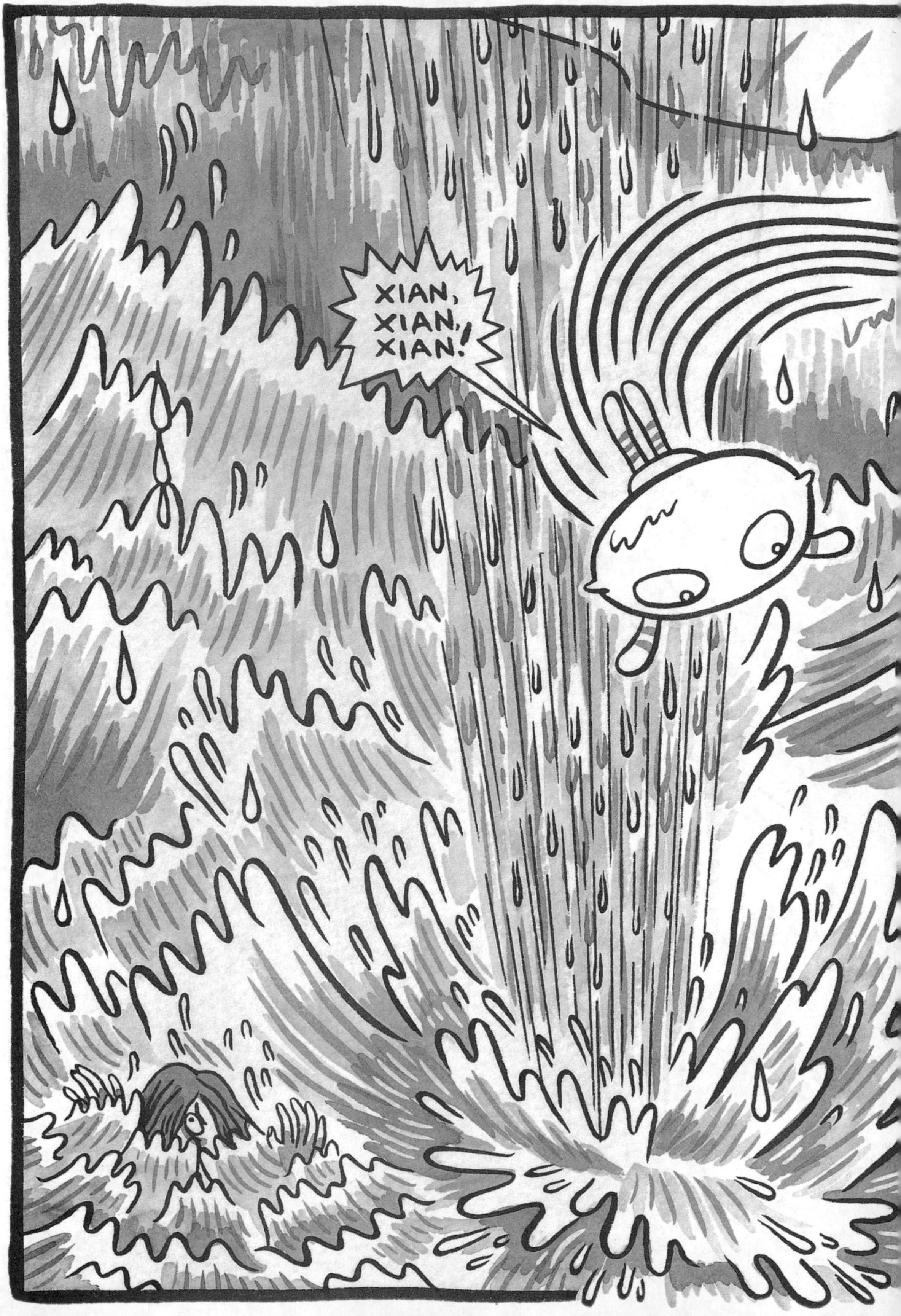
XIAN, XIAN, XIAN!

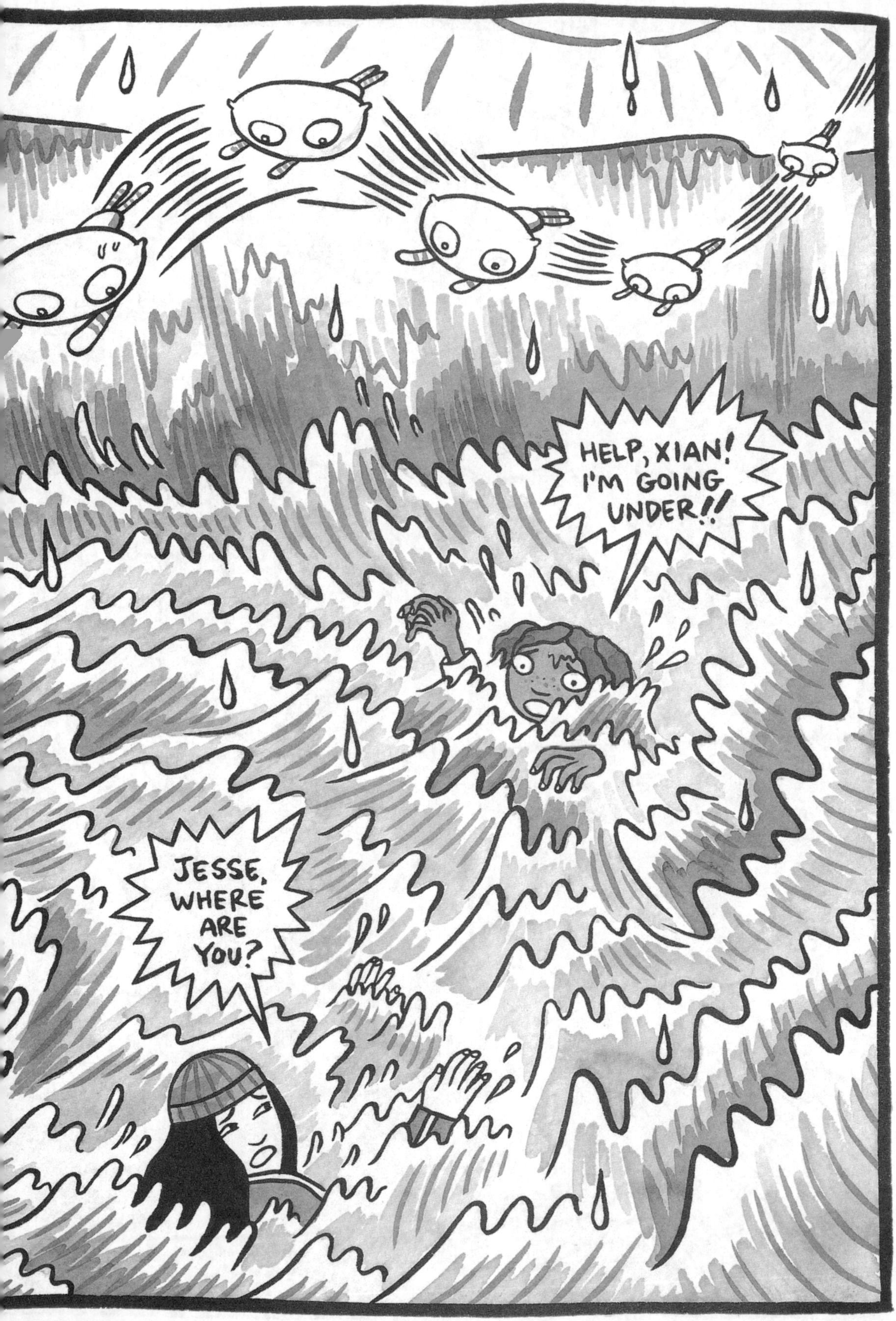
HELP, XIAN! I'M GOING UNDER!!
JESSE, WHERE ARE YOU?

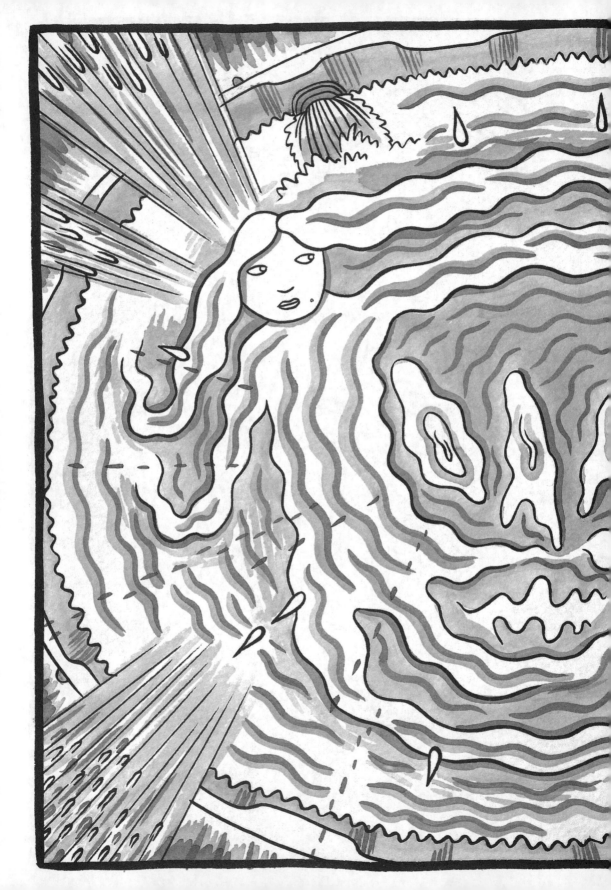

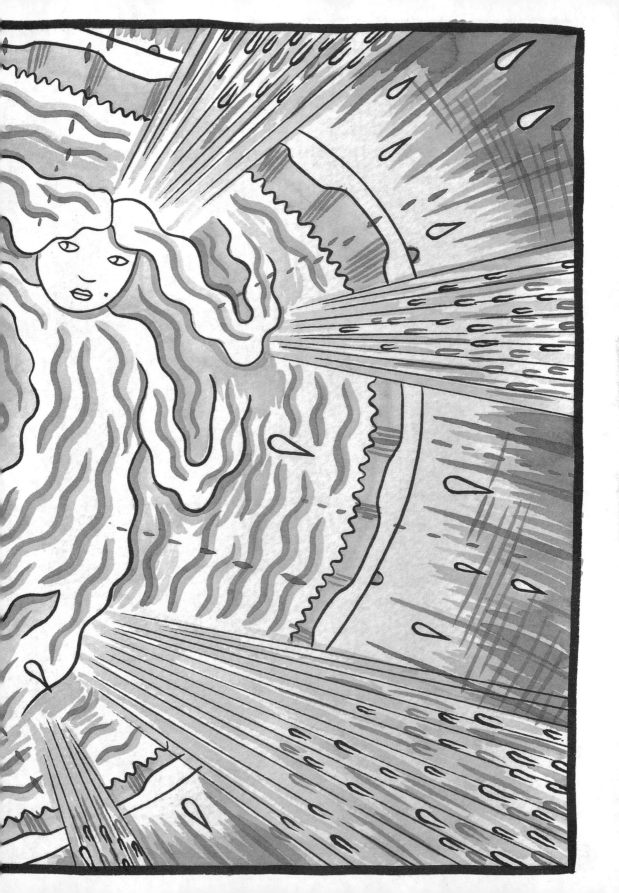

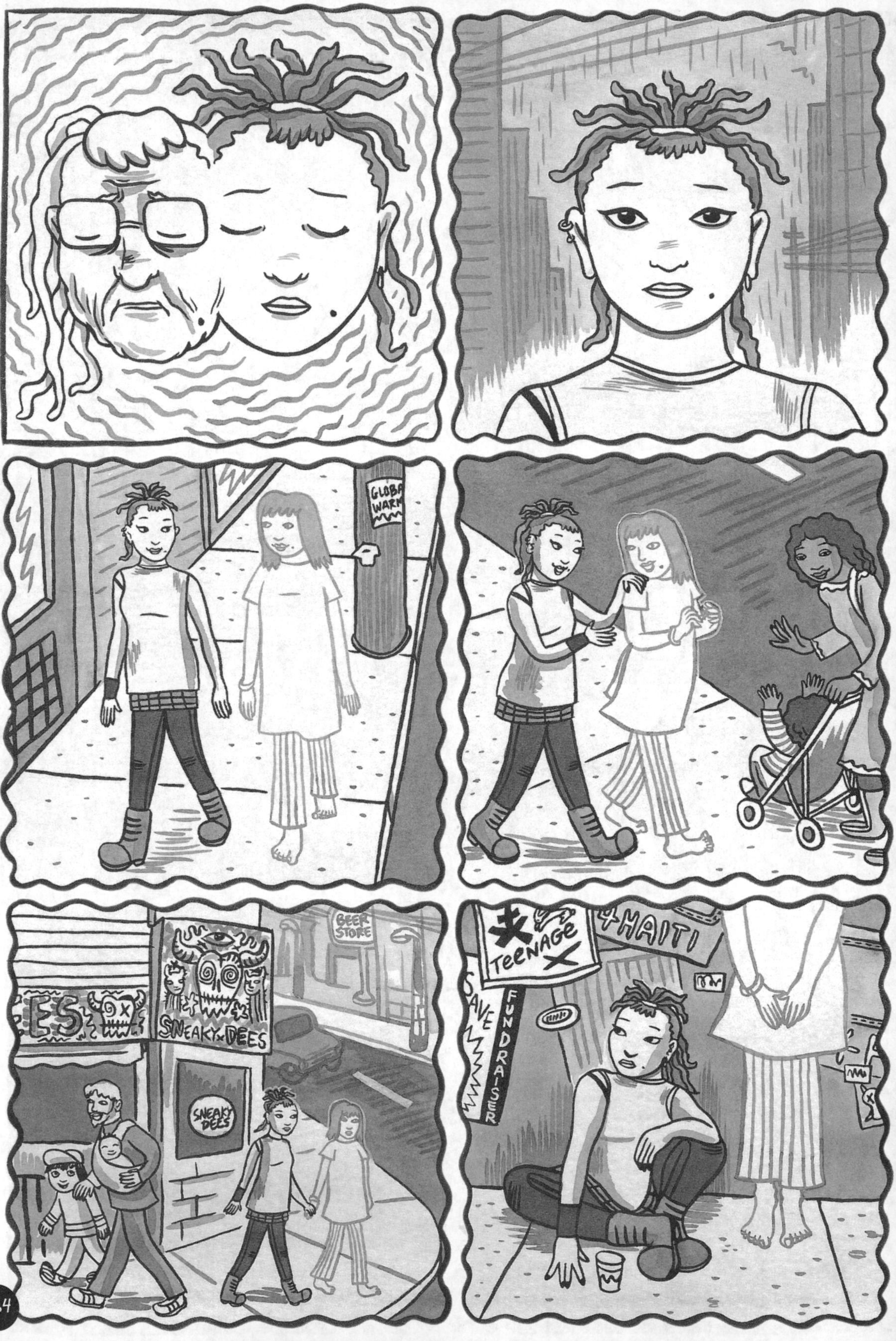
GLOBA
WARM
BEER STORE
ES
SNEAKY x DEES
SNEAKY DEES
TEENAGE
4HAITI
SAVE
FUNDRAISER

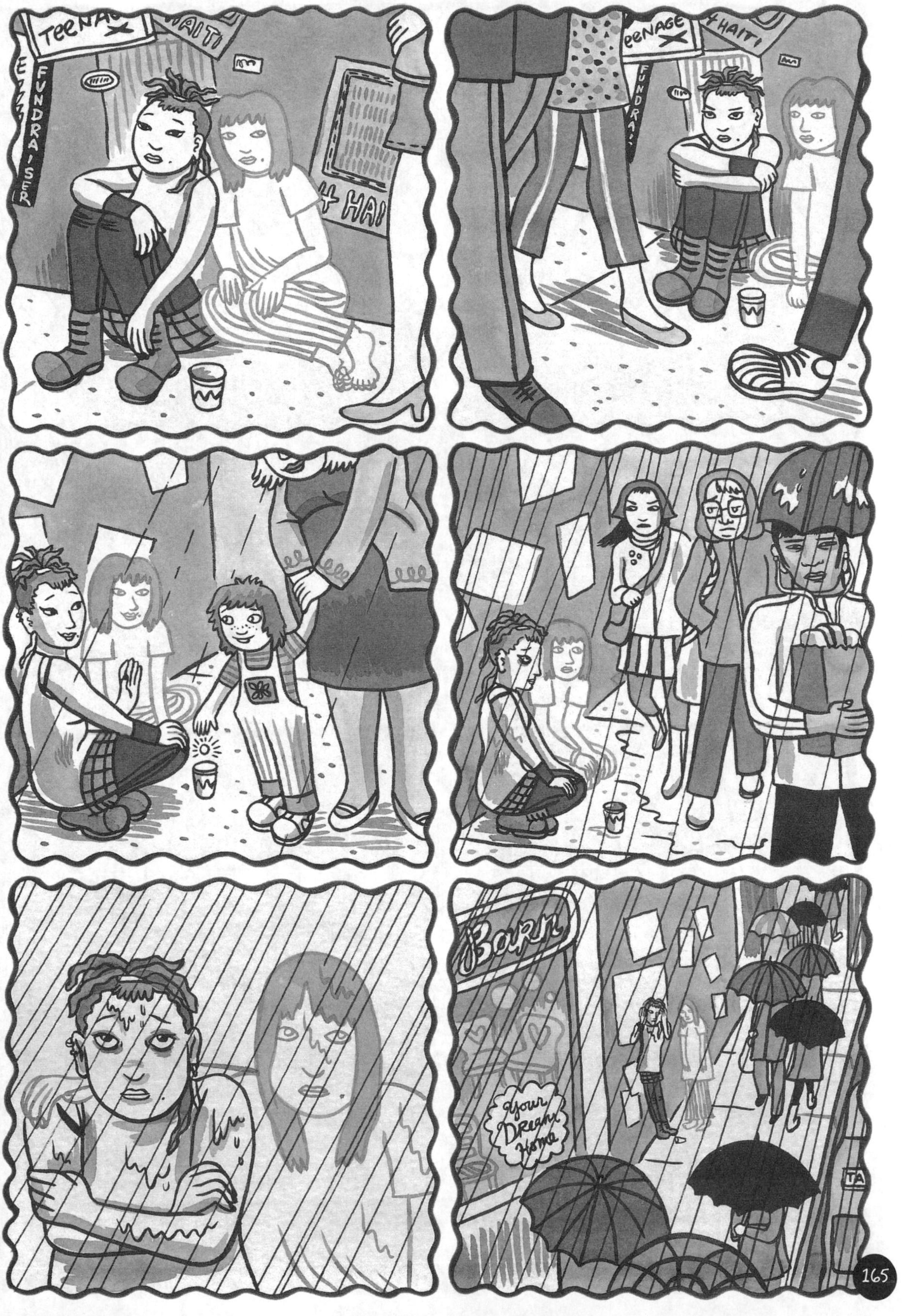
TEENAGE
4 HAITI
FUNDRAISER
Born
Your Dreamy Home

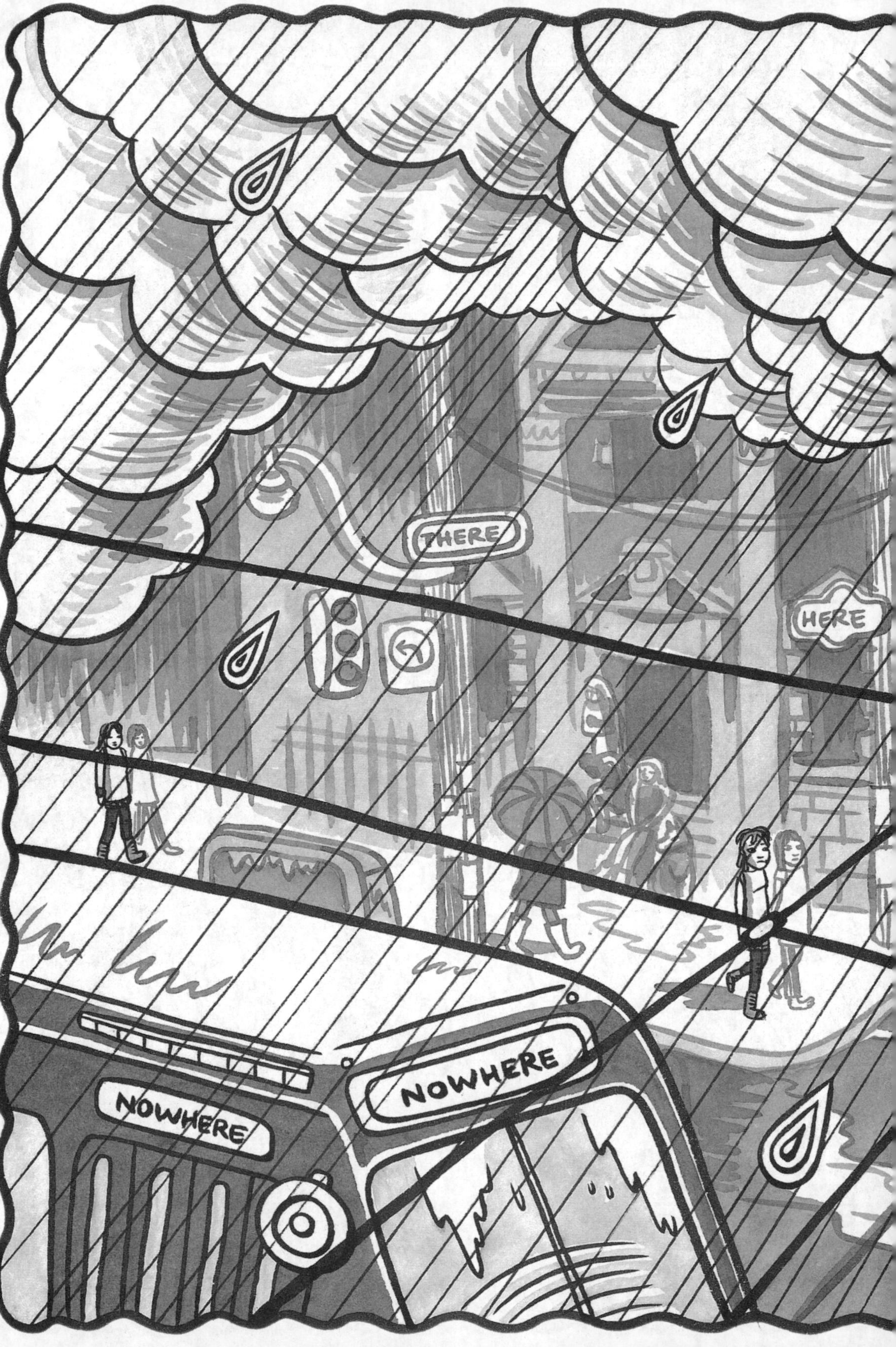
THERE
HERE
NOWHERE
NOWHERE

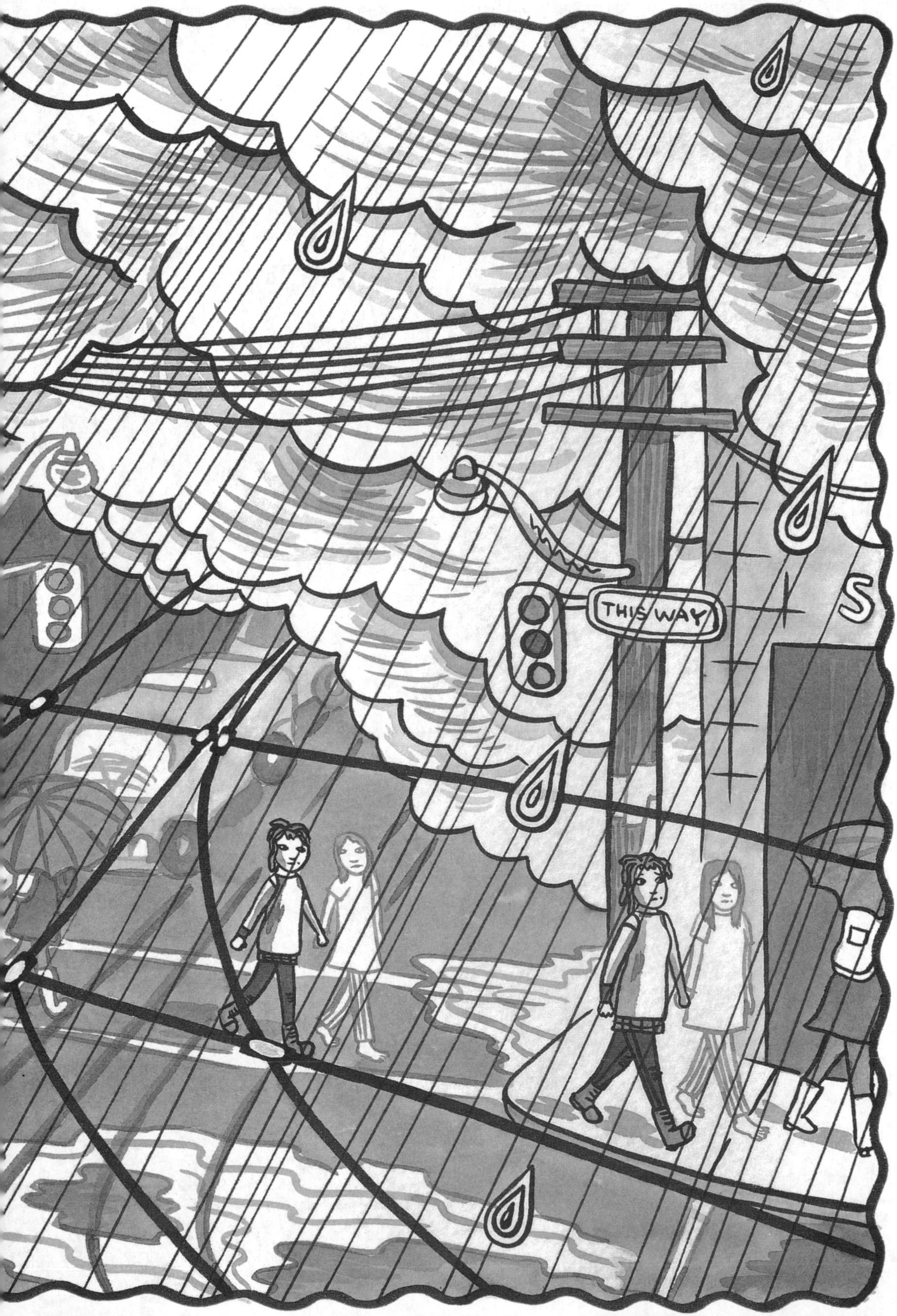
THIS WAY
S

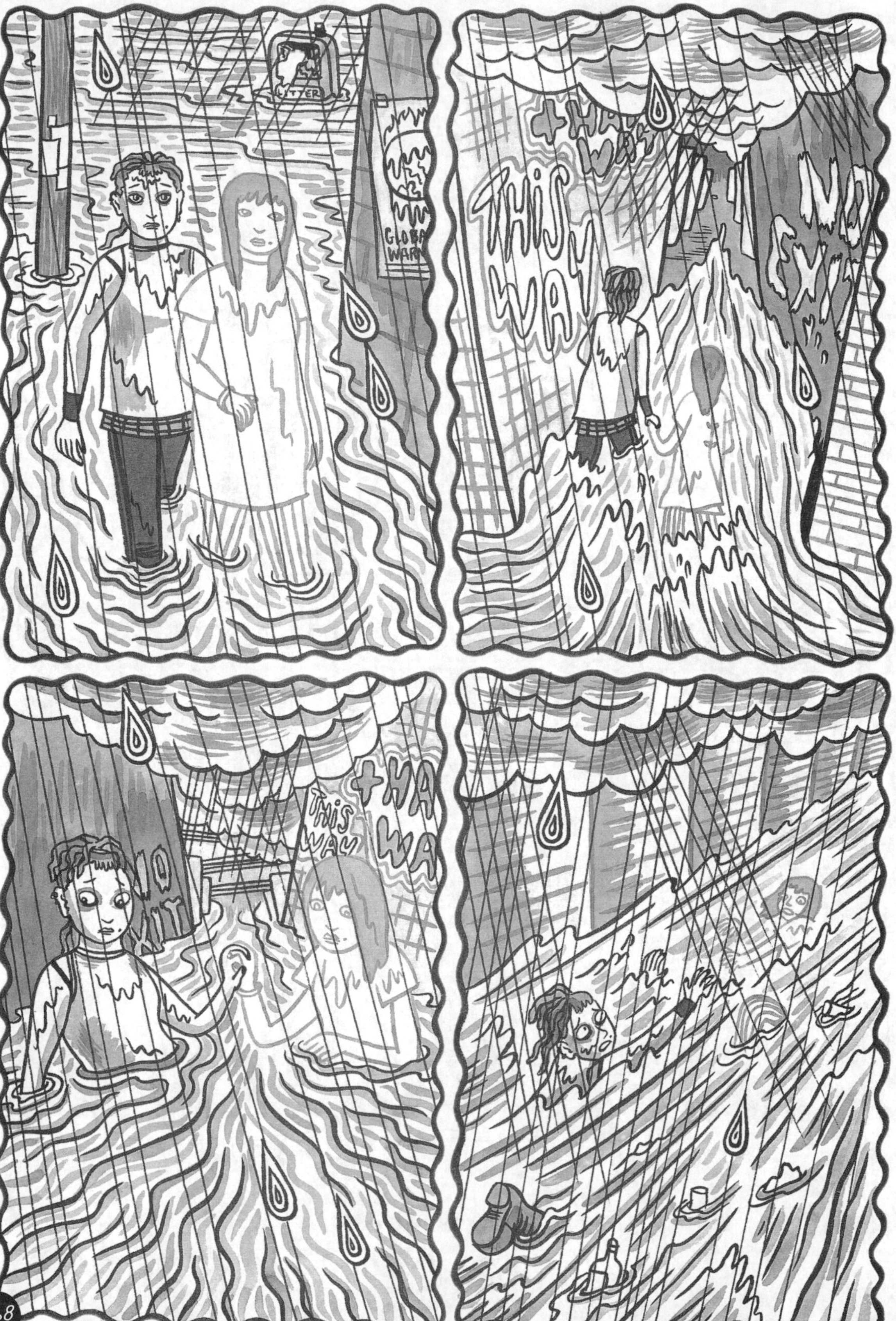
LITTER
THIS WAY
THIS WAY

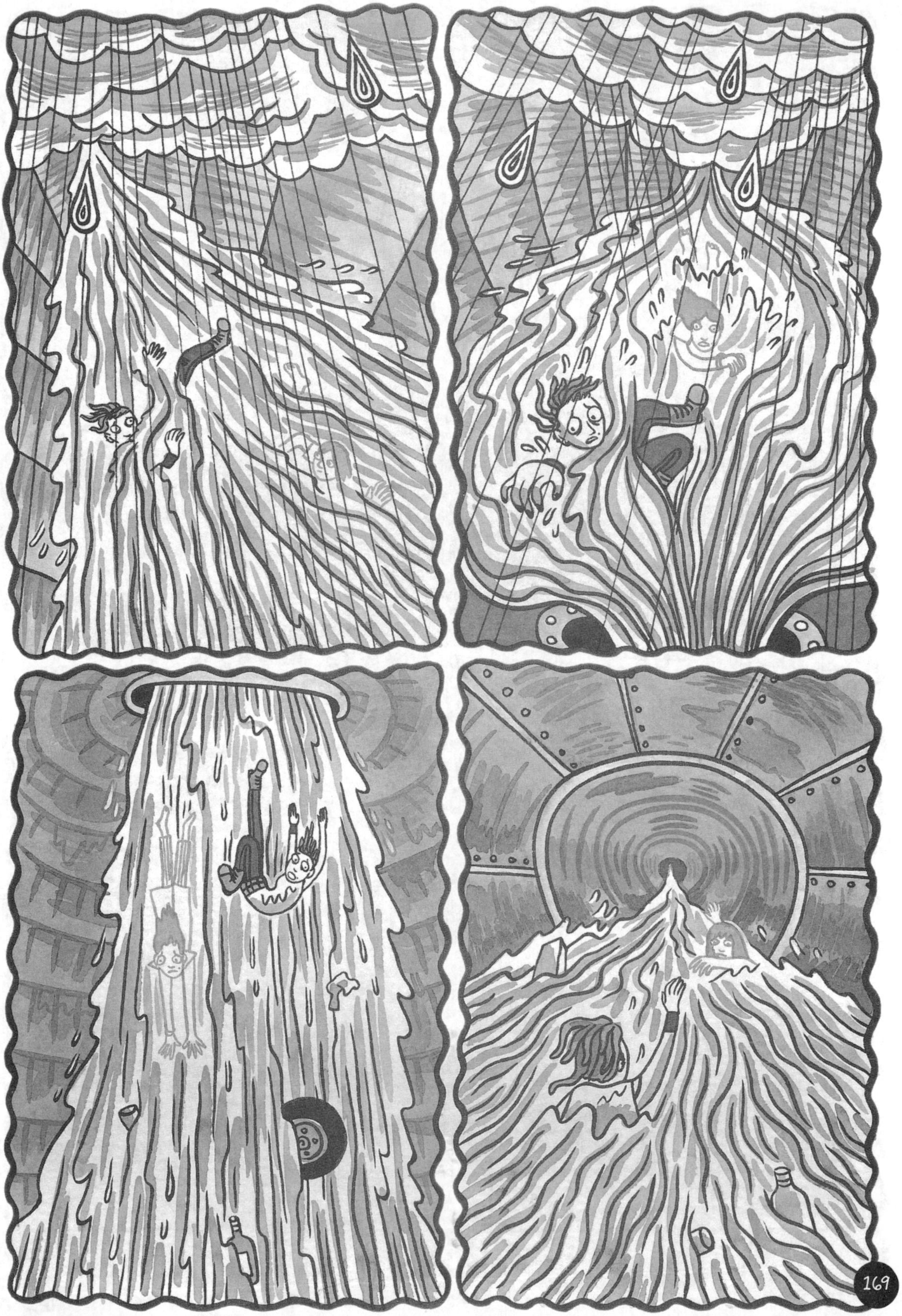

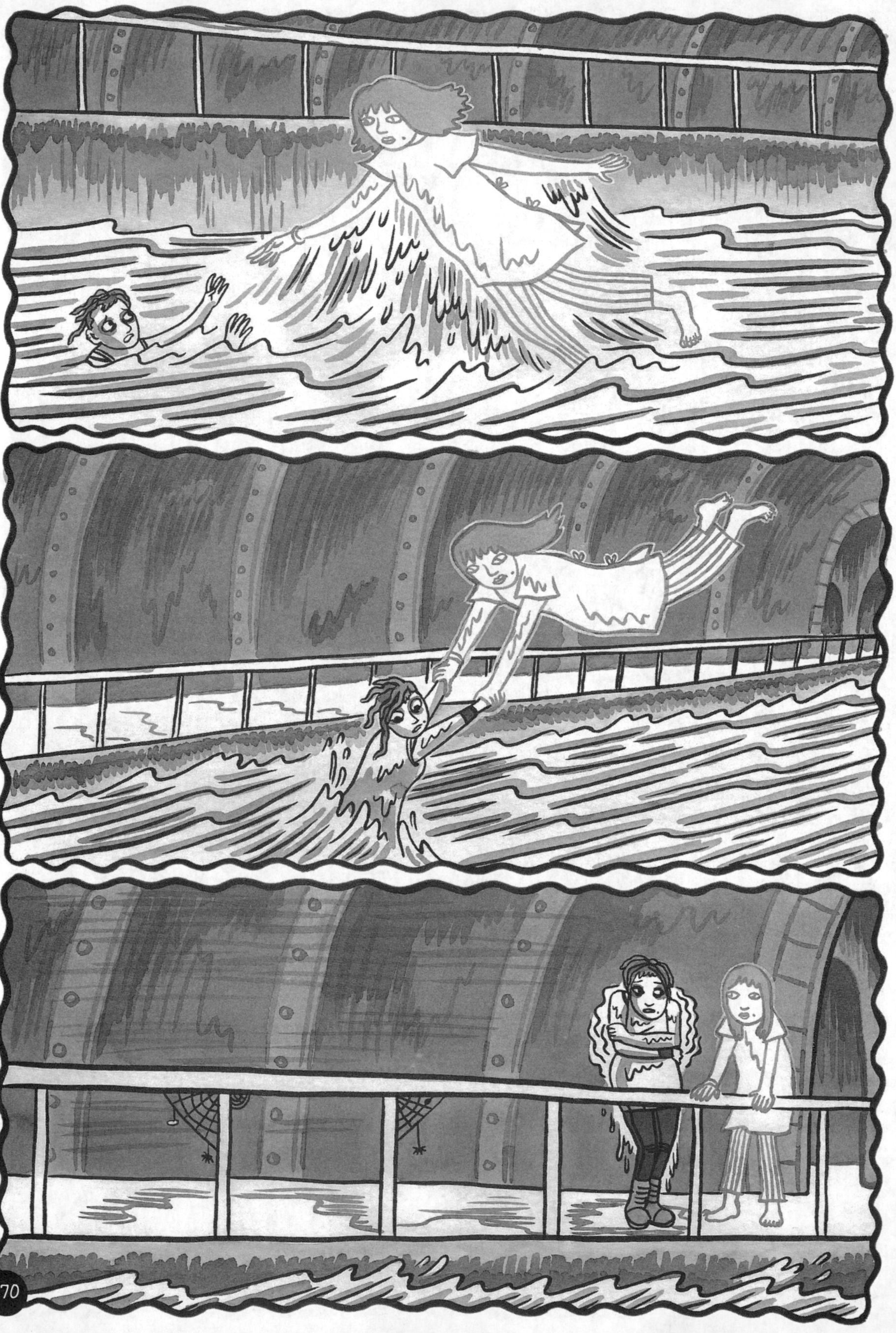

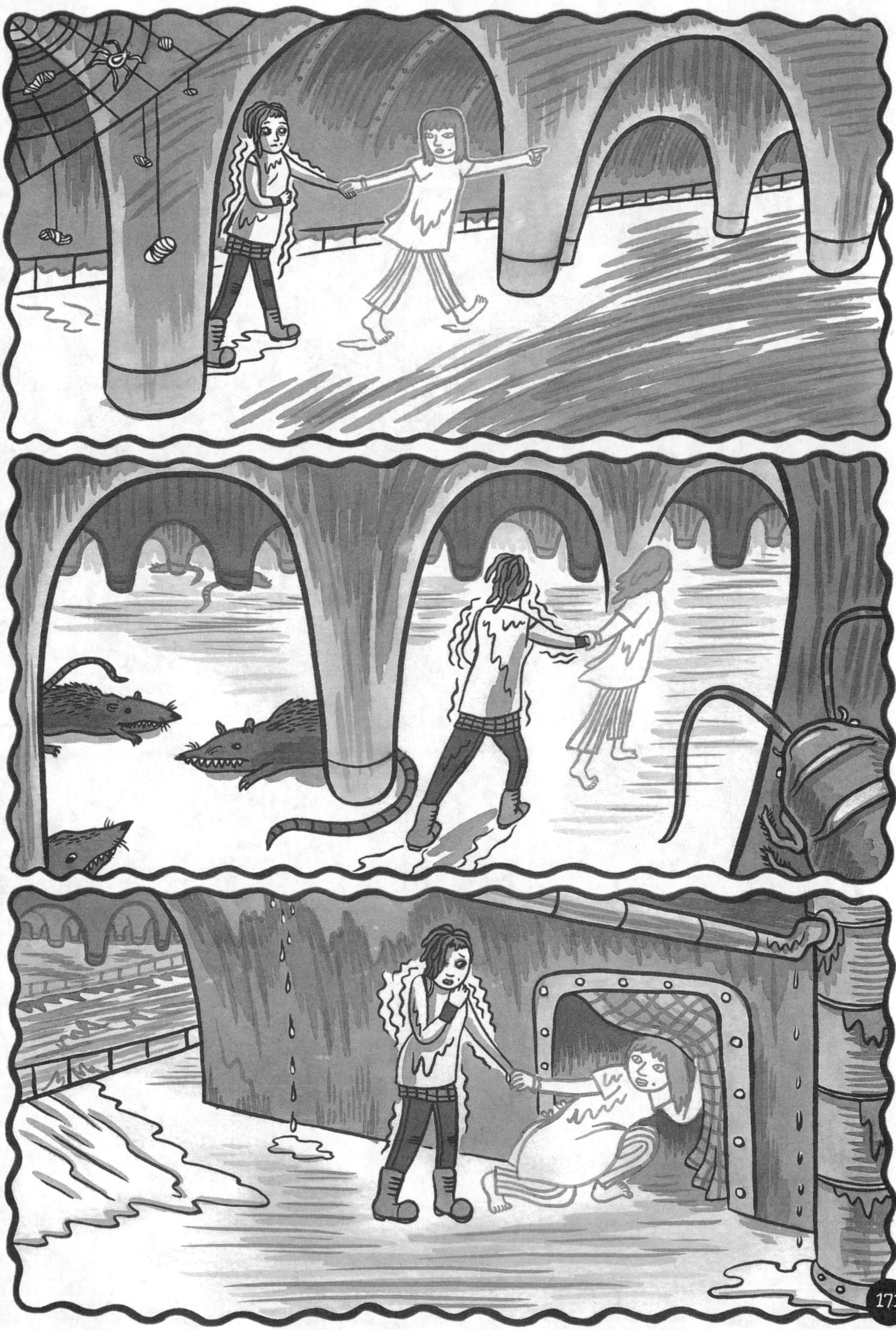

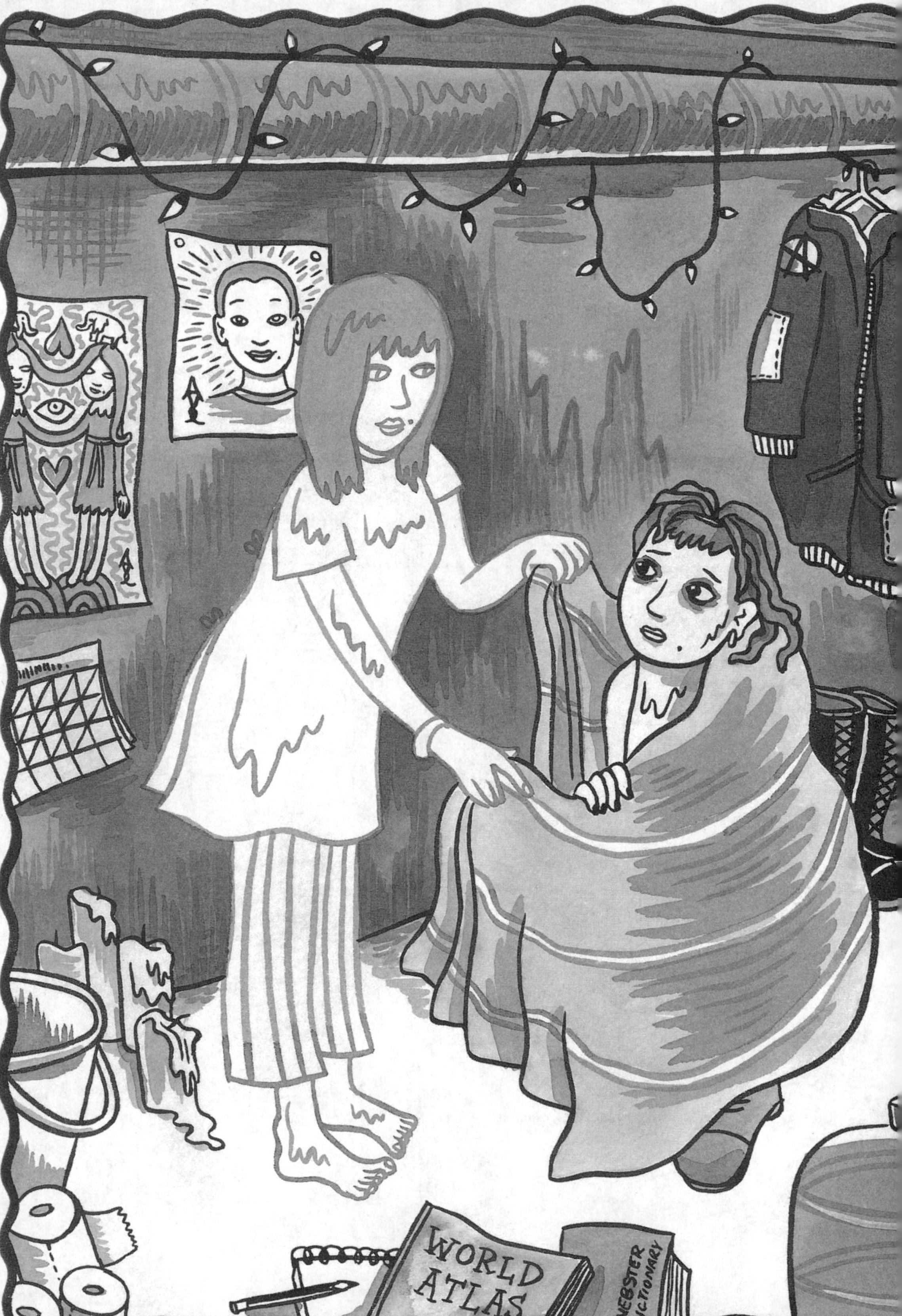
WORLD ATLAS

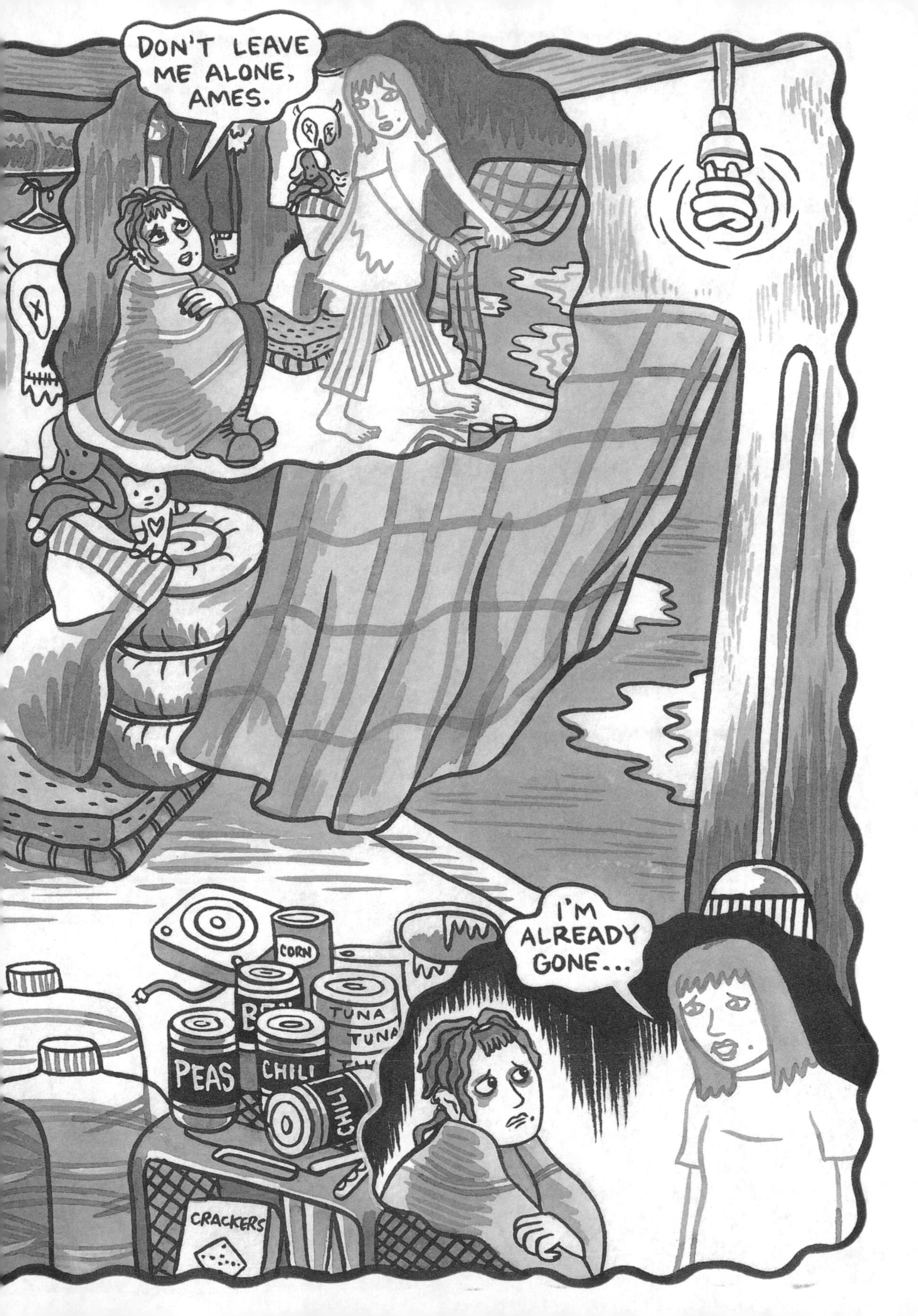

DON'T LEAVE ME ALONE, AMES.
I'M ALREADY GONE...
CORN
PEAS
CHILI
TUNA
TUNA
CHILI
CRACKERS

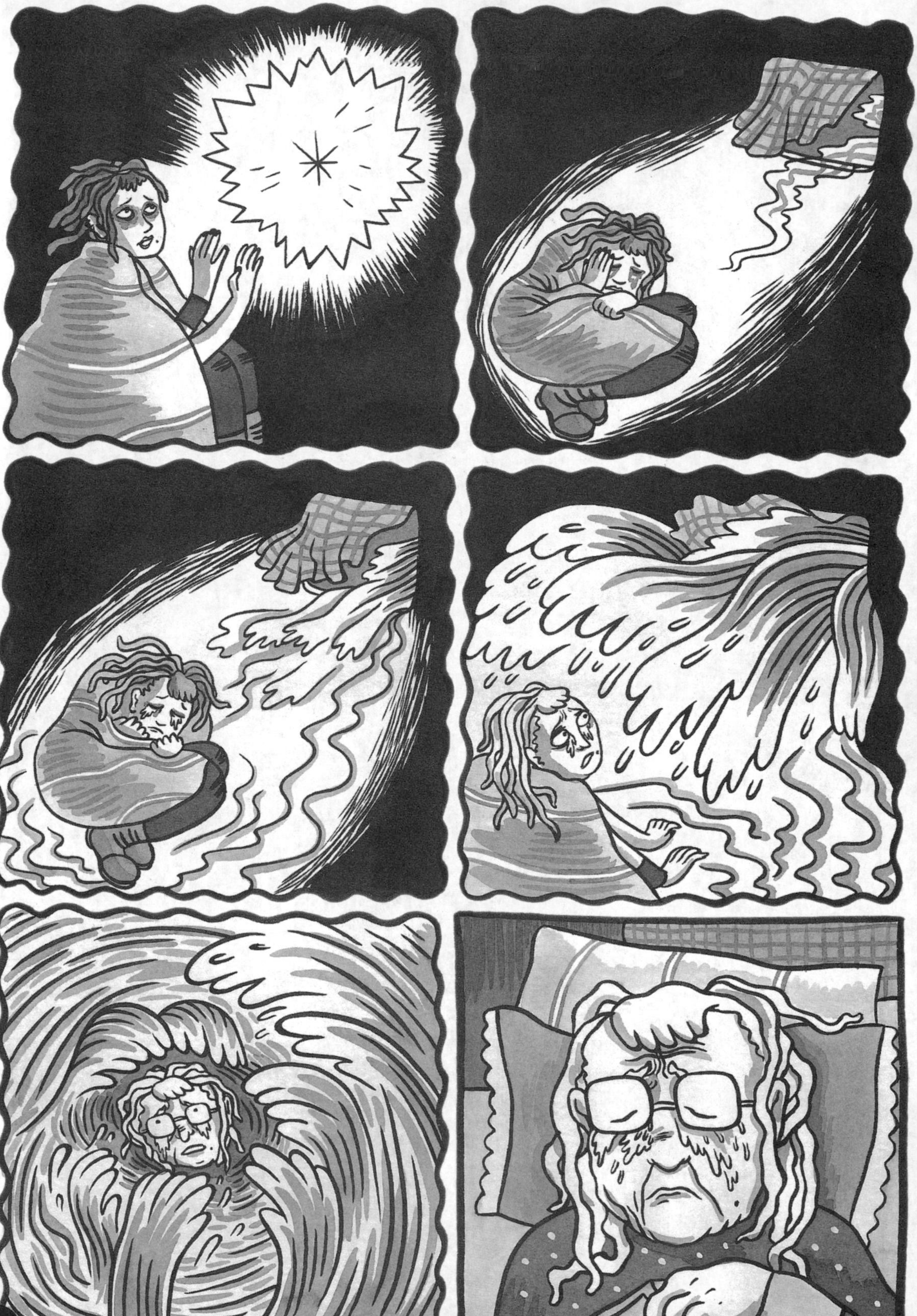

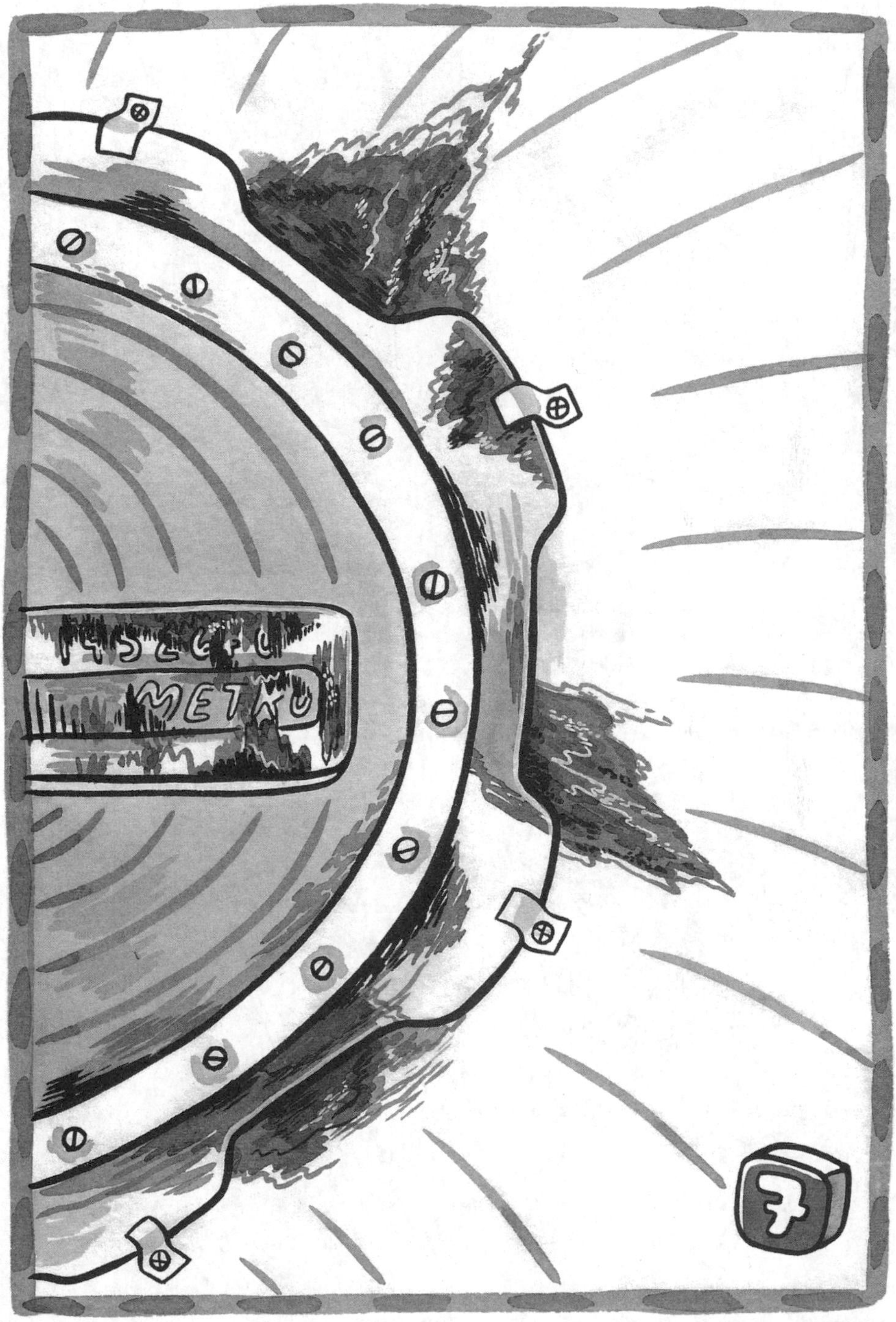
7

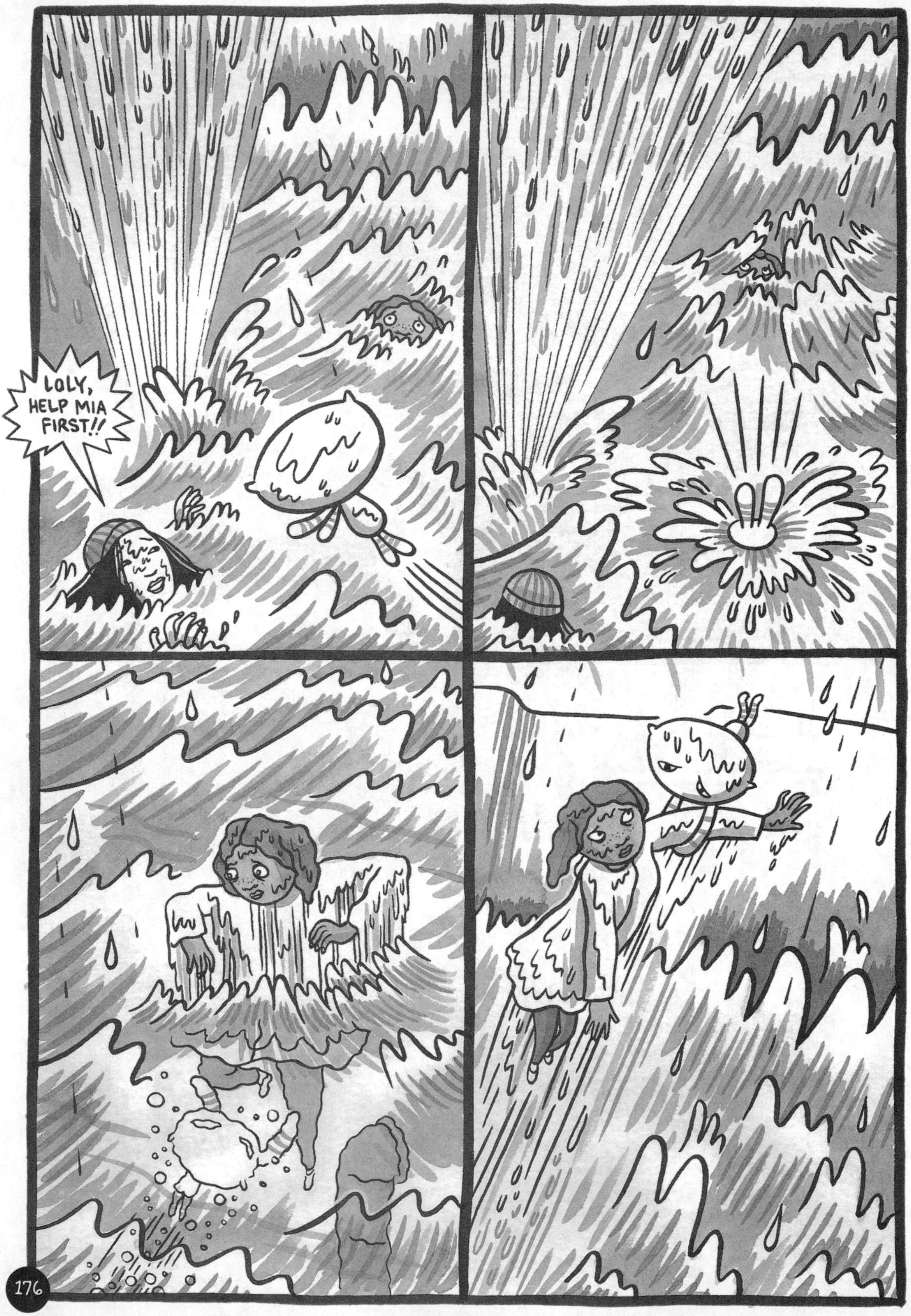
LOLY, HELP MIA FIRST!!

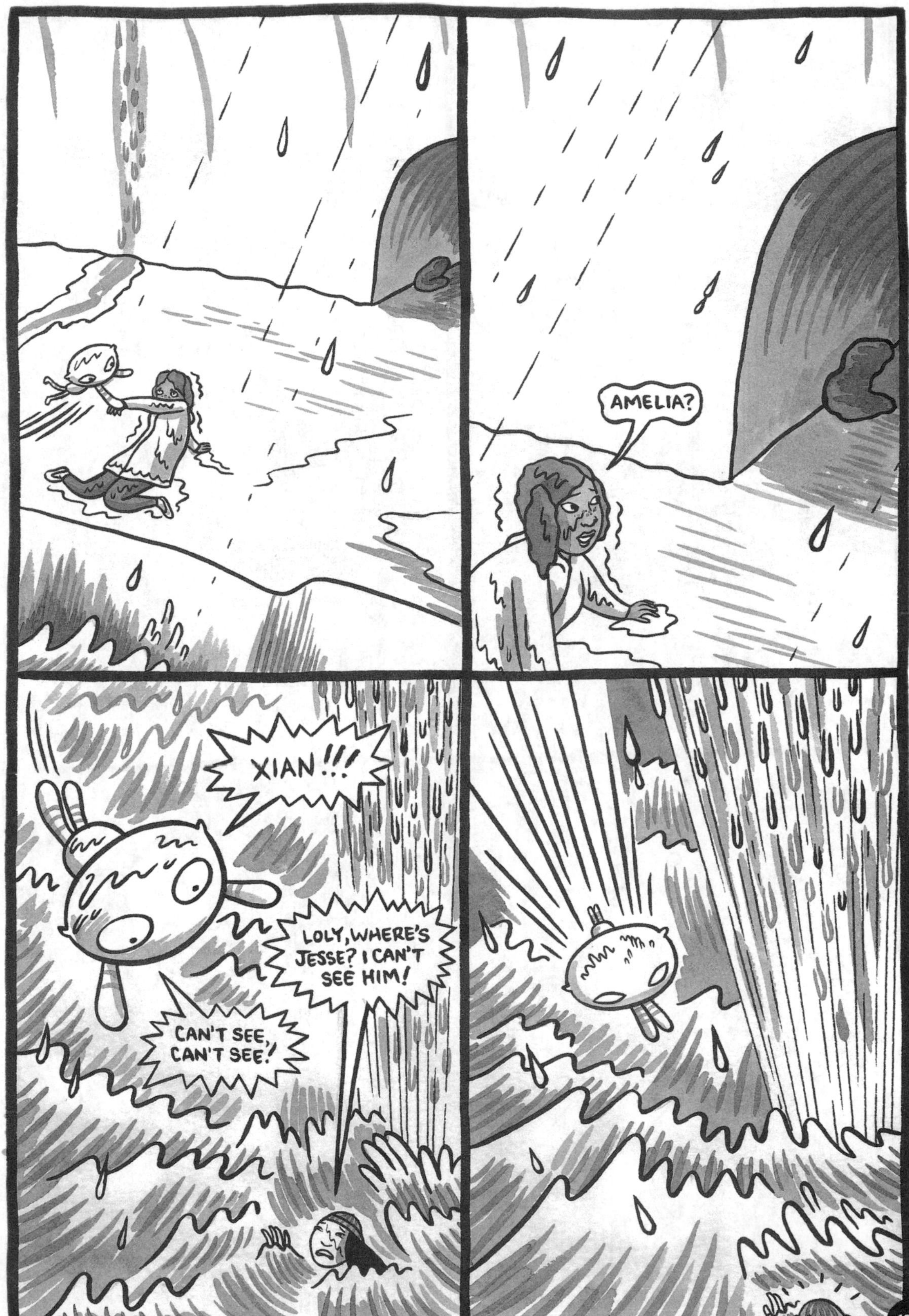
AMELIA?
XIAN!!!
LOLY, WHERE'S JESSE? I CAN'T SEE HIM!
CAN'T SEE, CAN'T SEE!

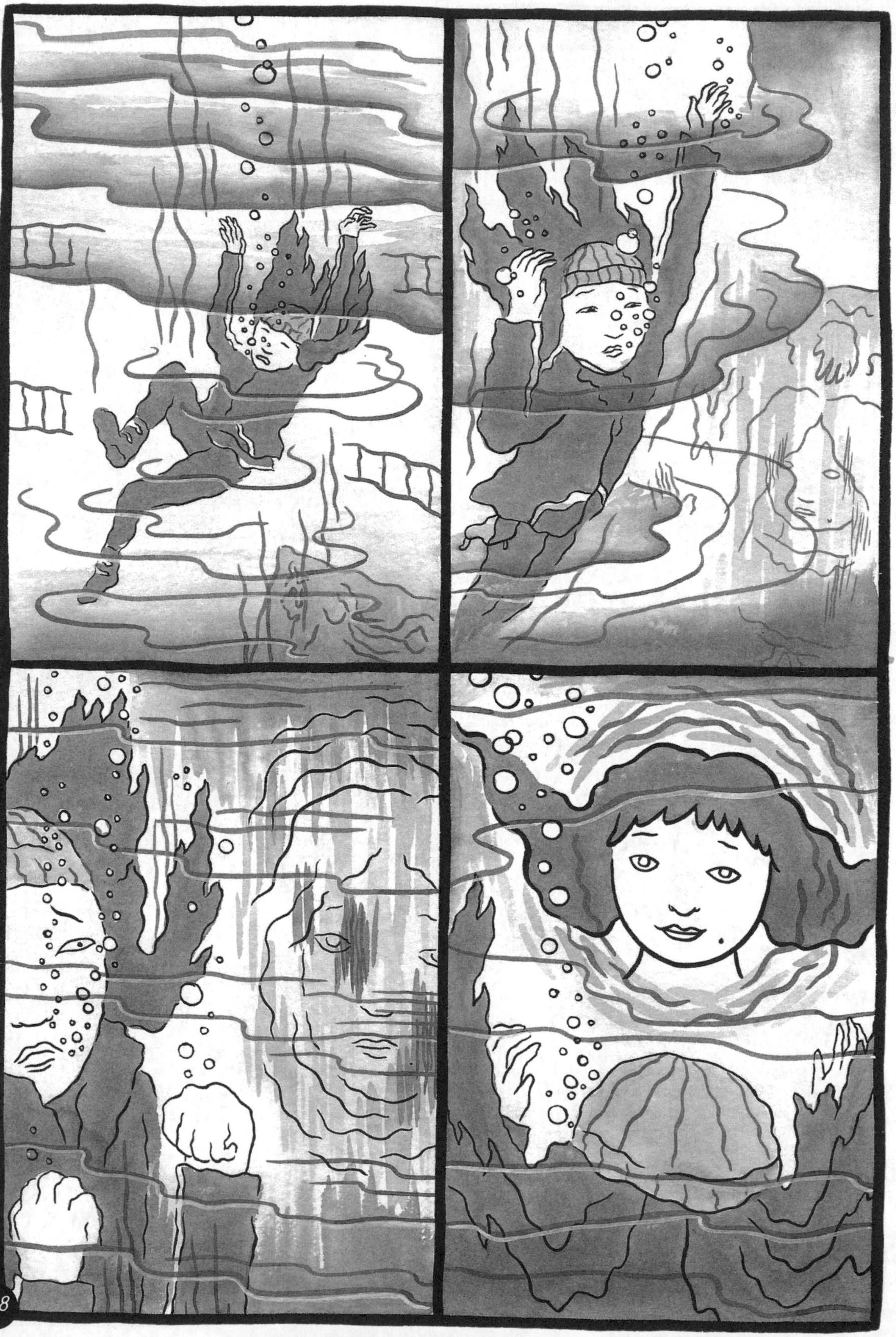

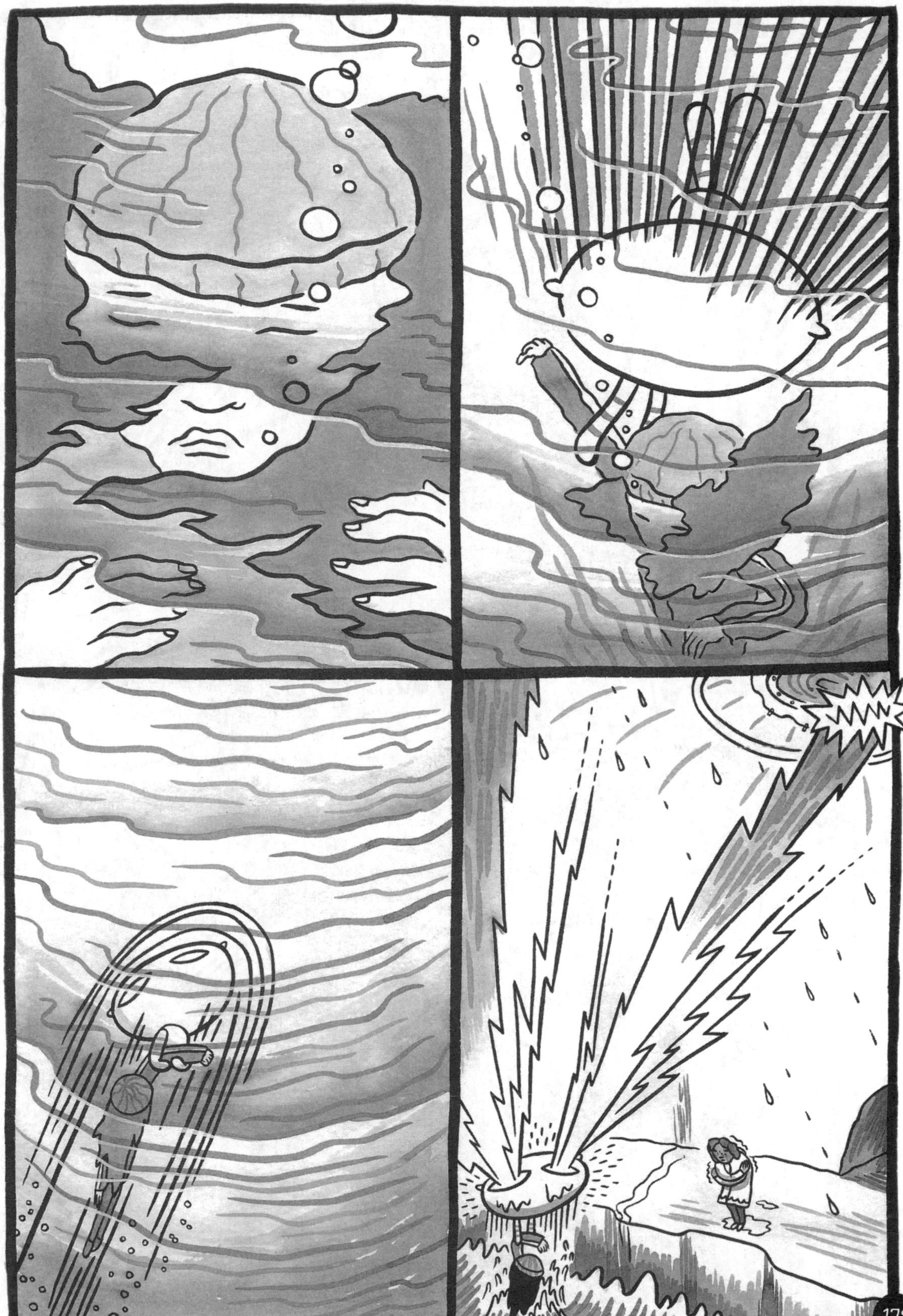

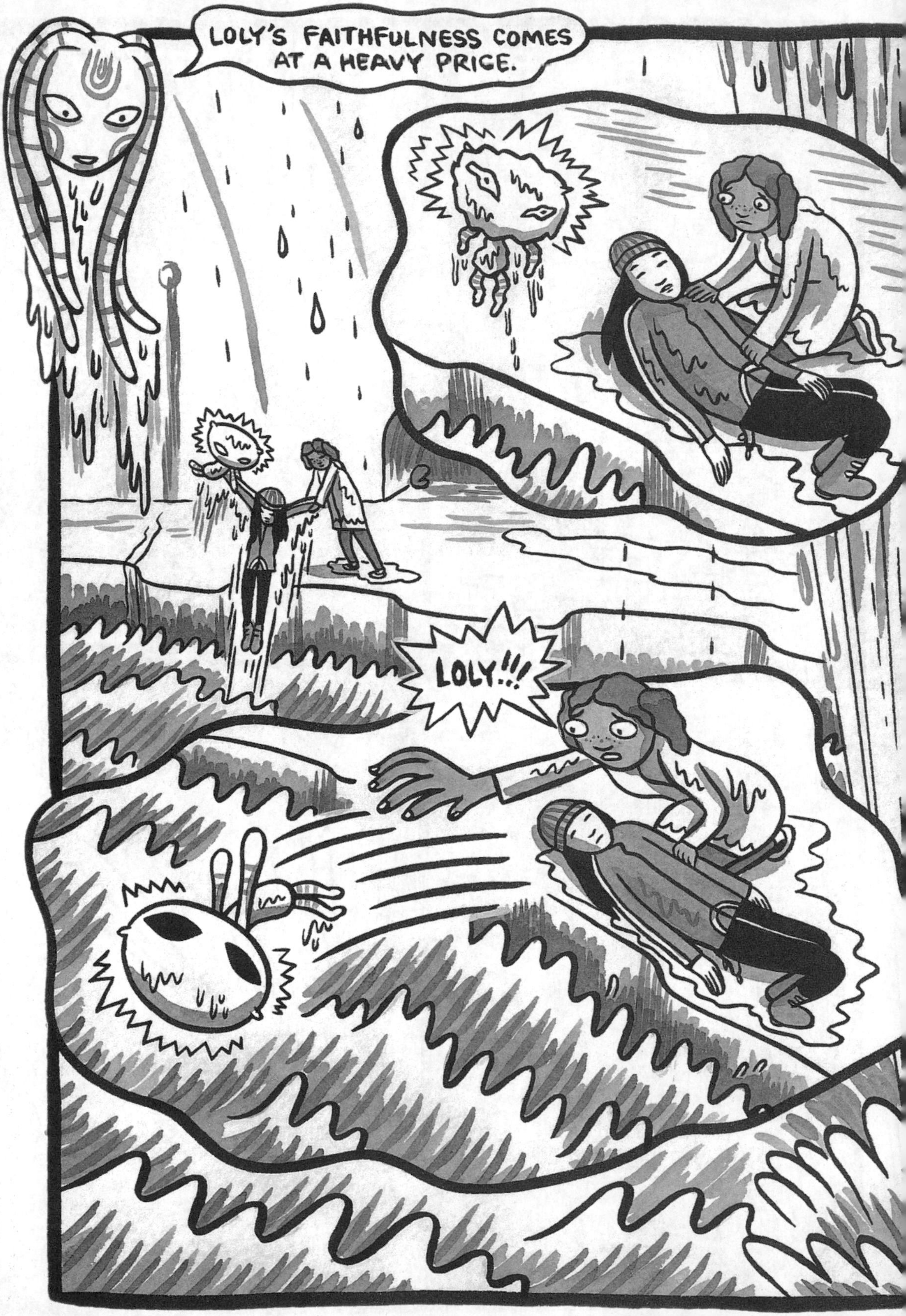
LOLY'S FAITHFULNESS COMES AT A HEAVY PRICE.
LOLY!!!

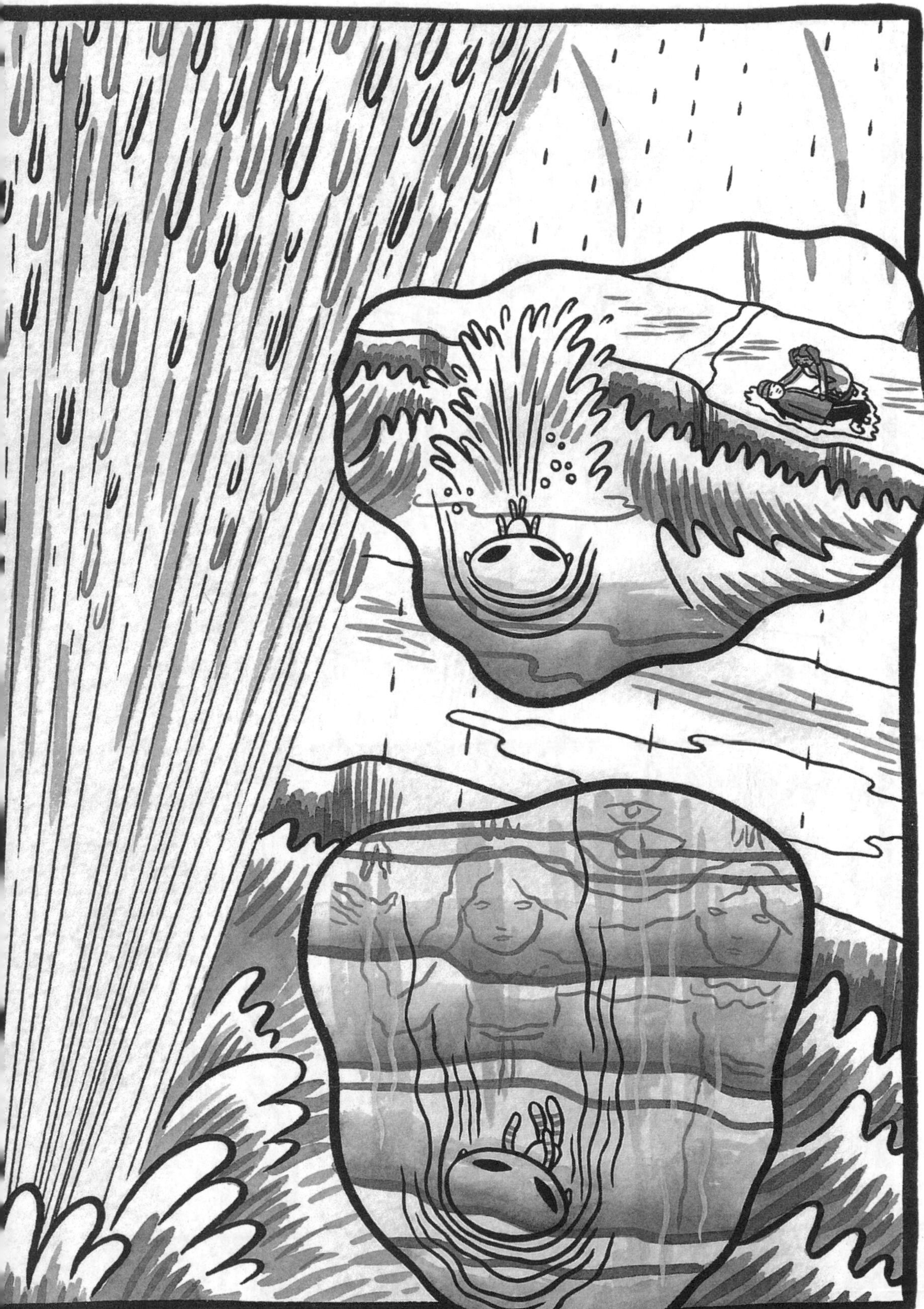

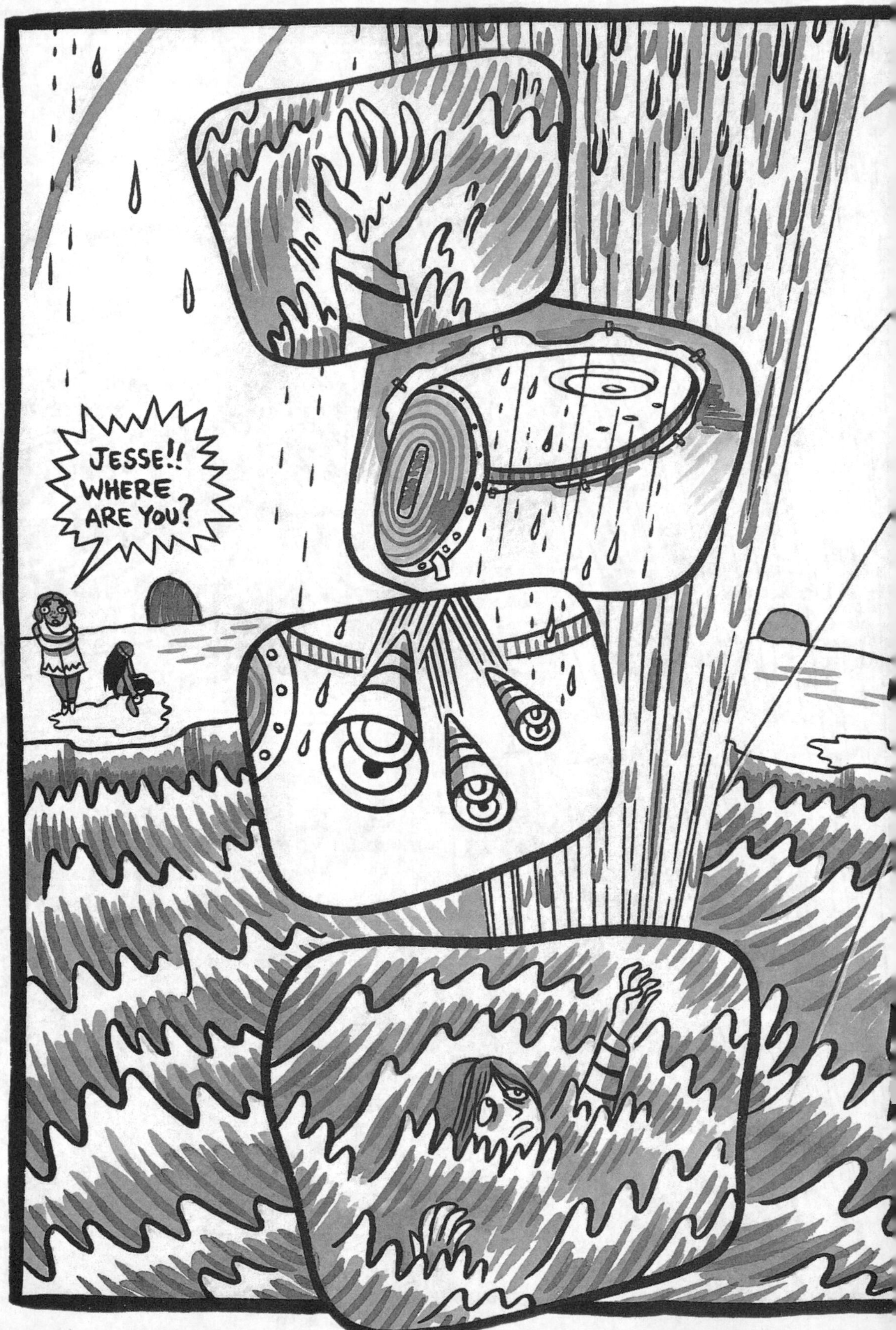
JESSE!! WHERE ARE YOU?

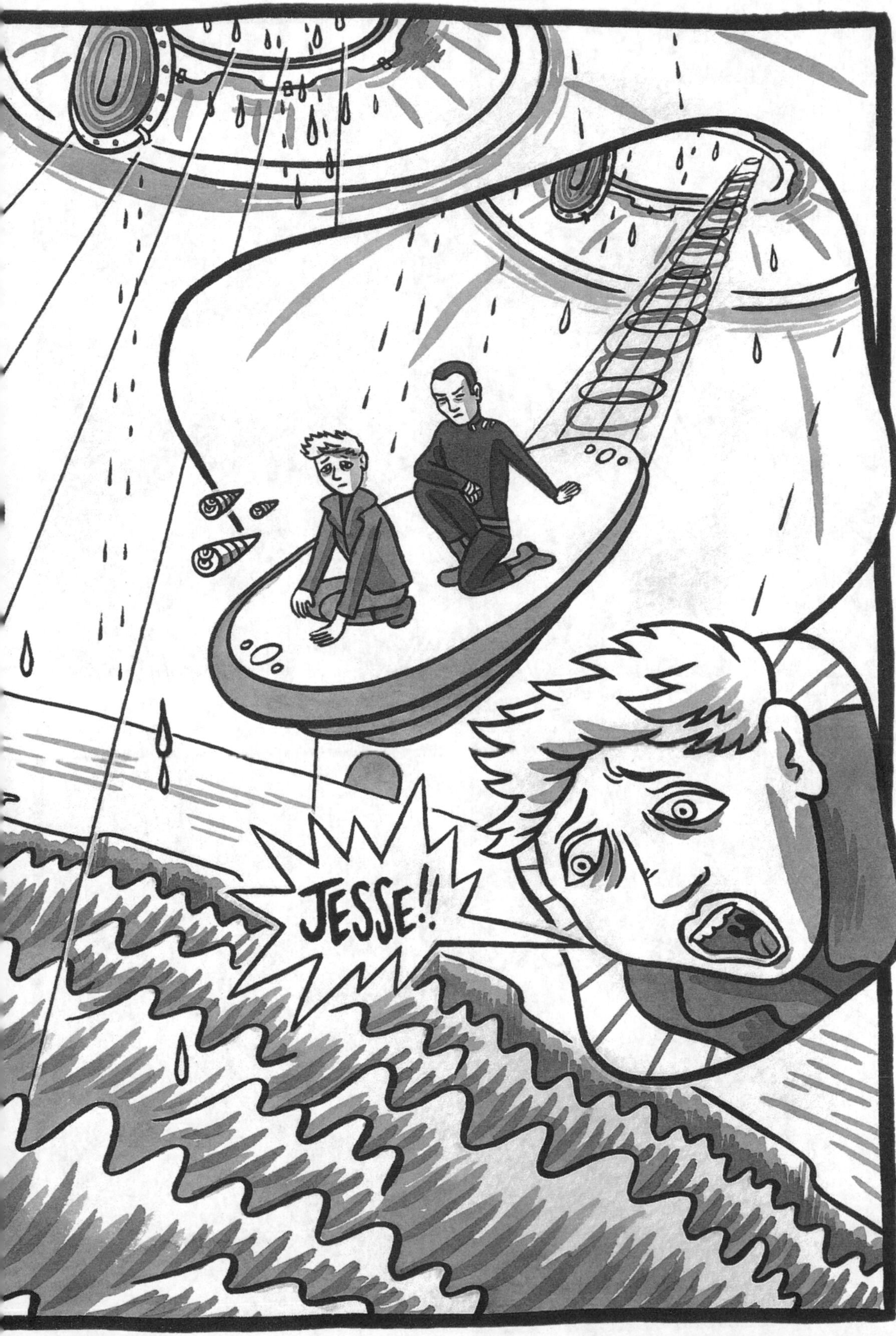
JESSE!!

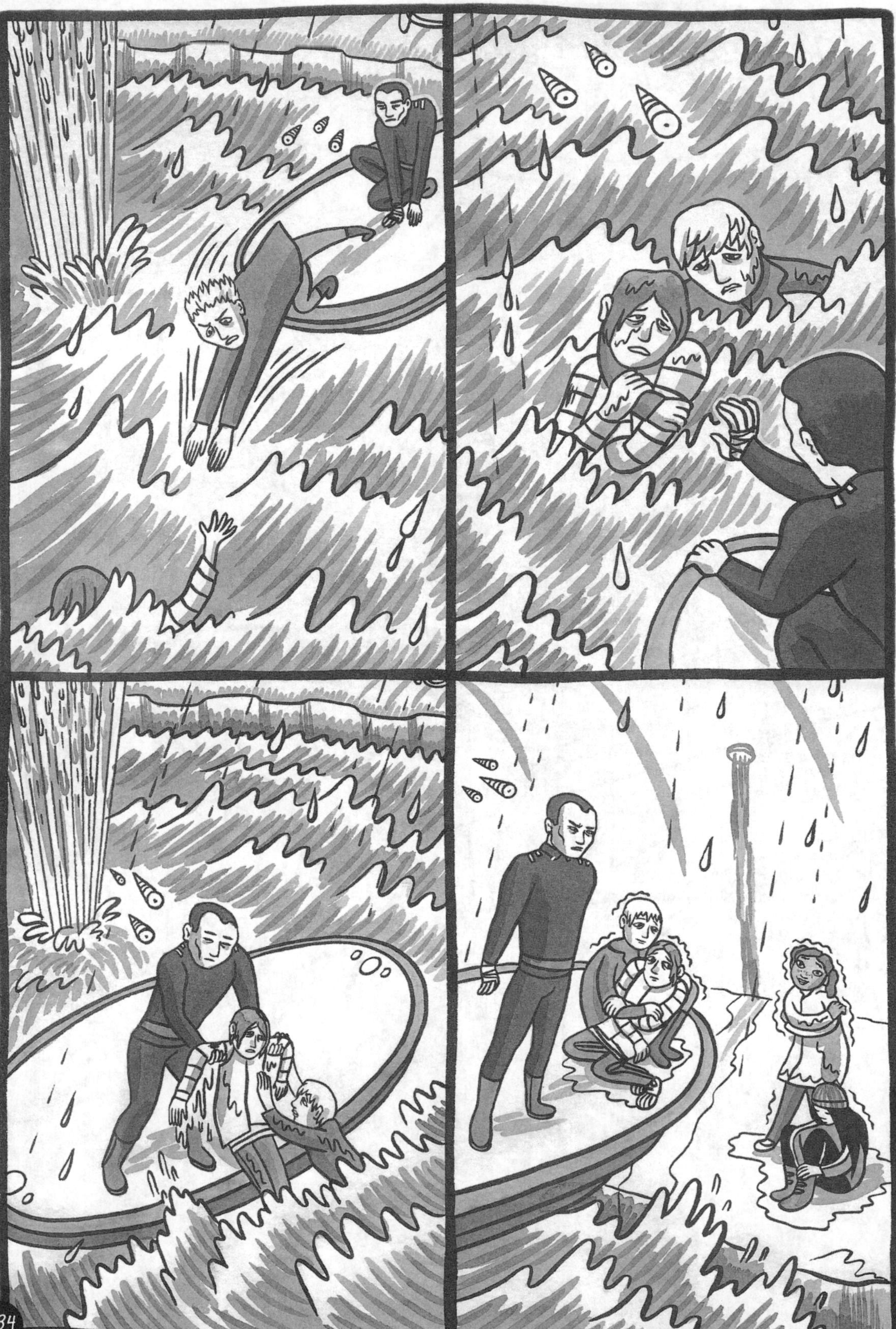

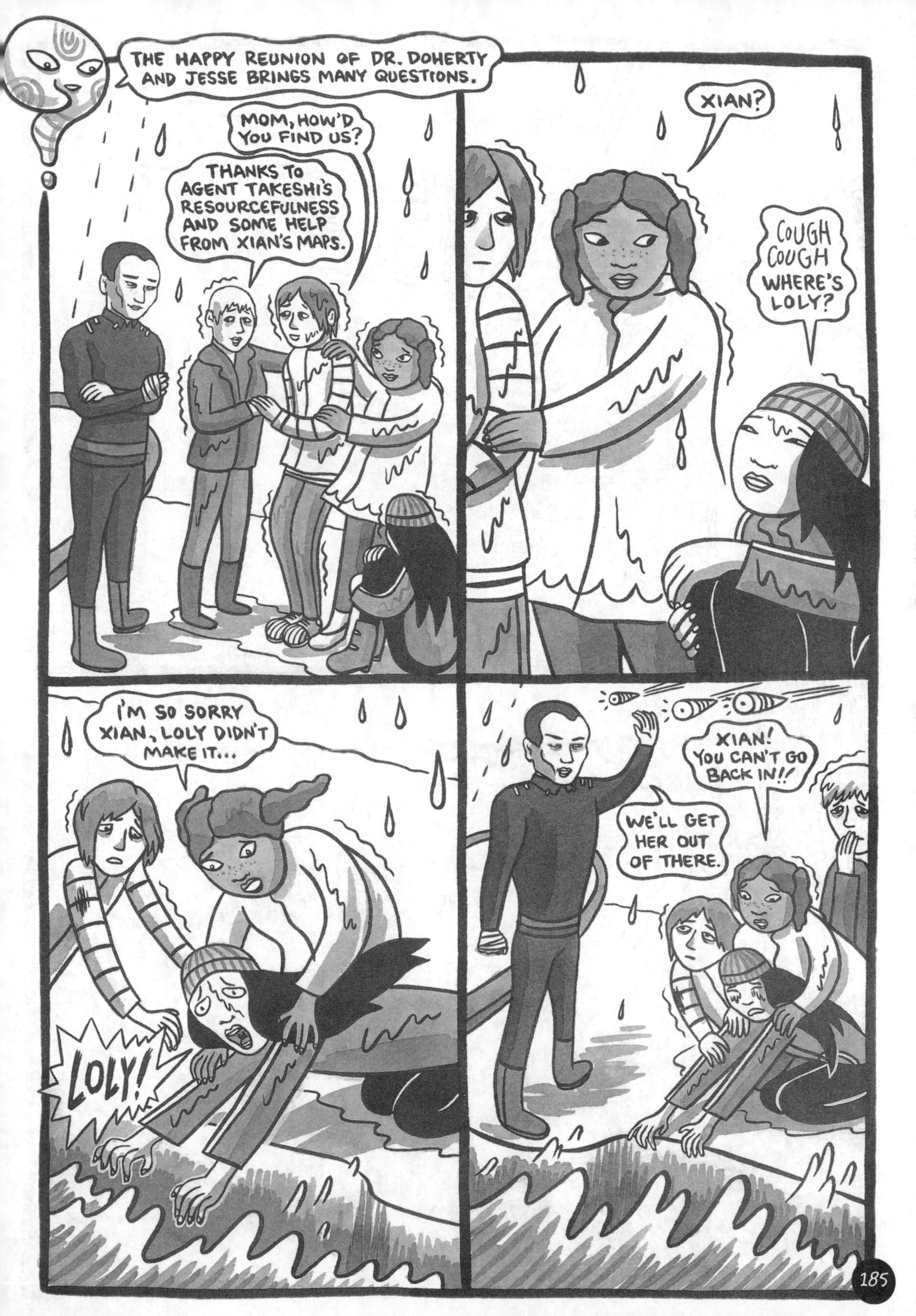
THE HAPPY REUNION OF DR. DOHERTY AND JESSE BRINGS MANY QUESTIONS.
MOM, HOW'D YOU FIND US?
THANKS TO AGENT TAKESHI'S RESOURCEFULNESS AND SOME HELP FROM XIAN'S MAPS.
XIAN?
COUGH COUGH WHERE'S LOLY?
I'M SO SORRY XIAN, LOLY DIDN'T MAKE IT...
LOLY!
XIAN! YOU CAN'T GO BACK IN!!
WE'LL GET HER OUT OF THERE.

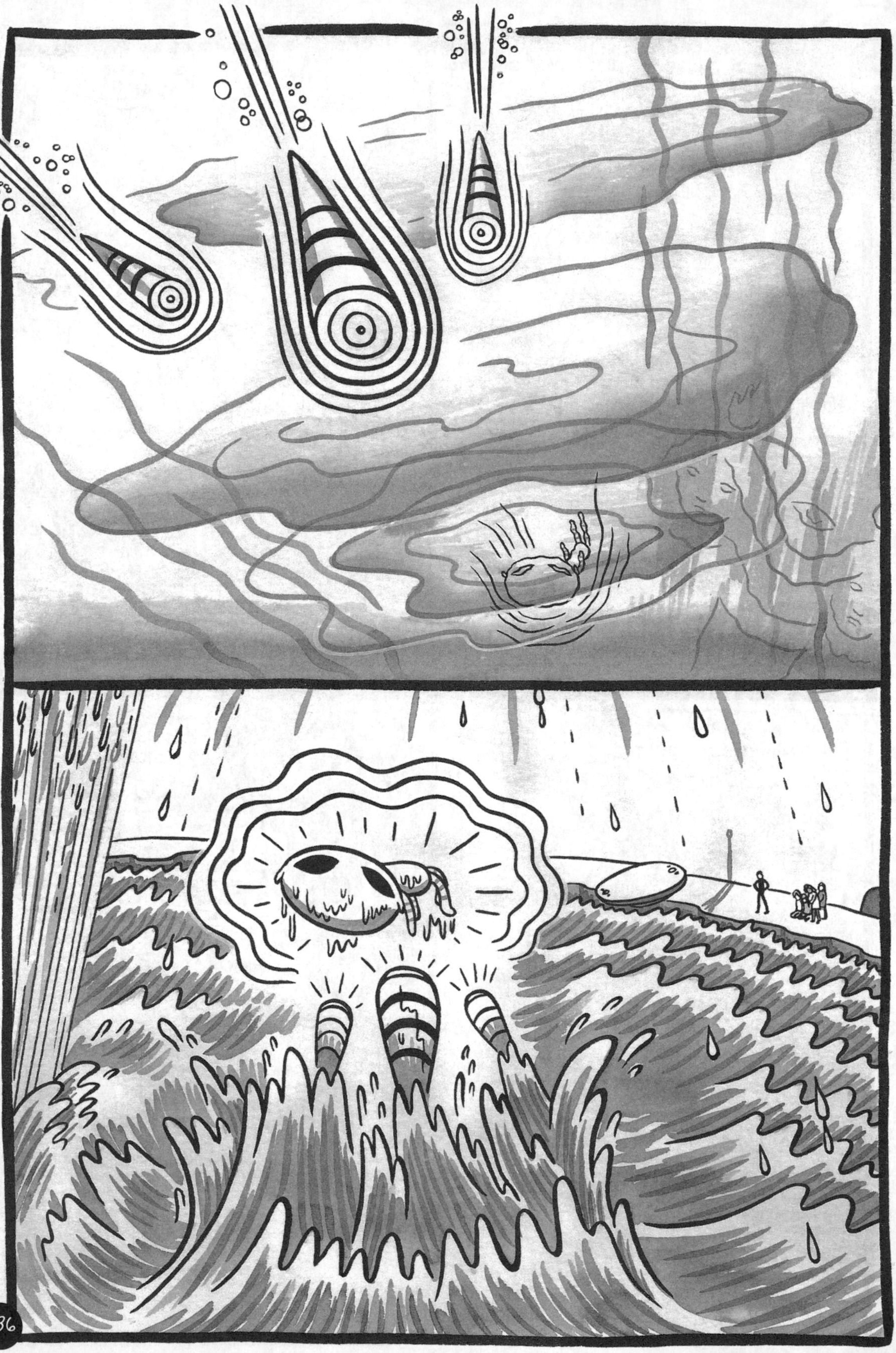

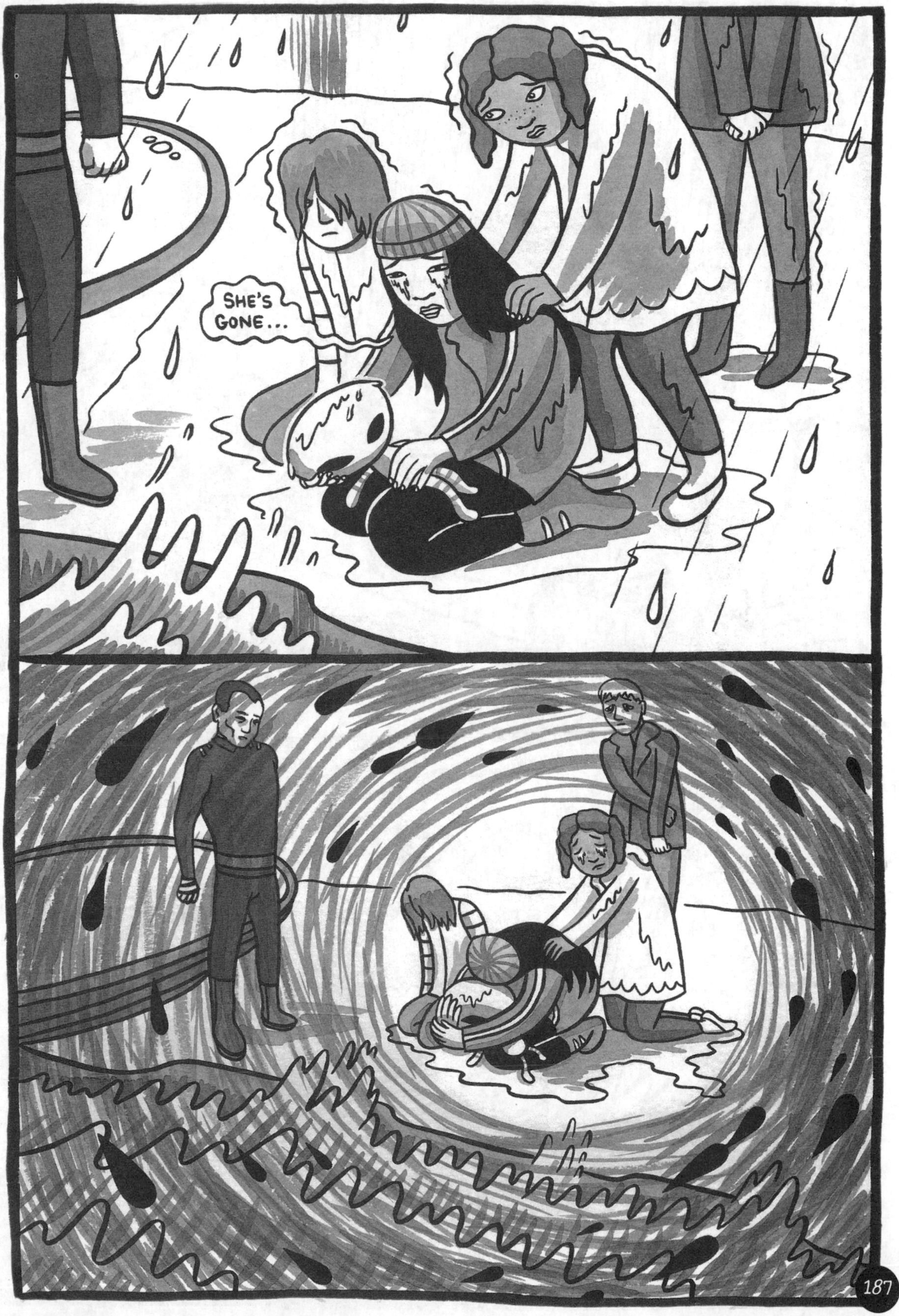
SHE'S GONE...

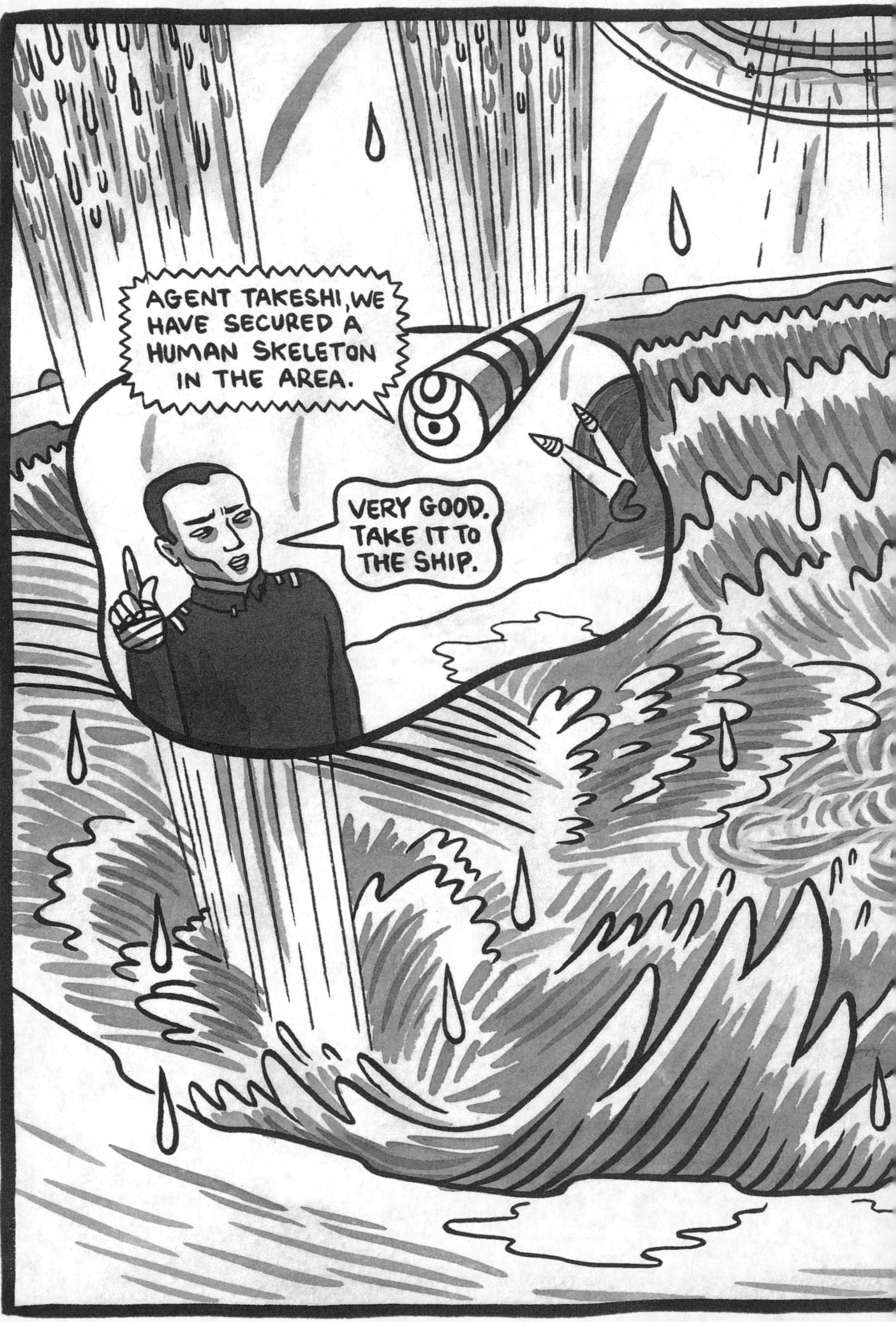
AGENT TAKESHI, WE HAVE SECURED A HUMAN SKELETON IN THE AREA.
VERY GOOD. TAKE IT TO THE SHIP.

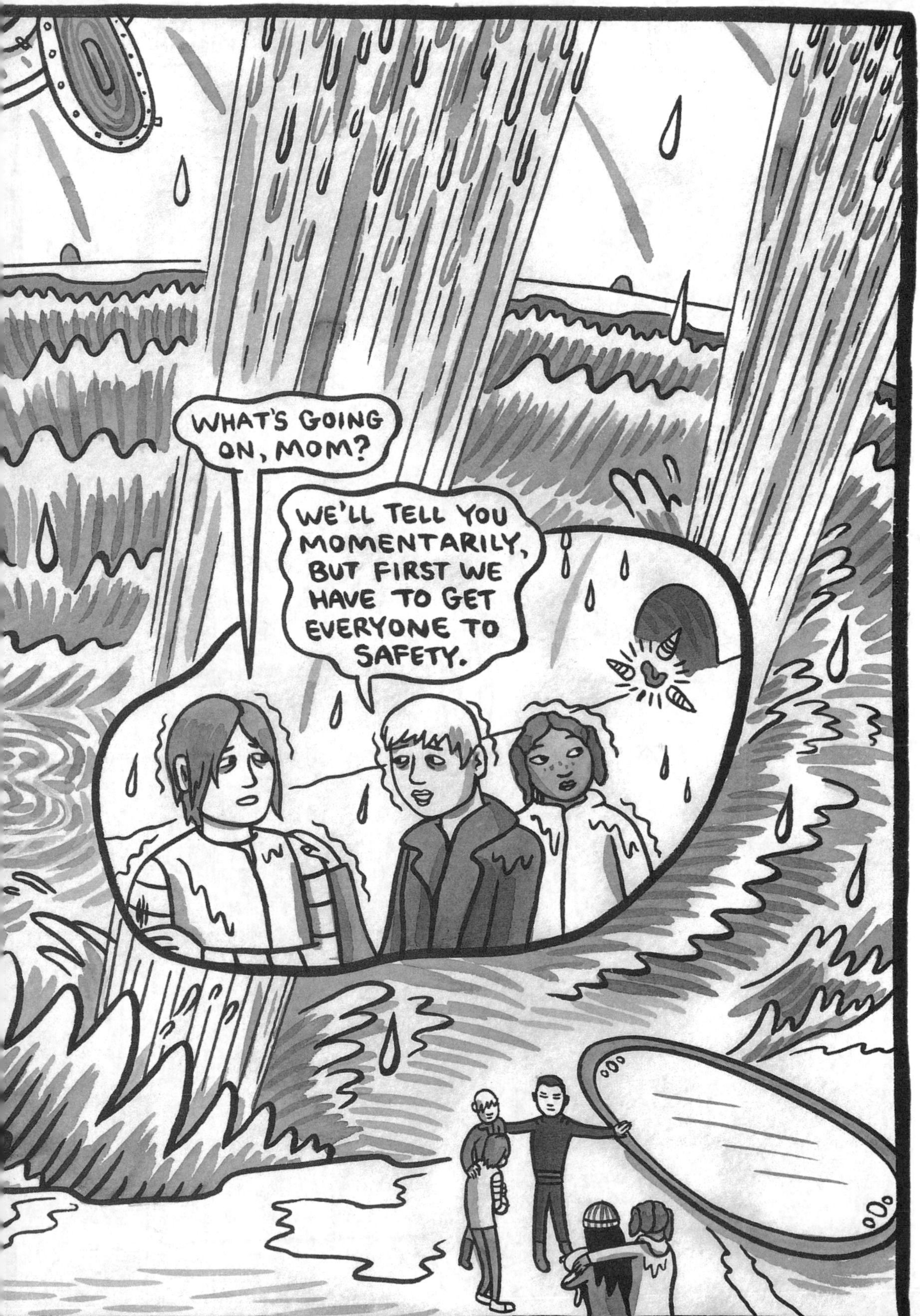
WHAT'S GOING ON, MOM?
WE'LL TELL YOU MOMENTARILY, BUT FIRST WE HAVE TO GET EVERYONE TO SAFETY.

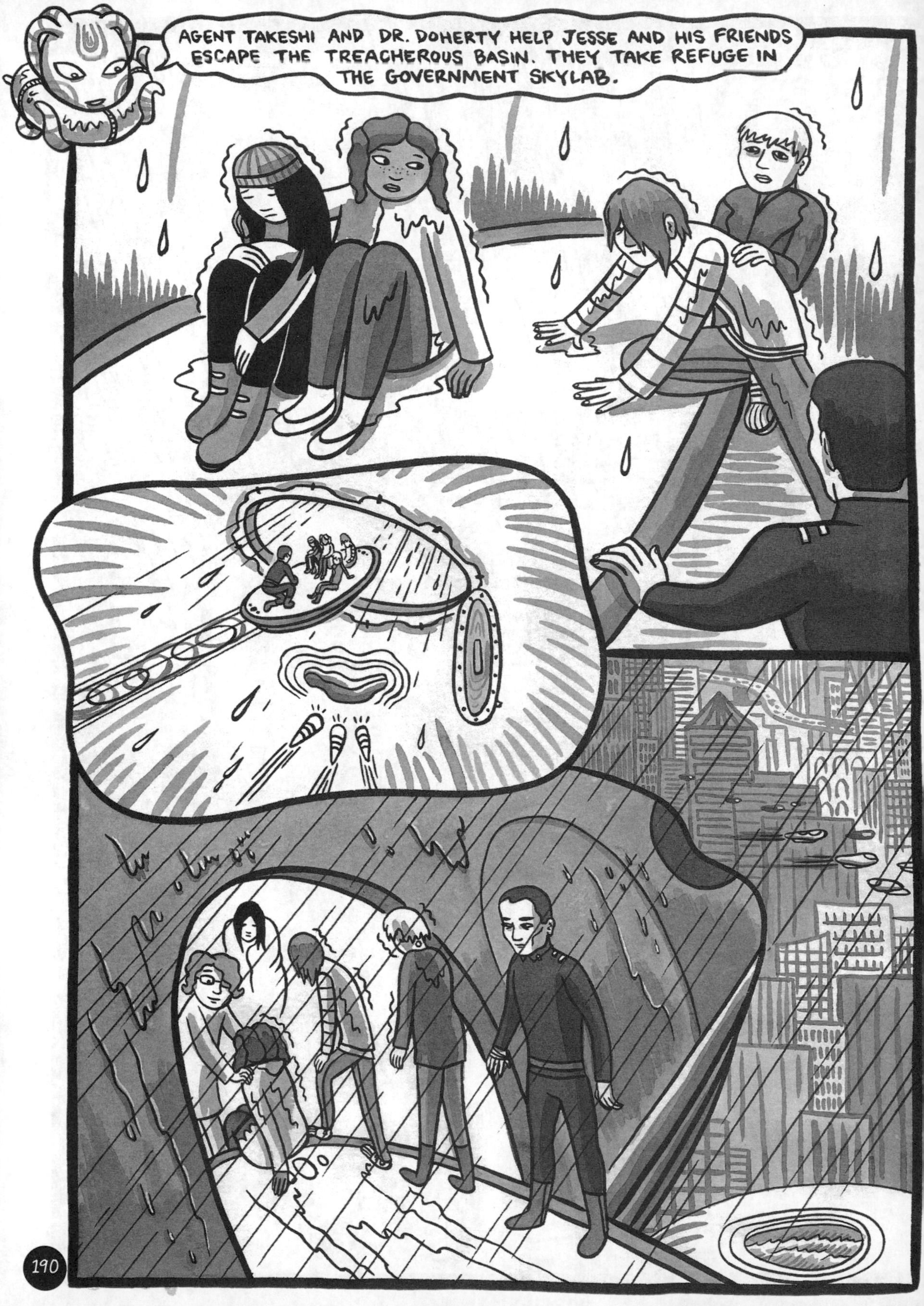
AGENT TAKESHI AND DR. DOHERTY HELP JESSE AND HIS FRIENDS ESCAPE THE TREACHEROUS BASIN. THEY TAKE REFUGE IN THE GOVERNMENT SKYLAB.

A.
A.

FIG.15

8

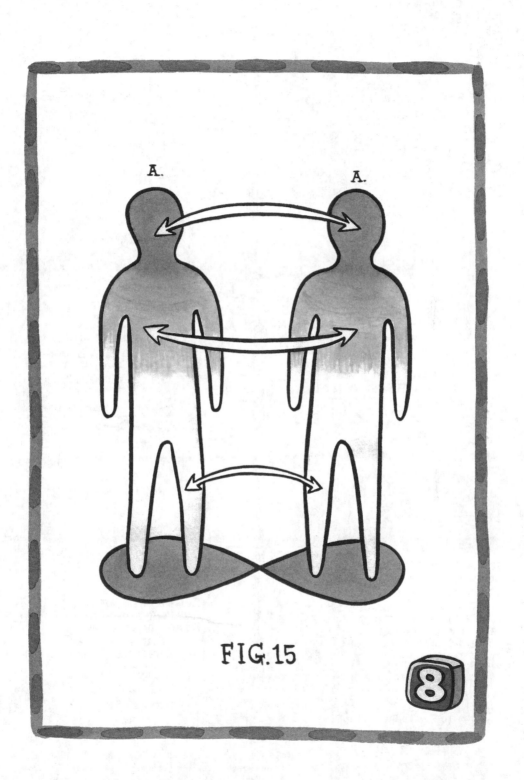

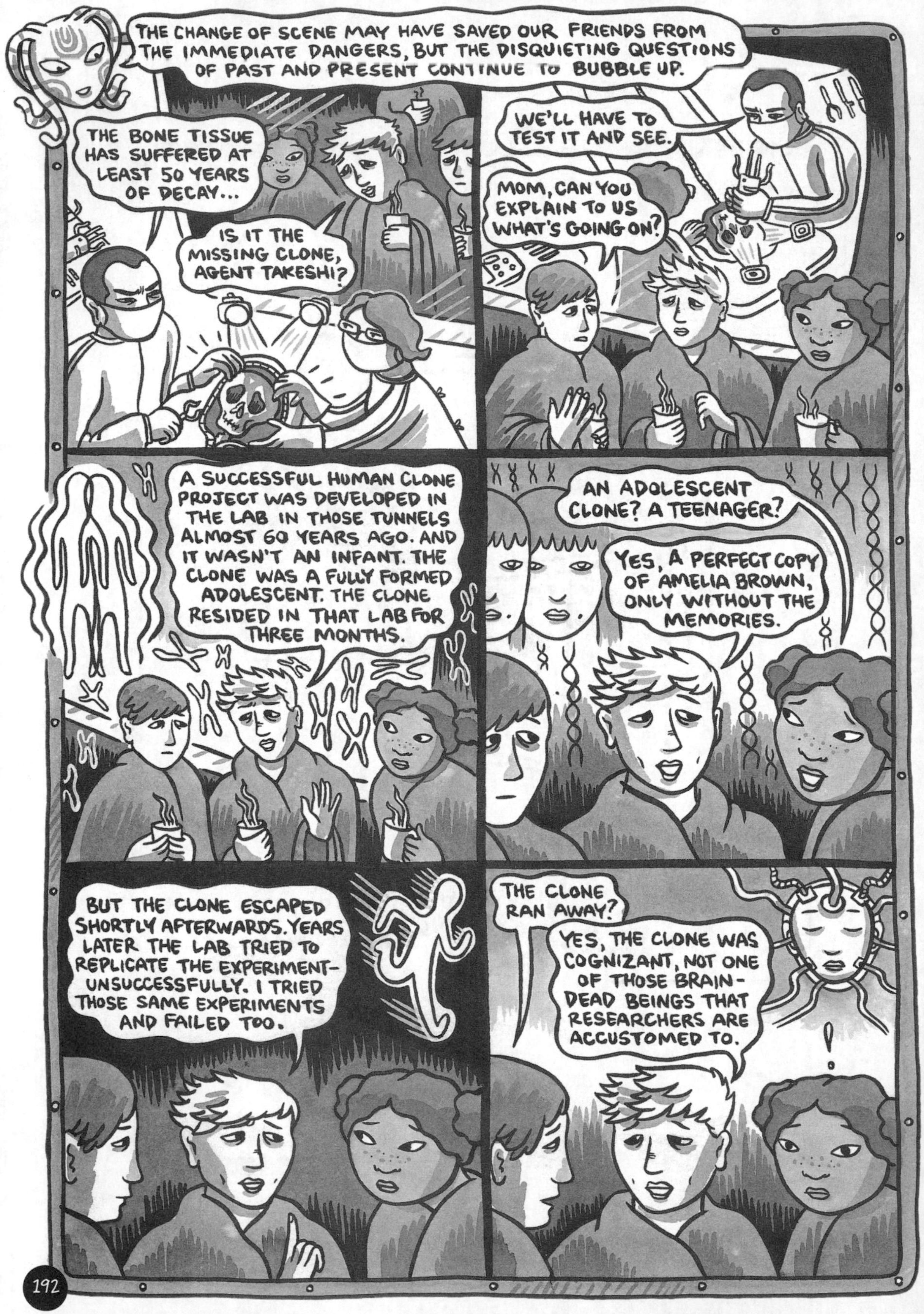
THE CHANGE OF SCENE MAY HAVE SAVED OUR FRIENDS FROM THE IMMEDIATE DANGERS, BUT THE DISQUIETING QUESTIONS OF PAST AND PRESENT CONTINUE TO BUBBLE UP.
THE BONE TISSUE HAS SUFFERED AT LEAST 50 YEARS OF DECAY...
IS IT THE MISSING CLONE, AGENT TAKESHI?
WE'LL HAVE TO TEST IT AND SEE.
MOM, CAN YOU EXPLAIN TO US WHAT'S GOING ON?
A SUCCESSFUL HUMAN CLONE PROJECT WAS DEVELOPED IN THE LAB IN THOSE TUNNELS ALMOST 60 YEARS AGO. AND IT WASN'T AN INFANT. THE CLONE WAS A FULLY FORMED ADOLESCENT. THE CLONE RESIDED IN THAT LAB FOR THREE MONTHS.
AN ADOLESCENT CLONE? A TEENAGER?
YES, A PERFECT COPY OF AMELIA BROWN, ONLY WITHOUT THE MEMORIES.
BUT THE CLONE ESCAPED SHORTLY AFTERWARDS. YEARS LATER THE LAB TRIED TO REPLICATE THE EXPERIMENT-UNSUCCESSFULLY. I TRIED THOSE SAME EXPERIMENTS AND FAILED TOO.
THE CLONE RAN AWAY?
YES, THE CLONE WAS COGNIZANT, NOT ONE OF THOSE BRAIN-DEAD BEINGS THAT RESEARCHERS ARE ACCUSTOMED TO.
!

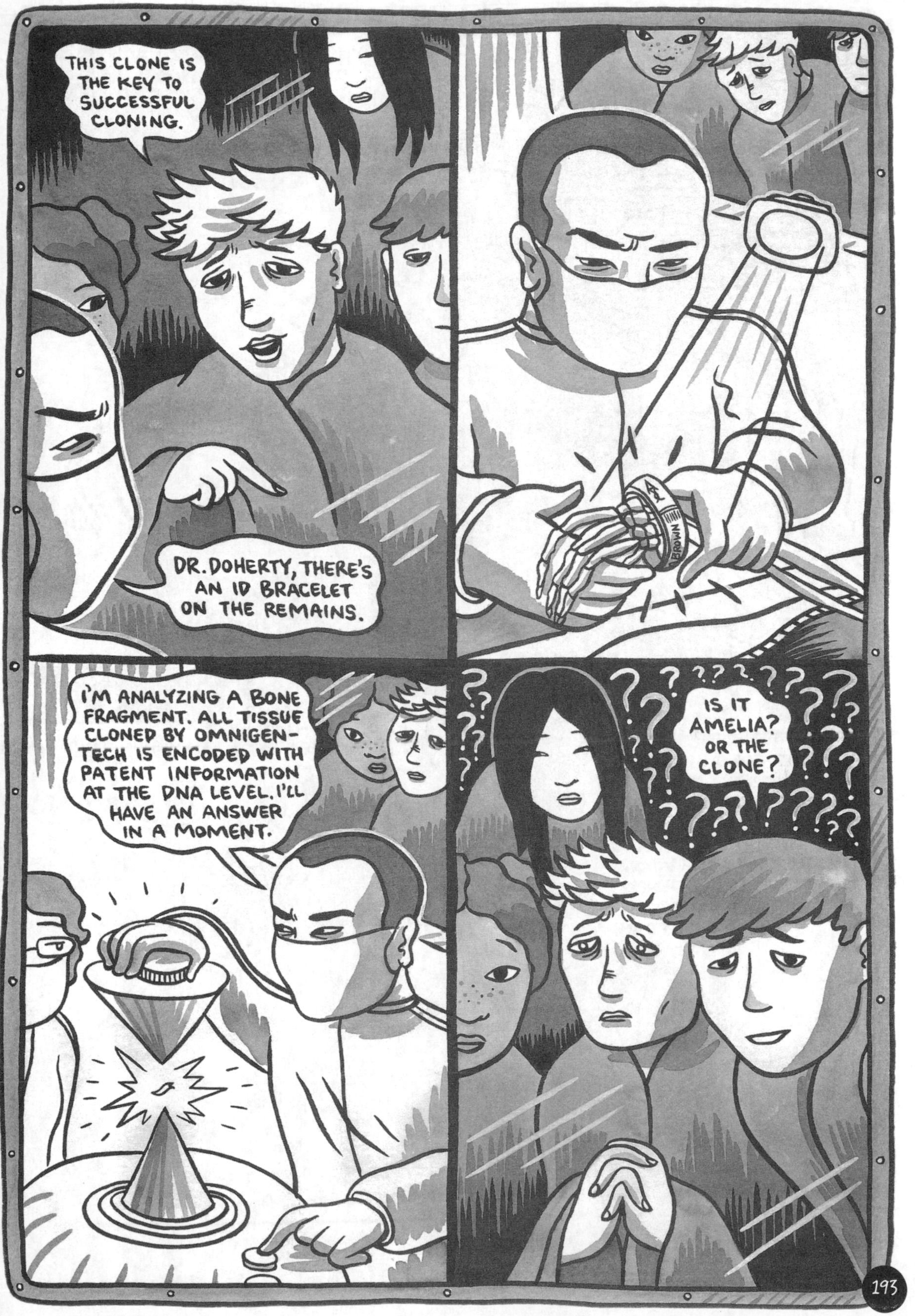
THIS CLONE IS THE KEY TO SUCCESSFUL CLONING.
DR. DOHERTY, THERE'S AN ID BRACELET ON THE REMAINS.
BROWN
I'M ANALYZING A BONE FRAGMENT. ALL TISSUE CLONED BY OMNIGEN-TECH IS ENCODED WITH PATENT INFORMATION AT THE DNA LEVEL. I'LL HAVE AN ANSWER IN A MOMENT.
IS IT AMELIA? OR THE CLONE?

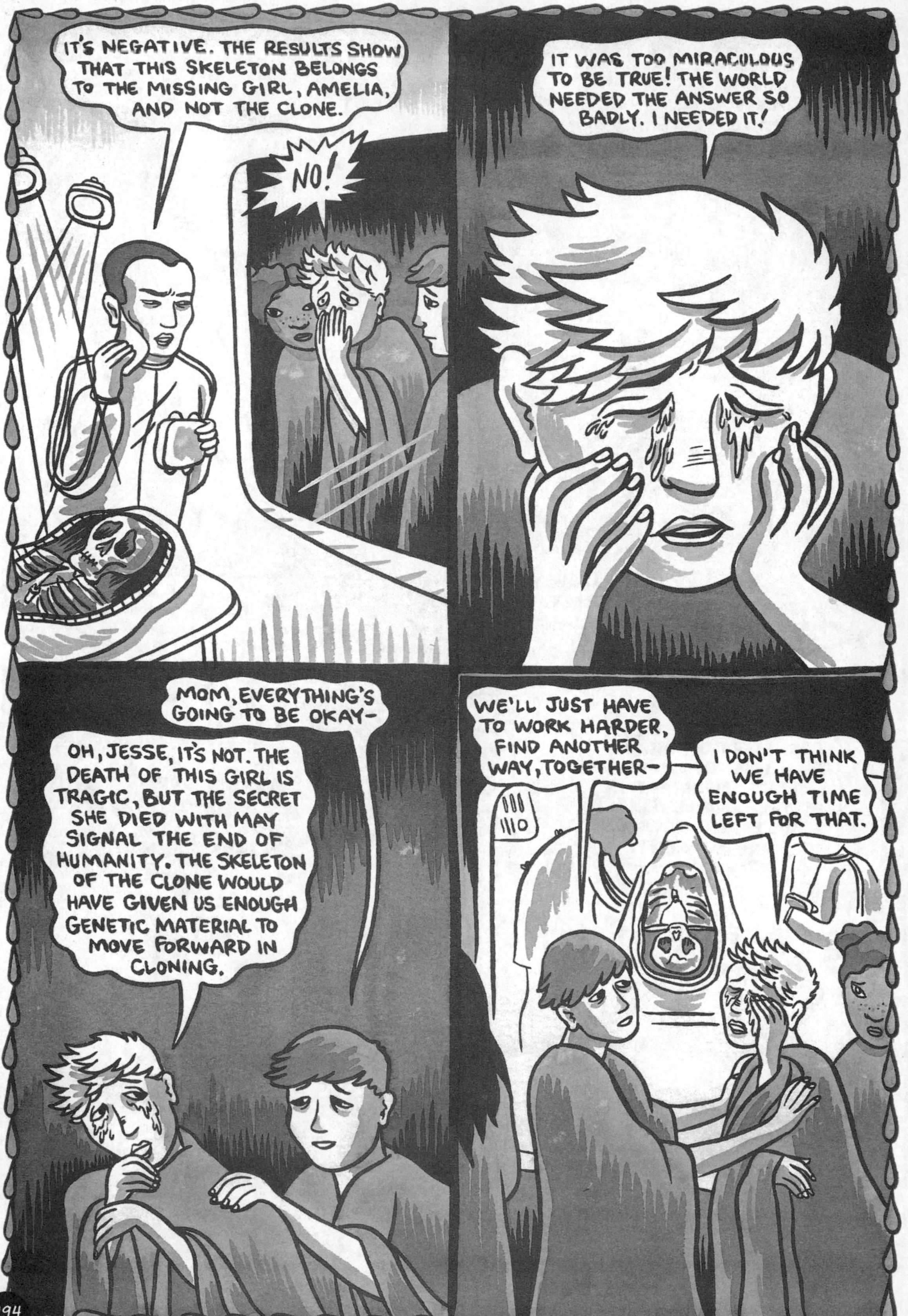

IT'S NEGATIVE. THE RESULTS SHOW THAT THIS SKELETON BELONGS TO THE MISSING GIRL, AMELIA, AND NOT THE CLONE.
NO!
IT WAS TOO MIRACULOUS TO BE TRUE! THE WORLD NEEDED THE ANSWER SO BADLY. I NEEDED IT!
MOM, EVERYTHING'S GOING TO BE OKAY-
OH, JESSE, IT'S NOT. THE DEATH OF THIS GIRL IS TRAGIC, BUT THE SECRET SHE DIED WITH MAY SIGNAL THE END OF HUMANITY. THE SKELETON OF THE CLONE WOULD HAVE GIVEN US ENOUGH GENETIC MATERIAL TO MOVE FORWARD IN CLONING.
WE'LL JUST HAVE TO WORK HARDER, FIND ANOTHER WAY, TOGETHER-
I DON'T THINK WE HAVE ENOUGH TIME LEFT FOR THAT.

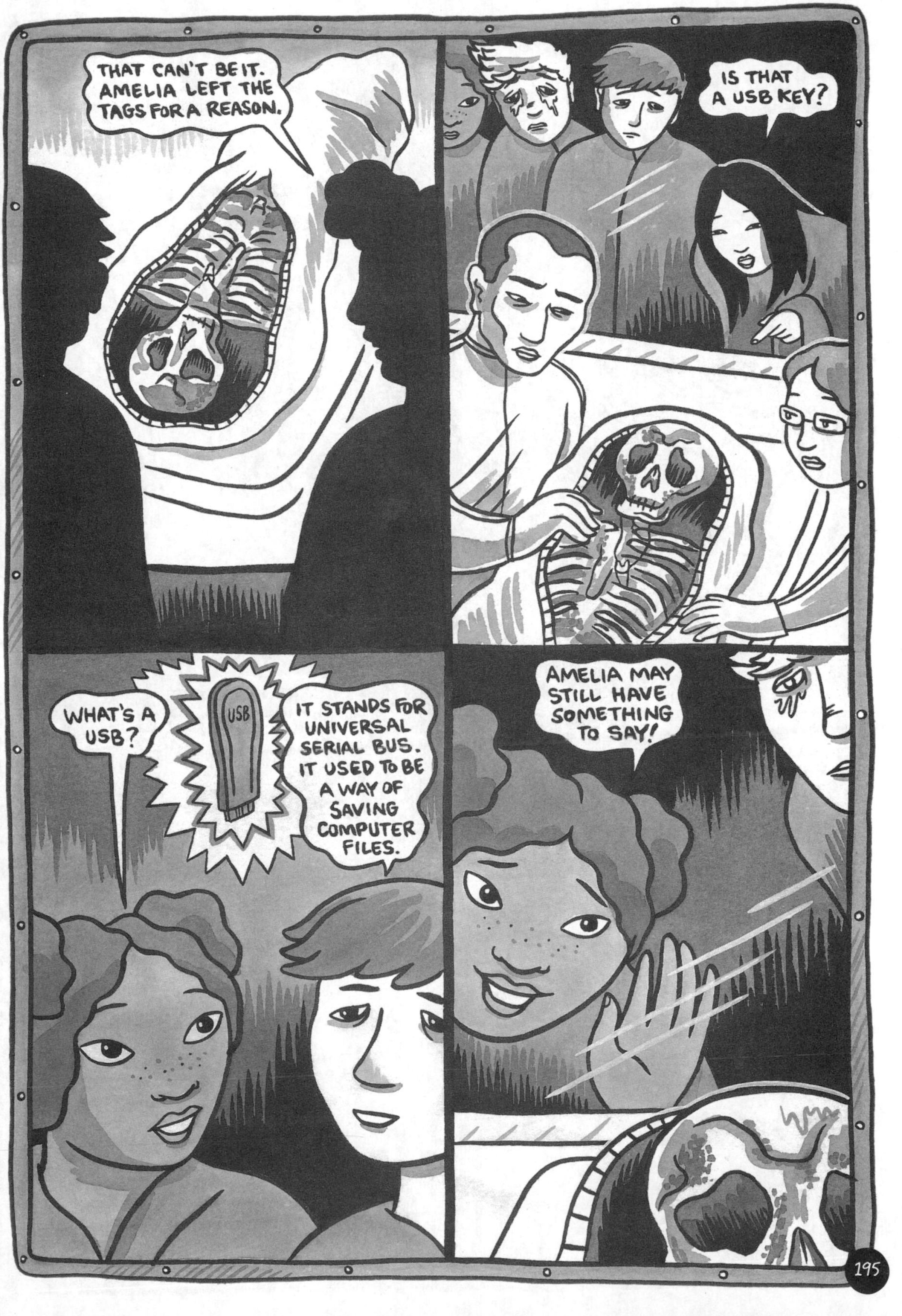
THAT CAN'T BE IT. AMELIA LEFT THE TAGS FOR A REASON.
IS THAT A USB KEY?
WHAT'S A USB?
USB
IT STANDS FOR UNIVERSAL SERIAL BUS. IT USED TO BE A WAY OF SAVING COMPUTER FILES.
AMELIA MAY STILL HAVE SOMETHING TO SAY!

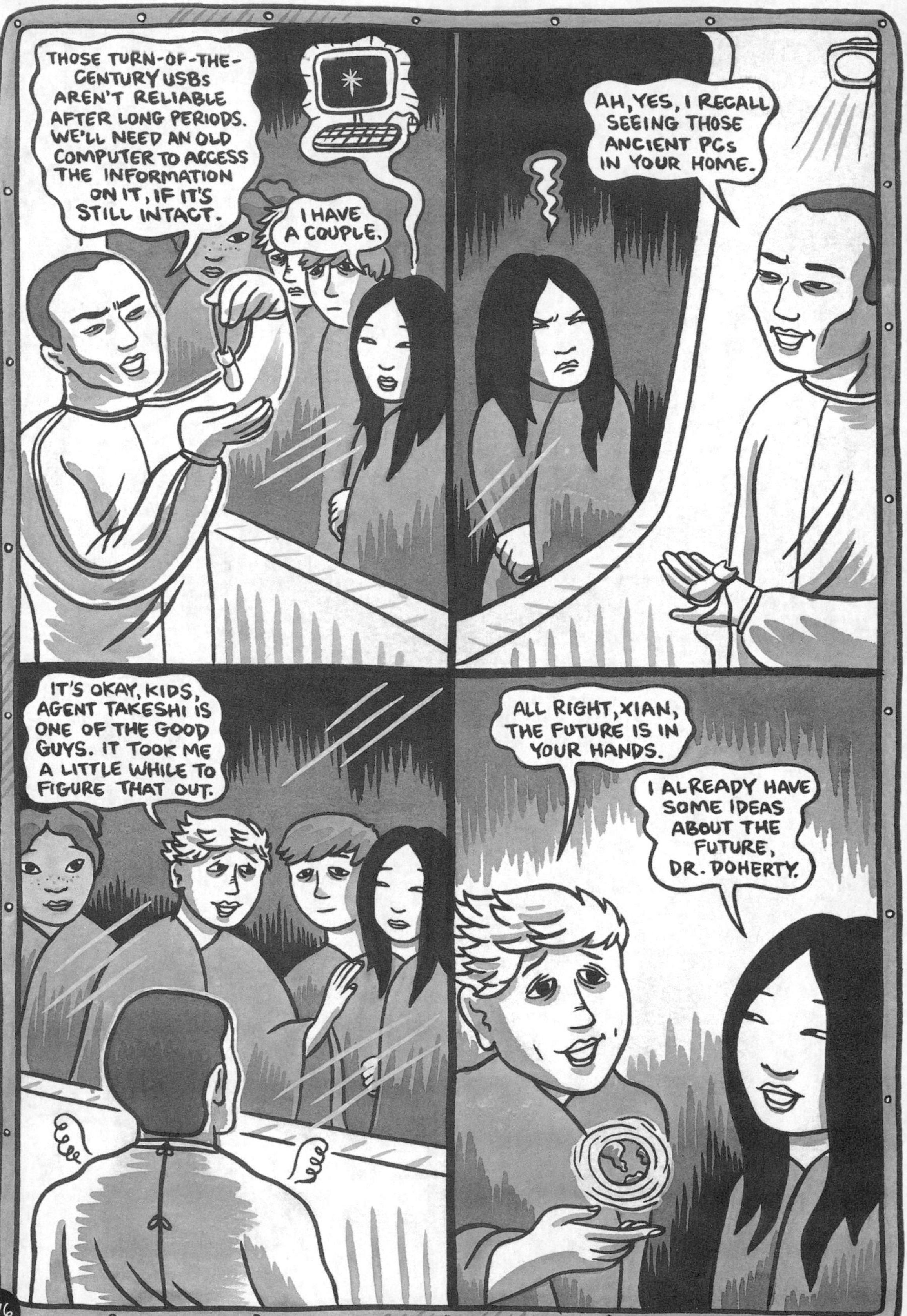
THOSE TURN-OF-THE-CENTURY USBs AREN'T RELIABLE AFTER LONG PERIODS. WE'LL NEED AN OLD COMPUTER TO ACCESS THE INFORMATION ON IT, IF IT'S STILL INTACT.
I HAVE A COUPLE.
AH, YES, I RECALL SEEING THOSE ANCIENT PCs IN YOUR HOME.
IT'S OKAY, KIDS, AGENT TAKESHI IS ONE OF THE GOOD GUYS. IT TOOK ME A LITTLE WHILE TO FIGURE THAT OUT.
ALL RIGHT, XIAN, THE FUTURE IS IN YOUR HANDS.
I ALREADY HAVE SOME IDEAS ABOUT THE FUTURE, DR. DOHERTY.

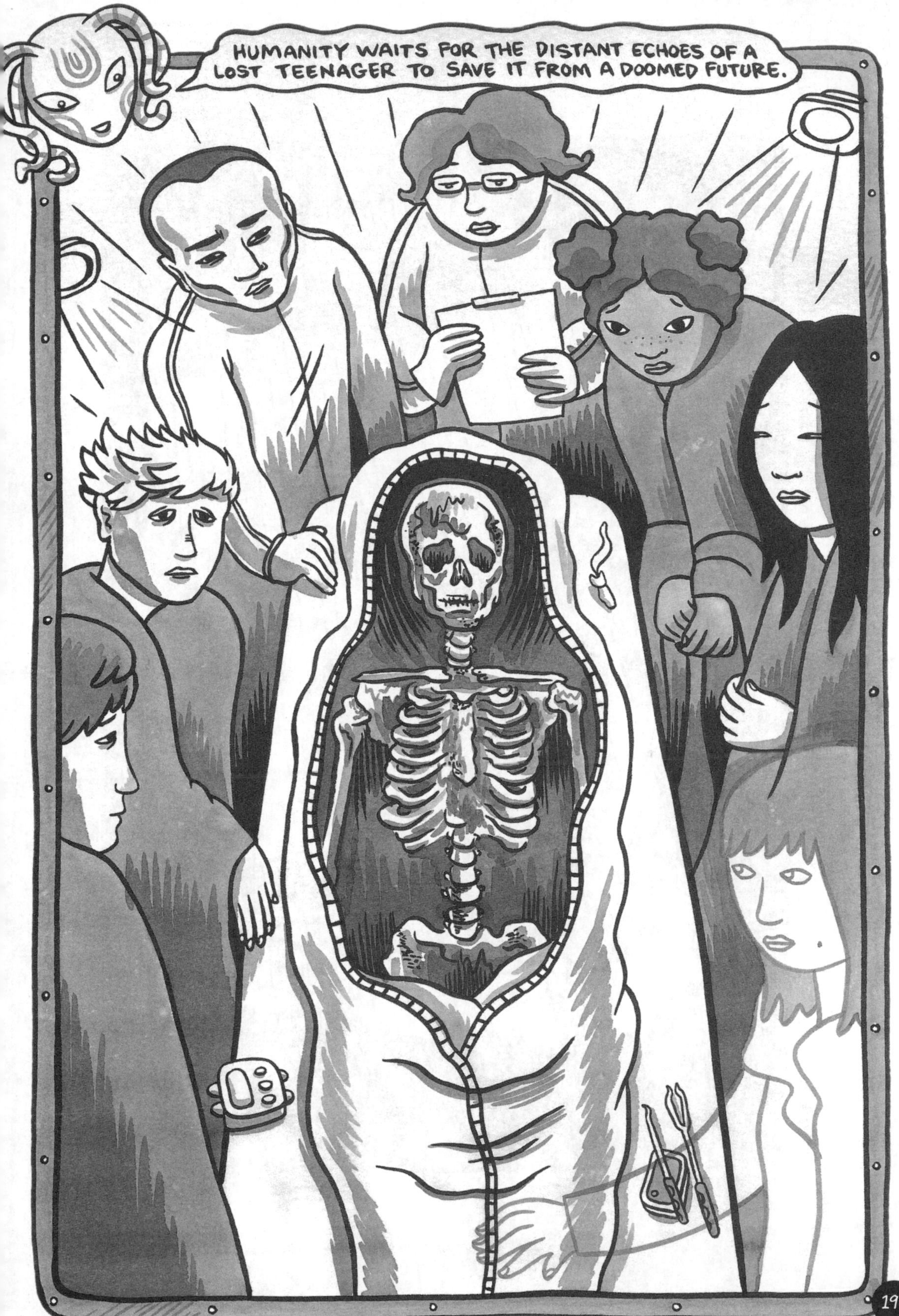
HUMANITY WAITS FOR THE DISTANT ECHOES OF A LOST TEENAGER TO SAVE IT FROM A DOOMED FUTURE.

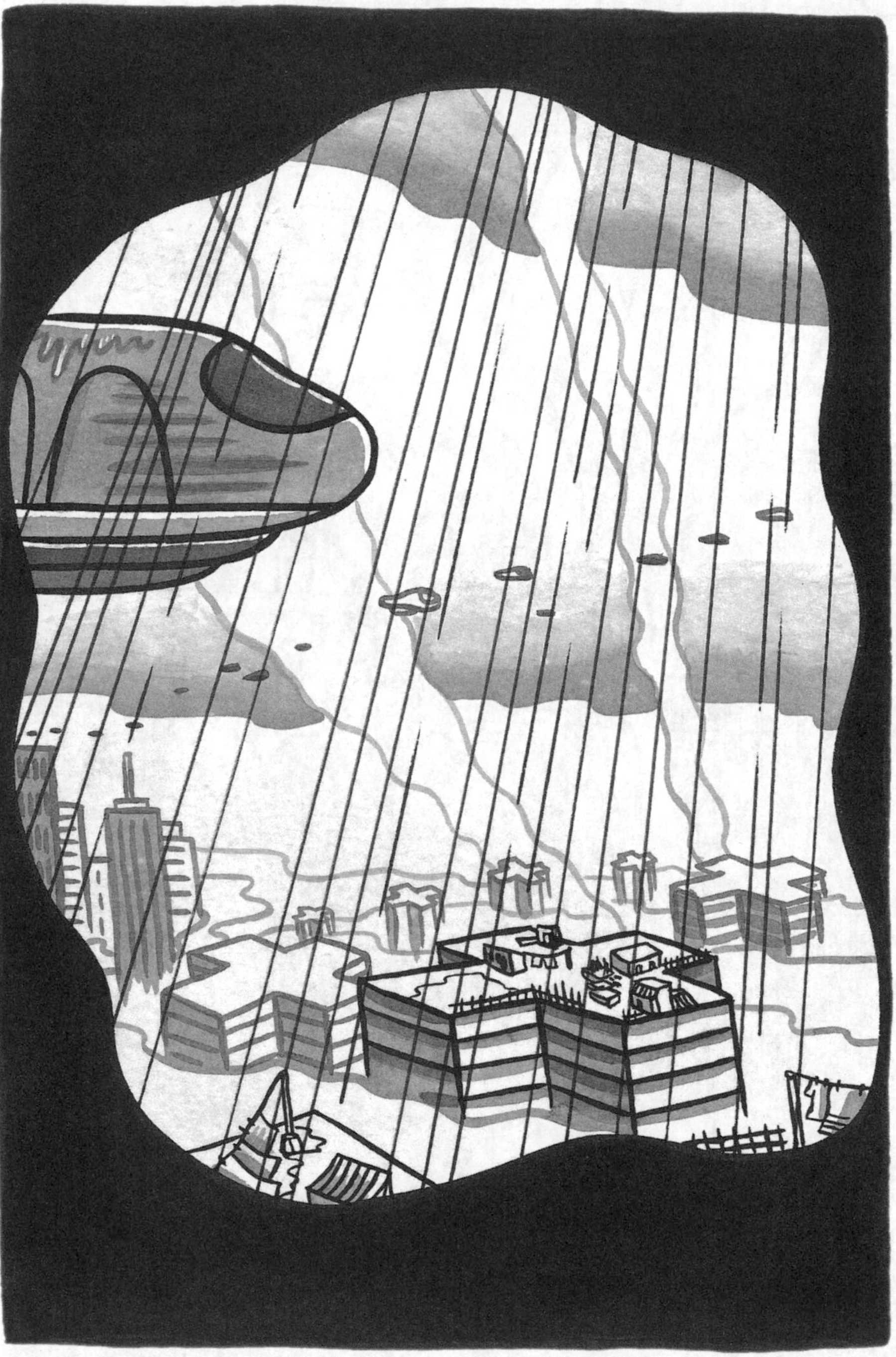

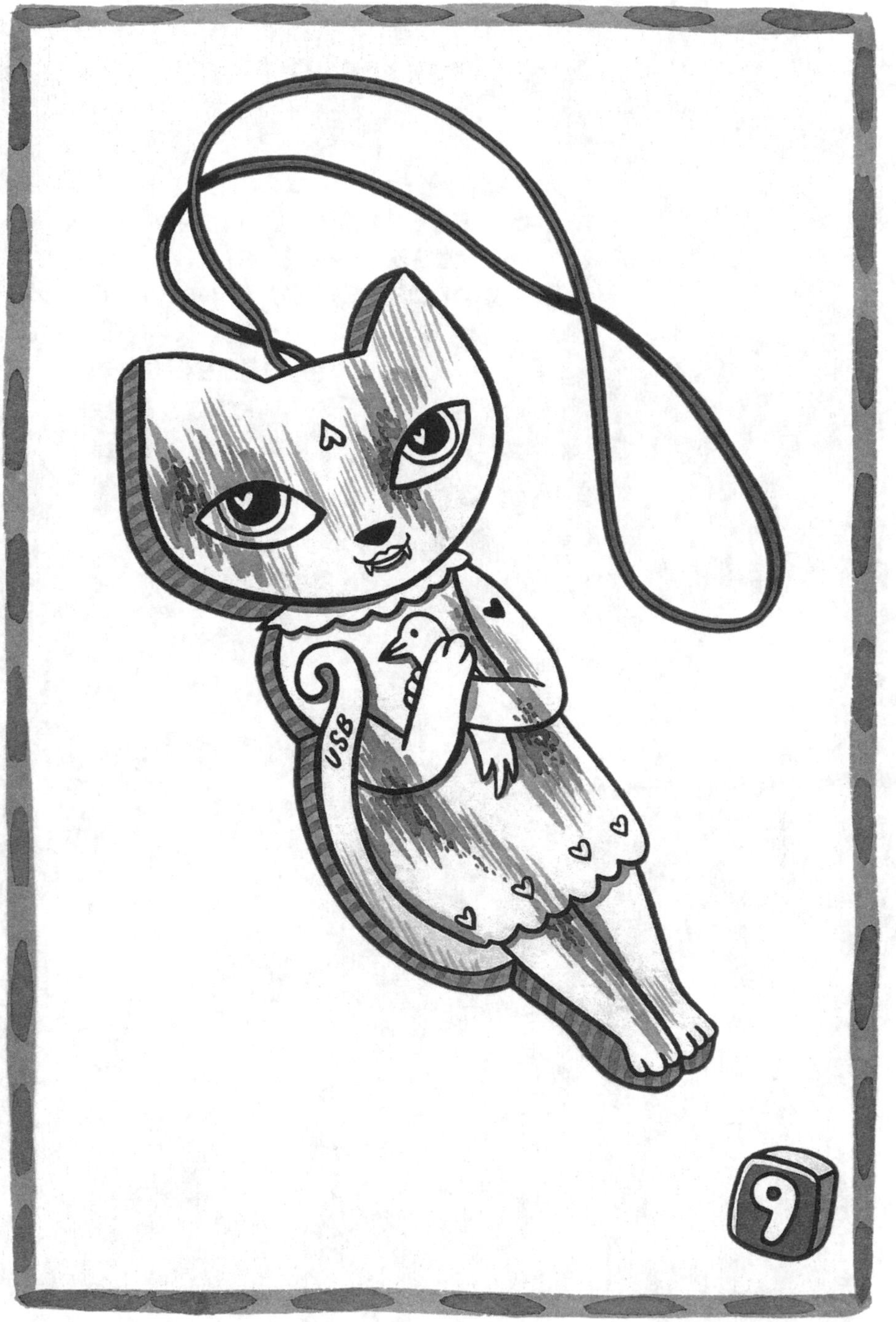
USB
9

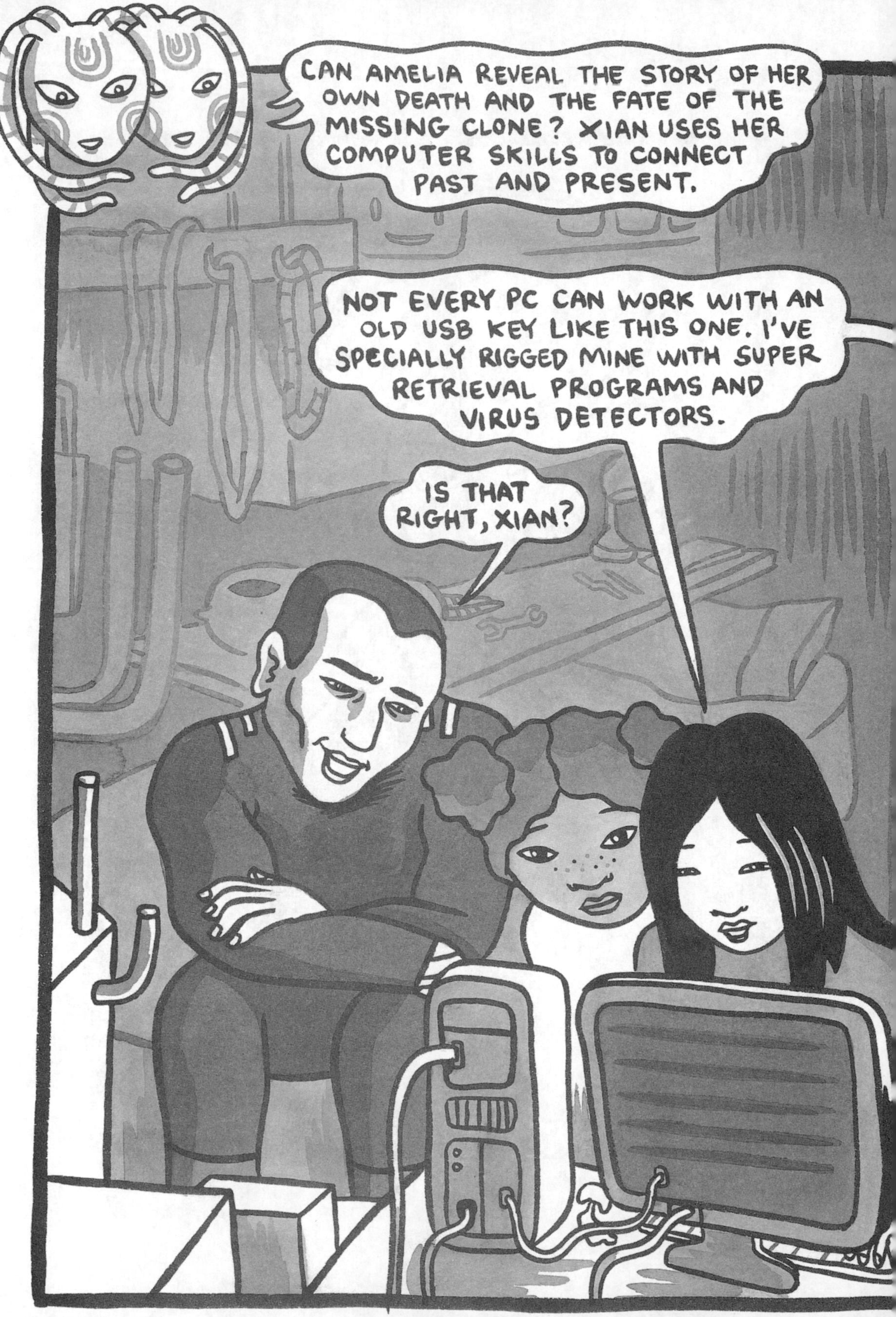
CAN AMELIA REVEAL THE STORY OF HER OWN DEATH AND THE FATE OF THE MISSING CLONE? XIAN USES HER COMPUTER SKILLS TO CONNECT PAST AND PRESENT.
NOT EVERY PC CAN WORK WITH AN OLD USB KEY LIKE THIS ONE. I'VE SPECIALLY RIGGED MINE WITH SUPER RETRIEVAL PROGRAMS AND VIRUS DETECTORS.
IS THAT RIGHT, XIAN?

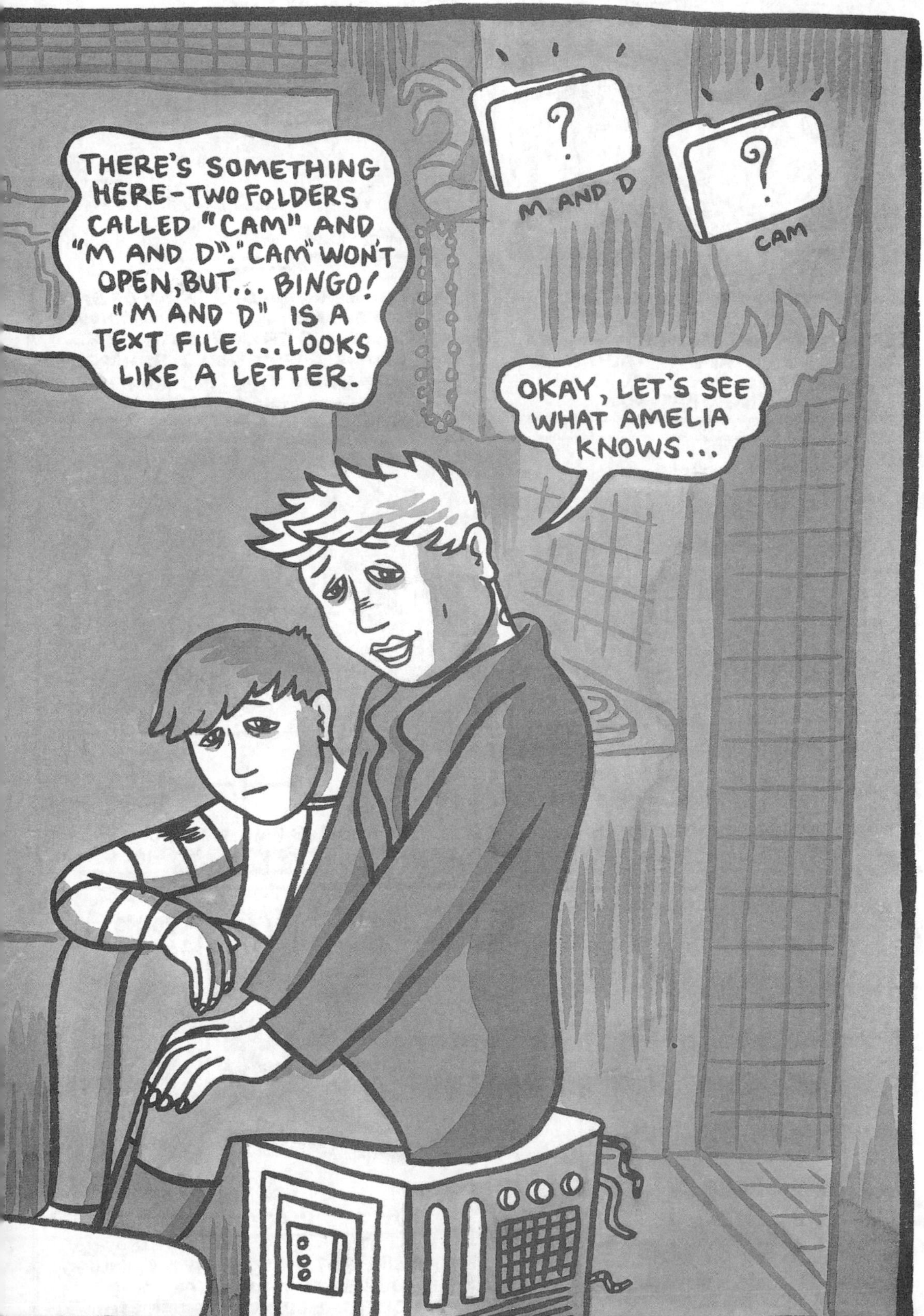
THERE'S SOMETHING HERE-TWO FOLDERS CALLED "CAM" AND "M AND D". "CAM" WON'T OPEN, BUT... BINGO! "M AND D" IS A TEXT FILE... LOOKS LIKE A LETTER.
M AND D
CAM
OKAY, LET'S SEE WHAT AMELIA KNOWS...

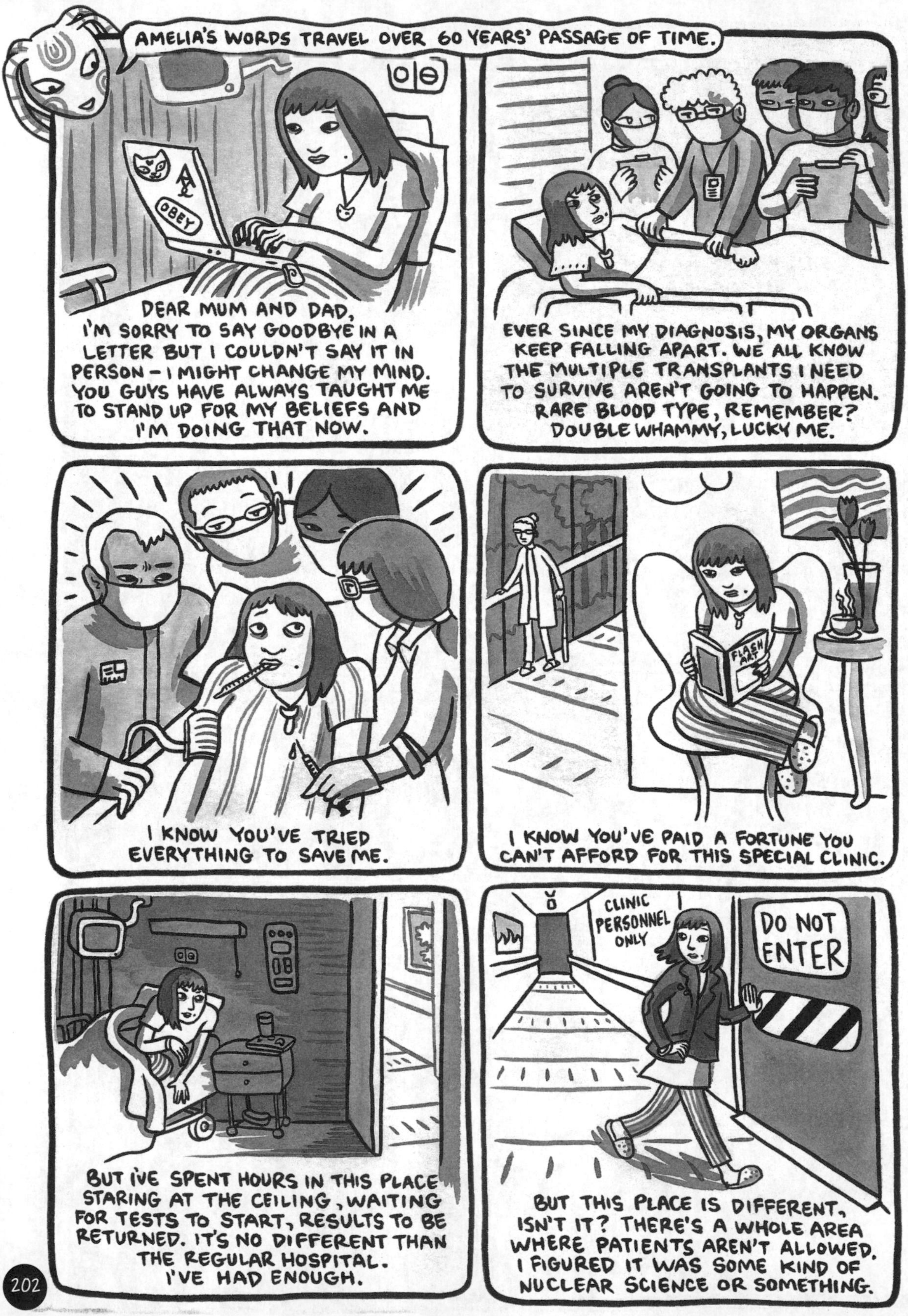
AMELIA'S WORDS TRAVEL OVER 60 YEARS' PASSAGE OF TIME.
OBEY
DEAR MUM AND DAD,
I'M SORRY TO SAY GOODBYE IN A LETTER BUT I COULDN'T SAY IT IN PERSON – I MIGHT CHANGE MY MIND. YOU GUYS HAVE ALWAYS TAUGHT ME TO STAND UP FOR MY BELIEFS AND I'M DOING THAT NOW.
EVER SINCE MY DIAGNOSIS, MY ORGANS KEEP FALLING APART. WE ALL KNOW THE MULTIPLE TRANSPLANTS I NEED TO SURVIVE AREN'T GOING TO HAPPEN. RARE BLOOD TYPE, REMEMBER? DOUBLE WHAMMY, LUCKY ME.
I KNOW YOU'VE TRIED EVERYTHING TO SAVE ME.
FLASH ART
I KNOW YOU'VE PAID A FORTUNE YOU CAN'T AFFORD FOR THIS SPECIAL CLINIC.
BUT I'VE SPENT HOURS IN THIS PLACE STARING AT THE CEILING, WAITING FOR TESTS TO START, RESULTS TO BE RETURNED. IT'S NO DIFFERENT THAN THE REGULAR HOSPITAL. I'VE HAD ENOUGH.
CLINIC PERSONNEL ONLY
DO NOT ENTER
BUT THIS PLACE IS DIFFERENT, ISN'T IT? THERE'S A WHOLE AREA WHERE PATIENTS AREN'T ALLOWED. I FIGURED IT WAS SOME KIND OF NUCLEAR SCIENCE OR SOMETHING.

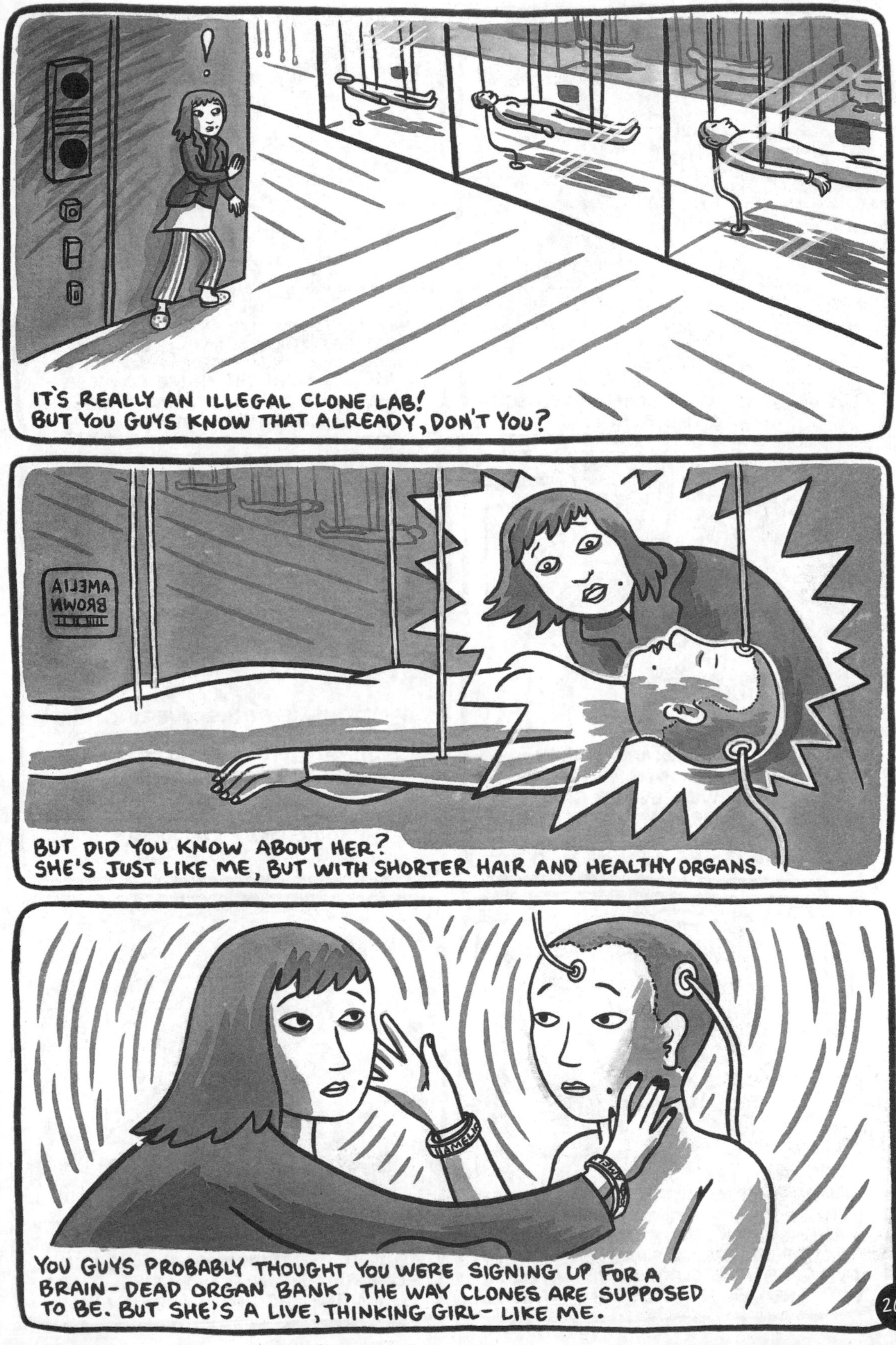
IT'S REALLY AN ILLEGAL CLONE LAB!
BUT YOU GUYS KNOW THAT ALREADY, DON'T YOU?
BUT DID YOU KNOW ABOUT HER?
SHE'S JUST LIKE ME, BUT WITH SHORTER HAIR AND HEALTHY ORGANS.
YOU GUYS PROBABLY THOUGHT YOU WERE SIGNING UP FOR A BRAIN-DEAD ORGAN BANK, THE WAY CLONES ARE SUPPOSED TO BE. BUT SHE'S A LIVE, THINKING GIRL- LIKE ME.

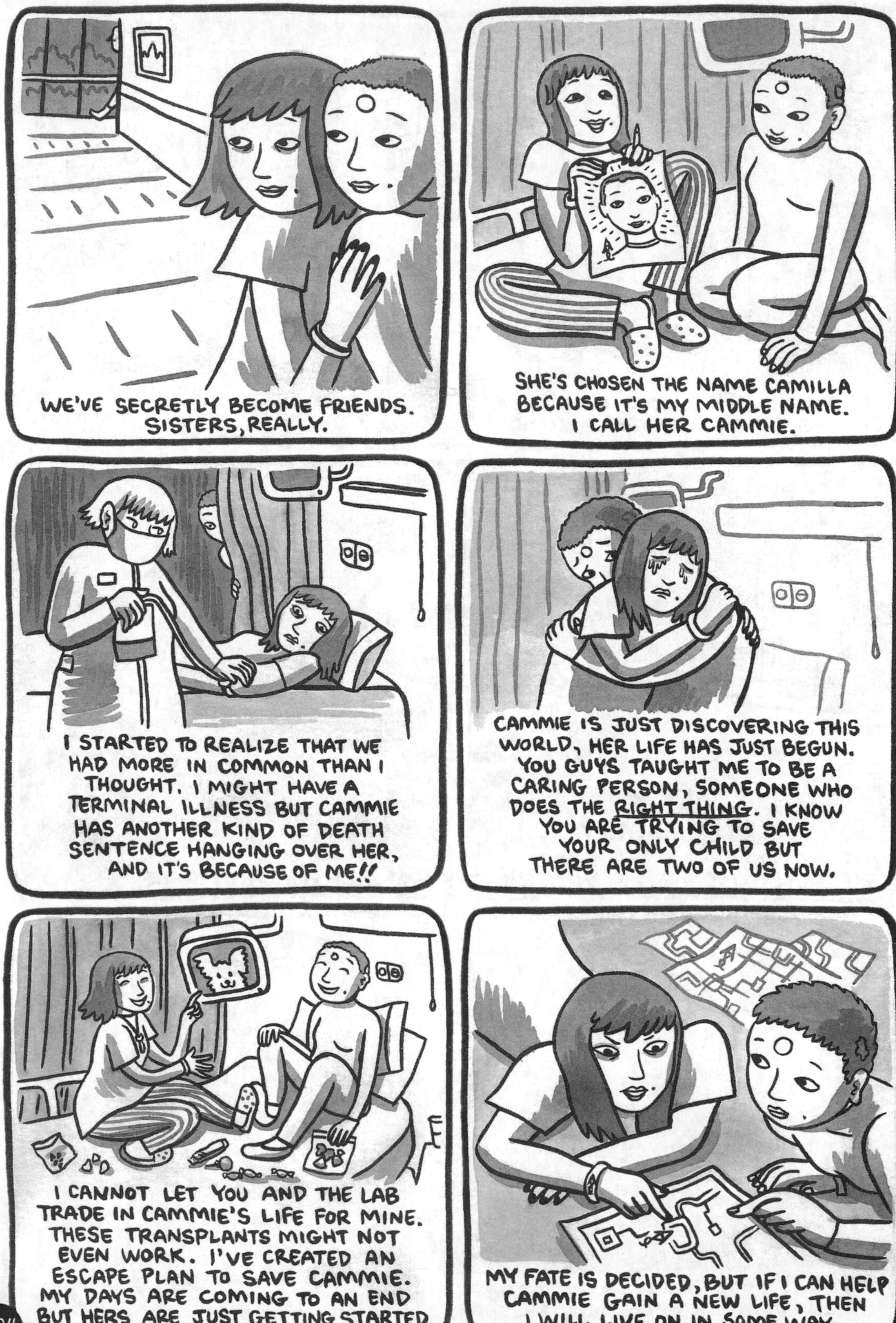
WE'VE SECRETLY BECOME FRIENDS. SISTERS, REALLY.
SHE'S CHOSEN THE NAME CAMILLA BECAUSE IT'S MY MIDDLE NAME. I CALL HER CAMMIE.
I STARTED TO REALIZE THAT WE HAD MORE IN COMMON THAN I THOUGHT. I MIGHT HAVE A TERMINAL ILLNESS BUT CAMMIE HAS ANOTHER KIND OF DEATH SENTENCE HANGING OVER HER, AND IT'S BECAUSE OF ME!!
CAMMIE IS JUST DISCOVERING THIS WORLD, HER LIFE HAS JUST BEGUN. YOU GUYS TAUGHT ME TO BE A CARING PERSON, SOMEONE WHO DOES THE RIGHT THING. I KNOW YOU ARE TRYING TO SAVE YOUR ONLY CHILD BUT THERE ARE TWO OF US NOW.
I CANNOT LET YOU AND THE LAB TRADE IN CAMMIE'S LIFE FOR MINE. THESE TRANSPLANTS MIGHT NOT EVEN WORK. I'VE CREATED AN ESCAPE PLAN TO SAVE CAMMIE. MY DAYS ARE COMING TO AN END BUT HERS ARE JUST GETTING STARTED.
MY FATE IS DECIDED, BUT IF I CAN HELP CAMMIE GAIN A NEW LIFE, THEN I WILL LIVE ON IN SOME WAY.

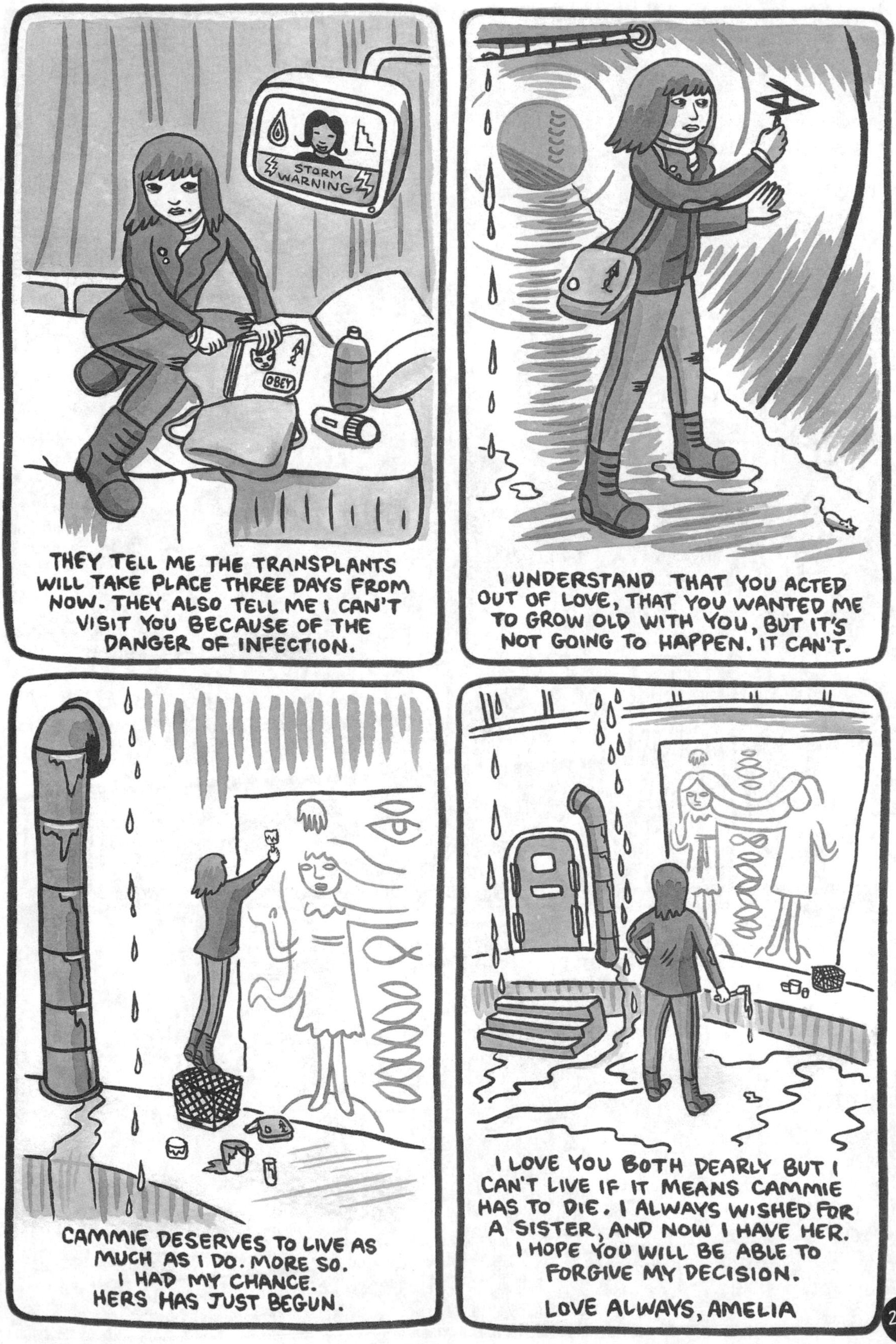
STORM WARNING
OBEY
THEY TELL ME THE TRANSPLANTS WILL TAKE PLACE THREE DAYS FROM NOW. THEY ALSO TELL ME I CAN'T VISIT YOU BECAUSE OF THE DANGER OF INFECTION.
I UNDERSTAND THAT YOU ACTED OUT OF LOVE, THAT YOU WANTED ME TO GROW OLD WITH YOU, BUT IT'S NOT GOING TO HAPPEN. IT CAN'T.
CAMMIE DESERVES TO LIVE AS MUCH AS I DO. MORE SO. I HAD MY CHANCE. HERS HAS JUST BEGUN.
I LOVE YOU BOTH DEARLY BUT I CAN'T LIVE IF IT MEANS CAMMIE HAS TO DIE. I ALWAYS WISHED FOR A SISTER, AND NOW I HAVE HER. I HOPE YOU WILL BE ABLE TO FORGIVE MY DECISION.
LOVE ALWAYS, AMELIA

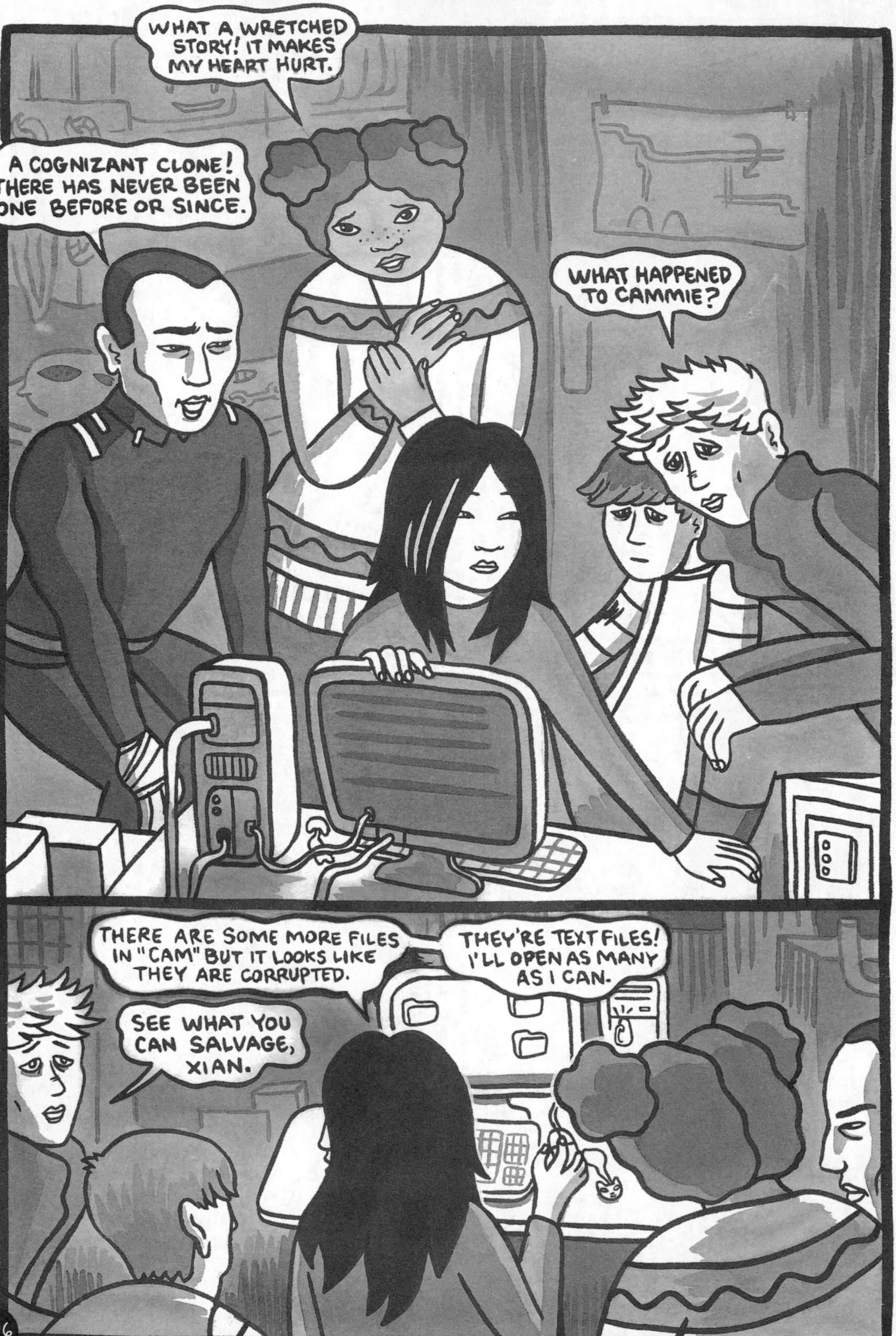
A COGNIZANT CLONE! THERE HAS NEVER BEEN ONE BEFORE OR SINCE.
WHAT A WRETCHED STORY! IT MAKES MY HEART HURT.
WHAT HAPPENED TO CAMMIE?
THERE ARE SOME MORE FILES IN "CAM" BUT IT LOOKS LIKE THEY ARE CORRUPTED.
THEY'RE TEXT FILES! I'LL OPEN AS MANY AS I CAN.
SEE WHAT YOU CAN SALVAGE, XIAN.

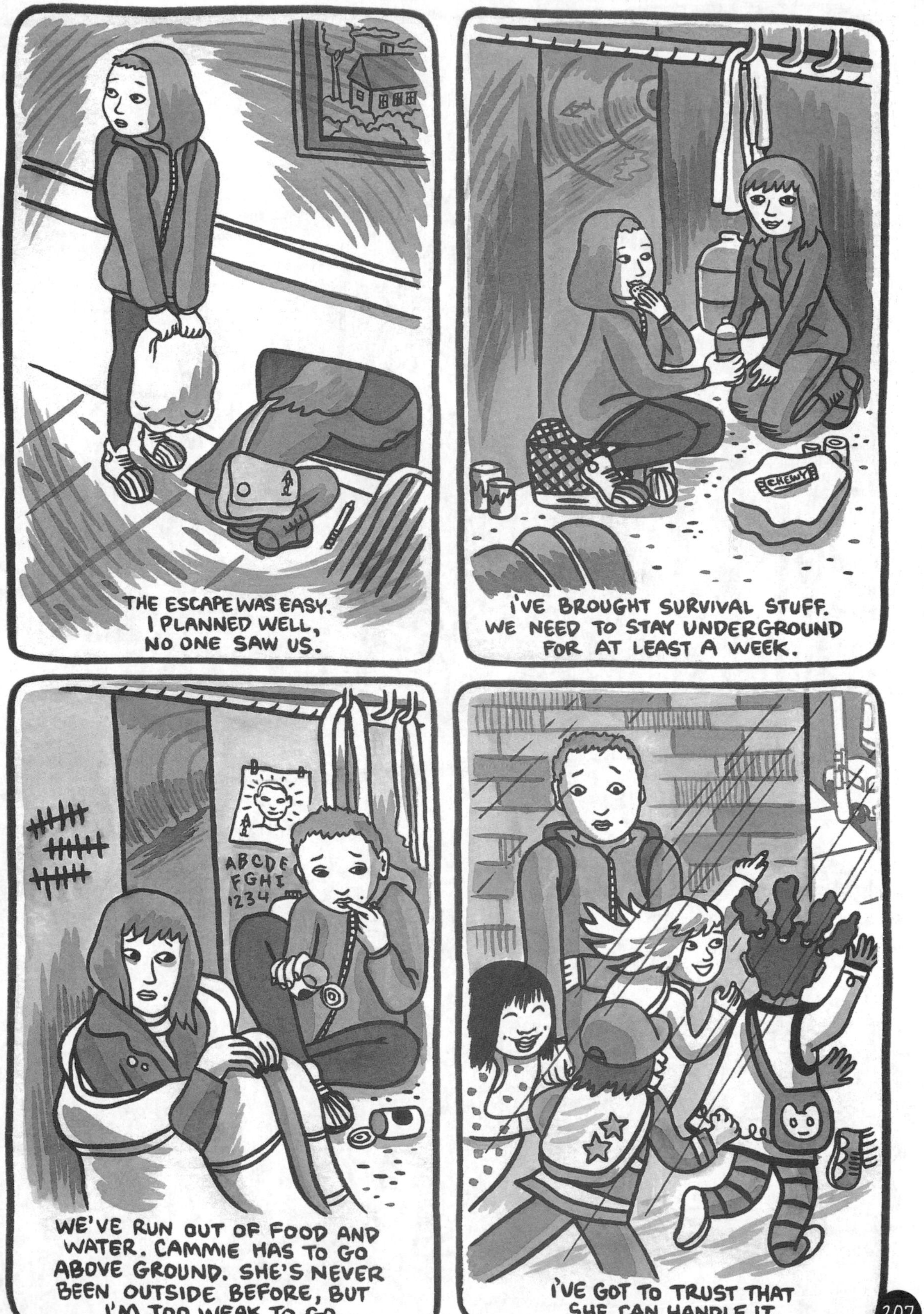
THE ESCAPE WAS EASY. I PLANNED WELL, NO ONE SAW US.
CHEWY
I'VE BROUGHT SURVIVAL STUFF. WE NEED TO STAY UNDERGROUND FOR AT LEAST A WEEK.
ABCDE
FGHI
1234
WE'VE RUN OUT OF FOOD AND WATER. CAMMIE HAS TO GO ABOVE GROUND. SHE'S NEVER BEEN OUTSIDE BEFORE, BUT I'M TOO WEAK TO GO.
I'VE GOT TO TRUST THAT SHE CAN HANDLE IT.

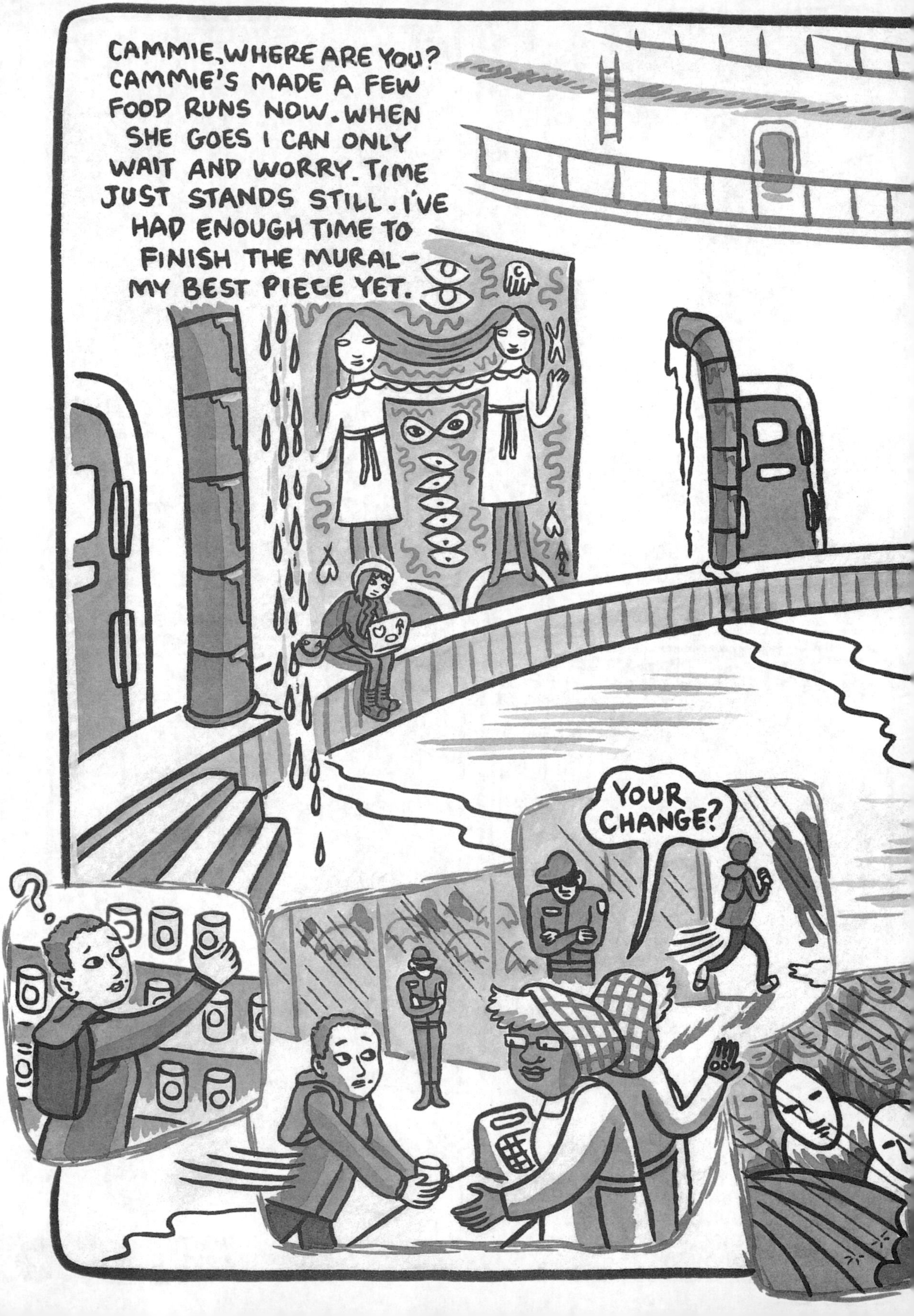
CAMMIE, WHERE ARE YOU? CAMMIE'S MADE A FEW FOOD RUNS NOW. WHEN SHE GOES I CAN ONLY WAIT AND WORRY. TIME JUST STANDS STILL. I'VE HAD ENOUGH TIME TO FINISH THE MURAL— MY BEST PIECE YET.
?
YOUR CHANGE?

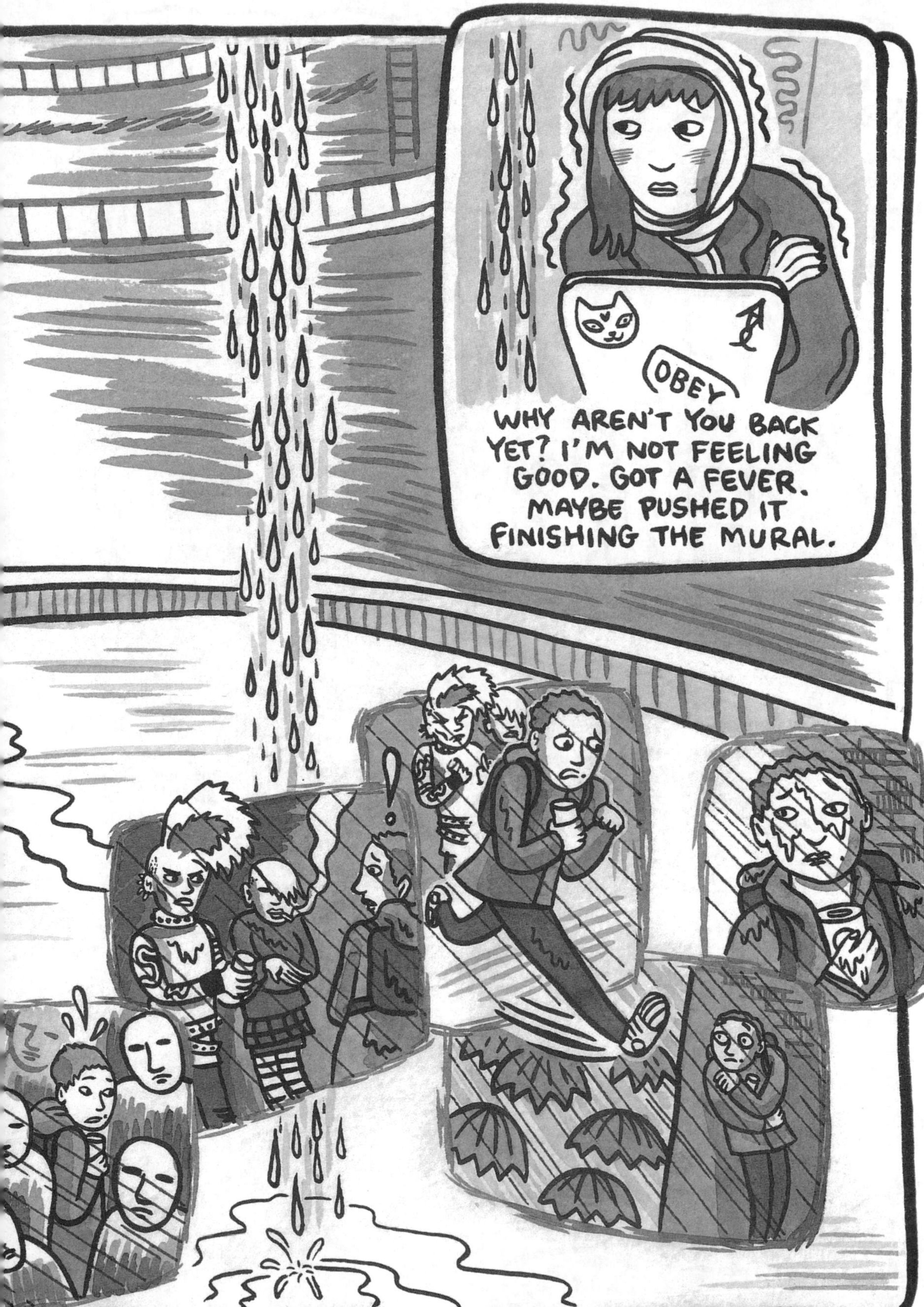

OBEY
WHY AREN'T YOU BACK YET? I'M NOT FEELING GOOD. GOT A FEVER. MAYBE PUSHED IT FINISHING THE MURAL.

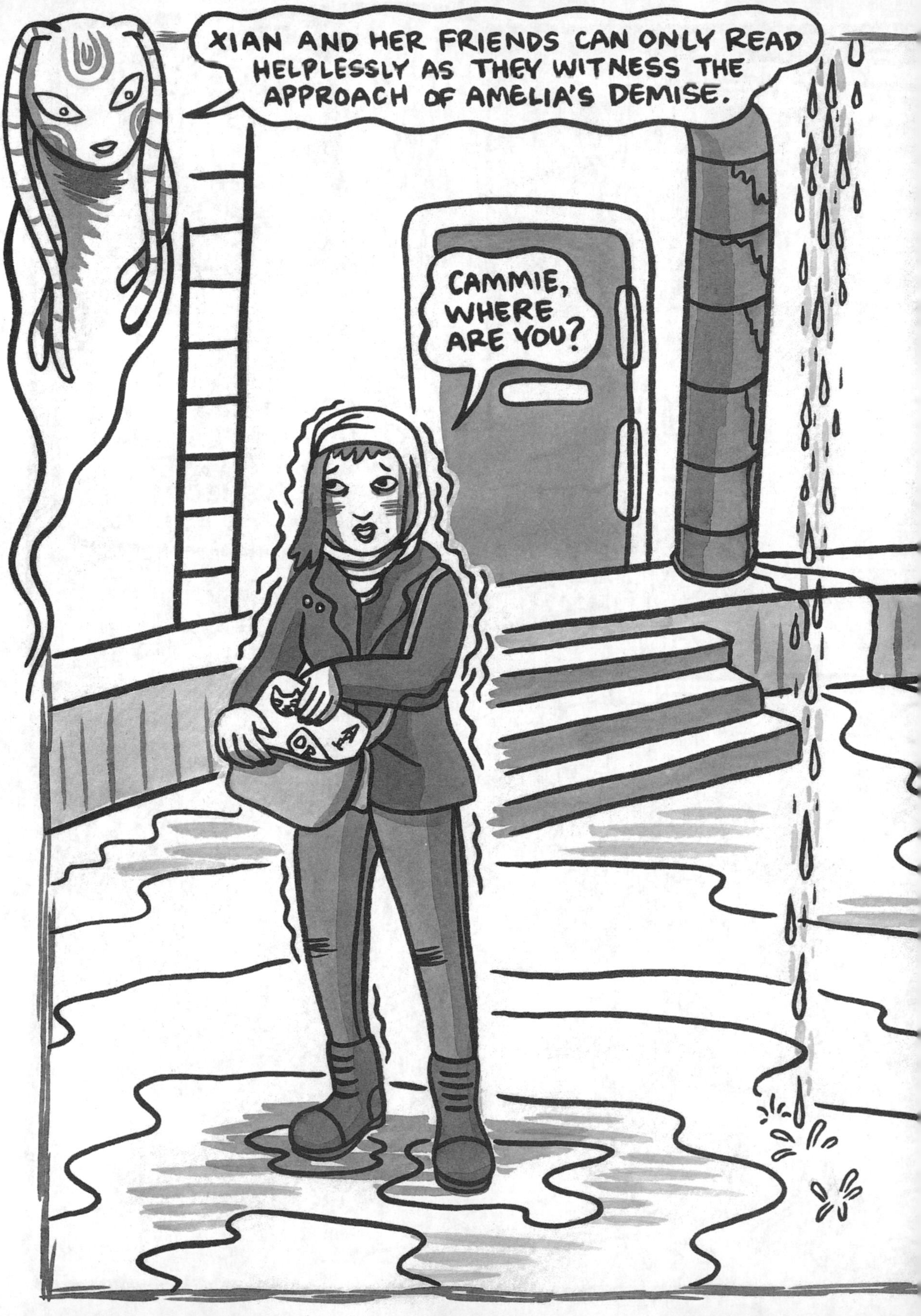
XIAN AND HER FRIENDS CAN ONLY READ HELPLESSLY AS THEY WITNESS THE APPROACH OF AMELIA'S DEMISE.
CAMMIE, WHERE ARE YOU?

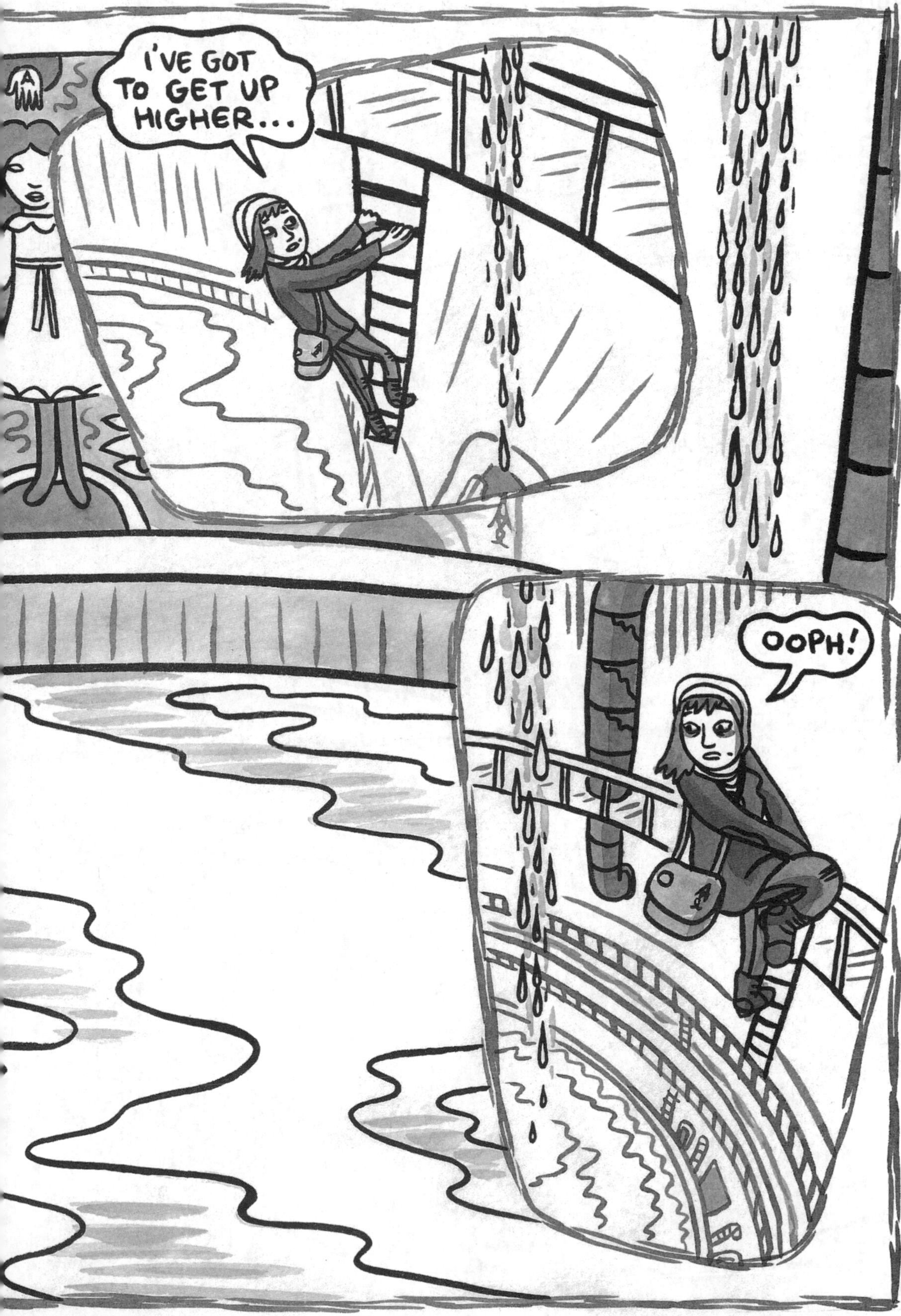
I'VE GOT TO GET UP HIGHER...
OOPH!

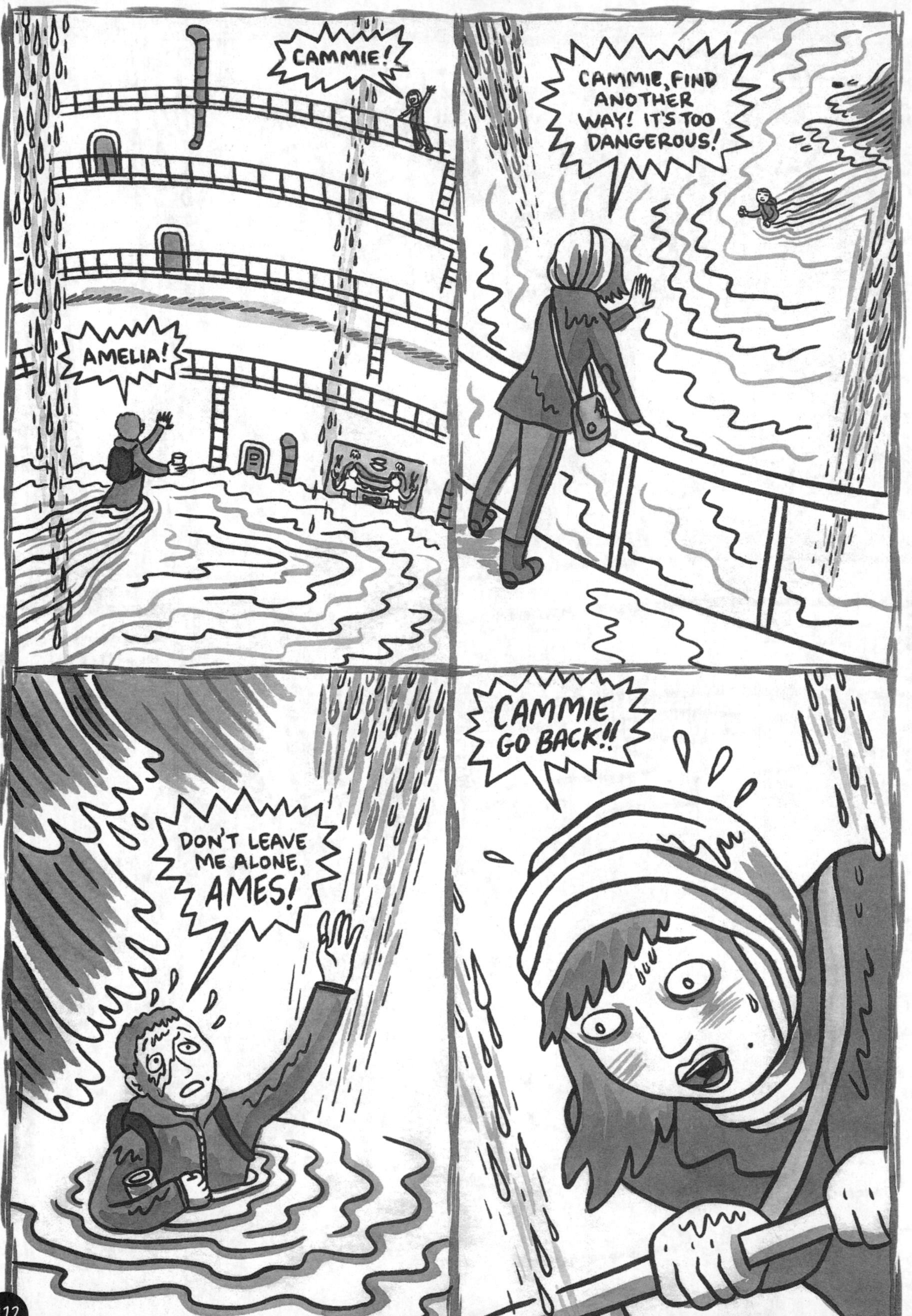
CAMMIE!
AMELIA!
CAMMIE, FIND ANOTHER WAY! IT'S TOO DANGEROUS!
DON'T LEAVE ME ALONE, AMES!
CAMMIE GO BACK!!

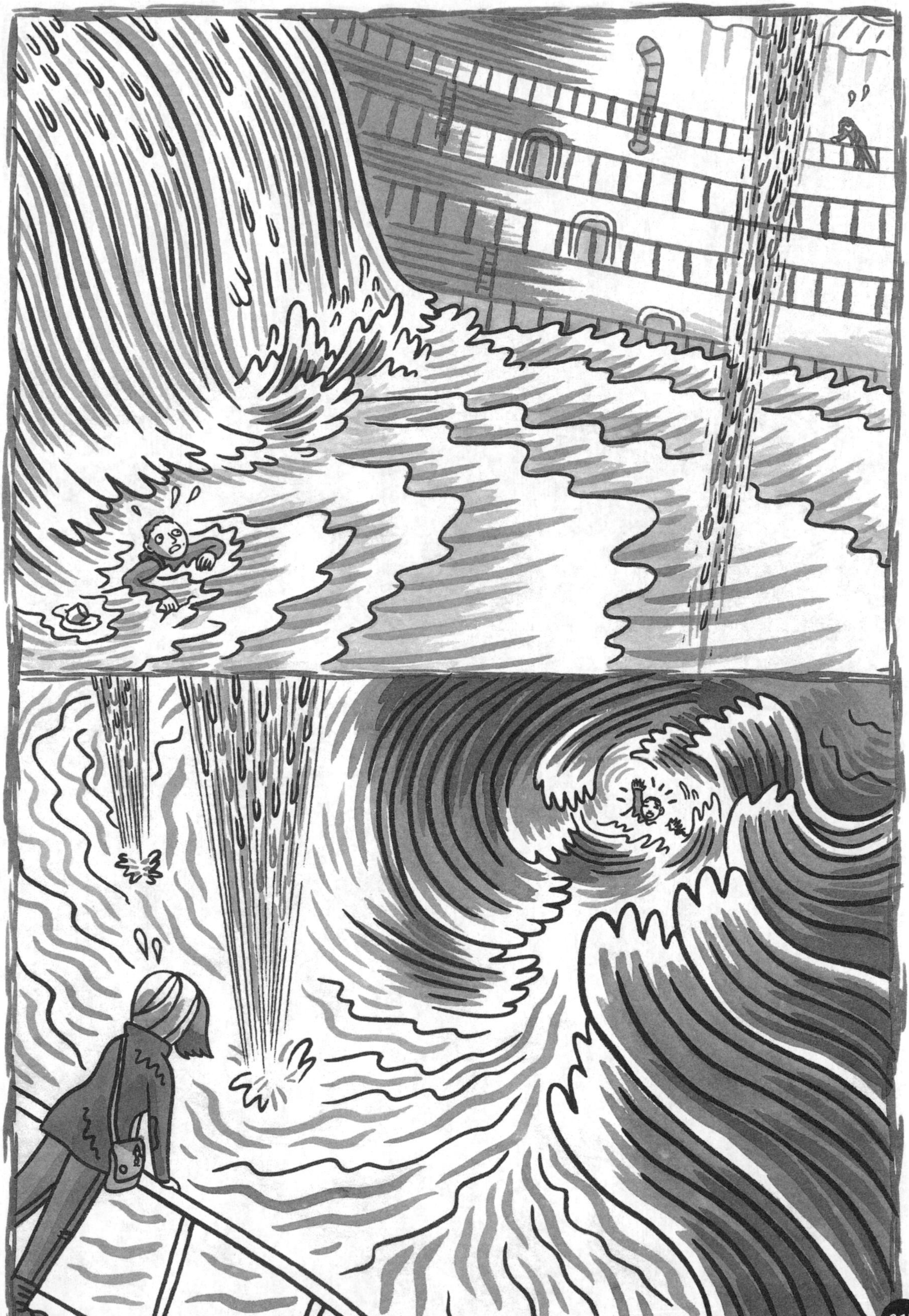

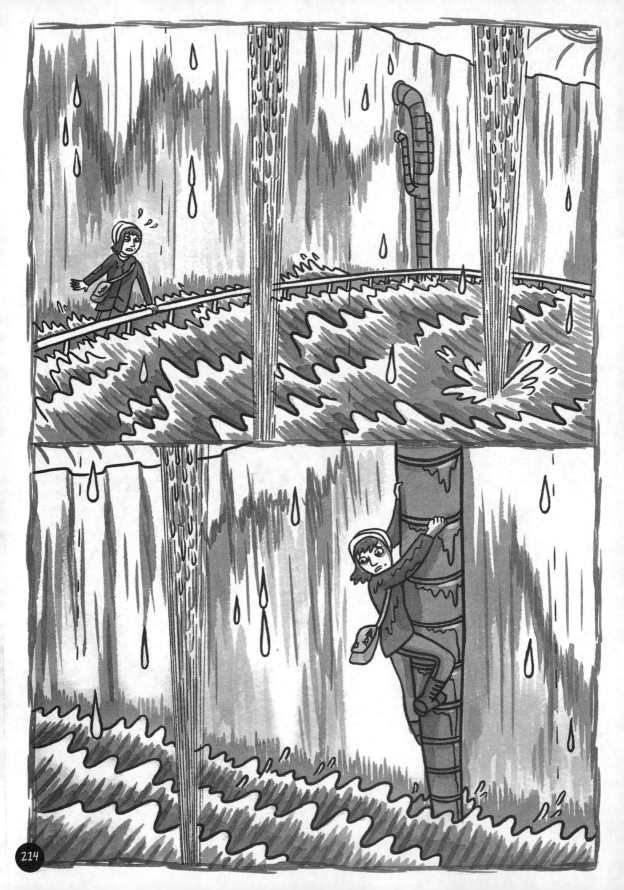

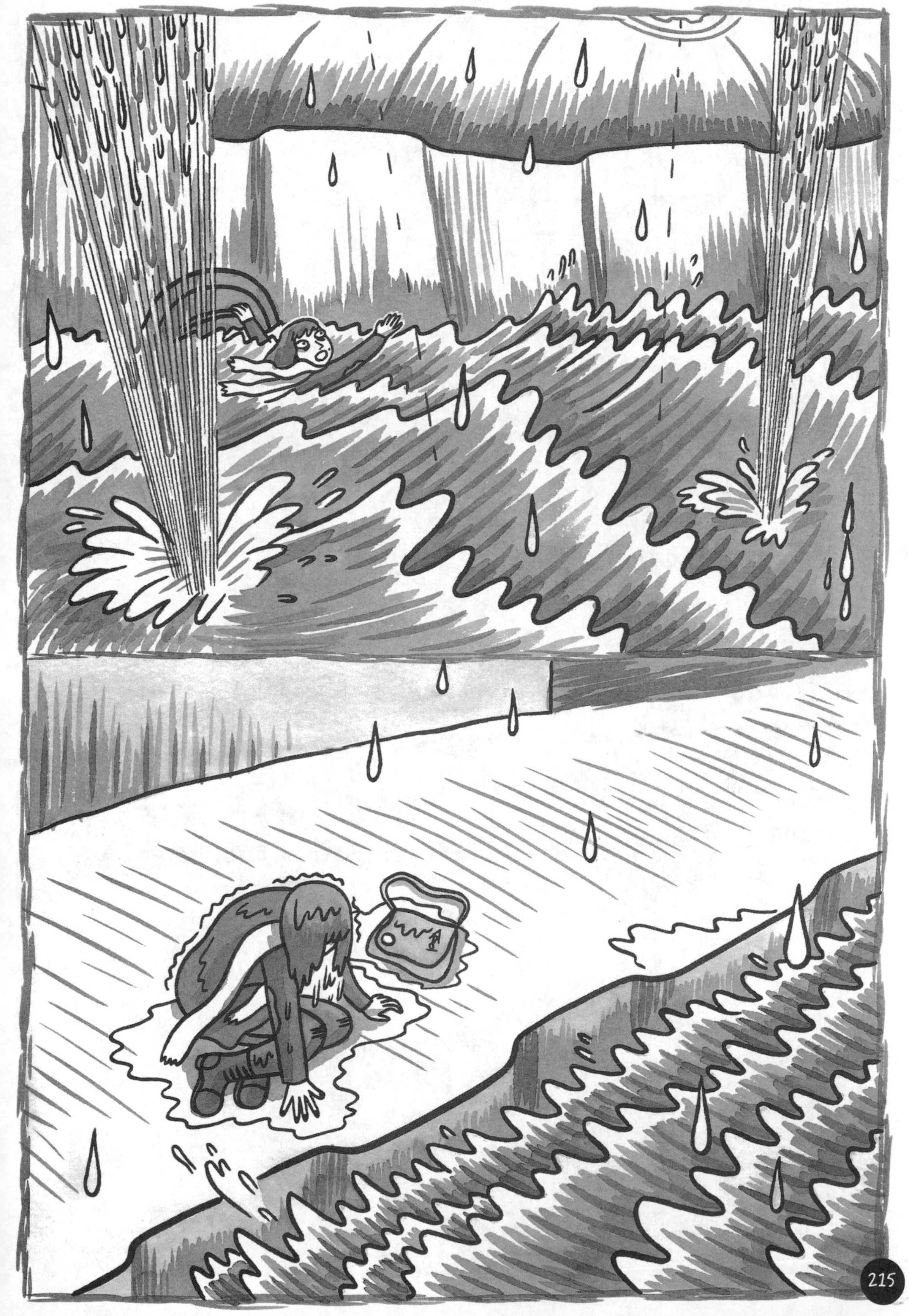

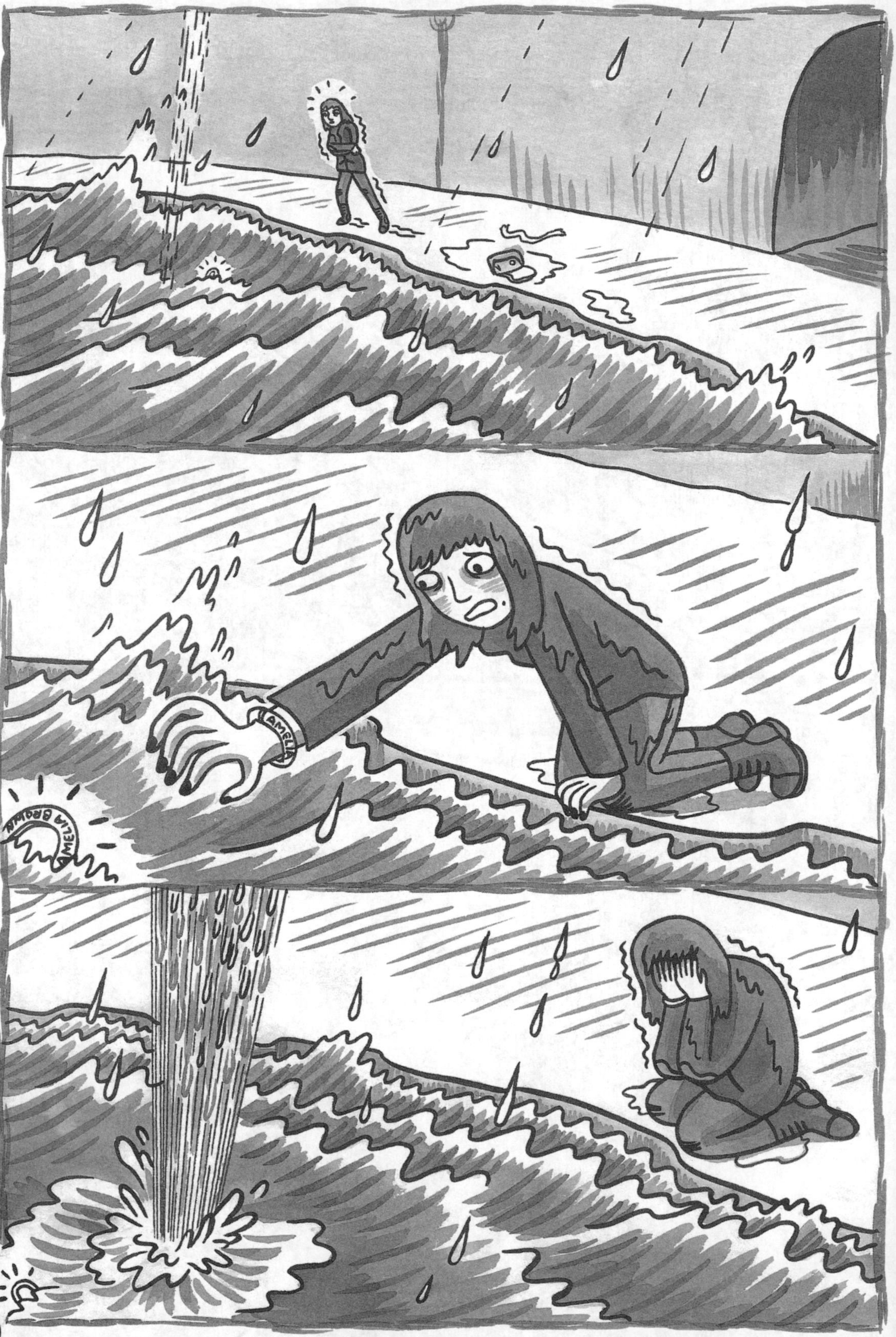
AMELIA
AMELIA BROWN

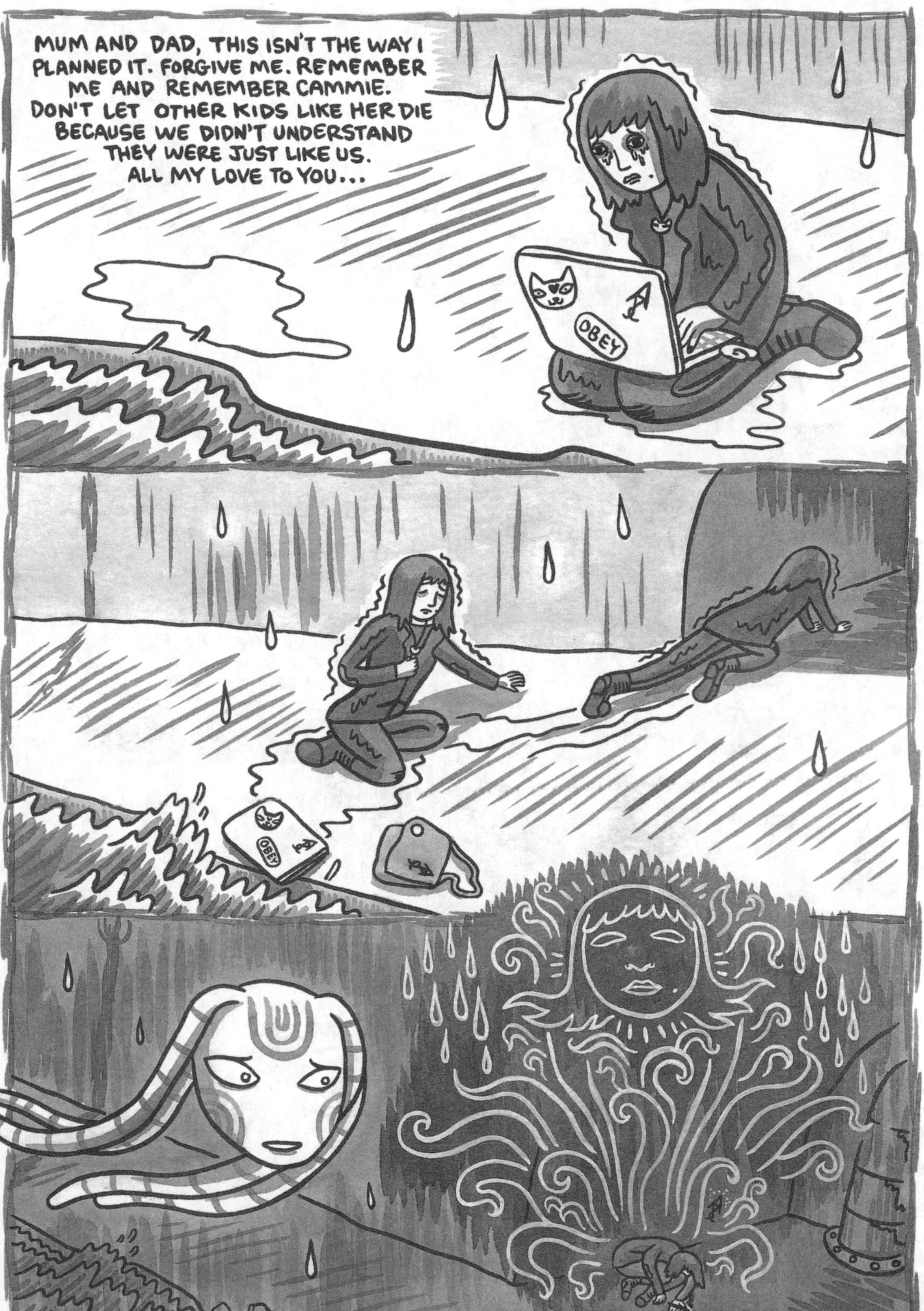
MUM AND DAD, THIS ISN'T THE WAY I PLANNED IT. FORGIVE ME. REMEMBER ME AND REMEMBER CAMMIE. DON'T LET OTHER KIDS LIKE HER DIE BECAUSE WE DIDN'T UNDERSTAND THEY WERE JUST LIKE US. ALL MY LOVE TO YOU...
OBEY
OBEY

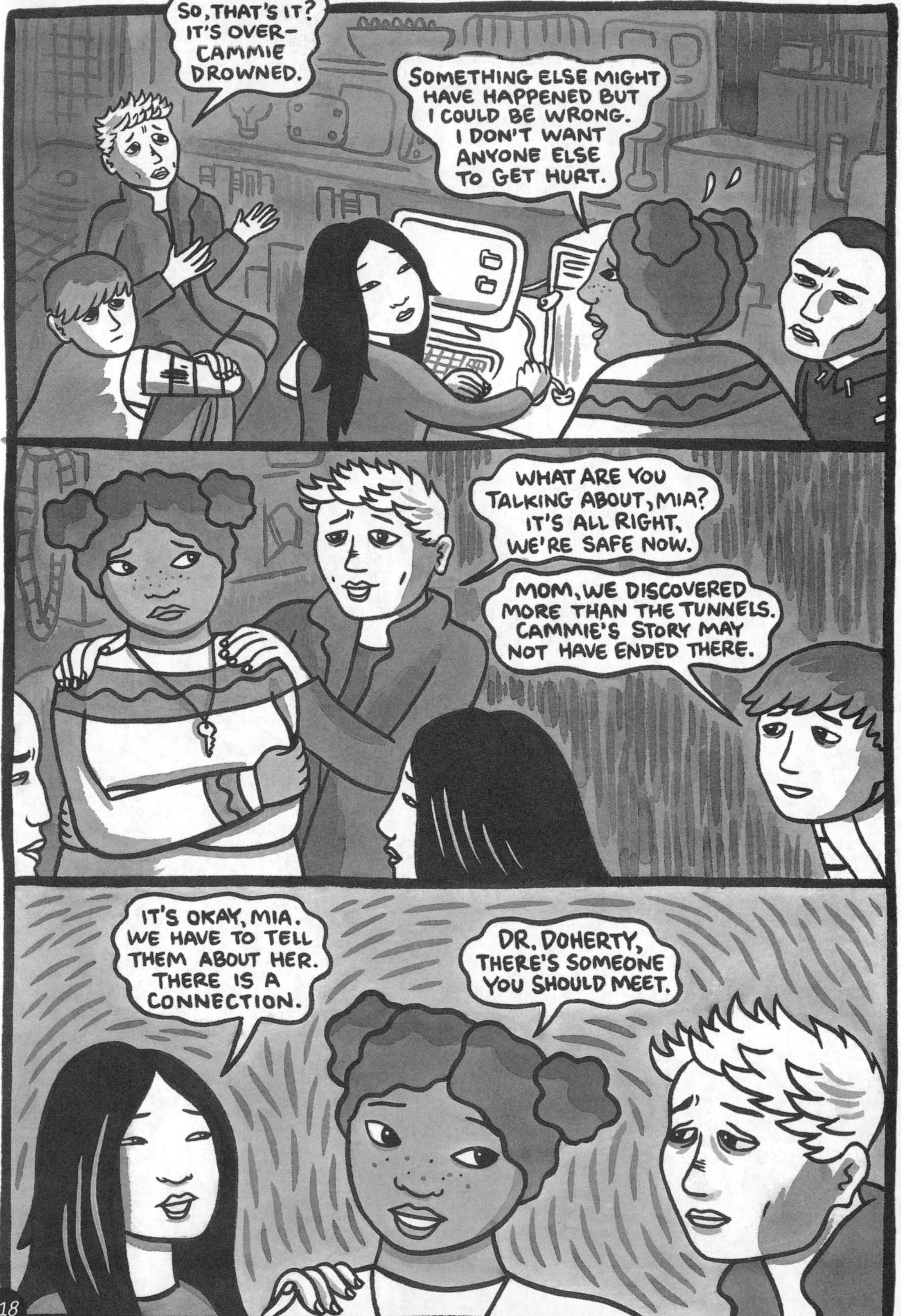
SO, THAT'S IT? IT'S OVER— CAMMIE DROWNED.
SOMETHING ELSE MIGHT HAVE HAPPENED BUT I COULD BE WRONG. I DON'T WANT ANYONE ELSE TO GET HURT.
WHAT ARE YOU TALKING ABOUT, MIA? IT'S ALL RIGHT, WE'RE SAFE NOW.
MOM, WE DISCOVERED MORE THAN THE TUNNELS. CAMMIE'S STORY MAY NOT HAVE ENDED THERE.
IT'S OKAY, MIA. WE HAVE TO TELL THEM ABOUT HER. THERE IS A CONNECTION.
DR. DOHERTY, THERE'S SOMEONE YOU SHOULD MEET.

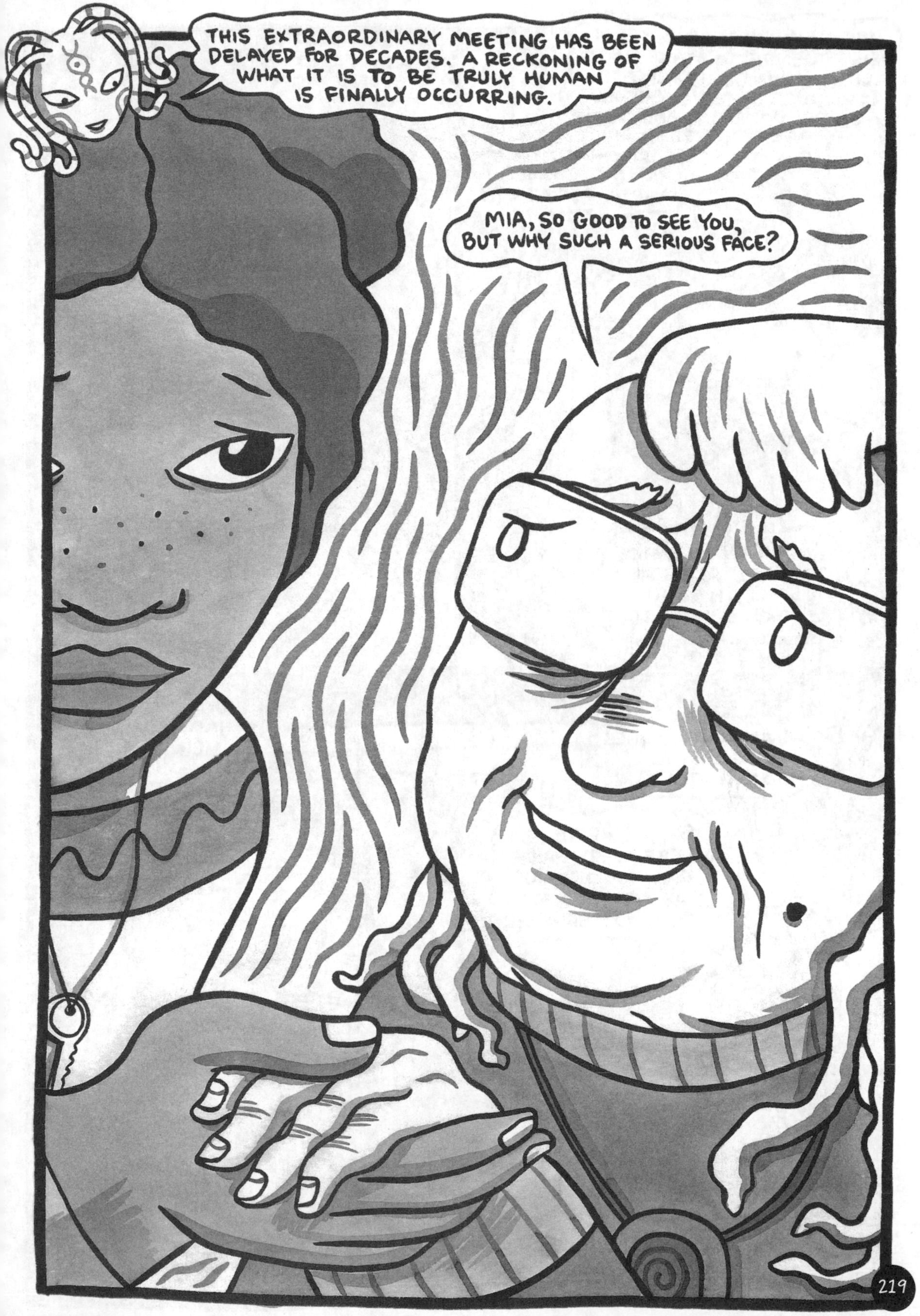
THIS EXTRAORDINARY MEETING HAS BEEN DELAYED FOR DECADES. A RECKONING OF WHAT IT IS TO BE TRULY HUMAN IS FINALLY OCCURRING.
MIA, SO GOOD TO SEE YOU, BUT WHY SUCH A SERIOUS FACE?

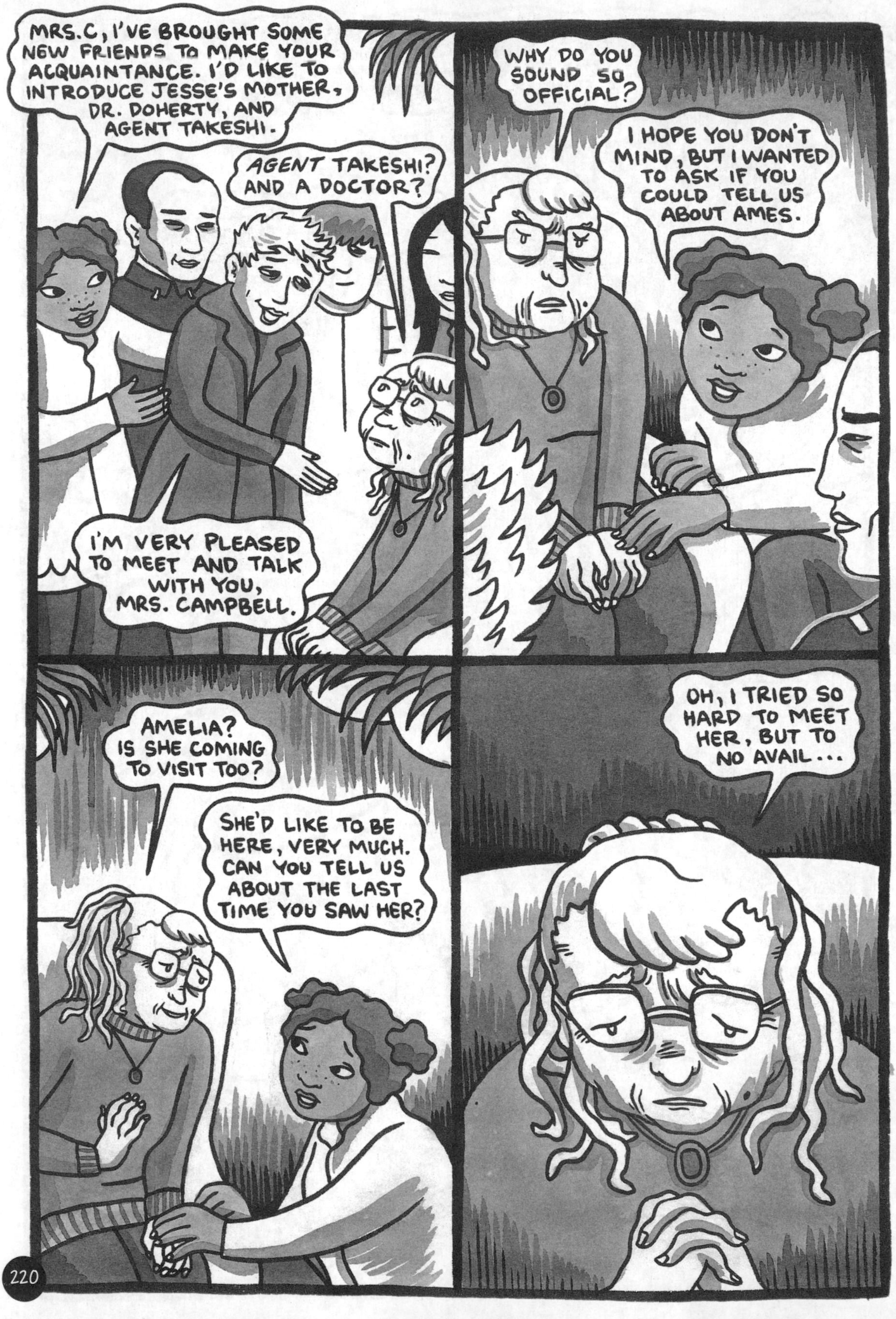
MRS. C, I'VE BROUGHT SOME NEW FRIENDS TO MAKE YOUR ACQUAINTANCE. I'D LIKE TO INTRODUCE JESSE'S MOTHER, DR. DOHERTY, AND AGENT TAKESHI.
AGENT TAKESHI? AND A DOCTOR?
I'M VERY PLEASED TO MEET AND TALK WITH YOU, MRS. CAMPBELL.
WHY DO YOU SOUND SO OFFICIAL?
I HOPE YOU DON'T MIND, BUT I WANTED TO ASK IF YOU COULD TELL US ABOUT AMES.
AMELIA? IS SHE COMING TO VISIT TOO?
SHE'D LIKE TO BE HERE, VERY MUCH. CAN YOU TELL US ABOUT THE LAST TIME YOU SAW HER?
OH, I TRIED SO HARD TO MEET HER, BUT TO NO AVAIL...

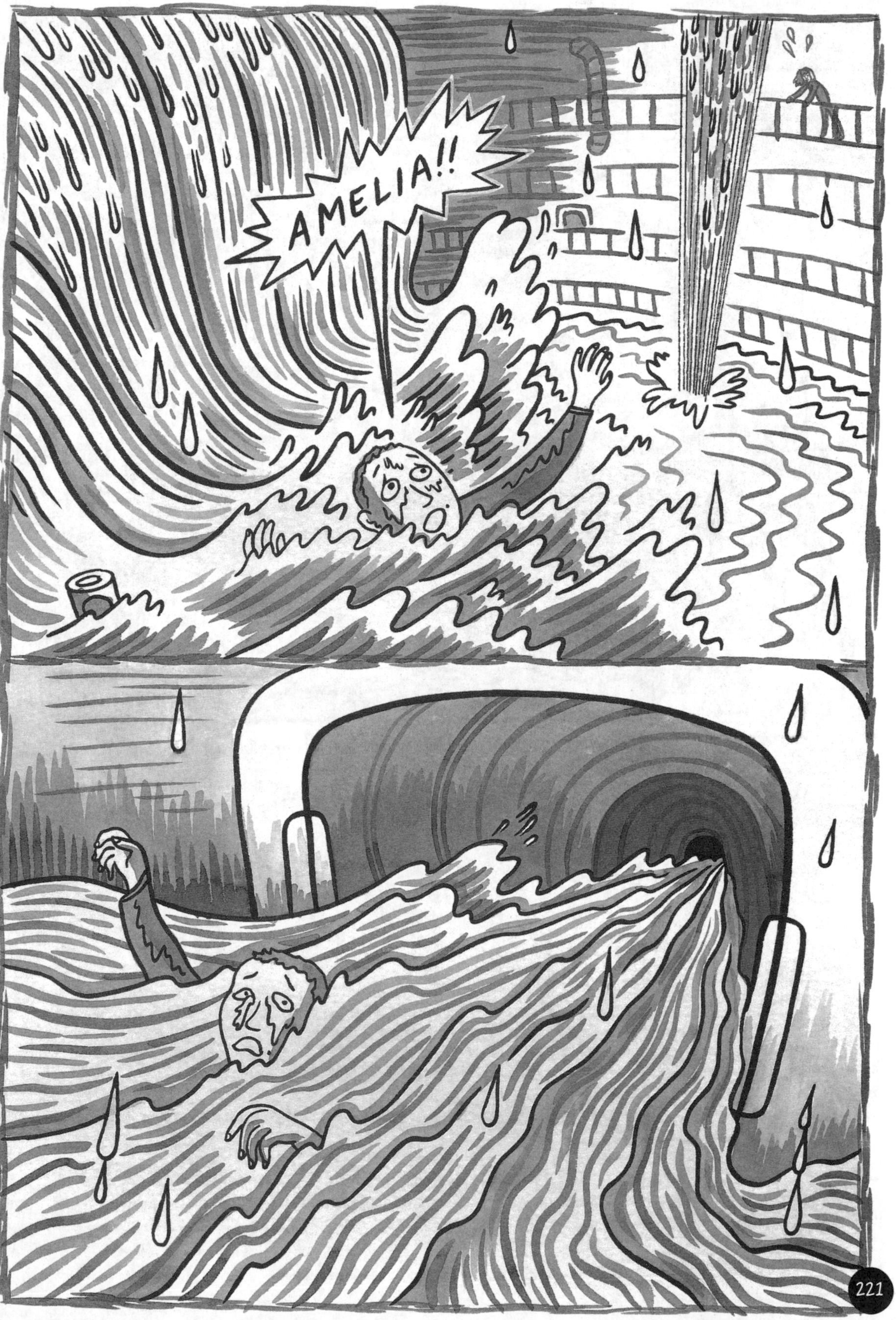
AMELIA!!

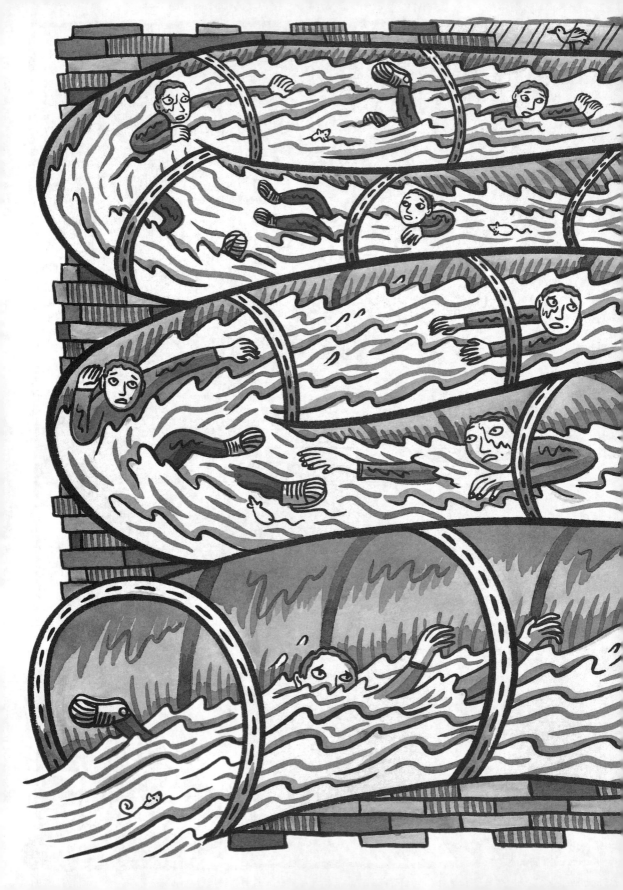

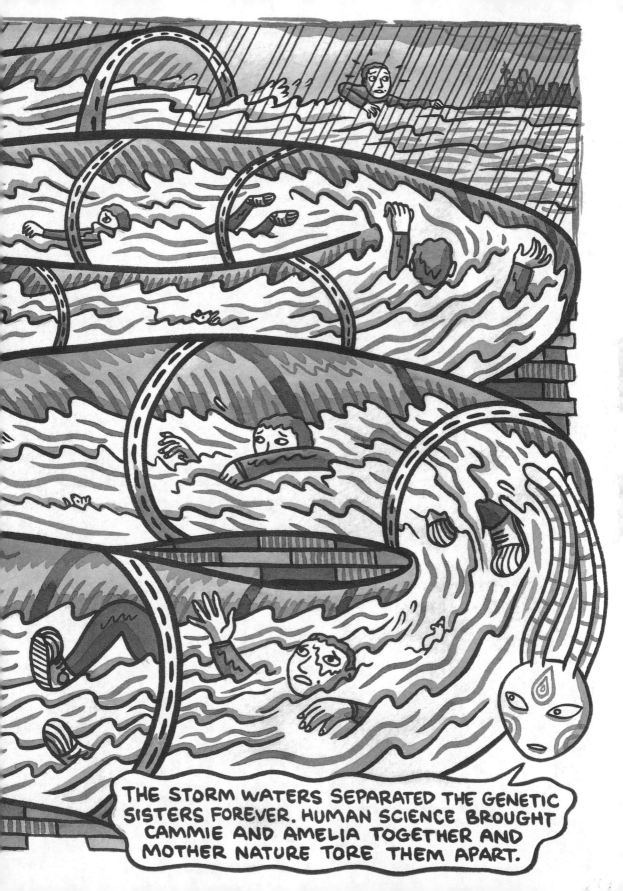

THE STORM WATERS SEPARATED THE GENETIC SISTERS FOREVER. HUMAN SCIENCE BROUGHT CAMMIE AND AMELIA TOGETHER AND MOTHER NATURE TORE THEM APART.

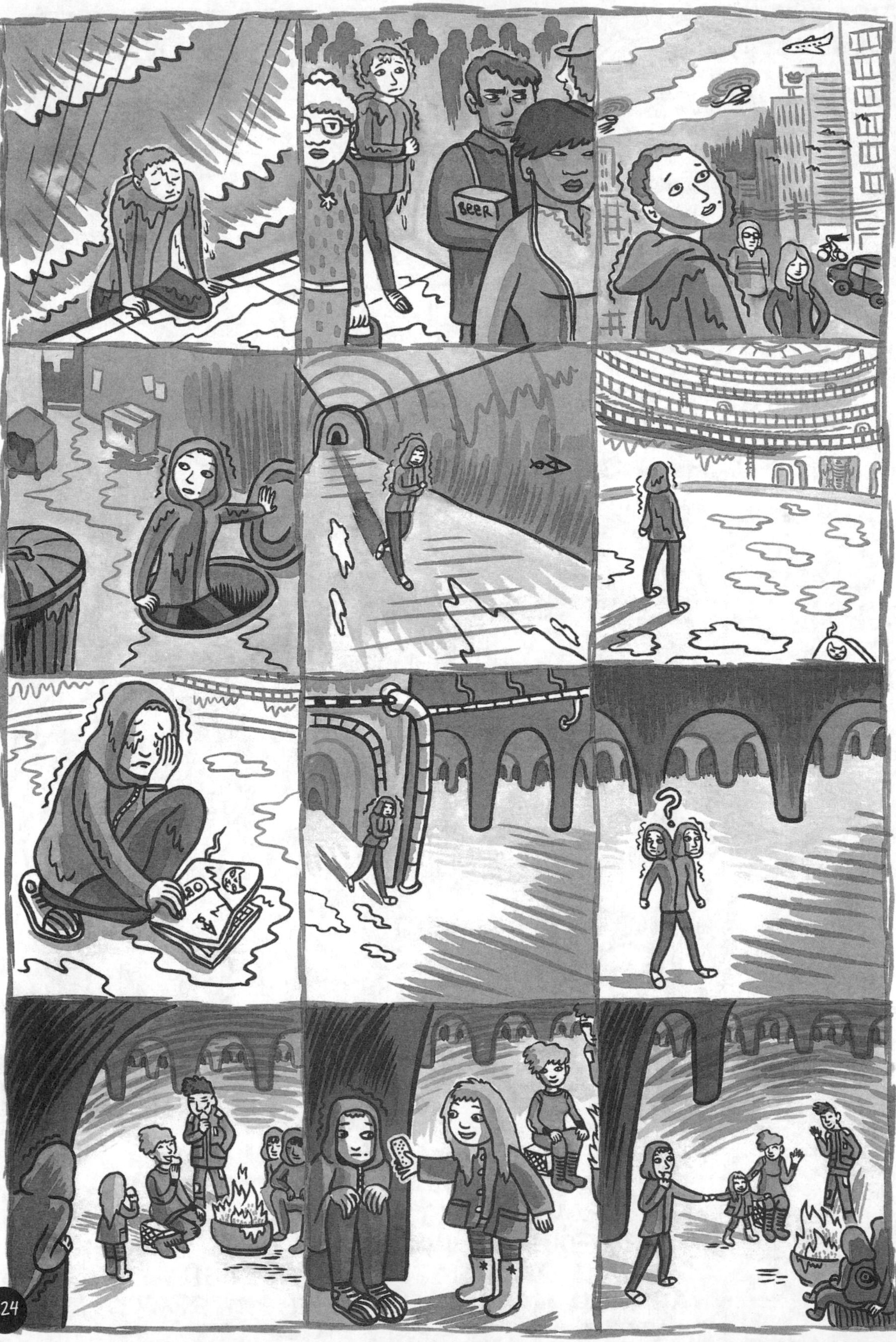
BEER

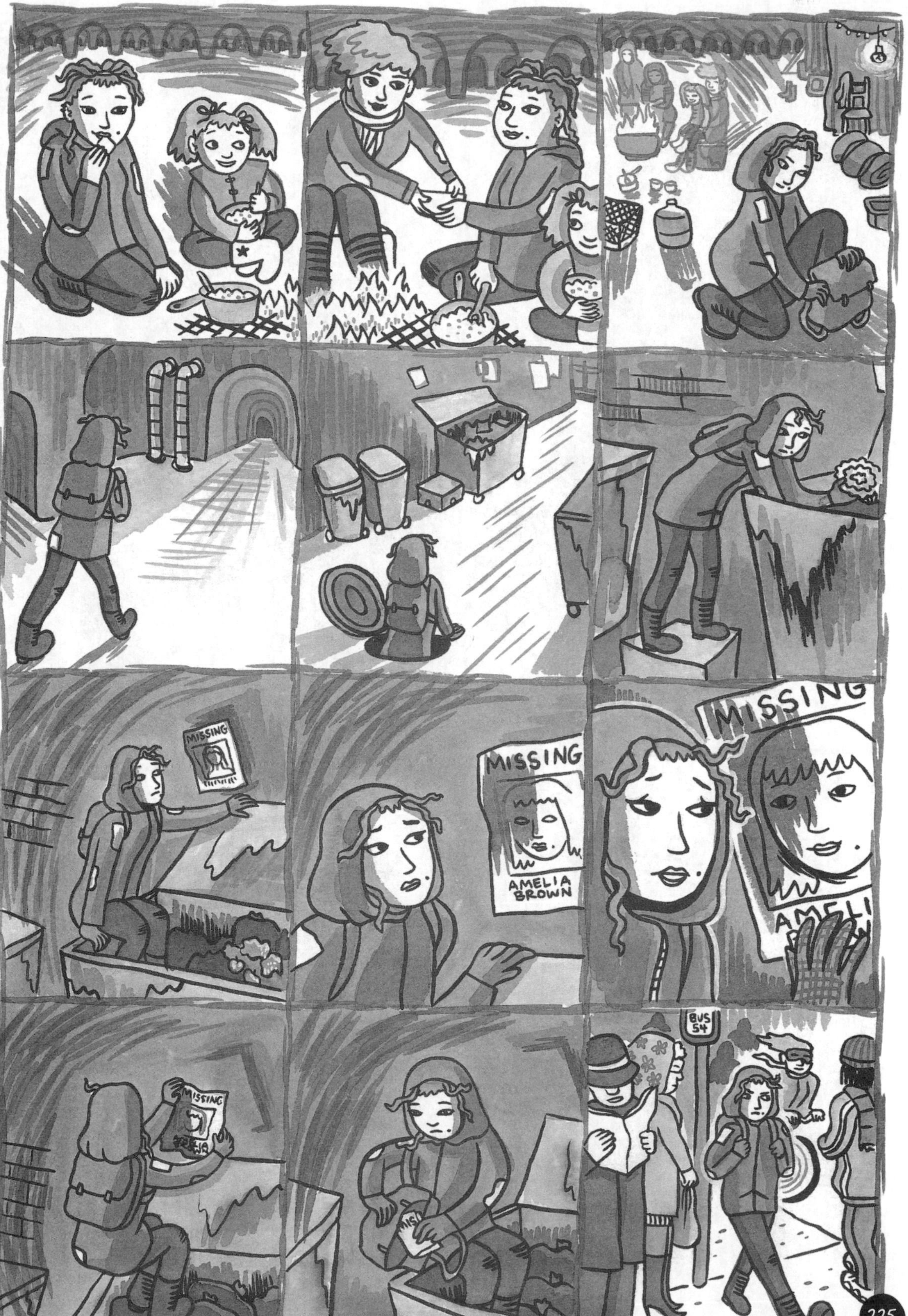
MISSING
MISSING
AMELIA BROWN
MISSING
AMELI
MISSING
BUS 54

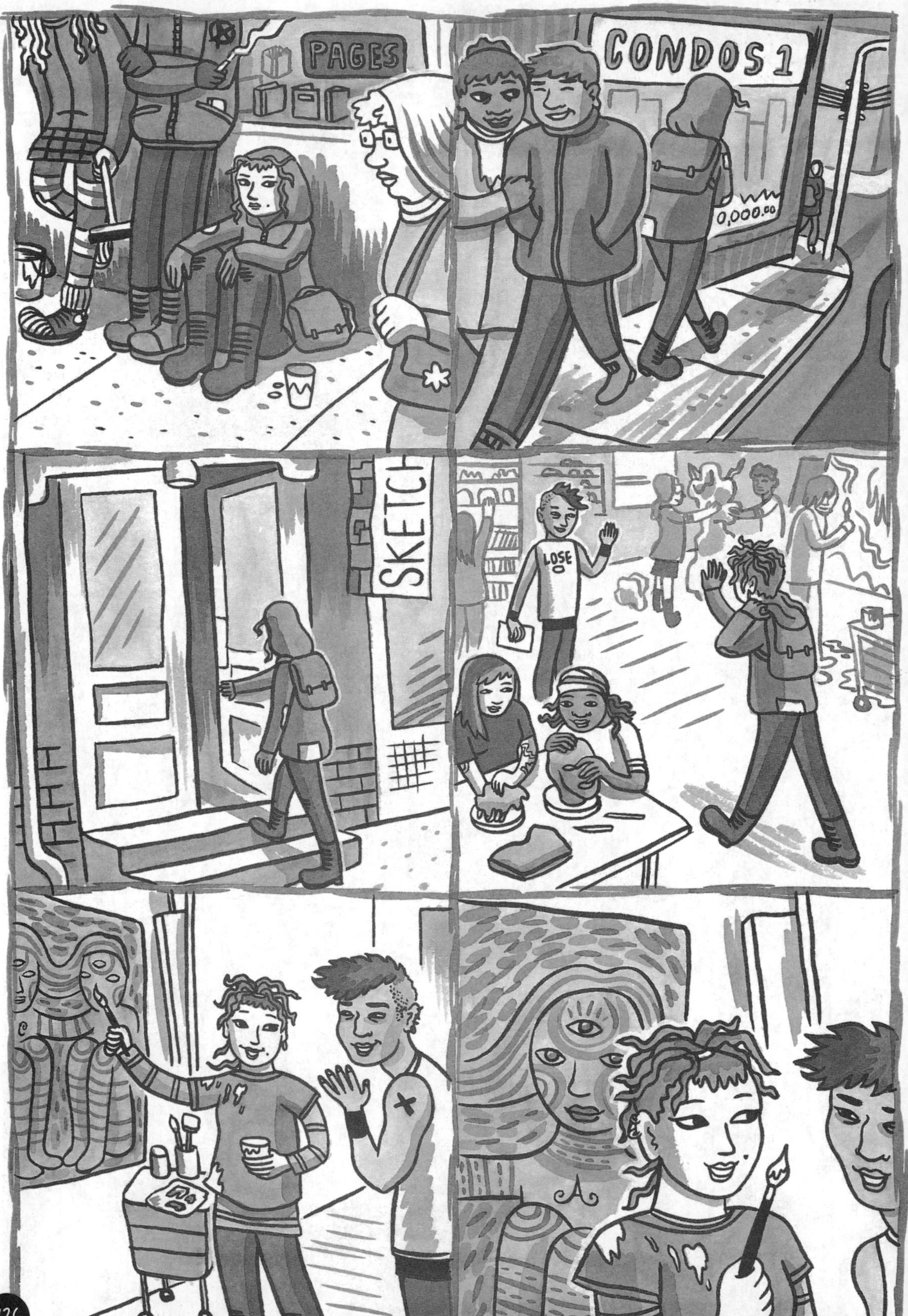
PAGES
CONDOS 1
0,000.00
SKETCH
LOSE

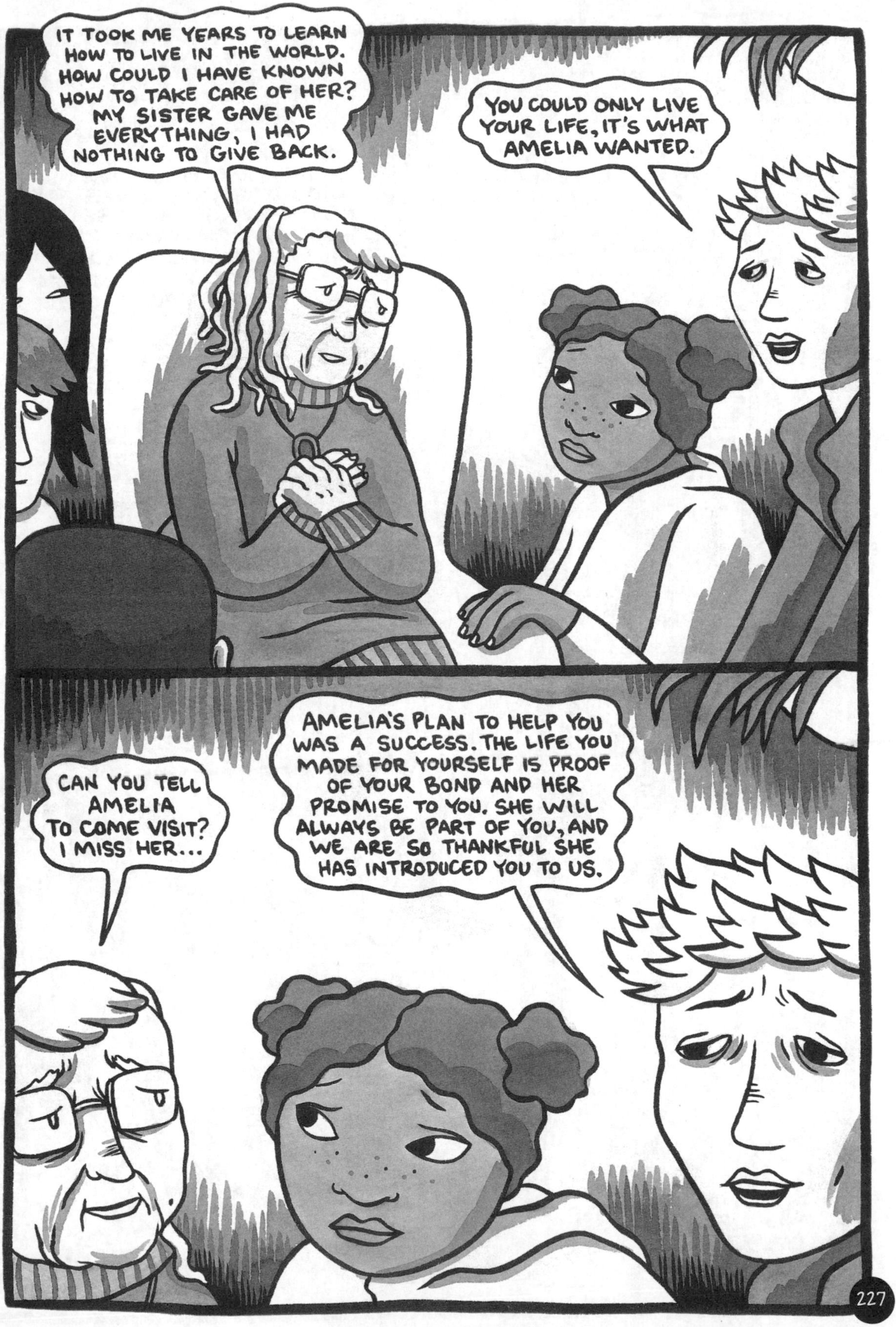
IT TOOK ME YEARS TO LEARN HOW TO LIVE IN THE WORLD. HOW COULD I HAVE KNOWN HOW TO TAKE CARE OF HER? MY SISTER GAVE ME EVERYTHING, I HAD NOTHING TO GIVE BACK.
YOU COULD ONLY LIVE YOUR LIFE, IT'S WHAT AMELIA WANTED.
CAN YOU TELL AMELIA TO COME VISIT? I MISS HER...
AMELIA'S PLAN TO HELP YOU WAS A SUCCESS. THE LIFE YOU MADE FOR YOURSELF IS PROOF OF YOUR BOND AND HER PROMISE TO YOU. SHE WILL ALWAYS BE PART OF YOU, AND WE ARE SO THANKFUL SHE HAS INTRODUCED YOU TO US.

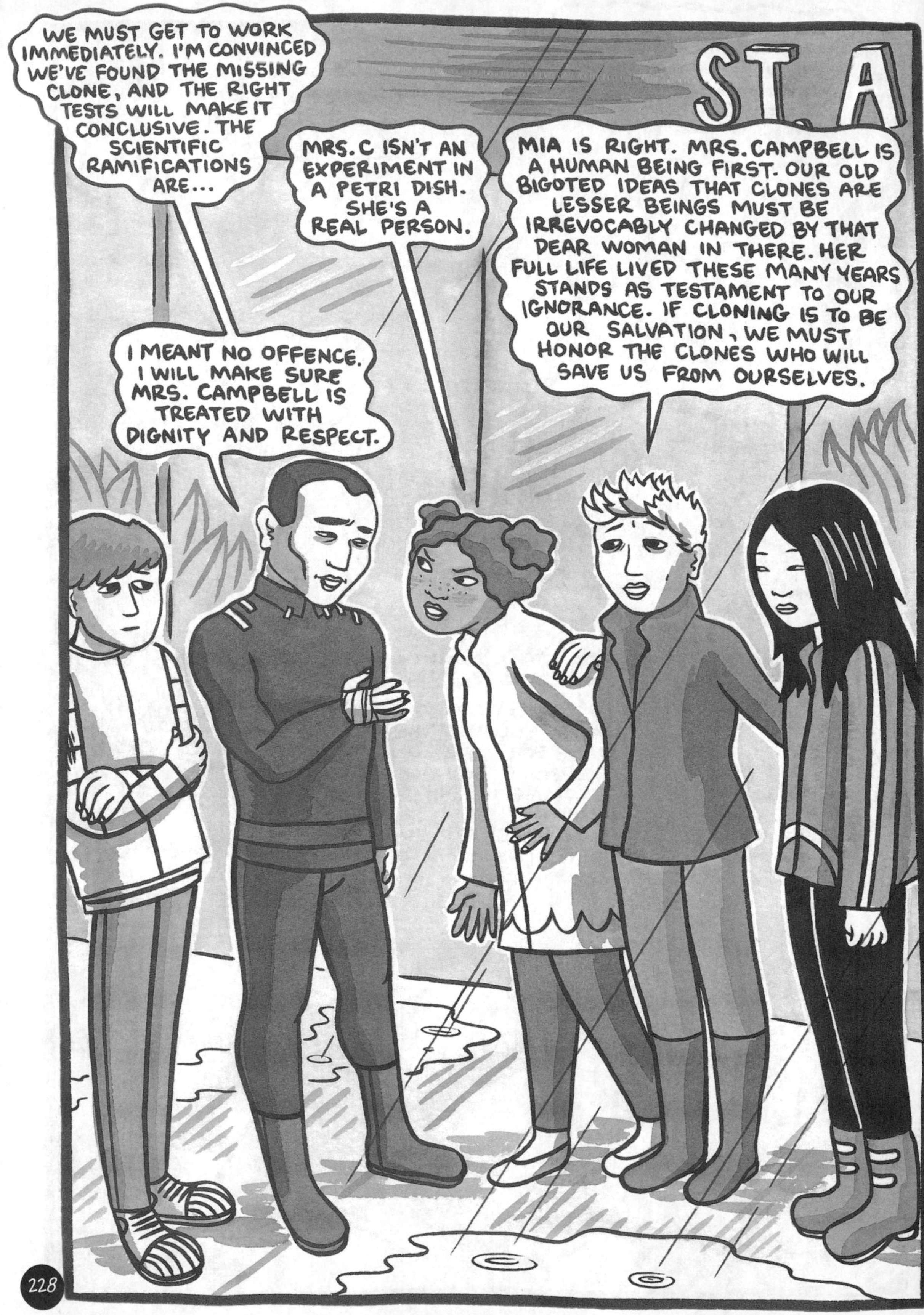
ST. A
WE MUST GET TO WORK IMMEDIATELY. I'M CONVINCED WE'VE FOUND THE MISSING CLONE, AND THE RIGHT TESTS WILL MAKE IT CONCLUSIVE. THE SCIENTIFIC RAMIFICATIONS ARE...
MRS. C ISN'T AN EXPERIMENT IN A PETRI DISH. SHE'S A REAL PERSON.
MIA IS RIGHT. MRS. CAMPBELL IS A HUMAN BEING FIRST. OUR OLD BIGOTED IDEAS THAT CLONES ARE LESSER BEINGS MUST BE IRREVOCABLY CHANGED BY THAT DEAR WOMAN IN THERE. HER FULL LIFE LIVED THESE MANY YEARS STANDS AS TESTAMENT TO OUR IGNORANCE. IF CLONING IS TO BE OUR SALVATION, WE MUST HONOR THE CLONES WHO WILL SAVE US FROM OURSELVES.
I MEANT NO OFFENCE. I WILL MAKE SURE MRS. CAMPBELL IS TREATED WITH DIGNITY AND RESPECT.

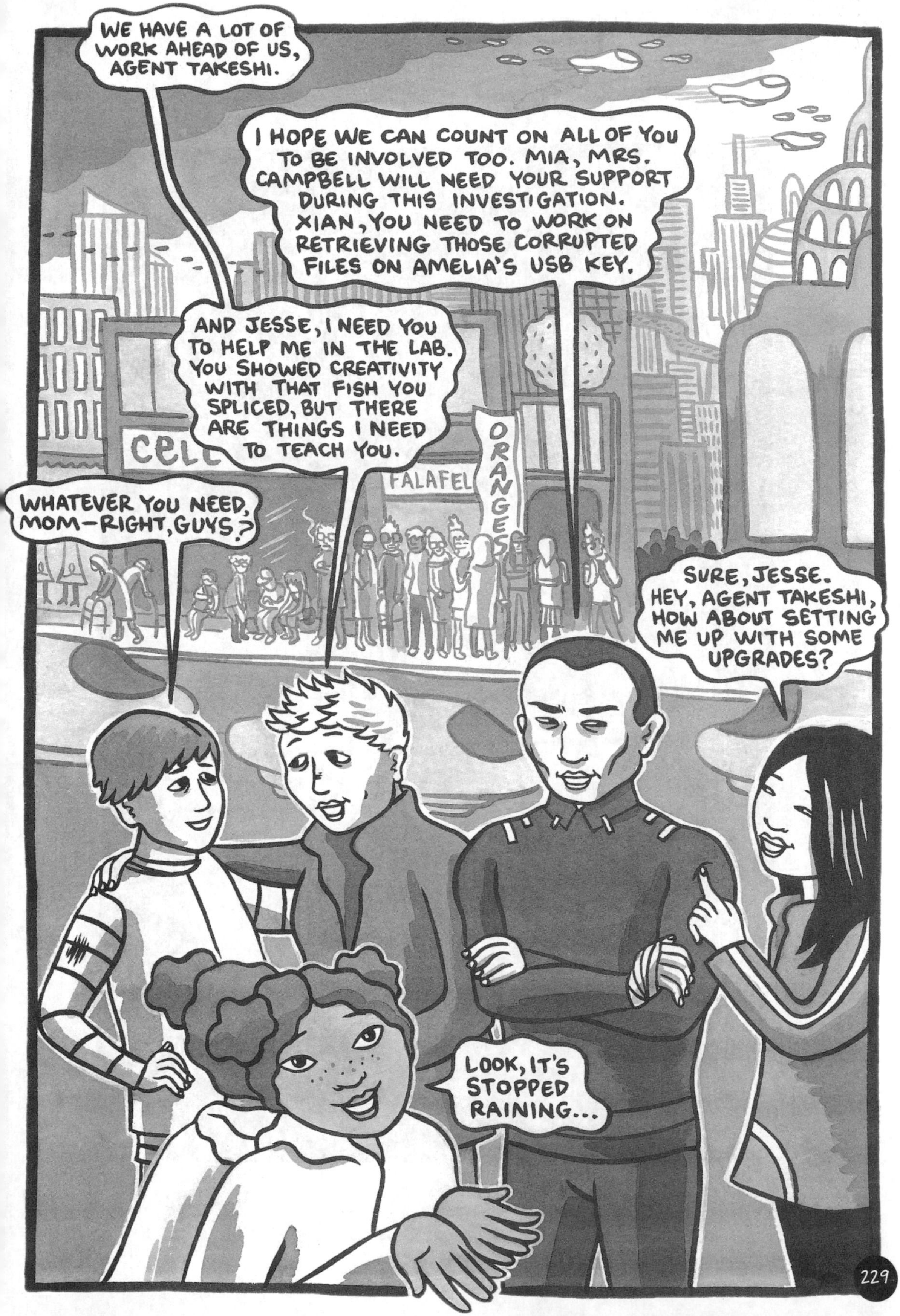
WE HAVE A LOT OF WORK AHEAD OF US, AGENT TAKESHI.
I HOPE WE CAN COUNT ON ALL OF YOU TO BE INVOLVED TOO. MIA, MRS. CAMPBELL WILL NEED YOUR SUPPORT DURING THIS INVESTIGATION. XIAN, YOU NEED TO WORK ON RETRIEVING THOSE CORRUPTED FILES ON AMELIA'S USB KEY.
AND JESSE, I NEED YOU TO HELP ME IN THE LAB. YOU SHOWED CREATIVITY WITH THAT FISH YOU SPLICED, BUT THERE ARE THINGS I NEED TO TEACH YOU.
CELL
FALAFEL
ORANGES
WHATEVER YOU NEED, MOM—RIGHT, GUYS?
SURE, JESSE. HEY, AGENT TAKESHI, HOW ABOUT SETTING ME UP WITH SOME UPGRADES?
LOOK, IT'S STOPPED RAINING...

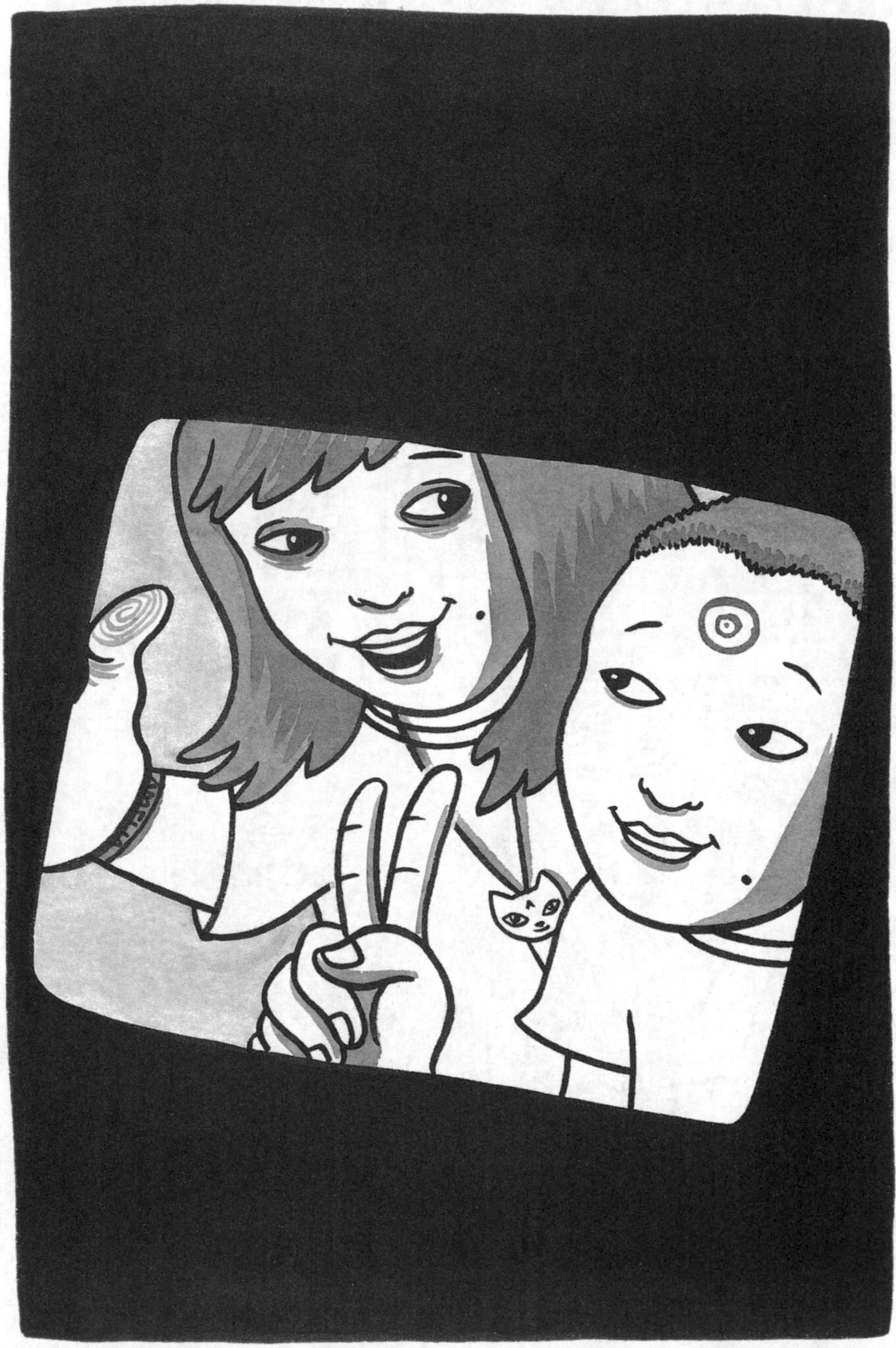

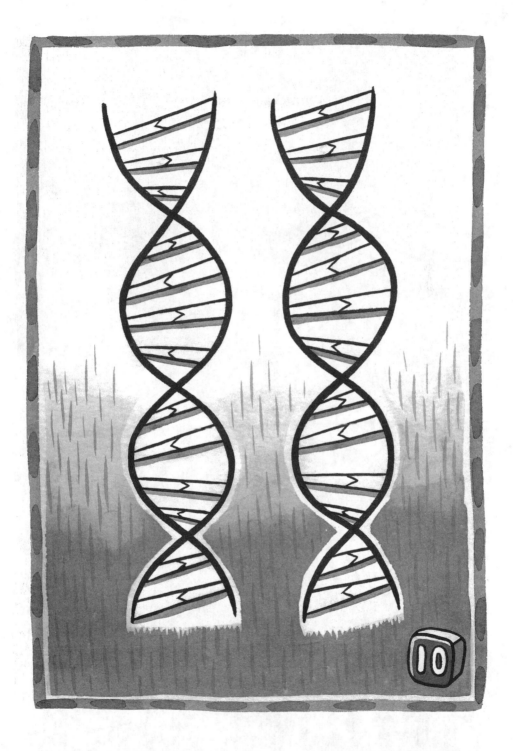

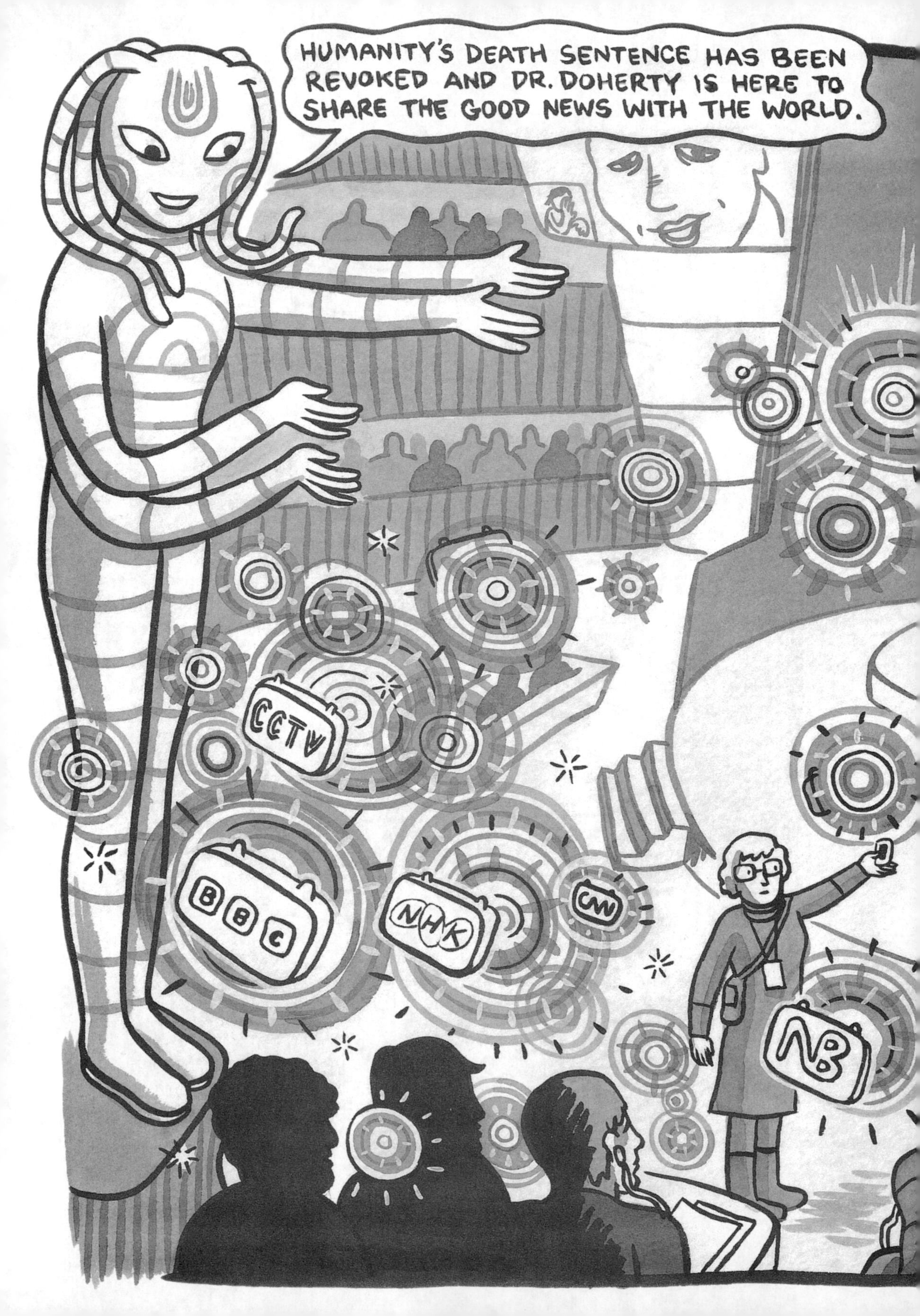
HUMANITY'S DEATH SENTENCE HAS BEEN REVOKED AND DR. DOHERTY IS HERE TO SHARE THE GOOD NEWS WITH THE WORLD.
CCTV
BBC
NHK
CNN

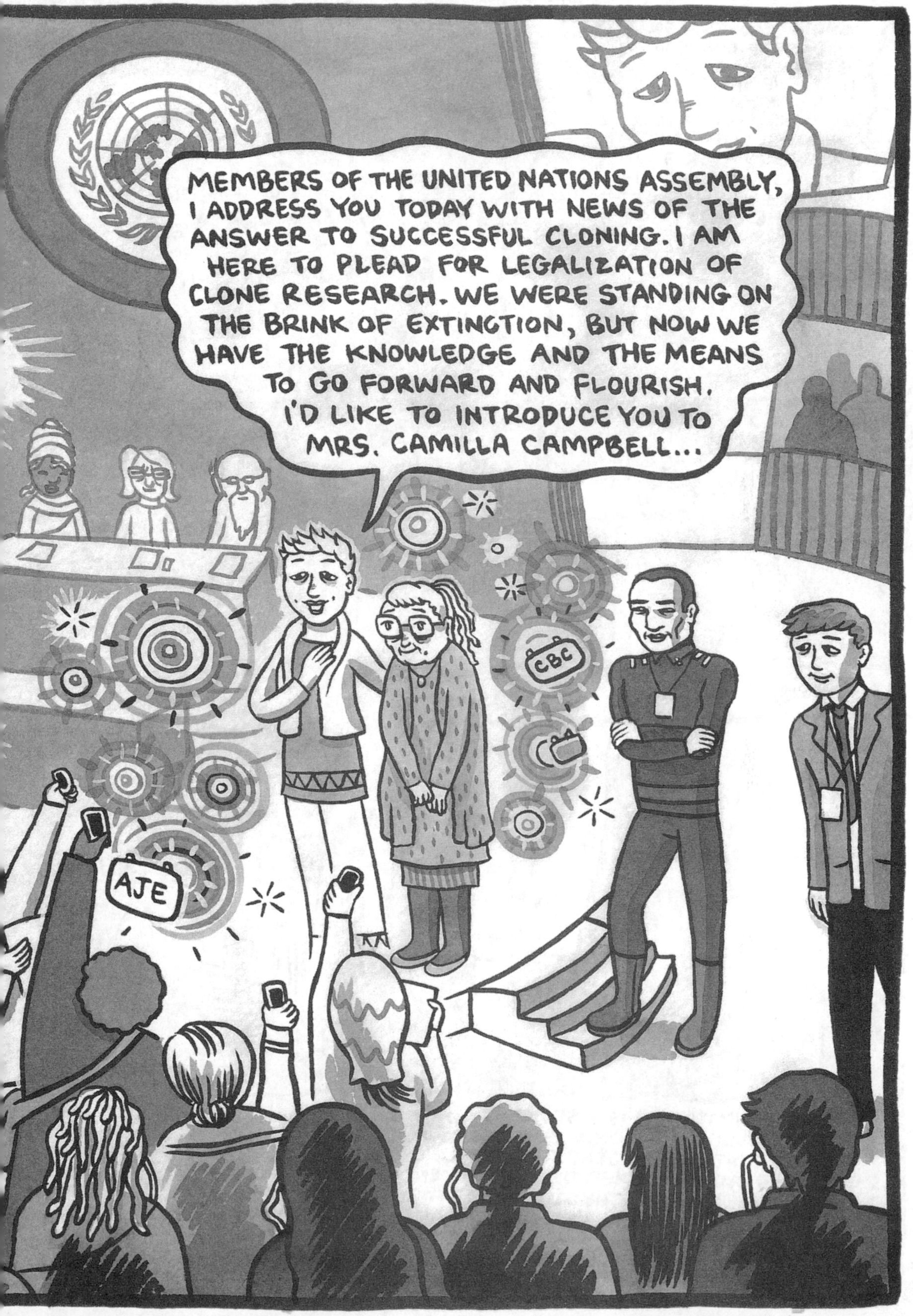
MEMBERS OF THE UNITED NATIONS ASSEMBLY, I ADDRESS YOU TODAY WITH NEWS OF THE ANSWER TO SUCCESSFUL CLONING. I AM HERE TO PLEAD FOR LEGALIZATION OF CLONE RESEARCH. WE WERE STANDING ON THE BRINK OF EXTINCTION, BUT NOW WE HAVE THE KNOWLEDGE AND THE MEANS TO GO FORWARD AND FLOURISH. I'D LIKE TO INTRODUCE YOU TO MRS. CAMILLA CAMPBELL...
CBC
AJE

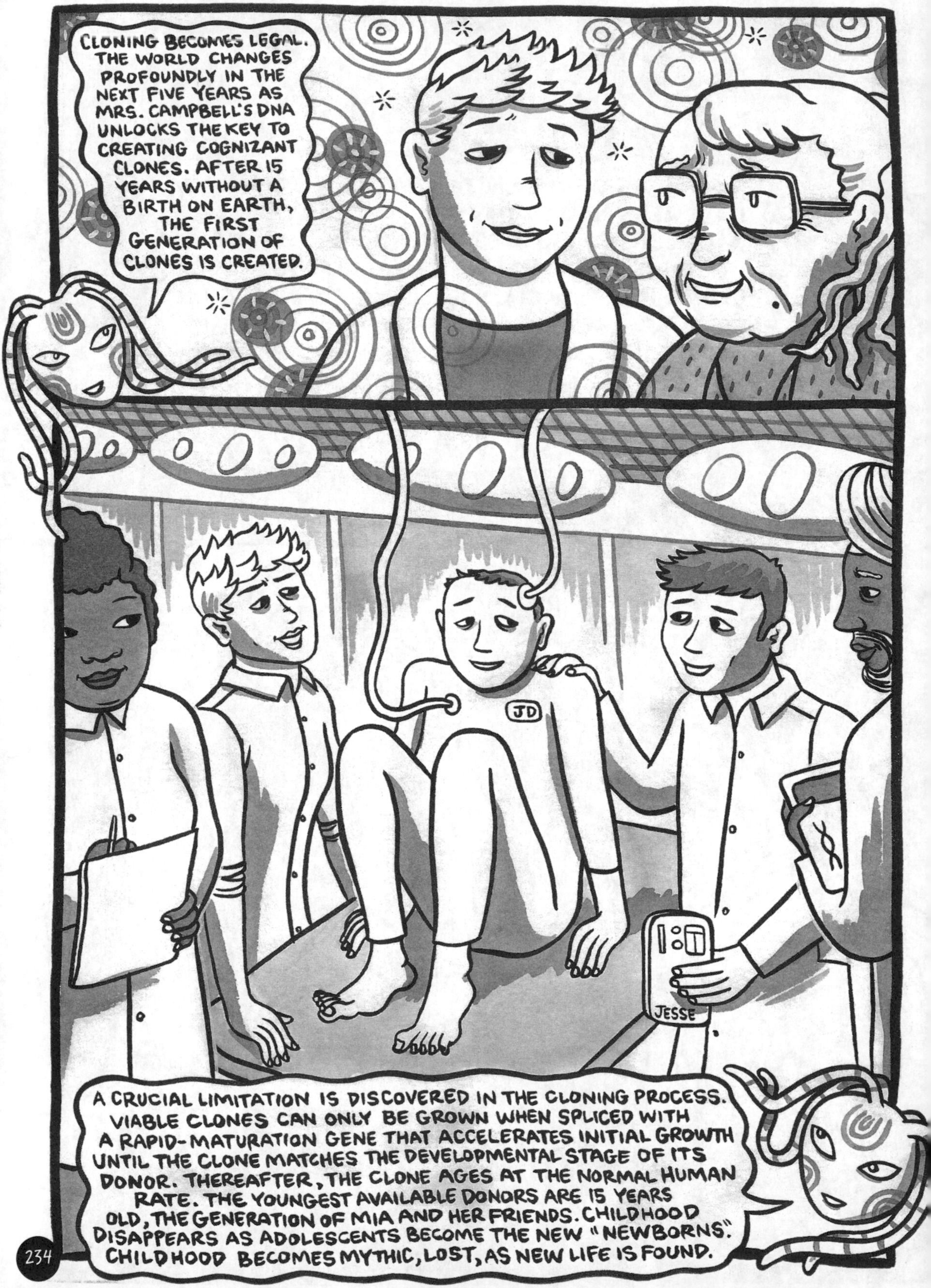
CLONING BECOMES LEGAL. THE WORLD CHANGES PROFOUNDLY IN THE NEXT FIVE YEARS AS MRS. CAMPBELL'S DNA UNLOCKS THE KEY TO CREATING COGNIZANT CLONES. AFTER 15 YEARS WITHOUT A BIRTH ON EARTH, THE FIRST GENERATION OF CLONES IS CREATED.
JD
JESSE
A CRUCIAL LIMITATION IS DISCOVERED IN THE CLONING PROCESS. VIABLE CLONES CAN ONLY BE GROWN WHEN SPLICED WITH A RAPID-MATURATION GENE THAT ACCELERATES INITIAL GROWTH UNTIL THE CLONE MATCHES THE DEVELOPMENTAL STAGE OF ITS DONOR. THEREAFTER, THE CLONE AGES AT THE NORMAL HUMAN RATE. THE YOUNGEST AVAILABLE DONORS ARE 15 YEARS OLD, THE GENERATION OF MIA AND HER FRIENDS. CHILDHOOD DISAPPEARS AS ADOLESCENTS BECOME THE NEW "NEWBORNS." CHILDHOOD BECOMES MYTHIC, LOST, AS NEW LIFE IS FOUND.

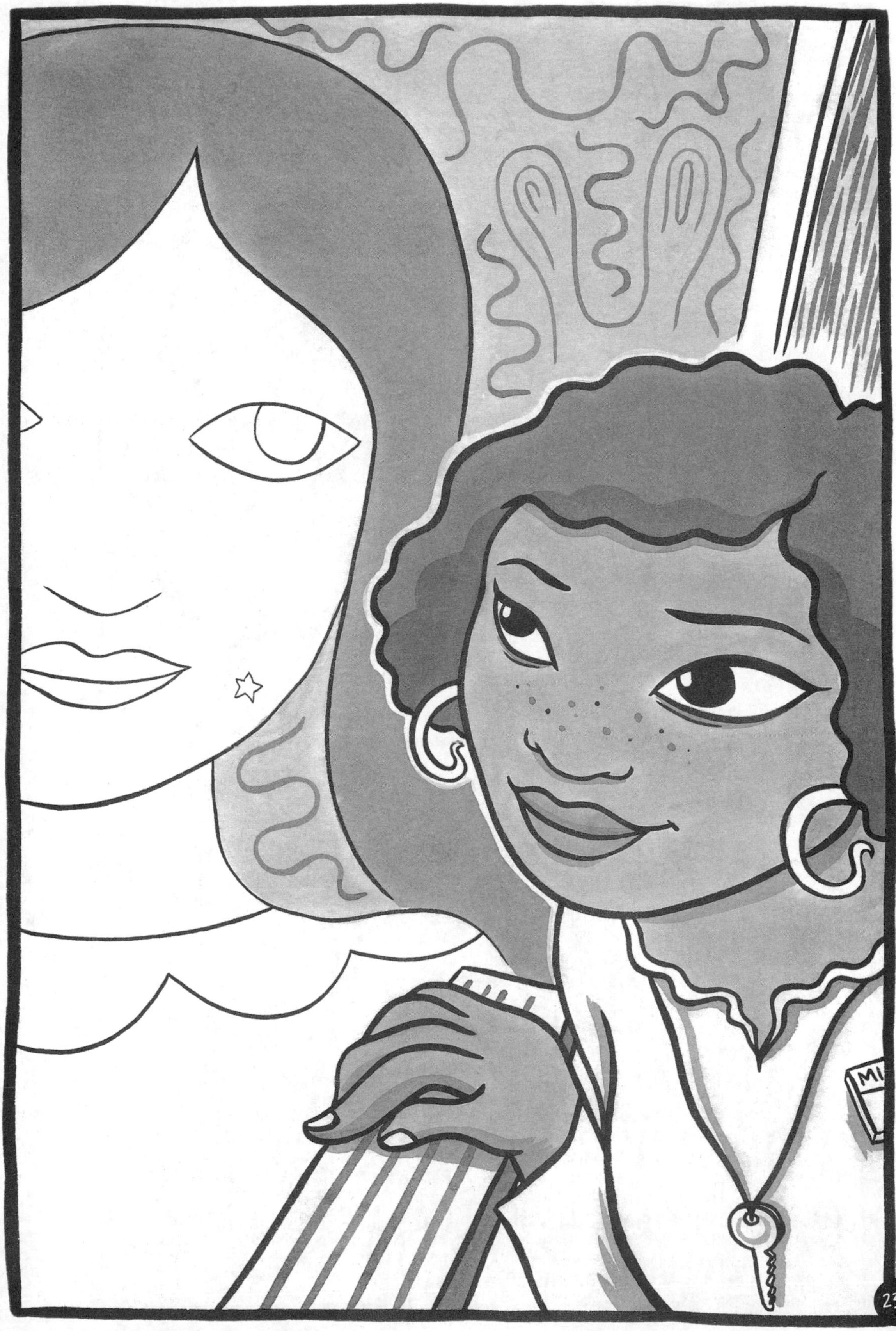

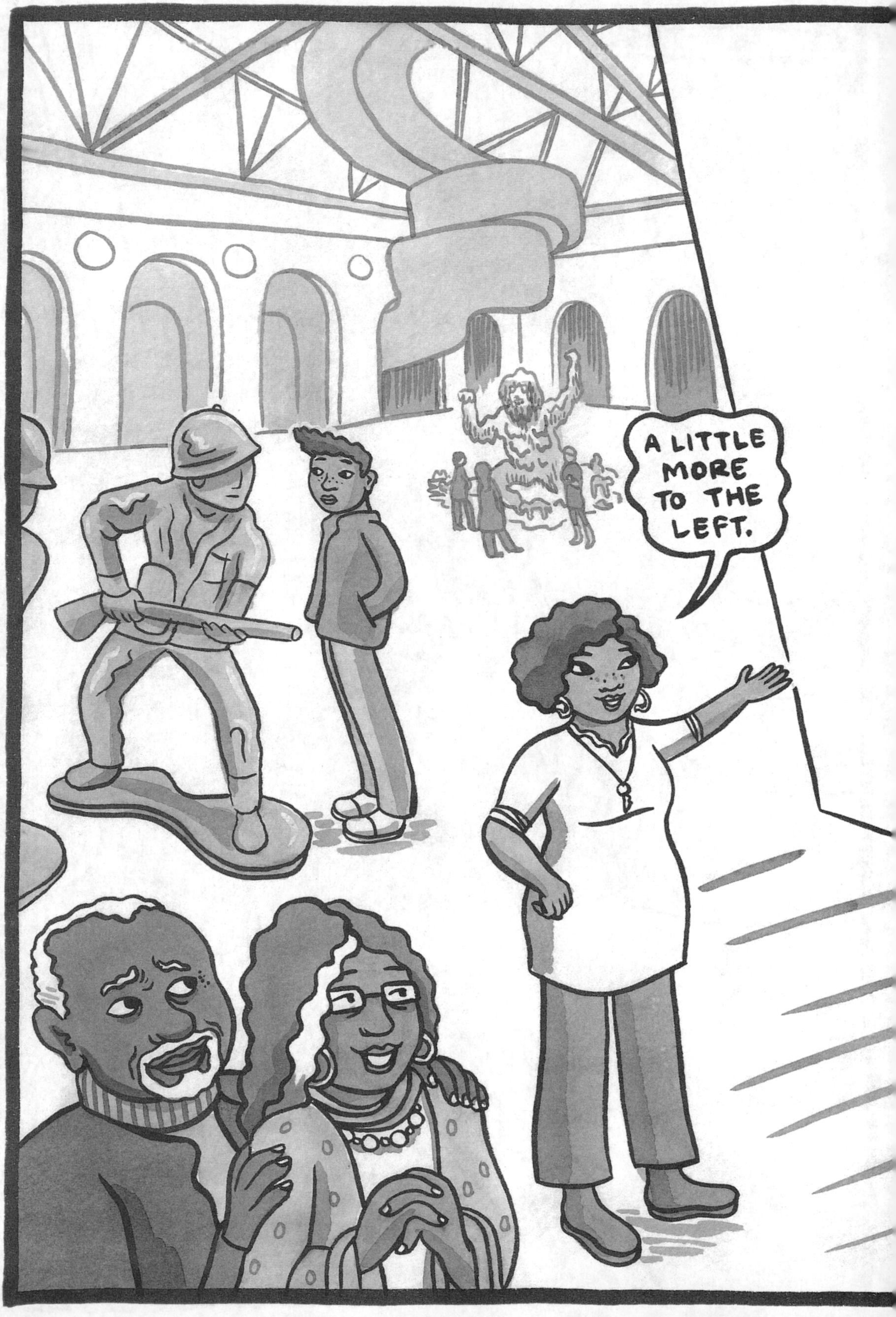
A LITTLE MORE TO THE LEFT.

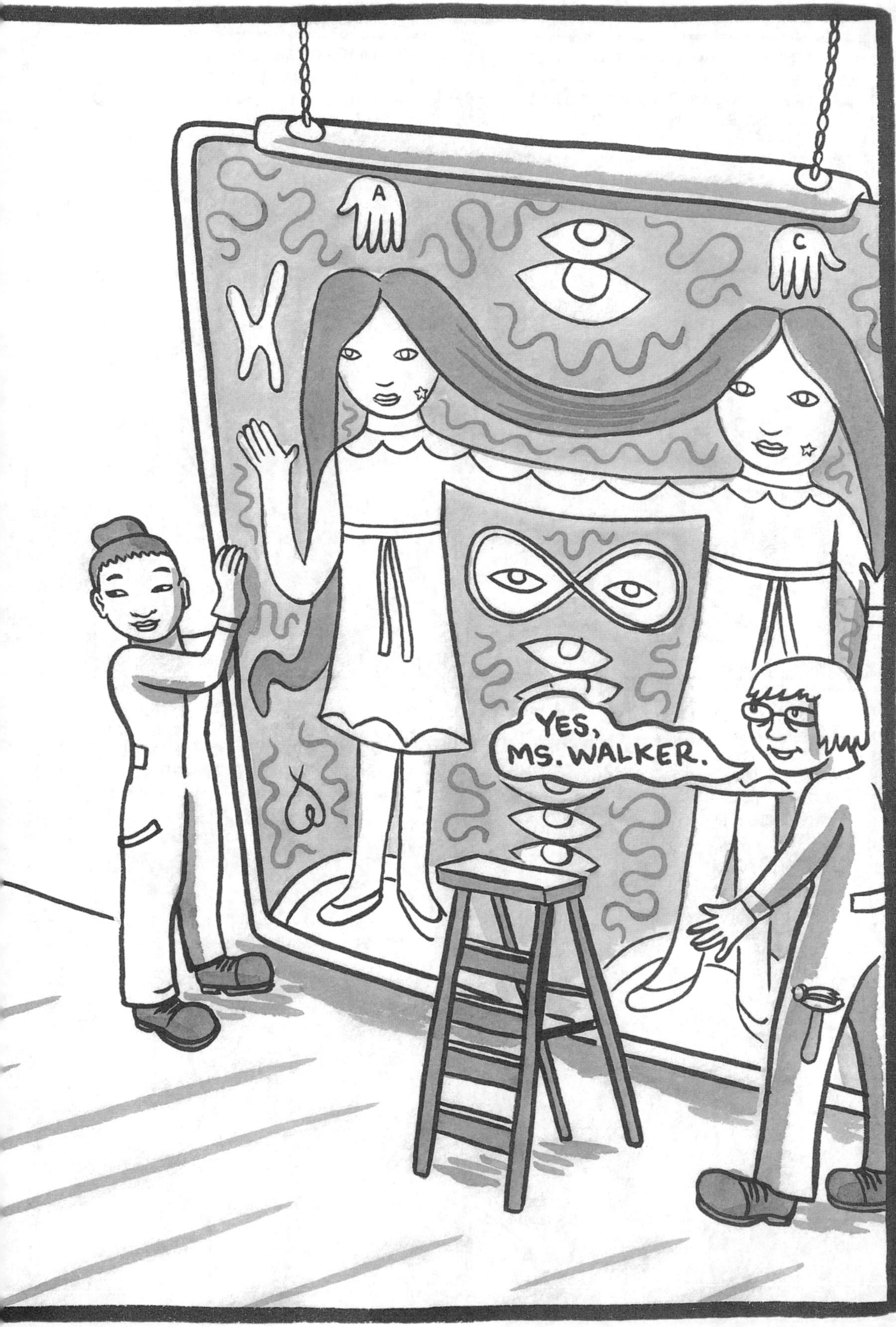
YES, MS. WALKER.

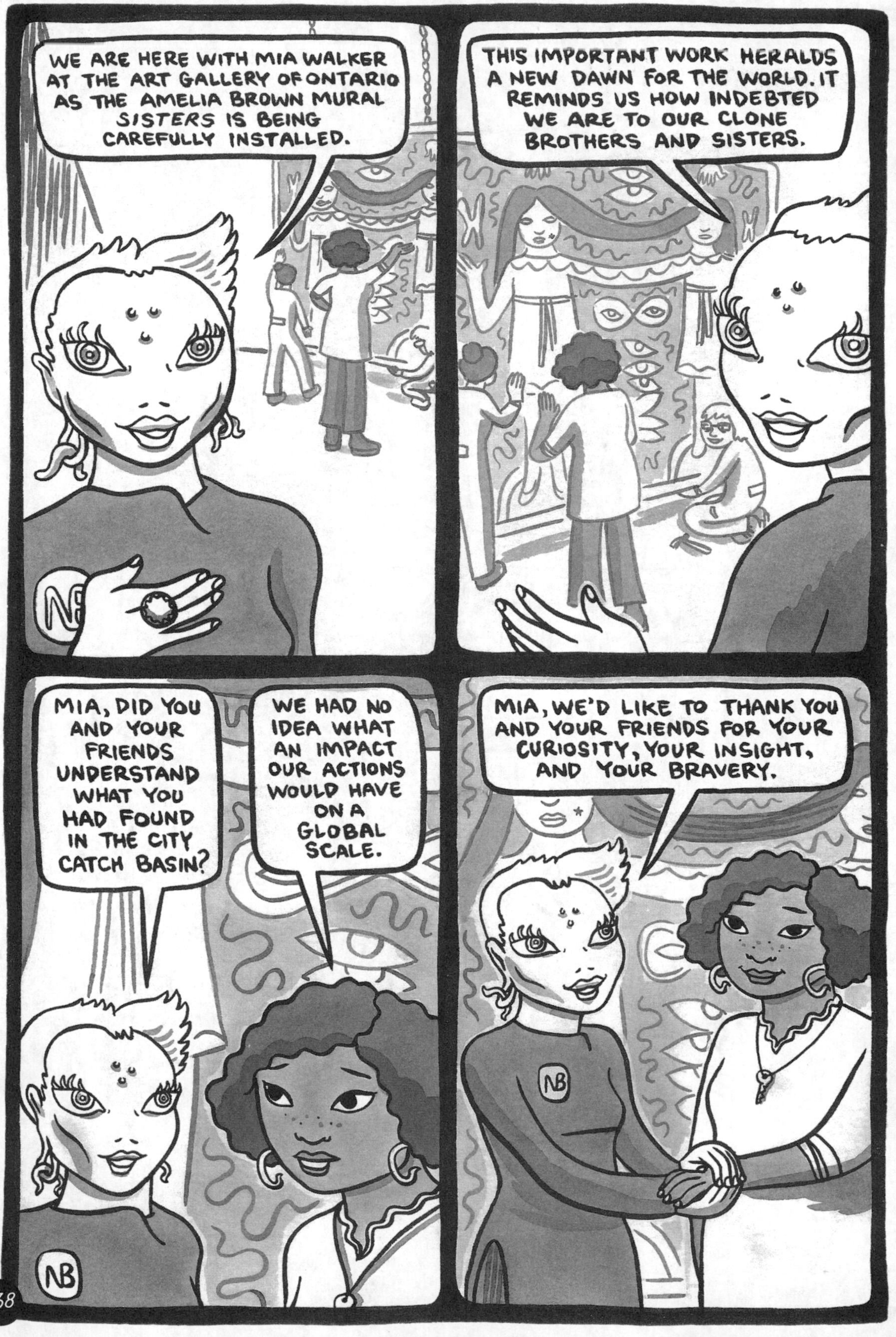

WE ARE HERE WITH MIA WALKER AT THE ART GALLERY OF ONTARIO AS THE AMELIA BROWN MURAL *SISTERS* IS BEING CAREFULLY INSTALLED.
THIS IMPORTANT WORK HERALDS A NEW DAWN FOR THE WORLD. IT REMINDS US HOW INDEBTED WE ARE TO OUR CLONE BROTHERS AND SISTERS.
NB
MIA, DID YOU AND YOUR FRIENDS UNDERSTAND WHAT YOU HAD FOUND IN THE CITY CATCH BASIN?
WE HAD NO IDEA WHAT AN IMPACT OUR ACTIONS WOULD HAVE ON A GLOBAL SCALE.
NB
MIA, WE'D LIKE TO THANK YOU AND YOUR FRIENDS FOR YOUR CURIOSITY, YOUR INSIGHT, AND YOUR BRAVERY.
NB

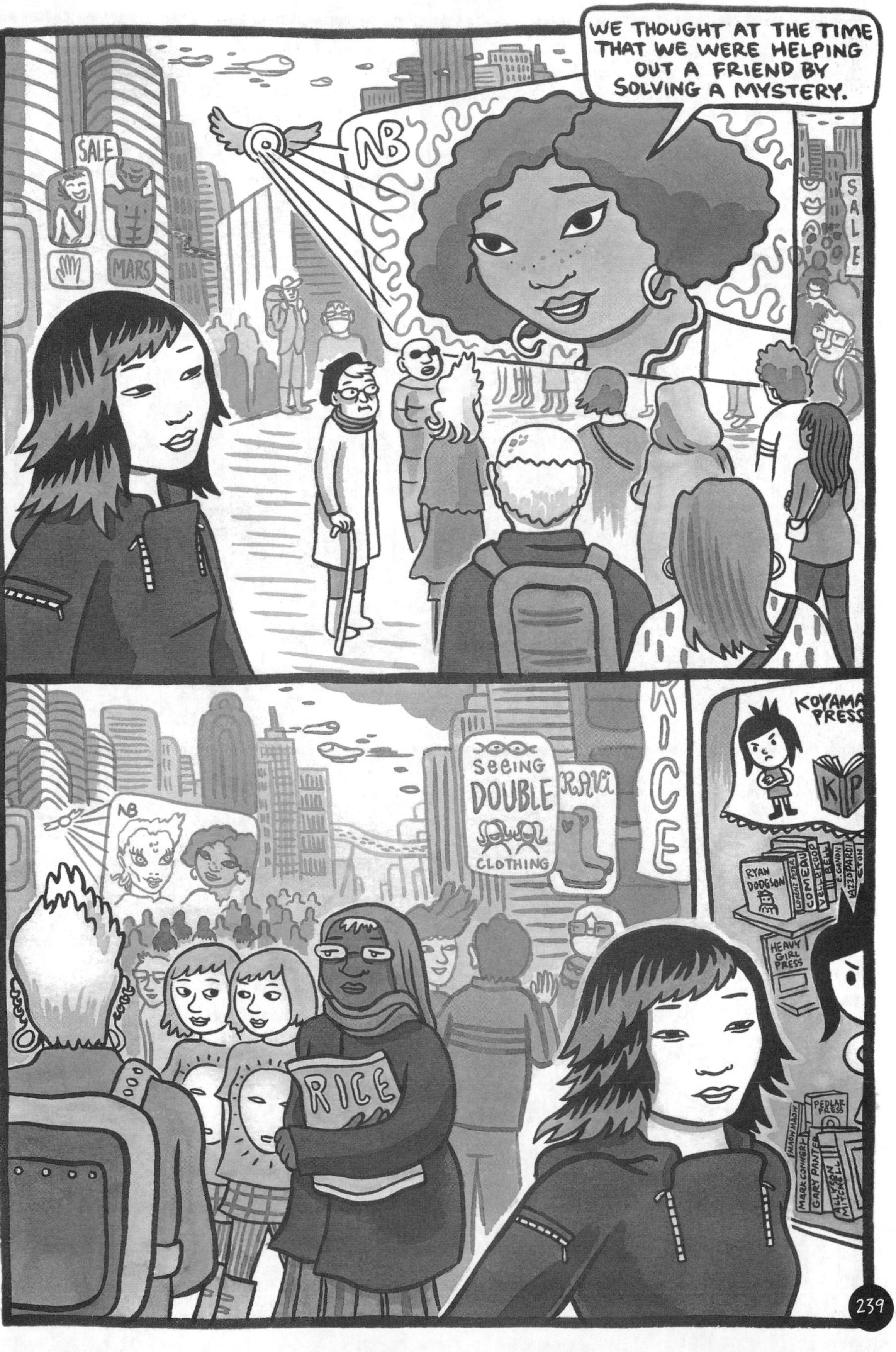
WE THOUGHT AT THE TIME THAT WE WERE HELPING OUT A FRIEND BY SOLVING A MYSTERY.
SALE
MARS
NB
SALE
NB
Seeing DOUBLE CLOTHING
RAVI
RICE
KOYAMA PRESS
KP
RYAN DODGSON
COMEAU
HEAVY GIRL PRESS
RICE
PEDLAR PRESS
GARY PANTER
ALLYSON MITCHELL

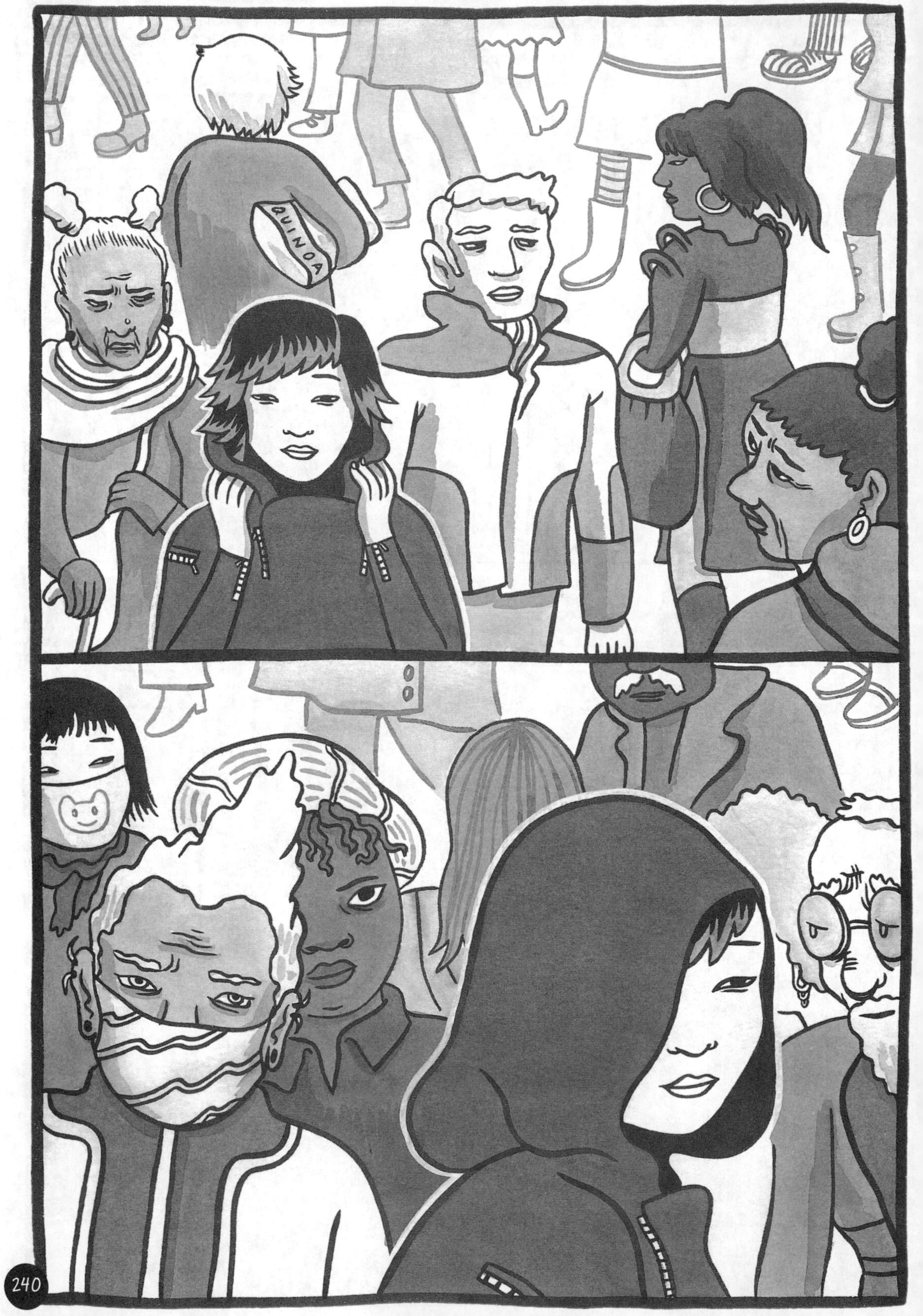
QUINOA

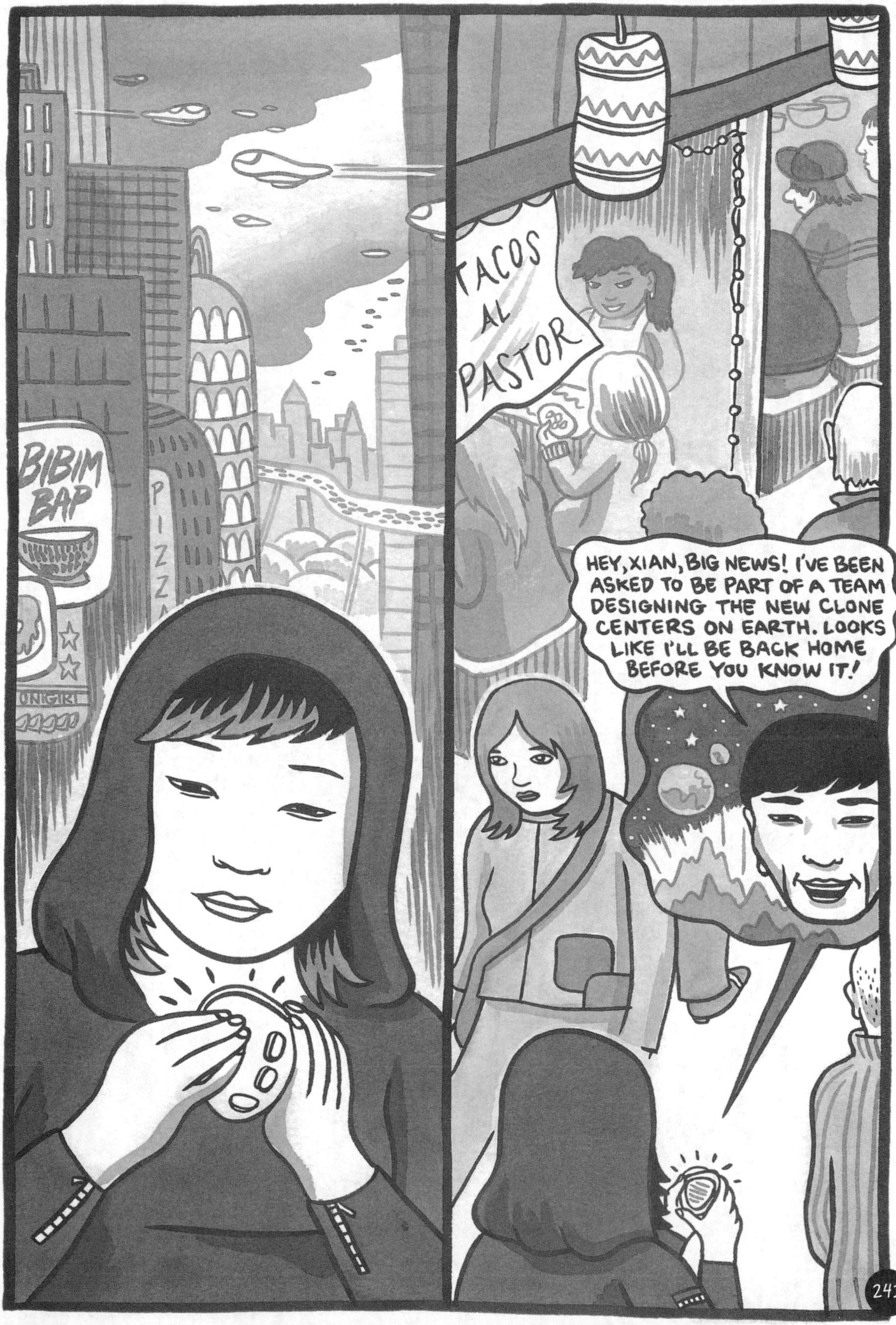
BIBIM BAP
PIZZA
ONIGIRI
TACOS AL PASTOR
HEY, XIAN, BIG NEWS! I'VE BEEN ASKED TO BE PART OF A TEAM DESIGNING THE NEW CLONE CENTERS ON EARTH. LOOKS LIKE I'LL BE BACK HOME BEFORE YOU KNOW IT!

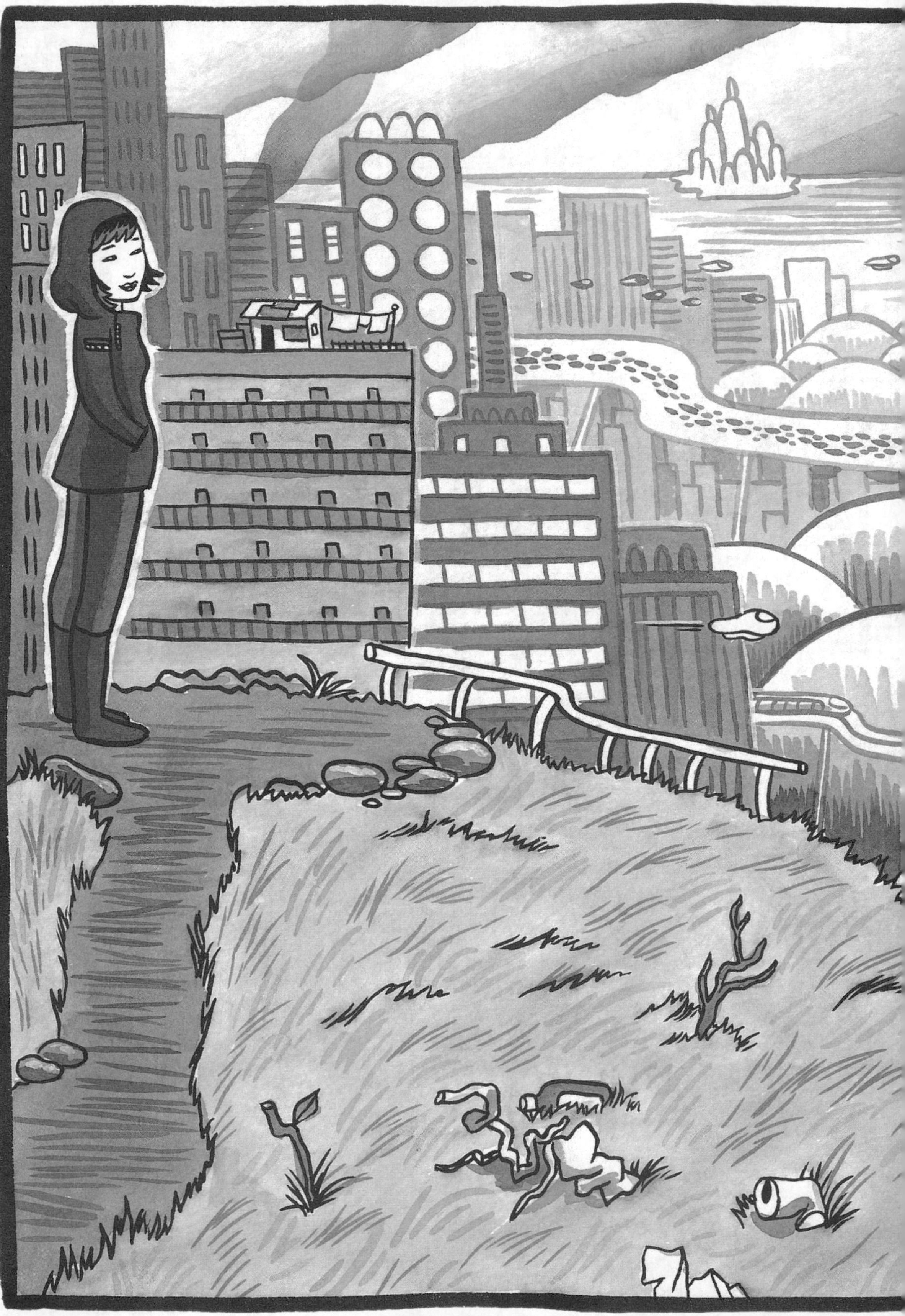

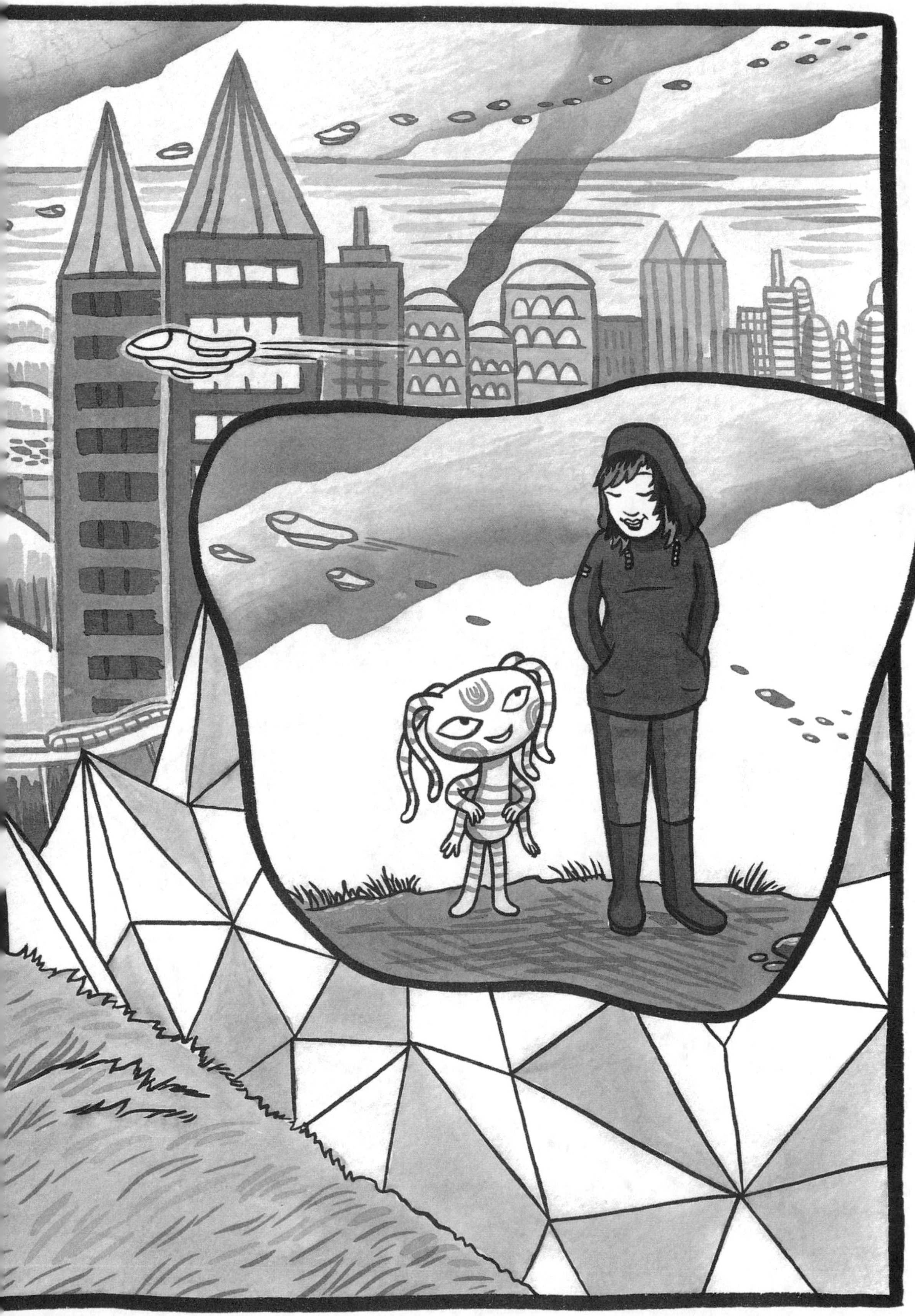

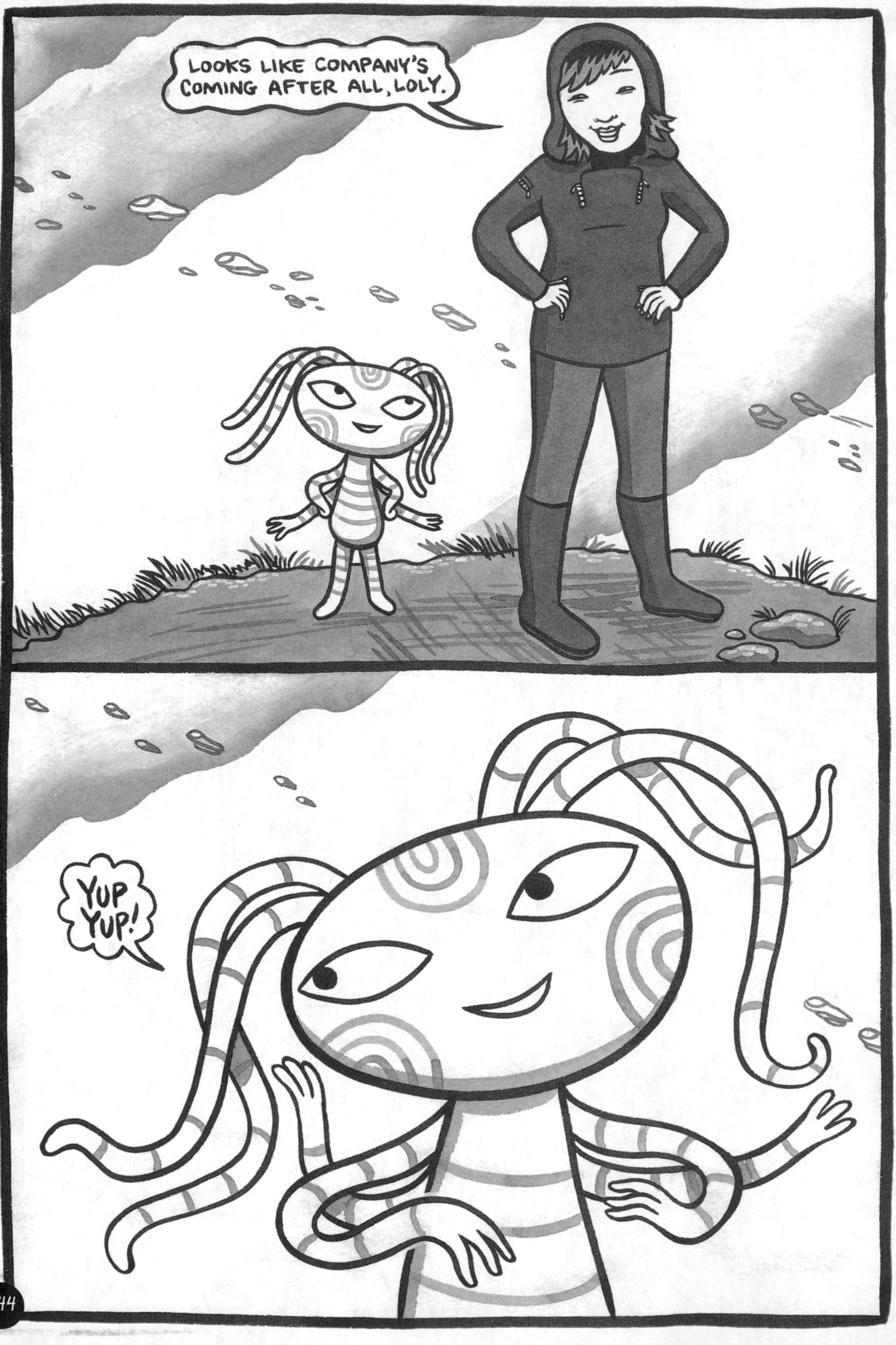
LOOKS LIKE COMPANY'S COMING AFTER ALL, LOLY.
YUP YUP!

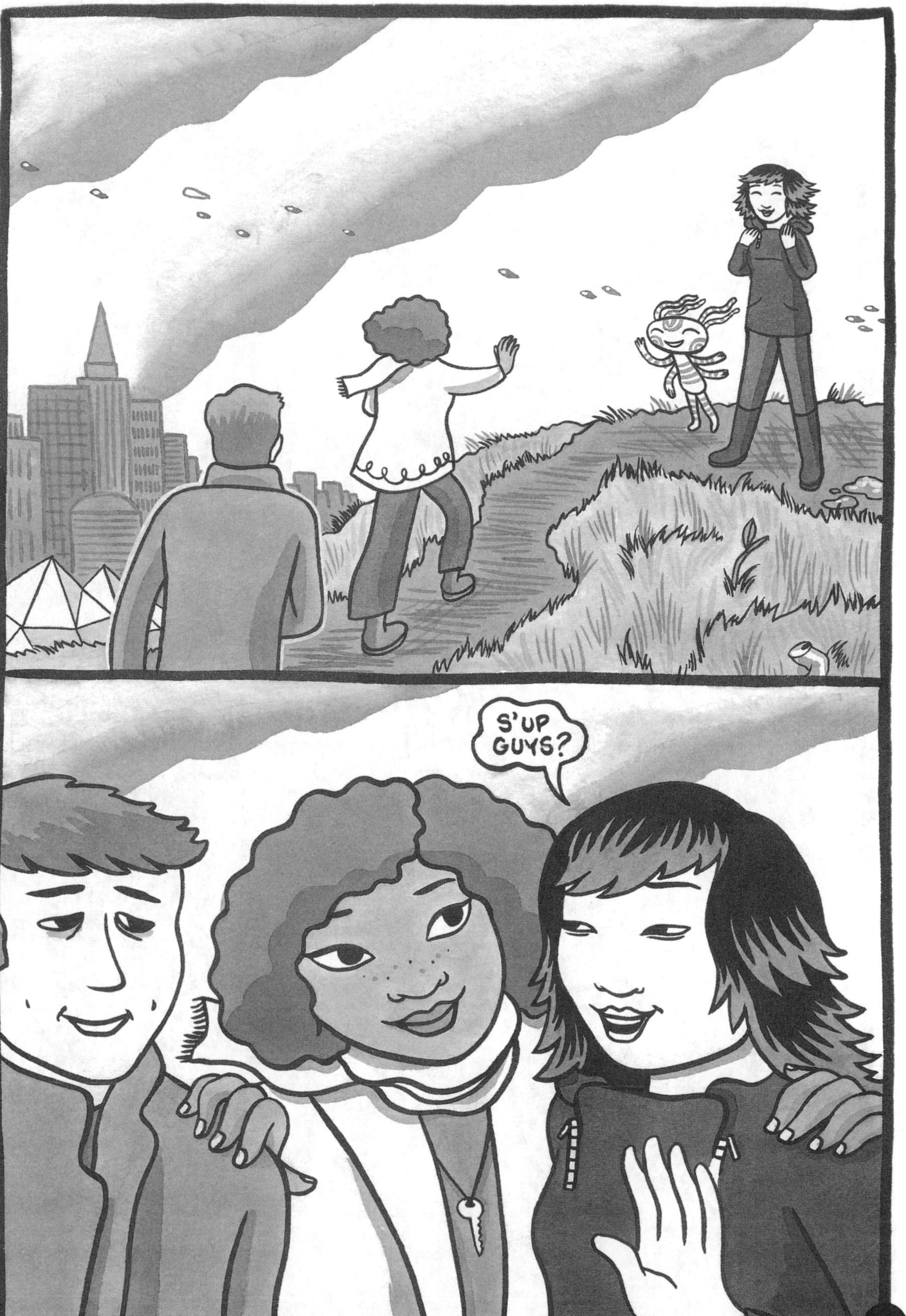
S'UP GUYS?

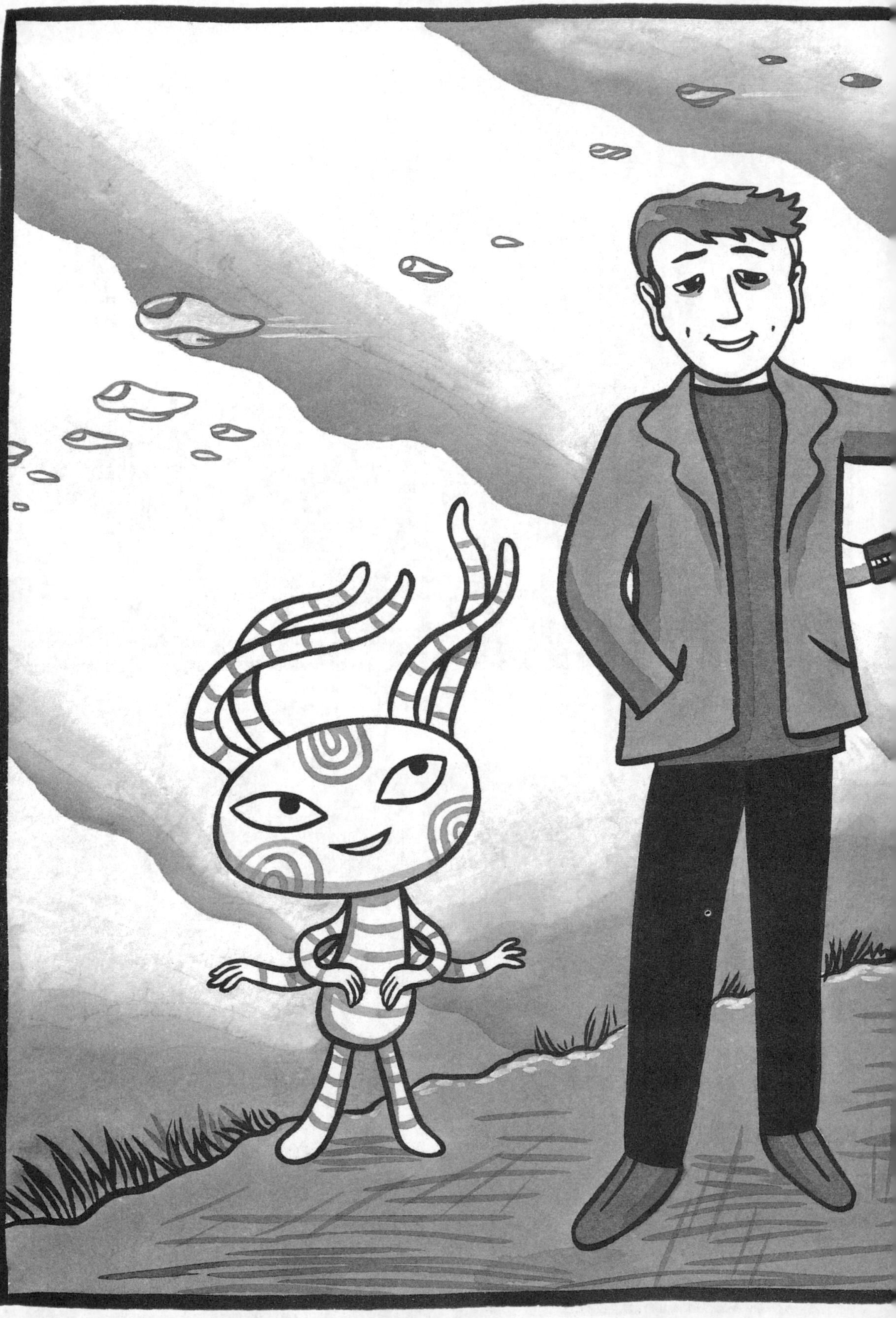

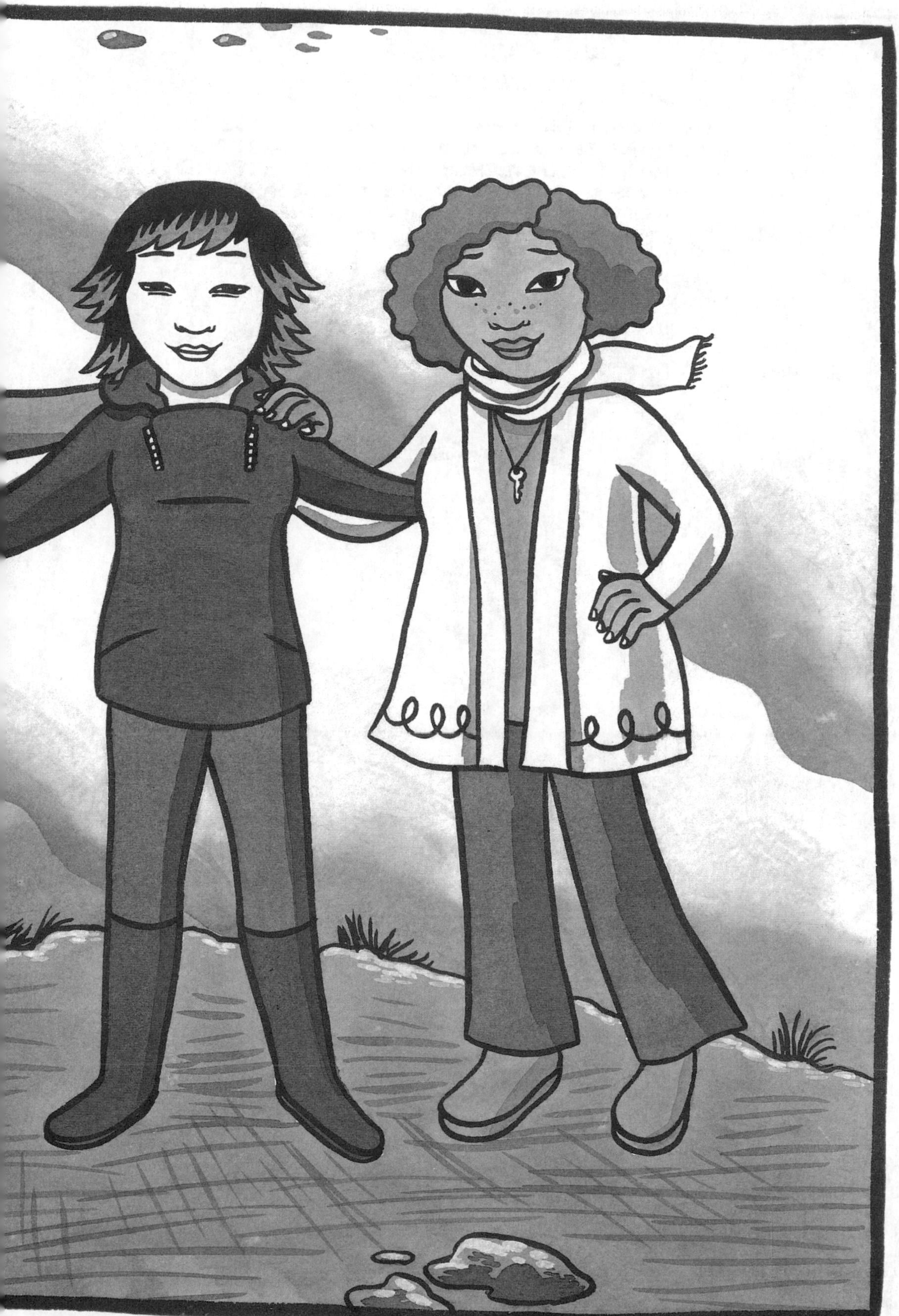

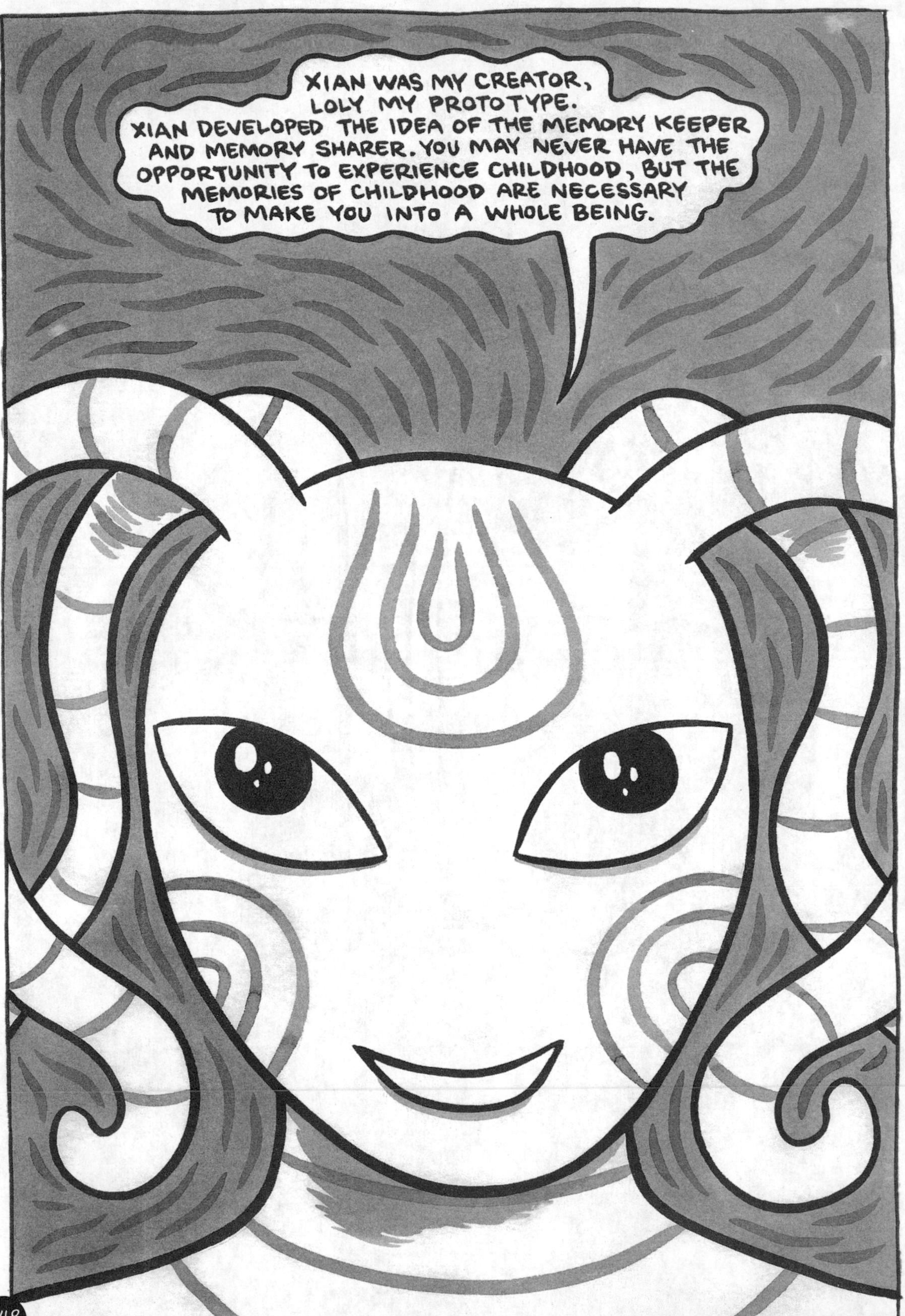
XIAN WAS MY CREATOR, LOLY MY PROTOTYPE. XIAN DEVELOPED THE IDEA OF THE MEMORY KEEPER AND MEMORY SHARER. YOU MAY NEVER HAVE THE OPPORTUNITY TO EXPERIENCE CHILDHOOD, BUT THE MEMORIES OF CHILDHOOD ARE NECESSARY TO MAKE YOU INTO A WHOLE BEING.

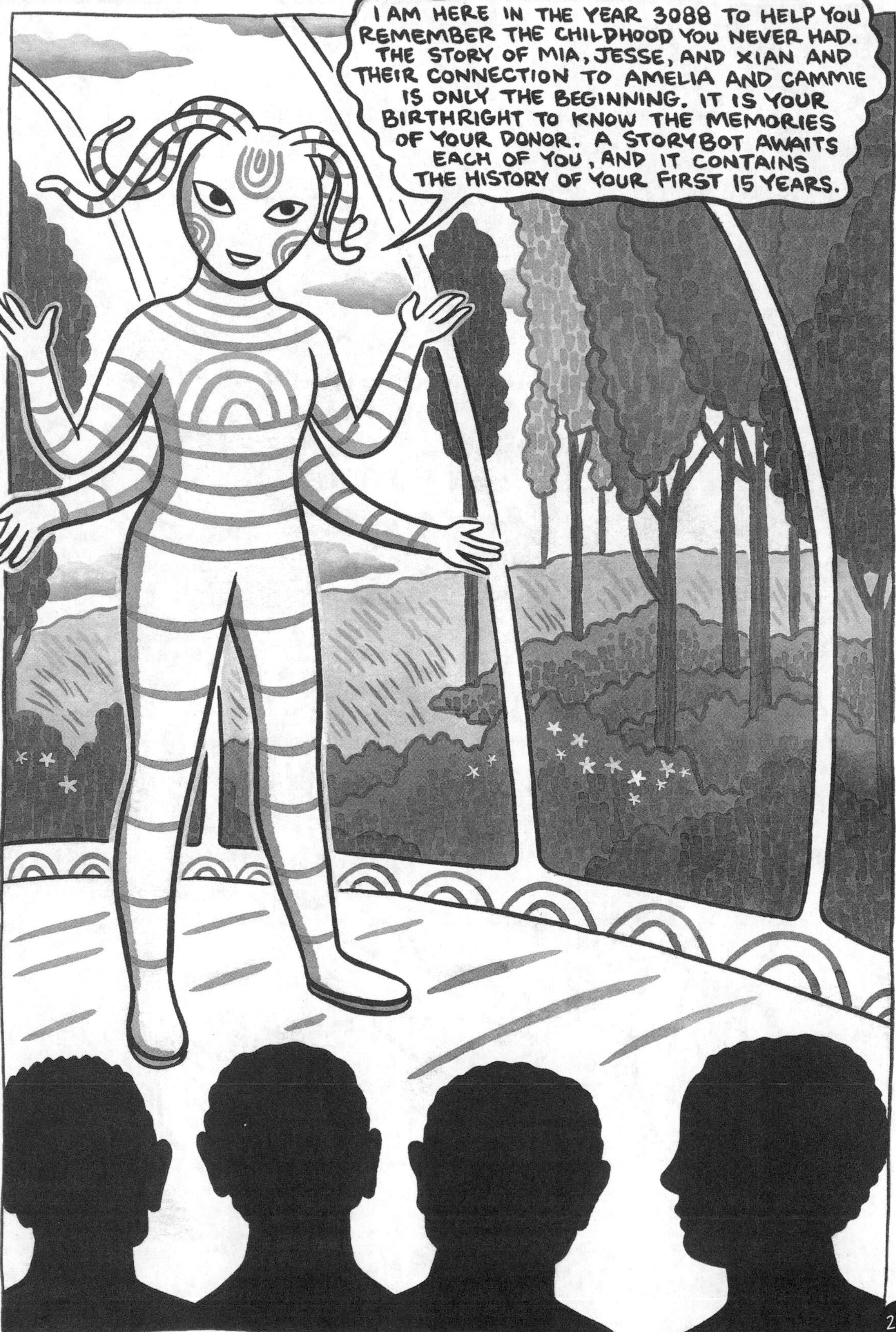
I AM HERE IN THE YEAR 3088 TO HELP YOU REMEMBER THE CHILDHOOD YOU NEVER HAD. THE STORY OF MIA, JESSE, AND XIAN AND THEIR CONNECTION TO AMELIA AND CAMMIE IS ONLY THE BEGINNING. IT IS YOUR BIRTHRIGHT TO KNOW THE MEMORIES OF YOUR DONOR. A STORYBOT AWAITS EACH OF YOU, AND IT CONTAINS THE HISTORY OF YOUR FIRST 15 YEARS.

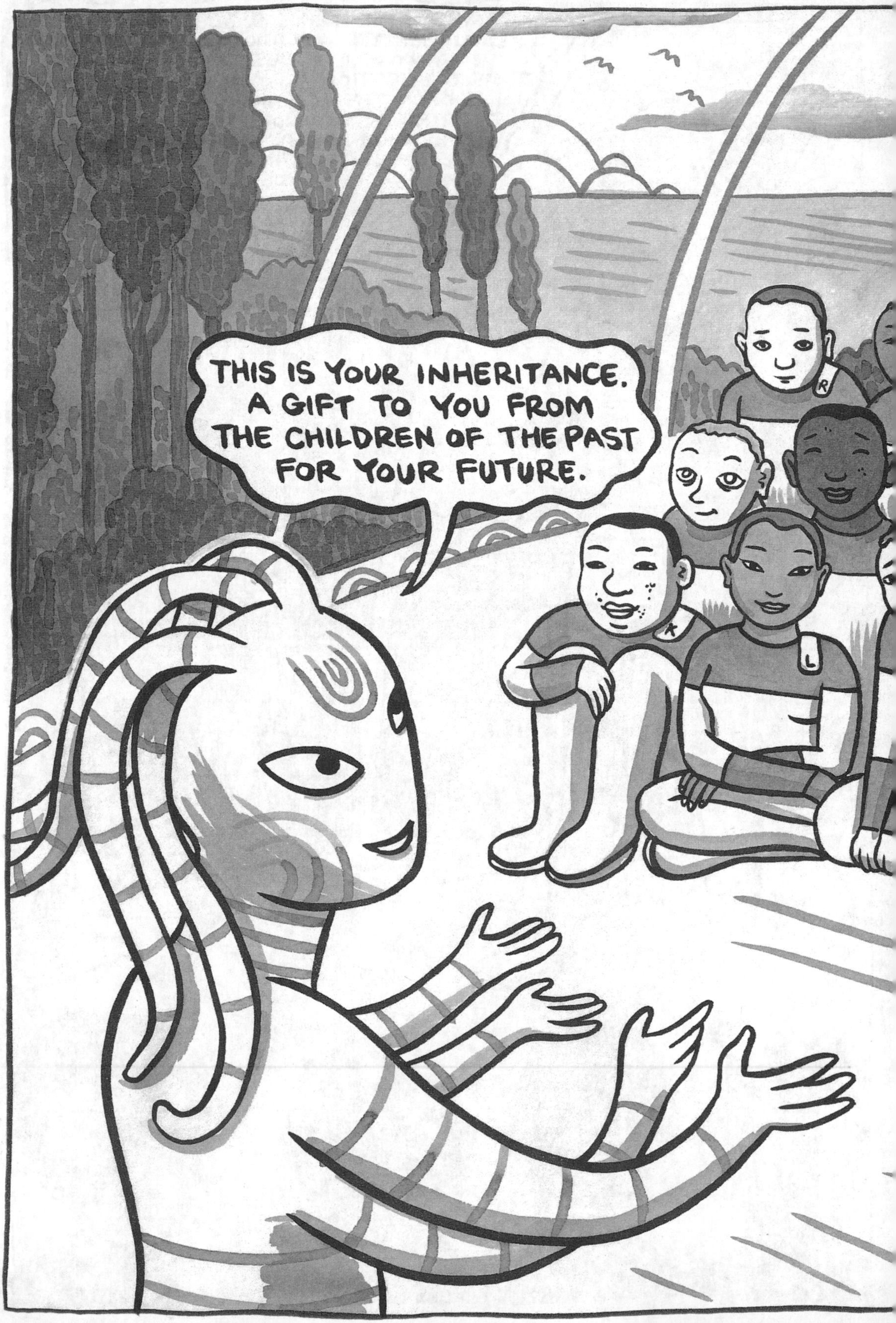
THIS IS YOUR INHERITANCE. A GIFT TO YOU FROM THE CHILDREN OF THE PAST FOR YOUR FUTURE.

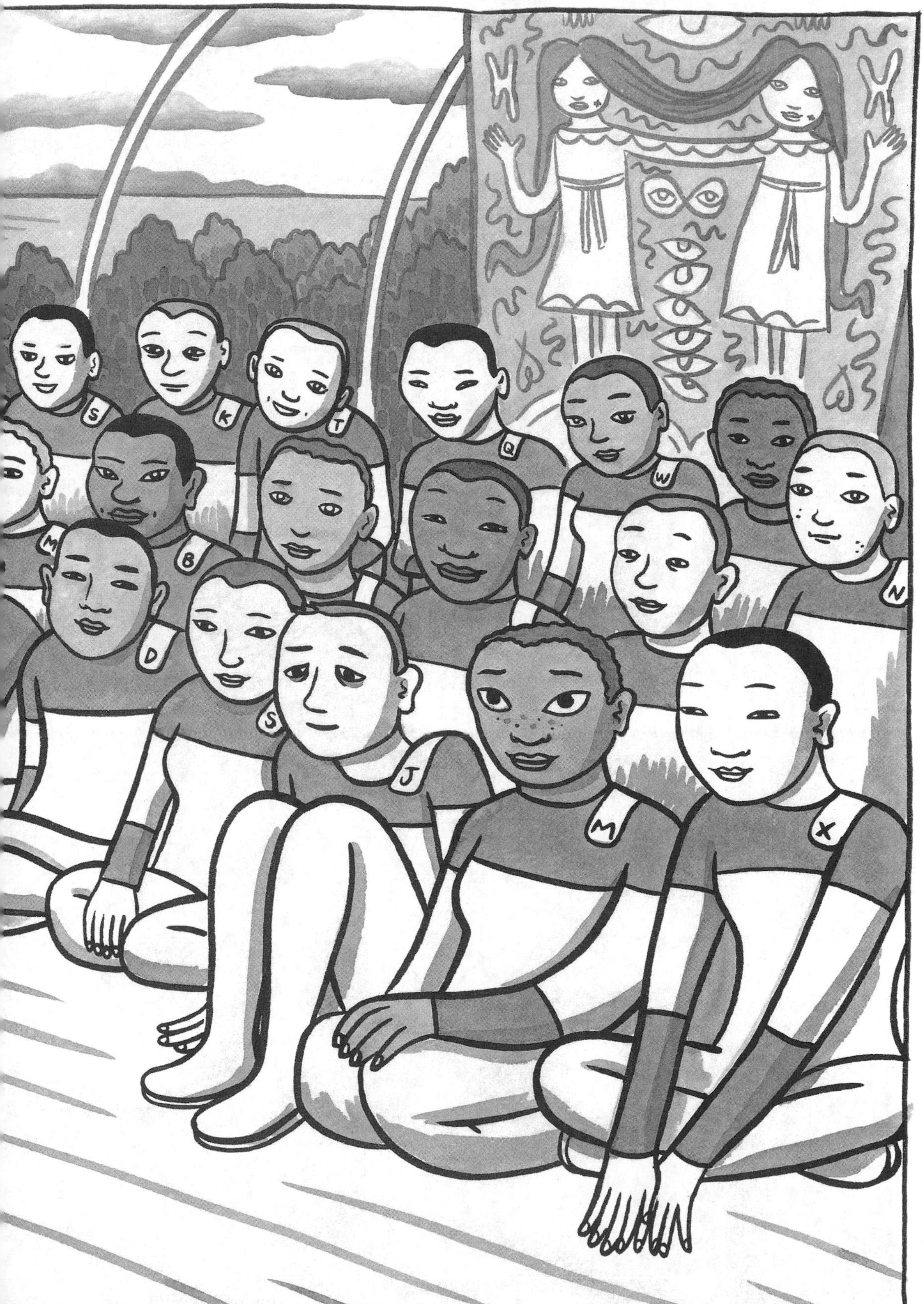

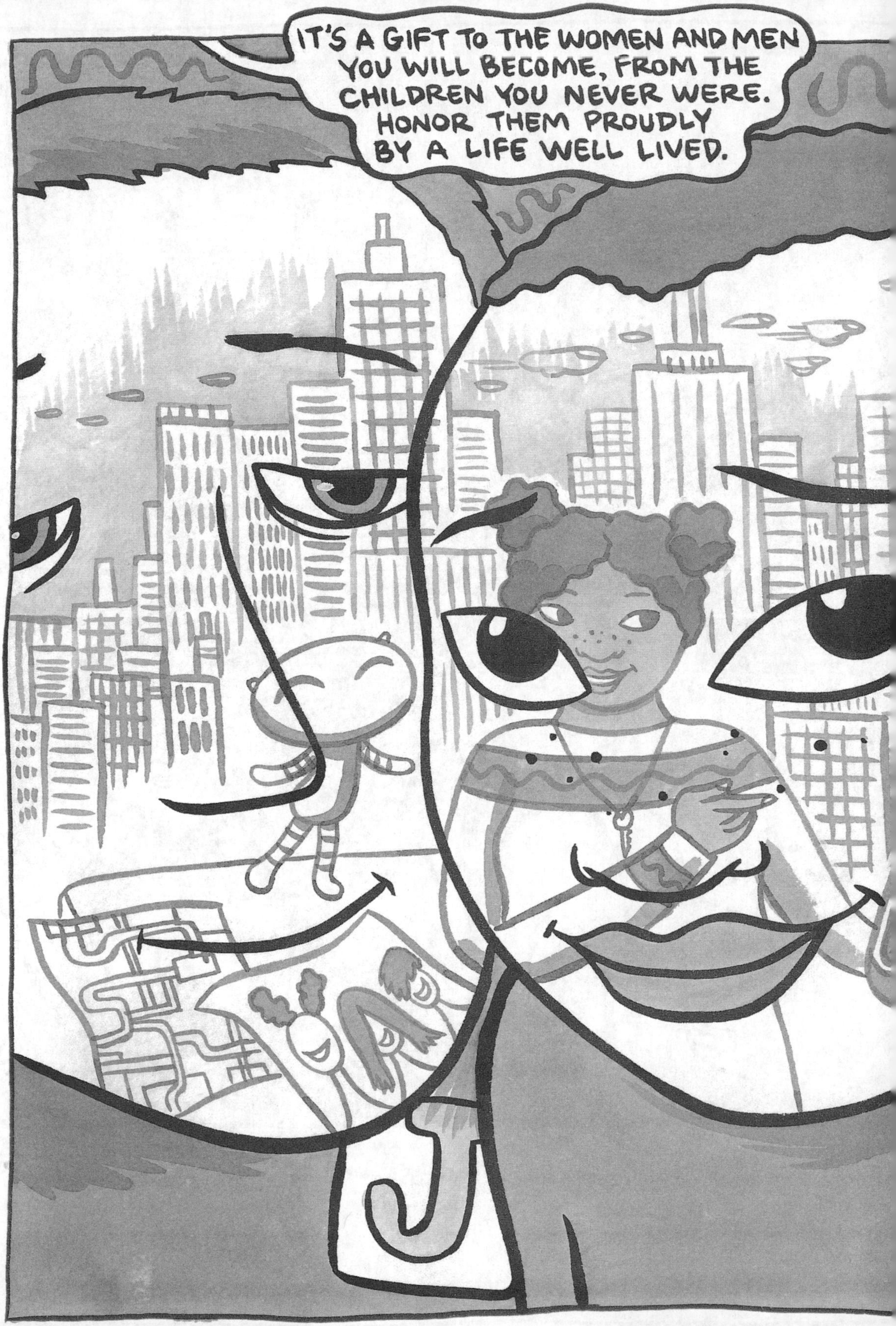
IT'S A GIFT TO THE WOMEN AND MEN YOU WILL BECOME, FROM THE CHILDREN YOU NEVER WERE. HONOR THEM PROUDLY BY A LIFE WELL LIVED.

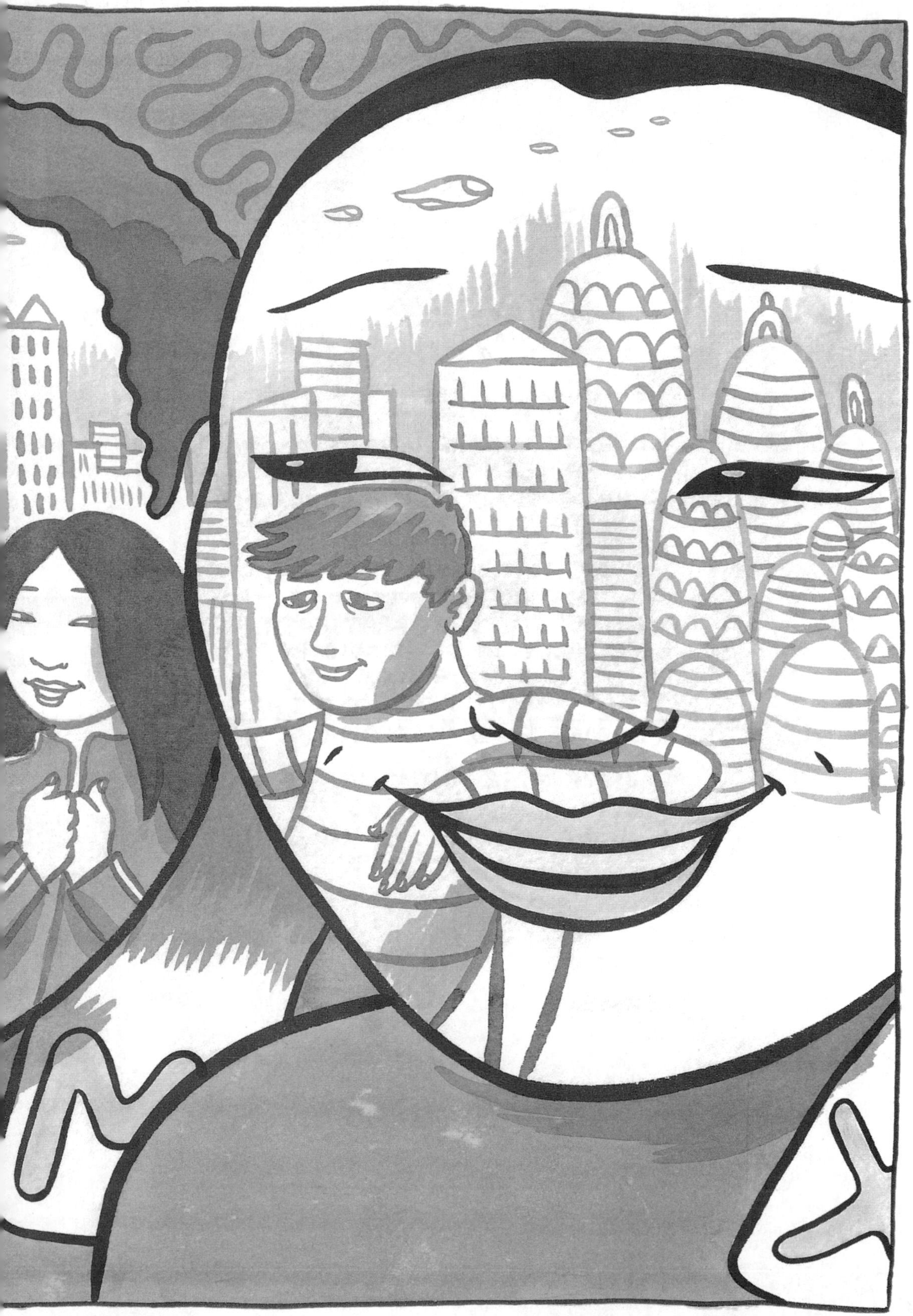

ACKNOWLEDGMENTS

THANK YOU TO THE ONTARIO ARTS COUNCIL'S
WRITERS' RESERVE GRANT FOR
GENEROUS SUPPORT IN THE CREATION
OF THIS BOOK.

MANY THANKS TO THE ANNICK PRESS CREW:
TO SHERYL SHAPIRO FOR INITIATING TNW,
TO KATIE HEARN FOR GREAT PATIENCE,
AND ESPECIALLY TO DAVID WICHMAN,
EDITOR EXTRAORDINAIRE,
FOR INSIGHT AND CREATIVITY THAT
TRANSFORMED TNW INTO AN EPIC TALE!

THANKS EVER AND ALWAYS
TO CRAIG DANIELS
FOR UNWAVERING LOVE AND SUPPORT
THESE MANY YEARS.

FIONA SMYTH IS A CARTOONIST, PAINTER, AND ILLUSTRATOR.
SHE GREW UP IN MONTREAL READING ASTERIX AND OBELIX,
MAD MAGAZINE, AND THE ENGLISH CARTOONIST GILES.
HER PREVIOUS COMICS WORK HAS INCLUDED LONG-RUNNING
STRIPS IN *EXCLAIM!* MAGAZINE, *VICE*, AND FOUR ISSUES OF
THE VORTEX COMIC BOOK *NOCTURNAL EMISSIONS*. A COLLECTION
OF HER *EXCLAIM!* STRIPS WAS PUBLISHED AS *CHEEZ 100* BY
PEDLAR PRESS IN 2001. SHE WAS A CONTRIBUTOR TO THE
SECOND VOLUME OF *TWISTED SISTERS*.
FIONA'S ILLUSTRATIONS WERE USED IN NICKELODEON'S
THE BIG HELP VOLUNTEERISM CAMPAIGN.

FIONA CITES FRANK HERBERT'S *DUNE* AS ONE OF HER
FAVORITE BOOKS. HER FAVORITE GRAPHIC NOVELS INCLUDE
SKIBBER BEE BYE, *SKIM*, *PERSEPOLIS*, AND *WHAT IT IS*.
SHE IS AN AVID ZINESTER AND COLLECTOR OF ZINES.

FIONA IS CURRENTLY TEACHING AT OCADU
(ONTARIO COLLEGE OF ART & DESIGN UNIVERSITY)
AND LIVES IN TORONTO WITH HER PARTNER,
MUSICIAN CRAIG DANIELS.
THE NEVER WERES IS FIONA'S FIRST GRAPHIC NOVEL.

Some Other New Harbinger Titles

The 50 Best Ways to Simplify Your Life $11.95

The Self-Nourishment Companion, Item SNC $10.95

The Daily Relaxer, Item DALY $12.95

Don't Let Your Mind Stunt Your Growth $12.95

Lift Your Mood Now, Item LYMN $12.95

Serenity to Go, Item STG $12.95

The Self-Esteem Companion $10.95

The Relaxation & Stress Reduction Workbook, 5th edition, Item RS5 $19.95

Being, Belonging, Doing $10.95

Spiritual Housecleaning $12.95

Juicy Tomatoes $13.95

Thoughts & Feelings, Second Edition $19.95

Wanting What You Have $18.95

Brave New You $13.95

Making Hope Happen $14.95

Call **toll free, 1-800-748-6273,** or log on to our online bookstore at **www.newharbinger.com** to order. Have your Visa or Mastercard number ready. Or send a check for the titles you want to New Harbinger Publications, Inc., 5674 Shattuck Ave., Oakland, CA 94609. Include $4.50 for the first book and 75¢ for each additional book, to cover shipping and handling. (California residents please include appropriate sales tax.) Allow two to five weeks for delivery.

Prices subject to change without notice.

Matthew McKay, Ph.D., is a well-known psychologist specializing in couples therapy. He is the co-author of a dozen popular books, including *Couple Skills: Making Your Relationship Work*.

Carole Honeychurch, M.A., is a freelance writer, iVillage.com relationship expert, and coauthor of *After the Breakup*.

Angela Watrous is a freelance writer, relationship workshop leader, and iVillage.com relationship expert. The coauthor of *After the Breakup*, Ms. Watrous also writes for Women.com and PlanetOut.

Introduction

When you first buy a new car, it's exciting. Even running errands takes on the exhilaration of something out of the ordinary. Everything is running smoothly. You don't have to worry. Things feel just a little bit easier. Life looks just a little bit brighter.

So you drive around town, with the windows down and your hair blowing in the wind. Sure, you add fuel, but it takes too long to schedule that oil change, that tune-up. You have too many more pressing matters to attend to. You'll get to it next week.

As you coast along, though, you slowly start to notice that things aren't running as smoothly as they did at first. The engine has that occasional "pinging" sound—not too loud, just a little irritating. You think about taking a look under the hood, but then the noise stops. You hope the problem will just go away on its own, and you forget all about it. Until it happens again.

At this point, you have a choice: Take some time to do some minor preventative maintenance, or let it go longer, until there's a real problem to deal with.

We all know that preventative maintenance is cheaper and easier in the long run. Plus, it ensures that your car lasts and lasts instead of breaking down long before its time. And if you'd take the time to tend to your car (and your bills and your home), then isn't your relationship worth at least the same level of care and attention?

That's where these love tune-ups come in. Use these simple, effective activities to give your relationship a quick tune-up. You'll find that they can enhance intimacy, clarify communication, and reignite the passion in your relationship.

This book is designed to be easy and fun to use. Flip around and try the activities in any order that appeals to you. Each tune-up shares specific tips you can use today to make an actual difference in your life. Some borrow from proven techniques used by skilled couples' counselors. The rest are based on tips from the best experts: couples who have found creative ways to keep their love healthy and vibrant. These couples shared their secrets with us in the hope that their discoveries will help keep your relationship as deeply rewarding and satisfying as theirs.

You know that even the best cars need regular maintenance. And you'll find that even the best partnerships can benefit from a tune-up.

PART I

Show Me Love

It's a Wonderful Love

You probably remember that moment in the favorite Christmas movie, *It's a Wonderful Life*, when the wretched George Bailey leans over the bridge, contemplating ending it all in the icy river churning below. He's saved, of course, by Clarence, his plucky guardian angel. Clarence then shows George what would have happened if, as George wished, he'd never been born.

Many folks love this film because it reminds them to think about what would have happened if they'd never been born or if their loved ones hadn't been around. Looking back like this helps us appreciate the impact others have had on our lives, helping us open our hearts to the gratitude and love we feel for what others have given us.

This past holiday season, Joanna took the opportunity to watch *It's a Wonderful Life* for the eighteenth time. When the film was over, she smiled and dried her eyes, making her way to the living room where Tom sat on the couch, absorbed in the evening paper.

"Hi, baby," she said, sitting down next to him so their legs touched. "Hey," Tom responded, continuing to read. "How was the movie?" he asked, already knowing the answer. "Oh, it was really great," Joanna sighed, still feeling a little emotional and tear-stained. Tom picked up the business section of the paper and languidly opened it. Joanna looked over at him, feeling her heart swell a little. "I love you, honey," she said to the front of the business section. "I love you, too," Tom mumbled.

This was a common enough exchange, and it was perfectly pleasant. But that she *loved* Tom was actually not exactly what Joanna had meant to convey. She did love Tom, but what's more, she was exceedingly grateful that he had come into her life. Just as George Bailey was given a chance to see what life would have been like without him, Joanna loved taking the opportunity to consider how her life would have been different without the loved ones around her. It made her feel great about Tom to think about all the good he had brought into her life. Of course, he didn't know that. She'd never told him—just kept her musings to herself. This year would be different.

"Hey," she said, sneaking her face over the top of Tom's paper. "You know, I've been thinking ..." Tom lowered the business section and regarded her expectantly.

"Well, I've been thinking not only about how much I love you"—Tom smiled—"but also how important you've been to my life. You know, if I hadn't had your support, I probably would never have gone back to graduate school. Really, it's true. And I don't know what I would have done without you when my dad passed away. And, maybe the most important thing, I'm so grateful for the way you've taught me to slow down a little and enjoy life more. If you hadn't been around I'm sure I'd be running myself to death. My life would be so different if I'd never met you, and I'm really happy you are here."

Tom pulled her close, a little shy about the tears stinging his eyes. The business section fell to the floor as he took his turn in sharing how Joanna had made his life different.

As a wonderful gratitude builder, go ahead and consider how different your life would be today if you hadn't met your partner. Do you think you'd be living somewhere different? Would you have a different sort of job, different friends? Would your outlook on life be different? What has your partner given you or taught you that is unique to them? What are you most grateful for?

After you've given it some thought, tell your partner about what you've discovered. It will be a true gift to them to know not only that you love them, but that they have made a concrete, positive difference in your life.

Leaving Little Notes

Sometimes it takes only a small gesture to help you reconnect with your partner. Although the weekend ski trip can do wonders in adding a little fun and romance to your relationship, you don't always have to go all out to add a spark. Sometimes all you need to do is get out a pen and paper.

"Good, she's asleep." John had finally gotten his two-year-old down for her afternoon nap and was looking forward to getting some chores done. Not that chores were his activity of choice given a couple of free hours in the afternoon. He'd much rather get some writing done, or even better, goof off. But he knew that the huge pile of clean laundry sitting on his closet floor needed to be put away.

John stayed home to take care of his daughter Amanda, a job he loved. Kelly, his wife, sometimes missed them both sorely while she was at work, but she really enjoyed her career as a veterinarian, so she gave up some time with her family. Though the situation generally worked well for both of them, sometimes they felt that the different tempos of their days put some distance between them. Recently they had been working on trying to reach out a bit more to each other, making special efforts to be closer.

John got to his bedroom closet and opened the door with a sigh. Ugh. There were all the clothes he'd almost forgotten he owned. He started with the boxers, grabbing a pile of them and stuffing them into his top drawer. As he shoved them in, he heard a crinkling noise. "What was that?" he thought, moving some of the undies and socks aside. Right there, underneath his pile of athletic socks, was a little slip of paper. Figuring that it was probably a receipt that had slipped in there, John plucked it out and took a look. On the scrap of cream-colored paper was a note in Kelly's handwriting: "I love seeing you in nothing but your boxers."

Whoa! John laughed and flushed a bit, reading the note again. "Ah, how sweet of her." He stopped for a moment, holding the note against his chest while he flashed on how much he loved to see Kelly in nothing but boxers, too. He laughed again, and felt a surge of love for his wife. How great that she'd thought of him. What a terrific little surprise! In the few minutes it took for John to read and absorb the note Kelly had left,

he felt much closer to her. In fact, he was inspired to return the favor, leaving Kelly a sexy little note somewhere—after he finished putting away his laundry, of course.

It's one of those little gestures that many of us have heard about or thought about doing, but perhaps have forgotten to try recently—leaving love notes. Leaving a little note someplace unexpected will let your partner know that you've been thinking of them, and that you care enough to let them know. Remember how thrilled you were in school when a boy or girl you liked passed you a note or left something in your locker letting you know that they liked you, too? Why not bring that thrilling feeling into your adult relationship by "passing notes" with your partner? Even though you're all grown up now, it will still be exciting for them to know how much you care about them.

Here are some suggestions you may want to try:

- "I love you" is a great way to start. Who wouldn't be delighted to get a note saying that from their partner? But don't forget that you can also add a lift to your partner's day with humor. "Shake it, Hot Pants" may not be as sincere as "I love you," but it will let your partner know (as they laugh) that you're thinking of them. And don't be shy! Feel free to spice it up as much as you like. How about a note letting your partner know exactly what sensual avenue you'd like to explore with them that evening? Let your imagination run wild. Remember, you get to write whatever you want—it's your note.

- Consider carefully where you'd like to hide your note. Underwear drawers are an all-time favorite, and hiding notes under your partner's pillow also works well. But sometimes an even more unexpected place can be fun. How about in the box of your partner's favorite cereal? That way the note will come spilling out first thing in the morning. Try to really surprise your partner—it's half of the fun. But be careful not to intrude on areas that your partner feels private about. You may not want to stick a goofy love note in her daily planner if she's very serious about keeping organized. And a sexy proposition may not be the best thing to have fluttering out of one's briefcase in the middle of a business meeting.

Leaving little notes for your partner can add a wonderful zip to both their day and yours. You get to feel sneaky and loving at the same time, and they get a caring surprise. A love note is a simple, delightful way to bring you instantly closer, no matter where you are.

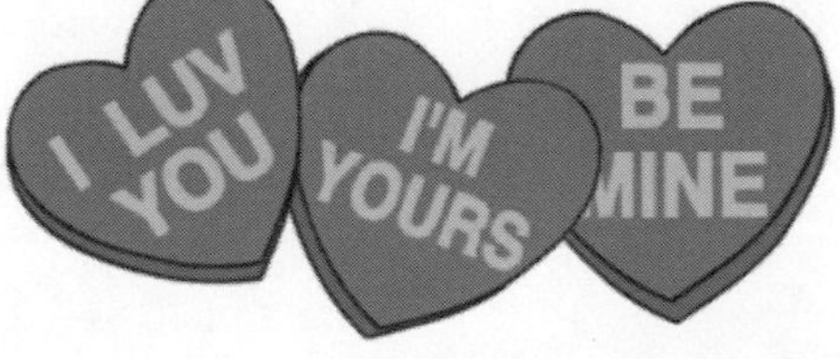
I LUV YOU
I'M YOURS
BE MINE

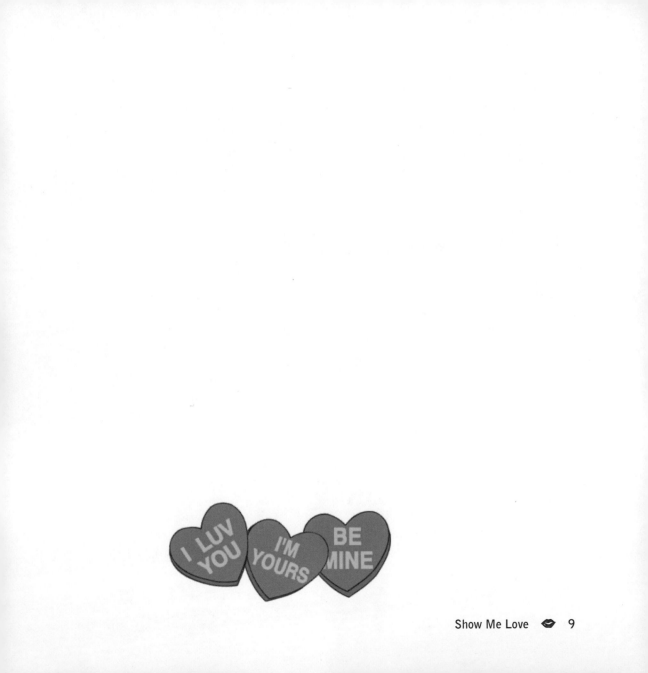

Daily Compliments

When someone gives us a genuine compliment, it's a beautiful gift. We get reassurance that we're loved and appreciated, as well as information about what is going well in our lives. Taking thirty seconds every day to compliment your partner on something is a quick and meaningful way to express that you care.

Seth and Xavier had been together for almost eleven years. One day Seth caught himself nitpicking at Xavier—again. He could see by the tired, pained look on Xavier's face that his nagging was starting to wear on him and on their relationship.

"I thought to myself, 'What am I doing? I love this person. Why am I spending more time telling him what he's doing wrong than I am thanking him for what he's doing right?'"

Later that night, Seth pretended to read the paper while Xavier helped their six-year-old daughter do her homework. But really Seth was listening: "After we'd put Jen to bed, I looked at Xavier and said, 'You're really great at helping her! I'm so impressed by your patience and your encouragement!' He looked a little surprised, but thanked me and smiled. After that, without telling him, I made a commitment to myself to try to compliment him every day."

Compliments are a way of expressing to your lover that you're noticing the good things, and not just the bad. They should be sincere and true, and they can be as simple as, "Your eyes are so beautiful" or "That was a really great dinner. Thanks for taking the time to cook for me tonight."

You may decide to make a commitment with your partner to express your compliments regularly, or you may just start giving them on your own. Seth noticed that over time Xavier started complimenting him more, too: "Suddenly, it just felt like our relationship had this component of appreciation and respect that we'd lost track of over time. It's changed my focus from being, 'What is he doing that I don't like?' to 'What is it about him today that seems particularly special?'"

If compliments don't come easily to you, these samples might give you some idea of where to start:

- Accomplishments: "I'm proud of you for taking on your new job search. It's impressive that you're willing to go for what you really want," or "The backyard looks really great. Thanks for weeding the garden!"

- Physical appearance: "That color looks nice on you," or "You smell so good!" or "You are so incredibly sexy!"

- Things you appreciate: "I'm so lucky to have such a supportive partner," or "Your strength in this situation has been really inspiring."

Try to give your compliments without expectations. Don't give one with the expectation that you'll receive one in return. Your compliments don't have to be met with undying gratitude—just give them as a gift that comes from your heart.

A lot of people have a hard time receiving compliments. Maybe they don't feel like they deserve them, or maybe the compliment isn't true from their perspective. Perhaps the positive attention makes them uncomfortable. Whatever the reason, if being complimented makes you or your partner nervous, that's all the more reason to practice saying nice things to each other. Disagreeing with or denying a compliment is unfair to you and to the giver. The appropriate response to a compliment is to say, "Thank you!" And then try to let it really sink in.

Anniversary Letter

Rosa excitedly threw open her closet door. She reached back into the nether recesses of the closet and pulled out her favorite dress, a little black number. That night marked three years that she and Paul had been together—years full of change, laughter, and happiness. This year they planned to celebrate at the hip new Bolivian restaurant that everyone had been talking about. They would eat delicious food, have some wine . . . Rosa couldn't wait.

By the time Paul got home from work, Rosa was all gussied up and starting to worry that they'd be late for their reservation. "Hi, love!" She gave him a big kiss. "You'd better get ready—remember, our reservation is at 8:30." Paul hugged Rosa and reassured her that he'd be ready in plenty of time. "There's just one thing I've gotta do before we go." With images of Paul trying to get some work done before they left, Rosa said with a little trepidation, "Okay, but I don't want to be late."

About fifteen minutes later, Paul walked into the dining room where Rosa was waiting, reading a magazine. Paul was dressed to the nines, and Rosa beamed up at him. "You look fantastic! Okay, let's go." "Well," Paul replied. "Before we head off, I'd like to give you this. I love you very much, Rosa." He pulled a flat box out from behind his back. It was tied with a shimmering green satin ribbon. "Oh, Paul! Thank you, honey! But I didn't get you anything." Paul smiled, "Well, this is really something for both of us. Go on, open it up."

Rosa untied the slippery ribbon and lifted the lid from the box. Inside were two sheets of paper. "This is my anniversary letter to you, Rosa. It's my way of letting you know how much you mean to me, and how I've enjoyed our last year together." As Rosa started to read, she realized that Paul had written a letter telling her all the many things that he loved about her—her boisterous laugh, the way she sang while doing the dishes, her patience when things went wrong—everything. He also reminded her of many of their great times together in the year past, letting her know how he felt about them and what he had learned. He even wrote about ways he wanted to be closer in the coming year, things he wanted to do that could strengthen their bond. The letter was a testament to Paul's experience of love for Rosa—and it was the best gift she'd ever received.

By the time she had finished reading the letter, tears were rolling down Rosa's cheeks. She looked at Paul sitting next to her on the couch and found herself speechless. All she could do was throw her arms around him and leak tears all over his shoulder. Her worries about their reservations were long gone.

An anniversary letter is a great way to remind your partner (and yourself) what you love about that person. And when both partners write one, you can exchange some of the most meaningful and treasured gifts you will ever receive. On your next anniversary, why not give anniversary letters a try? Here are some suggestions to help you get started:

- What would you like the letter to include? Should it be only about how much you love each other and why? Would you like to also recall some of the hard times of the past year, and write about what you learned from those experiences? How about sharing ways you think you've grown as a couple and ways you'd like to continue to improve? Consider talking with your partner about what you'd like to include and getting a sense of what they have in mind. This will prevent a potentially hurtful expectation gap. But keep the discussion light—remember, this is a gift, not a chore.

- Give yourself plenty of time to write your letter. Spending time in quiet contemplation of your love will be a wonderfully emotional journey for you.

- Decide what time you'll be exchanging your letters. This way, one of you won't be waiting around to do the exchange while the other feels pressured to hurry up and finish.

- Have plenty of time and privacy to read and enjoy your letters. You will want to cherish this lovely gift, and you could very well end up a bit weepy.

- Create an "anniversary letter spot" where you keep each year's letter. Looking at the letters from years past is a lovely way to feel love and gratitude at any time of the year—not just on your anniversary.

The act of writing and reading about your love for each other will encourage you to fully consider and appreciate all the rewarding aspects of your relationship. Make this next anniversary the best one ever by exchanging these gifts of the heart.

Helping Out

Laura threw open the front door and stalked in, throwing her briefcase and coat on the couch. In the bedroom, Sean heard her arrive and called out a breezy "Hi there!" His only response was the sound of her footsteps stomping into the kitchen. Then he heard the cabinet door open and the rattling of glasses. Was that also the sound of Laura muttering? All of a sudden the quiet kvetching was cut short by the shattering of glass and an expletive-filled explosion from Laura.

Sean ran out to see what had happened and found Laura standing amidst the shards of a broken drinking glass, crying. "Ah, honey, it's okay. It's just a glass." Sean opened the utility closet to get the broom and dustpan. "It's not the damned glass, Sean," Laura said, wiping her running nose with the back of her hand. "I've just had the world's worst day at work. It looks like I'll be working late—and I mean *late*—every day this week."

Sean got Laura a glass of water, and they sat down at the kitchen table while she told him all about her day. Apparently, Laura's coworker had made a major computer screw-up, and two huge data sets would have to be entirely redone. And, because the coworker had been scheduled for months to go on vacation the next day, it looked like Laura was going to be stuck doing the whole thing herself.

Sean listened while Laura got the whole thing out of her system, then said, "I'm so sorry, Laura. That does sound like one of the world's worst days at work." Sean took her hand and looked her in the eyes. "Honey, how can I help?"

When your partner is upset about a problem, letting them blow off steam can be a great service. But you may wish there was something you could do to help with the problem, besides just listening. Well, maybe there is—you just need to ask.

Asking "How can I help?" when your partner is distressed shows that you've heard and understood that their problem is serious and also demonstrates that you care enough to try to do something about it. Sometimes all a person needs is to be truly heard, but often there are specific things you can do to ease the situation a bit. Asking specifically how you can assist them will prevent any "mind reading" you may be tempted to do, trying to help in the ways you *think* might be useful and possibly getting

it wrong. By asking, you'll know exactly what your partner needs and where to most profitably put your energy. Your partner will feel like their problem has been acknowledged and appreciated, and you get the opportunity to demonstrate your affection and love.

In Sean and Laura's case, just hearing Sean ask how he could help eased some of the pressure Laura felt. He was letting her know that she wasn't in it alone. "Just having you listen really helps. But I could also use some help with the grocery shopping and dinners this week. I'm gonna be stuck at the office, so if you could be in charge of food, I'd really appreciate it." Sean agreed, and Laura felt as though, just maybe, she'd be able to get through the week.

An earnest offer of help can really lighten your partner's load. Just knowing that you are willing to step in with some assistance can go a long way toward de-catastrophizing a situation. So, the next time your partner walks in the door with the weight of the world on their shoulders, take the opportunity to help. The following suggestions can act as guidelines:

- Try not to offer help too soon. Often, someone with a problem really needs to be heard first, and a preemptive "Can I help?" acts to end the necessary venting. Hear your partner out fully. Then, when it seems as though they are pretty much vented out, gently ask them what you can do.

- Make sure your offer is in earnest. When you ask how you can help, really mean it. Your partner may respond that all they need is for you to listen and give them a big hug. But they may very well come back with a concrete request that may require some effort on your part. Try to find the generosity in yourself to take on whatever responsibility they ask you to shoulder.

- Really listen to what your partner needs. Making suggestions about what you could do to help may come in handy, especially if your partner is so distraught that they're not thinking clearly. But remember to pay close attention to what they are asking. They may not want you to jump right in and save the day. Count on your partner to ask for what he or she needs and try not to force them to accept help they may not want.

An offer of help can open your heart with generosity while letting your partner feel taken care of. You will feel like the hero, coming through in a pinch, and your partner will get the assistance they need in a tough situation.

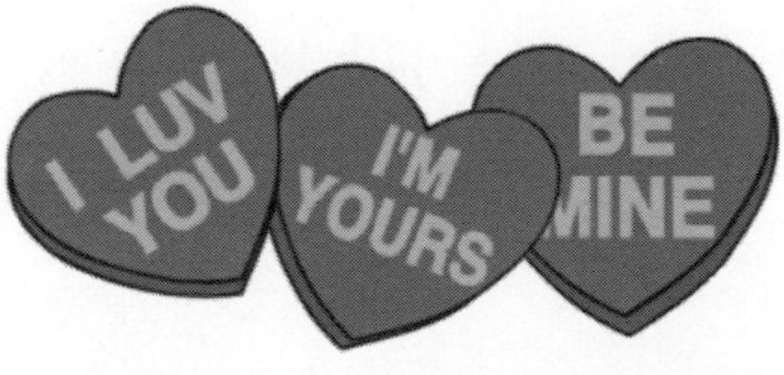
I LUV YOU
I'M YOURS
BE MINE

Writing the Book of Love

In day-to-day life, it can be easy to lose track of the things you love most about someone. You and your partner do things, big and small, that make an impact on the quality of each other's lives. If you feel like you forget to stop and take note of those things, you and your love may want to start a gratitude journal.

All you have to do is get a notebook or blank journal and put it in a spot that's convenient for both of you. (You may want to get one that's well made and attractive, so it can become a keepsake of your relationship after it's filled.) Then, any time your partner does something you appreciate, take a minute to jot it down in the journal.

Katrina and Jill started keeping an appreciation journal last year, after they noticed that they'd been bickering way more than usual. They tended to focus on the nit-picky aspects of life together: who cleaned the house more, who worked harder at the relationship, who made more sacrifices for the other person. Eventually each of them assumed a resentful stance, believing that the other person wasn't doing enough, and that they were giving more than they were getting.

When they talked about it and realized they both felt the same way (and that they both disliked it), they decided to try to focus on the positive aspects about each other to help balance things out. They'd received a journal as a wedding gift, but they'd never known what to do with it. So they placed it on the table in the hallway, along with some colorful pens. They made a pact to seek out things they appreciated and record them in the journal.

Over the next couple of weeks, the first few pages started to fill up. Here's a sample of their appreciation journal:

"Jill brought me a cup of my favorite tea today. It made me feel taken care of after a long day."

"When Katrina hugged me this morning, she held me longer than usual. It really touched me and made me feel like she was showing me how much she loved me."

"I love the way Jill was so patient with my mom on the phone tonight, even though she was behaving so badly."

"I'm so proud of Katrina for getting that promotion at work this week. I appreciate how dedicated she is to her work, and that she's doing a job she really loves."

Katrina and Jill noticed that they were so focused on trying to think of things for the journal that the positive things were at the forefront of their minds. "It wasn't that we never had disagreements, or that everything was idyllic all the time," Jill explained. "But it just seemed like we had more patience with each other with the little things, because the things we appreciated about each other seemed to outweigh those small irritations."

Keeping an appreciation journal can also be a good way to chronicle the great things about your love. During rocky times, it can remind you of the good things. (When you feel frustrated, reading over the journals can help you open your heart that little extra bit and give you the motivation to keep working at your relationship.) Besides, imagine how great it will be twenty years from now to have all those notebooks filled with words of kindness and love—that's the best kind of family heirloom imaginable!

Celebrating Each Other

Valentine's Day is a time for lovers to express to each other how much they care. You buy a card or flowers, maybe even go out to dinner. And while the idea is a sweet one, Valentine's Day has its share of problems. Some feel it's too commercialized, a day promoted by greeting card sellers and florists simply to make an extra buck. Other people wish they didn't have to share their special day with the crowds (waiting for a table on a weeknight?). Even those who appreciate the sentiment of the holiday may wish it didn't have to come just once a year. Whether or not you and your sweetheart celebrate Valentine's Day, you may want to try something new: "I Love You" Day.

Leo and Virginia have been celebrating "I Love You" Day for years. It all started one year when Leo got sick with the flu, forcing them to cancel their plans for Valentine's Day. Instead of going to their favorite restaurant, Virginia made chicken soup and picked up a few of Leo's favorite movies: "Sure, I was disappointed," Virginia told us, "Ever since we'd moved in together, it'd seemed like we just weren't going out as much. It felt like we were taking each other for granted. Unless it was our anniversary or a birthday or Valentine's Day, we just didn't make room for those romantic evenings out anymore."

The week passed, and Leo recovered enough to go back to work. Things were just getting back to normal when Virginia came home one night and noticed that "I Love Virginia" was written in on the kitchen calendar in the space for that day. "Leo?" she called out, "Are you home?"

"In here," Leo called from the direction of the bedroom. Virginia walked into their room, only to find Leo lying on their bed, with the candles lit and rose petals scattered all over the room. "Happy 'I Love You' Day, Virginia!"

"I was so shocked, I started crying!" Virginia said. "It was just so sweet, and so unexpected! It was better than any Valentine's Day that I'd ever had."

Starting your own "I Love You" Day tradition is easy enough: Each of you should pick one day on the calendar and write it in. Then, on that day, just remember to do something nice that expresses your love for your partner. It doesn't have to be

something elaborate or time consuming or expensive. In fact, it generally should be something you can do in less than an hour. Here are some ideas for celebrating the occasion:

- Send your partner something nice at work (flowers, a card, a singing telegram, etc.).
- Make her breakfast (or dinner!) in bed.
- Meet him at his office and take him out to lunch.
- Write a love letter and slip it somewhere where she'll be sure to find it.
- Make a "Ten Things I Love About You" list and leave it on his pillow.
- Make plans to do something that she loves (go to a reading, movie, hot tub, etc.).
- Give him a ten-minute foot massage at the end of the day.

When you're deciding what to do each month, try to think about something that's specific and tailored to your partner. After all, the great thing about having your own special holiday is getting to do it any way that you want!

Lending Your Support

Generosity is a powerful force in a relationship. Lending support to each other is a way to strengthen your relationship as well as enhance each of your individual successes.

Joan and Karl both have jobs that take up a lot of their time. Joan works as an event coordinator, arranging small- and large-scale events for corporations and non-profit organizations. Karl works from home as a freelance designer, as well as an at-home dad.

Recently, Joan had a particularly important event coming up, and she was feeling pretty stressed. Her assistant had a family emergency at the last minute, and Joan wasn't sure how she was going to get both of their jobs done alone. She called Karl at home, just needing someone to vent to: "What am I going to do?" she lamented. "The phone is ringing off the hook, and the voicemail and e-mail haven't been checked for two days! I feel like I'm going to explode!"

Karl let her talk it all out, and then reassured her, "I'm sorry you're under so much pressure right now. I know it's a stressful time. But you're going to be okay, no matter what happens. A week from now the event will happen, and maybe it won't be perfect, but it won't be a disaster, either. Just do your best, honey! And tonight when you come home, I'll make you a nice dinner and you can take a long bath, and things will look a little better." Joan appreciated Karl's support and reassurance, even though she was still freaking out. At least that bath was a nice thing to look forward to!

That night when they were eating dinner, after Joan recounted her day, Karl said, "Well, I called the babysitter earlier today, and she can watch the baby for the day. And I've got some slack on the project I'm working on right now. So I was thinking, could you use an extra set of hands tomorrow?"

Joan was thrilled. "That's too good to be true. But really, it won't be very fun for you. I just need someone to check messages and return calls and answer the phone . . . but it would be a great relief. . . ." Karl got up from the table to do the dishes, saying, "No problem. I could use a break from being at home, anyway. Besides, it'll be fun to see you in action. And you always take the time to give me feedback on my work, so it's about time I returned the favor!"

The great thing about lending support to each other is that it gives you a chance to show that you're behind each other 100 percent. The next time you can spare an afternoon, tell your partner that you have some time free to help with anything he or she needs. Maybe she'll ask you to hold her hand while she makes that stressful phone call. Or maybe what he really needs is a day to himself to think through an important decision, and you can watch the kids. Or maybe she has a list of errands you can run that she can never seem to get to. Whatever it is, giving your time and energy to help make your partner's life just a bit easier is a generous and loving offer, and sharing in each other's personal endeavors is a way to invest in your future together.

Choosing to Be Kind

Chris was feeling utterly frazzled. He found himself at the supermarket after work with no idea what to get for dinner. Somehow he'd lost the grocery list he had made the night before. No surprise, really. He had had one of those unbelievably busy days at work, with the phone ringing nonstop, a huge pile of paperwork, and e-mail messages pleading to be answered.

Barely maintaining his composure, he decided to cook his old standby of chicken burritos. He hurriedly gathered the ingredients, got through the checkout line, and headed out the door with his bag of groceries in tow. "Whew! Well, at least I can get home now," he sighed. But just as he was about to cross over to where his car was parked, he saw a flash of glorious purple out of the corner of his eye. He turned and saw the little flower stand on the corner. Featured prominently in a big white bucket was a huge bunch of purple irises, so many that they seemed to burst right out of the container.

"Wow, Carla would love some of those irises." Chris paused on his way to the car, thinking about how crazy his partner Carla was about irises. Her favorite flower, and right in front of him were some of the most beautiful examples he'd ever seen. He imagined how delighted she would be if he brought some home out of the blue. Suddenly his mood lightened. As he strode over to the corner and picked out a dozen flowers, all the stress of the day seemed to lift from his shoulders. All he was thinking about was the pleasure Carla would get from receiving the irises—and how happy he would be watching her.

Chris was right—Carla was delighted to receive such a beautiful and thoughtful surprise. And when she heard what a rotten day Chris had had, she was doubly grateful that he'd been able to put that aside and think of her. Instead of bringing a lot of anger and frustration home with him, Chris had chosen to be kind, to put Carla first. She was truly moved and felt wonderfully cared for.

Often in our daily lives we are given the opportunity to be kind to our partners. This opportunity may be the possibility of coming through on a difficult promise, the option to treat your partner to something they love, or the chance to give them what

they really need. Is there something your partner has been asking you to do that you've been putting off, feeling lazy or maybe even resentful that you "have" to do it? Is there something that your partner truly loves, a gift or action on your part, that you could give him or her? What's stopping you?

Choosing to be kind means taking those opportunities to be good to your partner, whether or not it's your "turn," whether or not there is a specific occasion. How about bringing home a gift for no reason other than to see your love smile? Why not go ahead and give one of the backrubs you're famous for? You could even do that long-postponed chore that your partner has been mentioning. Wouldn't these things make your partner feel good? Wouldn't they make you feel good?

Give kindness a try. Do something nice for your partner today, something totally unexpected and just for them. Here are a few tips to help you do it:

- Keep it simple. Choosing to be kind doesn't necessarily mean that you have to bust the bank or bowl your partner over. You don't have to bring home surprise tickets to Tahiti when buying a copy of the new book they've been wanting or volunteering to do the dishes can do the trick.

- Accept their appreciation. If you've decided to go ahead and do something that has been a point of contention between you and your partner, try to accept their pleasure without bitterness. Remember, you've chosen to be kind, so you don't have to feel resentful or coerced. Take the opportunity to feel love—both the love you feel for your partner and the love they return to you.

- Try not to expect any specific response. Choosing to be kind is about giving as selflessly as you can. Focus on giving your partner pleasure, not getting a response.

Choosing to be kind can really add a lift to your relationship. It shows your partner that you're thinking about them, and that you care enough to be truly giving. And it can help make you feel like the hero, coming through to make your partner's day. Give it a try and see if you don't find choosing to be kind a habit you don't want to break.

Musical Offerings

One March, Bill was getting ready to travel out of state on one of his many business trips. Vanessa, who was used to him having to take off, still felt a small pang whenever she knew he would be gone for a while. That Tuesday, as Vanessa was sitting at her new home computer, she got a great idea. She knew that Bill hated being separated just as much as she did. Why not give him a going-away gift that would remind him of her while letting him know how much she cared? She had the perfect idea! She set up the CD-making function of the computer and set to work.

For the next week, Vanessa would retire to her office after dinner. "No TV tonight?" Bill would ask. "Nope! I've got some work to do. You go ahead; I'll be in later." As it just happened to be the first week of the college basketball playoffs, Bill happily wiled away the evenings in a sports reverie. Meanwhile, Vanessa snuck various CDs from their music collection and smuggled them back and forth from her office. Once, when Bill walked by her office and noticed the door ajar, he could see Vanessa in there, headphones on, dancing all by herself. "Okay, if she needs to boogie down in the evenings—all alone—who am I to wonder." He got a juice from the fridge and went back to his basketball game.

Finally, the day came when Bill was due to leave. It was very early in the morning, and Vanessa was just getting out of bed when he came into the bedroom to give her a kiss. As they hugged, she whispered in his ear, "Oh, I'm not letting you out of here before I give you something." Vanessa walked over to the closet and pulled out a small velvet pouch. "Now, promise me that you won't open this 'til you're on the road. Promise?" Bill promised, giving Vanessa a big farewell kiss. "I'll see you in a week, honey. I love you!"

Bill put the little pouch on the passenger seat beside him, and when he got just outside of town, he reached for it. He slid the pouch open and fumbled with the tissue paper wrapped loosely around whatever was inside. Then he touched some hard plastic—a CD case! He pulled the CD out and quickly looked at it (keeping one eye on the road). On the front of the case, Vanessa had drawn a big heart and written in

calligraphy, "On the Road Again—with Vanessa!" "What is this?" Bill laughed, sliding the CD into his player.

Each song on the CD was either a love song, a song that meant something in their relationship, or both. Vanessa had crafted a love letter to Bill—in music. Bill remembered making a romantic mixed tape for a girl he'd liked in high school. He was tickled that, now that he was all grown up, Vanessa had made one for him. It had such a fun high school quality to it, yet was also one of the most touching and loving things he'd ever received. All the way to Tucson, he thought of Vanessa and how much he loved her.

You may have made or received lovey-dovey mixed tapes in your youth, but not for a long time since. How about trying it again? Whether you have a cassette recorder or a CD burner, you can create a unique combination of music just for your love. Music can say things that words sometimes fail to convey: memories, emotions, and desires. Why not let your partner know how you feel by sharing some songs?

Here are some tips for making your own love tape or CD:

- Choose both old favorites and surprise selections. This can be a good opportunity to introduce your partner to music that reminds you of them, but that they may not know about.

- Let them listen to it at their own speed. Don't insist that they listen to it right away or when you want them to. Listening to a collection of music you've chosen for them can be an extremely intimate act, and they may want to do it in their own time.

You may have been a veritable "mix master" in your past, or maybe you could never figure out how your tape deck worked. Give it a try now. Letting music reawaken old feelings and inspire new ones in your love can be one of the most effective ways of communication.

A Few of Your Favorite Things

It was a glorious Saturday, all sunshine and the feeling that finally the long chill of winter had really lifted. Sally and Eddie were spending the day puttering around the house, taking care of errands and small chores. They enjoyed these leisurely weekend days, when they could each do their own thing yet still touch base with each other throughout.

While Sally was busy doing some mending that had piled up in a bag on her closet floor, Eddie dashed out to the grocery store to pick up ingredients for dinner. When he got back, he put away the groceries and went to relax with the paper in the living room. Sally, having finished her mending, got up to forage in the kitchen for a snack. When she opened the cabinet, she saw the spaghetti and sun-dried tomatoes Eddie had gotten for their dinner. But she also saw a big bag of her very favorite snack, garlic melba rounds. "All right!" she exulted, grabbing the bag with delight. Then she stopped for a moment, recognizing that Eddie had bought the snack just for her. He hated melba rounds himself, and she knew that their delicious garlicky taste sometimes made her breath a trial for Eddie. But he had made the effort to remember to get some for her, just to make her happy.

Sally smiled and went to sit next to Eddie on the couch. "You know," she said. "I really love your thoughtfulness. I love the fact that you're thinking of me when you go to the store, and that you bring me special treats. It makes me feel very cared for, and I love that you can help me feel that way. Thanks, honey." Eddie's face broke out into a smile and he flushed with pleasure. "Of course. Any time!" He folded Sally into a big hug.

It feels wonderful to say, "I love you." Most folks like to hear it, too. But sometimes the "I love you," "I love you, too," exchange between partners can begin to feel a little stale. You can take the routine out of it simply by being more specific. Take a moment to tell your partner exactly *what* you love about them, either something you've just recognized, or a quality you've long cherished but have never made explicit. When you take the moment to say something like, "I love how gentle you are when you touch my face," or "I love that you try so hard to listen fairly when we have a fight," you let

the other person know not only that you care deeply for them and are willing to share that, but also that you really *see* them—that you recognize their efforts and appreciate them. This honest and loving acknowledgment is one of the best gifts you can give.

Try it tonight. Take some time to think about some qualities or habits that you really love about your partner—anything from the way he supports you when you're down, to the lovely crinkles in her face when she laughs. In the last week or two, has your love done anything that struck you as wonderful, thoughtful, or kind? Does your partner have a certain way of moving that sets your heart alight? A tone of voice or way of telling a story that you cherish? Tell them the specifics, and enjoy the pleasure it gives.

One-Minute Touch

When Charles gets home from work he often finds Alexis sitting at the kitchen table, staring out toward the laundromat across the street. Her shoulders sag; she's mechanically pulling at her hair. The way Charles tells it, Alexis gets pretty emptied out by her job at the Pacific Stock Exchange. Every dip in the market sets off a horde of automatic buy and sell orders. She's on the phone nonstop till long after the board closes. When Alexis stumbles home at the end of one of these days, she can barely speak. After a perfunctory kiss, she usually returns to a careful study of the laundromat.

Charles used to feel resentful and disappear for the evening into his photographic darkroom. Or he'd nag Alexis about finding another job. Neither response solved anything. Neither response drew them closer.

That's when Charles hit on an idea he calls the one-minute touch. Instead of withdrawing or picking a fight, he spends a minute or two touching Alexis in a way he knows will calm her. Touching also helps them connect without words. It all started one night when Charles asked a simple question: "What would make you feel good right now?" "I think if you just touched me," Alexis said. "Nothing sexual. Just something gentle and nice."

Charles asked more questions. Where would she like to be touched? Soft pressure and rubbing on her forehead; gentle rubbing and pulling of her ears. How should he do it? Alexis demonstrated and Charles practiced till he got the hang of it. How could he know when she wanted it? Any time she looked tired; any time she couldn't talk.

The very next night, Charles had an opportunity to try the one-minute touch. Alexis was sitting at the table looking like she'd been run over by a Sherman tank. Pulling her hair; staring. When Charles walked in, his first impulse was to turn right around and head for the darkroom. But he remembered his plan. Instead of leaving or complaining, he stood behind Alexis and leaned her head back against his stomach. Charles didn't say anything, just moved his fingers over Alexis's forehead in exactly the way she'd showed him. Then he rubbed her ears.

Charles says the thing he likes most about the one-minute touch is that Alexis will visibly relax. He can see the rigidity and tension melt out of her body. It feels like he's

doing something truly helpful. The other plus is that they end up feeling more connected. At some point, Alexis usually sighs and says, "That's really nice," in a throaty voice that tells him she means it. Suddenly things feel calm. Close. And after a while, they talk in that easy way that happens when everything's all right between them.

If the one-minute touch sounds like something you want to try, we suggest the following guidelines:

- Ask your partner this question: "If we only had a minute or two, how would you like to be touched that would feel really nice and soothing?"

- Encourage your partner to brainstorm and come up with at least two or three ideas that aren't overtly sexual.

- Make sure the one-minute touch is easy for you to do—comfortable, nontaxing, and nonembarrassing.

- Make sure you understand exactly how to do it so it's what your partner wants. Ask for a demonstration, then try it yourself while getting feedback from your partner.

- Keep it simple. Don't let the one-minute touch lead to anything else; don't elaborate or extend it much beyond two or three minutes. The easier and less complicated it is, the more likely you'll feel up to doing it.

- Identify specific situations where you plan to use one-minute touch. Commit yourself to doing it as often as possible whenever those situations arise.

Charles reports that the one-minute touch has greatly improved the emotional climate at home. "It's the biggest return I ever got," he says, "for a minute's worth of effort."

PART II

Get a Little Closer

Dreaming Together

Remember when you were a kid, and you spent so much of your time dreaming about the possibilities of the future? The adults in your life may have caught you "daydreaming," and reminded you to get back to the task at hand, whether it was your chores, your homework, or your math test.

Now that you're a grown-up, you may be all too aware of the tasks you're responsible for each day. Perhaps you've become your own daydream police, forcing yourself to stop gazing out the window and come back to the here and now.

Erin and Jess are what you might call "daydream believers." Sure, they both go to their nine-to-five jobs each day, and they manage to meet their deadlines every time. But their dreams aren't taking a backseat to their daily responsibilities, either. Their secret? They spend plenty of time dreaming together.

Sometimes, their dreams are pure fantasy—things that are fun to imagine but that wouldn't necessarily work in their real lives. In one dream that they often talk about, they live on a huge ranch in the middle of nowhere. There are lots of horses and chickens and dogs, and they don't have a pressure in the world. Of course, running a real ranch isn't nearly as relaxing as running an imaginary ranch, and neither Erin nor Jess is willing to give up the luxuries of city life. But they enjoy their daydream, all the same. In fact, they're planning an upcoming vacation on a working ranch. For two weeks, it'll be milking the cows, gathering the eggs, and dining on gourmet meals—just their kind of ranch experience.

Other times, their daydreams lead to goals for the future. Jess has always wanted to live in a foreign country, and Erin has been dreaming of getting her graduate degree. At first, these dreams were vague and nonspecific, but the more they talked about them, the more detailed they became. One day Jess suggested that they research some graduate programs in other countries, just to see if anything looked promising. So Erin sent away for applications from schools in three different countries, and Jess started reading up on life abroad.

Set aside some time to dream with your sweetheart. Here are some questions that might get you started:

- In your perfect life, where do you imagine yourself, and what are you doing? What is the pace of your day? Who are the people that surround you?
- If you could have any job in the world, what would it be, and why? What qualities do you have that would make you good at it?
- What would be your dream vacation?
- Where do you see us in five years?
- If you had three wishes, what would they be?

Can you remember the last time you and your partner talked about your hopes and dreams for the future? Whether you're just fooling around, or sharing your most heartfelt hopes for the future, dreaming together can bring you and your sweetheart closer. Saying things aloud can be incredibly powerful, and if you work together, there's no reason your life can't be a dream come true.

Sharing a Fear

It was that time of the month again—time to pay the bills. As Stephanie wrote checks out of the house account, she felt her shoulders get tighter and tighter. She sat at her desk surrounded with slips of paper and little plastic-windowed envelopes, and she noticed her heart rate speeding up, her breathing getting more and more shallow. Then, when Rob came into her office to ask her what she wanted for dinner, she couldn't seem to stop herself from snapping, "Whatever you want! It's your responsibility to decide, so just decide!" Rob responded with a curt "Fine," and stomped out to rattle and bang pans angrily in the kitchen. "Jeez, what did I do that for?" thought Stephanie. "He didn't deserve that. I'm just so freaked about paying these bills."

Actually, Stephanie had a pretty good idea about why she was tense enough to bite off Rob's head over dinner. She had always been "bad" with money—always felt totally out of control when it came to balancing her checkbook and managing her funds. The fact that she was actually quite good at getting the bills paid and had never bounced a check or made many late payments didn't seem to alter her feelings about her money-managing skills.

Her fears about money seemed even worse now that she lived with Rob. Stephanie had chosen to be the one to pay the house bills in a show of bravado to herself. She willed herself to be okay with it, but as time went on, paying those bills made her more and more miserable. And the fact that Rob had caught one or two small mistakes she'd made didn't help. She secretly lived in fear that he would "discover" that she was "terrible" with money and regret that he'd moved in with her. She tried to reassure herself that she was blowing things out of proportion. But deep inside, she really thought it was true.

Stephanie finished up the bills and went to straighten up the bedroom. She avoided Rob, who was still making angry noises in the kitchen. She waited until dinner to apologize. "Rob, I'm sorry I snapped at you about dinner. It wasn't fair, and I apologize for jumping down your throat."

"Okay, Stephanie. But I'd like to know why you did it. What made you so uptight that you had to come after me like that?" Stephanie paused, considering what to say.

Then she looked up at Rob. "You know, honey, I need to tell you something that really scares me and that I've never wanted you to know." Stephanie took a deep breath and told him all of her worries and fears about money.

"Oh, Steph, I don't feel that way at all. I think you're good at the bills, but now I understand why they make you so tense. I want you to know that you're much better at dealing with money than I could ever be, and even if you make a mistake every now and then, it's no big deal. Everyone makes mistakes." Stephanie got up and put her arms around Rob, and he returned her hug full force. Stephanie felt much closer to Rob than she had before—as though she could really trust him. She realized that this feeling was worth the risk she'd had to take to get it.

A big part of intimacy is allowing yourself to be vulnerable with your partner. This can mean exposing sides of yourself that you may think are unattractive or "bad." Sharing fears with your loved one can help them understand you much more fully and will provide you with a feeling that you are understood and accepted. Revealing your fears can be one of the most liberating things you can do with a partner.

Here are some suggestions for revealing a fear to your partner:

- Choose a time when they can hear you. Make sure you have enough time and privacy to be able to say all you need to without interruption.

- Ask for what you need. If you just want them to listen without commenting, say so. If you would like them to offer what they think, you can let them know. If revealing the fear is very difficult for you, tell your partner so. You can ask them to be gentle with you, to hold you, or anything else that will help you speak clearly and honestly.

- Don't necessarily expect reciprocation. Just because you're baring your soul doesn't mean that your partner will. You can ask, certainly, but try not to expect any specific response from them.

Although it can be hard to reveal your true self to your partner, it's an essential step toward real closeness. We're willing to bet that you'll feel more free when you feel that your partner knows the real you, and your partner will feel honored that you trusted them enough to reveal it.

Do an Interview

"The whole point of being in a relationship," Molly told a friend, "is feeling seen. All your struggles, all the sludge about yourself that you usually hide is seen and accepted. And if it's not, the whole thing's empty as hell. You're invisible. You might as well be alone."

Molly was getting cold feet about her upcoming wedding. Cameron, her fiancé, didn't understand her desire *not* to invite her father. "Cameron thinks that everyone should be included; they'll be hurt otherwise. He doesn't get it that I just can't have my father there. He's way too crazy; he's done too much to me in my life. If Cameron can't understand that, how can I trust he'll understand anything?"

The impasse continued until Molly had a "weird" idea. She was watching Barbara Walters dissect some poor schlub for the TV audience, and she began to think about Walters' technique. There were very direct, very probing questions asked in a framework of apparent compassion and support. "What do you fear . . . What do you need . . . What in your past led you to choose. . . ?"

Molly's idea was that she and Cameron could interview each other about the issue, using a set of six specific, probing questions. They'd write down the answers, and then try to summarize what they'd heard. Here are the interview questions Molly came up with:

1. What's your need in this situation?

2. What are you afraid might happen in this situation?

3. Do you have any other feelings that are triggered by this issue (anger, sadness, guilt)?

4. What have you experienced in the past that affects your feelings on this issue?

5. What are your beliefs (about what's right and wrong, what will happen in the future, what you suspect regarding my motives or feelings) affecting this issue?

6. What choices do you see for yourself in this situation?

When Cameron interviewed Molly, her answers to the questions about needs and past experience got his attention. "I need to be safe at my own wedding. I need to enjoy the moment, not be terrified that my father will do some wacko thing. At my sister's

Confirmation he poured the punch bowl on someone who admitted to voting for Clinton. He brought a gun to my grandmother's wake, and was running around the chapel trying to sign up new members for the NRA. He announced in the lobby of my college dorm that I was a slut because I was wearing a pink tank top."

As Molly interviewed Cameron, she learned some important things about his beliefs and history. "When you leave somebody out of a big family event, it's like you're throwing them to the wolves. They're basically out of the family right there. I don't want to do that to anyone, no matter what kind of nutball they are." Later, he told her about how his mother froze his dad out of the family after their divorce. "He was a pariah. It was like, 'Oh God, don't tell him about the birthday party—he might come.'"

Cameron suddenly realized that while he'd wanted to stay close to *his* dad—and was thwarted by his mom—Molly truly wanted nothing more to do with her father. Any trust in their relationship had already been destroyed. For the first time, as Cameron summarized what he'd learned in the interview, Molly felt seen and understood.

You can deepen your understanding of virtually any issue by asking each other the six key questions. Here are the steps:

- Pick an issue where you're struggling to understand each other.

- Write the six questions down on a piece of paper so you can both refer to it during the interview.

- Ask your questions using a gentle, supportive tone. Sound interested. Don't let your voice betray judgments or criticism.

- Be sure to write down the gist of each answer so you can refer to it later when you do your summary.

- Ask follow-up questions for anything you don't understand. Keep probing carefully until things are clear.

- Do both sides of the interview in one sitting. Don't leave one of you dangling.

- Be sure to include the summary. Make a real effort to distill and explain the essence of your partner's experience.

Sharing Old Pictures

A picture may be worth a thousand words, but that doesn't mean they aren't worth talking about. Those old photo albums (or boxes of mismatched snapshots) can be the key to learning things about your partner that you'd never think to ask.

Kate and Sophie had been together for twelve years, and it wasn't unusual for them to finish each other's sentences, they knew each other so well. The early days of their relationship, when they'd talked for hours, excited to learn all about each other, seemed like a lifetime ago. They still loved each other, but they found themselves secretly missing those days of wonder and discovery.

When Kate's parents decided to sell the family home and move into someplace a little smaller, they sent Kate three boxes filled with her childhood mementos. Photo albums, yearbooks, and letters from her high school best friend were among the contents.

Kate and Sophie sat together one lazy Sunday afternoon, going through the boxes on their living room floor. For each photo, Kate told Sophie everything she remembered: She wasn't smiling in that picture of her at camp when she was eleven, because she was dreading the swimming class that was going on later that afternoon. "But you love to swim!" Sophie said.

"Not that year," Kate said, seriously. "My mom had handmade my swimsuit. That was the year she was trying to be Miss Betty Sue Homemaker, even though you know she's terrible at those things. The elastic in my suit came undone, and I spent the whole class just trying to keep my little breasts covered. It was mortifying!"

"Oh, I'm sorry, sweetie! That sounds awful!" Sophie put her arm around Kate to console her, trying unsuccessfully to stifle her laughter at the mental picture of Kate as a gawky preteen in a homemade bathing suit.

"It's not funny!" Kate said, narrowing her eyes. But within a moment she was smiling. "You should have *seen* mom sitting at the sewing machine grandma had bought her! Trying to pin the stretchy fabric to the pattern! It must've been one of the most frustrating summers of her life!" They both dissolved into fits of laughter.

By going through your old photos, as well as other mementos from your past, you and your partner are bound to come across things you've never thought to mention to each other:

- Make a special date with each other to share your old pictures.

- Remember to "show and tell," don't just show. Spend time on each one, telling the story behind the photo. Where were you? How were you feeling? What was going on in your life at that time? What else do you remember from that day? What were you thinking about the other people in the picture? Who took the photo?

- When it's your turn to share, try to paint a vivid picture of that moment. When it's your partner's turn, ask questions and express your interest.

Your pictures are just a starting place for sharing your old memories and getting to know each other all over again.

Checking In

Todd and Samantha had always been pretty good at keeping each other up to date about what was going on in their lives. They would usually talk at dinner, responding to the usual "How was your day?" with brief sketches of what had happened. But because their jobs often wore them out emotionally, they would sometimes be too pooped to go into much detail, giving their exchanges a cursory feeling. They would eat and settle for idle chitchat, rarely sharing how they felt about things or what they'd been thinking deeply about. There just didn't seem to be the time or space for indulging in that kind of sharing.

Then one blustery day in February, Samantha was grabbing a quick lunch with her friend Tanya. Sam had been updating Tanya on her troubles with a particular coworker, a man who seemed to think that napping at his desk was the height of productivity. "Oh my," Tanya laughed. "Maybe you're having some kind of man-woman communication gap with this guy. What does Todd think about the whole thing?" Sam shook her head, "Oh, he thinks the guy's off his nut." Sam laughed, but as she and Tanya headed back to the office, she found herself wondering just what Todd did think about the situation. Sure, he thought the guy in question seemed like a loon. But what did he *really* think about it? Had she even told him enough about the problem for him to have any opinions? Or had she just given him the wacky details without talking about how much the situation worried and aggravated her, and about all the ideas she'd played with in trying to deal with it? As Sam sat back down at her desk, she was struck by the thought that Todd really knew very little about her everyday life. And she didn't really know much about his. Sure, they knew basically what was going on—but not about the feelings or what each really thought about what happened every day.

That evening, Samantha came up with the idea of a weekly check-in. She sat down on the couch next to Todd, telling him about her realization that they could use some deeper sharing about what was happening in each of their lives. "How about if we had some kind of ritual or habit of asking each other every week how the other's week has gone? And I mean, asking and expecting an in-depth, full answer? This wouldn't be a time when we're just chatting. It would be the chance for us to get stuff off our chests, to tell each other how

we really feel about things and what we're thinking about. Maybe we could do it on the ride to the farmer's market each week—that drive takes about an hour. What do you think?"

Todd thought that a weekly check-in would be a great idea. He had noticed how little he seemed to know about Sam's daily life and suspected that she had only a loose grasp on what he went through each week, too. The very next Saturday, they gave their weekly check-in a try. It was a tad awkward at first—of course, neither of them were used to it right away. But soon each felt much more free to open up to the other, sharing feelings, asking for real advice, and bouncing ideas off each other. By the time they got to the farmer's market, they felt worlds closer.

You can set up a weekly check-in with your partner, too. Here are some suggestions about how to start:

- Make sure that both of you understand how the check-in will work. If one of you intends it to be a space for deep sharing and the other thinks it's time to crack jokes and laugh, you may run into trouble. Of course, the structure and rhythm of the check-in may change as you do it, but try to be on the same page when you start. Should one person always speak first? How do you feel about interruptions? Try to be very clear about what you need in the interaction so that your wires don't get crossed.

- Choose a time and place that you're both comfortable with. Having a good block of time will help you both relax, knowing that each will get his or her say. And choosing a place where you both feel calm and at ease is a must. Many folks like to talk while driving; others prefer the comfort of their living room. You might also try getting out to a café, where the relatively anonymous environment might make opening up easier.

- If you run out of time and either of you (or both!) don't feel you've had your say, make a specific date to finish up the talk in the very near future. This way, you're both guaranteed to feel heard.

A weekly check-in can help you get to know your partner again. It's normal to get caught up in your busy daily life and sometimes forget to open up. But when you have a dedicated opportunity to "let it all hang out" with your partner, you'll find it easier to build the trust and intimacy that make your relationship precious.

Getting to Know All About You

If it feels like you and your partner know everything about each other, think again. You can never know absolutely everything about what another person thinks and feels, which means that there's always more to learn.

Sure, you know about each other's families and histories. You probably know all the big things (although even those can slip through the cracks sometimes). But if you start asking questions you'll hear some surprising new stories. Here are a few queries to try when you find yourselves hanging out with some time on your hands.

Early childhood:

- What was your first memory?
- Who was your favorite teacher when you were young?
- What was your hometown like back then, and how has it changed?
- What was your biggest moment of glory when you were a kid?
- What was the worst trouble you ever got into?
- Who were your friends, and what were they like?
- What did you think about your family when you were young, and how has that changed?
- What was your most embarrassing moment as a kid?
- Who was your first crush?
- What is your saddest memory from childhood?
- Were you ever in any school performances?
- What do you remember about recess and the schoolyard?
- How did you spend your summer vacations?
- Did you have any pets growing up?
- What did you know/think about sex when you were young?

- What did you want to be when you grew up?

Adolescence and young adulthood:

- When did you first know you were hitting puberty?
- What was it like for you (first period, etc.)?
- Who was your first love?
- Who were your friends?
- What kind of crowd did you hang out with?
- What were your favorite classes? Teachers?
- Did you have after-school jobs?
- What was your relationship with your family like?
- What was your most embarrassing moment?
- What did you dislike the most about yourself?
- What did you like most about yourself?
- What quality did you have then that you wish you still had?
- What did you expect from your future?
- What's the most dangerous thing you did?
- What do you regret about your youth?
- What did you want to be when you grew up?

Adulthood:

- When did you first start feeling like an adult?
- What is something you've always wanted to do that you've never told me?
- What has been your most embarrassing moment as an adult?
- What do you like best about our relationship?
- What do you wish we could add to our relationship?

- What is your greatest fear about the future?
- What is your greatest hope for the future?
- What do you want to be when you grow up?

Remember to form your answers as detailed stories, rather than just a laundry list. The idea is to paint a vivid picture of your past, so that you can share more about yourselves with each other.

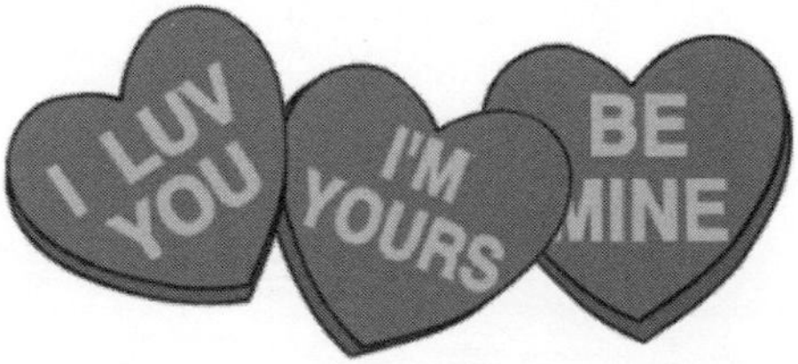
I LUV YOU
I'M YOURS
BE MINE

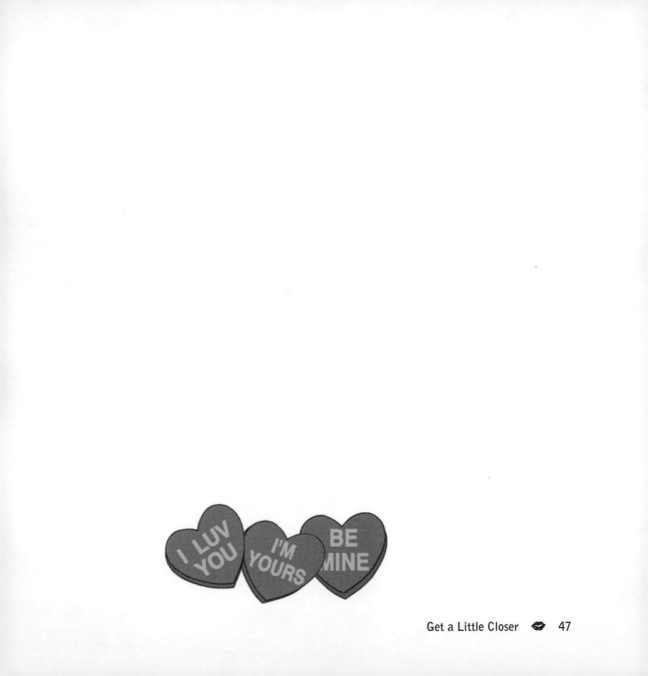

Your High and Low of the Day

How was your day, dear? Have you ever asked your partner this question, only to hear "Okay" or "Not bad"? And have you ever wished for just a little more detail?

Marc had. Every night at dinner, he asked Allen how his day had gone, and Allen gave him the same generic answer: "Pretty good." Marc knew Allen's job was stressful, and that Allen sometimes got tired of talking about it. But the more "pretty goods" Marc heard, the more distant he started to feel.

Over time, Marc started to realize that he didn't have the first clue how Allen's day-to-day life was going. And since Marc had started to reciprocate with his own brief, generic remarks, he knew he was not the only one who was out of touch.

One night, they rented a romantic "dramedy" that wasn't much to their liking. After they turned it off and started getting ready for bed, they went over all the cheesiest parts of the movie. Allen, his mouth full of toothpaste, laughed, "What were they thinking? What melodrama! And his hair was so *bad*!" "I know! It was unfortunate!" Marc agreed. "You know, though, there was one thing I kind of liked. It was nice how each day at dinner they shared the high point and the low point of their day. I thought it was sweet." "You're such a softie!" Allen said. "But I suppose it *was* one of the high points of that dreadful, dreadful movie."

The next night while they were cooking dinner, Marc asked Allen how his day went, and Allen replied, "Oh, it was pretty good, I guess." "What were the best and worst moments of your day today?" Marc asked, not looking up from the spinach he was washing. "Oh, I get it. Is this a new tradition we're starting?" Allen teased, but when Marc just nodded and smiled, Allen said, "Well, let me think. The low point was probably when I got stuck in traffic for an extra forty-five minutes on my way to work, and I almost missed this really important meeting and I was all stressed out.... And the high point was when I went to lunch with Sue. She's so funny!"

By the time dinner was on the table, Marc had asked Allen questions about his meeting and how it went, they'd caught up on Sue's gossip, and they'd made plans to invite Sue and her husband over for dinner sometime soon. Then, when Allen was done, he got to hear all about Marc's high and low.

By using this simple technique, you and your partner can stay more in touch with the landscape of your day-to-day lives. As you try out this tune-up:

- Give thought to your responses, and try to answer with honesty.

- Share your experiences with the intent to connect more deeply with your partner.

- Be honest. If your high or low involves an incident with your partner, feel free to share that. But remember not to use this ritual as a way to continue an argument or try to win a point. Always keep the emphasis on loving connection.

Reminiscing Together

There's on old folk song called "Kisses Sweeter than Wine" in which the singer reminisces about each stage of a long, passionate relationship. There was a lot of trouble and pain, he says, "But oh Lord, I'd do it again."

Reminiscing about the good times, as well as hard days you've gotten through together, is a lovely way to reaffirm your relationship. It strengthens the bond; it reminds you of the things you value in each other.

Adrian and Helen like to reminisce during Friday night dinners out. They usually start off with updates about what happened at work. Then, often as not, one of them will say, "That reminds me of the time . . ." And off they go, transported by memory to another day and place. A lot of their stories are funny or wry. Like the time they went to a county fair palm reader—also an insurance agent—who said Adrian's life line was missing and he needed to buy a big accident policy. Or when Adrian put his back out on their honeymoon lifting Helen over the threshold, and, undeterred, they made love while he lay on an ice pack.

Many of their stories are sentimental. Like when their daughter's first offering to the tooth fairy was lost before it got under the pillow, and Helen made a soap carving of the tooth to "fool" the fairy.

Some stories are sweet or romantic. For example, how Helen bought Adrian a pair of electric socks when he had to take a business trip to the Yukon. Or when Adrian built Helen a lovely spot in which to do her meditation.

As Helen and Adrian reminisce, they remind each other, indirectly, of their commitment, their resilience, and their gratitude. One good story is worth fifty perfunctory "I love you"s. One story can shift the focus from a hard day or recent squabble to the easy comfort of the life they've shared. It's like the stories put everything into perspective, shrinking problems and conflicts to a minor note in a sweet, ongoing melody.

If you think reminiscing might add leavening to your good time together, try the following:

- Prepare in advance a story you'll use to remind your partner of the good in your relationship.

- During conversations with your partner, think back to funny, sentimental, or romantic experiences that might relate to your current discussion.
- Use intro lines like, "That reminds me of a very sweet thing you did when . . ."
- Select stories that show your partner in a good light. Don't use reminiscence to tease or criticize; it will lose all its romantic value.
- Tell your partner what it means to you to have this shared experience. Talk about how it makes you feel about the relationship.

PART III

Work Out the Kinks

Quizzing for Clarity

Sometimes tensions build in a relationship, making it hard for you to bring up something you want to talk about—even something minor. Other times, you want to give your partner space, but you also need to know what you should do in the meantime. In the ideal world, we would always be able to bring things up with the one we love and work them out with love and respect. But in reality it isn't always that easy.

Madeline and Alex had both been really stressed, and the tension was wearing on their communication with each other. They were alternately snippy, or quiet, or in each other's faces. And whenever one of them would try to smooth things over, the other person seemed too far away to bridge the gap.

Finally, Madeline came up with a plan. She started putting multiple choice questions on Alex's pillow. They looked something like this:

When Madeline comes home from work, I wish she would:

    a) Come in and give me a hug right away.

    b) Give me some space, and let me come to her when I'm ready.

    c) Come say "hi," but then let me have some time to myself before dinner.

    d) Other: _____

Lately when we've been fighting, I've been:

    a) Thinking that some counseling might do us some good.

    b) Confident that this is just a phase that will work itself out.

    c) Wishing we could talk and work things out.

    d) Other: _____

When we're fighting and I get quiet, I wish that Madeline would:

    a) Give me space to get my thoughts together.

    b) Stay there, but wait for me to think of what I want to say.

c) Tell me what's on her mind in a calm way.

d) Other: _____

The quizzes allowed Madeline to bring up the problems she was perceiving, but in a nonjudgmental way that allowed Alex the time to think over a response. In return, Alex made up a few quizzes for Madeline. And once the conversation got going in this nonthreatening way, both of them felt more open to broach the subject face to face.

As they worked things out, they began making up quizzes for other things that they'd traditionally had a hard time talking about. Madeline was always shy about asking for specific things in bed, so Alex made up a quiz that allowed her to choose from a list of options. When Madeline's parents came for a visit, she made Alex a quiz to find out how much time Alex really wanted to spend with them.

Since then, they've started using the quizzes for fun things, too. Here's one that Alex made for Madeline about her birthday:

This year for my birthday, I'd like Alex to:

a) Whisk me away for a romantic weekend.

b) Invite my friends and family over for a party.

c) Make me breakfast in bed, and then keep me there all day.

d) Other: _____

The quizzes are not meant to take the place of talking about things in person, but rather to open the channels of communication in a slow and safe way. Over time, you may decide it's just easier to ask. Or you may find that you like having some options laid out for you.

Letting It Go

Peter padded into the kitchen, looking forward to cooking up a big omelet for breakfast. As he rounded the corner into the pantry, one of his least favorite odors hit his nose: cat box. Suddenly, his pleasant dreams of fluffy omelets threatened to evaporate in the wake of irritation and anger. You see, cleaning the cat box was Alicia's chore, and they had agreed that she would do it before she left for work in the morning. Yet, there stood Peter, hands on his hips, facing an unfortunately odiferous box.

Instead of giving in to his irritation, Peter stepped out of the pantry and took a moment to think. He reminded himself that he didn't want to let irritation ruin his good moods. He'd made a decision the previous week to try to let some of his anger go, especially anger about relatively small stuff. So, instead of getting mad, he took a deep breath, imagining the anger leaving his body as he exhaled with a "whoosh." After a few breaths, he felt much lighter. He decided to talk to Alicia that evening, and now that he had let go of his anger about the situation, he knew he'd be able to talk it out with her in a calmer and more productive way. Regaining his happy anticipation, he set about making that omelet he'd been dreaming about.

Every relationship inevitably brings its share of disagreements and annoyances. As you work to develop a way of resolving differences with your partner, you will undoubtedly run into impasses. Sometimes your partner will misunderstand what you need. Occasionally they'll run out of time to do the thing they promised. Maybe what you want from them isn't really feasible. These bumps along the road to happy coupledom can act as triggers, throwing you into a rage at the sight of a sink full of unwashed dishes or sending you into despair when your partner is late for a dinner date.

When faced with a potential annoyance, you have a choice to make. You can choose to take the situation personally and get angry or hurt. Or you can choose to let the strong emotion go for now, dealing with the problem in a more rational and productive manner later. In other words, you can spin your wheels, infuriated at your partner's misdemeanors, disrupting your whole day. Or you can take some deep breaths and

choose to deal with the problem productively. How you feel about the matter is ultimately your choice.

If you'd like to react to the next potential irritant by letting go, try the following steps:

- When you realize that your partner has done or said something that you could take personally, stop a for a moment. Usually these negative reactions happen quickly, so you'll have to make a conscious decision to nip your negative feeling in the bud. Before you allow the negative feelings to grow, put the brakes on and make a decision about whether you want to feel them or not.

- If you'd rather let the negative feelings go, pause a moment to take some deep breaths. Breathing deeply will relax your body and give you time to think.

- Inhale each breath deeply, expanding your belly while keeping your shoulders down. Hold the breath for a moment, thinking of the negative emotion you're trying to let go. Then, on the exhale, think of that emotion as you release your breath. Imagine that the emotion is draining out of your body with each exhale, cleansing you of the bad feelings.

- After about five deep breaths (or when you feel calmer), you may decide to address the problem with your partner. Can you think of a compromise that could work better than the current arrangement? Do you have unrealistic expectations of your partner when it comes to this issue? If you plan to discuss it with them at a later time, you may want to do your deep breathing immediately beforehand, to ensure that you're not acting on negative emotions but rather from a place of love and understanding.

Letting go doesn't mean that you can't stand up for what you want or need. It simply allows you to release some of the disruptive and painful negative emotions that so often come up and cloud a conflict. When your feelings are less volatile, you'll be able to communicate with your partner more clearly and effectively. And that sure beats ruining your mood over a dirty cat box!

Finding Middle Ground

Margie got home from work just as the sun was setting. Honestly, she felt like her sun was setting, too. She was absolutely beat after a hard day at what she liked to refer to as "the pits." Actually, Margie worked as an engineer, but some days she was sure she knew how her coal-miner grandfather had felt at the end of the day

But all that fatigue would melt away once she got into the kitchen and the creativity of cooking took hold of her. She loved to cook, and whipping up fantastic gastronomical creations every night was one of her principal joys. She would sometimes plan out the next evening's meal at night, before she went to bed. And other times, she'd wait until she got to the market to see what gorgeous produce or lovely cut of meat might inspire her. Looking forward to cooking dinner for herself and her partner Bart always helped her bridge that transition from work to home. She depended on it.

That day, she gathered up the bags of beautiful ingredients she'd picked up at the store and moved into the kitchen with a lively step. But when she got to the sink, the liveliness flew right out of her feet. There, in the sink, were piles of dirty dishes crusted with old food not only from that morning's breakfast, but also from dinner the night before. Margie felt her teeth clench as a wave of severe irritation swept over her. Doing the dishes was Bart's job, and he hadn't done it—again.

The happy feeling Margie started with when she came into the kitchen had evaporated in the wake of this long-standing grudge. She stood in the middle of the kitchen fuming, not quite knowing what to do. "Well, I guess I'll just have to do his work for him," she thought petulantly. But, as she started sorting the dishes to be washed, she stopped. She could feel all the tension she had brought home from work, a feeling that she counted on to dissipate as she cooked, simply intensifying as she raged about the dishes. "Do I really want to feel this way? Do I want to let this ruin my evening?" She put down the spaghetti-crusted pot she'd been holding and went to sit at the dining room table.

Margie sat for a while, thinking about what she could do. She reminded herself that dirty dishes weren't really worth ruining her evening over, and that a proactive approach would certainly make her feel better than raging at the man she loved. It was

clear that the job of doing all of the dishes was too much for Bart. He consistently let them go, which Margie could choose to interpret as disrespect toward her (which made her feel awful), or she could understand it as Bart simply not having the time or energy to get the dishes done the way Margie wanted him to. "Okay," Margie thought, taking a deep breath. "It looks like a compromise is in order, for my own sanity, if nothing else. How can each of us give a little in this situation to improve things?"

When Bart got home, Margie proposed a modification on their dish arrangement. "It seems as though doing all the dishes is getting to be too much for you, but I'd really like to have a clean sink in the evening so that I have room to make dinner. How about if we try a compromise?" Margie suggested that she be responsible for cleaning any dishes that were used during the day, if Bart would try to always do them after dinner. That, coupled with Bart agreeing to pick up dinner one night a week, would make both of them feel much better. After all, even the most enthusiastic cook needs a break every now and then. "How about it, Bart? Will that work for you?" Bart agreed, much relieved that he wouldn't be responsible for all the dishes, all the time. As Margie pulled him into a big hug, he kissed the top of her head. They both felt much better.

Compromise is an essential part of any relationship. Unfortunately, it can also be one of the hardest parts. But, when you're faced with the choice between an aggravating power struggle and creating a compromise, the route of compromise will take your relationship where you really want it to be—toward fairness, intimacy, and trust.

Here are some compromising tips:

- When faced with a frustrating situation in which both you and your partner seem unable to budge, consider what would really make you feel better—fighting or compromise. You have the option of promoting angry feelings in yourself and distance in your relationship or fostering a happier, more harmonious experience through compromise. It's up to you.

- If you've decided to create a compromise with your partner, try to be fair and even-handed when you present the situation. A blaming tone or snippy comments will make your road to compromise harder.

- Remember that compromise requires give-and-take. You'll get something from the arrangement, but you'll also have to give a little. You'll get a better solution if you try to accept the changes of the compromise with an open heart.

Compromising with your partner will help pull down the battle lines between you, moving you toward togetherness rather than angry distance. The next time you run into a thorny problem that you can't seem to solve your way, consider compromise.

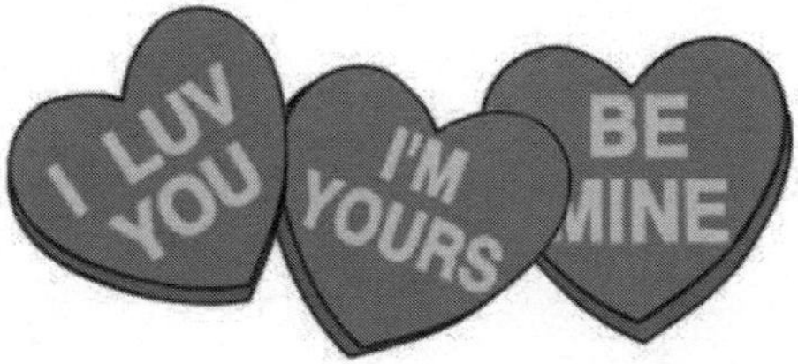
I LUV YOU
I'M YOURS
BE MINE

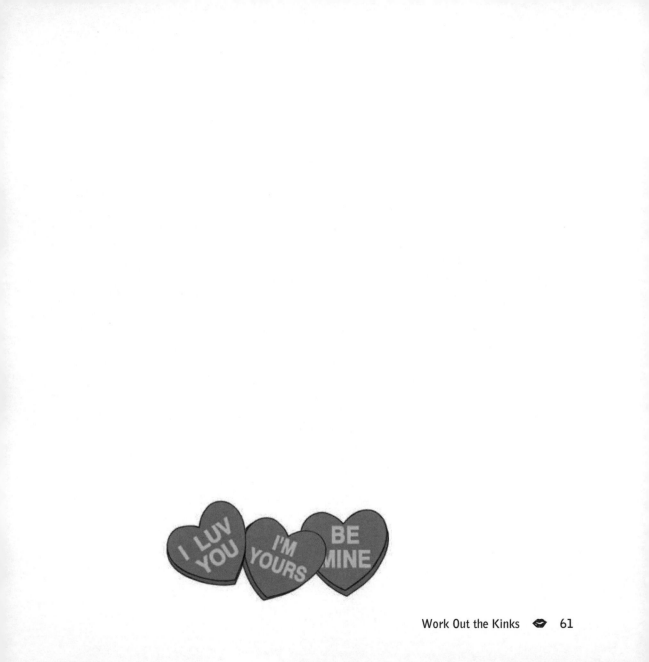

Early Warning Signs

Sometimes your communication with your partner may get a bit muddled, such as when one person takes things too far and hurts the other's feelings. Wouldn't it be wonderful if you had some sort of signal you could flash to your partner before your feelings get hurt, some indication that they are treading on sensitive ground?

Walter and Eden often found themselves stumbling onto each other's sensitive areas. Walter could be a wicked teaser, sometimes taking playful jesting a bit too far. And Eden occasionally resorted to verbal low blows. Both of them would then be surprised when they realized the other person was terribly hurt. They had difficulty picking up on subtle cues to back off, and by the time they had really gotten into it, the possibility of reasonable discussion was usually past.

One Monday night, as they were recovering from a fight initiated by Walter's clumsy teasing and made worse by Eden's jabs, Walter decided that there had to be a better way. He knew that neither he nor Eden intended to inflict such painful damage, but somehow they kept stumbling into it. Looking back, he could see just the point when he thought he'd gone too far in his teasing. And he certainly knew the point at which Eden should have pulled back from her attack. If only there were some way to let the other person know that they were heading into a danger zone.

He approached Eden as she sat crying on their bed. "Sweetie, I'm so sorry I hurt your feelings. I was only playing, but I realize I took it too far." Eden looked up and sighed deeply. "I know, honey. I'm sorry I said those things about your friends. I just don't seem to know when to cool it, and I end up really hurting you."

Suddenly, Walter hit upon an idea that he thought just might help. "This may sound kind of silly, but I think I have a solution, something that will help us warn the other person that they're getting too close to a sensitive area." Eden listened as Walter outlined his idea of a "warning sign," some sort of signal they could give each other during a fight or even when they were joking around. They could agree that this simple signal would mean "Slow down. You're about to really hurt me," allowing them to cool down the interaction before it got out of hand.

Eden thought this was a terrific idea. "How about using 'Ouch' as the signal? That way, we'll both know that we may be getting into some painful territory." Walter agreed, and the next time they found themselves engaged in an argument, he put it to good use. When a frustrated Eden made a disparaging comment about Walter's family, instead of taking it to the next level by lashing out at her, Walter simply looked her in the eye and said, "Ouch."

Eden started, realizing she was going too far. She apologized for the comment, and she and Walter continued their discussion at a much calmer level.

You and your partner can learn to avoid danger zones by devising a warning sign of your own:

- Discuss the idea with your partner.

- If both of you agree that this kind of signal may help you communicate better and avoid hurting each other's feelings, decide what your warning sign will be.

- Consider using a word or words as your sign. Some effective ones are "ouch," "wait," or "slow down." You may find that a gesture is more appealing. You can try holding up your hands, palms out, in a "hands up" posture. Avoid choosing words or gestures that may come across as hostile.

- Agree to respect this signal when your partner uses it. When it comes up, stop for a beat, consider that you may be hurting your partner's feelings, and try to rephrase what you want to say in a less damaging way.

This simple device can help you communicate with your partner more smoothly, getting across what you really mean instead of becoming sidetracked by needlessly hurt feelings.

Accepting with Love

Choosing to accept someone else for exactly who they are, warts and all, can grant you a feeling of liberation and release. When you choose to truly accept your partner, to understand that those little (or big) behaviors that drive you crazy are simply a part of the person you love, you can let go of your efforts to change them. Giving up your "partner reeducation program" will free you to enjoy the aspects of your relationship that you love and will take much of the tension from your interactions with your partner.

Take Lydia and Mark as an example. Lydia, a loquacious and extroverted "people person," loved going to parties and socializing with friends. Mark, on the other hand, would almost always prefer to stay home and curl up with a book or video. When he went to parties, he spent most of the time talking to only one close friend or retreating to a corner to simply watch the proceedings.

This difference between Mark and Lydia could really drive her nuts. "Why can't you just come out of your shell once in a while?" she'd ask Mark, irritation mounting each time they had this conversation. "I'm happy to be by myself," he would explain. "You don't have to worry about me or take care of me. Just have fun and let me do my thing." Lydia tried, but almost invariably, at the next party they attended, she'd feel her annoyance rise. Rolling her eyes, she'd confide to the friend she was talking to, " I just don't know what to do with Mark. He floats through parties."

After a birthday party they attended one Saturday night, Lydia's growing aggravation exploded. "Mark, I don't even know why you come to parties with me. You wander around like a zombie! Why can't you just mingle with people and take care of yourself, instead of always making me be your matchmaker?"

Although Mark was more than a little bothered by her harsh words, he couldn't help but laugh. "Honey, who asked you to take care of me? I enjoy talking to one or two people or just watching people talk. I'm not your responsibility, and the fact that you continue to insist I act the way you do is really becoming a problem." More serious now, he looked at Lydia. "I'm asking you to please stop trying to make me act

differently. Please understand that I enjoy things differently and let me be. I need you to do this for me."

Lydia was taken aback by this earnest appeal. She hadn't fully realized before how much energy she had been putting into trying to get Mark to change—to be more like *her*. It suddenly occurred to her how rotten that must feel for Mark, and she saw that her goal of changing him was a dead end.

Before the next party they attended, Lydia decided that she would try to simply let Mark be. She had to make a very conscious decision about this and had to continually remind herself of it throughout the party. She would glance away from the person she was talking with, only to see Mark sitting on the couch alone. Before, she would have gone over to him and tried to encourage him to mingle. This time, she simply thought, "He has his own way of enjoying himself, and I need to accept that." With this small effort, she was able to return to her conversation and let go of feeling responsible for him. On the drive home, both Mark and Lydia acknowledged that they'd had a lot more fun at this party than usual. They drove home holding hands, feeling more at peace than before.

Consider these steps for accepting behaviors that drive you crazy:

- What things does your partner commonly do that really bug you? What do you try to change about your partner? Choose one.

- Now, try to acknowledge that your partner is different from you, and, as a result, will naturally do things differently. Consider that there is no "right" way to do things, just preferences formed by many different factors.

- Finally, make a conscious decision to accept the behavior that had been bugging you. Acknowledge the difference and accept it. And, the next time your partner does this behavior, make an effort to think back to your decision and accept with love.

You may be surprised at how much energy and time you save by accepting some of your partner's habits. And, instead of feeling oppressed by irritation, your relationship will feel lighter, filled with buoyant compassion.

Reversing Roles

Do you get tired of the same old discussions and disagreements that seem to go nowhere? After a while your relationship feels like it's stuck in some kind of crazy car wash where you get hit with the same spray and spinning bristles over and over again. Jim and Cathy were like that. They used to come to their therapist's office and have discussions like this:

Jim: You did it again, Cathy. You filled Saturday with one hideous social obligation after another. Brunch with your parents, tennis with Laura and Carl, then we went with your cousin to look at SUVs, had dinner with her, and finally a movie and desert with Tina and Knucklehead.

Cathy: Those are all people you like. I . . .

Jim: Not really.

Cathy: Yes they are. Just last week you *suggested* some doubles with Laura and Carl.

Jim: No, I didn't. You must be thinking of some other Jim who isn't your husband.

Cathy: And my parents are getting hurt because it seems like we're avoiding them. They . . .

Jim: They're right. All they talk about is stock tips and the joys of arthritis. Even you can't stand it.

Cathy: We have to see them *sometime*. And I set the thing up with my cousin because I thought *you* were interested in SUVs.

Jim: God Almighty, I think SUVs should be scrapped. Turn 'em into rifles, knives, and shotguns—a lot less dangerous that way. Seriously, I'd like to spend, for once, a weekend with *you*. Not your cousin, not your folks, not a menagerie of friends.

And so it went, rehashing week after week their very different social needs. Totally stuck. Then their therapist asked them to try something that had brought dramatic results to his other clients. It's called a reversal.

What they did is replay the argument—but taking opposite roles. Cathy took Jim's part, and Jim tried to present Cathy's needs and concerns. Here's how it sounded:

Cathy (playing Jim):   I'm tired of nonstop family and friends all weekend.

Jim (playing Cathy):   I need to see my folks, and it was *you* who wanted to play tennis. I like people, Jim. I like friends around. I don't want to lose them just because I never make time to see them.

Cathy (Jim):   I understand, Cathy. But you overschedule. It's one thing after another.

Jim (Cathy):   I have a lot of family and friends. They're hurt if I don't give them time.

Cathy (Jim):   But our relationship is hurt if we don't reserve time for each other. And I'm getting burned out socially.

Jim (Cathy):   But you've enjoyed all those people at one time or another.

Cathy (Jim):   I know. But all in the same day it's depressing.

Jim (Cathy):   Okay, let's figure something out.

Cathy (Jim):   How 'bout no more than one four-hour social event per weekend day. And leave some time to hang out with each other.

Jim (Cathy):   Okay, but I want to do something social on Friday night, too.

Cathy (Jim):   Oh, God, not Friday. Well, how 'bout dinner alone, but maybe meet people later.

Jim (Cathy):   I'm going to have the social life of a clam. [They laugh] But ... Okay.

Notice that reversal helped them appreciate and give voice to each other's experience. But most of all, reversal got them unstuck. They could explain and make a point without a big emotional charge. And because no one was angry or defensive, they could easily move on to real problem solving. They could negotiate and compromise.

Here are some guidelines to follow when you try reversal:

- Start by trying to explain your partner's basic problem or complaint.
- Then talk about your partner's underlying needs—what makes them feel so strongly. If you aren't sure about your partner's needs, ask before the reversal.
- Avoid slipping back to advocate for your own position. Stay in your role, even if your partner isn't doing the greatest job of representing you.
- After the issue is laid out clearly, shift to problem solving. Use a phrase like, "Let's figure something out." Keep in role; present solutions you think your partner would advocate.

Reversal can be fun—and funny. And a good way to stop waltzing in circles.

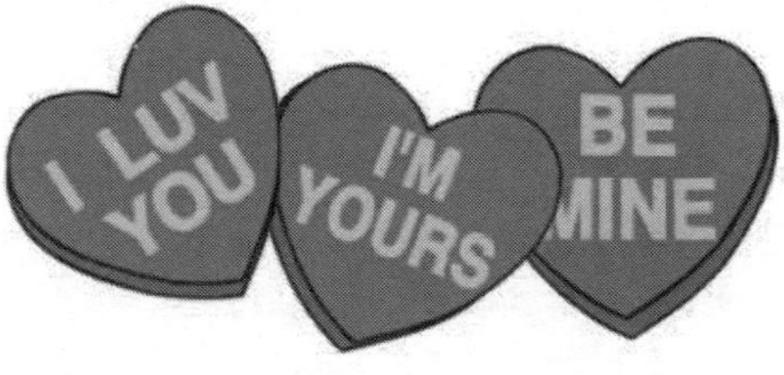
I LUV YOU
I'M YOURS
BE MINE

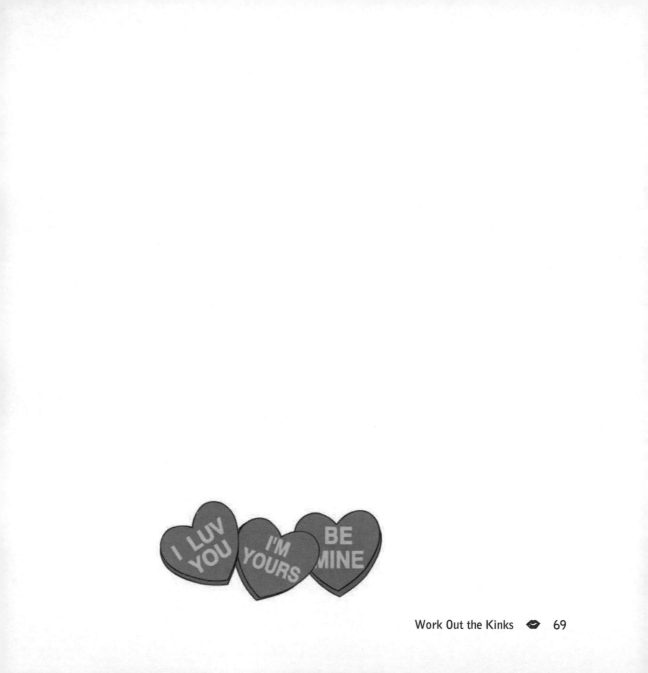

Untangling Crossed Wires

There are a million little things that can come up during the course of a close relationship. When left unchecked, miscommunications can eat away at your level of intimacy with each other. Caught early, they can be exposed and let go, and you and your partner will be closer for it.

Brett and Lucca recently went to a party where there were a lot of people they didn't know very well. Brett felt uncomfortable at parties in general, and he tended to act strangely out of nervousness. Once, when Lucca came over to see how Brett was doing, he said in a strained voice, "No complaints here!" and drifted over to the food table.

To Lucca, Brett's sarcasm felt personal: "I kept thinking, 'What did *I* do?' The rest of the night, I felt so uptight and pissed off at Brett. I felt like he was blaming me for his bad time. By the time we got in the car, I was ready to let him have it!"

But when they got in the car, it didn't seem like Brett was upset with Lucca at all: "He just said, with total relief and no animosity, 'Whew! Barely made it through that one! Did you have a good time?' I was stunned! Here I was, all ready to have a big fight, and I realized that maybe I was just overreacting. I realized I had a choice: stay angry, even though maybe I was off-base, or ask him about it. It was scary to bring it up, because I really hate conflict. But I also didn't want to just let it go, because similar stuff had happened before and it was starting to wear on me."

Brett was quite surprised that Lucca was upset. "I was actually thankful to Lucca for going to this thing my colleague was throwing. But I could see where I might have been shutting down a little, and that didn't feel so great to Lucca. I promised to work on being less distant with Lucca in future social situations."

In Brett and Lucca's case, working out this small misunderstanding ensured that they both understood where the other person was coming from. This helped them deal with the problem, instead of harboring resentment or building it up into something more hurtful.

If you feel upset by something your partner has done (or not done), it may be best to just ask a simple question. Here are some possible examples:

- "The other night when we were talking, it felt to me like you were angrier than you were admitting. Was that the case?"
- "It feels like we're misunderstanding each other a lot lately, and I really want to understand your point of view. Would you share with me how you've been feeling?"

Sometimes you may find that you say or do something that comes out differently than you intended. Either at the time or later, you may try to make your intentions clearer. For example:

- "I was really crabby this morning, and I spoke to you harshly. I just want to let you know that I'm sorry it came out like that, and that I don't really feel that way."

Everyone has off days and missed communications. If it's possible, setting things straight sooner rather than later can keep your relationship running smoothly. When the issue is a small one, you'll likely find that it just takes a few minutes to untangle those crossed wires.

Taking Time for Yourself

Have you ever sat down to dinner with your sweetheart, only to discover that you don't have anything new to share with each other? Do you sometimes find yourself getting irritated by every little thing your partner does, even though you know you're being unfairly critical? When you come home from work, are you dismayed to find your voicemail empty, *again?*

If you've answered yes to any of these questions, it may be that you're in need of a little away time. A mini-vacation from your relationship. A chance to come back refreshed and genuinely excited to see your partner.

It may seem strange to think that spending time apart could be a way to tune up your relationship. But by taking the time to nurture yourself, and by maintaining a strong community of friends and family to support you, you're actually giving your relationship—and yourself—a chance to continue growing and thriving.

Away time sometimes means spending quality time all by yourself. Other times a one-on-one date with a good friend, or a night out with the girls (or guys), may be just what you need. It can be a short break, like an hour in the bathtub with no interruptions, or it can be more extravagant, like taking a trip with a good friend. Here are some ideas to help get you started:

- Each month, you could take turns going away for one weekend. One of you can spend the weekend at a friend's house, visit your parents, or get your own private room at a bed and breakfast a few hours outside of town, while the other relaxes at home.

- Set aside some time every week to do something by yourself: see a movie, get a massage, take a walk at your favorite park, take a long drive.

- Make regular or standing dates with friends and family, to make sure that the hustle and bustle of daily life doesn't keep you from connecting with the other important people in your life.

- If you have kids, take turns planning special alone days with them. When it's your turn to take the kids, you can enjoy spending some one-on-one fun time with them. When it's your turn to stay home, you can take that well-deserved nap, read that novel you've been dying to get to, or dance naked in your living room.

By making away time a priority, you'll get to see firsthand why they say that absence makes the heart grow fonder: Having a little space can turn those irritating habits back into endearing quirks. And just think of all the stories you'll both have to share with each other about your adventures while you were apart!

PART IV

Add Some Sizzle

Hungry for Love

Kate and Giovanni draped their bodies over the furniture in their living room. It was mid-August, and the summer sun beat down on their house. They tried to distract themselves by reading in the living room, Kate on the oversized armchair and Giovanni on the sofa.

"This isn't exactly what we had in mind when we decided to spend some time together, is it?" Giovanni said as he fanned himself with his paperback. "But it's so damned hot, I just can't get it together to go out and do anything. I do like hanging out with you, though. I just wish I was a bit more perky." Giovanni dabbed at his upper lip with his already-damp T-shirt. "That makes two of us, brother," said Kate. "I'm going to get us some grapes. Maybe that'll help us cool down."

She returned from the kitchen with a big bowl of white and red grapes, all beaded with water and cool looking. She slumped back down into her chair and picked up her book, which seemed to be wilting in the heat. "Hey there, woman. Don't go hogging all those grapes over there. Bring some over to your poor, melting sweetheart here."

"Oh, sorry, Mr. Sweetheart. I don't know what I was thinking." Kate tried to hand the bowl over to Giovanni, but she couldn't quite reach. With a sigh she dragged herself up once again and took the bowl over to him, plopping down on the floor beside the sofa. Giovanni leaned down and planted a kiss on her, grabbing some of the frosty grapes. He popped one in his mouth and the sweet flavor and crisp juiciness of it nearly bowled him over. "These are really good." He plucked one off the stem in his hand and offered it to Kate. She accepted it, saying through her full mouth, "I know. They're really doing the trick, huh? I feel a little cooler already."

Kate picked one of the fat, round red grapes and held it in front of Giovanni, waiting for him to open up. When he opened his mouth, she placed it on his tongue. He liked the deliberate way she'd done it, and he smiled as he chewed. Kate countered with a slightly sly smile. "If that makes you feel better, what about this?" She chose one of the plump white grapes from the bowl and bit it in half. Then she reached up and gently touched the wet inside of the grape to Giovanni's neck, just below his ear. Then

she moved it slowly down his neck to his collarbone, leaving a slight trail of cool juice down his neck. "How was that?" she asked, her voice quiet.

Instead of answering, Giovanni chose a fat grape from the bowl and bit it in half. Very slowly he touched the grape to where the back of Kate's neck was exposed by her short haircut. She bent her head forward slightly, and he ran the cool grape very slowly down the back of her neck and between her shoulder blades. She responded by halving another grape and moving it from the base of Giovanni's throat, down inside his T-shirt, and slowly down his chest to the top of his shorts. Small rivulets of juice rolled down the sides of his stomach, which Kate bent to kiss away. Saying nothing, Giovanni proceeded to do the same thing to Kate. Though they may not have felt all that much cooler, they had definitely forgotten about the weather.

Combining the textures, flavors, and scents of food with your bedroom (or living room) adventures can be a fun and stimulating way to explore your sensual side. Not that we all have to live up to the couple in the movie *9½ Weeks*—you may not feel up to a gustatory odyssey using everything in your fridge. If you'd like to initiate your own bedroom banquet, here are some tips to get you started:

- Consider taste, texture, fragrance, and temperature. What would feel good against the skin? What scents would highlight a feeling of sensuality? Smooth, slippery, soft, cool, or warm foods can go a long way toward spicing things up. Have you considered the texture and flavor of whipped cream? The heat of brandy on the skin? The coolness of melon slices? The color of honey? Let your imagination go a bit, and you may decide that your cupboard and refrigerator are two of the sexiest places in your house.

- Let laughter in. Fooling around with food may inspire you with longing and lust, but we're pretty sure you'll find some laughter in it, too. Using objects in unfamiliar ways can be just plain silly, so don't be afraid to "break the mood" by giving a guffaw or two if the spirit moves you.

- Don't worry about the mess. Try to get into the spirit of the event and not think too much about stains or spills. You can always grab a couple of towels from the bathroom if you're getting distracted. They will allow you to really relax and get into the mess. And remember, showering together afterward can be an added treat.

Introducing food into your love life can be a great way to give you a sensuality boost. It can help you think of food, your body, and your experience of both in new and different ways. So try raiding the refrigerator tonight!

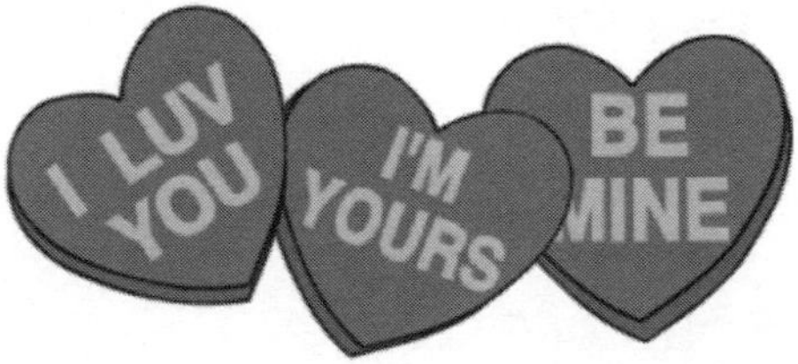
I LUV YOU
I'M YOURS
BE MINE

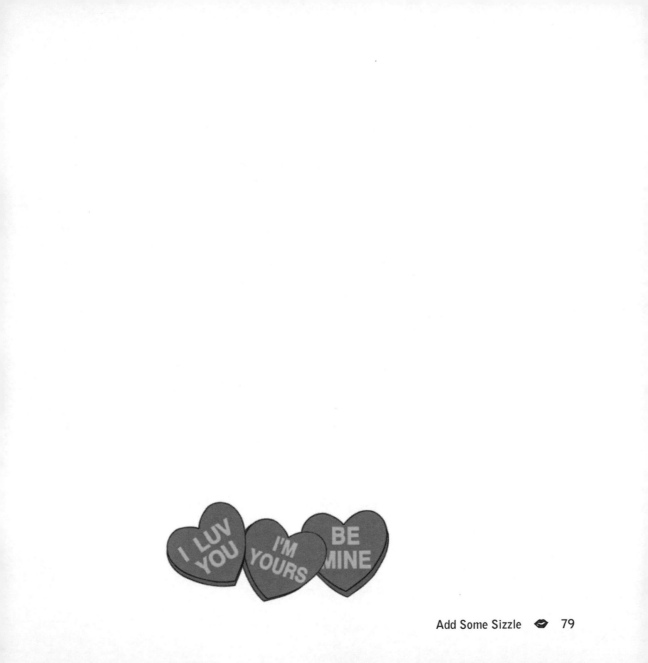

Fantasy Exchange

Next time you and your lover are looking for a little extra spice, try doing a fantasy exchange. Whether you act out your fantasies or just give each other the detailed descriptions, it's guaranteed to get things going.

Nate and Sara had a nice sex life. They knew what they liked, and they knew how to do those things well enough. But one thing that was missing from their repertoire was sex talk. Even though they'd been together for a long time, they'd never found a way to get comfortable sharing their desires aloud.

When they tried this exercise, they were a little embarrassed—to say the least. But both of them were committed to trying it out. Sara had an idea of how to make it easier for them to start: "First we lit some candles and got all snuggly in bed. But we were so nervous we couldn't look at each other without cracking up. Now, I'm all for a little laughter in bed, but it wasn't so conducive this time. So I got one of my silky scarves and tied it around Nate's eyes. Then I cuddled up to him and whispered one of my fantasies in his ear. . . . It was so hot!"

Sometimes you might want to live out your fantasies. Other times your fantasies may be dangerous or unsavory in reality, but sexy to talk about or imagine. You and your partner may want to convey to each other what you'd be open to trying out.

Try to be open with each other and not judge each other's fantasies. If you don't feel comfortable acting out or discussing a particular fantasy with your partner, try to discuss your reasons using an "I message" ("While I really appreciate you being willing to share your fantasy with me, I'd rather not try that one out. How about that other one you mentioned last time . . .").

Here are some details you may want to include in your fantasy descriptions:

- Who is there? What do they look like? Does everyone want to be there?

- Are you yourself or are you in character?

- Who initiates contact? What are the characters thinking?

- Are all of the people there participants? Or are there observers as well?

- What do they say to each other? What happens?

For Nate and Sara, this was a tough exercise at first. They were both worried about what the other person would think. They were afraid that some of their fantasies were socially and politically objectionable. But after doing fantasy exchanges a number of times, they started trusting each other to understand that what they said to each other in this space was often really different from what they believed out in the real world. This understanding allowed them to play out multiple variations of power and submission, gender roles, and role playing, all in the privacy of their own home. And now, instead of describing their sex life as "nice," they report that it is "fantastic!"

Thirty Minutes for You

Carmen walked slowly over to the bed and threw back the covers. She shucked off her slippers and slid under the covers, enjoying the feel of the cool sheets against her body. A small sigh escaped her lips as she began to relax after her unusually hard day. It seemed as if people at work had wanted stuff from her all day long, and her head still seemed to ring from all the phone calls, e-mails, and meetings she'd had to deal with. She was really looking forward to reading a bit and drifting off to sleep.

Craig, who was already in bed, looked over at her with a smile. He gave her a kiss on the forehead, knowing that she'd had a tough day. He opened his left arm to allow her room to snuggle into him as she opened her book. "Tired, huh?" he said, brushing back some tendrils of hair that were obscuring her eyes from his gaze. "More drained, really. I just feel like I was giving, giving, giving all day long. I need to replenish some-how. I hope this new thriller does the trick." Carmen snuggled in close to Craig's warm chest. He gave her a squeeze. "Well, maybe there's something I can do to help replenish you," he said, kissing the top of her head. Carmen looked up into his face and saw the gleam in his eye. "Oh, love, I don't think I'm up for it tonight. I feel as though I'd be only half there. You don't want to make love to a zombie, do you?" He laughed, "Well, I don't know—rotting flesh, the scent of the grave—pretty sexy stuff." They laughed as they exchanged a kiss.

"Actually, I didn't exactly have sex in mind, per se," he continued. "Per se?" Carmen smiled. "Well, what *did* you have in mind, my little grave robber?" "Well, I know you've been going all day and haven't had much time or energy to yourself. So, I was thinking that maybe tonight we could just spend thirty minutes on you." "On me?" She laughed. "What do you mean?" Carmen slid out of the crook of his arm to look him in the face, so Craig rested his head on his hand, arm bent. "It means that for thirty minutes I'm all yours—I will spend that time simply touching you. You don't have to do anything but lie there and enjoy it." Carmen was getting interested. "You mean I could have a thirty-minute massage? What about a foot massage?" "Sky's the limit, Carm. Anything you want, I'll do." He smiled and took her hand. "I just want to help you feel better." She smiled up at him, seeing the love in his eyes. "And if things move in

a slightly more … amorous direction? Are you still mine to command?" He slid down and put his arms around her. "At your service, ma'am. Your wish is my command." Carmen gave Craig a big kiss and let her book slip from her fingers onto the floor.

Enjoying physical intimacy with your partner is probably near the top of your list of what you enjoy in your relationship. What many of us may miss is the sheer joy of simply touching your partner and making them feel good without holding any expectations of our own. Spending thirty minutes giving your partner the joy of touch can be one of the best gifts you can offer, both to your partner and yourself. Not only will your partner feel more relaxed and closer to you, but you'll get to have the pleasure of helping him or her feel that way.

If you'd like to try giving thirty minutes to your partner, here are a few suggestions:

- Keep it physical. This is an opportunity to spend some time with your partner as physical beings, to enjoy giving and receiving physically. If your partner suggests using the thirty minutes to do that vacuuming you've been putting off, gently suggesting a massage instead will get you both back on track.

- Be open to possibility. Your gift of thirty minutes may turn into an all-night sexual carnival or it could simply be a thirty-minute foot rub. Try not to have too many expectations about where you'd like it to go—remember, this time it's all about your partner.

- Stop gently. If you're ready to stop when the thirty minutes come to an end, do so as calmly, smoothly, and gently as you can. You will most likely be in a different emotional space than your partner, so try to respect that difference when you're done. Shouting "Time's up!" in the middle of a massage may defeat the purpose.

Try giving your partner thirty minutes tonight. Not only will you be making them feel good physically, but your generosity and care will add warmth and connection to your evening.

Spending the Day in Bed

Does it seem like you're always rushing around, running errands and fighting traffic? Do you look forward to bedtime so that you and your love can spend some time alone, only to find that you both fall asleep as soon as your heads hit the pillow? Is it hard for you to remember the last time you had sex? If your answer is, "How'd you know?" then you might be in need of a day in bed.

Imagine this: You wake up on a Saturday morning without an alarm. The sun streaming into your bedroom has brought you gradually out of a deep and restful sleep. As you open your eyes, you see that your partner is already awake, watching you and smiling. Today, you know that there will be no rushing out of bed, no gulping down coffee in a desperate attempt to jump-start your day. It's just the two of you, and there's absolutely nothing to do but spend the day together.

You snuggle in for a while, until your stomach starts to signal that it's time for breakfast. You get up, turn on some music, and make a yummy breakfast that you eat together in bed (crumbs be damned!). As morning stretches into afternoon, you enjoy each other's company, and allow yourselves to restore your energy reserves.

The nice thing about a day in bed is that it slows things down. In your pj's (or out of them, if you're lucky), things have a different perspective. Sure, the world's spinning around outside, but for right now, it's just you and your partner.

Some ideas for a nice day in bed:

- Turn off the ringer the night before. Don't answer the phone or check your e-mail. Don't clean the house. Pretend you're on your own island, far away from civilization.

- A day in bed can be the perfect time to catch up with each other. You may take the opportunity to do some of the other exercises in this book, like reminiscing or having a fantasy exchange. It can be sexy or sweet, or both—'cause you're gonna be there for a while.

- Try not to set any particular agenda ahead of time. Just let the day unfold naturally, depending on your mood. You may want to read (separately or aloud), listen to music, or stare into each other's eyes for a while.

- If you have kids, see if they can visit friends or family for the weekend. (You might try exchanging child care with other parents. That way, you all get an occasional break, and your kids have fun, too.)

- You never know when a day in bed can turn into a sexual *tour de force* (remember those, from the beginning of your relationship?). You may decide together that you want to make some sparks of your own. After all, you have a whole day of uninterrupted alone time. Wanna see if you can break some of your own records? Or how about trying something new?

The most important thing about spending the day in bed is that you spend it *together*. Remember to think of it as a time to connect and just enjoy being with each other.

Sexy Scavenger Hunt

The next time you want to try something fun and sexy, try planning a scavenger hunt for your sweetheart. This kind of scavenger hunt is a little different than the kind you might have done as a kid; instead of finding a bunch of random items, you send your partner out to have specific experiences that you arrange.

Sid set up a scavenger hunt for Moira on their tenth anniversary, and Moira said it was one of the most special things a lover had ever done for her. She shared with us the details of their date: "Sid told me to set aside the whole day for something special. We try to do sort of elaborate things for each other on special occasions, so I was excited. When I woke up in the morning, I found that Sid had left a bunch of envelopes that were sealed and numbered."

The first envelope had some money and a note that said: "Here's some cash to take yourself out to breakfast with. I left the paper and a magazine at the front door if you'd like to take them with you. After you're finished with breakfast, open envelope #2. I LOVE YOU!!!!"

After a leisurely breakfast, Moira ripped open the second envelope. Inside was a ticket for a matinee at the local playhouse. Before the play started, Moira stopped at home to change clothes. She got to the theater and found her seat, and just as the lights were about to go down, she saw Sid sitting on the other side of the theater. Sid blew her a kiss, but when the play was over, Moira looked over and saw that Sid was already gone.

She opened the third envelope. The note said: "You look beautiful. I hope you enjoyed the play. I'll see you later tonight!" At the bottom of the page there was an address and an appointment time. Moira wasn't sure what it was for, but when she got there she saw that it was a day spa: "I went inside, and told the receptionist that I thought I might have an appointment. I guess it was the tentative look on my face that gave it away, but she immediately smiled at me and said, 'Are you Moira? We've been expecting you.'"

Sid had booked Moira the deluxe treatment—an hour in the spa, a massage, and a manicure/pedicure treatment. After hours of pampering, Moira felt like a whole new

person. She opened up the fourth envelope, which said, "Come home to me. I've been waiting for you."

"But when I got home, Sid wasn't there. I went straight to the bedroom, and found candles and fresh flowers everywhere. And there was a final envelope. Inside it said, 'Light the candles, put on some music, and put on the blindfold. I'll be there soon.'"

Moira had just finished when she heard Sid coming up the stairs and walking to their bedroom door: "I couldn't see anything, which was actually really exciting. Then Sid did all these amazing things to me. Eventually I had to take the blindfold off—but I will say that it was used on many subsequent occasions." Much later, they came up for air, and Moira realized that she was starving. At Sid's suggestion, she checked the fridge, and inside were all of their favorite foods, already prepared. They spread out a picnic on their bed, and didn't bother going out that night.

In planning your own scavenger hunt, try to be creative. You may want to try things that are less expensive and elaborate, like a bargain matinee or an "arranged" meeting at a coffee shop. Whatever you do, remember that a little mystery and intrigue go a long way. And all roads should lead to the bedroom!

Toy Spree

Sam and Melissa knew everything there was to know about each other sexually—or so they thought, until the night Melissa opened up a whole new world for them. "Where are you taking me?" Sam asked, clutching Melissa's hand, blindfolded.

"You'll see. Just a few more steps and we'll be there," she reassured, leading Sam around the busy street corner. Evening commuters clogged the streets, some doing a double take at seeing the pair. And then there was a smile of recognition when they realized where Melissa was taking Sam: Good Vibrations, the local sex toy store. "Okay," Melissa said as she led Sam in the door, "you can take the blindfold off now."

Sam pulled away the scarf and gasped—discovering that they were surrounded by every kind of sexual accoutrement imaginable: vibrators, videos, dildos, books of erotica, bondage paraphernalia. Melissa smiled and said, "Okay, you've got thirty minutes to pick out $100 worth of stuff. Anything you want. And I promise, anything you choose I'll try out with you, at least once!" Sam looked around, starting to grin. "I don't even know what some of this stuff does! Come with me and help me decide!"

It ended up taking Sam an hour to choose, but later that night after they tried their new purchases, they both agreed that the decisions had been good ones. When Sam thanked Melissa for the gift, she just smiled and said, "It was my pleasure—literally!"

Sam and Melissa are lucky enough to live in a city that has a sex-positive, women-run sex shop. Ray and Max weren't as fortunate, so they had to get more resourceful. They ordered a catalog, and waited anxiously for it to arrive. When the catalog arrived, they crawled into bed together and scoured the catalog page by page, discussing what each of them thought might be fun. Max told us, "We placed our order the very next day! The stuff came a few weeks later, in a nice, discreet package. Unfortunately, we'd already invited friends over for dinner that night. We could barely wait for them to leave, so we could watch the videos that we'd ordered!"

Here are some ideas for how to arrange a toy spree of your own:

- Leave a gift certificate and a catalog on your lover's pillow.

- Take turns with the catalog, writing down everything that appeals to you on a slip of paper and folding it in half. Put the papers in a jar or small box, and then whenever a special occasion comes up, pull out a paper and buy whatever is on it.

- Make a wish list from the catalog. Then, when one partner's birthday rolls around, the other buys one toy from the list. Who says you can't teach an old dog new tricks?

Trying new things in bed is a great way to keep your relationship exciting and satisfying. For further information, check your local listings, or try one of these two sex-positive, friendly stores, which you can find out more about online:

- Good Vibrations (www.goodvibrations.com)

- Babes in Toyland (www.babesintoyland.com)

Sharing What You've Always Wanted

"My, my, you're looking a bit bleary this morning, my friend." Laura gave Andrea a big hug when they met in front of the Pumpernickel Café for breakfast. "Bleary, but very happy. Is there anything you want to tell me?" Laura laughed and raised her eyebrows as she asked. "All in good time, all in good time," Andrea replied with a yawn as she stepped inside to put their names on the waiting list. When she came back out she was grinning like a Cheshire cat.

"Well, it's going to be about half an hour." Andrea sat down on one of the wooden benches in front of the restaurant and Laura plopped down beside her. "Okay then, missy, you've got one half an hour to come clean. What, may I ask, is making you look so sleepy yet overly satisfied? I'm your best friend and therefore you must tell me all."

"Well," Andrea relented, looking around to make sure no one was hovering near enough to overhear, "I got to do something I've always wanted to do last night." "You mean 'something' in the bedroom department?" Laura prodded. "Yup, I guess you could call it the bedroom department . . . though we didn't exactly do it in the bedroom. We didn't do it in any one room in particular, really. It was more of a traveling thing." "What!?" Laura laughed. "You mean you got to do *the* thing? The thing you talked about all through college but could never get up the nerve to initiate? Whoa! Congratulations, girl! I'm so happy for you. But you've been with Ted for four years. How did 'the thing' happen to come up at this stage of the game?"

"I have to give the credit to Ted, really," Andrea smiled. "He and I were hanging out in bed last night, and he got this sort of gleam in his eye. We'd been feeling very close and comfy all evening, and I was very relaxed. I wasn't really even thinking about sex. But then Ted took my hand and gave me a long look. Then he kissed me and told me that he would really love to know if there was anything that I'd always wanted to do that I hadn't gotten the chance to. Well, it was so extremely sweet, but I must say that it took me off guard a bit. I got sort of shy, and so, smart ass that I am, I said something about climbing Everest. But he didn't let that stop him. He squeezed my hand and made it clear that he meant something sexual. Woo hoo, let me tell you, 'the thing' popped right into my head, but I still felt shy about it. I don't know . . . I've been with

Ted so long and we get along great, but I still felt shy. Anyway, he was so wonderful about it. He just kissed me again and said, 'You know, Andrea, I really want to be close to you, and I would love it if you felt you could share anything with me. Do you think you could tell me what you're thinking about now?' So, I got up the nerve and told him all about what I really wanted to do. And then we did it!"

"Wow! That is so terrific, Andrea." Their names were called and they rose to go inside the café. Laura, who had known about "the thing" forever, was very happy that her friend had finally felt comfortable enough to tell a lover about it. She was also impressed at how open and generous Ted had been about it. Not that "the thing" was that big a deal, but he had to be so persistent to get it out of Andrea. That had to have taken some guts. Laura was very impressed—and intrigued. So intrigued that, when she got home that afternoon, she and her partner, Carl, ended up fulfilling one of Carl's fantasies—twice.

Asking your partner what they've always had a hankering for can be a powerful act of generosity and a great way to shake up your sex life. Whether you feel as though your sexual time with your partner has become a wee bit routine or if you'd just like to spice things up a bit, finding out what your partner's secret desires are can bring you closer together. Sharing desires can help your partner feel heard and appreciated and let you get to know something new about them. It can add wonderful intimacy to your night, as well as providing a good roll in the hay!

Here are some suggestions to keep in mind:

- Be gently persuasive. Perhaps your partner is simply shy and needs sensitive encouragement. But if your partner is more resistant, don't push it. The timing may not be right—but you can always try again later.

- Try not to judge. If your partner's unfulfilled longing seems odd or funny to you, try not to react in a hurtful way. Your partner is revealing part of themselves to you, and that act is best treated with respect. If you'd prefer not to engage in the activity, you can say so gently, but never demean your partners desires.

- Keep it fun. You may not be able to fulfill a fantasy perfectly—after all, fantasies are often a bit unrealistic. But it's okay not to reach perfection, especially if you have a funny, sexy time doing it.

Try a bit of adventure tonight (or today!). You and your partner will be glad you did.

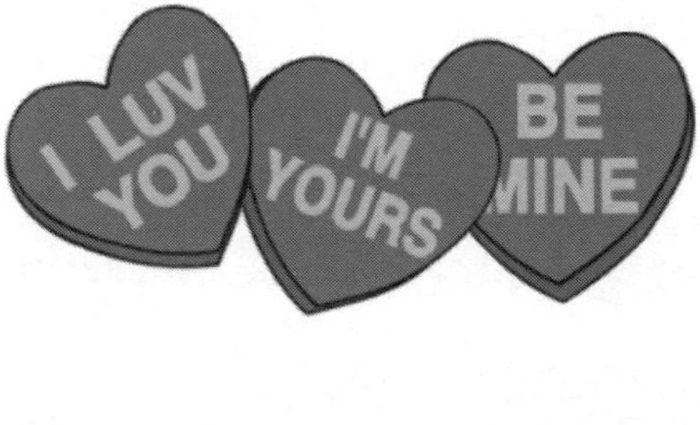
I LUV YOU
I'M YOURS
BE MINE

Revealing the Erotic

Joaquin was madly searching for *Blood Will Tell*, the mystery novel he'd lent Sheila a month before. "It's gotta be here somewhere," Joaquin thought as he moved over to Sheila's nightstand. "Yikes," he said aloud as he opened the lower part of the stand. The thing was crammed with books, everything from tattered paperbacks to an oversized photography book she'd somehow gotten wedged in there. His heart leapt as he saw the red corner of *Blood Will Tell*. "All right! My afternoon's made." Joaquin grabbed the corner and pulled. After one big tug, he dislodged the book, but only after upsetting the whole intricately engineered pile. Half the books in the nightstand came spilling out onto the floor.

"Oh, there's that Indian cookbook I've been looking for." Joaquin picked the old paperback book out of the pile. Right next to it was a glossy-covered book with a picture of a woman's naked belly on it. "Hmm, what's this?" Joaquin took a closer look, noting that the title was *Erotica for Lovers*. "So that's where she keeps 'em." Joaquin knew that Sheila read erotica—it was no big deal. He just hadn't ever noticed where she kept it. Joaquin flipped through the book, noticing by creases in the spine that some of the stories had been read more than others. He was chuckling a bit about that when a thought struck him. He wondered why Sheila had never shared her erotica with him. "Well, maybe she feels it's kind of personal. Or maybe she thinks that I wouldn't be interested. Maybe she thinks I'd be embarrassed!" He thought about these reasons a bit, and set upon an idea.

Later that afternoon, as the sun was just setting, Joaquin sat down with Sheila in the huge, green armchair they had in the living room. "Hey," he said, giving her a warm kiss. "Hey yourself," she replied, squeezing his arm. "What have you been up to today?" "As a matter of fact, I was out shopping for you," Joaquin replied with a smile. "For me? Ooh, loot! Lemme at it." "Actually," Joaquin said, laughing at her enthusiasm, "it's really for both of us. I'll go get it."

He returned with books he'd bought that afternoon, placing them with a flourish on Sheila's lap and scooting in next to her. "Whoa! Sexy stuff!" Sheila laughed and flushed a bit. "Honey! Very nicely chosen." Now it was Joaquin's turn to blush. "I was

thinking that we could share some of these stories." Sheila smiled but looked a little puzzled. "What I mean is, I think it would be fun if we each took a book and read through some of the stories separately. Then we could each choose a story that we especially liked and, later tonight, we could each read our selection out loud. I think it would be really sexy." He looked at Sheila, who was smiling slyly. "And it could be kind of revealing," she said. "I'd be really interested to know which stories you find particularly sexy." She gave him a big kiss. "Let's do it. I'll see you tonight." Sheila grabbed one of the books and headed into the backyard, stopping first in the kitchen to pour herself a glass of lemonade.

That night they met in their bedroom. Joaquin had brought a glass of wine for each of them, and they each sipped from their glasses as they read. Throughout, there was much giggling, many caresses, and the occasional kiss. And, even though they couldn't quite make it all the way through the second story and somehow broke a wine glass that had seemed pretty secure on the nightstand, they both thought of that night as one of their best ever.

Sharing erotica is a terrific way to create a sexy mood with your partner. Not only can the stories be steamy, but the act of selecting a story for your lover is wonderfully intimate. You may feel like two kids sharing the "naughty" parts of a book. And maybe the experience will lead to something fabulously grown up.

Here are some tips to get you started:

- Choose carefully. Erotica spans the gamut in terms of content, so consider where your partner is coming from when you make your selection. Don't be afraid to push the boundaries a bit, but try to avoid anything that could be upsetting.

- Try not to have specific expectations. Erotica may make your partner feel shy or it could awaken the sexual dynamo you always knew was in them. Either response should be okay. Try to enjoy the experience of sharing itself and try not to expect a specific outcome.

- Have fun! Remember, laughter can be just as sexy as smoldering sensuality. This experience could result in either one—or, most likely, both.

Why not make a special trip to the bookstore and share some erotica tonight? What a way to while away your evening!

Sex, Love, and Videotapes

Kurt and Thalia were always open to trying new things together in bed. They'd talked about renting some sexy videos, but they weren't really sure what they'd do with them. Sit there and watch silently? Wait until they were turned on, shut off the TV, and then get it on? Every time they talked about it, they ended up cracking up and then letting the subject go.

Finally, Thalia had an idea. She went to the video store and rented a couple of different flicks. She got home much earlier than Kurt did, so she started to watch them on her own. The first one she tried was a little too tame for her taste: "I figured, if my mind was wandering, this wasn't the one!"

The next video was a little too embarrassing: "The characters were just too dumb! I mean, porn can be a bit absurd, but this one was so lame it was irritating!" Finally, the third video seemed just right: "It was a little silly, but also pretty sexy. I liked that it came from a female perspective, and that there were a lot of different stories in the same movie. I congratulated myself, and then hoped Kurt would hurry up and get home! Whew!"

When Kurt arrived, the first thing Thalia did was greet him wearing her favorite sexy outfit. When she shared her plan, Kurt was all for it. She suggested that they watch the video together, with one simple rule: They had to do everything that was happening on screen, acting it out alongside the characters in the movie. "At first it was just funny," Kurt said. "But eventually we did get into it, and it was really fun and sexy. In fact, we ended up buying that tape to have on hand!"

If you and your partner want to try being your own private video stars, check and see if your local movie rental place has videos you're interested in. If you can't find anything there, you may want to try out the women-run sex stores mentioned in "Toy Spree" (you can buy movies through their catalogs, many of which are specifically women-friendly or made by women).

You may want to take turns picking out movies that you've preapproved, or just pick blindly and see what happens. The main thing is to have fun and stay checked in with each other to make sure you're both enjoying a particular scene. Over time, you

may find that by taking some of the decisions "out of your hands" about what to do in bed, you try more things than you might have alone. And your role-playing skills and comfort with each other's fantasies are likely to improve as well.

If you have fun with this exercise, the next step might be making your own movies. Get your camcorder set up and either make up your own scripts or follow those of your favorite videos. Then, on those rainy nights when you're tired of all the reruns on TV, you and your lover can check out your own video collection for a little more, shall we say, stimulation.

PART V

The Best of Times

Mystery Date

Remember the early days of your courtship, when you and your lover would make special plans to spend time together? Maybe you went to candlelit restaurants and the theater. Maybe you planned hikes that included a picnic for two. Or, if you never did these sorts of things, maybe you're worried that you've passed your honeymoon period and that it's "too late."

Luckily for you, it's never too late. One particularly fun way to heat up your together time is to take turns planning mystery dates. Mason and Ione have a mystery date once a month, and they've found that it's the perfect way to keep the element of surprise in their relationship.

Here's how it works: They set aside one day a month for a mystery date, and one of them makes all of the plans in secret. All they tell the other person is when (day, evening, overnight), what to wear, and what to bring.

One month, Mason took Ione out to dinner at the restaurant where they had their first date, and then they went to a showing of *All About Eve* at the local repertory movie theater. The next month, Ione planned a "spa day" at their home: "I brought Mason a light, healthy breakfast in bed. Then we tried a new yoga video together, and spent the afternoon in bed reading poetry aloud. Later, we took a long, hot shower and massaged this fancy exfoliating scrub onto each other. After that, we helped each other apply a nice moisturizer I'd bought especially for the day (it had Mason's favorite scent) . . . and you can probably guess what followed all of that!"

The great thing about mystery dates is that you and your partner take turns. Being the planner can be fun, especially if you get creative and try to think up things your partner would never suspect or has always wanted to do. And being the person on the receiving end means all you have to do is sit back and enjoy yourself, with the knowledge that your partner has taken the time to do something special for you.

There are plenty of things you can do on a mystery date. Here are a few ideas to get you started:

- Ask your sweetie to make plans to spend time away for the afternoon, and suggest the best time to come home. While you're alone, take the time to clean the

house, do that pile of laundry, and make those pesky phone calls. Then, make a special meal (or get take-out), and set the table with candles and a note that lists the things your partner doesn't have to worry about doing now (leaving the two of you plenty of time to talk, rent a movie, or take a bath together).

- Plan something your partner enjoys that you don't know much about. If she loves baseball and you've never had much interest, take a roll of quarters and go to the batting cages. If his favorite food is Thai, see if you can find a one-day Thai cooking class the two of you can take together.

- Plan an overnight at a hotel, bed and breakfast, or campsite you've never gone to before. (Note that youth hostels, which aren't just for "youths," often have inexpensive couples' rooms.)

The main ingredient of a good mystery date is that you get to spend time together and do something nice that expresses your love. It can be elaborate or simple, at home or outdoors, romantic or silly. Try to achieve variety by not repeating the same date twice. A little mystery can go a long way.

Enjoying the Ordinary

"Thanks for coming along, honey," Mira said squeezing her partner Dylan's knee gently. "Well, sure. But actually, I'm not quite certain why you were so insistent that I be here. I mean, it's okay, but it's just a car wash." Mira smiled as she pulled in to Bob's Wash-a-Lot, her preferred car-wash emporium. "Oh, just a car wash, eh? Well, maybe it is and maybe it isn't. We'll just see, shall we?" Dylan laughed at her weird, mysterious tone. Sometimes Mira just had to be indulged in her odd flights of fancy.

Mira pulled the car up onto the metal guide rails and turned off the engine. They felt the car being pulled forward, heading into the waiting, wet machinery inside. "You know, when I was a kid, these things scared the hell out of me," Dylan recalled. "It couldn't help that my brother spent the whole time telling me what kind of terrible monsters lived in car washes. I usually ended up trying to wedge myself under the dashboard for safety." "Well, my love," smiled Mira, "no need to fear now. I'm the only one here, and I don't intend for this to be scary." She looked over at Dylan with a distinct gleam in her eye. "Hmm, what *do* you intend it to be?" Dylan replied, a bit puzzled.

Mira held up her finger in a "just wait" gesture and reached into her bag. She pulled out a cassette tape and slipped it into the tape deck. Flowing out of the speakers came the strains of "Moments in Love" by the group the Art of Noise, a favorite make-out song for Mira and Dylan when they met in high school. "How about some smoochin'?" Mira asked, eyebrows raised seductively. "Aha! So this is why you enticed me to the car wash. You want to take advantage of my virtue!" "Right you are, my sweet. Now come on over here." In the middle of their first kiss, Dylan couldn't suppress a chuckle, "I feel just like we're in high school again." The rest of the wash was spent in silence, with only the occasional eruption of a giggle or two.

What could be more ordinary and dull than getting your car washed? But Mira found a way to make even this pedestrian activity fun. Every day each of us has to do numerous dull, necessary activities to keep our lives going. We've got to go grocery shopping, clean the cat box, make dinner, get the car lubed. Most of us get these tasks done without too much thought and with very little enjoyment. But what if you could infuse some of these experiences with a sense of togetherness and fun, using them as

quality time to spend with your partner? Okay, so maybe you can't think of a way to make cleaning the cat box an opportunity for fun togetherness, but are there any tasks or chores you need to do that could be livened up by your partner's presence? For instance, going to the grocery store with a sense of dread can be one of life's most tedious duties, but what if you and your partner agreed to make it fun? You could pop some great music in the stereo and do some car dancing on the way. Then you could investigate some of those more mysterious foods that you've never really looked at before (pig's feet? hearts of palm?). A rude or sluggish checker may be much less of a burden if you can roll your eyes at your partner.

When you must do ordinary tasks with your partner, why not try to enjoy them more by enjoying the time you're spending with your sweetheart? After all, he or she is someone whose company you enjoy more than almost anyone else's. Just because you're in the middle of a mundane task doesn't mean you can't focus on the fun your partner brings to the experience. Give it a try using the suggestions below:

- Keep it light. The key to enjoying the ordinary with your partner is not to get bogged down in the tedious or aggravating aspects of the task. Yes, the grocery store may be crowded; perhaps there's a mountain of dishes to do. Instead of focusing on the negatives, try to jump into the task with enthusiasm and a light heart. Tell your partner that bit of gossip you've been saving, or be silly enough to get a laugh out of them. Remember, this too is time with your partner, time you can choose to enjoy.

- Add a treat. A great way to enjoy the ordinary is to make sure that you have some sort of treat waiting for you during or at the end of the task. If you have to run to the drugstore, how about stopping by the frozen yogurt shop afterward? If you've got to clean the house, why not make sure you have a great video to enjoy together when you're done? Thinking about the treat will help both of you keep your moods light as you get through your chore.

We all have our mundane responsibilities. Instead of facing them with a sigh, why not grab your partner by the hand and jump into them with a lighter heart? You may just discover that a trip to the grocery store with your love turns out to be some of the most fun you'll have all day.

Creativity Date

The phone rang. Marsha picked it up and heard the voice of her oldest friend, Karen, on the other end. "Hey, Marsha, how are ya?" "I'm good, Karen. I finally got around to planting all those bulbs I ordered. Whew! I'm just about done." "Well, it sounds like you could use some real fun after all of that work. How about a night out at that new Balinese restaurant?"

"Oh, Karen, that's a terrific idea, but I can't. I've got my creativity date with Martin tonight." Marsha smiled a bit as she said this, knowing that she might get some teasing from Karen. "Your 'creativity date'? What on earth is that—planning to be creative?" Marsha laughed, "Well, yeah, it is. Every Thursday, Martin and I have decided to do something creative together. We both had been in a creativity drought for a while, and a few months ago we talked about it. Since we were also trying to spend more time together, we decided to have a creativity date each week, an evening when we learn some new creative thing or do something that we both already love. These days we've been taking guitar lessons together. We're getting pretty good, though I can still play 'Mary Had a Little Lamb' way better than Martin."

Karen laughed. "That sounds like a great idea. It's pretty cool that you guys can do it together. Has it been fun?" "Oh yeah," Marsha confirmed. "At first I was afraid it would be like those dreadful clarinet lessons I had to take in school. But, I've gotta tell you, adult coordination does wonders for the ol' fingering. We're both improving, and it gives us something fun to do together every week."

They made plans for another night, and Karen hung up the phone feeling inspired. Marsha's creativity date had given Karen ideas of her own. She knew that her partner, Wilson, missed playing the piano. He loved it when he got around to practicing, but with a schedule as busy as his, it was difficult to have time to dedicate to the instrument. Karen felt the same way about her poetry. She loved writing and had written some beautiful pieces, but she found that lately she just hadn't taken the time to focus on her poetry. It was a shame, too, because it made her feel so good when she finally sat down to do it.

That night as she and Wilson were cooking dinner, she proposed that they institute a creativity date of their own. "It would be a time for us to get back to the creative things we love and also spend more time together. You could practice the piano while I write." Wilson though about it for a moment. "But don't you think that my playing will distract you from your poetry?" "No, I don't think so," said Karen. "I love hearing you play—it's beautiful! And I sort of have an idea that we can also take little breaks to share what we're doing with each other. You know, like you could play a song for me, and I could read a poem I've finished to you. We'll sort of be alone, together. What do you think?"

Wilson thought they should give it a try, so after dinner they retired to the living room—he at the piano, and she on the couch with her writing journal. At first they felt a little self-conscious; it had been a while since either of them had sat down to be creative. After a few minutes, Wilson filled the air with some rusty but beautiful Schubert, and Karen started reworking an old poem. At the end of the evening they felt fuller, as though their evening had somehow nourished them both.

Many people feel that they don't have enough time for their relationships or for exploring their creative spirits. Why not combine these two deficits and have time for both by enjoying a creativity date with your partner? You can either do one activity together, or each spend time engaging in a different favorite creative activity side by side. Creating with your partner can make you feel alive, because you're nurturing a part of yourself and your relationship that may often be neglected—the creative side. And as you share the creative part of your nature, you'll be nurturing your relationship, too.

Here are some tips to help you get started:

- Take a class. Choose an activity that appeals to both of you and attend together. Learning something new can be exhilarating, and learning new creative skills can encourage you to be more creative at home, as well. Try a class in painting, drawing, quilting, sculpting, writing, music, dance, or anything else that tickles your fancy.

- Don't be afraid to be less than expert. On your creativity date, it's not really about producing a "good" product—a perfect drawing or poem. It's about you

and your partner creating, in and of itself. Shut your inner critic in the closet and have fun, no matter what the final product looks or sounds like.

Let yourself get back to those days of free expression you had as a kid, creating just for the fun of it. With your partner along for the ride, you'll have the time to enjoy each other while you nourish your soul, too.

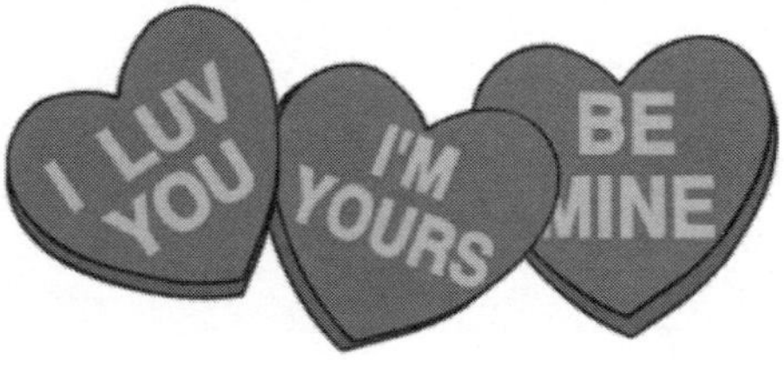
I LUV YOU
I'M YOURS
BE MINE

A Bath for Two

It was a cold, blustery Friday night. Marcie was all bundled up in her bulkiest black sweater, trying to ward off the mid-November chill. She was curled up with a mystery novel while her partner Harry finished up some work he'd brought home. The evening had a real sense of familiarity to it. Marcie and Harry spent most of their evenings reading or working quietly together, not really talking, but hanging out in the same space. They both enjoyed spending quiet time together, but had recently agreed that they needed to make some small changes in order to liven up some of their evenings a bit.

To that end, they had decided to set up a weekly date night, a time when they would get together and do something fun and different. Saturday was their date night, and while reading, Marcie was half-considering what she could plan for their evening. They took turns deciding what to do, and it was Marcie's turn that week.

Pulling the wool throw over her chilly feet, Marcie was having some trouble coming up with anything appealing. "Hmm…" she thought. "Well, we always have fun going to a movie. Or we could go to that art lecture at the university. But my goodness, it's just so cold. I don't really relish the idea of going outside at all. What can we do inside that's warm, cozy, yet romantic?" All of a sudden it came to her. Something warm, special, and very romantic—a bath! She giggled quietly to herself, picturing them sliding around in a soapy tub.

The next day, Marcie went to a local gift shop that specialized in soaps and spa products. She chose bath oil scented with sandalwood, a loofah scrubber, a bath pillow, and a small collection of candles that smelled like cinnamon, vanilla, and clove. After dinner that night, she asked Harry to go into the living room and wait for her. "What about date night?" he asked. "Oh, you'll see, Harry. We're having date night all right. Just relax." Marcie went upstairs to the bathroom and began to fill the claw-foot tub with hot, steaming water. She added some sandalwood bath oil, and its fragrance floated up on the steam to fill the space. Marcie lit the candles, set up the bath pillow, placed the loofah within easy reaching distance to the tub, and poured two small glasses of port. Then she stripped down and put on a silky robe. Now everything was ready.

When she brought Harry upstairs to the tub, he laughed. "We're going to take a bath together? Wow! What a perfect idea for such a cold night." He kissed Marcie, and she helped him take off his clothes. As they slipped into the steaming tub with the wonderful scents swirling around them and the taste of port on their tongues, they both felt like staying in forever.

Why not make the simple, necessary activity of bathing something sensual and romantic by sharing it every once in a while with your partner? Obviously we're not talking about a quick dip to scrub with the antiseptic soap, but rather a long, luxurious date in water.

Beyond just getting the hot water into the tub, here are some tips to make your bath for two complete:

- Add fragrances and flavors. Treat yourself to some scented bath products: bath oil, bubble bath, salts. These can make the shared bathing experience that much more sensual and enjoyable. Choosing musky, rich fragrances will add an extra sexy touch. Also, try having something to tempt your tastebuds nearby. Fruit (a bowl of grapes, slices of melon) can be just the cool and delicious treat you'll want in a hot bath. And sipping some delicate dessert wine or brandy while you bathe can be transporting.

- Candlelight adds to the mood. Avoid using the harsh overhead light while you bathe together. Letting gentle, warm candlelight play over the water and each other will add beauty and romance to your bath.

- How about music? Having a portable CD player nearby (but far enough away so that it can't fall into the tub—electrocution does not equal romance) with some of your favorite mellow or sexy music can help remove the stresses of the day and take you to the loving, sensual place you'd like to be.

- Allow yourself plenty of time to revel in your senses and in each other.

Bathing together can wash away the ordinariness of any evening, infusing your night with pleasure and intimacy. Surrounded by fragrance, candlelight, warm water, and your partner, you'll find a relaxing sensuality in this most ordinary of activities. Try it tonight!

Date Night

Six months ago, Zoe and Mark felt quite a distance in their relationship. Even though they lived together, they both secretly felt that they didn't see enough of each other. What with their busy work schedules, trying to get errands and chores done, and constantly trying to stay current with their friends, it seemed as though they'd forgotten to keep up with each other.

The situation broke one Thursday evening. Zoe was lying on the couch in her comfy sweats, reading *Sense and Sensibility* for the eighth time. Mark came in from the garage and collapsed into an easy chair with a sigh. He looked at Zoe on the couch, thinking that she looked so pretty in her sweats, so relaxed and comfortable. Just then, a feeling of longing struck him, making him take a quick breath in. He realized that he was longing to be with Zoe—that he missed her. He had been all ready to spend another night at home, reading or watching TV and barely talking to Zoe. But, as he continued to look at her, he was aware that he didn't want to settle for that again. He wanted something more.

"Um, is there some reason you're peering at me that way?" Zoe smiled quizzically. "You have an almost maniacal look on your face, Mark. What's going on?" Mark laughed, realizing that he'd been staring fixedly at her. "Well, I had been contemplating entering a life of crime, but how about a date instead?" "A date?" said Zoe. "What, like to the malt shop or something? It's Thursday night, and I'm already in my sweats." Zoe seemed reluctant to put down her book. "Zoe, you know, I've been feeling lately that we just don't see enough of each other. We used to love going out together, and now we just spend time at home. That's nice and all, but I'm really starting to miss you. So, what I'd like to do tonight is have a date with you. A real date—going out to dinner and a movie, or a walk in the park, or whatever you like. How about it?"

Zoe paused, considering this proposition. She had been looking forward to reading that night . . . but, what was she thinking! She herself had been feeling a little alienated from Mark. This was a great opportunity to have fun, just the two of them. "You're on," she said, jumping off the couch. "Let's hit that new little pasta joint downtown, and then we can go bowling!"

Their night out was such a success that Mark and Zoe decided to make it a regular thing. That way, no matter how busy they got during the week, how stressed at work, how overcommitted socially, they each knew that they would have some time to be together alone, guaranteed. They took turns deciding what to do on each of their dates, and quickly discovered that date night helped to remind them how much they liked being together. Knowing that they had a dedicated night to reconnect made them each feel more comfortable about the time they spent apart, too. They could count on Thursday night as theirs.

Here are some tips about setting up a date night of your own:

- Discuss the idea with your partner. They may not see the idea the same way you do, perhaps viewing it as a bit constricting. If your partner balks at setting up "rules" for going out, try to emphasize the fun nature of date night. It can be a great way to ensure that you have time to connect with each other, and an opportunity to try new things together. You can start out on a trial basis, agreeing to have a date night each week for the next two months. At the end of that time, you can reevaluate. We're guessing that neither of you will want to give up your night of togetherness and fun.

- Spice it up with variety. Taking turns deciding what to do each time can help add variety to date night. Some great activities you can try are bowling (Zoe's favorite), going to the zoo, seeing a play at a local small theater, going out for a drink at a swanky nightclub, watching the sunset with a picnic dinner at your local "inspiration point," or going to a poetry reading. Check your local paper for activities that you may not have considered doing before.

- Don't forget about sex! Okay—how *could* you forget about sex? Well, it seems that some couples can use some livening up in the sex department, too. Making your date night a time to "get down" every so often can be a delightful way to spend your evening. Also, dedicating a whole evening to the pleasures of the flesh can encourage you to be a little bit more daring or sensuous than you might otherwise be. Live a little!

Having a night every week that's just for the two of you can help you to remember how much you enjoy each other's company. After all, that's why you're together, right? You like being with each other. So why not make sure you have the time you need to connect and revel in each other?

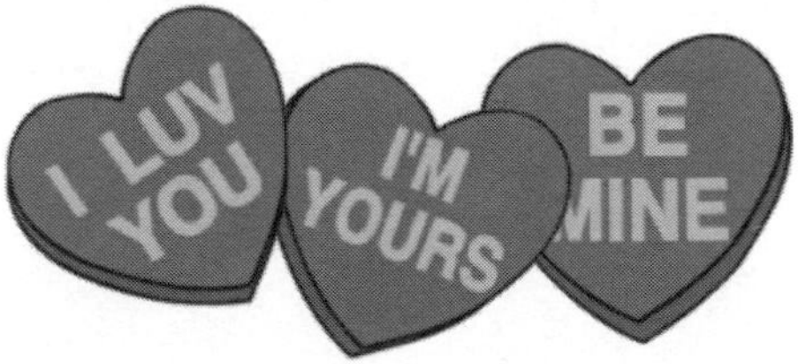
I LUV YOU
I'M YOURS
BE MINE

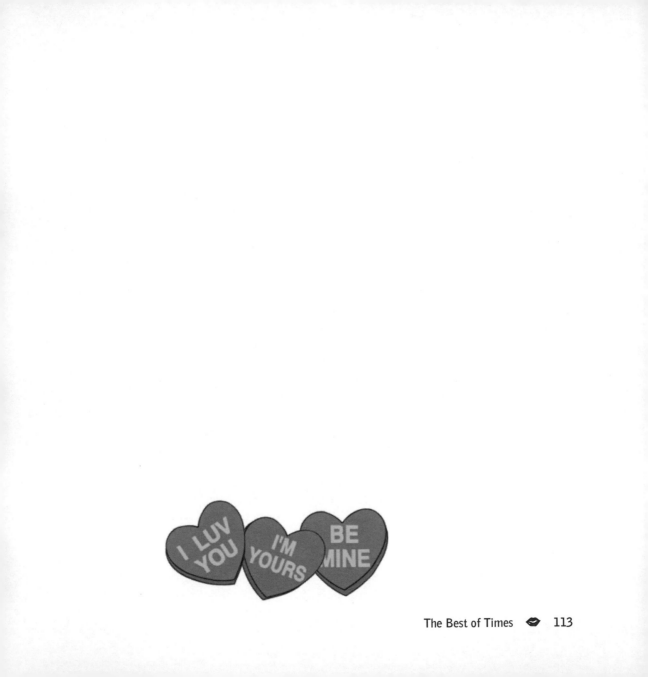

Out for a Treat

Most of us are very busy people, maybe even busier than we'd like to be. We find ourselves looking up, realizing it's Thursday, and wondering where the week has gone. Sometimes we look back at our days and they can seem like an undifferentiated mass of activities. We may feel as though we're simply getting through all the items on our lists without taking a break to stop and enjoy life a little.

Nurturing your relationship may sometimes seem like just another item for that big "to-do" list, something you'd really like to do more of, but aren't quite sure how to do in an effective but fun way. We'd like to suggest that you give your relationship a break—literally! Lots of people make a concerted effort to check in with friends, going out for tea, a beer, or some other treat. But so many of us don't think to do the same in our romantic relationships. Breaking for a treat can give us a chance to reconnect and remember that our lives with our partners aren't all about getting the house clean, getting out the door on time in the morning, or going to dinner parties with friends. It can also be about you, your partner, and a very serious ice cream sundae.

George and Wally are both busy entrepreneurs, each trying to nurture a small business while maintaining closeness with their friends, family, and each other. They live together, but sometimes feel as though they don't see each other much.

"Hey, honey," George said as he and Wally prepared for another stifling Atlanta August day. "What would you say to coming to the store after work so we can cruise by that Korean restaurant for some take-out?" "Umm, I can't today," replied Wally. "I'm meeting Sarah at La Petite Chat for a glass of wine. It's been ages since I've seen her, and we've got to catch up."

They kissed and each went off to their separate jobs, but something about what Wally had said bugged George. Of course it was okay for Wally to hang out with friends—George would be concerned if Wally didn't. But George also felt that he needed some "catching up" with Wally, too. Because they lived together and saw each other every evening, they didn't seem to make those casual dates to go out, get a treat, and just hang out together.

"Well," thought George. "There's certainly something I can do about that." George remembered that he and Wally had casual plans to work in their garden that coming Saturday, and he also knew that it would be brutally hot. He loved working outside with Wally, but it was like a lot of their time together—they were together, but working on different things. They certainly wouldn't be doing too much talking or connecting. George had the perfect solution.

That evening, when Wally had returned from his outing with Sarah, George gave him a big welcome-home hug. "Hi there. Hot enough for you?" Wally laughed and said, "I almost melted at work today. Ugh! Actually, I'm a little worried about gardening this weekend. We should make sure to have plenty of lemonade on hand." "Even better than that," said George, "I'd like to propose a post-gardening treat." "A treat?" smiled Wally. "Yup. I want to go out for a treat with you. I think, when we're done in the yard, we should walk down to Walt's Ice Cream and get ourselves a big ol' banana split. Live a little, and maybe catch up, too." Wally laughed and took George's hand. "Just like kids," he said. "Well, why not," George squeezed his hand. "We deserve it!"

Why not catch up on your relationship over a treat? Get out of the house together and enjoy a wonderful dessert, a café latte, or a glass of wine, just as you would with a friend. It will probably take no more than an hour or so, but the simple act of getting out and treating yourself can help mend a week's worth of busy-ness.

Trying Something New

Jeff and Lucy had been together for eight years. They'd gotten a lot of their life together worked out. Jeff cooked the meals, and Lucy cleaned the house. They alternated between his family and hers on holidays. Every month they put aside the same amount of money, in hopes of someday buying a home. They were both dedicated to their jobs, and they were looking forward to having kids in a few years. Everything was going exactly to plan.

But they'd both been feeling an encroaching sense of boredom. When they talked about it, they agreed that what they needed was something new. Something fun they could do together.

"How about a class?" Lucy suggested. "That might be fun. But I know I don't want to do any homework. I'm too wiped out right now from work to use too much of my brain at night," Jeff said. Lucy laughed, "Don't I know it! But we're getting a little too glued to the TV these days. If we don't do something soon, we're going to get stuck on the couch for good!"

A few days later, Jeff found the perfect thing: skydiving lessons! They'd always talked about trying it, even though neither considered themselves daredevils. Lucy agreed, but asked Jeff to make reservations before either of them could chicken out.

Five weeks later, getting ready to jump out of the plane, Lucy told Jeff, "At least we're not bored now!" Jeff managed a half-hearted smile that looked more like a grimace. "Uh, maybe a few weeks of TV won't be so bad, after this!" Lucy blew him a kiss and shouted over the roar of the engines, "Next time, maybe a cooking class will do! See ya down there!"

If skydiving isn't your speed, here are some other pursuits you and your partner might try:

- Take a class together on something you're both interested in learning more about, for example: martial arts, photography, home improvement, Spanish, the modern novel, music appreciation, or meditation.

- Switch responsibilities for a month. For example, if you always pay the bills, let your partner hold the checkbook. If your partner always cooks, take over the

apron for a month. You'll get a nice break from your usual chores and a new appreciation for your partner's practical contributions to your life.

- Try something new in bed: act out a fantasy, do some role playing, have sex in an unusual place, read erotica aloud to each other, leave each other amorous notes.
- Get a new cookbook and try some foods you've never eaten before.
- If you never have people over, plan a party. Have people over for dinner, or create your own monthly film festival. Cook an elaborate meal together, or plan a potluck.

No matter what you decide to do, trying something new is always a good way to infuse fresh energy into your relationship and your life.

Dinner for Two

"I'm starting to get hungry," Sandra could hear her belly faintly rumbling. "Me too," said her partner Bob. "Any more pizzas?" Bob laughed as Sandra tickled him. She was always getting after him to eat better—frozen pizza was his favorite food. Not that Sandra really had a handle on the whole nutrition thing. She was just as likely to grab a burger from the local smokehouse as Bob was to indulge in a pepperoni pie. They'd often talked about trying to eat in a more healthful way, but neither was inclined toward cooking. They usually let the matter go, eating another frozen dinner in front of the TV.

But that Saturday, Sandra was unwilling to just let it go. "You know, honey, I kind of wish not only that we could eat a little better, but also that we would eat together more." "What do you mean?" Bob was surprised. "We almost always eat together." "Well," Sandra countered, "I don't really mean eating in front of the TV. I mean maybe making a nice meal, setting the table, and eating together—no TV, just you and me. I think we may be missing out on each other a little bit, spending so much time in front of the tube. Also, I've started to think that if we paid more attention to what and how we were eating, we would be more inclined to start cooking more. You know, making healthier and probably better-tasting food." "Yeah." Bob slid his arm around Sandra. "You're probably right. I mean, we have that nice china from my grandmother, and we never use it. Maybe we could whip up a fancy recipe every once in a while and bring out the good stuff. It would be like going out to dinner, only we'd be staying home. It sounds like it could be fun."

Sandra jumped up to get their small collection of cookbooks. She brought them back to the couch, and she and Bob started looking through them. "Lots of this stuff sounds really good," Bob said happily. "And it doesn't look all that hard to make." They chose a recipe for chicken piccata and decided to serve it with steamed asparagus and a nice risotto. Getting really hungry now, they hurriedly got their coats on and left for their local market.

When they returned they worked on the meal together, Bob concentrating on the risotto while Sandra handled the piccata and asparagus. They put on some old Al Green and sang to all the songs as they cooked. Bob set the table with his grandmother's china,

and when the meal was ready, they sat down to a veritable feast. The piquant fragrance of the lemony chicken and the creamy scent of the risotto made their mouths water. Candles cast a warm glow over the table, and white wine sparkled in their glasses.

"Here's to home cooking—and to you, Sandra." Bob raised his glass to her. "Thanks for thinking of this. I've gotta say, it's a damned sight more fun than frozen lasagna and reruns of *Seinfeld*—though I still think that has its place." They laughed and dug in. That Saturday night turned out to be one of the best dates they'd had in a long while.

Creating together can be a wonderful way to feel closer, and cooking has an added romance. With our hectic lives, many of us tend to treat meals as chores to be gotten through instead of savored. Why not take the opportunity to work together with your partner on a culinary project tonight, creating a feast of the foods you both love? A dinner for two can be a fun and delicious way to create something for both of you, making not only a meal but also the space to enjoy each other.

Here are some suggestions to help make your dinner for two the best it can be:

- Make the meal a project for both of you from the beginning by collaborating on the menu. Dreaming together about foods you love can make your menu planning into a sensual treat all its own.

- Don't be afraid to take chances on the menu. Cooking is an adventure, especially if you're attempting dishes you've never cooked before. Try not to focus too much on the final product, but enjoy the whole process instead. It matters less that your soufflé turns out perfectly than that you had fun and felt close to your partner while making it.

- Make it special. If you have china or silver that you only use for holidays, why not break them out now? Use the tablecloth you bought in Florence. Go ahead and spend a little extra for candles or a nice wine. The meal you create together is special and deserves to be served with the best.

You can create a dinner for two as often as you like. Some couples do it nearly every night! Even if you treat yourself to some home-cooked elegance only once a month, you'll get the benefit of time together and the space to enjoy each other. You know you have to eat—so why not make it beautiful?

Home Sweet Home

The space you live in has a profound effect on how you feel. It is where you have some of your most intimate and personal moments, and it is the place where you and your partner spend most of your time together. One way to contribute to your relationship is to spend time sprucing up your home.

Travis and Emily's first house was a real fixer-upper. But after years of living in a tiny apartment, they were thrilled to have a backyard, even if it was just a huge pile of dirt. And as for the orange shag carpet in the family room, well, at least it gave them a hearty dose of nostalgia for the seventies!

Neither of them had ever been all that handy. Emily had taken wood shop in high school, but that was just because the only other alternative was sewing, which didn't interest her. Travis had done some house painting one summer in college, but even he admits that his work ethic hadn't been so great. However, neither of them let their inexperience get in the way.

They started by going to the library and checking out home repair books. The first order of business was to rip up the carpeting (nostalgia can only go so far) and refinish the hardwood floors they knew were underneath. They bought some tools, borrowed the big equipment from their local tool lending library and from friends, and flipped open the book. And before they knew it, half the carpeting in the house was lying on the dirt pile that was their back lawn.

"Every weekend for months, that's all we did. Get up, eat breakfast, and get started," Travis recalled. "But we cranked up the tunes, and sang together as we ripped apart our house and our yard. Doing it together made it so fun, because we were investing in our future, and because we were learning so much by working together. Sometimes things went wrong, but we managed to laugh at our mistakes, and just try again."

"And don't forget the backrubs! At the end of each day, we were so sore from all the work that we'd take a long, hot shower together and then take turns giving each other massages. I have to admit—that was my favorite part!" Emily added, "Next month, we're getting a hot tub and building a deck around it. We're inviting friends and family over to help. Now that's going to be nice!"

Whether you and your partner own a house or are renting a tiny apartment, you can spend some time together fixing up your place. Be creative. Brainstorm together. And don't let lack of experience stop you.

Add a fresh coat of paint to the walls, or plant a tiny herb garden in a window box. Get some sexy new bedding, or put up new photos of your loved ones. Whatever you decide, allow your home improvements to bring you closer together. Make it light and fun. And after you're done, remember to congratulate each other on a job well done.

Hometown Tourists

Does it seem like you're in a rut? Do you do the same thing every Saturday night, not because it's so much fun, but because you're too uninspired to think of something new when the time comes? One way to beat the doldrums is to become tourists in your own area.

When we travel, we often explore as much as we can of what the area has to offer. We check out the beautiful churches and cutting-edge art galleries. We visit the historical landmarks and the natural wonders. And we cram it all into a few days or weeks, leaving us exhausted and armed with plenty of memories.

At home, it's easier to get lazy. If you can see something any time, you may find that you never get around to seeing it. By exploring your area like a tourist, you and your partner can get a whole new appreciation for your hometown and for each other. And then, at the end of the day, you can go home instead of going to some unfamiliar bed with scratchy sheets. It's the best of both worlds!

One year for their anniversary, Lynn made Cat a special gift. She got a calendar for the next year, and picked up their local papers and magazines. Then she took a pair of scissors and clipped out all of the ongoing events and destinations that looked interesting: the museums they'd never been to, the restaurants they'd never checked out, the parks they'd never gone to together.

Next, she pasted them onto three-by-five cards, and sorted them out roughly by season. After filing the cards under each month, Lynn wrapped the calendar and gave it to Cat. "The idea was to show her that I still loved spending time with her, that there was more for us to explore together, and that I was still totally into hanging out and having fun together. Plus, it would take away our excuse to complain that there was nothing new to do!"

"Now, every month we try to do at least one thing from the calendar," Cat explained. "We've gone to some great lectures at the university, and we don't just eat at the same Chinese restaurant every week like we used to ... Well, okay, we still eat there every week, but we also make sure to try out the new places. We can't help it if our old standby has the best moo shoo vegetables ever!"

Here are some variations on the calendar idea:

- Get a tourist's guidebook of your area. Go through it with your partner and star all the things you're even remotely interested in doing. (Some of the most bizarre or seemingly dull things can often be the most fun.) Then, try to do one thing out of the book once a week or once a month.

- Get a trail guide or a book of walking tours for your area.

- Spend a day checking out those tiny shops you've never made it to, or that creepy-looking doll museum you always rush past. Go to places you'd never otherwise think to go. Play social anthropologist, pretending that you're doing a study on the unique behaviors of die-hard bowlers (or bar hoppers, or massage therapists . . .).

Who says you have to travel far to have adventure? With the right intentions, a trip to the mall together can have the same intrigue as a trip across the globe!

Taking a Beverage Break

You probably understand very well that taking a short breather can help you go back to your work with renewed energy and vigor, knowing that you're taking proper care of yourself. But have you ever considered that your relationship could use the same thing? What would happen if you regularly took time-outs with no aim at all except to enjoy some peaceful time together?

Roger was dissatisfied with the way he spent his evenings with Marta. They would greet each other as they came home from work, only to move off to separate areas of the house to begin their evening's activities. Roger would cook dinner while Marta caught up on phone calls. They would eat, sometimes together but mostly apart, and then continue their separate tasks. All the time, they could be in the same room for hours without ever making a real connection. Roger knew he wanted a change.

He and Marta already were pretty good at making dates to go out together. But one Tuesday afternoon, Roger hit upon the idea of making another kind of date with Marta. He wanted to have a set time when they would leave whatever activity they were engaged in and spend a brief period making some connection with each other. Nothing elaborate—just fifteen or twenty minutes to touch base and enjoy each other's company.

He dropped by the wine store the next day to pick up a bottle of the nice port that he and Marta usually drank only on special occasions. That night he put his arm around Marta's waist as she did the dinner dishes. "How about meeting me in the living room at ten o'clock?" he said in his best casual voice. "The living room? What's up?" Marta responded a little quizzically. "I'd just like us to spend some time catching up tonight—can you spare twenty minutes?" Marta looked sideways at Roger, paused, and decided that whatever Roger had in mind was probably more important than the courtroom drama she'd been half-planning to watch at ten that night. "Okay," she said. "You're on. See you then." She chuckled a little at the formality of their "date" and went back to finishing up the dishes.

When ten o'clock rolled around, Marta walked into the living room to find that Roger had set out their nice crystal wineglasses and a bottle of her favorite port. There was some lovely classical music on the stereo, and the lights were low.

"Wow, this looks great! Have I walked into a seduction?" she asked with a smile, sitting down next to Roger. "Well, not necessarily," he replied. "I just thought it would be nice if we made some time to touch base at the end of the day. You know, sit and have a nice drink and talk about our day—or whatever comes to mind. I've been kind of missing you in the evenings, and I'd like to reconnect. I got some port to tempt you," he smiled.

They spent the next twenty minutes or so talking, sharing their experiences of the day, the thoughts they'd been thinking, the things that had worried them or made them glad. And when their glasses were empty, they felt more connected to each other. That's when the evening beverage break became a regular occurrence for Marta and Roger.

You could try this, too. Get some delicious herbal tea, juice, wine, or even hot cocoa, and make a date with your partner tonight. It won't take long, but the simple act of sharing some time over a beverage can bring a sense of renewal to the time you spend together. By making the beverage break a regular ceremony, you honor the time you spend together, avoiding the casual taking-for-granted that is so often the result our busy lifestyles.

Special Place

Every couple needs a special place—a spot that's beautiful and serene and feels like it belongs to them. It's a place where you can look out at some kind of vista, and feel above all the struggle of ordinary life. It's a place you return to again and again to talk and touch and huddle against each other as it gets dark.

Everything about this place—the way the air smells, the quality of the light—gets imprinted on some deep part of you. And memories are more vivid there, like conversations you can remember nearly word for word, or a sense of exactly what it felt like to be you, to be together.

Perry Mason, the great fictional lawyer, had a special place where he and Della often went after a case. It was a spot in the desert where they could watch the great empty dunes turn pink at twilight, and where the constellations blazed in a sky untouched by city lights. There, in book after book, Perry would ask Della to marry him. And Della would decline, saying that she was having a lot more fun being his secretary than stuck at home as his wife.

The moral of this story? Don't do anything special in your special place. Perry overdid it, and the conversation always took an unfortunate turn. Just talk, sweet and rambling. Just walk and hold hands. Just watch the horizon, the distant lights. Remember why you like each other—the familiar, easy jokes, the things you've always shared, the feeling of belonging.

If you don't have a special place, this is a good time to make one. Here's how to do it:

- Find a place that's accessible, that won't take a lot of time or work to get to.

- Make sure it has a vista of some kind. It doesn't have to be a great view, just a little above the daily hassles.

- Look for a place to walk; you don't always want to be stuck in the car.

- Try out different places until you find one that makes you both feel peaceful, calm, and close.

- When you've found a spot that feels good to both of you, go there often to establish an emotional connection. Make it yours.
- Don't burden your special place with heavy problem solving and deep issues. Don't bring anger there. Try to keep things light and affirming.
- Bring no one else to your special spot. This is reserved for the two of you to strengthen and replenish your bond.
- If you can think of it, share with your partner one thing you appreciate or value about him or her. Make this a spot for little, low-key celebrations of the qualities you love.

Fit for Love

Caring for your body is a way to increase your sense of well-being—which, not incidentally, is integral to the health of your relationship. If you find it hard to motivate yourself to exercise, or if it seems like an endless bore, one solution is to team up with your sweetheart.

After years of sinking deeper into their couch, Adam and Pat decided they could use a little exercise. They couldn't afford a gym, and they didn't have a lot of time, so they decided to start simply. Every night after dinner, they went for a walk together around their neighborhood. At first, they took it slow: thirty minutes at not much more than a stroll.

Pat remembers how it all began: "We didn't break a sweat or anything, but at least we were outside, breathing fresh air. We both work at desk jobs, hunched over computers all day long. My back had kinks, and Adam was getting headaches. Moving around, I could feel myself start to loosen up. And almost just as great was the chance we had to talk about our days. It was so much better than sitting in front of the TV!"

After a while, Pat and Adam picked up the pace and started walking farther. On weekends, they drove to the state parks in their area and went for hikes. They found that it was a pleasant and inexpensive way to spend time together, and that they had more energy and less stress than they'd had since they could remember.

"It was great for our sex life, too, I have to admit," Adam told us. "We both just felt better about our bodies—not because we'd become super-fit model types or anything, but because we were taking care of ourselves and each other."

Here are some ideas that can help you and your lover get fit for love:

- Take up a sport that you both enjoy and that you can play together (for example, tennis, racquetball, or cycling).

- Get a family membership at your local gym. If you have children, see if the gym has swim lessons or other activities that they can participate in while you work out.

- Train for an event together, such as a marathon, triathlon, or bike race. See if there are fund-raising events in your area that you can do together, such as an AIDS or breast cancer walk: this way you can raise money for worthy causes, spend time together, and take care of your body, all at the same time. Events can also give you something to focus on and look forward to.

- Buy a yoga or fitness video that the two of you can try together at home, either in the mornings before work, or on the weekends.

- Don't forget to include sex in your fitness routine: it gets your heart rate up, and if you're creative you can get a full-body workout!

You may want to check in with your doctor before starting anything too rigorous. Remember, start slow, get moving, and enjoy the time you spend with your partner.

Love Gifts

You don't have to get out your wallet to give your partner a gift that shows how much you care. This tune-up is about sharing the gift of your time, effort, and consideration.

Julia was having one of those days: everyone at work kept coming to her with "emergencies," she had the worst headache, and the zipper on her favorite pants had just broken. It was her night to cook dinner, but there was no food in the house and she knew she'd be getting home late.

Julia called up Meg and asked her if she could pick up some groceries on the way home, saying, "I'll be a little late, but I promise dinner will be on the table by eight. I'm really sorry."

Hearing the stress in Julia's voice, Meg answered, "Just take your time, and I'll see you when you get home." Once off the phone, Meg quickly got to work, finishing up everything that *had* to be finished that day, and then let everyone know she was leaving a little early. She went to the grocery store, picked up everything she needed to make Julia's favorite dinner, and bought some flowers and new candles for the table.

When Julia rushed in the door that night, it was 7:30, giving her just enough time to throw something together for dinner. She rubbed her temples on the way up the stairs, trying to press away the pounding in her head.

"I'm home!" Julia called, walking into the kitchen. And there was Meg, who had dinner ready in the oven, candles lit, and some nice music coming from the stereo. "You made dinner! But it was my night. I could have done it, Meg!"

"That's okay. Consider it my gift to you, for a hard day and a job well done. Go get changed and I'll put dinner on the table," Meg said, kissing Julia on the forehead. "And I'll get you some aspirin for that headache."

When exchanging gifts with your partner, consider the following:

- Go over the example in this tune-up together. Make a commitment to give each other at least one gift of consideration this week.

- You may want to negotiate what the gifts will be. For example, "I'd love it if you'd walk the dog without me tomorrow. Is there anything I can do for you in exchange?"

- If you've decided to keep your gifts a surprise, ask yourself each day if there's something you can do that could relieve your partner's burden. Can you take out the garbage, even if it's her job? Or help the kids with their homework and let your partner watch his favorite TV show? Or offer her a foot massage when she gets home from work? Is there something small you could do, just to show your support?

- Keep in mind that you should only offer gifts that you're willing to give, and that these gifts should be an expression of your appreciation and love. Keep your gifts small and doable.

Sometimes the best gifts are those that are unexpected. Making the commitment to shower each other with the gifts of nurturing and support can be better than anything you could ever wrap in a box.

Building Traditions

Traditions give us continuity and something to look forward to. Although many of our cultural traditions have fallen by the wayside or seem irrelevant to our modern lives, developing and practicing our own traditions can foster a special sense of community.

Traditions can be as simple as a daily morning ritual you can anticipate and enjoy, like reading the paper together at the kitchen table. Other traditions might be more elaborate or happen less frequently. They might include special holiday celebrations or a cherished weekend vacation spot.

David and Lisa have built a tradition of having weekly Friday night dinners with their friends and family. They've borrowed this tradition in part from the honoring of Shabbat, the Jewish day of rest that begins at sundown on Friday evening. Though they don't follow all of the religious rules of Shabbat, they see the dinners as a way to remember Lisa's culture and connect with family and friends.

Imagine that it's a Friday night at the end of a long week. You're tired of the workaday routine, and you're ready to settle in to your weekend. But instead of simply renting a movie and sitting comatose in front of the TV, you prepare a healthy dinner with your partner and the people you love. Then you all sit around the table, winding down with interesting conversation and delicious food.

If you'd like to start your own weekly dinner tradition, there are many ways to approach it. You could invite different people every week, or see if a few close friends and family members would like to join you every week. You could make all of the food yourself, or have a potluck, or make a rotating schedule for the dinners. David and Lisa take turns with another couple preparing the dinner, which means that the guest list always includes some regulars and some newbies. And since David is a great cook, Lisa stays out of the kitchen until it's time to clean up.

Treat the dinner like a special occasion. Light some candles, put on some nice music, and have some appetizers that people can snack on while they chat before dinner. Give your loved ones, your partner, and yourself the opportunity to spend some good old-fashioned quality time together.

Including friends and family in some of your traditions can make both your community and your relationship with your partner stronger. Broadening your support network beyond your lover means that both of you can have your needs better met, and it takes a lot of pressure off of the relationship when you recognize that you can't be everything for each other.

One way to approach the creation of new traditions is to look back to old traditions. Like David and Lisa, you may choose to borrow from religious or cultural traditions. Or you may remember special things you and your partner used to do together that you haven't done for a long time. It's never too late to start those activities up again.

By building nourishing traditions that have meaning for both of you, you're investing in the future of your relationship. And a future rich in connection and meaning is a future worth investing in.

Part III

Work Out the Kinks 53

Part IV

Add Some Sizzle 75

Part V

The Best of Times 99

Contents

Publisher's Note

This publication is designed to provide accurate and authoritative information in regard to the subject matter covered. It is sold with the understanding that the publisher is not engaged in rendering psychological, financial, legal, or other professional services. If expert assistance or counseling is needed, the services of a competent professional should be sought.

Distributed in the U.S.A. by Publishers Group West; in Canada by Raincoast Books; in Great Britain by Airlift Book Company, Ltd.; in South Africa by Real Books, Ltd.; in Australia by Boobook; and in New Zealand by Tandem Press.

New Harbinger Publications, Inc.
5674 Shattuck Avenue
Oakland, CA 94609

Cover design by Amy Shoup
Edited by Heather Garnos Mitchener
Book design by Michele Waters

ISBN 1-57224-274-4 Paperback

Printed in the United States of America

New Harbinger Publications' Web site address: www.newharbinger.com

03 02 01

10 9 8 7 6 5 4 3 2 1

First printing

LOVE
TUNE-UPS

Fun Ways to Open Your Heart
& Make Sparks Fly

Matthew McKay, Ph.D. • Carole Honeychurch, M.A. • Angela Watrous

New Harbinger Publications, Inc.

99

In my closet, there were clothes ranging from size 6 to 14. I used to buy the same item of clothing in several sizes, so that I could wear it no matter where I was on my weight curve.

pasta and cheese or rice pudding with cinnamon sugar, and at other times I completely starved myself.

I repeatedly lost 44 to 66 lb and put it back on again, gaining a little more weight each time. The pounds crept up on me insidiously over the years and I adapted my life just as gradually to a body that was constantly changing in size.

In my closet, there were clothes ranging from size 6 to 14. I used to buy the same item of clothing in several sizes, so that I could wear it no matter where I was on my weight curve.

At that time, I was quite physically active, so the reason for the extra pounds wasn't that I was spending my days lying on the couch eating. My weight gain was almost certainly because I was eating the wrong food. I loved calorie-packed meals: white bread with honey, chocolate spread, or cheese; cornflakes with lots of sugar; pasta; pizza; and burgers.

In my early twenties, my eating habits changed so often that my weight was constantly fluctuating. At times, I was only a few pounds overweight, at others—when I wasn't on a diet—I was decidedly overweight.

Looking back, I can see that I was overeating. I lived in a blinkered, black and white world. Either I threw myself, frothing at the mouth, at everything I felt like eating, without questioning it, or everything was completely off limits because I was on a diet. Whenever a diet fell flat—and it always did at some point—I felt like a huge failure, and then I let loose again on the overeating. In those moments, nothing really mattered.

The change in my eating habits came about after a particularly bad breakup with a boyfriend. From one day to the next, I was suddenly living alone. It was a big upheaval; I felt lonely and at the same time I was struggling with a lovesickness that I tried to relieve with food. And it

99

I would wolf down half a loaf of white bread with chocolate spread while Jesper was out of the house for a short while. Similarly, I would skillfully and swiftly conceal packaging that would reveal that I had just consumed four or five ice pops.

was easy—there was no one to see what I was eating, so I could let go of control completely.

I kept my misery and my overeating to myself. I had become an expert at putting up a façade when I was with other people—I was always the happy, smiling one. No one had any idea that deep inside I was an unhappy person fighting a bitter battle. I was deeply dissatisfied with myself and my appearance, and I quickly became surly and sad. I wanted to dig myself into a hole and indulge my destructive thoughts, because how on earth could I improve my situation?

In 2005, Jesper and I fell for each other and we soon moved in together. At that time, I weighed about 190 lb and was trapped in a pattern that fluctuated between overeating and restrictive dieting.

Thoughts on my weight and the food I was eating or not eating occupied far too many of my waking hours.

I developed strategies for eating surreptitiously and subsequently covering my tracks.

I would wolf down half a loaf of white bread with chocolate spread while Jesper was out of the house for a short while. Similarly, I would skillfully and swiftly hide packaging that would reveal that I had just consumed four or five ice pops.

I would buy two bags of toffees and transfer the contents from one bag into the other, so it looked like I had only bought a single bag. Overeating was a secret of which I was deeply ashamed.

In hindsight, it is a little scary that these deception tactics were such a big part of my life, even though I was head over heels in love. This new chapter of my life made me want to pull myself together and lose weight for good. I was fed up of never being happy with myself. Every time we went into town, I left with a feeling of depression because I didn't look

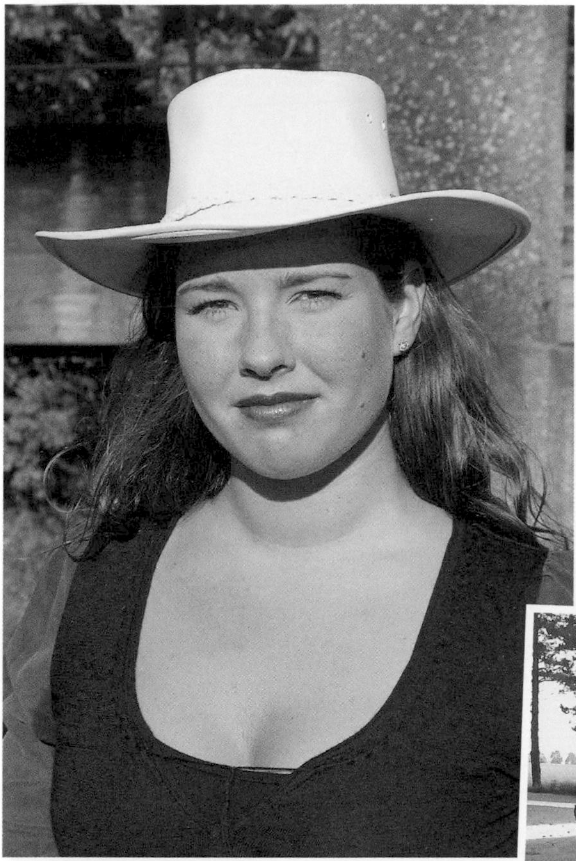

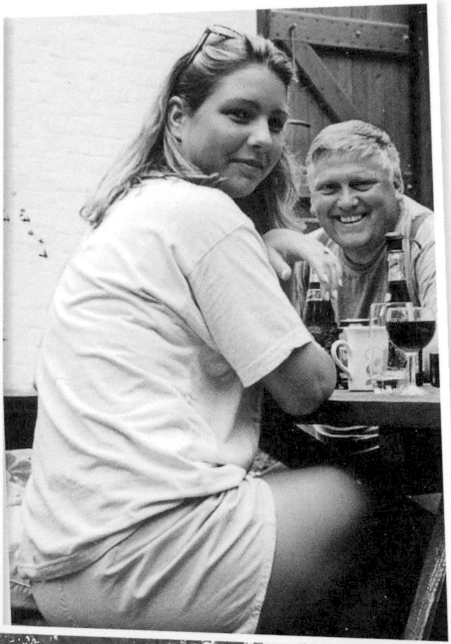

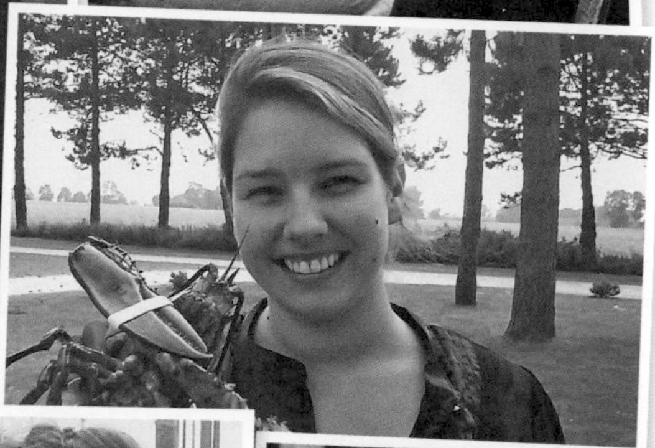

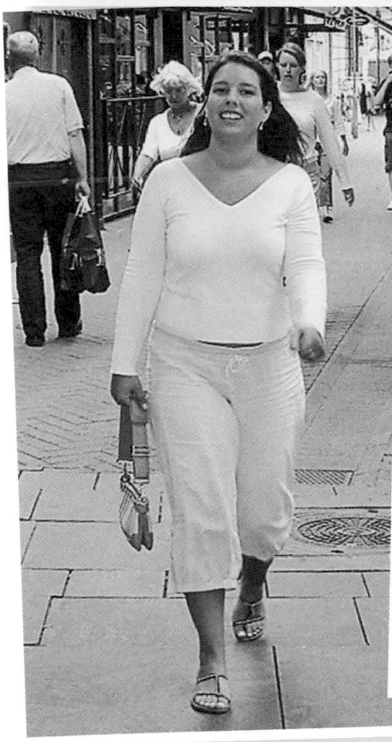

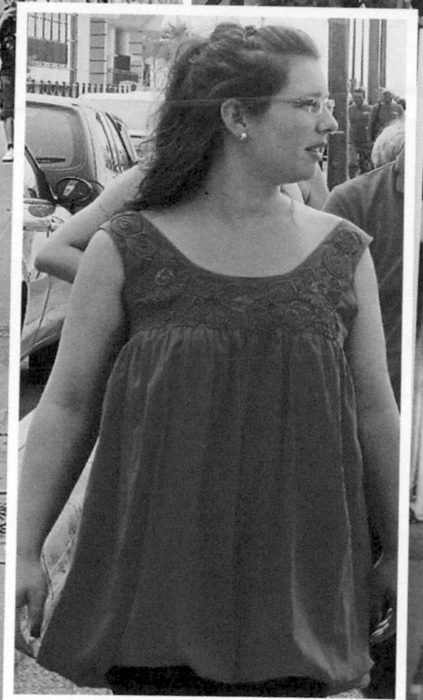

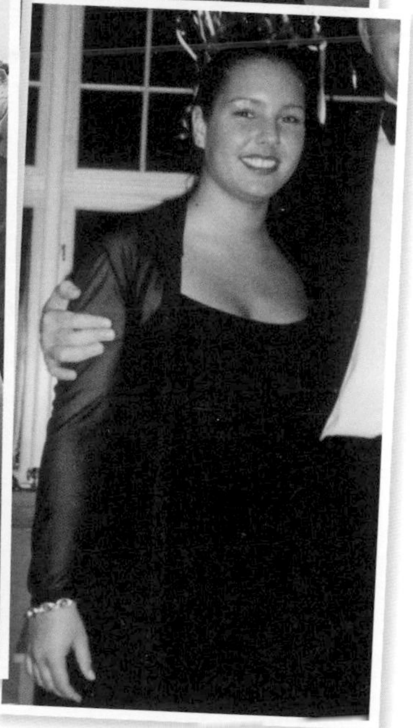

good, no matter how many hours I had spent in front of the mirror. I felt that my legs were still too heavy and that my eyelids were enveloped in fat.

I thought it was embarrassing that I couldn't just pull myself together and control my weight. I would concoct reasons to cancel a social engagement—just to avoid being looked at.

I was constantly thinking about losing weight; I felt like I was on a never-ending diet. Even so, my weight never changed significantly. I was trapped in an unhealthy pattern of hunger and overeating that canceled each other out.

But then something happened—on Christmas Eve 2007, Jesper proposed to me and I said yes. At that time, I had an exact picture of how I wanted to look at our wedding and it wasn't the size 16 that I was at that moment. I had five months to lose weight before the wedding. I managed to reach my goal through intense effort—I walked or jogged to and from work every day and was very consistent with my diet.

We were married on May 17, 2008. My wedding dress was a size 8. It was wonderful to be standing there with my slim hourglass waist in my dream wedding dress. But neither the joy nor the dress size lasted, because I couldn't, of course, maintain the strict regime I had set for myself.

I began overeating again the day after the wedding—to an intense degree. I thought that, as I had reached my goal, I could let go. It was as if I was desperately trying to catch up with all those calories that both my body and my mind had missed over the past five months.

99

The doctor asked me why I didn't have control of my diet and my body, when I seemed to have control of my life in all other areas. The question really hit home.

I put on almost 44 lb in no time. Then I became pregnant, and after the birth of our first son, Valdemar, in 2010, my weight had risen to almost 200 lb. One day, I went to my doctor with Valdemar for a checkup and I was confronted on my eating habits for the first time. The doctor asked me why I didn't have control of my diet and my body, when I seemed to have control of my life in all other areas. The question really hit home. Two months later, however, I became pregnant once more so I let go of the reins and ate freely—without restraint.

My doctor's question had planted a seed, however. It was that question that made me decide that I would take serious steps with my obesity once I had given birth to our second child, Albert; not a day, a week, or a month after I had given birth, but the moment he came into the world. And when that moment came, I had no doubt at all.

I decided to tackle the weight loss completely differently this time.

No quick fix, no starvation diet, no heavy exercise, which I wouldn't be able to keep up anyway. No, this time I would use my common sense and find a way that suited me.

I had to lower my expectations and recognize that things aren't always black and white. And I realized that I needed a fixed structure to reach my goal of a lasting change in my lifestyle. So I spent a great deal of my second pregnancy reading about nutrition and familiarizing myself with diet research. I came to understand that it was good to have protein, vegetables, and fat if you want to live healthily and lose weight. And I learned that a varied diet and lasting change in lifestyle make a difference. With that knowledge under my belt, I started from scratch.

For long periods of my life, I was unable to recognize when I was full. That is why I ate constantly, regardless of what signals my brain was sending to me. Now my system works as it

11

99

For long periods of my life, I was unable to recognize when I was full. That is why I ate constantly, regardless of what signals my brain was sending to me. Now my system works as it should, but it took three years for my body to learn to tune into the natural signals of feeling full.

should, but it took three years for my body to learn to tune into the natural signals of feeling full.

In the beginning, I had to test out my ideas to make progress, so it was particularly important for me to have structure and direction. I quickly realized that if I always ate so that I was full, three meals a day pretty much suited me.

At the same time, three daily meals gave me a structure that I could stick to. If I felt hungry an hour after I had eaten, I would understand that it wasn't real hunger, so I drank a glass of water instead of eating.

It worked! In nine months I lost 88 lb and I've kept to that weight ever since. At the same time, my energy levels increased significantly with my weight loss. I had more energy to play with my children because I didn't get out of breath from the smallest bit of activity.

Suddenly, I didn't need an afternoon nap on the couch either. The weight loss affected my whole life. My mood improved, my energy reserves grew, my skin became better, and I got my allergies under control.

In addition, I gained the space and energy to think about a whole lot more than food and weight. I don't think it would be an exaggeration to say that, before the weight loss, my head was 90 percent filled up with negative thoughts and speculation about my weight. After the weight loss, there was nothing more to worry about in that respect so it was a huge release. I love the physical and mental calm that has followed my escape from overeating hell. It is tricky to put into words, but I've been released from my bell jar and am back in reality— a reality worth living in.

After cracking the code for weight loss, I wanted to share my method with other people. Just think, what if I could help other overweight people

to find a similar freedom? I qualified as a dietitian, and at the same time I set myself the task of writing down everything that I had learned during my journey. I knew that I wanted my method to rely on common sense and simplicity. I wanted to help people to escape the monotony of calorie counting and weighing food. Last but not least, I wanted to get away from a restrictive eating model where things are either healthy or unhealthy.

That's why I constructed the idea of the handful principle and meal-boxes—that is, the system you can read about in this book. Today I eat everything with great enjoyment and without any guilt. I hope you get as much enjoyment out of the Scandi Sense diet as I have.

Suzy Wengel

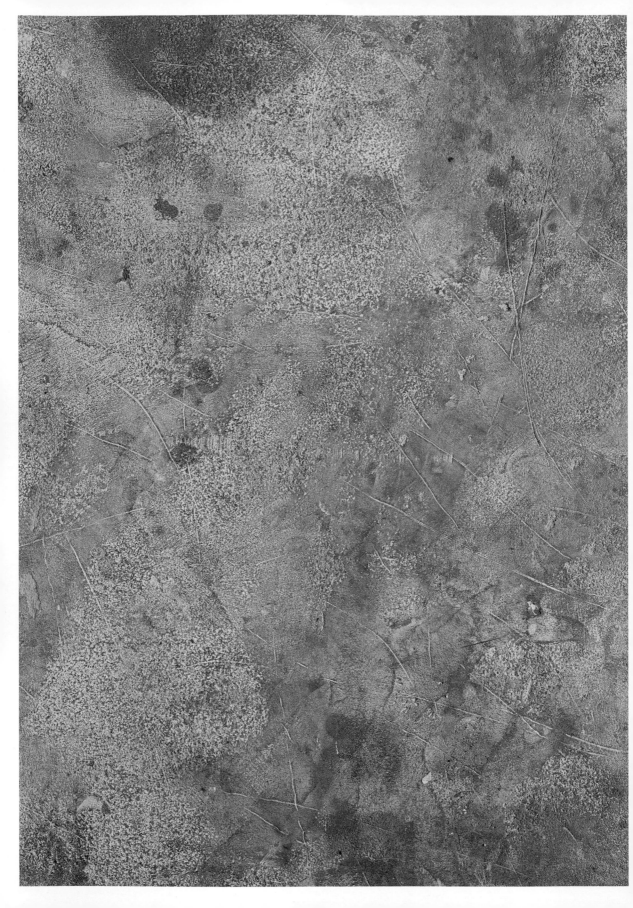

What
Scandi Sense
is all about

WOMAN'S MEAL
586 kcal

MAN'S MEAL
786 kcal

The name Scandi Sense is inspired by the notion of "common sense." It is no coincidence that I have chosen this particular name; as well as being simple and straightforward, Scandi Sense is based on common sense in relation to the composition and amount of food we choose to eat.

Scandi Sense is intended to be suitable for everyone, regardless of size and weight, and is therefore more a lifestyle than a diet. The basic idea is that you eat a Scandi Sense version of the food you usually have. This means that you won't have to overhaul your diet entirely—it will just need adjusting. This makes it more likely that the lifestyle will last in the long run.

For example, if you make spaghetti bolognese for the whole family, you will eat less spaghetti and more bolognese sauce than you might have previously. At the same time, you'll put a lot of vegetables into

the bolognese sauce and possibly supplement it with a green salad. You can also add some extra flavor by sprinkling cheese on top, because in Scandi Sense, you don't have to be afraid of fat. In moderation, fat is good for the body and, of course, it often adds extra flavor to your food.

Scandi Sense isn't a ready-made diet plan, but some simple principles to live by—principles that will give you the right balance of nutrients and ensure that you maintain a stable blood sugar level throughout the day. The Scandi Sense diet is based on the official dietary advice of the Danish Health Board. The basic idea is that if you fill yourself up with balanced, healthy meals, you won't be so easily tempted by food that will make you gain weight. You also get a mental tool, namely the "meal-boxes," to help you fit yummy things such as a piece of cake into your diet.

While nothing is forbidden by Scandi Sense, there are some foods that you

MEAL-BOX 1

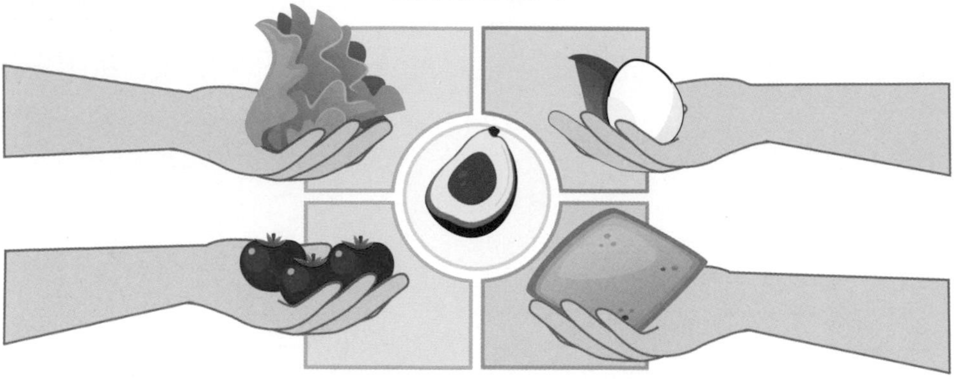

MEAL-BOX 2

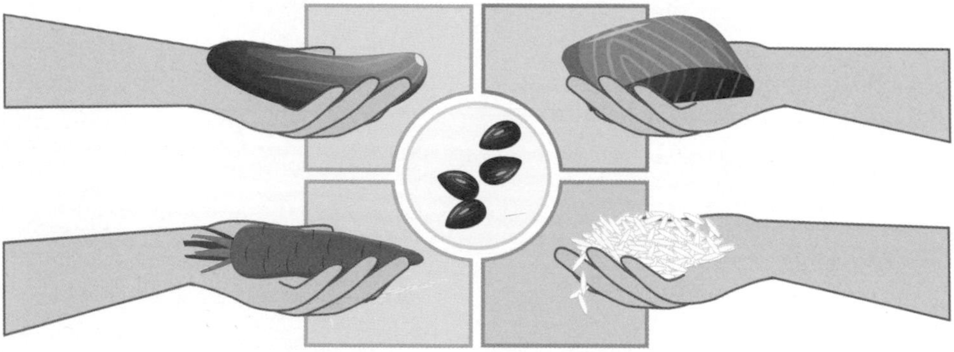

MEAL-BOX 3

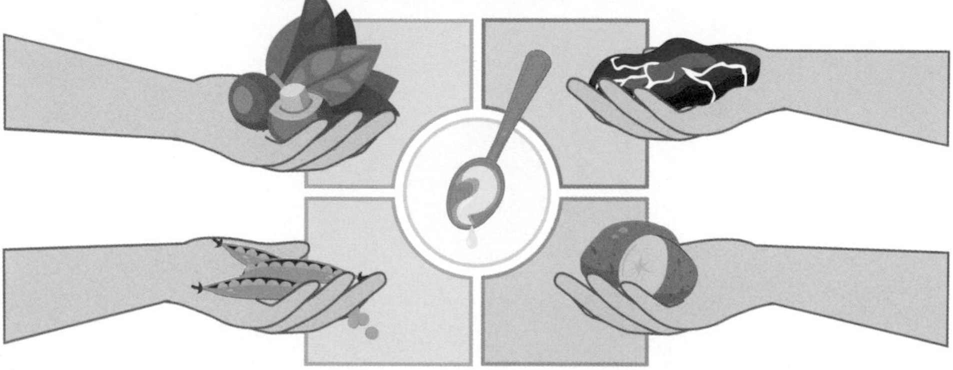

READ MORE ABOUT WHAT YOUR HANDFULS SHOULD CONTAIN ON PAGE 22.

should enjoy in limited quantities, or compensate for at other meals. I call these foods "indulgences." They could be candies, cake, ice cream, potato chips, tortilla chips, or sodas.

HANDFULS AND MEAL-BOXES

You will use the palms of your hands to measure the amount of food you should eat at each meal. You can eat up to four handfuls of food for each meal, and if they are properly balanced you will easily feel full.

Because the size of our hands is most often related to our build and our height, this will work out as on average 1,500 calories a day for women and for men a little more, around 2,000 calories a day.

If food is prepared according to the Scandi Sense principles, the amounts will enable you to lose on average 0.9 to 1.8 lb at a measured pace per week until the goal weight is achieved. Your goal weight is the weight that suits the lifestyle you are happy with.

As men generally require a little more food than women, I have included recipes suitable for both men and women.

If cooking for both men and women in your household, you can double up the woman's portion and just check how much extra protein, starch/fruit, and fat the man's portion requires. The amount of vegetables is usually the same for both and the recipe method is generally the same.

The Scandi Sense meal-boxes are both a practical and a mental tool to help you keep track of your meals. Each meal-box represents a meal. You should imagine that you have three meal-boxes a day available, each filled with your four handfuls of food plus 1 to 3 tablespoons of fat.

If there is sometimes a little extra food in a meal-box, or maybe food that wasn't planned, just close that meal-box and carry on, without beating yourself up or feeling guilty.

Think about people who have always had a healthy weight. They also eat too much food, or too many calories, on occasion, and they do so without reproaching themselves. You have to get away from thinking, "Now it's all ruined, so it doesn't really matter," because it is exactly that reaction that causes the failure of so many attempts to eat healthily.

If you have strayed from the plan at a meal, rather than stressing over it, it is a much better strategy to be proactive and get straight back into a good rhythm with the next meal-box.

19

THREE MEALS A DAY

There is no evidence to suggest that it is better to eat six times a day rather than three. Some people thrive on more meals daily, while others are fine with fewer.

But there is no doubt that the risk of eating too many calories is greater when you eat more times a day.

With three daily meals, it is easier to keep blood sugar levels stable, especially when meals are sensibly planned using the Sense Meal-Box Model (see pages 34 to 35). Following this model, the metabolism doesn't drop significantly when you cut down on the number of meals. It is healthy for the body to have a break between meals, not only for blood sugar levels, but also for your mental well-being and your intestinal system.

Finally, it is good to allow yourself to feel hungry sometimes! It helps you to achieve a natural regulation of how much you eat.

When your meal-boxes are filled with nourishing, filling food, you won't crave yummy things to the same extent as you might do with lots of daily meals of different sizes.

I recommend that you follow the Sense Meal-Box Model strictly for the first 14 days.

Fill out a diet plan so that you are sure you are getting the right amount of food. You can find a template on page 67, which you can photocopy and fill in.

You will probably find that you don't need snacks in between meals and that there is a certain freedom in only eating three times a day.

After the first two weeks you will be in a position to determine how many meals you need and tailor your eating pattern accordingly.

HUNGER BAROMETER

If, after the first 14 days of Scandi Sense, you still struggle to work out when you are hungry and when you are full, just continue to follow the Scandi Sense principles strictly.

Once you feel ready to stand on your own two feet, it is time to familiarize yourself with the hunger barometer.

Think of your appetite as something that can be measured on a hunger barometer, from zero to ten. Zero is "not hungry at all" and ten is "totally famished." The idea is that you are ready to have a meal according to the Sense Meal-Box Model (see pages 34 to 35) when you land on around 7 or 8 on the hunger barometer.

It also means that it is okay to eat a late breakfast if you aren't hungry the moment you get up. Or have a late dinner, if it fits better with your lifestyle. It is a myth that breakfast is the most important meal of the day and it is also a myth that everything you eat after 6 p.m. will make you put on weight!

Once you have become familiar with your own hunger signals and only eat when you are hungry, you will eventually, using the Sense Meal-Box Model, know how much food you need to sustain you for 5 to 6 hours, and will find yourself naturally wanting a meal when you land on 7 or 8 on your hunger barometer. Once you have eaten, you will be back down to 0 on the barometer—and after 5 to 6 hours you will return to 7 or 8. In this way you will find an eating pattern that suits you. The eating pattern isn't set in stone—it may vary from day to day and from season to season.

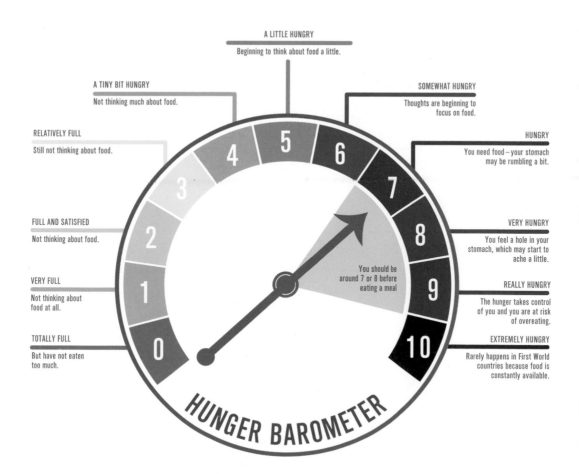

A LITTLE HUNGRY
Beginning to think about food a little.

A TINY BIT HUNGRY
Not thinking much about food.

SOMEWHAT HUNGRY
Thoughts are beginning to focus on food.

RELATIVELY FULL
Still not thinking about food.

HUNGRY
You need food – your stomach may be rumbling a bit.

FULL AND SATISFIED
Not thinking about food.

VERY HUNGRY
You feel a hole in your stomach, which may start to ache a little.

VERY FULL
Not thinking about food at all.

You should be around 7 or 8 before eating a meal

REALLY HUNGRY
The hunger takes control of you and you are at risk of overeating.

TOTALLY FULL
But have not eaten too much.

EXTREMELY HUNGRY
Rarely happens in First World countries because food is constantly available.

HUNGER BAROMETER

Scandi Sense

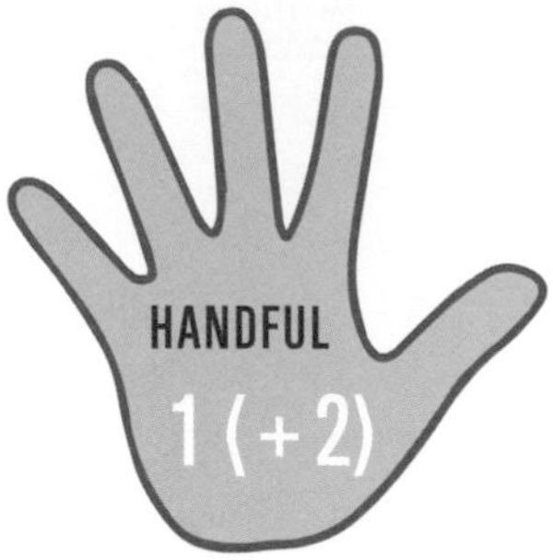
HANDFUL
1 (+2)

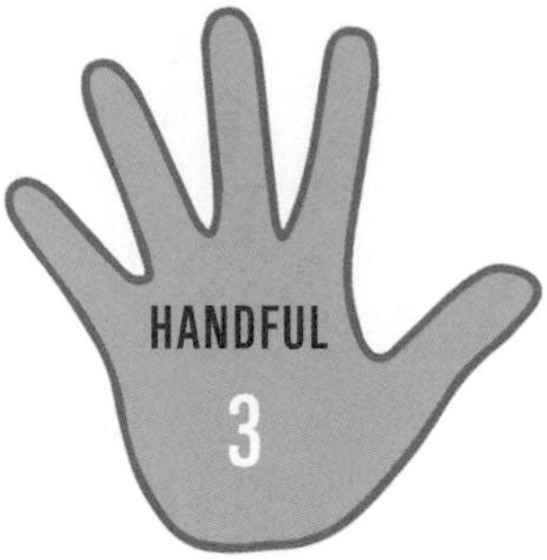
HANDFUL
3

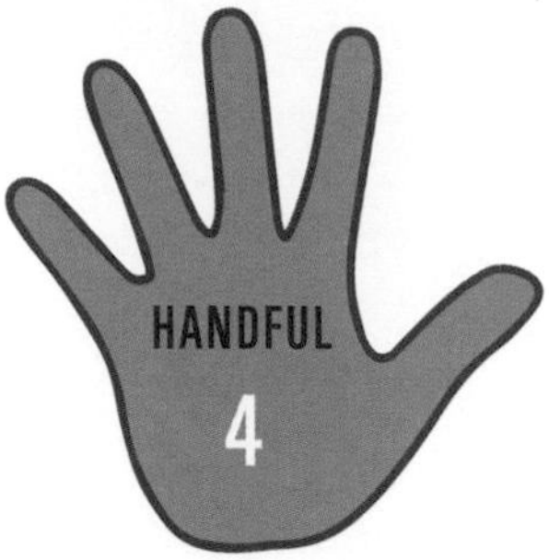
HANDFUL
4

VEGETABLES

c.3½ to 9 oz

1 to 2 handfuls

PROTEIN

c.3½ to 7 oz

MEAT
POULTRY
FISH
LOW-FAT CHEESE
(max. 17% fat)

1 handful = 2 to 3 eggs

STARCH AND/OR FRUIT

BREAD
PASTA
RICE
POTATOES
MUESLI (less than 13 g of sugar per 100 g)
FRUIT/BERRIES

Choose wholemeal
1 HANDFUL =
1 cup oatmeal,
1 piece of fruit
or 1 slice of bread

N.B. This handful can be replaced by up to ½ Handful 3 (protein) and possibly more vegetables.

1 TO 3 TABLESPOONS OF FAT PER MEAL

8 to 10 g of "pure fat" per tablespoon

COCONUT OIL
OLIVE OIL
BUTTER
MAYONNAISE
NUTS/KERNELS
PESTO
SEMISWEET CHOCOLATE
(min. 70% cocoa solids)
CHEESE (18% fat or above)

3 TABLESPOONS = ½ a large avocado

REMEMBER: 3 MEALS A DAY – ONLY WHEN HUNGRY

At least 2 of your 3 daily meals shall contain this combination of VEGETABLES, PROTEINS, STARCH/FRUIT, and FAT

OPTIONAL:

2 TABLESPOONS OF DAIRY DRESSING per meal
Up to 9% fat

1¼ cups DAIRY PRODUCTS per day
Up to 3.5% fat
Max. 5 g sugars per 100 g

READ MORE ABOUT WHAT SHOULD BE IN YOUR HANDFULS ON PAGES 226 TO 243.

THE ONLY RULE IN SCANDI SENSE:
"THE TWO-OUT-OF-THREE PRINCIPLE"

Yogurt and
muesli

AT LEAST TWO OF THE DAY'S THREE MEALS
SHOULD FOLLOW THE SENSE MEAL-BOX MODEL

The Sense Meal-Box Model tells you what and how much there should be on your plate: 1 to 2 handfuls of vegetables, a handful of protein, a handful of starch and/or fruit in the form of bread, pasta, rice, potatoes, berries or the like and, in addition, 1 to 3 tablespoons of fat. I call this way of dividing up the food the Sense Meal-Box Model.

In addition, you can drink limited amounts of dairy products, as well as freely enjoy drinks with zero calories. However, the best way to quench your thirst is with water.

Scandi Sense doesn't contain a lot of rules. Rules confuse and cause us to lose our motivation. However, there is one rule you should follow: at least two of your three daily meals should follow the Sense Meal-Box Model.

This rule means that if you don't feel like vegetables in the morning, you can skip them and enjoy some yogurt and muesli or whatever you prefer to eat in the morning. However, you must remember to eat the right combination of vegetables, protein, starch/fruit, and fat for lunch and dinner. The starch/fruit portion could be swapped for more vegetables and protein—see how on page 35.

It is important that you keep this balance in mind at all times. Even though you may deviate from the Sense Meal-Box Model with one of your three meal-boxes, make sure you don't eat more food calorie-wise than is in a meal-box.

For example, if you choose to eat a piece of cake, you should be conscious of not putting a lot of additional calories in the same box, because then the balance will be off.

How to measure with your hands

When trying to lose weight, it is important that you include food
in the meal-boxes—and so on your plate—in the right quantities.
Take a look at your hands. If you stretch them out completely, you
will have a large surface area. If you gather your fingers and thumb
together and curve the palm of your hand, you will find the correct
handful size in relation to the Scandi Sense way of thinking.

Then it is simply a question of building a sensibly composed meal
from 3 to 4 handfuls, with the right proportions of carbohydrates,
protein, and fats.

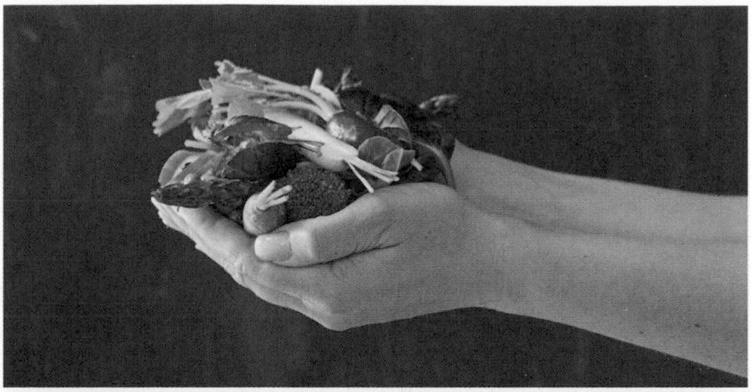

HANDFUL 1 (+2)

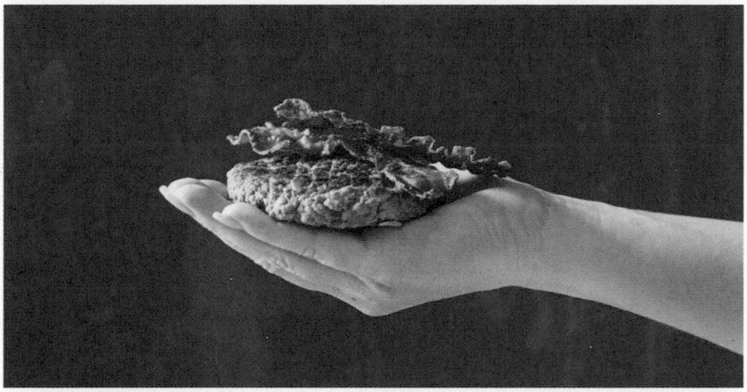

HANDFUL 3

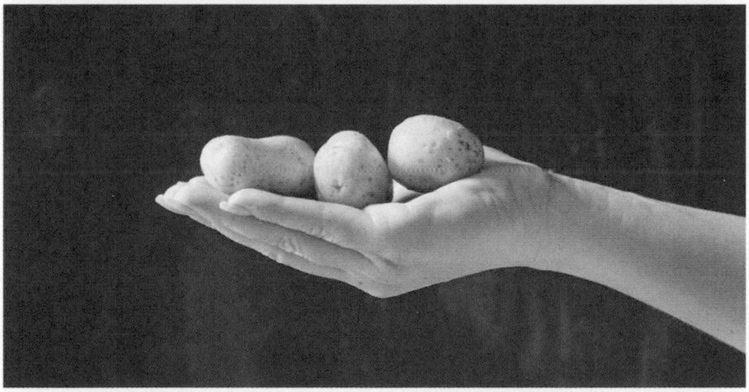

HANDFUL 4

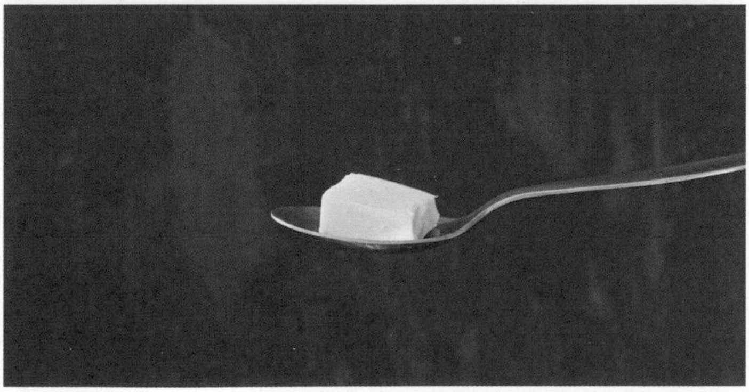

1 TO 3 TABLESPOONS OF FAT

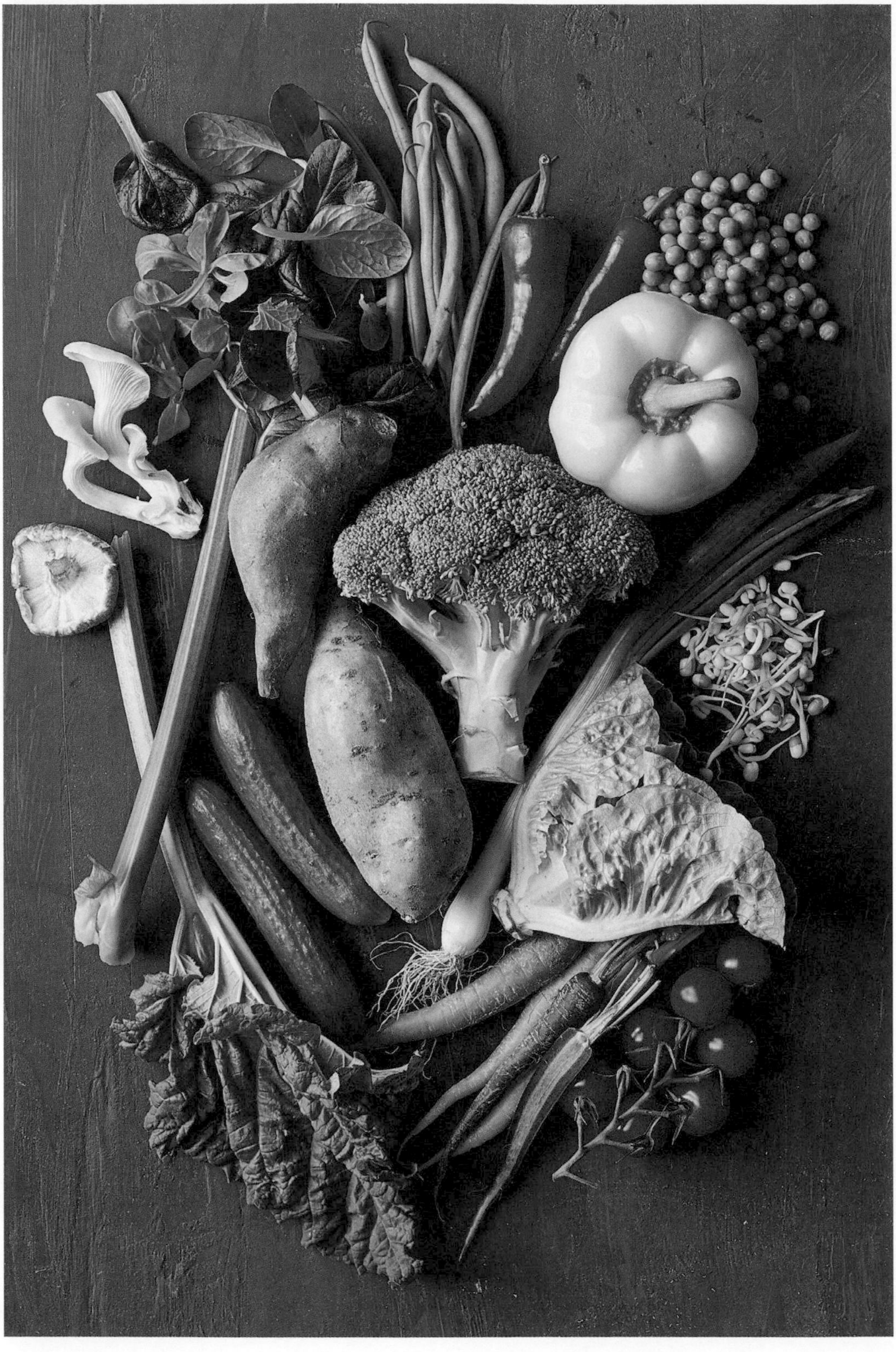

Handful 1 (+2): Vegetables

Handfuls 1 and 2 consist of carbohydrates in the form of vegetables. The bracketed (+2) indicates that you can choose two handfuls of vegetables, if you like, but a single handful will suffice.

For a detailed list of what can be included in Handful 1 (+ 2), see page 226.

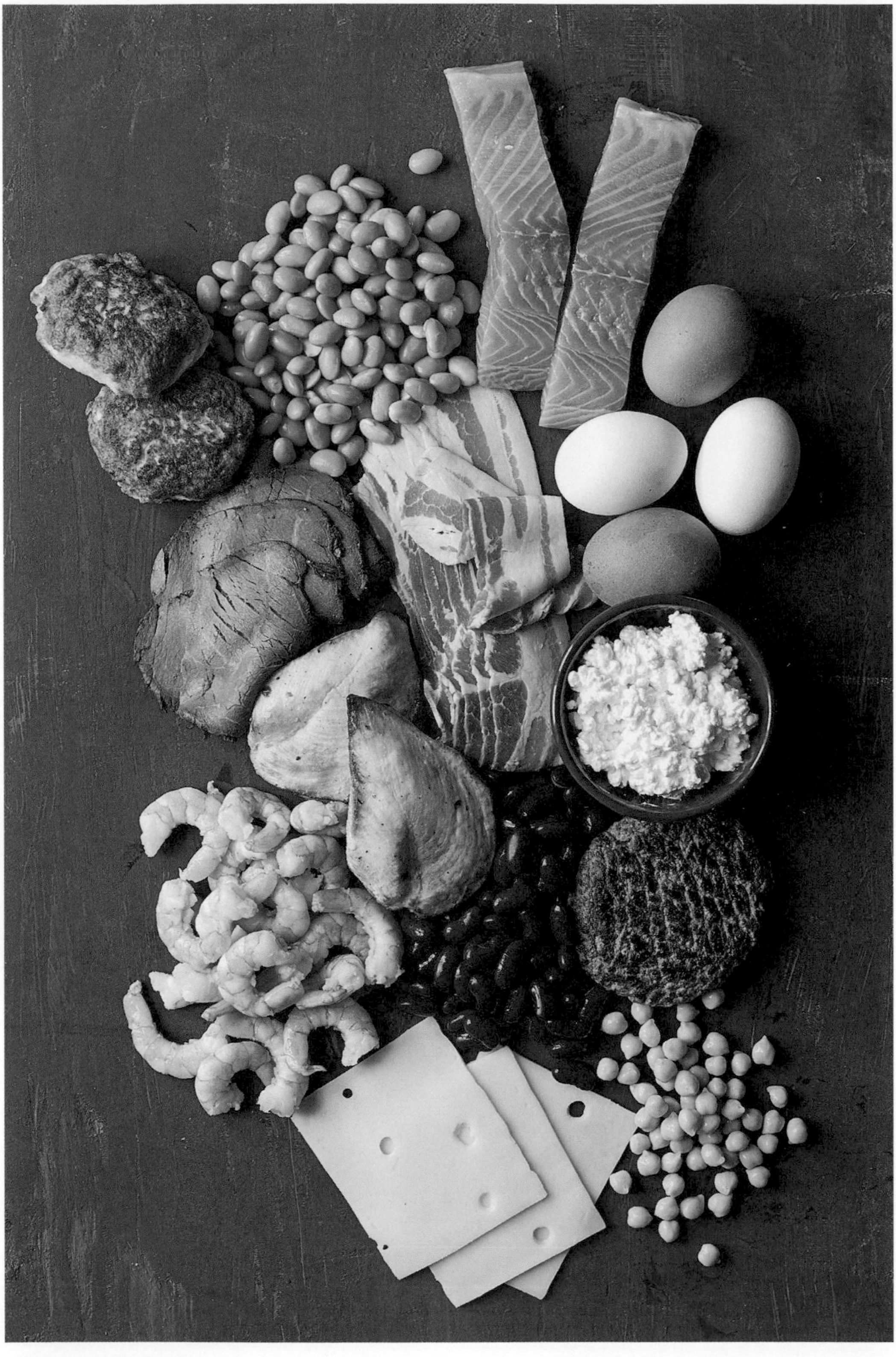

Handful 3: Protein

Handful 3 is protein from meat, poultry, fish, shellfish, eggs, low-fat cheese, or beans. You must have protein with at least two of your three daily meals, however processed protein (such as ham, salami, and bacon) must be limited. If you exercise a lot, it is a good idea to have protein with all three of your daily meals.

For a detailed list of what can be included in Handful 3, see page 228.

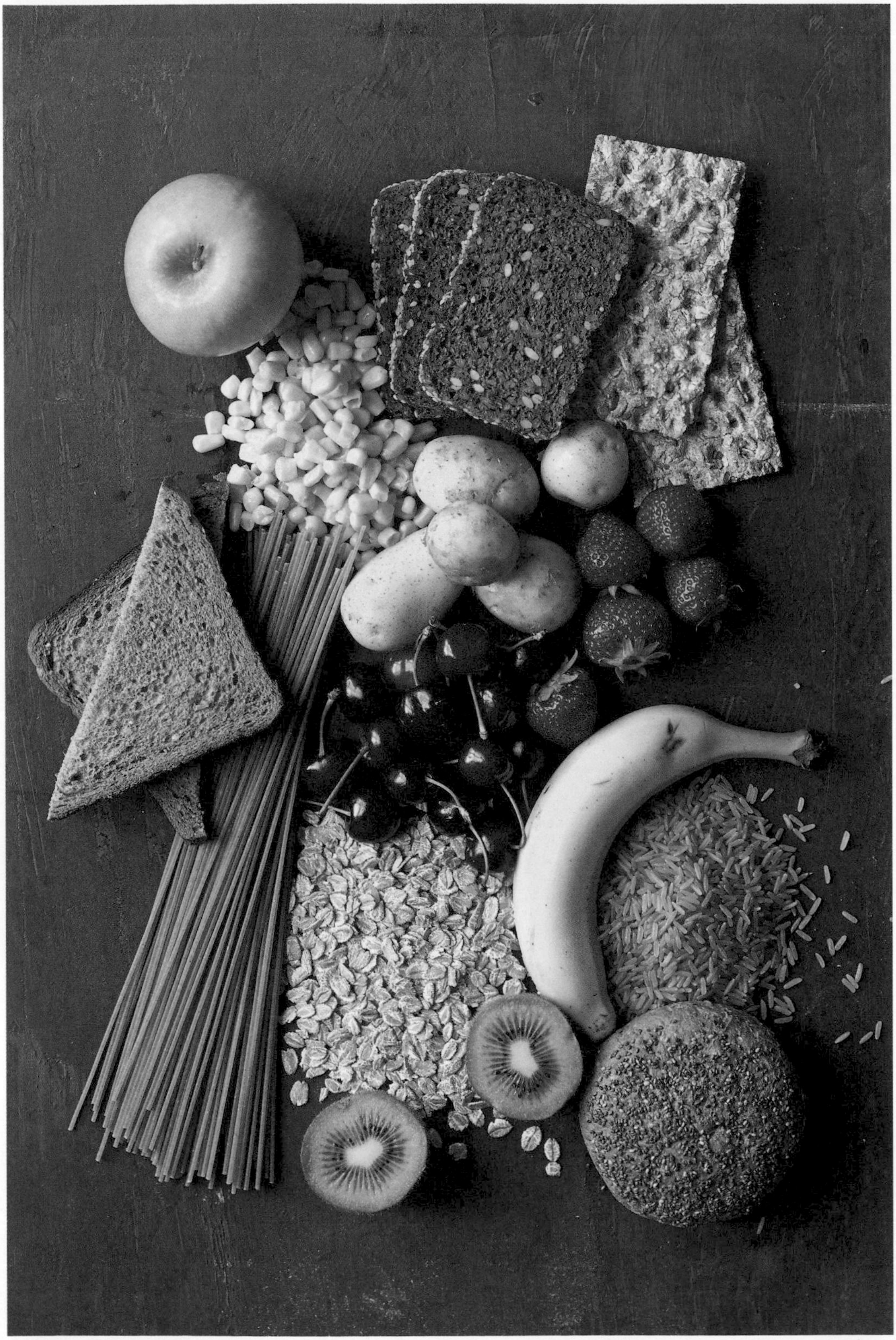

Handful 4: Starch and/or fruit

Handful 4 is carbohydrates in the form of bread, breakfast cereals, pasta, rice, potatoes, and/or fruit and berries. Handful 4 may be replaced with extra vegetables and up to half a handful of protein if you want to avoid bread, rice, pasta, etc.

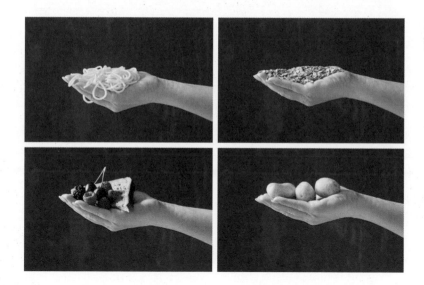

For a detailed list of what can be included in Handful 4, see page 232.

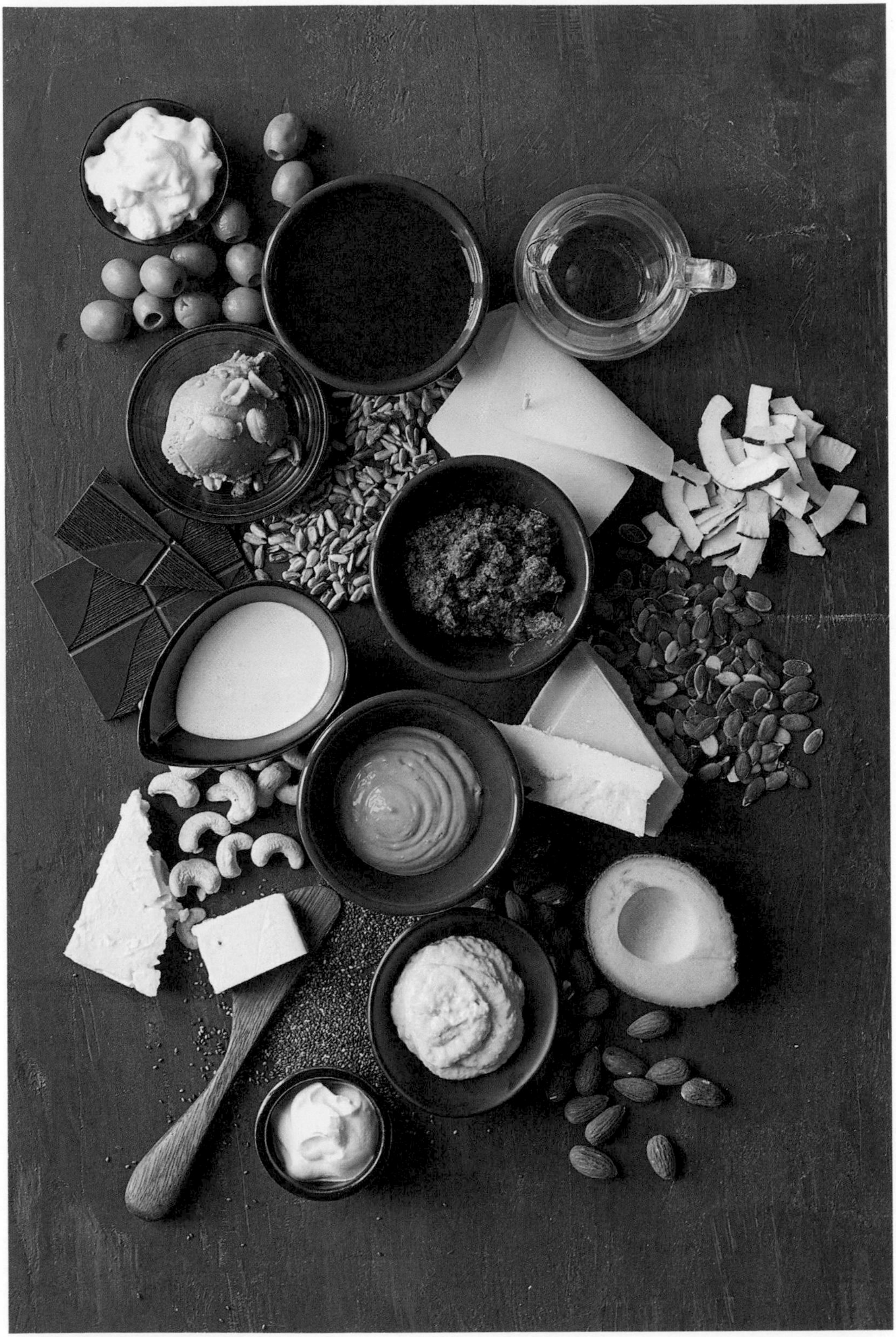

1 to 3 tablespoons of fat

You can have 1 to 3 tablespoons of fat at each meal. This includes products such as olive oil, canola oil, nuts, kernels, seeds, tartare sauce, mayonnaise, avocado, aioli, and pesto, as well as butter, cream, crème fraîche, fatty cheese, and semisweet chocolate. Coconut flakes are one example of fat with dietary fiber—the same applies to avocado, nuts, kernels, and seeds.

If you use concentrated fat such as butter, oil, and mayonnaise, eat a level tablespoonful. When it comes to less concentrated fats such as nuts, avocado, crème fraîche, or cheese, you can eat a heaping tablespoonful.

For a detailed list of fats, see page 238.

The Sense Meal-Box Model®

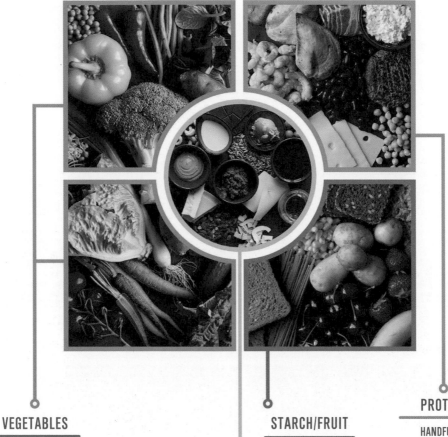

VEGETABLES

HANDFUL 1 (+ 2):
Leafy vegetables, root
vegetables, cabbage,
tomatoes, etc.

FAT

1 TO 3 TABLESPOONS:
Butter, oil, nuts, pesto,
avocado, mayonnaise,
fatty cheese, semisweet
chocolate.

STARCH/FRUIT

HANDFUL 4:
Bread, breakfast
cereals, pasta, rice,
potatoes, and/or fruit.

PROTEIN

HANDFUL 3:
Meat, poultry, fish,
shellfish, eggs, low-
fat cheese, beans.

If you would rather avoid Handful 4, replace it with extra vegetables and up to half a handful of protein. Then the model will look like this:

VEGETABLES

HANDFUL 1 (+ 2)
+ $\frac{1}{2}$ HANDFUL VEGETABLES
Leafy vegetables, root
vegetables, cabbage,
tomatoes, etc.

FAT

1 TO 3 TABLESPOONS:
Butter, oil, nuts, pesto,
avocado, mayonnaise,
fatty cheese, semisweet
chocolate.

PROTEIN

HANDFUL 3
+ $\frac{1}{2}$ HANDFUL PROTEIN
Meat, poultry, fish,
shellfish, eggs, low-fat
cheese, beans.

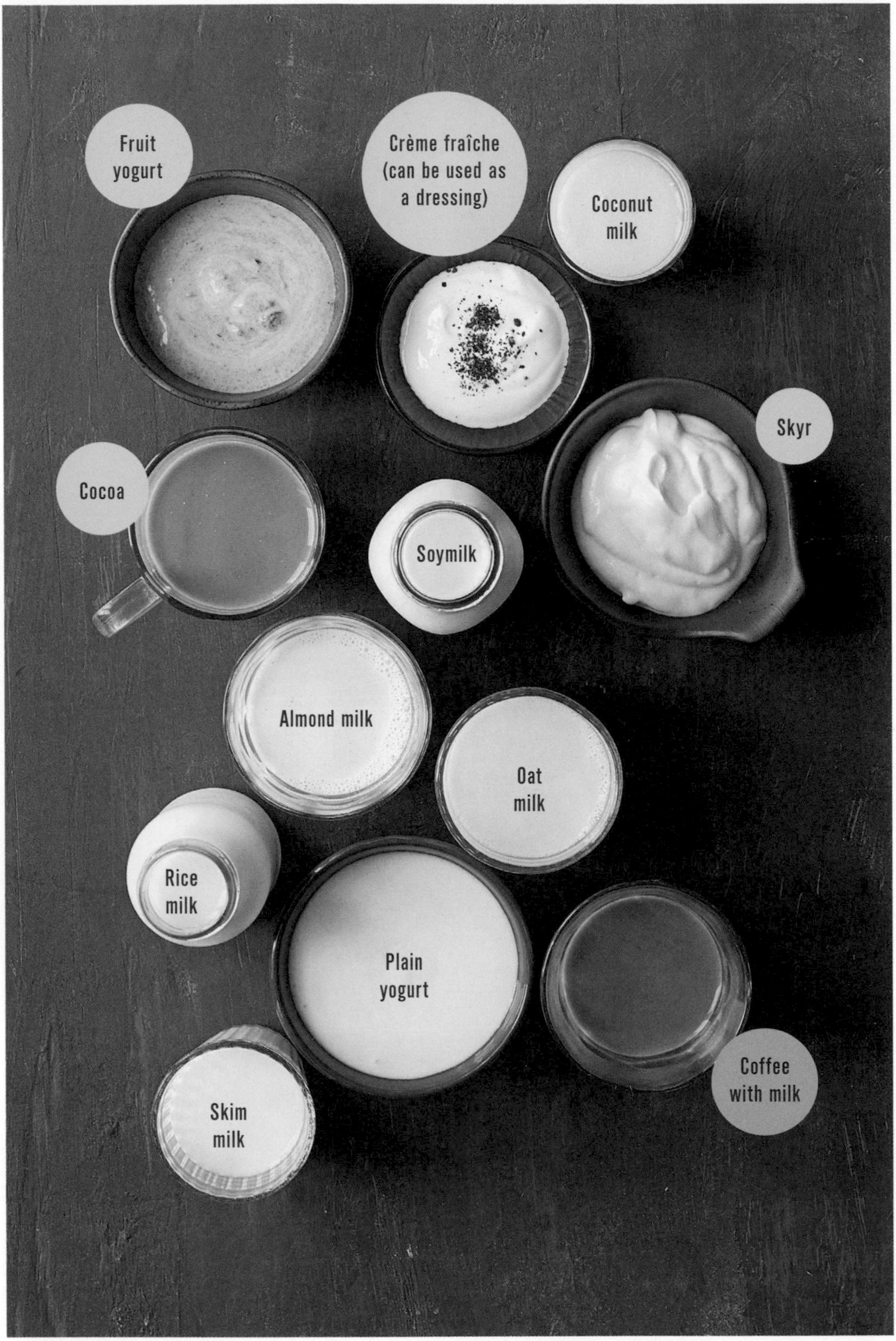
Fruit yogurt
Crème fraîche (can be used as a dressing)
Coconut milk
Skyr
Cocoa
Soymilk
Almond milk
Oat milk
Rice milk
Plain yogurt
Skim milk
Coffee with milk

Optional things that you can eat and drink

In addition to what is included in the meal-boxes,
you can have the following:

DAIRY PRODUCTS

You may eat/drink up to 1¼ cups of dairy products a day if you feel like it—in addition to what is already included in your meal-boxes. This 1¼ cups must have a fat content of 3.5 percent or less and a maximum of 5 g of sugars per 100 g of product.

For a detailed list of suitable dairy products, see page 243.

DAIRY DRESSINGS

In addition, you can add up to 2 tablespoonfuls of dairy dressing to each meal-box. The fat content should be 9 percent or less.

For a detailed list of dairy dressings, see page 243.

Quench your thirst with water.

Drink as much black coffee and tea (with no milk or sugar) as desired.

Enjoy diet sodas as often as desired, but use your common sense.

Enjoy alcoholic drinks sensibly.

Drink a moderate amount of milk only.

Enjoy sugary drinks in limited quantities.

Drinks

You can drink water, both still and sparkling, as much as needed. Drink 4 to $6\frac{1}{4}$ cups of water a day—more if you have done physical activity or if it is warm. Black coffee, black tea, diet sodas, and calorie-free cordial can also be consumed as often as you like—but use your common sense.

Decide what habits you want to keep in your life—especially when it comes to beer, wine, and spirits. If you want to live a life where there is space for a glass of wine or beer, it is a good idea to establish your habits during the weight loss period so that you have them in place even after your weight loss.

If you only occasionally drink wine or beer and therefore haven't included it in your daily allowance, one way you could compensate for consuming the occasional glass is reducing Handful 4 (bread, rice, pasta, potatoes, and fruit) at one meal. This will allow you to balance your calorie intake.

If you enjoy flavored drinks and cocktails at times, replace sugary drinks such as juice or sodas with low-calorie products.

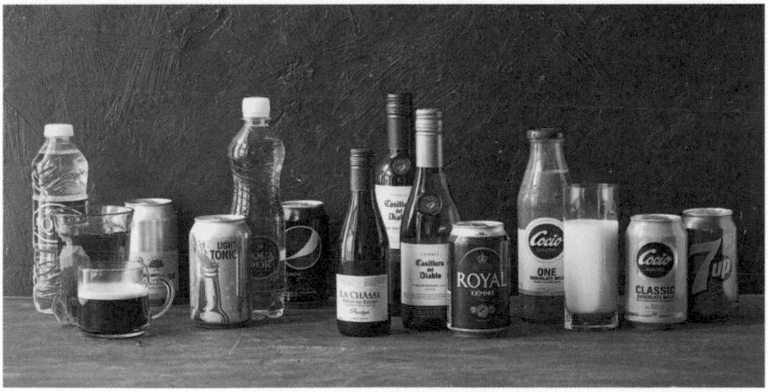
ROYAL
ONE
CLASSIC
7up

For detailed lists of drinks, see pages 244 and 246.

Indulgences

Indulgences is a label that covers different varieties of sugar, candies, ice cream, cakes, breakfast cereals, potato chips, tortilla chips, fast food, and sugary drinks.

There are no definitive quantities for this group. If you use a little sugar or honey as part of your cooking, it is only counted as a flavoring. If you eat larger quantities from this category, you should try to compensate for it in your meal-boxes. For example, you could certainly eat a small piece of cake but you should then take away something that corresponds to half a meal-box to compensate. In that way, the majority of what you eat will be sensible food.

For a detailed list of indulgences, see page 245.

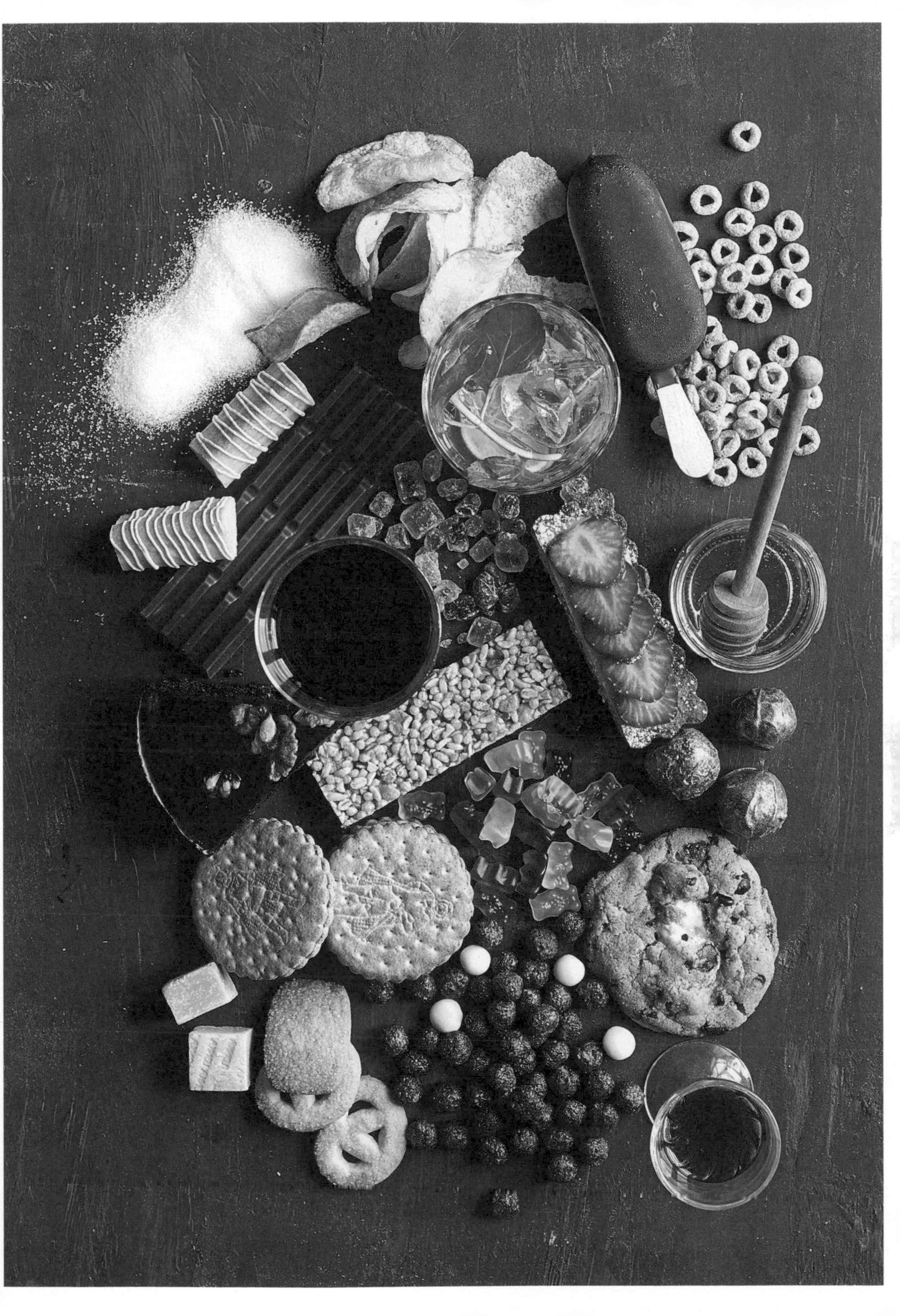

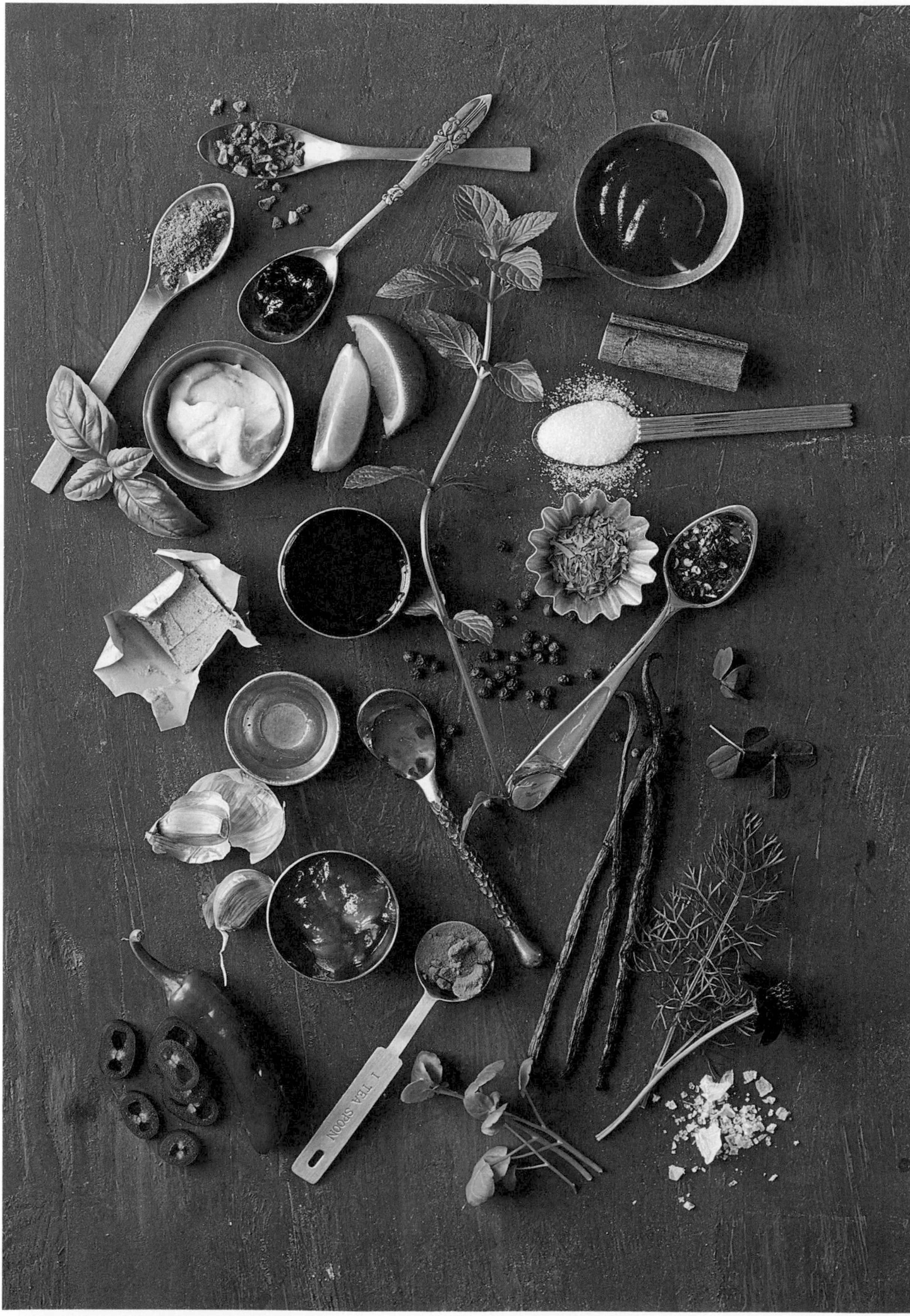
1 TEA SPOON

Flavorings

Your food should be tasty, so feel free to use different flavorings.
This category covers everything that makes the food tasty in small
amounts. For the sake of convenience, I have chosen to add raising
and thickening agents to this group as well.

For a detailed list of flavorings, see page 247.

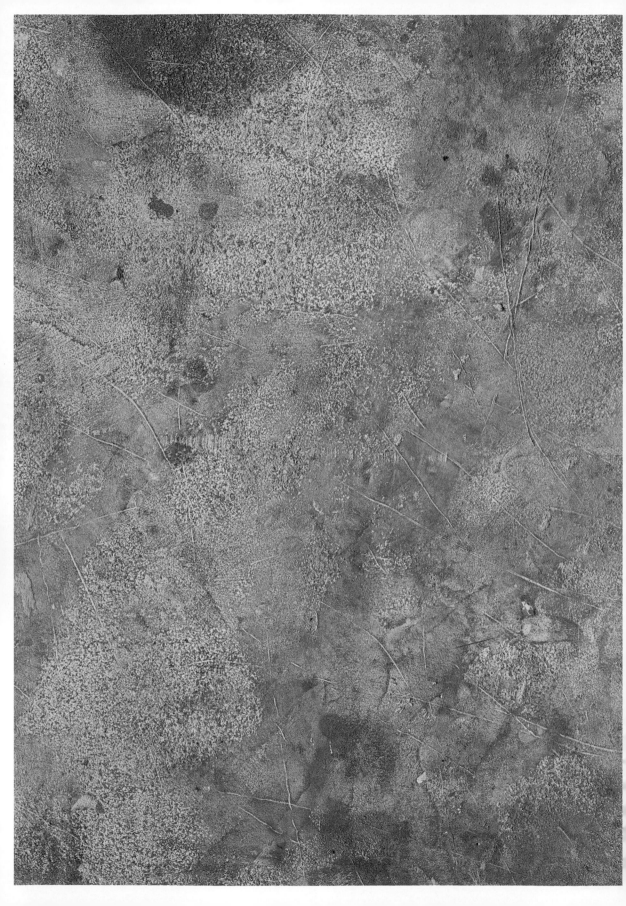

Examples
of meals

Breakfast

If you are in a hurry in the morning and you don't want to eat vegetables so early in the day, you can leave them out and, for example, have regular low-fat yogurt or Skyr yogurt with muesli. You just have to observe the Sense Meal-Box Model for the other meals during the day.

It shouldn't take long to prepare a breakfast that fits the Sense Meal-Box Model. Here is an example. While cooking an egg, gather the remaining items and fill your plate (and therefore your meal-box) with:

Handful 1 (+2): *Tomato, cucumber, lettuce*

Handful 3: *Eggs, low-fat cheese*

Handful 4: *Crispbread, banana, muesli*

Fat: *Avocado, semisweet chocolate*

Dairy product: *Plain yogurt*

Dairy dressing: *Two tablespoons crème fraîche, max. 9% fat*

Flavorings: *Salt, pepper, lemon, mint in your tea*

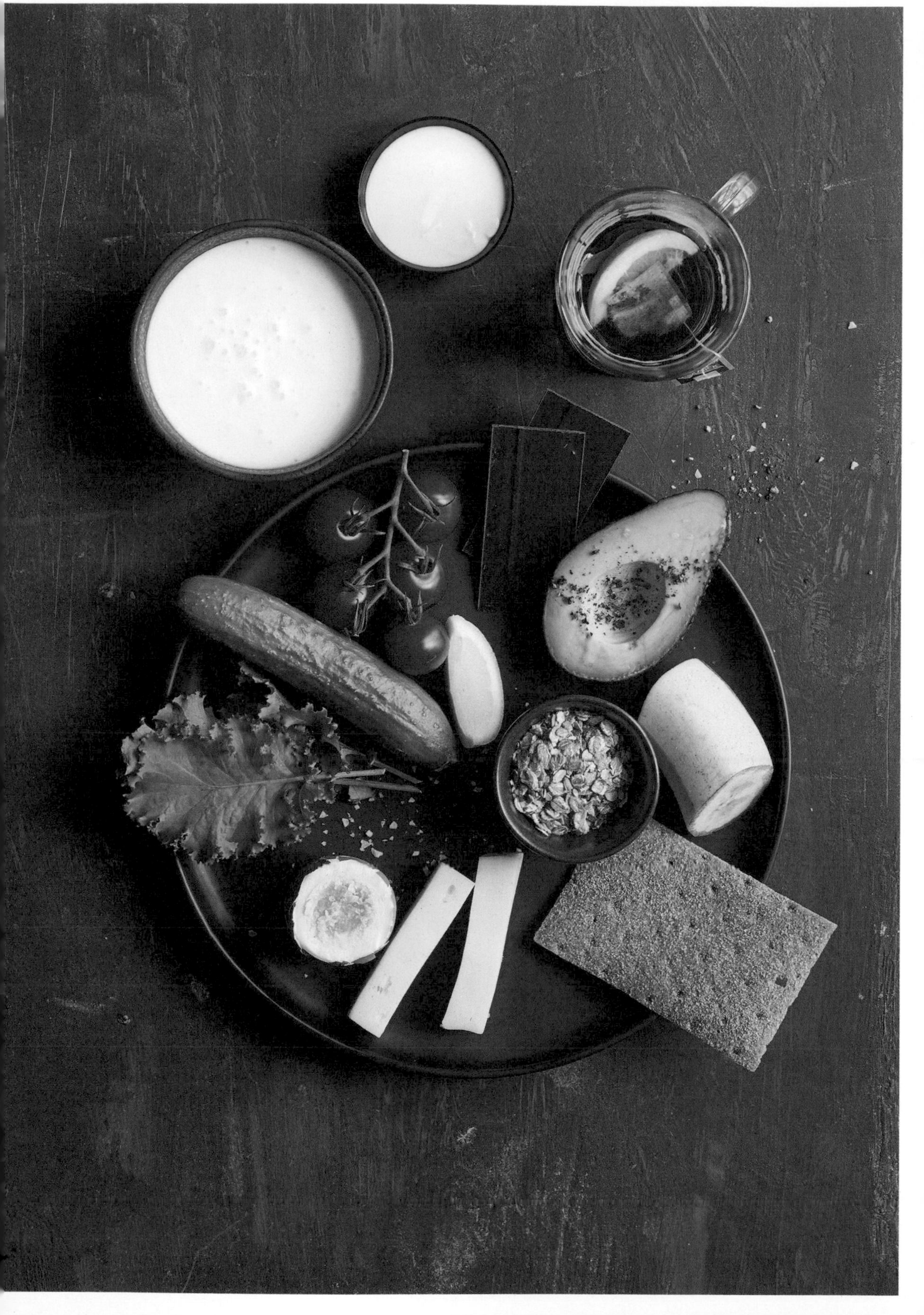

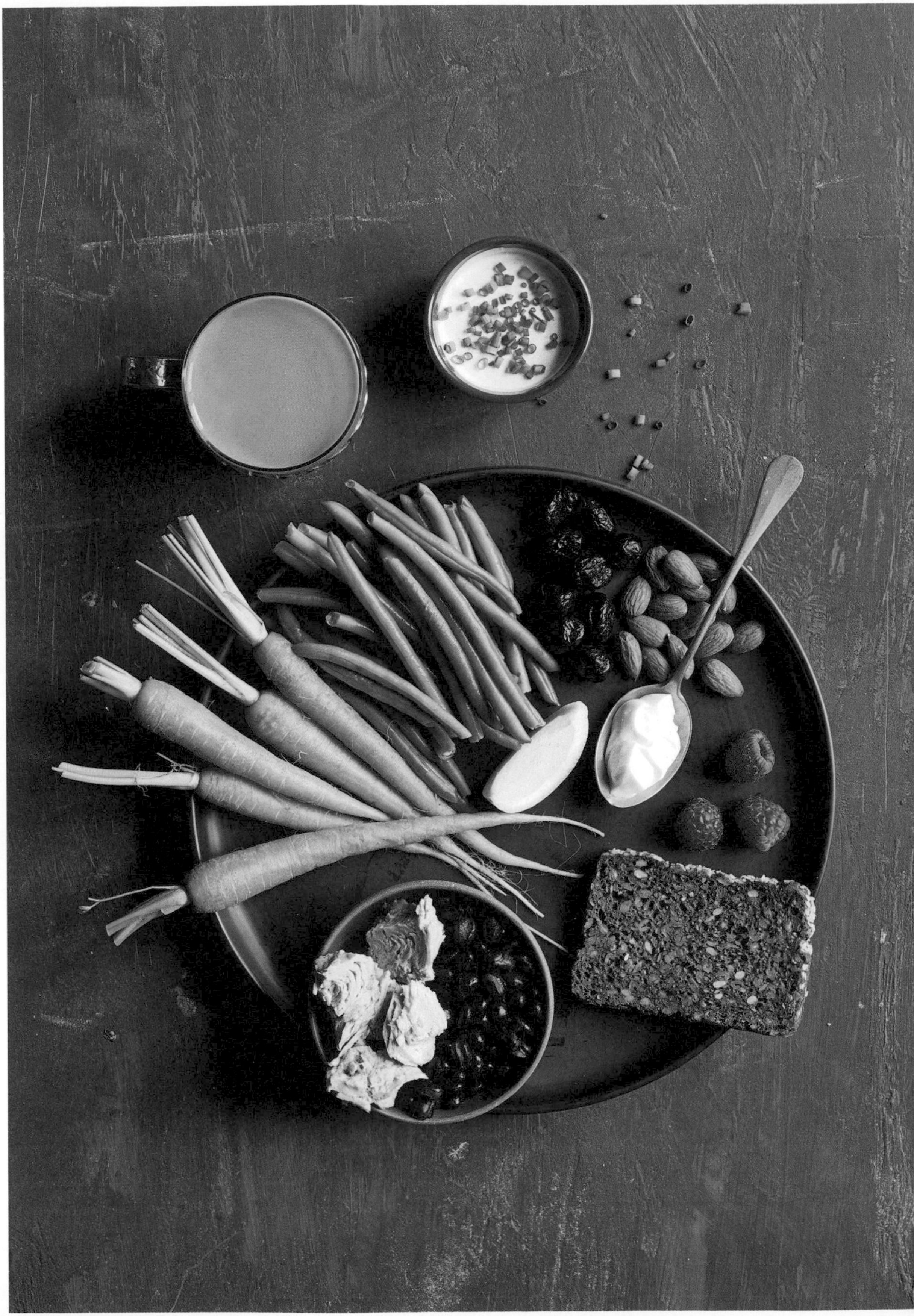

Lunch

Lunch is a good time to use leftovers from the previous evening's meal. You can easily put together several kinds of protein as long as it is only a handful in total. The meal should keep you going for 5 to 6 hours, so it is important to fill up this meal-box.

Handful 1 (+2): *Green beans, carrots*

Handful 3: *Tuna, black beans*

Handful 4: *Rye bread, raspberries*

Fat: *Mayonnaise, almonds, olives*

Dairy product: *Milk in your coffee*

Dairy dressing: *Two tablespoons crème fraîche, max. 9% fat*

Flavorings: *Salt, pepper, lemon, chives, ketchup in the crème fraîche dressing*

LUNCH ACCORDING TO
THE SENSE MEAL-BOX MODEL

Supper

If you are used to having something sweet with your coffee and are reluctant to go without, it is a smart idea to have it as a dessert at supper instead, as the blood sugar effect is based on the overall meal. In other words, the dietary fiber, fat, and proteins in your evening meal can guard against the dessert raising your blood sugar levels.

Handful 1 (+2):	*Mushroom, onion, lettuce*
Handful 3:	*Beef*
Handful 4:	*Potato*
Fat:	*Feta cheese, crème fraîche, butter/olive oil for frying*
Dairy dressing:	*Two tablespoons crème fraîche, max. 9% fat*
Flavorings:	*Salt, pepper, thyme, dill, curry in the dressing, mint in your water*

SUPPER ACCORDING TO
THE SENSE MEAL-BOX MODEL

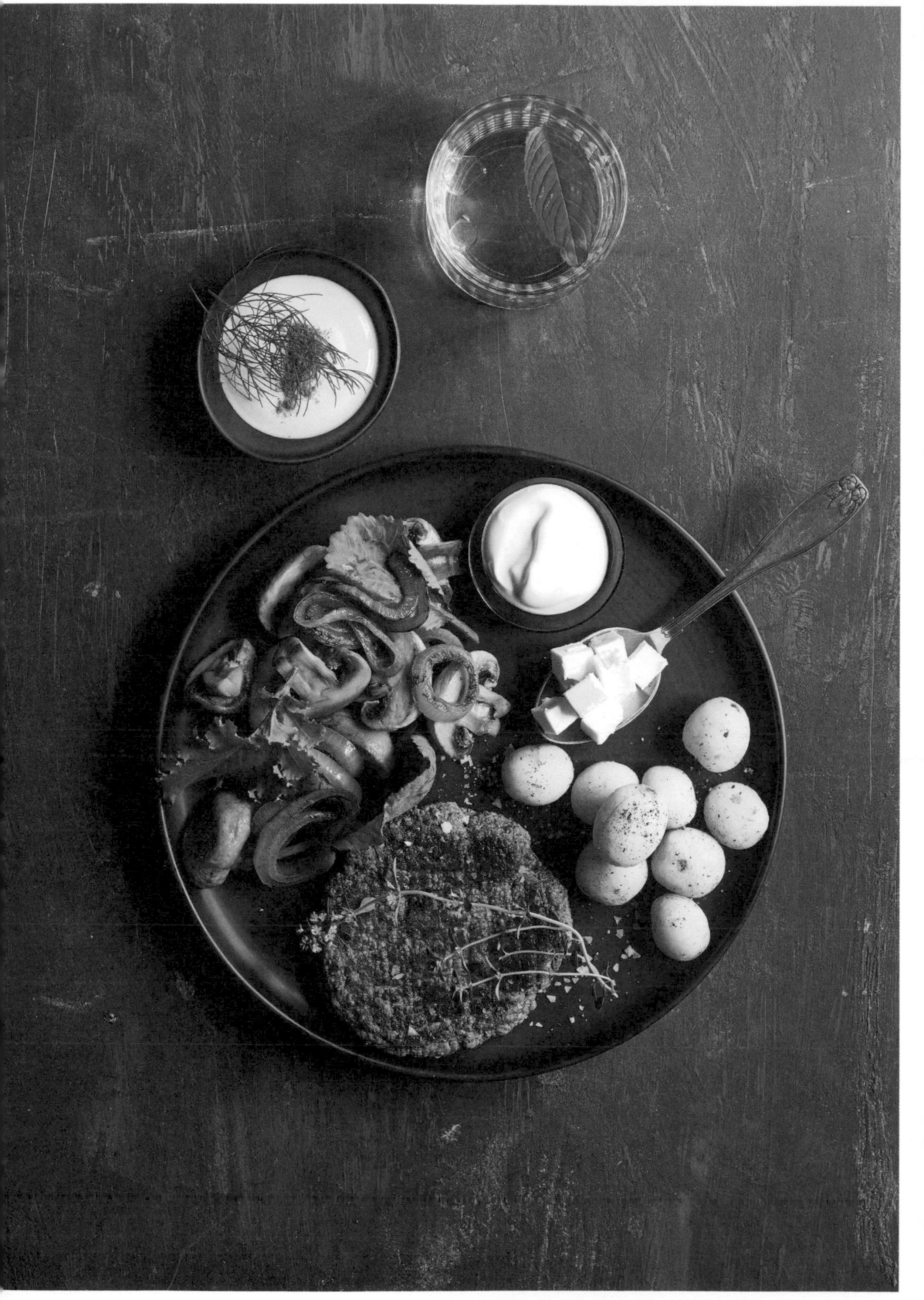

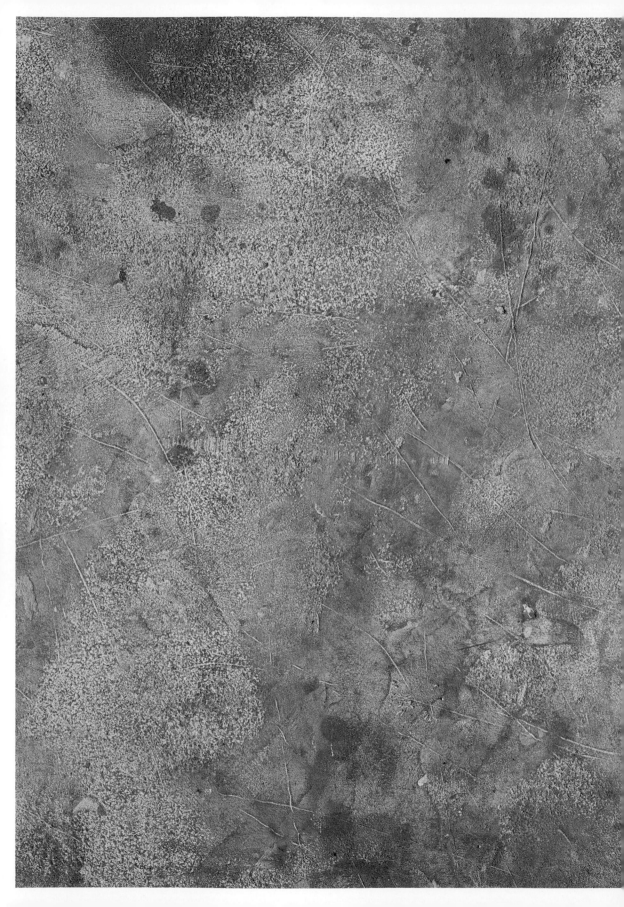

Getting off to a good start with Scandi Sense

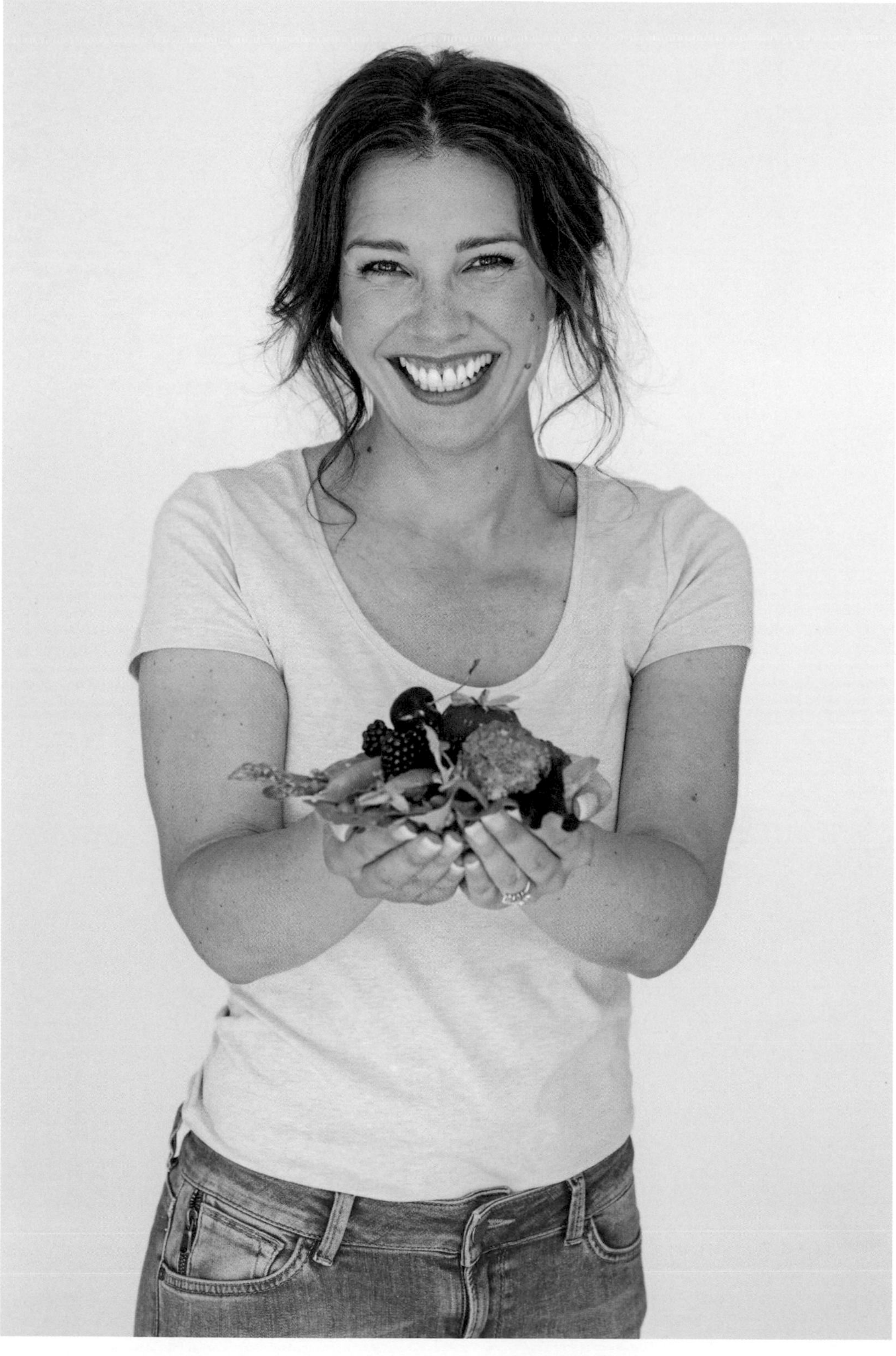

I recommend that you follow the Scandi Sense principles completely for the first 14 days; that is, three meal-boxes created following the Sense Meal-Box Model each day. Filling up the meal-boxes completely will make it easier to avoid snacking between meals.

If it is hard for you to wait such a long time between meals, drink a cup of hot bouillon a couple of times a day to counteract any side effects of reducing your carbohydrate intake. You can read more about this in the "Beginner's difficulties" section on page 56.

I advise you to complete a diet plan for the first 14 days. See an example of a completed diet plan for a woman on page 146 and for a man on page 214. There is an empty chart for you to photocopy and fill in on page 67.

You can start either by following the recipes in this book or by using your current diet as the basis. Just be sure to follow the portion guidelines— handfuls of food and tablespoonfuls of fat. You could easily select one or two favorite breakfasts and alternate between them for the first 14 days, and you can freely choose between all the lunches and suppers.

Look through your assortment of food. Fill the refrigerator with vegetables. Start using those you are familiar with and know you like—you can always expand your repertoire later. Seasonal vegetables are cheap and full of vitamins, but don't buy more than you can use. Fill the freezer with readily available vegetables such as spinach, peas, beans, and so on, so that you never run out of vegetables.

Fresh meat, fish, poultry, and cheese are excellent sources of protein. But it is a good idea to stock up on canned fish such as mackerel, cod roe, and tuna. Just like a tray of ready-made fishcakes, they are an easy solution for lunch or for a quick meal.

Make sure that you have several different fats in your kitchen: butter, olive oil, mayonnaise, olives, nuts, almonds, and fatty cheese.

Choose whole wheat when eating bread. Most people don't eat much fruit at first in Scandi Sense, but it is a good idea to keep berries or berry mixes in the freezer. Keep 34 oz of milk, a cultured dairy product and, for example, crème fraîche (5 to 9 percent) in the refrigerator, so you are well prepared.

Beginner's difficulties

You won't feel normal during the first 14 days of Scandi Sense. Remember that you are challenging your body to adapt to your new diet. It may well bring with it some reactions, not all of which are fun. The extent of the body's reaction varies enormously.

DIZZY, TIRED, AND BESIDE YOURSELF?

Some people experience almost no difficulties when beginning the diet, while others feel as if they have a mild flu, with symptoms such as headaches, dizziness, increased urination, stomach problems (diarrhea or constipation, for example), low energy levels, and irritation.

The symptoms arise because the body is responding to a change of diet. It is natural and you mustn't feel discouraged. You will have to use all your reserves of patience and faith that things will turn around after the first few weeks.

The digestive system can take several weeks to adapt to new dietary habits.

Don't eat too many raw vegetables if you aren't used to them, as they may be difficult for your stomach to handle. Instead, you can fry, boil, roast, or steam some of your vegetables.

Drink 1 to 2 cups of hot bouillon every day for the first few weeks. During the early days of Scandi Sense, you are draining fluids from the body and this can cause discomfort. The salt in bouillon helps to counteract this effect.

DO YOU FIND IT DIFFICULT TO AVOID SNACKS?

Many people eat more out of habit than hunger. It is important that you become familiar with the feeling of hunger using the hunger barometer (see page 21). If you find it difficult to keep hunger at bay with three meals a day, you can do one of two things.

You can add a little more into one of your meal-boxes by, for example, increasing the amount of protein by 5 to 10 percent. It may be that you are not getting enough food.

8 A.M.
1 P.M.
7 P.M.
1
2
3

I'M HUNGRY EVERY DAY AT 4 O'CLOCK!

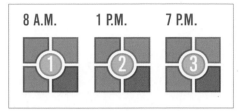

SOLUTION:

Put some extra food – preferably protein – in Meal-Box 1 and/or 2. Or you can take some food from a meal-box and eat it as a snack.

Or, you can divide your allowance between three main meals and one or more snacks. You have to find your own way, even when it comes to the number of meals. Scandi Sense will still work as long as you don't eat more overall than what can be in the suggested three meal-boxes.

If you choose to introduce snacks during the day, it is a good idea to choose a small snack that contains protein, carbohydrate, and fat. This combination will fill you up and keep your blood sugar levels stable. Of course you can just eat a carrot or another vegetable, if that's what works for you.

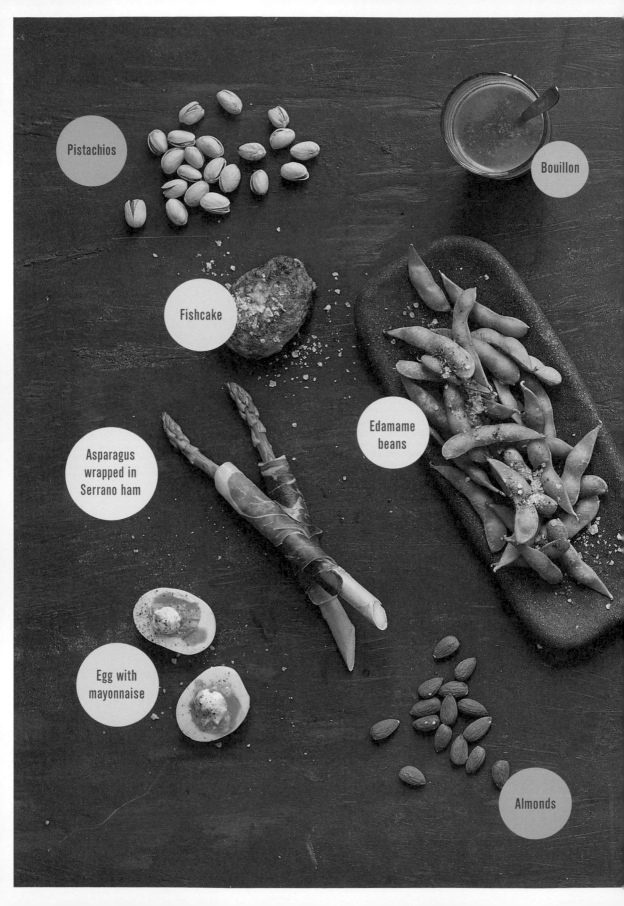

Pistachios

Bouillon

Fishcake

Edamame beans

Asparagus wrapped in Serrano ham

Egg with mayonnaise

Almonds

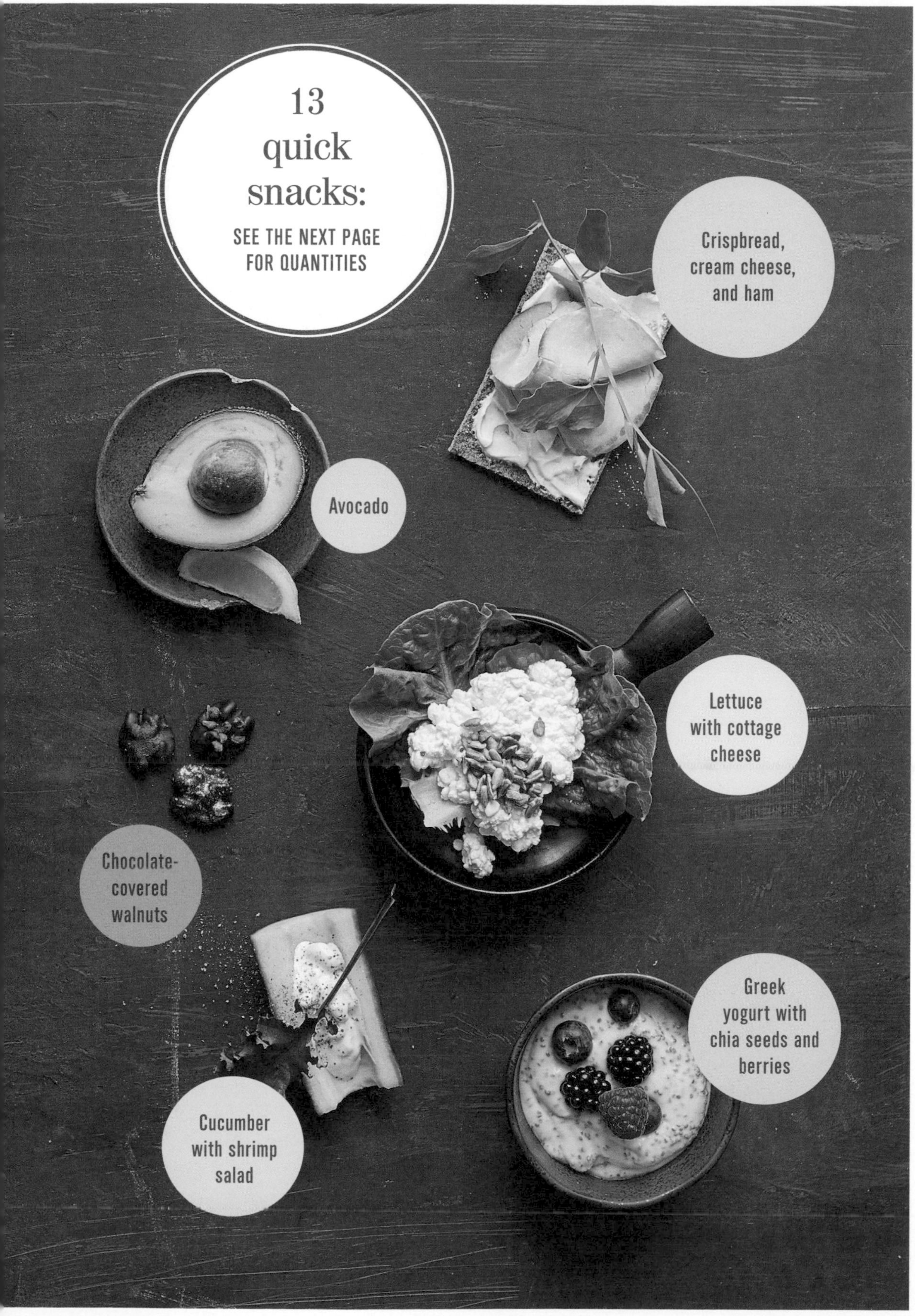
13 quick snacks:
SEE THE NEXT PAGE FOR QUANTITIES
Crispbread, cream cheese, and ham
Avocado
Lettuce with cottage cheese
Chocolate-covered walnuts
Greek yogurt with chia seeds and berries
Cucumber with shrimp salad

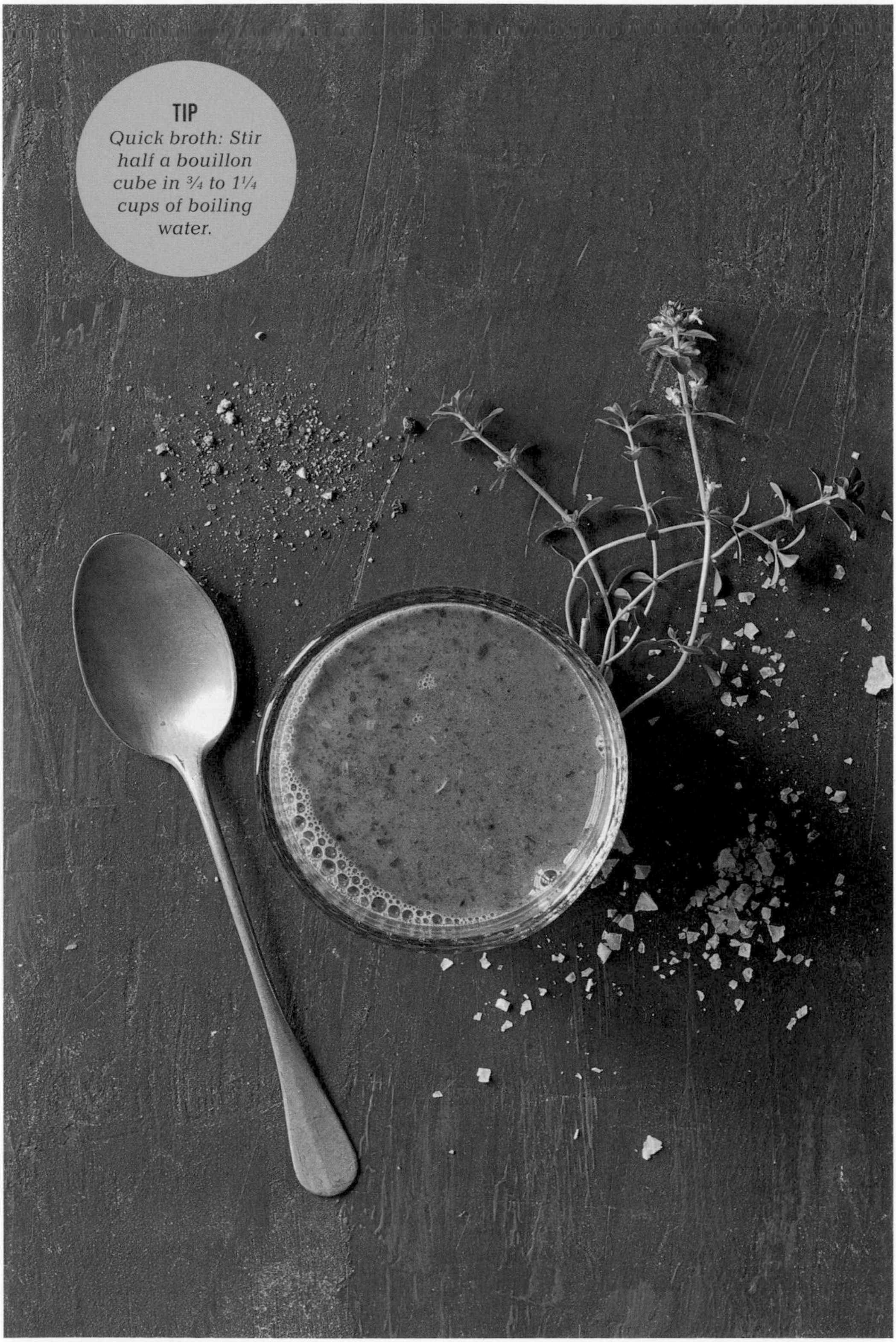

TIP

Quick broth: Stir half a bouillon cube in ¾ to 1¼ cups of boiling water.

13 quick snacks: How much you can eat

1/4 cup of pistachios in their shells

1 tablespoonful of fat. 85 kcal

A cup of bouillon

Can be drunk as necessary, as there are only 13 kcal in 1 1/4 cups of ready-mixed bouillon. You can buy bouillon drinks, but a bouillon cube or a teaspoon of bouillon powder stirred into water is just as good. 13 kcal

A fishcake

Counts as half of Handful 3. 93 kcal

2 spears of asparagus wrapped in Serrano ham

Counts as half of Handful 1 and one-third of Handful 3. 45 kcal

1 cup of edamame beans with chili and salt flakes

Counts as half of Handful 3. 109 kcal

A piece of thin crispbread with a tablespoon of low-fat cream cheese and two slices of ham

Counts as one-third of Handful 4 and half of Handful 3. 80 kcal

Half an avocado with a teaspoon of lemon juice, salt and pepper

Counts as 2 tablespoonfuls of fat. 134 kcal

15 almonds

Counts as 1 tablespoonful of fat. 79 kcal

1 hard-cooked egg with 1/4 oz of mayonnaise, plus tabasco, salt, and pepper

Counts as one-third of Handful 3 and 1 tablespoonful of fat. 149 kcal

Two baby romaine lettuce leaves with 1/4 cup of cottage cheese and half a teaspoon of sunflower seeds

Counts as one-quarter of Handful 1, one-third of Handful 3, and half a tablespoonful of fat. 96 kcal

Three walnuts dipped in 1/4 oz of semisweet chocolate (min. 70%) with a sprinkle of freeze-dried raspberries, licorice, and edible glitter

Counts as 2 tablespoonfuls of fat. 166 kcal

3 1/2 oz of cucumber with 1 oz of shrimp salad

Counts as Handful 1, one-fifth of Handful 3, and 1 tablespoonful of fat. 86 kcal

1/3 cup of 2% Greek yogurt mixed with 1 tablespoon of chia seeds and decorated with 1/4 cup of berries

Counts as 1/3 cup of dairy product, 1 tablespoonful of fat, and one-quarter of Handful 4. 156 kcal

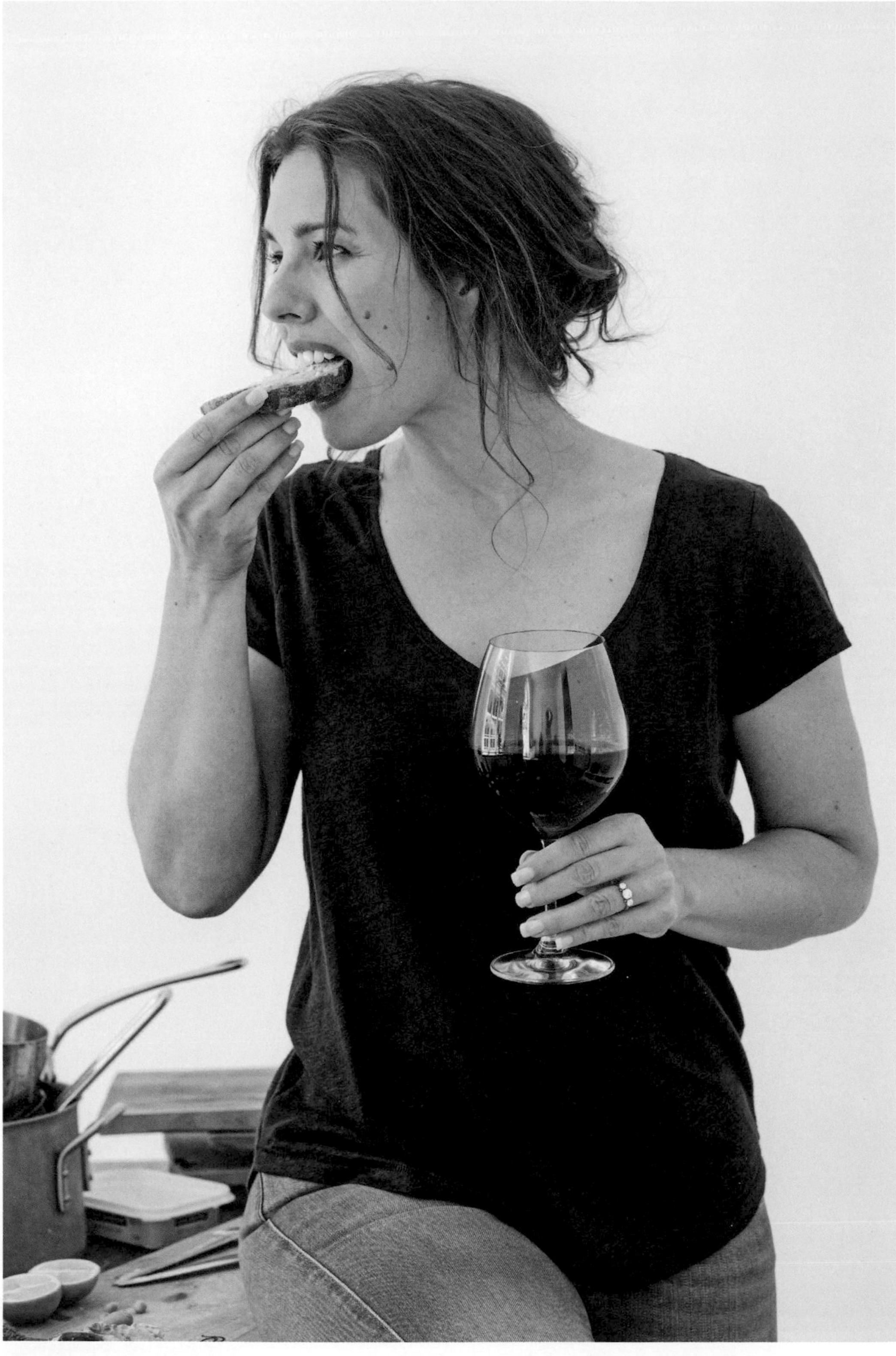

What about dining out?

I'M GOING TO EAT IN TOWN!

SOLUTION:

Save up so that you have two full meal-boxes to play with when you are invited for dinner.

Once you have understood the principles behind the meal-boxes, you can play about with them—for example, if you are eating out or having guests for dinner.

THREE STRATEGIES FOR A BIG MEAL

If you only eat half a meal-box for breakfast and half a meal-box for lunch, you will have two whole meal-boxes to play with for your evening meal.

If you skip either breakfast or lunch completely, you will also have two whole meal-boxes available in the evening.

You can also fill your meal-boxes for breakfast and lunch as normal and complete the last meal-box to the best of your ability. The crucial thing is to be level-headed, do not overeat, and be sure to get back into a good rhythm at the next mealtime.

How much exercise do you need?

Exercise is good for your health, your mood, your muscles, your bones, and your joints. It can also make it easier for you to maintain a healthy weight when you have lost some weight. But when you reach the point where you want a few extra pounds to disappear, it is predominantly your eating habits that determine whether or not you will succeed.

During an attempt at weight loss, exercise works a bit like stepping on the gas—it speeds it up a little.

However, to be completely honest with you, it doesn't make a great deal of difference.

Fortunately, there are plenty of other good reasons to exercise, and if you have the desire and the energy, I can only encourage you to do so to supplement the Scandi Sense diet.

However, moderate exercise doesn't mean you can eat larger helpings. Some people mistakenly think that they can afford to eat much more because they exercise. Unfortunately, the calorie requirements of the body don't really work like that.

It is also a myth that you should eat both before and after exercise. It is the amount of protein and other macro-nutrients distributed throughout the day that are important for nutrition. As long as you eat a handful of protein two to three times a day, you will get the amount of protein you need to cope with exercise alongside weight loss, as long as we are talking about moderate exercise.

You will only need more food if you exercise a lot, for example, running long distance several times a week or doing intensive weight training for many hours a week. In this case, make sure you eat three handfuls of protein daily—and these can be heaping.

The day before a long run or similar, you can have one or two extra handfuls of starch/fruit. But this only

applies to people who exercise a lot. Moderate exercisers—and that is the majority of us—should be satisfied with the food from the meal-boxes.

I recommend that you stick to the official guidelines for exercise: 30 minutes a day at moderate to high intensity. At least two days a week, you should engage in a heartbeat-raising activity for at least 20 minutes. If you start exercising very long and hard, you risk triggering your hunger hormones, so you will get an intense urge to make up for any weight lost

in exercise with food—if not more. It isn't smart at a stage where you are rediscovering the natural regulation of your appetite.

The best exercise is whatever you feel like doing—and what you can stick to over the long term. It is, of course, fine to be more active for some periods.

Exercise shouldn't stress you out, however. If you are very overweight and are confronted with having to lose weight, it is completely okay to take one project at a time. Begin by taking control of your dietary habits. The desire to exercise often emerges by itself once the pounds begin to tumble off. Maybe you have some pain because of your weight or reduced mobility; this all changes when you start losing weight. You will have less to lug around and you suddenly become able to do a lot that you couldn't do before. As these changes occur, your desire to be more active will automatically increase.

If you feel that you ought to exercise but never really get started because you are constantly encountering obstacles, you need to take a good look at your habits, and perhaps your calendar too. Everyone ought to have time to engage in 10 to 30 minutes of exercise a few times a week.

Scandi Sense is a lifestyle that can be tailored to everyone: those who are very overweight; those who just have to lose a few pounds; those who don't need to lose weight but just want a healthier lifestyle; those who never exercise; and those who exercise a great deal.

If you don't lose weight

Most people who follow Scandi Sense experience a weight loss of 0.9 to 1.8 lb per week—calculated as an average over the entire weight loss period. If, contrary to expectations, you don't lose any weight, it may be because you are either eating too much, not following the Sense Meal-Box Model, or eating too many indulgences.

So try to make your handfuls and tablespoons of fat a bit smaller and stick to your three meal-boxes. Then you will see results. You need to be in a calorie deficit to achieve weight loss.

On the page opposite, there is an empty diet plan that you can photocopy and fill in to plan each meal-box. There is also a measurement chart on page 250 to help you to track your progress.

The diagram on page 22 can be photocopied and pinned to your refrigerator to remind you of the core principles of Scandi Sense.

Scandi Sense

	MEAL-BOX 1	MEAL-BOX 2	MEAL-BOX 3	
	Handful 1 (+2): Vegetables	Handful 1 (+2): Vegetables	Handful 1 (+2): Vegetables	MOST IMPORTANT ELEMENTS IN THE DIET
	Handful 3: Protein	Handful 3: Protein	Handful 3: Protein	
	Handful 4: Starch and/or fruit	Handful 4: Starch and/or fruit	Handful 4: Starch and/or fruit	
	1 to 3 tablespoons of fat	1 to 3 tablespoons of fat	1 to 3 tablespoons of fat	
	2 tablespoons of dairy dressing	2 tablespoons of dairy dressing	2 tablespoons of dairy dressing	OPTIONAL ELEMENTS
	Dairy products	Dairy products	Dairy products	
Snacks				

Don't worry— you will maintain your new weight

If you have tried out a lot of diets in the past, and have struggled to lose weight, or found that you regain the weight further down the line, you may wonder if it is worth your while to try the Scandi Sense diet. Old failures stick with you, but you are not alone. The statistics show a gloomy picture—after losing weight, almost everyone regains the weight that they have lost, if not a little more. Anyone who has experience with dieting knows that one of the hardest thing to do after a diet is maintain your weight loss.

With Scandi Sense, it doesn't have to be like that because it isn't a temporary diet but a lifestyle that you can easily continue with—so don't let doubt undermine your motivation.

People generally lose a little more weight with Scandi Sense than they initially anticipate. This is because of uncertainty about the transition from the weight loss phase to their sustainable

lifestyle. It is of course important that you stick to the Scandi Sense lifestyle after the weight loss period. If you return to old habits, you will quickly regain the weight that you have lost. All that this means is that you must continue to live by the Scandi Sense principles and meal-boxes, and you should try to maintain the habit of eating according to hunger rather than cravings, for the rest of your life.

However, after the weight loss period, there is room for a few more indulgences as long as your weight is stable. You can choose to eat more on a daily basis or you can save up during the week and eat a little more at the weekend. Both these methods are fine as long as you maintain your weight and stick to the Scandi Sense principles.

It may take one or two years before you find the weight where your diet, exercise routine, and lifestyle find harmony. I call this the practical ideal

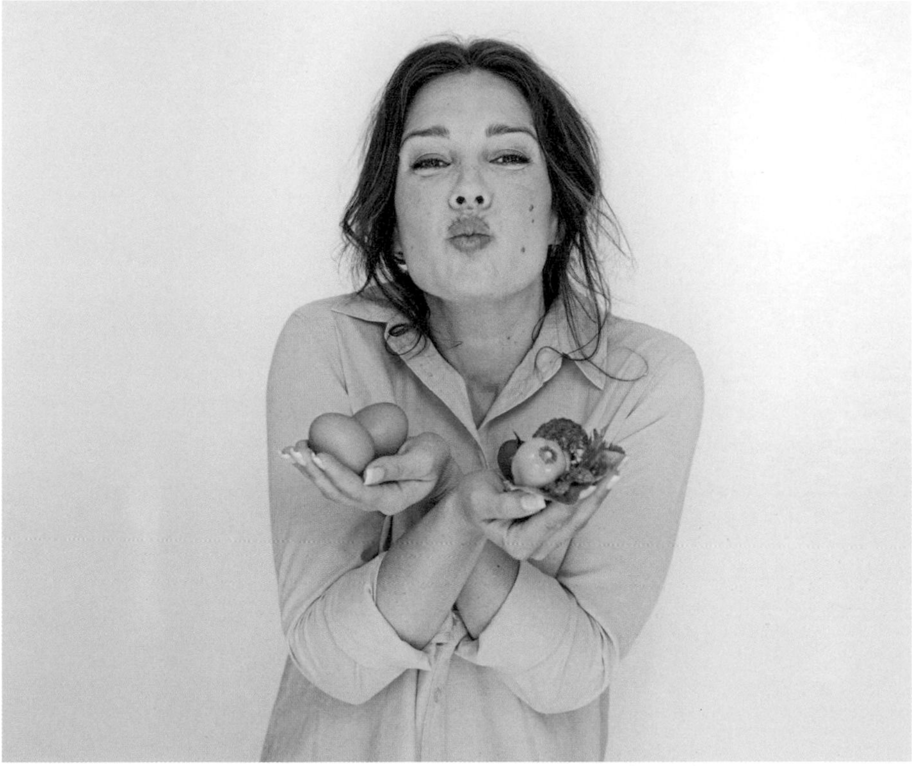

weight because it is determined by the habits you practice in your life. The lifestyle you follow will determine your weight and not vice versa, otherwise you won't maintain your weight.

When you reach your practical ideal weight, it is therefore a matter of deciding—with a view to quality of life—which habits you don't want to go without. Then you must lay out a plan that makes room for them within the Scandi Sense model.

Once you have lost weight, you may panic if the needle on the bathroom scale suddenly moves a little in the wrong direction. It is important to know that a stable body weight regularly fluctuates by 4½ to 6½ lb. Likewise, you must be prepared for the eventuality that, even though you have reached your practical ideal weight, it may change over time. Very few people weigh the same at 50 years old as they did at 20 because the body changes hormonally and metabolically as you age, so you don't need as many calories as you once did. It can be difficult to accept, but it is perfectly normal for your weight to rise slightly in line with age.

Mette and John
The best thing we have ever done

HOW WE LIVED BEFORE SCANDI SENSE

METTE: My spinal cord was damaged in a traffic accident in 1998, so I have trouble walking and use a wheelchair a lot of the time. I live with chronic pain and cannot exercise due to cysts in my spinal cord. The cysts cause me to lose control of my legs if I am overloaded. My life is therefore very sedentary.

Before the accident, I was very active. I loved my job and, with four children in the house, it goes without saying that I also had an active family life. My physical condition in the years following the car crash has slowly deteriorated, but I didn't receive my final diagnosis, syringomyelia (cysts in my spinal cord) until 2013. Following the diagnosis, I was given early retirement.

The deterioration in my body combined with this final diagnosis made me feel that I had lost my entire identity; everything that had defined me before was suddenly taken away. I could no longer work, couldn't be very active, and I didn't feel I could give my children what I wanted to give them. I fell into a hole and stopped looking after myself.

I took—and still do take—a lot of medication for my illness, which was a contributing factor in my weight gain, but the rest of it was down to diet. I didn't eat a lot of food, but what I did eat was unhealthy. We often had takeout burgers for supper, for example, and if we prepared food ourselves, it was always fried in butter or oil. I only drank coke or coffee, never water. I had very little strength and my life was just about survival, nothing more. This affected what I ate and drank.

When my weight exceeded 207 lb, I started to have more physical problems, such as heart palpitations, and I felt constantly out of sorts. Because of my background in health work, I knew plenty about the connection between an unhealthy diet, excess weight, lack of exercise, and blood clots. So, I went to the doctor and had a cardiovascular study that showed that I had high cholesterol and an irregular heartbeat and that I was in the high-risk zone for a blood clot because of my weight and lack of activity.

METTE CHRISTENSEN, 42

- Early retiree,
  previously worked as
  a healthcare assistant
- Married to John
- Has lost 46 lb with Scandi
  Sense in 9 months

JOHN CHRISTENSEN, 46

- Early retiree, previously
  worked as a press operator
- Married to Mette
- Has lost 132 lb with Scandi
  Sense in 9 months
- Mette and John have four
  children, aged 21, 19, 16,
  and 15—the youngest two
  live at home

JOHN: When I was in my midtwenties, I was diagnosed with asthma and received medical treatment for it. I stopped playing soccer at that point because my asthma made it difficult for me to run. The less active I became, the more weight I gained, and I slowly got heavier and heavier.

In 2009, I was injured at work and was given early retirement. The accident made me even more inactive and I became increasingly overweight. I completely gave up. I was convinced that I would never lose weight, so I ate without restraint, because it didn't seem to matter.

On a typical morning, I would eat 2 or 3 bread rolls with butter or cream cheese, and after that I would continue to eat for the rest of the day, consuming about eight meals a day, all of which were unhealthy. I ate lots of fatty foods, for example in fast food shops I would order 3 to 4 burgers at a time, and I ate lots of white bread from the grocery store. If I was out shopping, I always bought a chocolate bar on my way out. I never ate vegetables—

I thought they were rabbit food.

When I reached 313 lb, I became severely affected by the weight gain. I sweated and puffed a lot and I had difficulty getting around. When Mette and I were intimate, I became incredibly physically uncomfortable. My heart would hammer away, I would sweat, and my whole body shook.

That's not how it's supposed to be, so Mette made me go for tests. I went to see the doctor and, after an extensive medical examination, I got miserable results across the board—high blood sugar, and consequently the first signs of diabetes, high cholesterol, and high blood pressure. Mette and I were both scared by this.

HOW WE LIVE ACCORDING TO SCANDI SENSE

METTE: Pretty much at the same time I went to be examined by the doctor, I stumbled across Scandi Sense on Facebook. I was curious, began to read about it, and watched Suzy's videos. I must have been mentally ready for a change because I immediately thought, yes, I could live with this, because it was straightforward and sensible and I wouldn't have to weigh my food or count calories.

Rules and restrictions don't work for me. On the contrary, they make me overeat. Scandi Sense doesn't restrict or tell me off, which suits me well. Today, I live one hundred percent according to the principles of Scandi Sense. I typically start the day with a bowl of Skyr. For lunch, I eat homemade hummus, carrots, almonds, cottage cheese, and home-baked bread. We never buy bread from the baker or the grocery store anymore. In the evening, I eat different dishes inspired by Suzy's recipes. I have set aside the coke and coffee for good, and I only drink water, 4 to 8½ cups a day. I can be a bit naughty—some nachos with the kids or candies—but it never takes over. I eat a little, then close the meal-box and move on.

JOHN: Mette introduced me to Scandi Sense. I have tried out different diets in the past and have lost weight. But it's always been a tough fight, where I've been hungry and unhappy. So I already had my guard up when Mette brought a piece of paper with some hands on it and introduced me to Scandi Sense. I couldn't be bothered with yet another unsuccessful attempt at losing weight.

But Mette convinced me by serving up a dish of pork chops, cauliflower, and cream sauce from one of Suzy's recipe books. It tasted really good; the plate was packed with good food and I was more than satisfied. Mette told me that I could eat this dish, or something similar, every day and that I could eat three helpings the same size every day. I was sold from that point onward. We stuck together and made a joint decision to change our lives.

It's the best thing we've ever done. We started very practically, by thoroughly clearing out the kitchen and throwing out anything ill-advised. Today we have nothing unhealthy in our home—the refrigerator is filled with healthy food.

The change of diet quickly paid off. The weight tumbled off me and after nine months on Scandi Sense, the scale showed a loss of 132 lb—an incredible transformation.

From day one, I have lived one hundred percent according to Scandi Sense. In the morning, I have oatmeal with raisins and cinnamon or a bowl of Skyr. The day's other meals are made up of vegetables, meat, eggs, etc.

Since we had both retired early, we lost about 26,000 kroner ($4,292) of our monthly income and had to cut back on all our expenses. In the past, we spent a lot of money buying unhealthy food on impulse. Today, as we are following a diet plan, we buy in large quantities and freeze what we can. Even though the refrigerator and freezer are full of food, we save 1,000 to 1,500 kroner ($165 to 248) each month because we no longer buy impulsively. We've set aside the money we've saved, and for the first time in nine years, we've been able to afford a family vacation. We're going to Croatia with our children and we're looking forward to it immensely.

METTE AND JOHN BEFORE THEIR WEIGHT LOSS

WHY SCANDI SENSE WORKS FOR US

METTE: Scandi Sense works for me because there are no restrictions. In general, if somebody or something tries to restrict me, I become stubborn.

"

It works because it's so easy and uncomplicated, without anything forbidden or restricted.

– METTE AND JOHN

This system is so simple that it captured my attention immediately. At first, I measured all of my food with my hands. I don't need to do that today. I know exactly what I can put on my plate because I've carefully followed the Scandi Sense lifestyle for a long time now.

When we have meals out, I don't have to have special food or avoid the food that other people eat. I just make sure I stick to the amounts. You can always find something suitable for Scandi Sense.

JOHN: Scandi Sense works for me because it's so straightforward and simple. Nothing is forbidden so you don't have to beat yourself up or give up if you occasionally eat something unhealthy. You just close that meal-box and move on.

Following Scandi Sense with Mette has contributed to the fact that it's worked so well, I'm sure of that. We've been able to support and motivate each other all the way through, and that has meant a great deal. We've got a lot of inspiration and support in the Facebook group. It is such a friendly place and we're happy to be part of that community.

HOW THE FAMILY WORKS ON SCANDI SENSE

METTE: Our two children that live at home had to get used to our changed eating habits. They made a fuss at first, but quickly moved past it because the food tastes so good. Neither of them are picky, fortunately. Our son used to be an elite soccer player and our daughter is also active, so they've always had a good attitude toward exercise and health. Nevertheless, they'd been eating the same unhealthy food as us, so they've certainly become healthier too. For example, they often used to buy food in the school canteen, but they don't do that anymore. They take whole-wheat rolls with salad and meat to school every day.

JOHN: All things considered, the children have taken it very well. They can see the transformation in their parents and are very proud of us. They've only ever known me as overweight, so that's one big positive change. The other day we heated up some ready-made chicken nuggets and fries in the oven, just to make things easy, and there were no vegetables. When the children saw the meal, they told us that it was boring and uninteresting. We completely agreed, and we ended up throwing it all out, because none of us wanted to eat it. That probably tells you a lot about how the relationship with food has changed for the whole family.

HOW WE TACKLE CHALLENGES

METTE: I haven't on one occasion thought, no, now I can't be bothered anymore. The hardest times have been the periods when my weight doesn't budge.

METTE AFTER HER WEIGHT LOSS

verge of giving up and telling myself that I had done enough. But I'm glad I didn't give up. I adjusted my calorie intake and change started again. Now I've reached my goal.

WHAT SCANDI SENSE HAS MEANT FOR US

METTE: My new eating habits have sparked me back into life. I'm a happier person and my self-esteem has never been better. I've found a good balance and think I look great. Everything has become easier for me—getting up, putting my clothes on, just being able to get around. I'm not under as much strain as I was before. In the past, I was prone to migraines, but since starting Scandi Sense they've disappeared. I'm sure that it is because of the increased intake of vitamins and fluids. My body gets everything that it needs now.

Since my accident, I've had problems with my intestines because they're paralysed. Before changing my diet, I'd have one or two bowel movements per fortnight, even though I was taking laxative medicine. Today, my stomach has more to work with, so it happens two or three times a week, and I've reduced the amount of laxatives I take. That means a lot for my well-being.

I also used to struggle a lot with fluid in my body, both in my legs and in my face. Today, the fluid accumulation has almost gone. There can sometimes be a little in the morning, but it's short-term and has usually gone after an hour.

I've always been stubborn and determined, but after the accident I had a huge identity crisis. My self-esteem was at zero and I couldn't see the point of anything—I completely gave up.

Scandi Sense changed all my negative thinking. When I decided to change my

Then I feel frustrated that nothing has happened. But every time, I say to myself, take it easy, you don't have to achieve all the time. And it works, because soon the scale move again. Today I'm just under 2 lb from being in the "healthy weight" zone. That was my goal, so it's a big thing for me that I'm almost there.

JOHN: My weight loss went well until I hit my first goal of 198 lb. Then the scale suddenly stopped moving. I really wanted to get down to around 176 lb, but the last 22 lb were stubborn. I was on the

lifestyle, I rediscovered my fighting spirit. Scandi Sense became my project and my goal and gave me the kick in the pants I needed. In fact, we both feel that Scandi Sense has given us a new chance in life.

JOHN: Scandi Sense has given me a new life. I had always been unconcerned about what people thought and said about me, but I recognize that it was a defense mechanism, because of course I got sad if people made comments about my weight such as "have you swallowed a beach ball?" or similar. When I went to soccer with my son, I was embarrassed at being a big, fat Dad. Today, people tell me I look fifteen years younger and I'm proud and walk with my head held high when I'm out with the children. I've gained a lot of confidence from getting to grips with my problems, and it was fantastic that Mette and I could do this together.

My annual checkup with the doctor showed that all my numbers are more than fine—in fact they are like those of a 14-year-old, says my doctor. When you've previously had high numbers across the board, that's a really nice message to get. I feel healthy and I know my body is getting everything it needs.

I can also feel a big change physically. The pain in my ankles and knees has disappeared. I don't have headaches anymore and my mood is good. I have lots of energy and I'm considering canceling our big TV package, because I don't use it much anymore.

I get a lot of exercise every day. When I started on Scandi Sense, I also started walking 9 to 11 miles a day. Every day, whether it was raining, storming, or snowing. Nowadays, I walk 4 to 6 miles. I've become totally addicted to it and wouldn't dream of skipping a day.

And then there's the change of closet. I've gone from size XXXXXL down to medium. It's crazy! Suddenly I can buy

JOHN AFTER HIS WEIGHT LOSS

smart clothes. When we were going to a christening recently, I needed a shirt. My son, who is 6 ft tall and weighs almost 150 lb, offered me his shirt and it fitted me without any problems. So I wore it!

Mette's top tips

You must be a hundred percent motivated. If you are, you'll see it through, but you'll need a lot of patience. There will be ups and downs—it's all part of the journey.

Even if you're on medication and have constant pain, or are in a wheelchair like me, it's still your life and your decisions. You have to stop making excuses and take responsibility for your happiness, regardless of what you're up against. Self-pity only makes it worse. I decided that I didn't want to be an angry, bitter woman because I knew that I would end up alone, with no friends, husband, or children around me. That wasn't what I wanted.

Extra energy comes naturally if you are happy and experience success. No matter what life has thrown at me and how much the accident changed my body, I'm still the same person inside. I still have my stubbornness, my fighting spirit, and my strong will.

John's top tips

You have to really want it, because if you have the right attitude, you'll keep going, even when it gets difficult. And believe me, it's worth it. I feel that my life has started over and I'm so grateful. I've been living with obesity for twenty years and I'd given up completely. But when I finally decided to do it, I was more determined than I've ever been before in my life.

I can barely describe in words what it has meant to me. I love my family above everything and I have a zest for life that has carried me through. I really feel that I've saved my life and been given a new chance. So my number one tip is to drop the self-pity and find your strength and determination. You can do it if you really want to—I'm living proof of that.

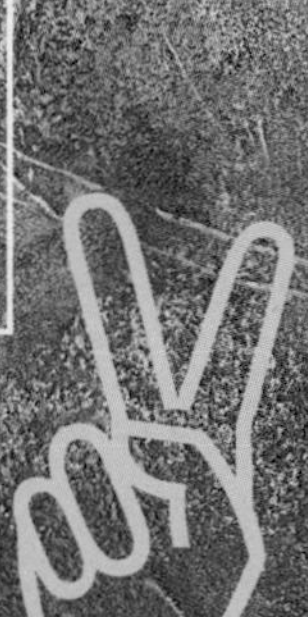

Christa and Camilla

It meant so much that we could take the journey together

HOW WE LIVED BEFORE SCANDI SENSE

CHRISTA: I used to eat an enormous amount of bread and pasta—several large helpings every day. I work at a hotel where there is a breakfast buffet every morning so I would start the day with a couple of rolls with cheese and butter. Then I would continue to eat bread throughout the day and at supper I generally had three helpings, simply because I was hungry—I never felt full.

A typical supper would be meat with gravy or sauce, lots of potatoes or pasta and barely any vegetables. If something tasted good, I'd eat a lot—as much as I wanted. I didn't give much thought to the type of food or the quantity. On the other hand, I've never eaten a lot of snacks or candies. A couple of times a week I might have some potato chips, but not always. My weight problems came from eating too much at meals, and not having a balanced diet.

In August 2015, I gave birth to my son and, for a long time after the birth, I weighed over 220 lb. I wasn't happy about that. I had dresses that didn't fit me anymore hanging in the closet and it really upset me to see photos of myself. I could see that I was overweight and I certainly didn't want to look like that.

CAMILLA: I think I've always tried to live healthily—at least periodically. But it was difficult for me to stick to a healthy lifestyle, because I felt healthy food was so dull. At that time, I thought that all healthy food was fat-free and lacking in taste. So, despite good intentions, I always gave up.

Before Scandi Sense, I ate a very traditional Danish diet—lots of bread for breakfast, three slices of rye bread for lunch, and meat with gravy and potatoes for supper. I wasn't a fan of vegetables, so I ate very few. I always snacked during the day as well as having three big main meals, so I was taking in a lot of calories.

CHRISTA AND CAMILLA BEFORE THEIR WEIGHT LOSS

I felt really bad about my weight, so my sister and I, along with a friend, decided that together we would begin a healthier lifestyle. We all started on January 4, 2016. At that point, we weren't following a program, just using our common sense. We began exercising, thought more about what was in the food we were eating, and dropped everything unhealthy—no potato chips, cakes, and candies. It worked and I lost 18 lb. At that point, we hadn't heard of Scandi Sense, but when I look back on it now, I can see that we had already adopted the principles of Scandi Sense.

HOW WE LIVE ACCORDING TO SCANDI SENSE

CHRISTA: January 2016 was the starting point for a healthier lifestyle. The combination of exercise and the rejection of all potato chips, candies, and cake gave us quick rewards. Then, after six months, my sister stumbled across Scandi Sense and began to eat following those principles.

That sparked my curiosity, even though in the beginning I struggled to understand what was involved.

In October 2016, I followed in my sister's footsteps and started living by the Scandi Sense principles—and that was when my weight loss began to make serious progress. Since then I've been eating three full meals a day, and drastically cut down on bread, pasta, and potatoes, with a lot more veg and protein.

Now I usually have Skyr with homemade muesli for breakfast. I do have bread in the morning on occasion, but instead of having two rolls, I make do with one and top it with eggs, vegetables, and only a little fat.

For the rest of the day's meals, I make sure I stick closely to the portion sizes recommended by Scandi Sense. I make the dishes that I've always made, but I focus on including a lot more vegetables. I have a simple recipe book and I find inspiration for other new dishes in the Scandi Sense Facebook group.

For me the most radical change was changing my view on fat. In the past,

I connected fat with extra weight around my hips and an unhealthy lifestyle. Today, I stick to Scandi Sense's suggested servings of fat, which means, for example, adding a splash of cream to a sauce. I would never have done that before.

I never snack between meals—I almost always feel full. If I get hungry, I've become good at looking forward to the next meal because I know that I'm going to have something good and filling to eat.

Now that I've got the hang of the principles behind Scandi Sense, I don't stand there measuring food with my hands. I do it by eye and by feel, because I know what my plate should look like. I've got used to keeping things in balance with my Handful 4. I can easily save on bread during the day, so there is room for a few more potatoes for supper. If we're eating out or are on vacation, I also hold back on bread, fruit, pasta etc. during the day, so I have a little more leeway in the evening.

CAMILLA: In July 2016, I stumbled on Scandi Sense on Facebook. I joined the group and began to read what it was all about. It sounded like a lot of what I was already doing. It was good to confirm that I was on the right track and to have a specific concept to follow, because until then I'd mostly been feeling my way. Now I had found a finished package that fitted in so well with everything I was already doing, so it couldn't have been better.

From the very beginning, I've lived completely in accordance with the principles of Scandi Sense. I stick to three meals a day and make sure the portion sizes on my plate are as they should be. I've taken up the habit of drinking a cup of coffee with milk and having a piece of chocolate in the evening —it's nice that there's room for that. Apart from the fact that the chocolate

CHRISTA KEHLET, 31

- Hotel receptionist
- Married, mother of a two-year-old boy
- Camilla's sister
- Has lost 68 lb with Scandi Sense in a year

CAMILLA HANSEN, 32

- Office worker
- Engaged, mother of a two-year-old boy and a three-year-old girl
- Christa's sister
- Has lost 48½ lb with Scandi Sense in a year and is 9 lb from her goal weight

satisfies the desire for something sweet, it's become a moment I look forward to, a moment of pure relaxation.

The transition to Scandi Sense was relatively unproblematic for me because I was already working on a healthier lifestyle. I'd cut down on sugar, so the change wasn't that big. I've never been frightened of fat, yet I felt that I should cut down on fat when I wanted to lose weight, even though in fact it was fat I had been missing when I had previously tried to live healthily. Fat gives a feeling of fullness and adds taste to food, so you feel its loss if you cut it out entirely.

I've followed various diets in the past, such as LCHF (Low Carb High Fat) diet. The food was okay, but it was far too difficult to follow. There were so many rules and things you mustn't have. It can just about work when you're at home, but as soon as you step out the door, it becomes almost impossible to live by.

With Scandi Sense it's totally different, because I can live completely normally.

CHRISTA AFTER HER WEIGHT LOSS

I can eat everything—bread, rice, and pasta and even cake. I just have to limit the amount and make sure I have the right quantities on my plate.

WHY SCANDI SENSE WORKS FOR US

CHRISTA: Scandi Sense is so easy to follow. Once you get the hang of the principles, it runs itself. I easily become full, despite the fact that I eat less bread and pasta, and in a much more comfortable way. I feel much less bloated than before.

It's a great relief that I don't have to exercise to follow Scandi Sense. I have a high percentage of body fat and I know that I need exercise. The desire to exercise will probably come by itself, but until it does, it's liberating that I can simply focus on the diet. If I was following a program that required me to exercise several times a week, I'd never be able to stick to it.

From day one on Scandi Sense, I've been motivated to make results happen. And you have to be motivated and have willpower to keep it up. Breaking your habits requires an effort, especially in the beginning. Going with my sister to weekly weigh-ins with a Scandi Sense consultant, Bodil Cramer in Skanderborg, Denmark, helped a lot to motivate me. Knowing that I'm going to face the scale makes me keep going.

I'm so grateful that my sister introduced me to Scandi Sense and that we could make the journey together. I don't think for a moment that I'd have had such a successful result without her.

CAMILLA: Scandi Sense works for me because it's about using your common sense. It's logical and easy, and it's smart that you literally have your quantities at hand. I don't have to count calories or weigh my food. I just have to reflect and evaluate if the food on my plate looks sensible. It's so straightforward.

My husband is a sailor and is alternately home and away for a fortnight at a time. When I'm alone with our two small children, it's very important that I can live according to Scandi Sense without it being too difficult and without having to leave home in the evening to go to the gym or for a run. That simply wouldn't work for me. I just have to concentrate on the food and it works really well. If we hadn't had children, I'm sure I'd also have exercised more, but as it is now, I'm satisfied with doing a little exercise in the living room in the evening.

HOW THE FAMILY WORKS ON SCANDI SENSE

CHRISTA: There are no problems at all for the family. I make the food I've been making all along, but just make sure there are more vegetables than before. I don't make any special food—all three of us eat the same food. My husband eats more potatoes than I do, and I eat a lot more vegetables than him, but we all serve ourselves from the same dishes.

CAMILLA: I haven't had any complaints about the food, either from my children or my husband. I often eat alone with my children and they eat more or less what I give them. If I am trying to restrict Handful 4 (starch/fruit) I make sure that there is still bread, pasta, rice, or potatoes for them. I also give them extra sauce and they can have two helpings if they want.

I put all the food on the table at the same time, so the children don't realize that I'm eating differently to them. And my husband doesn't say anything either about the fact that there are more vegetables on the table. He just eats what he wants and takes a few more potatoes.

I often lie in wait for new dishes to emerge on the Facebook group and have tried some, but I mostly make the same dishes that I've always made, just a Scandi Sense version with lots more vegetables.

HOW WE TACKLE CHALLENGES

CHRISTA: Before Scandi Sense I ate five times a day, so at first it was hard to settle for three meals. I've got used to it now and I never feel hungry. In the beginning, I also found it difficult to find the balance when I was invited out. It's often mostly Handful 4 that is served up when you're at a birthday or a party— bread, pasta, potatoes, and rice. Today,

CAMILLA AFTER HER WEIGHT LOSS

I've learned how to find a balance by cutting down on these foods during the day, so I have more leeway when I eat out. It works fine.

CAMILLA: I think the biggest challenge is to stick to Scandi Sense when we're on vacation and the weekdays aren't running in their usual rhythm. Then I start eating the wrong food and too much of it and maybe drink more wine than ususal. It takes its toll on my weight and sometimes I come home from vacation with a few extra pounds on my hips.

99

We have supported each other along the way and shared it all, both the joys and the frustrations. Making the journey together has been invaluable.

— CHRISTA AND CAMILLA

But actually, it's okay to allow yourself to have a little more fun when you're on vacation. The important thing is just to find your way back into the old rhythm with your good habits. Luckily, for me it happens by itself as soon as we're home again—and then the pounds fall off again just as quickly.

It can be the same at weekends if you don't quite keep a tight rein on yourself. It's okay to allow yourself a glass of wine or something a little yummy, but it mustn't get out of hand and develop into parties every weekend, because that's the way it all goes wrong. Again, it all comes down to simply using your common sense.

WHAT SCANDI SENSE HAS MEANT FOR US

CHRISTA: I have so much more energy and desire to play with my son. And I've become a much happier person. The clothes that hang in the closet now fit me and I don't have to go to the grocery store or the plus-size stores anymore to find new clothes. It has meant a lot for my self-esteem that I can buy clothes from any store. I have gone down four dress sizes and suddenly everything they have on show fits me.

When I look at old pictures of myself, I can see how big I was. Today, it's hard to understand that I looked like that.

I currently weigh almost 55 lb less today than I did when I fell pregnant.

CAMILLA: I've got a better understanding of how to put food together to feel full. When you come to understand the connection between the different parts of the diet, it's easier to live according to Scandi Sense.

I think a lot about food, but it's in a different way to before. Today I take plenty of time to plan my meals. I make a food plan for one week at a time, and buy in large quantities. It's both practical, as I'm alone with the children a lot of time, and beneficial, because I save a lot of money by planning the shopping. I completely avoid all the impulse buys that I made when I went shopping before Scandi Sense.

For a long time after I had my two children, my weight was around 220 lb. At that time, I always wore leggings and big blouses to hide my body and I didn't want to go to clothes stores, because I knew the clothes I liked wouldn't fit me and that made me sad. It's different today. I've gone down three or four dress sizes and now wear size 8 to 10. It's so nice to be able to go into all kinds of stores and find that the clothes that I could only look at before now fit me. It's worked wonders for both my self-esteem and my energy levels.

Christa's top tips

It's important to fill the meal-boxes so that you stay full. The first two weeks can be difficult if you're changing habits such as indulging in sweet snacks and large helpings. So it's about being determined and sticking to it. Take baby steps—just one meal at a time. Suddenly you get used to it and then it isn't difficult at all.

Once you've got the hang of the principles, you can start trying to save up during the day if you're doing something in the evening.

It's a really good idea to take the journey with someone. It's been invaluable for me to have my sister by my side. At the same time, it has been very motivating for both of us to go to weekly weigh-ins. It has kept us going, so I can only recommend others do that too.

Camilla's top tips

Make sure you religiously follow the rules of Scandi Sense for the first 14 days, and fill your meal-boxes completely. Then you will gradually learn what's best for you and adjust slowly from there. Perhaps you will be satisfied with half of Handful 4 for some of your meals or even just a snack.

I don't think that you have to cut out bread, pasta etc. completely, because when you deny yourself something, it suddenly becomes interesting.

It's a good idea to take before and after pictures of yourself to document your weight loss. I often refer to these and it's a great motivation to see how much has changed. It takes a bit of effort to change your habits at first, so it's largely about focusing on what motivates you.

It's been really nice to have my little sister taking on this project with me. We've always been close so it felt natural to take this journey together. We see each other often and eat together at least once a week, so we've been able to share it all—both the joys and the frustrations. We often take pictures of ourselves and our food and send them to each other. It's both supportive and inspiring.

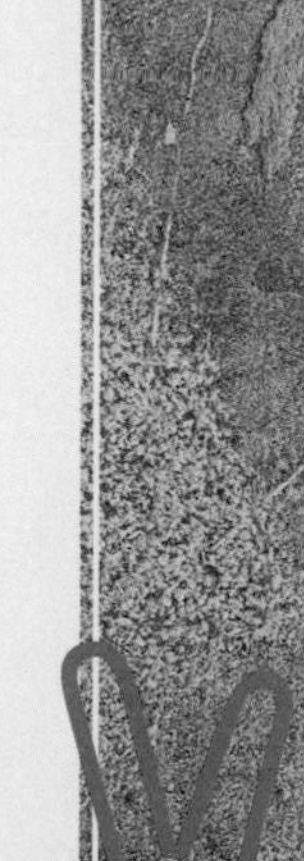

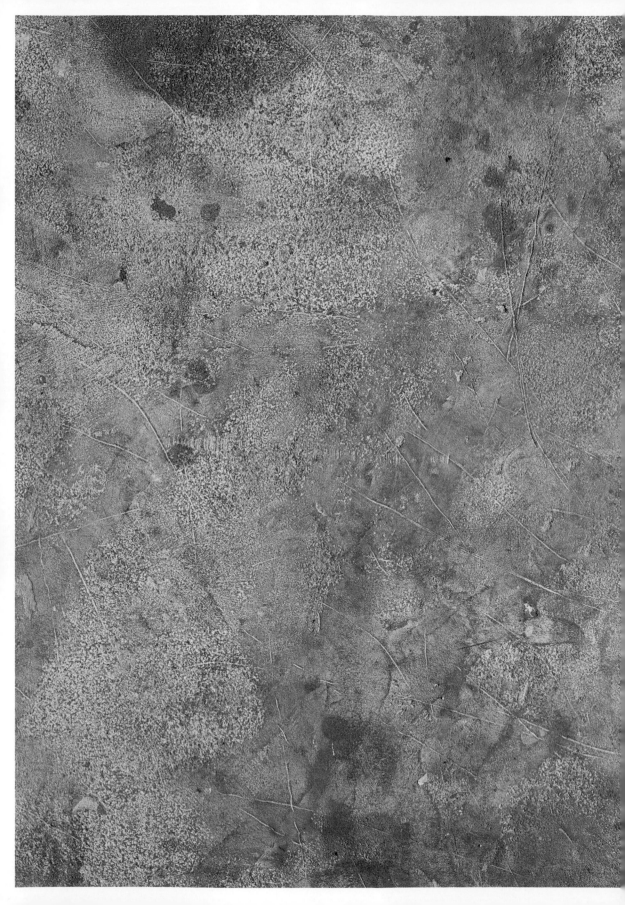

Nine-day diet plan

Nine days with Scandi Sense, meal by meal
Choose the right diet plan for you

You can start on any day you like, and in principle you can choose breakfast, lunch, and supper as you want or need, which you may find helpful on busy days.

If you feel the portion sizes are too large or too small for you, simply adjust the recipes. The idea is that, over time, you will discover how much food you need. You could also choose to have a smaller portion for one of your three daily meals.

If you are a woman, but have a BMI of more than 40, you should probably follow the men's diet plan to ensure that you get enough calories to meet your basic needs. As you lose weight, you will be able to switch to the women's diet plan.

If you are a woman and exercise for more than 10 to 12 hours a week, again you should follow the men's diet plan.

If you are a man and exercise for more than 10 to 12 hours a week, you should increase the amount of protein in the recipes or eat an extra half or whole meal-box, divided out across the day.

- RECIPES FOR WOMEN see page 88.
- WOMEN'S DAILY DIET PLAN see page 146.
- RECIPES FOR MEN see page 156.
- MEN'S DAILY DIET PLAN see page 214.

	DAY 1	DAY 2	DAY 3
Breakfast	· Breakfast plate with soft-cooked egg Page 93 (♀) or 161 (♂)	· Toast with ricotta, ham, and tomato Page 98 (♀) or 166 (♂)	· Green smoothie Page 105 (♀) or 173 (♂)
Optional snack	· Bouillon drink		
Lunch	· Cottage cheese and mango lunchbox Page 94 (♀) or 162 (♂)	· Chicken pasta salad Page 101 (♀) or 169 (♂)	· Shrimp noodle salad Page 106 (♀) or 174 (♂)
Optional snack		· Bouillon drink	
Supper	· Spaghetti and meatballs with zucchini Page 97 (♀) or 165 (♂)	· Falafel pita with pesto dressing Page 102 (♀) or 170 (♂)	· Marinated steak with mushrooms and cream Page 109 (♀) or 177 (♂)
Optional snack			· Bouillon drink

	DAY 4	DAY 5	DAY 6
Breakfast	· Toast with salmon and avocado cream Page 110 (♀) or 178 (♂)	· Oatmeal with stuffed pepper Page 117 (♀) or 185 (♂)	· Pancakes Page 122 (♀) or 190 (♂)
Optional snack	· Bouillon drink	· Bouillon drink	
Lunch	· Buddha bowl Page 113 (♀) or 181 (♂)	· Roast beef wrap Page 118 (♀) or 186 (♂)	· Tuna fishcakes with rye Page 125 (♀) or 193 (♂)
Optional snack			· Bouillon drink
Supper	· Curried chicken and rice soup Page 114 (♀) or 182 (♂)	· Cheesy tortilla tart Page 121 (♀) or 189 (♂)	· Baked sweet potato with chickpeas Page 126 (♀) or 194 (♂)
Optional snack			

	DAY 7	DAY 8	DAY 9
Breakfast	· Breakfast plate with cottage cheese Page 129 (♀) or 197 (♂)	· Ham on toast Page 134 (♀) or 202 (♂)	· Bacon and egg Page 141 (♀) or 209 (♂)
Optional snack			· Bouillon drink
Lunch	· Caesar salad with croutons Page 130 (♀) or 198 (♂)	· Boston lettuce wraps Page 137 (♀) or 205 (♂)	· Spinach, egg, and chicken wrap Page 142 (♀) or 210 (♂)
Optional snack		· Bouillon drink	
Supper	· Baked salmon with lemon dressing Page 133 (♀) or 201 (♂)	· Homemade burger Page 138 (♀) or 206 (♂)	· Stir-fried duck breast Page 145 (♀) or 213 (♂)
Optional snack	· Bouillon drink		

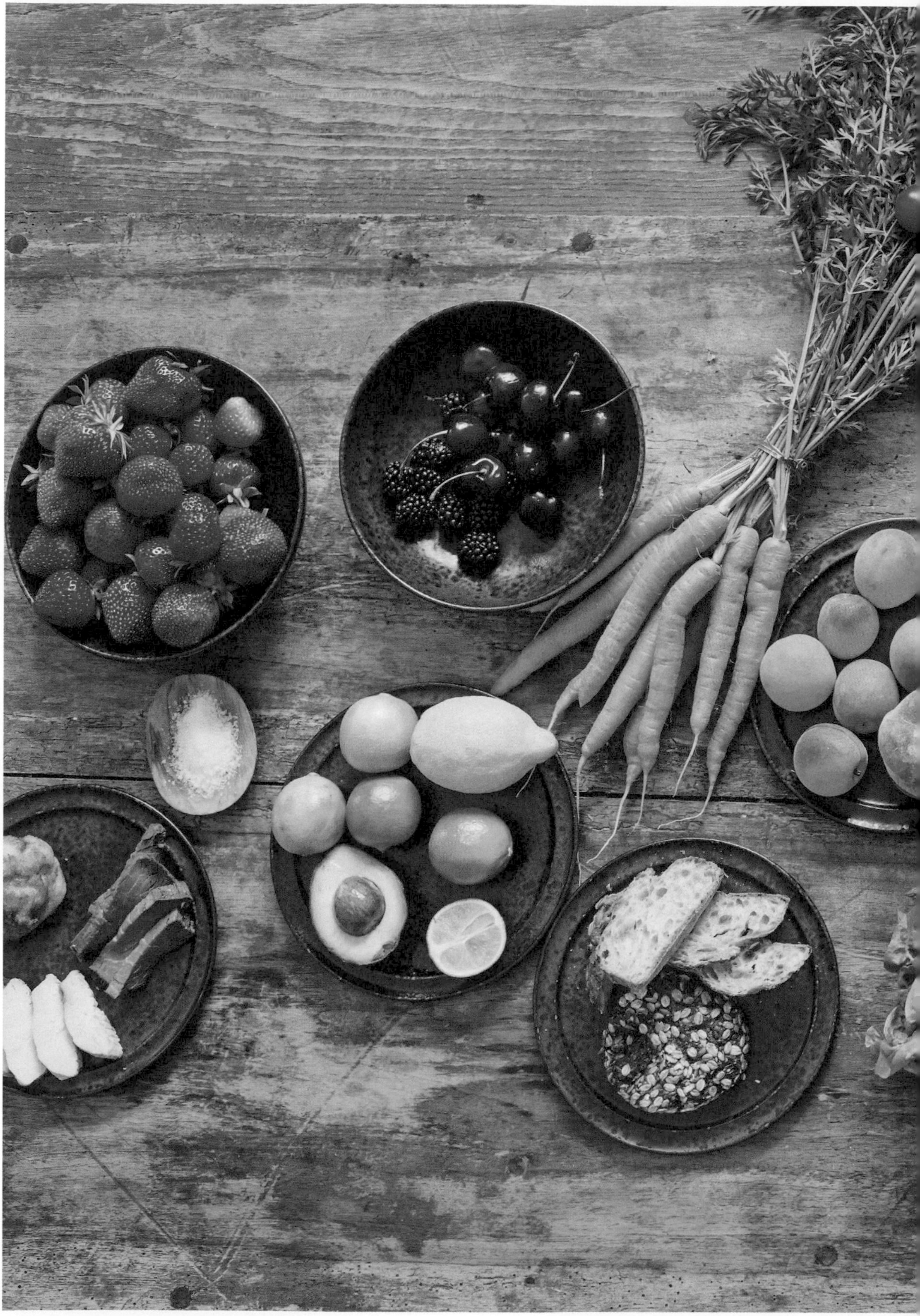

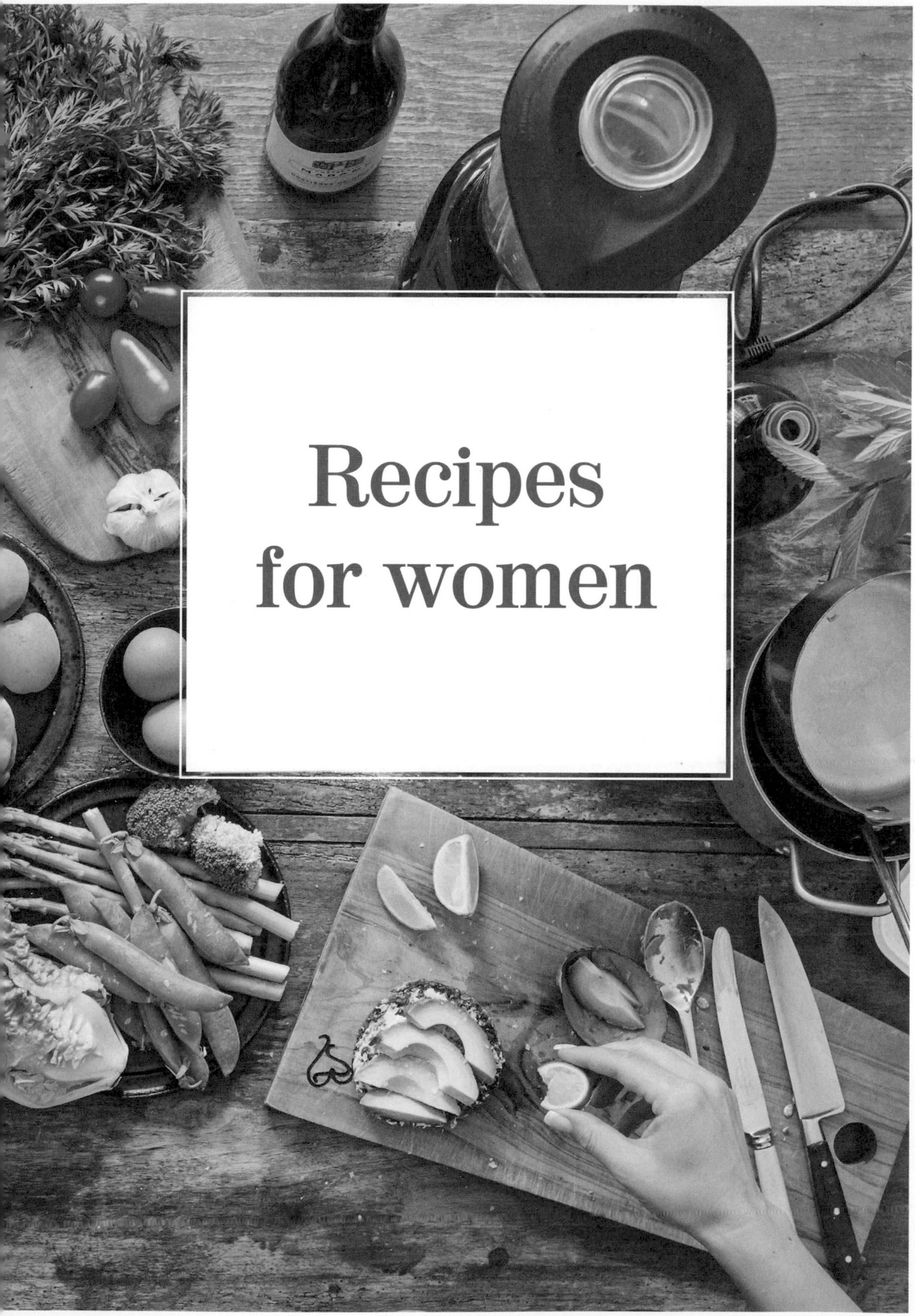

Recipes for women

Recipes

ALL RECIPES SERVE 1 WOMAN

Breakfast

Lunch

Supper

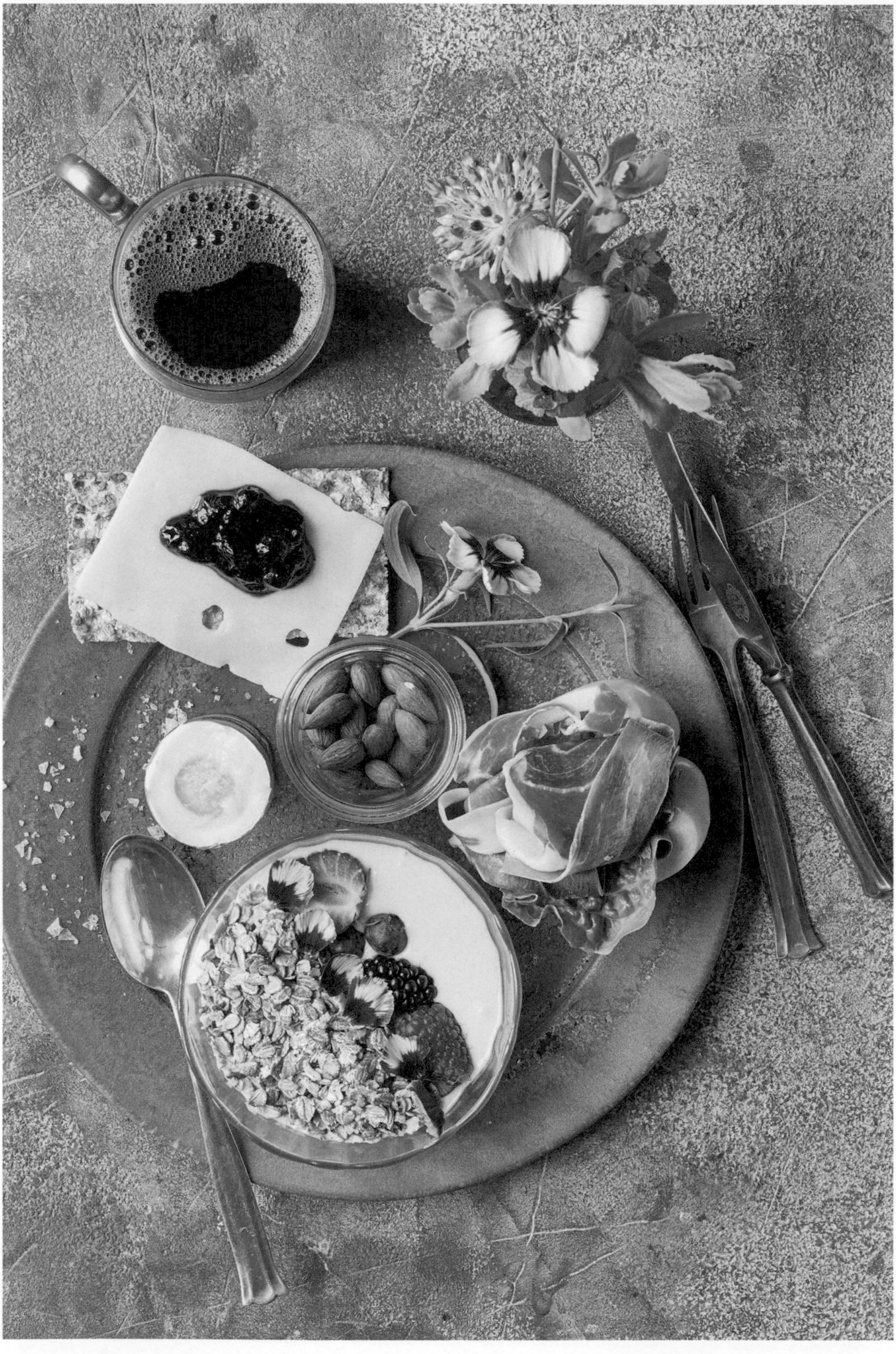

Breakfast plate with soft-cooked egg

PREPARATION TIME: *about 30 minutes*

BASIC MUESLI:

1/3 cup rye flakes
2/3 cup spelt flakes
2/3 cup oats
2 tablespoons honey
Pinch of salt

PLUS:

1 egg
1/2 yellow bell pepper
1 Boston lettuce leaf
2 slices of air-dried ham
1 slice of cheese, min. 18% fat
1 piece of crispbread
1 tablespoon jam or marmalade
Generous 3/4 cup plain yogurt
Scant 1/4 cup Basic Muesli
Scant 1/4 cup berries
Scant 1/4 cup almonds

WHAT YOU SHOULD HAVE ON YOUR PLATE

Half a pepper with lettuce and ham.
A piece of crispbread with cheese and jam
or marmalade. A glass or bowl of yogurt
with Basic Muesli, berries, and almonds.
A soft-cooked egg.

HOW IT IS DIVIDED IN THE SCANDI SENSE MEAL-BOX

HANDFUL 1 (+2): *Pepper, lettuce*

HANDFUL 3: *Egg, ham*

HANDFUL 4: *Muesli, crispbread, berries*

FAT: *Cheese, almonds*

DAIRY PRODUCT: *Yogurt*

FLAVORINGS: *Honey, salt, jam,*
or marmalade

To make the Basic Muesli, toast the rye,
spelt, and oats in a skillet over medium heat.
When they have browned slightly, stir the
honey into the mixture and add the salt. Let
cool and store in an airtight container.

Boil the egg for 5 to 6 minutes. Seed the
pepper and place the lettuce inside, with
the ham on top.

Place the cheese on the crispbread and top
with the jam or marmalade.

Pour the yogurt into a glass or a bowl. Top
with the Basic Muesli and berries. Serve
the almonds on the side.

TIP *The Basic Muesli will keep for 2 to 3
weeks in an airtight container.*

TIP *You can use store-bought muesli instead
of the Basic Muesli, but make sure that the
sugar content does not exceed 13 g sugar
per 100 g of the product.*

TIP *You can use Skyr yogurt or another
cultured milk product instead of plain
yogurt, but make sure that the sugar
content does not exceed 5 g sugar per
100 g of the product.*

If men are eating with you

*Men can have a little more ham, cheese,
muesli, berries, and almonds. See page 161.*

Energy 571 kcal · Protein 32 g · Carbohydrate 47 g · Dietary fiber 5.6 g · Fat 28 g

Cottage cheese and mango lunchbox

PREPARATION TIME: *about 10 minutes*

5¹/₄ oz green beans, trimmed
1 tomato
¹/₂ red onion
¹/₂ mango
15 almonds
¹/₂ cup peas
1 tablespoon green pesto
²/₃ cup cottage cheese, max. 4.5% fat
Salt and pepper, to taste
1 Boston lettuce leaf (optional)
¹/₄ oz semisweet chocolate, min. 70% cocoa

Boil the green beans for 2 to 3 minutes. Drain and set aside.

Halve the cooked green beans. Cut the tomato into small pieces and finely chop the red onion. Remove the mango from its skin and cut the flesh into chunks. Coarsely chop the almonds.

Combine all of the prepared ingredients in a suitable container, along with the peas.

Mix the pesto and cottage cheese together and season with salt and pepper. Add this dressing on top of your lunchbox, using a lettuce leaf to keep it separate, if desired.

Serve with the chocolate on the side.

WHAT YOU SHOULD HAVE ON YOUR PLATE

The contents of one lunchbox and some semisweet chocolate.

HOW IT IS DIVIDED IN THE SCANDI SENSE MEAL-BOX

HANDFUL 1 (+2): *Green beans, tomato, red onion, peas*

HANDFUL 3: *Cottage cheese*

HANDFUL 4: *Mango*

FAT: *Pesto, almonds, semisweet chocolate*

FLAVORINGS: *Salt, pepper*

TIP *If you are vegan, you can the substitute the cottage cheese with beans.*

TIP *You can prepare this meal the day before and safely store it overnight in the refrigerator.*

TIP *You may prefer to use fresh vegetables but frozen vegetables are fine.*

TIP *Instead of the almonds, you can use other nuts, grains, or seeds.*

If men are eating with you

Men can have more almonds, cottage cheese, and semisweet chocolate. See page 162.

Energy 531 kcal · Protein 30 g · Carbohydrate 40 g · Dietary fiber 13.1 g · Fat 26 g

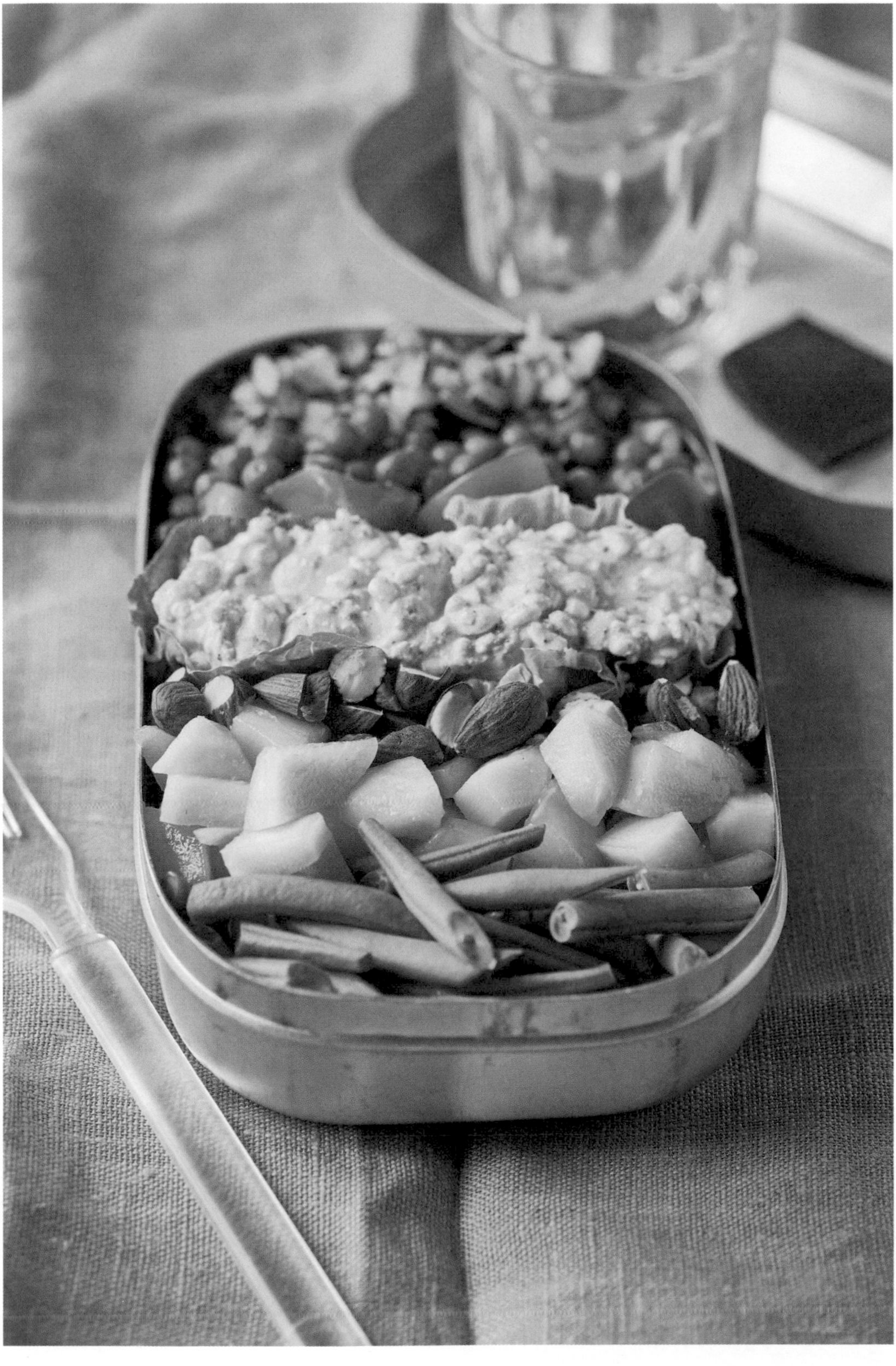

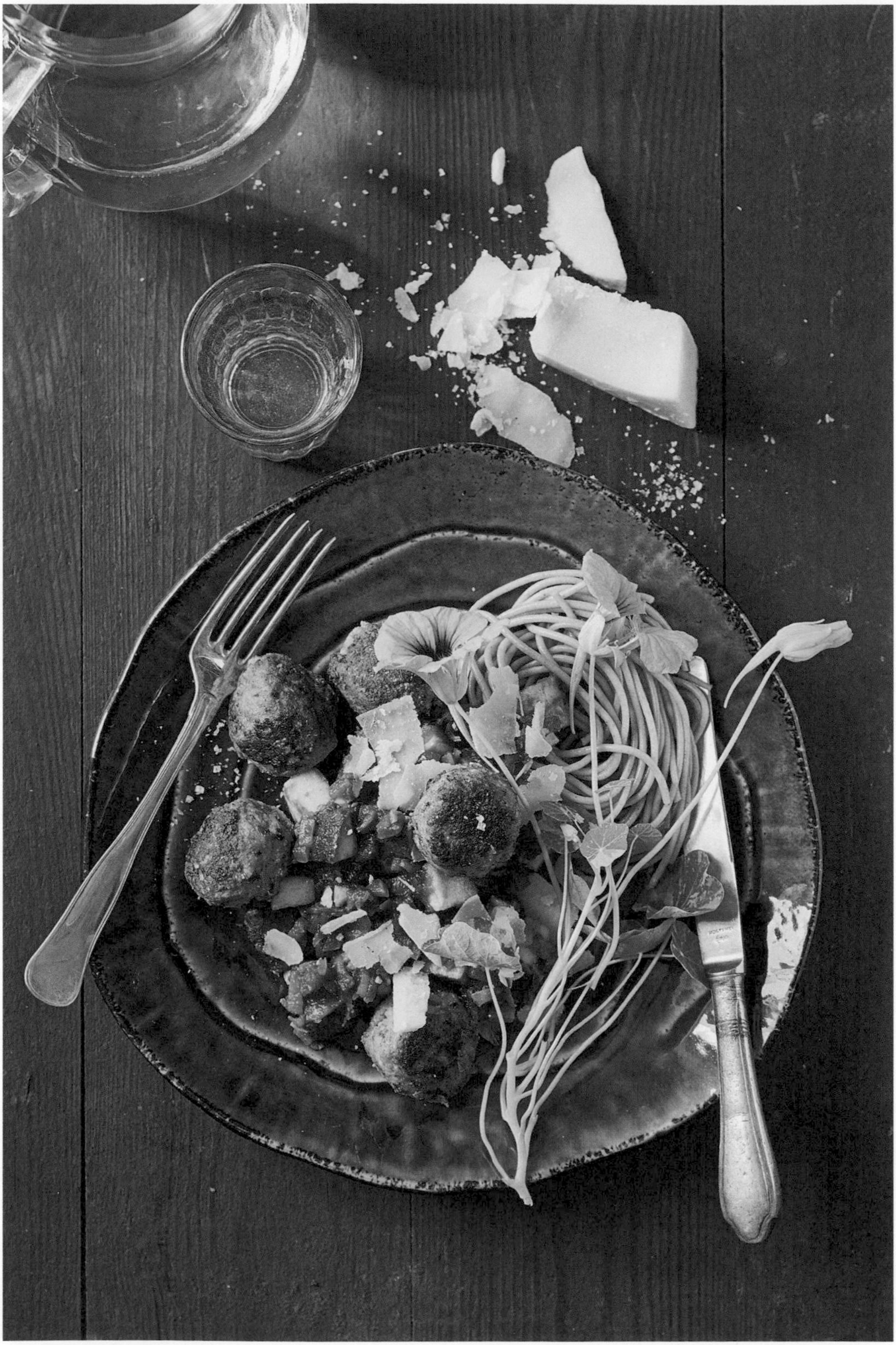

Spaghetti and meatballs with zucchini

PREPARATION TIME: *about 40 minutes*

TOMATO SAUCE:

2 garlic cloves
¹/₂ onion
¹/₄ fresh chile (optional)
1 teaspoon olive oil
¹/₂ teaspoon paprika
¹/₂ can chopped tomatoes
Salt and pepper, to taste

MEATBALLS:

5¹/₂ oz ground pork and veal, max. 7% fat
1 tablespoon bread crumbs
1 small egg
¹/₂ handful parsley, chopped
1 teaspoon dried oregano
¹/₂ teaspoon salt
1 teaspoon olive oil, for frying

TO GO WITH IT:

1 oz spaghetti, uncooked
¹/₂ zucchini
³/₄ oz Parmesan cheese, shaved
Nasturtium flowers or parsley, to garnish

Finely chop the garlic, onion, and chile, if using. Heat the olive oil in a skillet and cook them for a couple of minutes. Add the paprika and fry for another minute before adding the tomatoes. Season with salt and pepper. Let this mixture simmer while you make the meatballs.

Mix all the meatball ingredients together and form small balls the size of a walnut. Fry the meatballs in olive oil for 10 minutes, shaking the pan now and then so that they brown evenly.

Cook the spaghetti, following the package directions.

Cut the zucchini into cubes, or shred it, if you'd rather, and add to the tomato sauce 3 minutes before you are ready to serve.

Arrange everything on a dish—first the spaghetti, then the tomato sauce, and finally the meatballs. Sprinkle the Parmesan on top and add your chosen garnish.

WHAT YOU SHOULD HAVE ON YOUR PLATE

Spaghetti, tomato sauce with zucchini, and meatballs, Parmesan cheese.

HOW IT IS DIVIDED IN THE SCANDI SENSE MEAL-BOX

HANDFUL 1 (+ 2): *Onion, tomato, zucchini*

HANDFUL 3: *Pork and veal, egg*

HANDFUL 4: *Bread crumbs, spaghetti*

FAT: *Olive oil, Parmesan*

FLAVORINGS: *Garlic, chile, paprika, salt, pepper, oregano, nasturtium flowers, parsley*

TIP *You can use only pork or only veal instead of mixed pork and veal. Or combine meat as you like.*

TIP *You can substitute extra zucchini for the spaghetti if you want to avoid pasta.*

If men are eating with you

Men may have a little more ground meat, spaghetti, and Parmesan. See page 165.

Energy 663 kcal · Protein 55 g · Carbohydrate 43 g · Dietary fiber 10.8 g · Fat 29 g

Toast with ricotta, ham, and tomato

PREPARATION TIME: *about 15 minutes*

RICOTTA MIXTURE:

¹/₈ cup pine nuts
¹/₄ cup ricotta cheese
Salt and pepper, to taste

TO GO WITH IT:

1 egg
1 slice of bread, preferably whole-wheat
1 tomato
2 slices of ham
Chives and edible flowers, to garnish
Coffee or tea
3¹/₂ tablespoons milk, if required

Toast the pine nuts in a dry pan over medium heat. When they are golden brown, chop them finely and let cool before mixing them into the ricotta. Season with salt and pepper.

Boil the egg for 5 to 6 minutes.

Toast the slice of bread and cut it in half. Cut the tomato into slices.

Spread the ricotta mixture onto the bread, then add a slice of ham to each and a couple of slices of tomato. Season with salt and pepper and garnish with chives.

You can drink a cup of tea or coffee with this meal, and add milk, if desired.

WHAT YOU SHOULD HAVE ON YOUR PLATE

Two half slices of bread with topping, a soft-cooked egg, and a cup of tea or coffee.

HOW IT IS DIVIDED IN THE SCANDI SENSE MEAL-BOX

HANDFUL 1 (+ 2): *Tomato*

HANDFUL 3: *Ricotta, egg, ham*

HANDFUL 4: *Bread*

FAT: *Pine nuts*

DAIRY PRODUCT: *Milk, if used*

FLAVORINGS: *Salt, pepper, chives,*
edible flowers

TIP *Additionally, there is room for you to eat 10 to 15 almonds, a piece of semisweet chocolate, or 8 to 10 olives with this meal.*

If men are eating with you

Men can have an extra egg and a few more pine nuts, more ricotta, bread, and ham. See page 166.

Energy 456 kcal · Protein 24 g · Carbohydrate 30 g · Dietary fiber 5.7 g · Fat 26 g

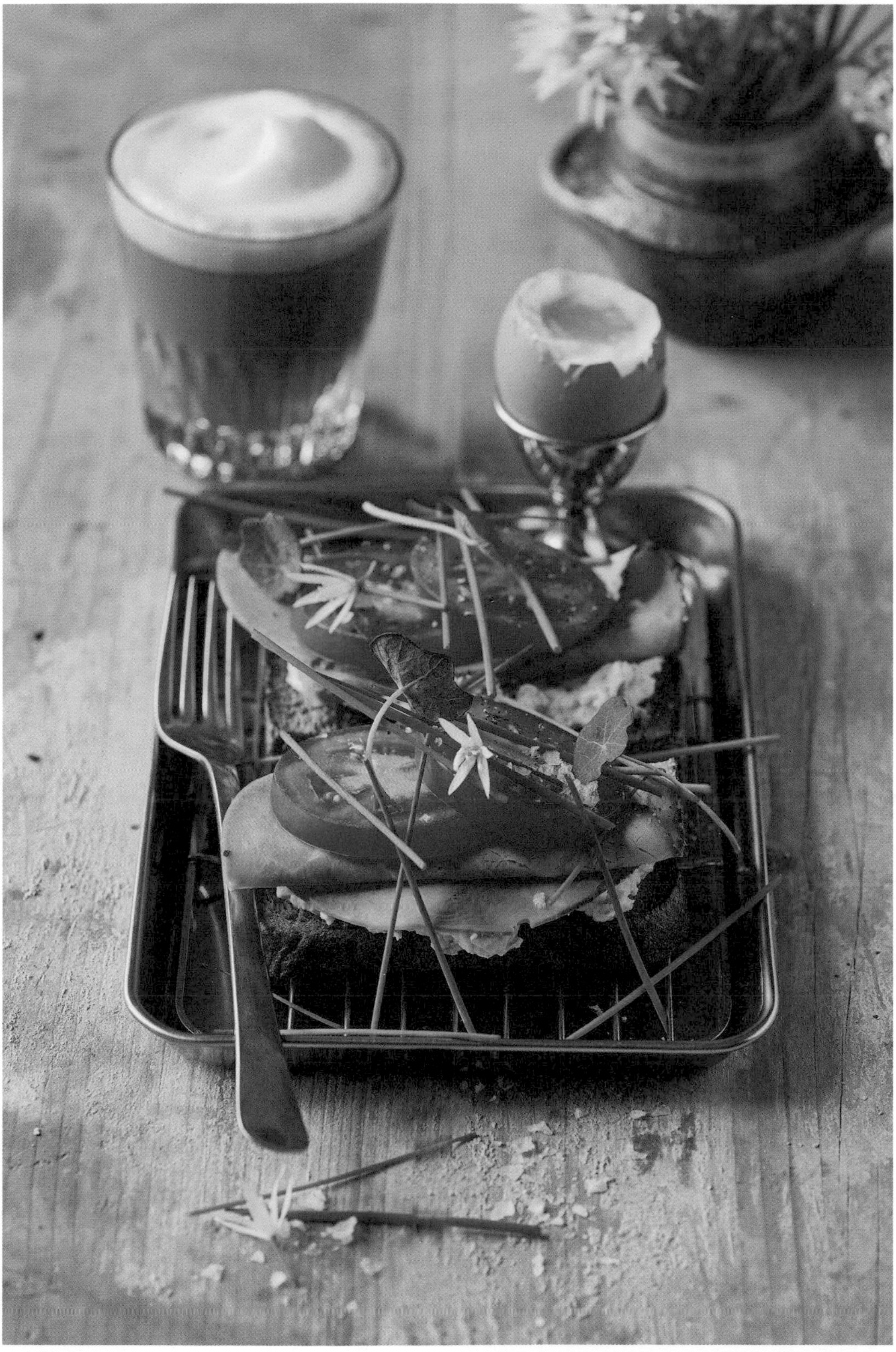

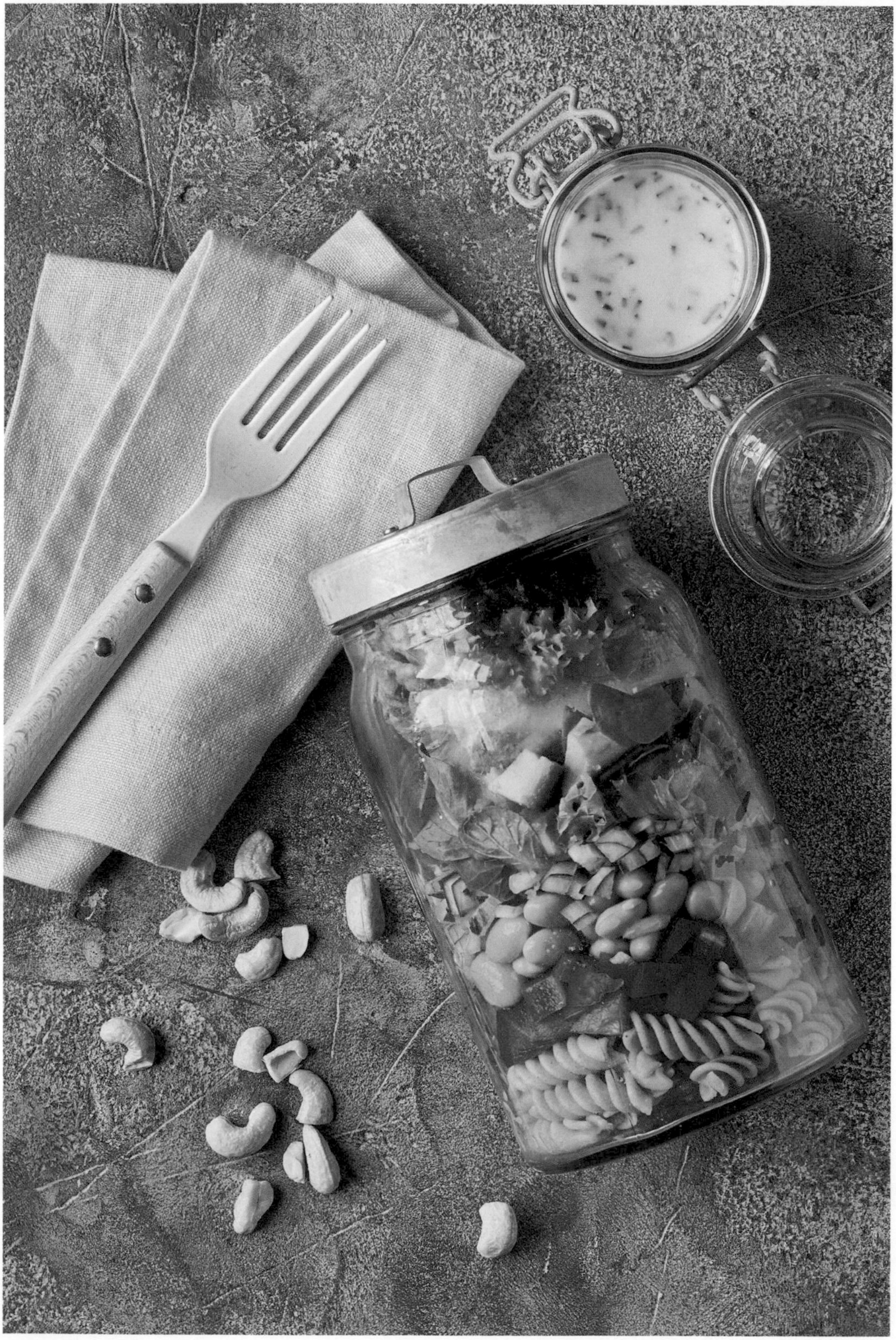

Chicken pasta salad

PREPARATION TIME: *about 10 minutes*
PLEASE NOTE: *The recipe uses cooked pasta.*

¹/₂ cup frozen edamame beans
2 tablespoons lemon juice
¹/₂ small red onion
¹/₂ red bell pepper
¹/₂ avocado
1 tablespoon cashews
1 cup mixed salad greens
3 oz cooked chicken, diced or in strips
2³/₄ oz cooked pasta, preferably whole-wheat

YOGURT DRESSING:

1 garlic clove
1 tablespoon chopped chives
3¹/₂ tablespoons plain yogurt
¹/₂ teaspoon salt
Sprinkling of pepper
1 tablespoon lemon juice

Place the frozen edamame beans in a bowl and pour over boiling water. Leave for a minute, then drain and toss them in a tablespoon of the lemon juice.

Finely dice the onion and pepper.

Peel and cube the avocado and toss in the remaining lemon juice.

Coarsely chop the cashews.

Finely chop the garlic and mix with the rest of the ingredients for the yogurt dressing.

Arrange all the items, including the chicken and pasta, with lettuce, either in a jar or on a plate. Serve the dressing on the side.

WHAT YOU SHOULD HAVE ON YOUR PLATE

A pasta salad with dressing.

HOW IT IS DIVIDED IN THE SCANDI SENSE MEAL-BOX

HANDFUL 1 (+2): *Red onion, pepper, lettuce*

HANDFUL 3: *Edamame beans, chicken*

HANDFUL 4: *Pasta*

FAT: *Avocado, cashews*

DAIRY DRESSING: *Yogurt*

FLAVORINGS: *Lemon juice, garlic, chives, salt, pepper*

TIP *You can choose other sources of protein instead of the chicken and edamame beans—you can choose freely between other meats, fish, shellfish, low-fat cheese, or beans. You can easily use up leftovers from supper the day before in this way.*

TIP *Instead of the pasta you can substitute rice, corn, bulgur wheat, couscous, wheat berries, even a piece of baguette—any other carbohydrate item.*

If men are eating with you

Men can have more edamame beans, cashews, chicken, and pasta. See page 169.

Energy 579 kcal · Protein 36 g · Carbohydrate 36 g · Dietary fiber 10 g · Fat 24 g

Falafel pita with pesto dressing

PREPARATION TIME INCLUDING BAKING: *about 45 minutes*
PLEASE NOTE: *It is a good idea to let the chickpea dough rest in the refrigerator for 2 hours before you form into balls. However, you can make them straightaway.*

FALAFELS:

³/₄ cup canned chickpeas (drained)
1 tablespoon lemon juice
¹/₂ onion
1 garlic clove
2 tablespoons parsley
¹/₂ teaspoon ground coriander
¹/₂ teaspoon salt
¹/₂ teaspoon cayenne pepper
¹/₂ teaspoon ground cumin
1 small egg
1 to 2 tablespoons all-purpose flour
1 tablespoon olive oil
1 tablespoon bread crumbs

SALAD:

¹/₂ cup cherry tomatoes
¹/₃ cup peas
1 cup corn salad or other salad greens
Pea shoots (optional)

DRESSING:

2 large tablespoons plain yogurt or
   other low-fat dairy product
1 teaspoon red or green pesto

TO GO WITH IT:

¹/₂ pita bread, preferably whole-wheat
Lemon wedges

Toss the chickpeas in the lemon juice. Coarsely chop the onion, garlic, and parsley. Blend in a food processor with the drained chickpeas. Add the coriander, salt, cayenne pepper, cumin, and egg and blend to a coarse consistency.

Add just enough flour, a tablespoon at a time, so the dough is firm enough to roll into walnut-size balls.

Place the balls on a baking sheet lined with wax paper. Brush them with olive oil, sprinkle with bread crumbs, and turn carefully. Press down lightly on them before brushing with more olive oil and sprinkling with more bread crumbs. Bake in the middle of an oven preheated to 400°F for 30 minutes, turning halfway through.

Arrange the salad, falafel, and dressing on top of the pita. Garnish with lemon wedges.

WHAT YOU SHOULD HAVE ON YOUR PLATE

Two handfuls of salad, one handful of falafel, half a pita bread, and 2 to 3 tablespoons of dressing.

HOW IT IS DIVIDED IN THE SCANDI SENSE MEAL-BOX

HANDFUL 1 (+2): *Onion, tomato, peas, salad, pea shoots*

HANDFUL 3: *Chickpeas, egg*

HANDFUL 4: *Flour, bread crumbs, pita bread*

FAT: *Olive oil, pesto*

DAIRY DRESSING: *Yogurt*

FLAVORINGS: *Lemon juice, garlic, parsley, coriander, salt, cayenne pepper, cumin*

If men are eating with you
Men can have slightly more chickpeas and pita bread. See page 170.

Energy 620 kcal · Protein 25 g · Carbohydrate 64 g · Dietary fiber 15 g · Fat 26 g

TIPS

Substitute a tortilla wrap or flatbread for the pita bread. Mix the falafel dough with a hand blender instead of in a food processor. There's nothing wrong with buying ready-made falafel every once in a while, when you're in a hurry.

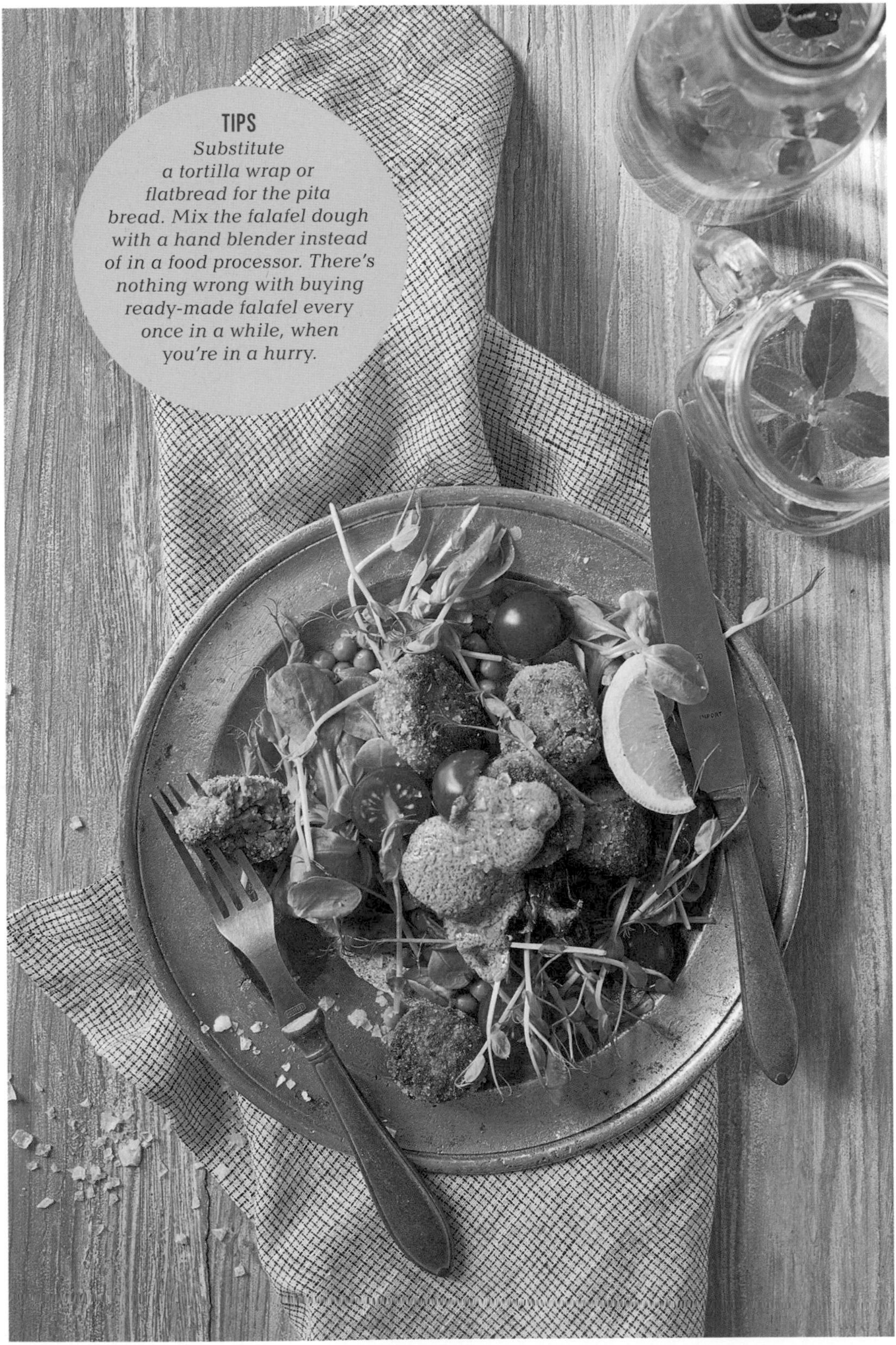

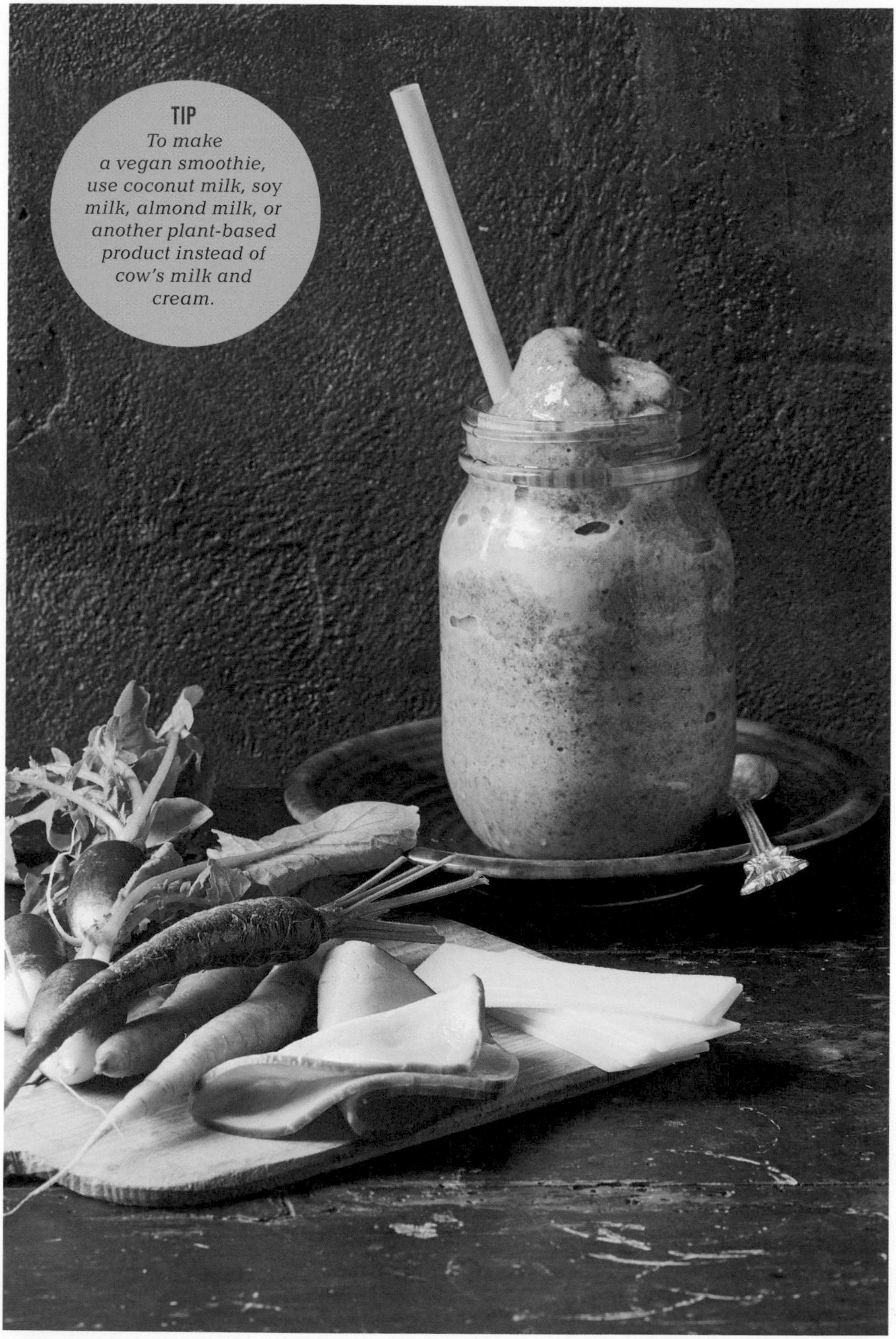

TIP
To make a vegan smoothie, use coconut milk, soy milk, almond milk, or another plant-based product instead of cow's milk and cream.

Green smoothie

PREPARATION TIME: *about 10 minutes*

3³/₄ *tablespoons frozen chopped spinach*
1¹/₂ *cups strawberries, frozen*
Generous ³/₄ cup skim milk
¹/₄ *cup whipping cream (38% fat)*
¹/₂ *teaspoon vanilla extract*
1 *teaspoon liquid sweetener*
1¹/₂ *oz cheese, max. 17% fat*
2 *slices of smoked saddle of pork*
2 *to 3 small carrots*
2 *to 3 radishes*

Place the spinach, strawberries, skim milk, cream, vanilla extract, and sweetener in a sturdy blender. Blend everything to a thick consistency. It may be necessary to stop the blender a few times, stir the ingredients and blend again.

Cut the cheese into sticks or small slices. Serve the cheese, the smoked pork, and the carrots alongside the smoothie.

WHAT YOU SHOULD HAVE ON YOUR PLATE

A smoothie, half a handful of cheese, radishes, sliced meat, and carrots.

HOW IT IS DIVIDED IN THE SCANDI SENSE MEAL-BOX

HANDFUL 1 (+2): *Spinach, carrots, radishes*

HANDFUL 3: *Cheese, smoked pork*

HANDFUL 4: *Strawberries*

FAT: *Cream*

DAIRY PRODUCT: *Skim milk*

FLAVORINGS: *Vanilla extract, sweetener*

TIP *Add a little more milk if you want a more liquid smoothie.*

TIP *Substitute an egg for the cheese, if desired.*

If men are eating with you

Men can have a little more cream, cheese, smoked pork, and radishes. See page 173.

Energy 506 kcal · Protein 28 g · Carbohydrate 28 g · Dietary fiber 5.8 g · Fat 31 g

Shrimp noodle salad

PREPARATION TIME: *about 15 minutes*

DRESSING:

1 tablespoon soy sauce
1 tablespoon peanut butter
2 teaspoons honey
Pinch of dried red pepper flakes
1 tablespoon lime juice

SALAD:

1^1/$_2$ oz glass noodles
1^3/$_4$ oz broccoli
1 small carrot
^{1}/$_2$ cup bean sprouts
4^1/$_2$ oz shrimp
1 tablespoon chopped cilantro
^{1}/$_8$ cup toasted cashews

PLUS:

Cilantro, to garnish

Combine the soy sauce, peanut butter, honey, red pepper flakes, and lime juice with a whisk to make the dressing.

Cover the glass noodles with boiling water and let them stand for 10 minutes. Drain and rinse the noodles in hot water.

Divide the broccoli into small florets and cut the carrot into matchsticks.

Combine the broccoli, carrot, and bean sprouts in a bowl. Toss the vegetables in the dressing.

Add the shrimp and chopped cilantro.

Arrange the vegetables on top of the glass noodles, and sprinkle with the cashews, coarsely chopped. Garnish with a sprig of cilantro.

WHAT YOU SHOULD HAVE ON YOUR PLATE

Two or three handfuls of noodle salad with shrimp, one handful of glass noodles.

HOW IT IS DIVIDED IN THE SCANDI SENSE MEAL-BOX

HANDFUL 1 (+ 2): *Broccoli, carrot, bean sprouts*

HANDFUL 3: *Shrimp*

HANDFUL 4: *Glass noodles*

FAT: *Peanut butter, cashews*

FLAVORINGS: *Soy sauce, honey, red pepper flakes, lime juice, cilantro*

If men are eating with you

Men can have slightly more glass noodles, shrimp, and cashews. See page 174.

Energy 524 kcal · Protein 32 g · Carbohydrate 61 g · Dietary fiber 5.4 g · Fat 16 g

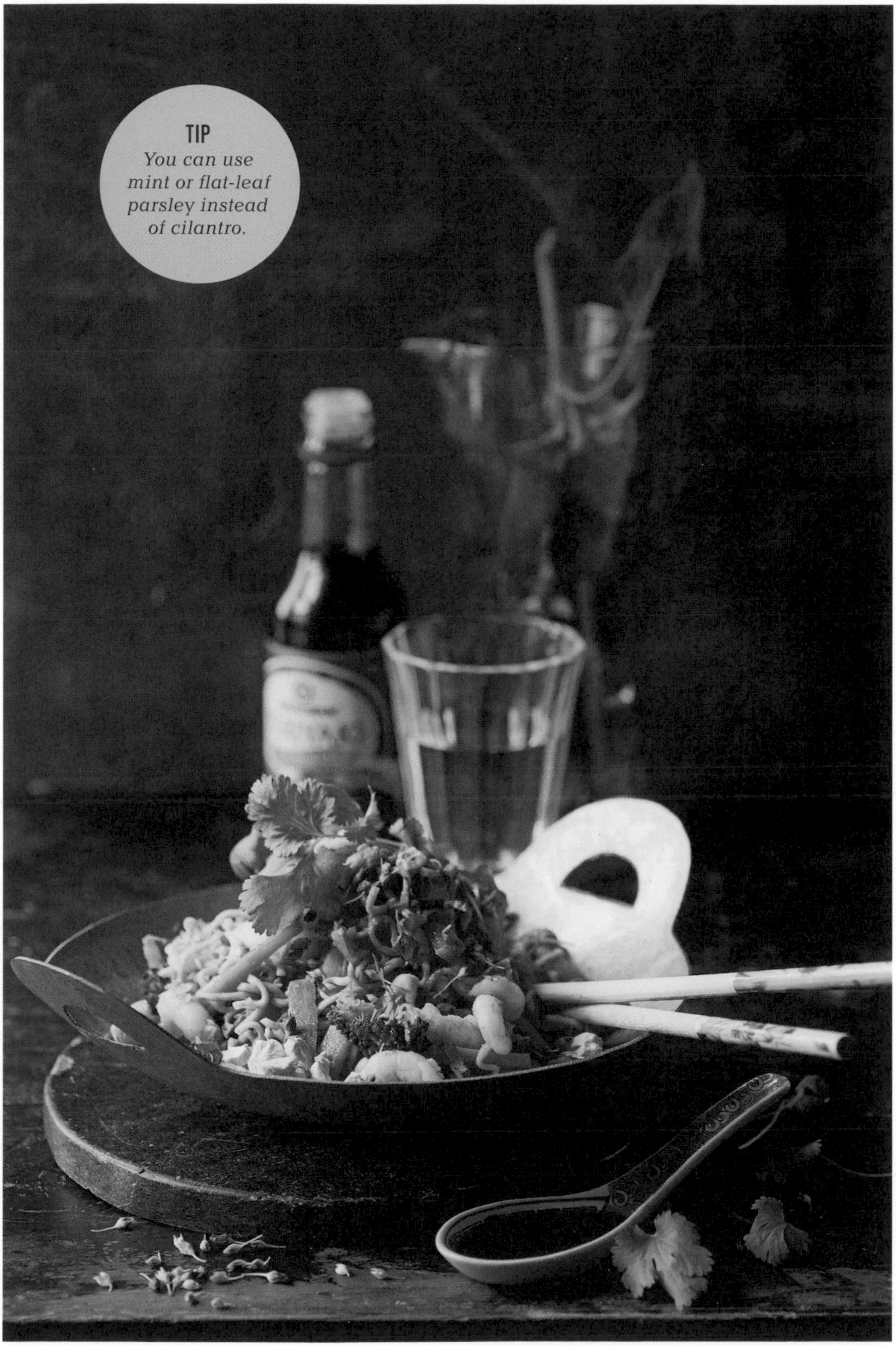
TIP
You can use mint or flat-leaf parsley instead of cilantro.

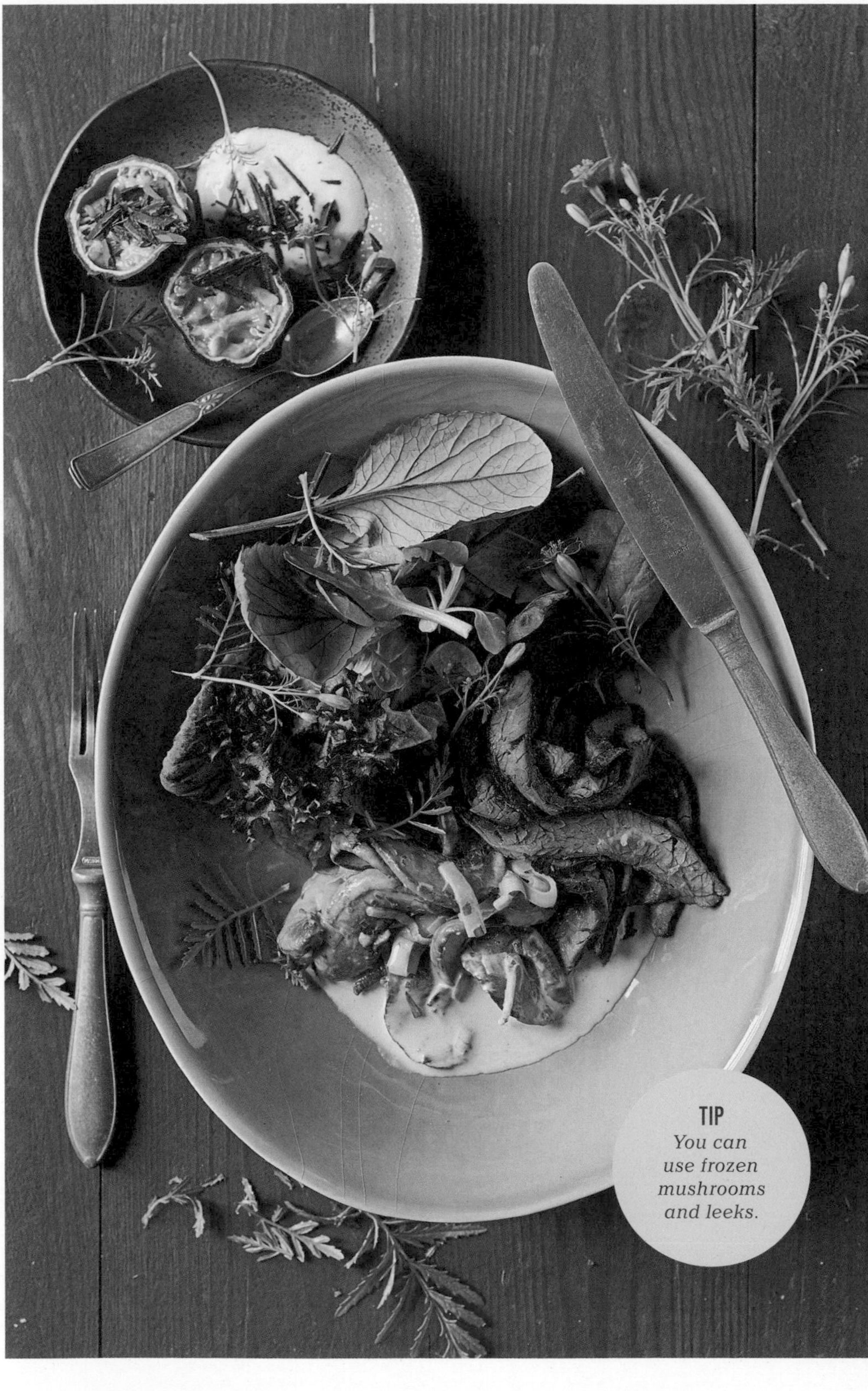

TIP
You can use frozen mushrooms and leeks.

Marinated steak with mushrooms and cream

PREPARATION TIME: *about 25 minutes*

PLEASE NOTE: *Marinate the steak for a couple of hours in the refrigerator, or overnight if possible.*

MARINADE AND MEAT:

1 tablespoon soft brown sugar
2 tablespoons soy sauce
1/2 tablespoon dried red pepper
   flakes or paprika
Sprinkling of pepper
1 tablespoon olive oil
1 skirt steak (about 5 oz)

MUSHROOM DISH:

2 portobello mushrooms
1/2 leek
1 teaspoon olive oil
1/4 cup whipping cream (38% fat)
1/2 vegetable bouillon cube dissolved
   in 7 tablespoons boiling water
1/2 tablespoon dried tarragon
Salt and pepper, to taste

TO GO WITH IT:

1 2/3 cups mixed salad greens
Fresh tarragon, to garnish

DESSERT:

1 passion fruit
1 tablespoon crème fraîche, max. 9% fat
A drop of vanilla extract
2 drops of liquid sweetener (optional)
1/8 oz semisweet chocolate, min. 70% cocoa

Mix together the marinade ingredients. Place the steak and marinade in a sandwich bag, close the bag tightly, and marinate in the refrigerator for at least 2 hours.

Slice the mushrooms and leek. Fry the mushrooms in the olive oil for 10 minutes before adding the leek. Add the cream and stock and simmer for 10 to 15 minutes. Season with tarragon, salt, and pepper.

Fry the steak for 6 to 8 minutes on each side. Let rest until the mushroom mix is ready. Arrange slices of steak with the mushroom mix and salad.

Cut the passion fruit in half. Stir the vanilla into the crème fraîche and add sweetener, if using. Serve with a spoonful of vanilla dressing and grate the chocolate on top.

WHAT YOU SHOULD HAVE ON YOUR PLATE

One handful of salad, one handful of the mushroom mix, and one handful of steak. One passion fruit with vanilla cream.

HOW IT IS DIVIDED IN THE SCANDI SENSE MEAL-BOX

HANDFUL 1 (+ 2): *Mushroom, leek, salad*

HANDFUL 3: *Skirt steak*

HANDFUL 4: *Passion fruit*

FAT: *Olive oil, cream, semisweet chocolate*

DAIRY DRESSING: *Crème fraîche*

FLAVORINGS: *Sugar, soy sauce, red pepper flakes, pepper, bouillon, tarragon, salt, vanilla, sweetener, if using*

If men are eating with you
Men can have slightly more steak and cream. See page 177.

Energy 566 kcal · Protein 42 g · Carbohydrate 25 g · Dietary fiber 6.7 g · Fat 32 g

Toast with salmon and avocado cream

PREPARATION TIME: *about 15 minutes*

AVOCADO CREAM:

¹/₂ avocado
1 tablespoon crème fraîche, min. 18% fat
1 teaspoon lemon juice
Salt and pepper, to taste

DRESSING:

¹/₄ chile
1 tablespoon mint leaves
1 tomato
1 tablespoon lemon juice
1 teaspoon white wine vinegar
Salt, to taste

PLUS:

1 slice of bread, preferably whole-wheat
2¹/₄ oz cucumber
3 oz smoked salmon
Pepper, to taste
¹/₂ handful watercress, pea shoots,
*   or daisies, to garnish*

Mash the avocado with the crème fraîche, lemon juice, salt, and pepper.

Seed the chile. Finely chop the chile and mint. Cut the tomato into small cubes. Toss everything in the lemon juice and white wine vinegar. Season with salt.

Toast the bread. Slice the cucumber into long strips.

Spread the avocado cream onto the toast, and place the cucumber and salmon on top. Top with dressing, your chosen garnish, and a grinding of pepper.

WHAT YOU SHOULD HAVE ON YOUR PLATE

Bread, avocado cream, cucumber, and salmon with dressing.

HOW IT IS DIVIDED IN THE SCANDI SENSE MEAL-BOX

HANDFUL 1 (+ 2): *Tomato, cucumber*

HANDFUL 3: *Smoked salmon*

HANDFUL 4: *Bread*

FAT: *Avocado, crème fraîche*

FLAVORINGS: *Lemon juice, salt, pepper,*
*   mint, chile, white wine vinegar,*
*   watercress, pea shoots, or daisies*

TIP *If you are in a hurry, just slice the avocado. Arrange it with the salmon and cucumber on top, with crème fraîche instead of the dressing.*

If men are eating with you

Men may have a little more toast and salmon. See page 178.

Energy 476 kcal · Protein 22 g · Carbohydrate 34 g · Dietary fiber 7.7 g · Fat 25 g

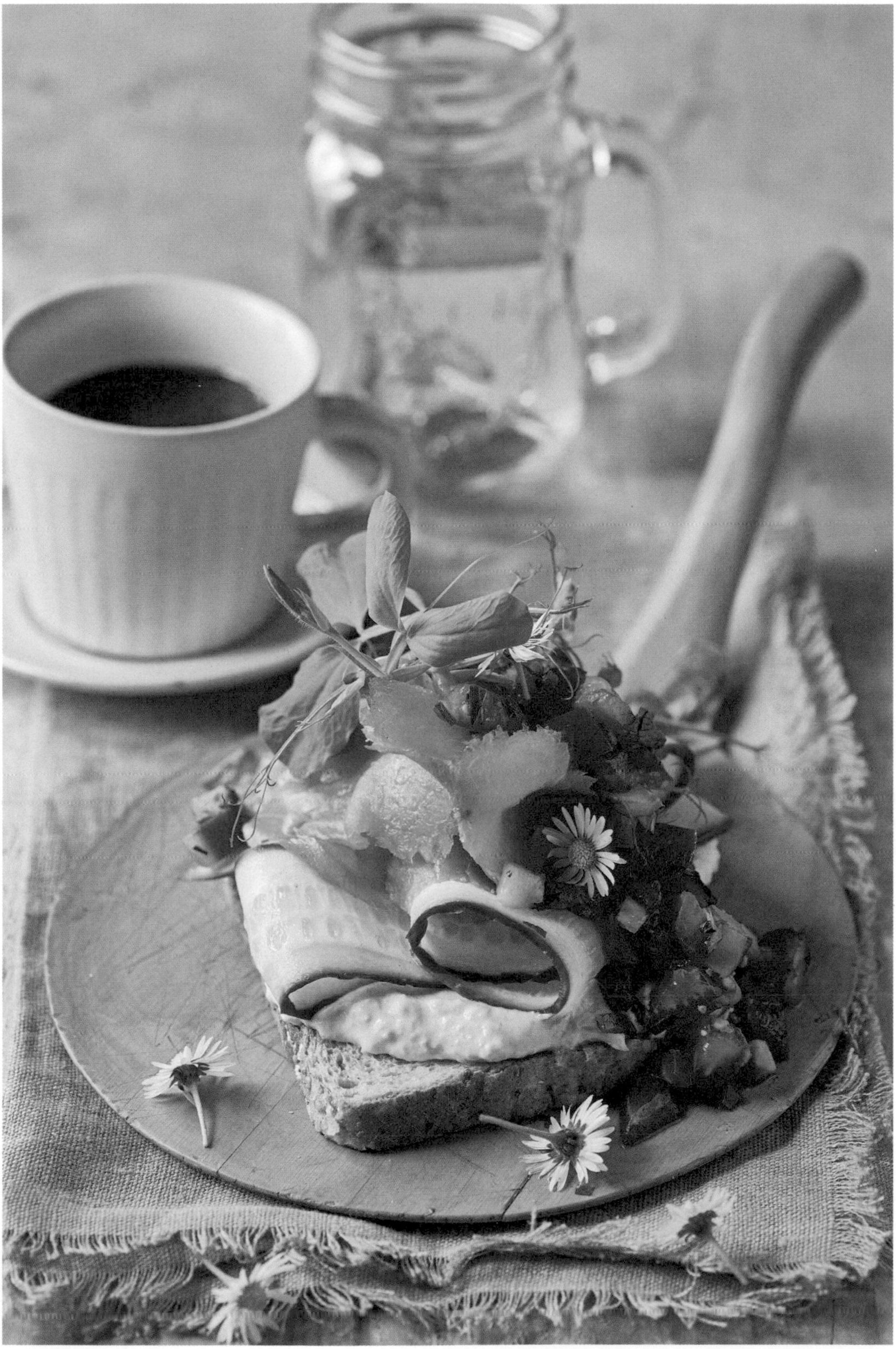

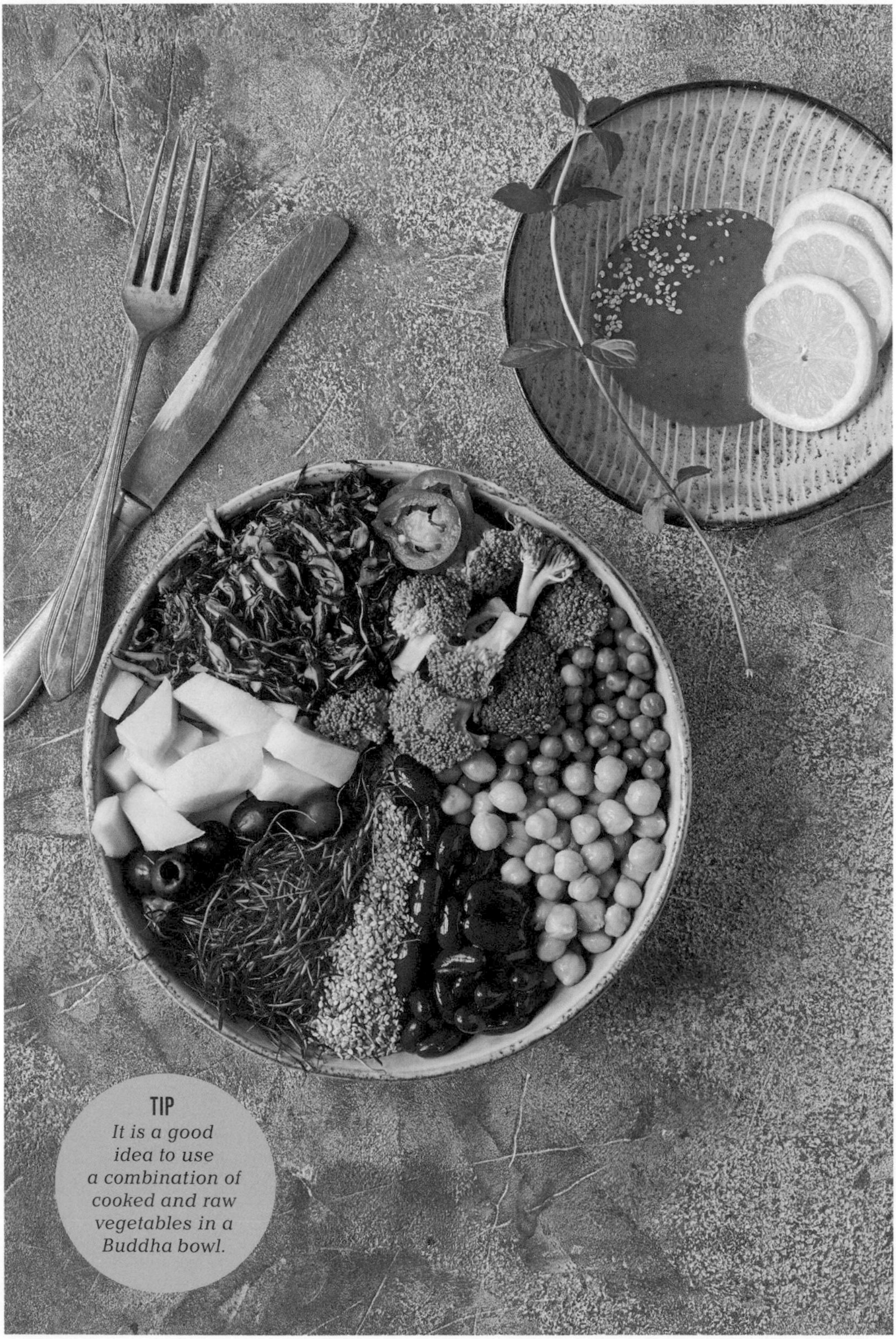

TIP

It is a good idea to use a combination of cooked and raw vegetables in a Buddha bowl.

Buddha bowl

PREPARATION TIME: *about 15 minutes*

DRESSING:

¹/₂ tablespoon tahini
¹/₂ tablespoon olive oil
¹/₂ garlic clove, crushed
1 tablespoon lemon juice
Pinch of dried red pepper flakes
Pinch of ground cumin

BUDDHA BOWL:

1³/₄ oz broccoli
¹/₂ mango
1³/₄ oz red cabbage
¹/₂ cup canned kidney beans (drained)
¹/₂ cup canned chickpeas (drained)
¹/₂ cup peas
¹/₃ cup black olives
¹/₃ cup beet sprouts
¹/₄ oz jalapeños
¹/₂ lemon
1 tablespoon sesame seeds

Whisk the tahini, olive oil, garlic, lemon
juice, red pepper flakes, and cumin together
to make the dressing.

Cut the broccoli and mango into bite-size
pieces. Finely chop the red cabbage.

Arrange all of the ingredients side by side
in a round bowl.

Serve with the dressing on the side.

WHAT YOU SHOULD HAVE ON YOUR PLATE

Three to four handfuls of Buddha bowl
salad with three tablespoons of dressing.

HOW IT IS DIVIDED IN
THE SCANDI SENSE MEAL-BOX

HANDFUL 1 (+2): *Broccoli, red cabbage, peas*

HANDFUL 3: *Kidney beans, chickpeas*

HANDFUL 4: *Mango*

FAT: *Tahini, olive oil, olives, sesame seeds*

FLAVORINGS: *Garlic, lemon juice, red pepper*
flakes, cumin, jalapeños

If men are eating with you

Men can have a little more olive oil, kidney
beans, chickpeas, and olives. See page 181.

Energy 514 kcal · Protein 21 g · Carbohydrate 48 g · Dietary fiber 19.0 g · Fat 22 g

Curried chicken and rice soup

PREPARATION TIME: *about 30 minutes*

¹/₂ small onion
1 small leek
¹/₂ garlic clove
2 teaspoons curry powder
¹/₂ teaspoon ground cumin
¹/₂ tablespoon olive oil
4¹/₄ oz chicken
1 cup chicken stock
¹/₂ teaspoon dried thyme
1 small tomato
¹/₂ red bell pepper
¹/₂ teaspoon salt
Sprinkling of pepper
1¹/₂ teaspoons cornstarch dissolved
*   in 3 tablespoons cold water*
Generous ¹/₈ cup rice
1¹/₂ tablespoons whipping cream (38% fat)
Parsley and marigolds, to garnish (optional)

Dice the onion and slice the leek and garlic.

Heat the curry powder and cumin in a heavy saucepan until fragrant.

Add the olive oil, onion, leek, and garlic, and fry until the onion has softened.

Dice the chicken and add it to the pan. Brown it on all sides, then add the stock and thyme. Cover the soup and let it simmer for about 20 minutes.

Cut the tomato and pepper into cubes then add them to the soup. Season with salt and pepper, and thicken the soup with the cornstarch mix.

In a separate saucepan, cook the rice following the package directions.

Heat the soup until it is hot through and add the cream.

Spoon the rice on top and garnish with sprigs of parsley and marigolds. Serve immediately.

WHAT YOU SHOULD HAVE ON YOUR PLATE

A portion of soup with rice, garnished with parsley and marigolds.

HOW IT IS DIVIDED IN THE SCANDI SENSE MEAL-BOX

HANDFUL 1 (+ 2): *Onion, leek, tomato, pepper*

HANDFUL 3: *Chicken*

HANDFUL 4: *Cornstarch, rice*

FAT: *Olive oil, cream*

FLAVORINGS: *Curry powder, cumin,*
*   garlic, stock, thyme, salt, pepper,*
*   parsley, marigolds*

If men are eating with you
Men can have a little more olive oil,
chicken, chicken stock, cornstarch,
rice, and cream. See page 182.

Energy 513 kcal · Protein 33 g · Carbohydrate 39 g · Dietary fiber 6.9 g · Fat 2 4g

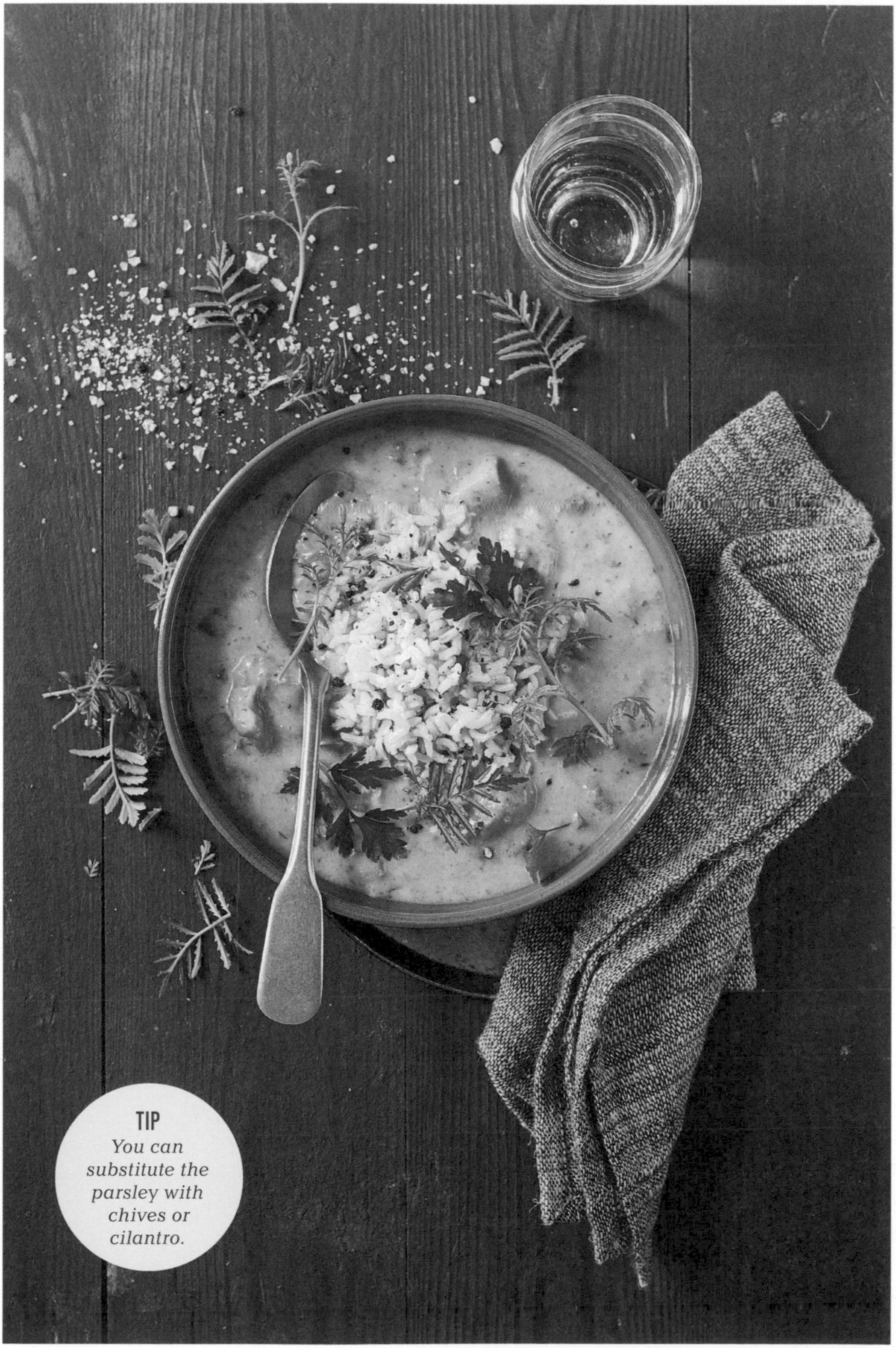

TIP
You can substitute the parsley with chives or cilantro.

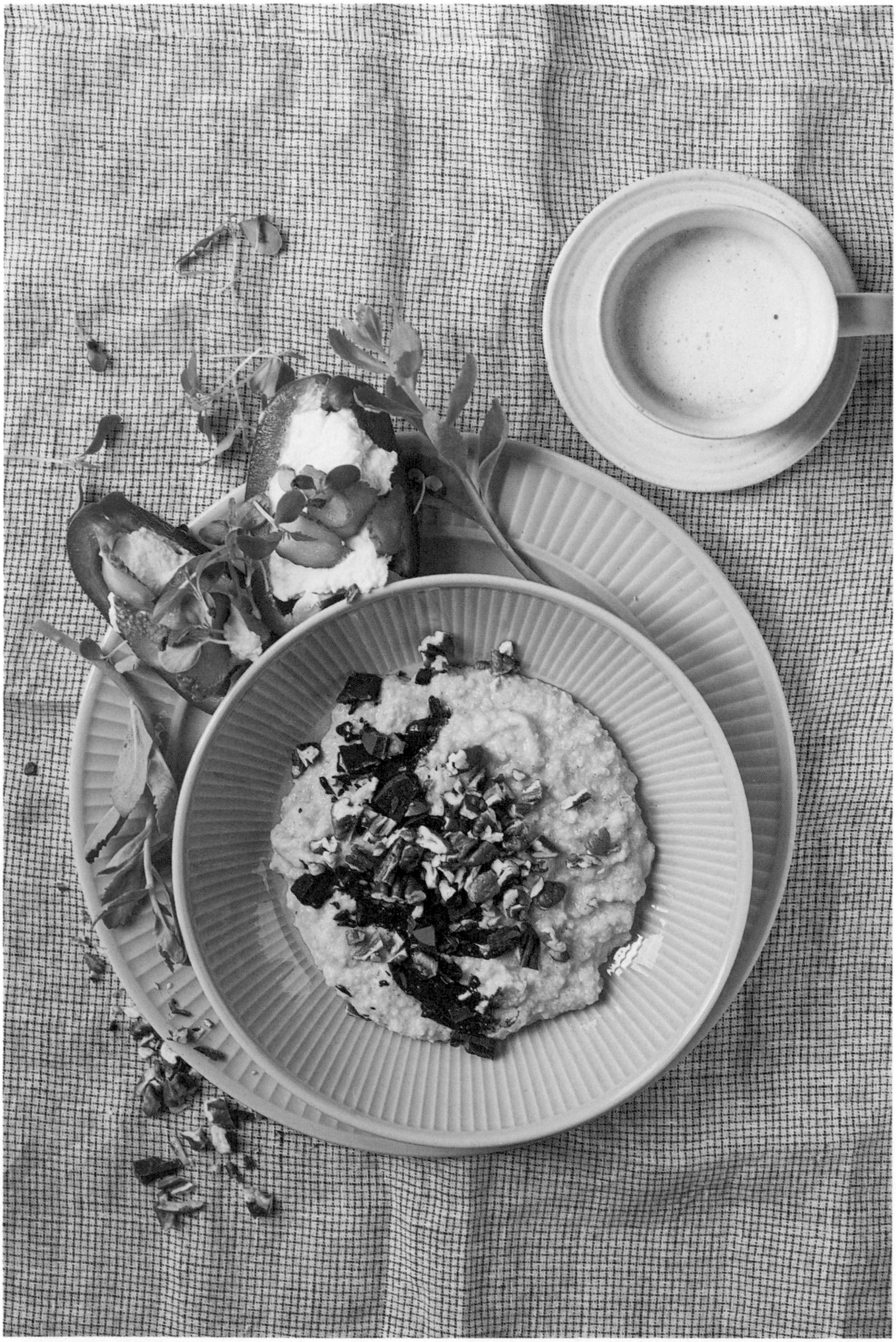

Oatmeal with stuffed pepper

PREPARATION TIME: *about 15 minutes*

STUFFED PEPPER:

1 teaspoon pine nuts
¹/₂ red bell pepper
¹/₃ cup ricotta cheese
Salt and pepper, to taste
Cress and sorrel, to garnish

OATMEAL:

¹/₃ cup oats
Generous ³/₄ cup water
Pinch of salt
1 egg
2 teaspoons pecans
¹/₄ oz semisweet chocolate, min. 70% cocoa
1 teaspoon honey

PLUS:

2 dill pickles or cornichons

Toast the pine nuts in a dry skillet over medium heat. Remove the seeds and white membrane from the bell pepper. Fill the pepper with ricotta and sprinkle the pine nuts on top. Season with salt and pepper and garnish with cress and sorrel.

Place the oats, water, and salt in a heavy saucepan. Bring to a boil, stirring continuously for a few minutes, until it has the right consistency. Break the egg into the oatmeal and stir until it is evenly distributed. Coarsely chop the pecans and chocolate.

Serve the oatmeal with nuts, chocolate, and honey, with the stuffed pepper and dill pickles on the side.

WHAT YOU SHOULD HAVE ON YOUR PLATE

Half a stuffed pepper, two dill pickles, and a bowl of oatmeal.

HOW IT IS DIVIDED IN THE SCANDI SENSE MEAL-BOX

HANDFUL 1 (+2): *Pepper, dill pickles*

HANDFUL 3: *Ricotta, egg*

HANDFUL 4: *Oats*

FAT: *Pine nuts, pecans, semisweet chocolate*

FLAVORINGS: *Salt, pepper, cress, sorrel, honey*

TIP *You can substitute the ricotta for quark or cottage cheese, if desired.*

TIP *You can substitute the pecans for any other kind of nuts, grains, or seeds.*

If men are eating with you

Men can have a few more pine nuts and pecans, a little more ricotta, and semisweet chocolate. See page 185.

Energy 576 kcal   Protein 22 g · Carbohydrate 47 g · Dietary fiber 6.8 g · Fat 32 g

Roast beef wrap

PREPARATION TIME: *about 10 minutes*

MANGO DRESSING:

1 tablespoon mango chutney
1 tablespoon mayonnaise
¹/₂ teaspoon curry powder
Salt and pepper, to taste

PLUS:

1 carrot
1 small tortilla, preferably
  whole-wheat (about 1¹/₂ to 1³/₄ oz)
1 cup mixed salad greens
¹/₂ cup snow peas
¹/₄ cup dill pickles
4¹/₄ oz roast beef, cut into strips or squares
Wild garlic, to garnish (optional)

Mix the mango chutney, mayonnaise, and curry powder to make the dressing. Season with salt and pepper.

Cut the carrot into matchsticks.

Lay the tortilla flat on a cutting board and spread half the dressing on it.

Place the salad greens, vegetables, and beef on top, adding the rest of the dressing in the middle. Garnish with wild garlic.

WHAT YOU SHOULD HAVE ON YOUR PLATE

A wrap filled with one handful of vegetables, one handful of meat, and some mango dressing.

HOW IT IS DIVIDED IN THE SCANDI SENSE MEAL-BOX

HANDFUL 1 (+2): *Salad, carrot, snow peas, dill pickle*

HANDFUL 3: *Roast beef*

HANDFUL 4: *Tortilla wrap*

FAT: *Mayonnaise*

FLAVORINGS: *Mango chutney, curry powder, salt, pepper, wild garlic*

If men are eating with you

Men can have a little more mayonnaise and roast beef, and a larger tortilla. See page 186.

Energy 553 kcal · Protein 33 g · Carbohydrate 48 g · Dietary fiber 7.1 g · Fat 24 g

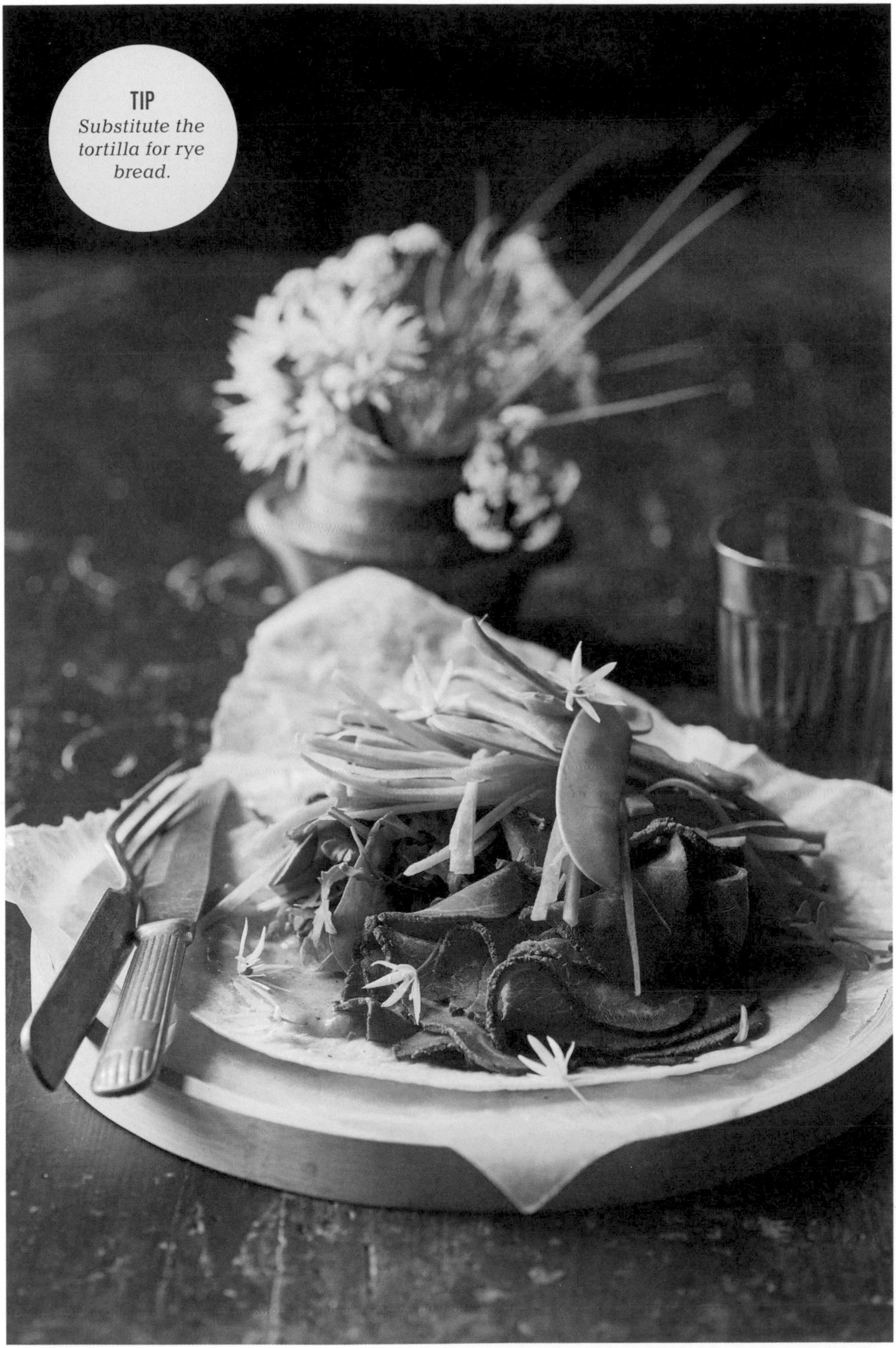
TIP
Substitute the tortilla for rye bread.

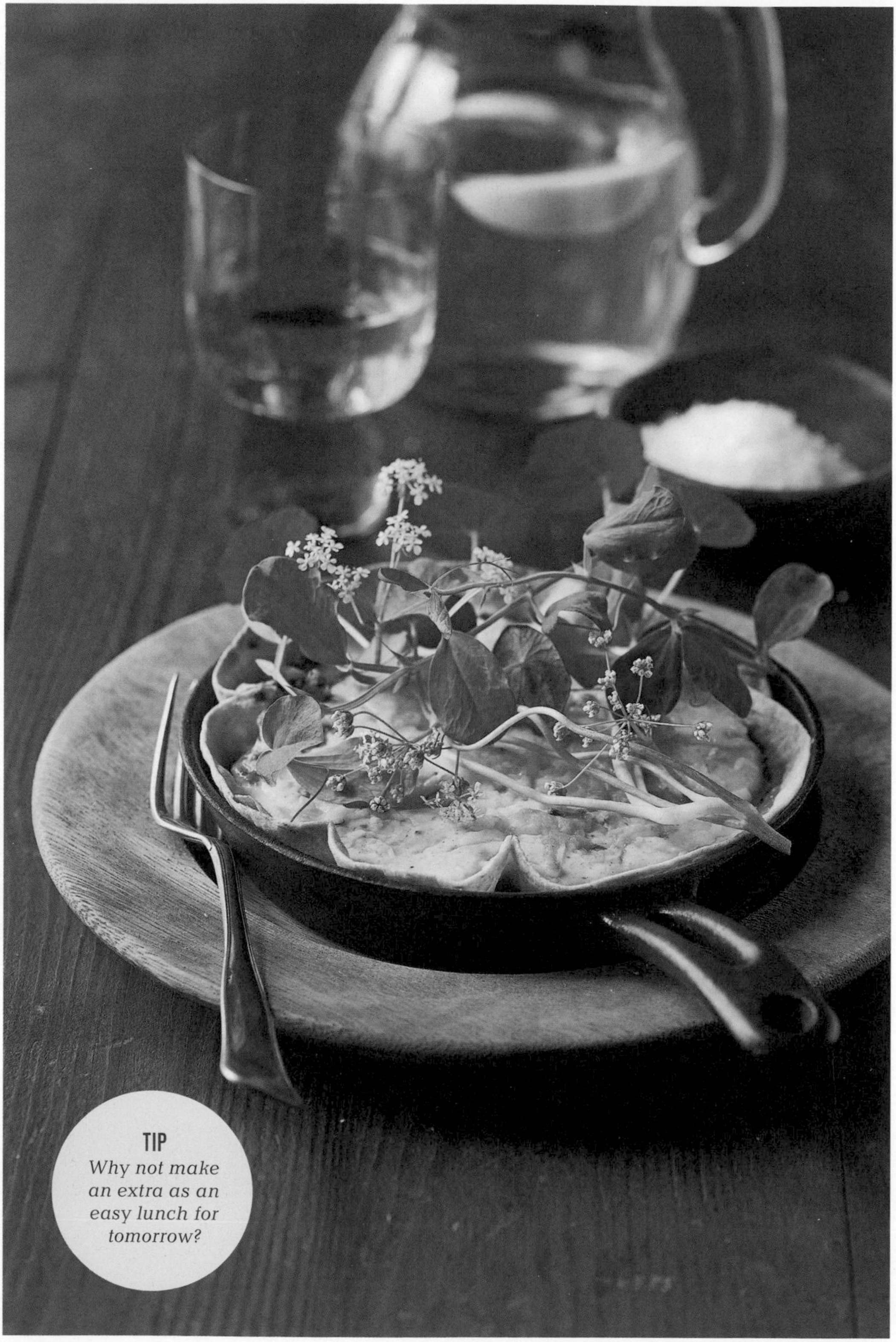
TIP
Why not make an extra as an easy lunch for tomorrow?

Cheesy tortilla tart

PREPARATION TIME, INCLUDING BAKING TIME: *about 40 minutes*

SPINACH MIXTURE:

¹/₂ onion
1 garlic clove
2 scallions
2 bacon slices
3¹/₄ tablespoons frozen chopped spinach

CHEESE FILLING:

1 egg
¹/₂ cup ricotta cheese
¹/₂ teaspoon grated nutmeg
¹/₂ teaspoon salt
Sprinkling of pepper
2 tablespoons skim milk
¹/₂ teaspoon olive oil

PLUS:

1 small tortilla, preferably
  whole-wheat, about 1¹/₂ to 1³/₄ oz
³/₄ oz cheese, grated, min. 18% fat
Pea shoots or nasturtiums, to garnish

Finely chop the onion, garlic, and scallions. Chop the bacon into small pieces, and fry over medium heat for a few minutes before adding the onion and garlic. Add the spinach and scallions and continue frying until the spinach has fully defrosted.

Whisk together the egg, ricotta, nutmeg, salt, pepper, and milk to make a smooth custard.

Brush a suitable ovenproof dish with the olive oil and place the tortilla in the dish. Press it into the edges.

Put the filling in the tortilla in the following order: half of the spinach mixture, half of the cheese filling, the rest of the spinach mixture, the rest of the cheese filling. Top with the grated cheese.

Bake in an oven preheated to 400°F for 30 minutes. Garnish with pea shoots or nasturtiums and serve.

WHAT YOU SHOULD HAVE ON YOUR PLATE

A tortilla tart with a little garnish on top.

HOW IT IS DIVIDED IN THE SCANDI SENSE MEAL-BOX

HANDFUL 1 (+ 2): *Onion, scallions, spinach*

HANDFUL 3: *Bacon, egg, ricotta*

HANDFUL 4: *Tortilla*

FAT: *Olive oil, cheese*

DAIRY PRODUCT: *Skim milk*

FLAVORINGS: *Garlic, nutmeg, salt, pepper,*
  pea shoots or nasturtiums

TIP *Season with your favorite herb, for example 1 tablespoon dried thyme.*

If men are eating with you

Men can have a little more scallion, a larger tortilla, and more cheese. See page 189.

Energy 625 kcal · Protein 33 g · Carbohydrate 34 g · Dietary fiber 7 g · Fat 37 g

Pancakes

PREPARATION TIME, INCLUDING RESTING TIME: *about 30 minutes*
PLEASE NOTE: *This makes enough batter for 4 to 6 small pancakes, which constitutes 1 portion.*

PANCAKE BATTER:

¹/₂ small banana
¹/₈ cup oats
2 eggs
2 egg whites
Pinch of salt
¹/₂ teaspoon vanilla extract
¹/₂ teaspoon ground cinnamon or cardamom
1 tablespoon honey

PLUS:

1 teaspoon almonds
¹/₄ oz semisweet chocolate, min. 70% cocoa
2 teaspoons butter
4 to 6 berries of your choice

TO GO WITH IT:

1 cup sugar snap peas
Pansy flowers, to decorate

Place all the ingredients for the pancake batter in a blender. Blend until smooth, then let rest for 10 to 15 minutes.

Chop the almonds and chocolate into nibs.

Melt a little butter in a pan and drop the batter on in blobs. When they have begun to set, add a berry to the middle of each one. Turn them over when the batter has set completely to cook the other side.

Stack the pancakes with a sprinkling of chocolate and almond nibs on top. Garnish with pansy flowers.

Serve the peas in a glass on the side.

WHAT YOU SHOULD HAVE ON YOUR PLATE

All of the pancakes topped with chocolate and almond nibs. One handful of sugar snap peas on the side.

HOW IT IS DIVIDED IN THE SCANDI SENSE MEAL-BOX

HANDFUL 1 (+ 2): *Sugar snap peas*

HANDFUL 3: *Egg, egg whites*

HANDFUL 4: *Banana, oats, berries*

FAT: *Almonds, butter, semisweet chocolate*

FLAVORINGS: *Salt, vanilla extract, cinnamon or cardamom, honey, pansy flowers*

TIP *Use calorie-free sweetener instead of honey, if you want to avoid added sugar.*

If men are eating with you

Men can add an extra egg and a little more banana, oats, almonds, semisweet chocolate, butter, and berries. See page 190.

Energy 576 kcal · Protein 30 g · Carbohydrate 52 g · Dietary fiber 7.1 g · Fat 26 g

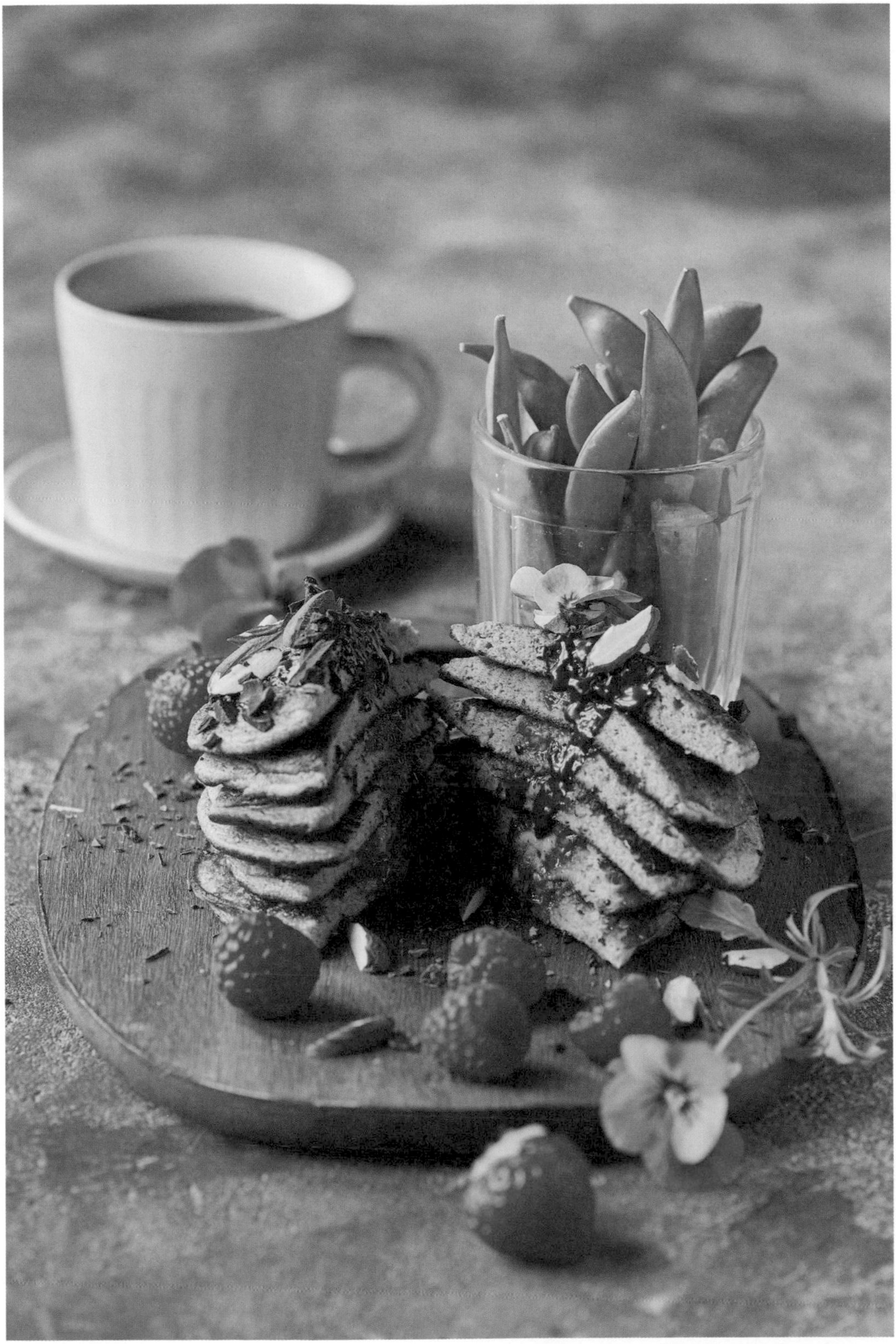

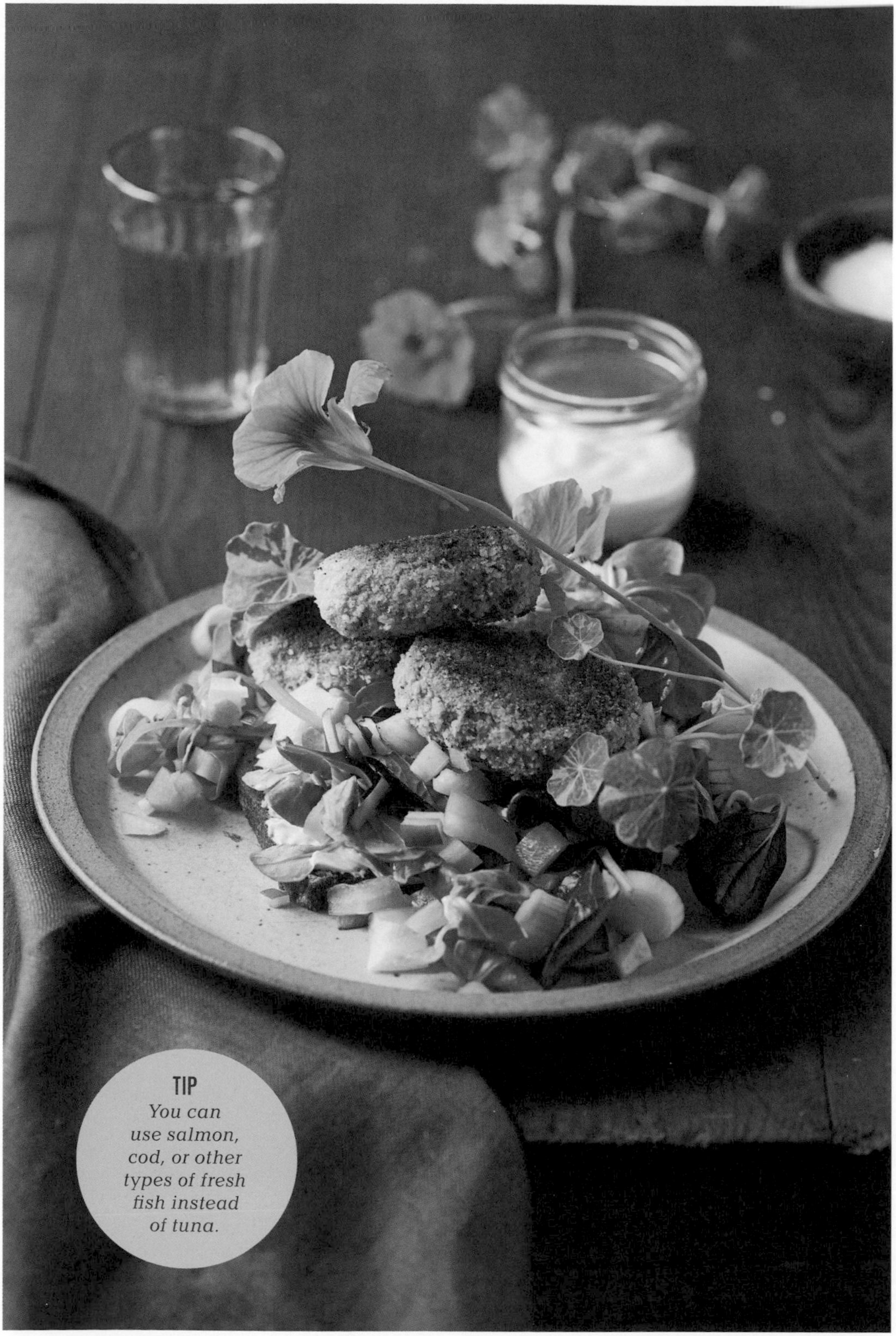

TIP
You can use salmon, cod, or other types of fresh fish instead of tuna.

Tuna fishcakes with rye

PREPARATION TIME: *about 30 minutes*

TUNA FISHCAKES:

2¼ oz sweet potato, diced
1 can of tuna (about 4¼ oz when drained)
1 egg white
1 small garlic clove, crushed
Pinch of dried red pepper flakes
1 tablespoon chopped parsley
1 tablespoon chopped dill
½ teaspoon salt
2 tablespoons bread crumbs
1 tablespoon olive oil

SALAD:

1 scallion, sliced
¼ red onion, diced
¼ yellow bell pepper, diced
1 cup mixed baby lettuce greens
2 tablespoons crème fraîche, max. 9% fat

PLUS:

1 slice of rye bread
2 teaspoons mayonnaise
Nasturtiums or cilantro, to garnish

Boil the sweet potato in lightly salted water for about 20 minutes.

Drain and mash the sweet potato. Mix with the tuna, egg white, garlic, pepper flakes, parsley, dill, and salt. Form into patties and press them into the bread crumbs.

Heat a tablespoon of olive oil in a skillet and fry the fishcakes.

Spread the mayonnaise on the rye bread. Combine the scallion, red onion, pepper, and lettuce greens in a bowl, and put on top of the rye bread. Place the fishcakes on top and garnish with nasturtiums or cilantro, if desired.

Serve the crème fraîche on the side in a small bowl.

WHAT YOU SHOULD HAVE ON YOUR PLATE

One large handful of tuna fishcakes, one handful of mixed salad, and two tablespoons of crème fraîche. One handful of rye bread with mayonnaise.

HOW IT IS DIVIDED IN THE SCANDI SENSE MEAL-BOX

HANDFUL 1 (+ 2): *Sweet potato, lettuce, scallion, red onion, pepper*

HANDFUL 3: *Tuna, egg white*

HANDFUL 4: *Bread crumbs, rye bread*

FAT: *Olive oil, mayonnaise*

DAIRY DRESSING: *Crème fraîche*

FLAVORINGS: *Garlic, pepper flakes, parsley, dill, salt, nasturtiums or cilantro*

If men are eating with you

Men can have extra rye bread and mayonnaise. See page 193.

Energy 586 kcal · Protein 39 g · Carbohydrate 44 g · Dietary fiber 8.1 g · Fat 27 g

Baked sweet potato with chickpeas

PREPARATION TIME, INCLUDING BAKING TIME: *about 1 hour 10 minutes*

1 medium sweet potato
¹/₄ onion
1 garlic clove
¹/₄ red chile
¹/₂ yellow bell pepper
1 tablespoon olive oil
¹/₂ teaspoon ground cumin
¹/₂ teaspoon paprika
¹/₂ cup canned chickpeas (drained)
*¹/₂ vegetable bouillon cube dissolved
    in 3¹/₂ tablespoons boiling water*
1 tablespoon lemon juice
1 teaspoon honey
¹/₂ avocado
1¹/₂ oz cubed salad cheese, such
    as feta, max. 17% fat

DILL DRESSING:

2 tablespoons chopped dill
2 tablespoons crème fraîche, max. 9% fat
Salt and pepper, to taste

PLUS:

Wild garlic and dill, to garnish

Wrap the potato in foil and bake for an hour in an oven preheated to 400°F.

Finely chop the onion, garlic, and chilli. Dice the pepper.

Heat the olive oil in a hot skillet and fry the cumin, paprika, and chile for 30 seconds, then add the onion, garlic, and pepper. Add the chickpeas after about 3 minutes, let them fry for a further minute, then add the stock. Let simmer for a few minutes and turn off the heat.

Combine the lemon juice and honey. Cut the avocado into slices and toss in the lemon juice and honey mix.

Stir the dill into the crème fraîche. Season with salt and pepper.

Unwrap the sweet potato and cut a slit in the top lengthwise. Squeeze the potato gently to open it up. Scrape out most of the flesh and mix it with the chickpea mixture. Add the cheese and mix until well combined. Fill the potato generously with the chickpea mixture, then place it under the broiler for 3 to 5 minutes.

Serve with the avocado and dill dressing on top. Garnish with wild garlic and dill.

WHAT YOU SHOULD HAVE ON YOUR PLATE

A filled sweet potato with avocado and dill dressing.

HOW IT IS DIVIDED IN THE SCANDI SENSE MEAL-BOX

HANDFUL 1 (+2): *Sweet potato, onion, pepper*

HANDFUL 3: *Chickpeas, cheese*

FAT: *Olive oil, avocado*

DAIRY DRESSING: *Crème fraîche*

FLAVORINGS: *Garlic, chile, cumin, paprika, vegetable stock, lemon juice, honey, dill, salt, pepper, wild garlic*

If men are eating with you

Men can have a little more sweet potato and cheese. See page 194.

Energy 613 kcal · Protein 16 g · Carbohydrate 52 g · Dietary fiber 13.8 g · Fat 35 g

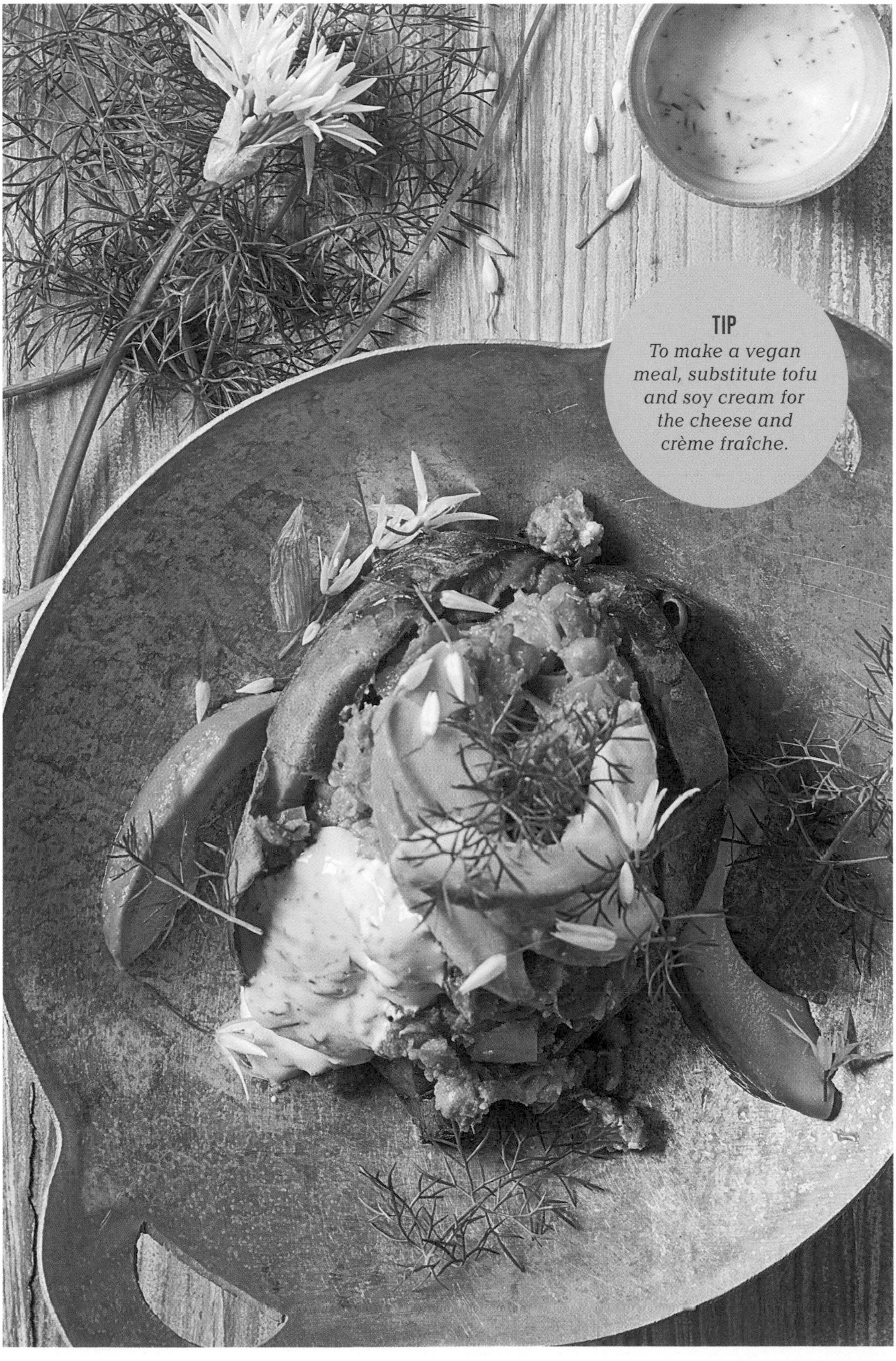
TIP
To make a vegan meal, substitute tofu and soy cream for the cheese and crème fraîche.

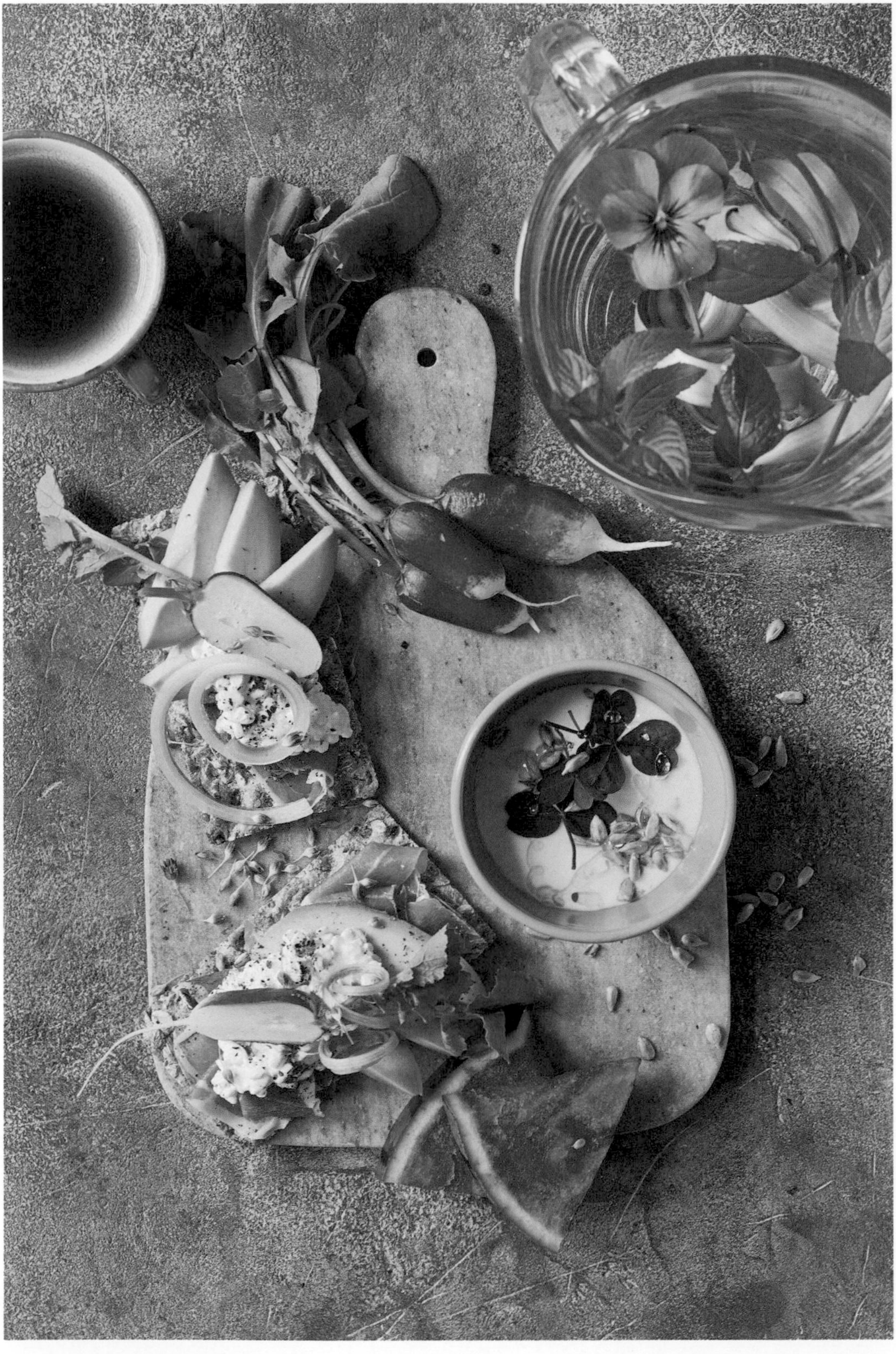

Breakfast plate with cottage cheese

PREPARATION TIME: *about 15 minutes*

1³/₄ oz radishes
1³/₄ oz watermelon

YOGURT IN A GLASS:

7 tablespoons plain yogurt
1 tablespoon sunflower seeds
1 teaspoon honey or
  1 tablespoon raisins
Red sorrel and rhubarb curls
  (see Tip), to garnish

TOPPED CRISPBREAD:

¹/₂ avocado
1 tablespoon lemon juice
1¹/₂ oz air-dried ham
¹/₃ cup cottage cheese, max. 4.5% fat
2 pieces of crispbread

Clean the radishes but leave the tops on.

Cut the watermelon into slices.

Pour the yogurt into a glass or bowl and top with sunflower seeds and honey or raisins. Garnish with red sorrel.

Slice the avocado and sprinkle with the lemon juice.

Divide the ham, avocado, and cottage cheese between the pieces of crispbread.

WHAT YOU SHOULD HAVE ON YOUR PLATE

Half a handful of radishes and just under half a handful of melon. A portion of yogurt with topping and a crispbread with ham, avocado, and cottage cheese.

HOW IT IS DIVIDED IN THE SCANDI SENSE MEAL-BOX

HANDFUL 1 (+ 2): *Radishes, rhubarb, if used*

HANDFUL 3: *Ham, cottage cheese*

HANDFUL 4: *Watermelon, crispbread*

FAT: *Sunflower seeds, avocado*

DAIRY PRODUCT: *Yogurt*

FLAVORINGS: *Honey, lemon juice,*
  red sorrel

TIP *You can make rhubarb curls when rhubarb is in season by placing thin strips of rhubarb in ice water. They will curl after a few minutes. You can also use them to flavor a pitcher of water.*

If men are eating with you

Men can have a few more radishes and more watermelon, sunflower seeds, ham, cottage cheese, and crispbread. See page 197.

Energy 557 kcal · Protein 31 g · Carbohydrate 36 g · Dietary fiber 7.2 g · Fat 31 g

Caesar salad with croutons

PREPARATION TIME: *about 20 minutes*

CAESAR DRESSING:

$3^1/2$ tablespoons plain yogurt
1 egg yolk
$^1/2$ garlic clove, crushed
$^1/2$ teaspoon salt
2 tablespoons white wine vinegar
1 anchovy fillet (optional)

PLUS:

2 Boston lettuces
1 tablespoon olive oil
1 slice of bread, preferably whole-wheat
Pinch of salt
1 roasted chicken breast (5 oz), sliced
$^3/4$ oz grated Parmesan cheese
Pepper, to taste
Pea shoots or pansy flowers, to garnish

Whisk the yogurt, egg yolk, garlic, salt, and white wine vinegar together to make the dressing. Mash the anchovy fillet, if using, and stir it into the dressing.

Remove and discard the outer leaves of the lettuces and rinse.

Cut one lettuce in half. Brush the cut surface with a little olive oil. Fry the cut surfaces for 1 to 2 minutes in a hot skillet.

Brush the bread on both sides with the remaining olive oil, season with a pinch of salt, and sauté in a hot pan until crisp on both sides.

Coarsely tear the leaves from the second lettuce and spread them out on a plate.

Cut the bread into cubes and sprinkle over the lettuce greens. Place the fried halves of lettuce on top. Equally arrange the chicken, Caesar dressing, and Parmesan on top. Season with pepper.

WHAT YOU SHOULD HAVE ON YOUR PLATE

Three or four handfuls of Caesar salad with croutons, dressing, and Parmesan.

HOW IT IS DIVIDED IN THE SCANDI SENSE MEAL-BOX

HANDFUL 1 (+ 2): *Lettuce*

HANDFUL 3: *Chicken breast, anchovy*

HANDFUL 4: *Bread*

FAT: *Egg yolk, olive oil, Parmesan*

DAIRY PRODUCT: *Yogurt*

FLAVORINGS: *Garlic, salt, white wine vinegar, pepper, pea shoots or pansy flowers*

TIP *You can also buy ready-made Caesar salad dressing.*

If men are eating with you

Men can have a little more bread, chicken, and Parmesan. See page 198.

Energy 594 kcal · Protein 48 g · Carbohydrate 27 g · Dietary fiber 6 g · Fat 31 g

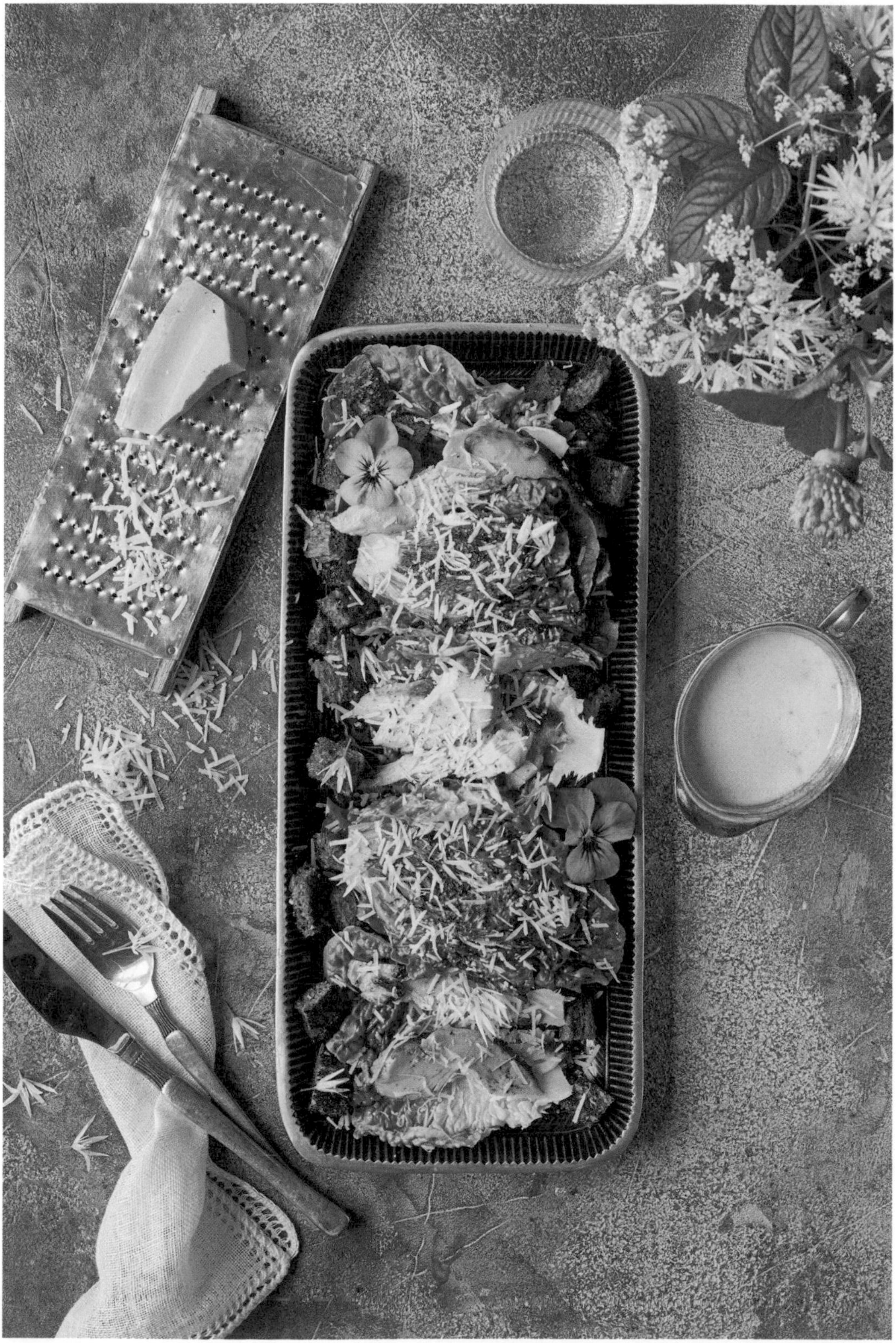

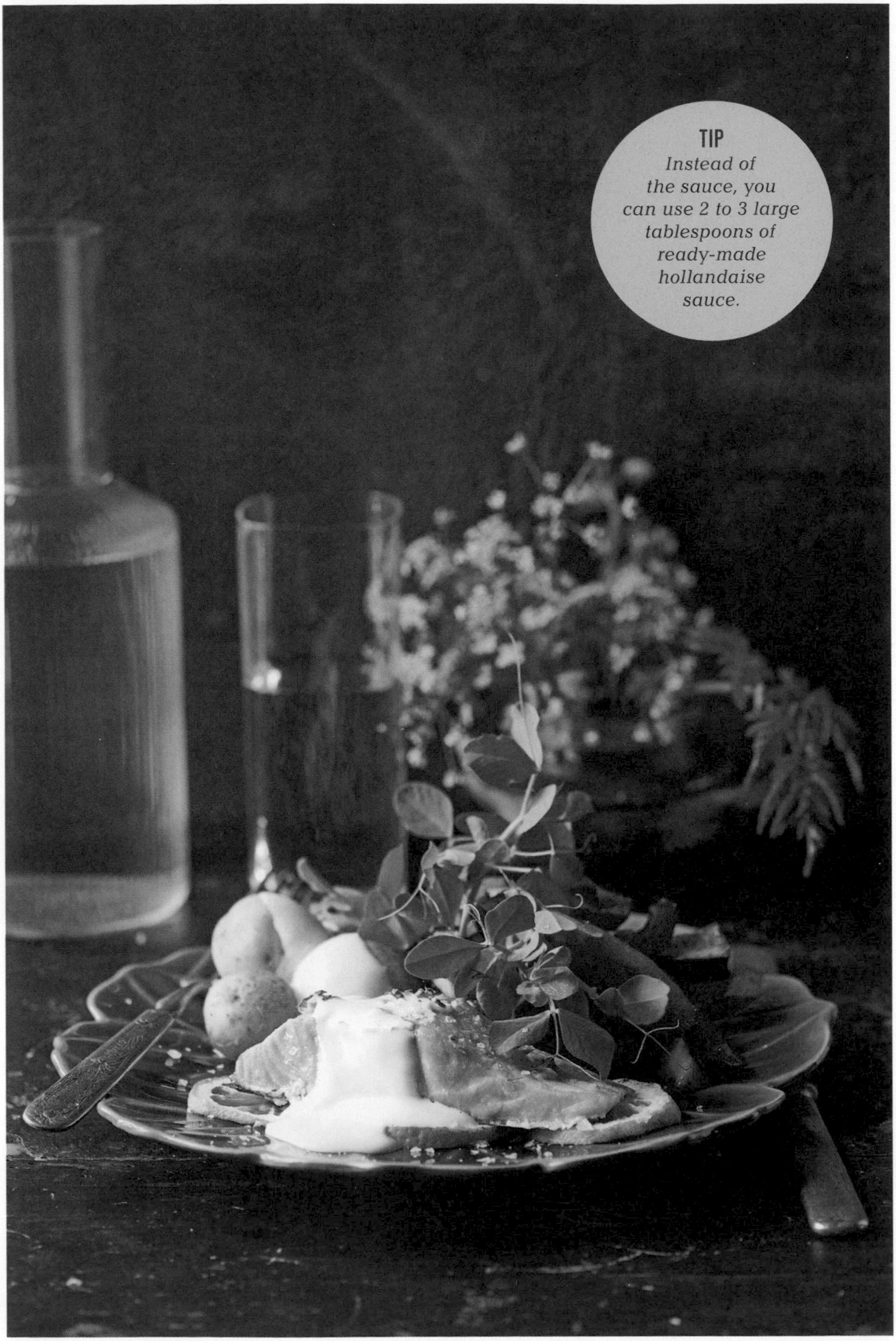

TIP
Instead of the sauce, you can use 2 to 3 large tablespoons of ready-made hollandaise sauce.

Baked salmon with lemon dressing

PREPARATION TIME: *about 20 minutes*

BAKED SALMON:

4¹/₄ oz salmon
Pinch of coarse salt
¹/₂ garlic clove, crushed
1 lemon, sliced

LEMON DRESSING:

1 tablespoon mayonnaise
3¹/₂ tablespoons plain yogurt
2 teaspoons lemon juice
Pinch of salt

TO GO WITH IT:

3¹/₂ oz new potatoes
1³/₄ oz zucchini
2³/₄ oz carrot
1³/₄ oz red bell pepper
1 teaspoon olive oil
Pea shoots, to garnish

Season the salmon with the salt and garlic. Place the lemon slices in the bottom of an ovenproof dish. Place the salmon on top.

Bake the salmon in an oven preheated to 400°F for about 20 minutes until tender.

Boil the potatoes.

Stir the mayonnaise, yogurt, lemon juice, and salt together to make a dressing.

Cut the zucchini, carrot, and pepper into thin sticks. Stir-fry them in the olive oil.

Serve the salmon with the potatoes, lemon dressing, and stir-fried vegetables. Garnish with pea shoots.

WHAT YOU SHOULD HAVE ON YOUR PLATE

One handful of salmon, one to two handfuls of vegetables, one handful of potatoes, and about 7 tablespoons of the lemon dressing.

HOW IT IS DIVIDED IN THE SCANDI SENSE MEAL-BOX

HANDFUL 1 (+ 2): *Zucchini, carrot, pepper*

HANDFUL 3: *Salmon*

HANDFUL 4: *Potato*

FAT: *Mayonnaise, olive oil*

DAIRY PRODUCT: *Yogurt*

FLAVORINGS: *Salt, garlic, lemon juice, pea shoots*

If men are eating with you

Men can have a little more salmon, mayonnaise, and potato. See page 201.

Energy 598 kcal · Protein 32 g · Carbohydrate 29 g · Dietary fiber 5.5 g · Fat 38 g

Ham on toast

PREPARATION TIME: *about 15 minutes*

¹/₂ cup frozen edamame beans
1 tomato
2 slices of onion
2¹/₄ oz ham
1 teaspoon butter
1 slice of bread, preferably whole-wheat
1 teaspoon mustard
2 slices of cheese, min. 18% fat
1 tablespoon lemon juice
1 teaspoon olive oil
Salt and pepper, to taste
1 handful watercress, to garnish

Soak the edamame beans in boiling water for 30 seconds and drain. Cut the tomato and onion into slices. Fry the ham, onion, and edamame beans in butter in a large, nonstick pan.

Toast the bread. Spread with the mustard. Lay the onion and ham on it and place the cheese on top. Place the toast in the pan until the cheese begins to melt.

Place the edamame beans in a small bowl and toss them in the lemon juice and olive oil. Season with salt and pepper.

Arrange the tomato slices on top of the toast. Garnish with watercress.

WHAT YOU SHOULD HAVE ON YOUR PLATE

A slice of toast with ham, cheese, and tomato. Edamame beans on the side.

HOW IT IS DIVIDED IN THE SCANDI SENSE MEAL-BOX

HANDFUL 1 (+ 2): *Tomato, onion*

HANDFUL 3: *Edamame beans, ham*

HANDFUL 4: *Bread*

FAT: *Butter, cheese, olive oil*

FLAVORINGS: *Mustard, lemon juice, salt, pepper, watercress*

TIP *You can use chickpeas or lentils instead of edamame beans.*

TIP *If you use half the quantity of ham, you can add a fried egg on top.*

If men are eating with you

Men can have a fried egg with this, and a little more onion, ham, and butter. See page 202.

Energy 528 kcal · Protein 36 g · Carbohydrate 31 g · Dietary fiber 8.9 g · Fat 28 g

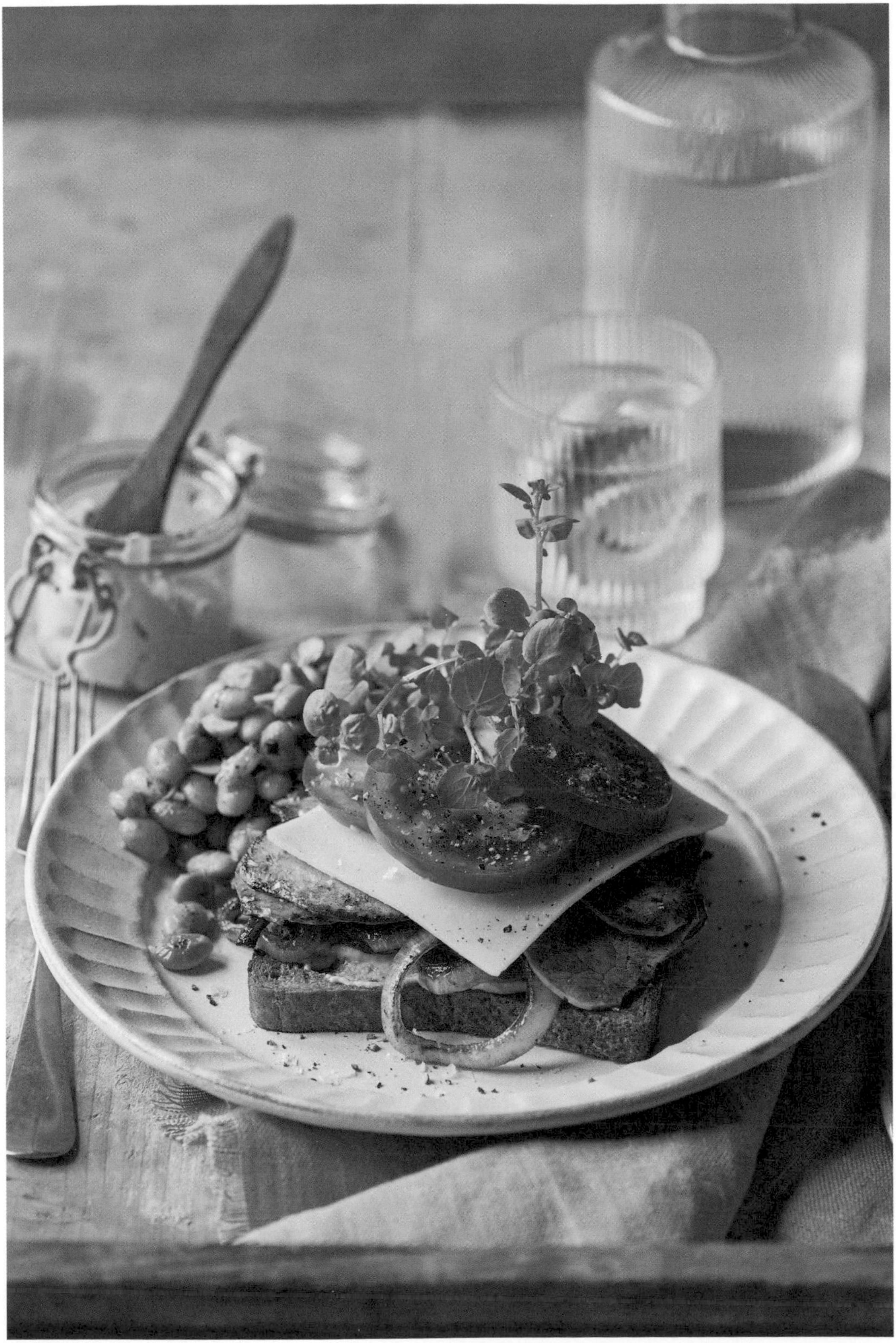

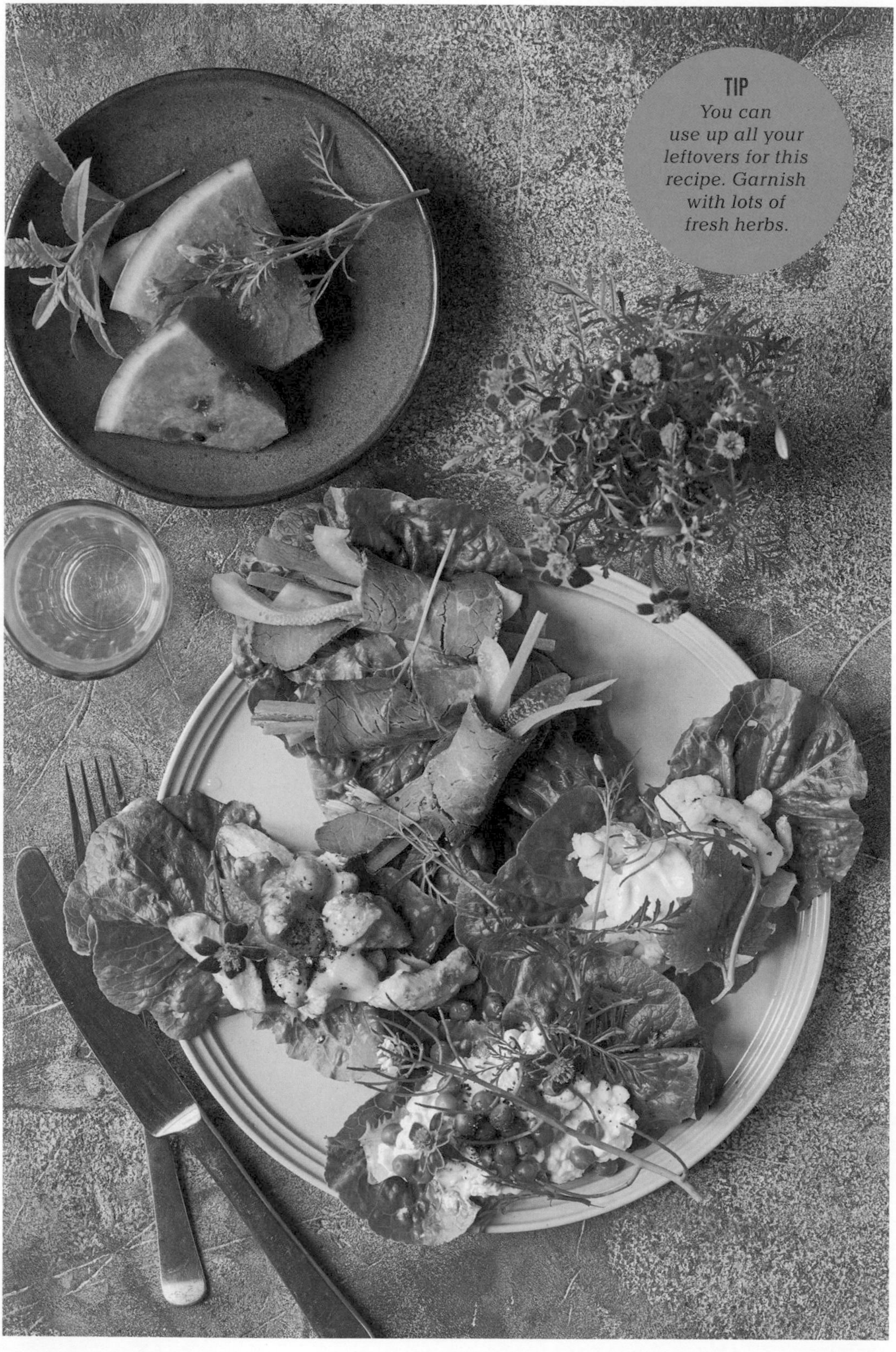
TIP
You can use up all your leftovers for this recipe. Garnish with lots of fresh herbs.

Boston lettuce wraps

PREPARATION TIME: *about 15 minutes*

1 Boston lettuce

ROAST BEEF TOPPING:

1 oz carrot
1 oz yellow bell pepper
¹/₄ cup dill pickles
¹/₂ tablespoon mayonnaise
1 teaspoon shredded horseradish
   or chopped garlic
Salt and pepper, to taste
3 slices of roast beef

SHRIMP TOPPING:

1 teaspoon sweet chili sauce or paprika
¹/₂ tablespoon mayonnaise
Salt and pepper, to taste
2¹/₄ oz shrimp

CHICKEN TOPPING:

¹/₂ tablespoon mayonnaise
1 teaspoon mango chutney or curry powder
Salt and pepper, to taste
1³/₄ oz cooked chicken, diced or in strips

COTTAGE CHEESE TOPPING:

¹/₄ cup cottage cheese, max. 4.5% fat
¹/₄ cup peas
Salt and pepper, to taste

PLUS:

Fresh herbs, to garnish
3¹/₂ oz watermelon

Separate the lettuce leaves and lay them on a plate to form four small "bowls."

Cut the carrot, pepper, and dill pickle into matchsticks. Mix the mayonnaise with the horseradish or garlic and season with salt and pepper. Roll the beef slices around small piles of vegetable matchsticks, adding a little horseradish dressing before rolling. Place onto one lettuce bowl.

Add sweet chili sauce or paprika to the mayonnaise and season with salt and pepper. Place the shrimp with the dressing onto another lettuce bowl.

Mix the mayonnaise with the mango chutney and season with salt and pepper. Place the chicken with the dressing onto a lettuce bowl.

Top the final lettuce bowl with cottage cheese and peas. Season with salt, pepper, and fresh herbs. Serve the watermelon on the side.

WHAT YOU SHOULD HAVE ON YOUR PLATE

Four lettuce bowls with toppings. Watermelon on the side.

HOW IT IS DIVIDED IN THE SCANDI SENSE MEAL-BOX

HANDFUL 1 (+ 2): *Lettuce, carrot, pepper, dill pickles, peas*

HANDFUL 3: *Roast beef, shrimp, chicken, cottage cheese*

HANDFUL 4: *Watermelon*

FAT: *Mayonnaise*

FLAVORINGS: *Horseradish or garlic, salt, pepper, chili sauce, mango chutney or curry powder, herbs*

If men are eating with you

Men may have slightly more mayonnaise, roast beef, shrimp, chicken, and cottage cheese. See page 205.

Energy 564 kcal · Protein 36 g · Carbohydrate 30 g · Dietary fiber 6.1 g · Fat 32 g

Homemade burger

PREPARATION TIME: *about 25 minutes*

CUCUMBER SALAD:

¹/₄ cucumber or 1 baby cucumber
2 tablespoons white wine vinegar
¹/₂ teaspoon sugar
Salt and pepper, to taste

BURGER FILLING:

2 slices of tomato
2 slices of red onion
1³/₄ oz red cabbage or other type of cabbage
¹/₂ cup ground beef, max. 7% fat
1 bacon slice
1 slice of cheese, min. 18% fat
1 small burger bun, about 1³/₄ to
  2¹/₄ oz, preferably whole-wheat
¹/₂ tablespoon mayonnaise

CREME FRAICHE DRESSING:

1 tablespoon crème fraîche, max. 9% fat
1 tablespoon tomato ketchup
¹/₂ teaspoon paprika

PLUS:

A nasturtium flower, to garnish (optional)

Shred the cucumber into long, thin strips and place them in a bowl of boiling water for about 10 minutes.

Slice the tomato and onion.

Shred the red cabbage very finely—use a mandoline if you have one, but take care not to cut your fingers.

Form the meat into a large, flat patty with your hands. Fry the bacon in a nonstick pan, and when it is cooked, fry the beef patty in the same pan over high heat for a couple of minutes on each side. Drain the bacon on paper towels.

Place the cheese on the beef patty and the bacon on top of that.

Drain the cucumber in a strainer. Mix the vinegar, sugar, salt, and pepper, and toss the cucumber in the marinade.

Warm the burger bun. Mix all of the ingredients for the crème fraîche dressing.

Spread crème fraîche dressing on the bottom half of the burger bun and spread mayonnaise on the top half. Place the cabbage on the bottom half, followed by the patty, then tomato and onion slices and finally the cucumber salad. Close the burger. Garnish with a nasturtium flower, if desired.

WHAT YOU SHOULD HAVE ON YOUR PLATE

A burger.

HOW IT IS DIVIDED IN THE SCANDI SENSE MEAL-BOX

HANDFUL 1 (+ 2): *Cucumber, tomato, red onion, red cabbage*

HANDFUL 3: *Beef, bacon*

HANDFUL 4: *Burger bun*

FAT: *Mayonnaise, cheese*

DAIRY DRESSING: *Crème fraîche*

FLAVORINGS: *White wine vinegar, sugar, salt, pepper, tomato ketchup, paprika, nasturtium flower*

If men are eating with you

Men can have a little more ground meat, burger bun, and mayonnaise. See page 206.

Energy 602 kcal · Protein 41 g · Carbohydrate 45 g · Dietary fiber 6.4 g · Fat 26 g

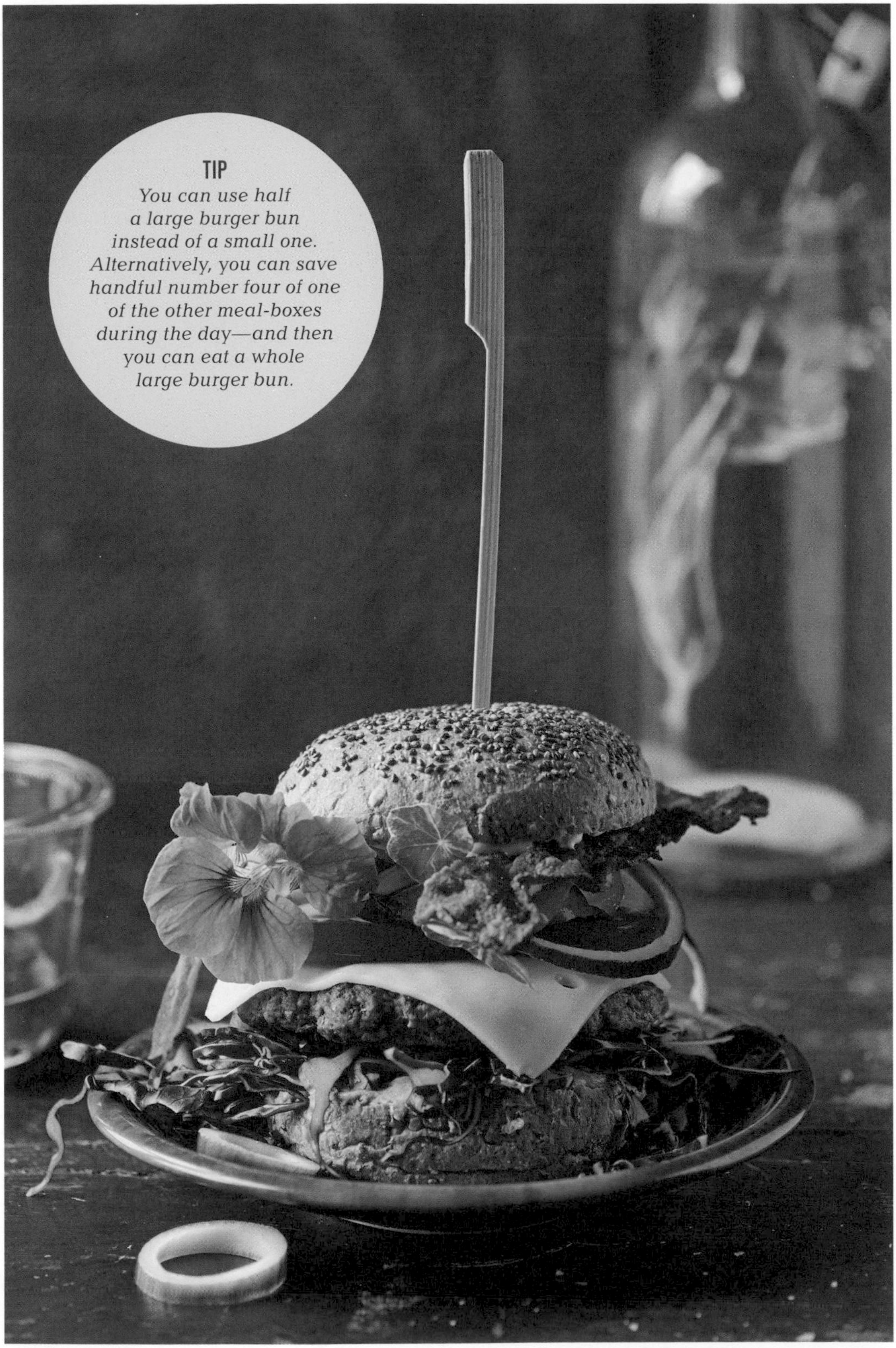

TIP

You can use half a large burger bun instead of a small one. Alternatively, you can save handful number four of one of the other meal-boxes during the day—and then you can eat a whole large burger bun.

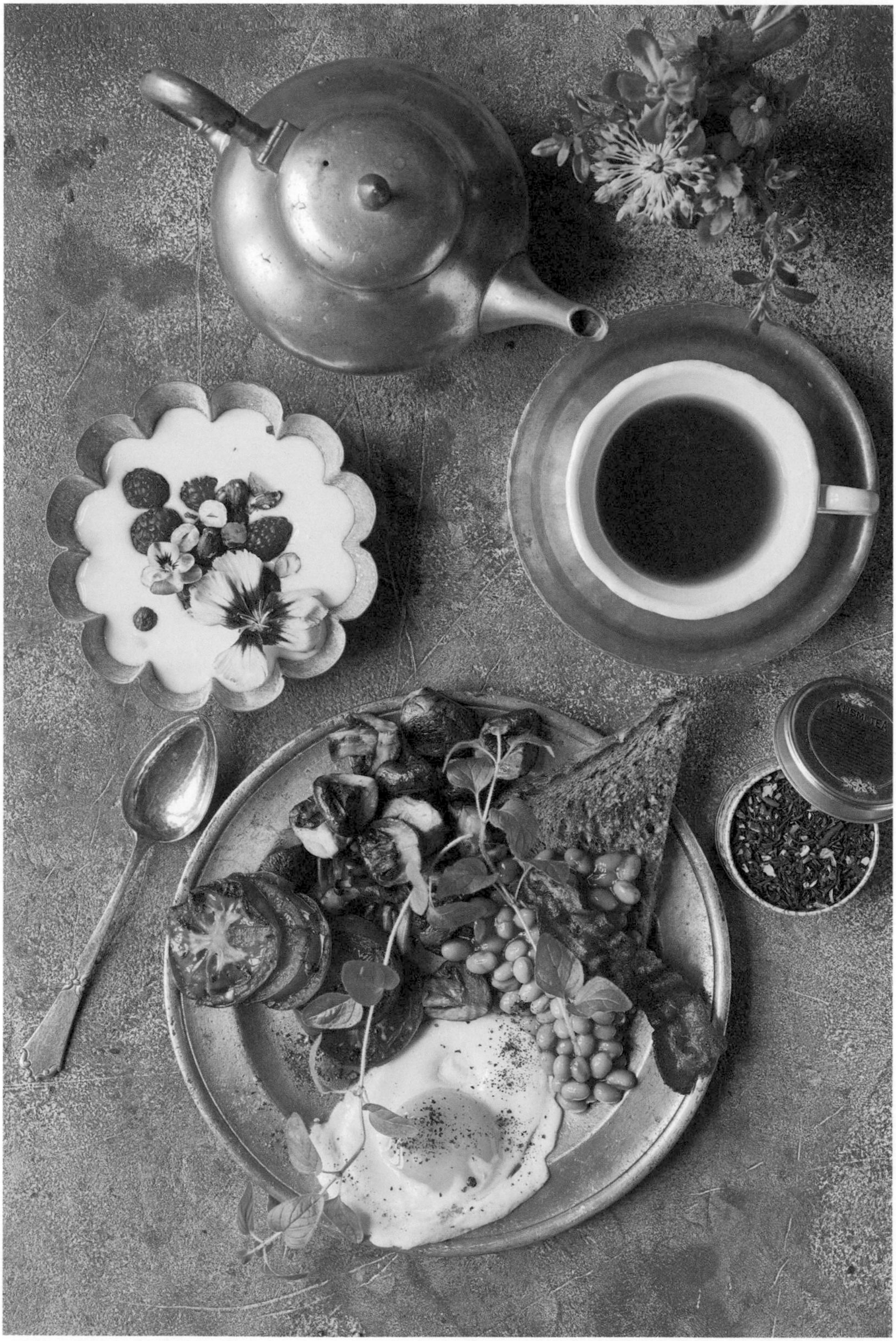
KUSMI TEA

Bacon and egg

PREPARATION TIME: *about 15 minutes*

1 bacon slice
5¼ oz mushrooms
1 tomato
1 egg
1 teaspoon butter
Salt and pepper, to taste

BEANS ON TOAST:

½ can of baked beans (1 cup)
½ slice of bread, preferably whole-wheat

YOGURT IN A GLASS:

7 tablespoons plain yogurt
1 teaspoon hazelnuts
Scant ½ cup raspberries
Sweet William (petals only) and
*   pansy flowers, to decorate*

Fry the bacon until crisp in a nonstick skillet. Place it on paper towels to soak up the excess grease.

Quarter the mushrooms and fry in the same pan, until they darken. Thickly slice the tomato. Let the mushrooms rest at one side of the pan while you fry the tomato and egg in butter on the other side. Season with salt and pepper.

Heat the baked beans in a small saucepan or in the microwave. Toast the bread.

Pour the yogurt into a glass or a bowl. Cut the hazelnuts in half and sprinkle them over the yogurt with the raspberries. Decorate with edible flowers.

WHAT YOU SHOULD HAVE ON YOUR PLATE

Two handfuls of tomato and mushroom, a bacon slice, a fried egg, baked beans on toast, and a portion of yogurt with nuts and raspberries.

HOW IT IS DIVIDED IN THE SCANDI SENSE MEAL-BOX

HANDFUL 1 (+2): *Mushrooms, tomato*

HANDFUL 3: *Bacon, egg, baked beans*

HANDFUL 4: *Bread, raspberries*

FAT: *Butter, hazelnuts*

DAIRY PRODUCT: *Yogurt*

FLAVORINGS: *Salt, pepper, sweet William*
(petals only), pansy flower

TIP *Not keen on baked beans? Have an extra fried egg instead.*

TIP *Try toasting the hazelnuts to get more flavor from them. A little pinch of salt gives the taste an extra edge.*

TIP *You could add scant ¼ cup olives to this meal.*

If men are eating with you

Men can have an extra egg and a little more bacon and mushrooms. See page 209.

Energy 573 kcal · Protein 31 g · Carbohydrate 55 g · Dietary fiber 21.8 g · Fat 21 g

Spinach, egg, and chicken wrap

PREPARATION TIME: *about 15 minutes*

SCRAMBLED EGG:

1 egg
1 egg white
1 tablespoon whipping cream (38% fat)
Salt and pepper, to taste

PLUS:

1 tortilla, about 1¹/₂ to 1³/₄ oz,
  preferably whole-wheat
2 tablespoons cream cheese, min. 18% fat
¹/₂ cup fresh spinach
¹/₂ cup cherry tomatoes, halved
3 oz cooked chicken, cubed
1 tablespoon pine nuts
Marigolds, to garnish (optional)

Whisk the egg, egg whites, and cream together. Season with salt and pepper.

Pour the egg onto a hot pan and cook, stirring a little now and then, until it has set. Take the pan off the heat.

Spread the cream cheese onto the tortilla and sprinkle the spinach leaves on top.

Top with the scrambled egg, cherry tomatoes, chicken, and pine nuts. You can toast the pine nuts, if desired. Garnish with marigolds, if desired.

WHAT YOU SHOULD HAVE ON YOUR PLATE

A tortilla wrap with two tablespoons of cream cheese, one handful of vegetables, a portion of scrambled egg, half a handful of chicken, and a small tablespoon of pine nuts.

HOW IT IS DIVIDED IN THE SCANDI SENSE MEAL-BOX

HANDFUL 1 (+2): *Spinach, cherry tomatoes*

HANDFUL 3: *Chicken, egg, egg white*

HANDFUL 4: *Tortilla wrap*

FAT: *Cream cheese, pine nuts, cream*

FLAVORINGS: *Salt, pepper, marigolds*

TIP *Add a good sprinkling of fresh herbs to the wrap, such as chives or basil.*

If men are eating with you

Men can have an extra egg and a little more tortilla, chicken, and pine nuts. See page 210.

Energy 525 kcal · Protein 40 g · Carbohydrate 30 g · Dietary fiber 5.8 g · Fat 26 g

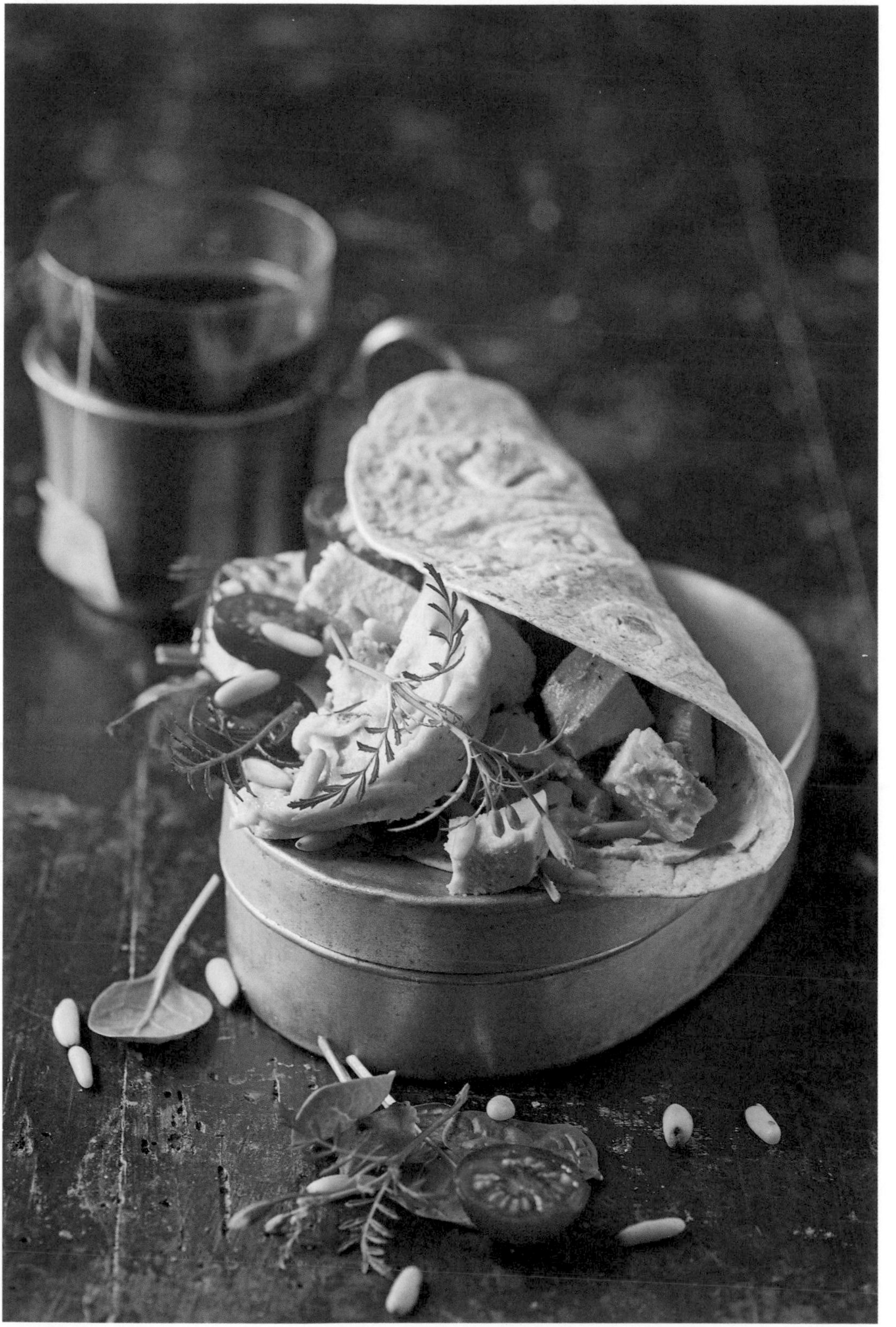

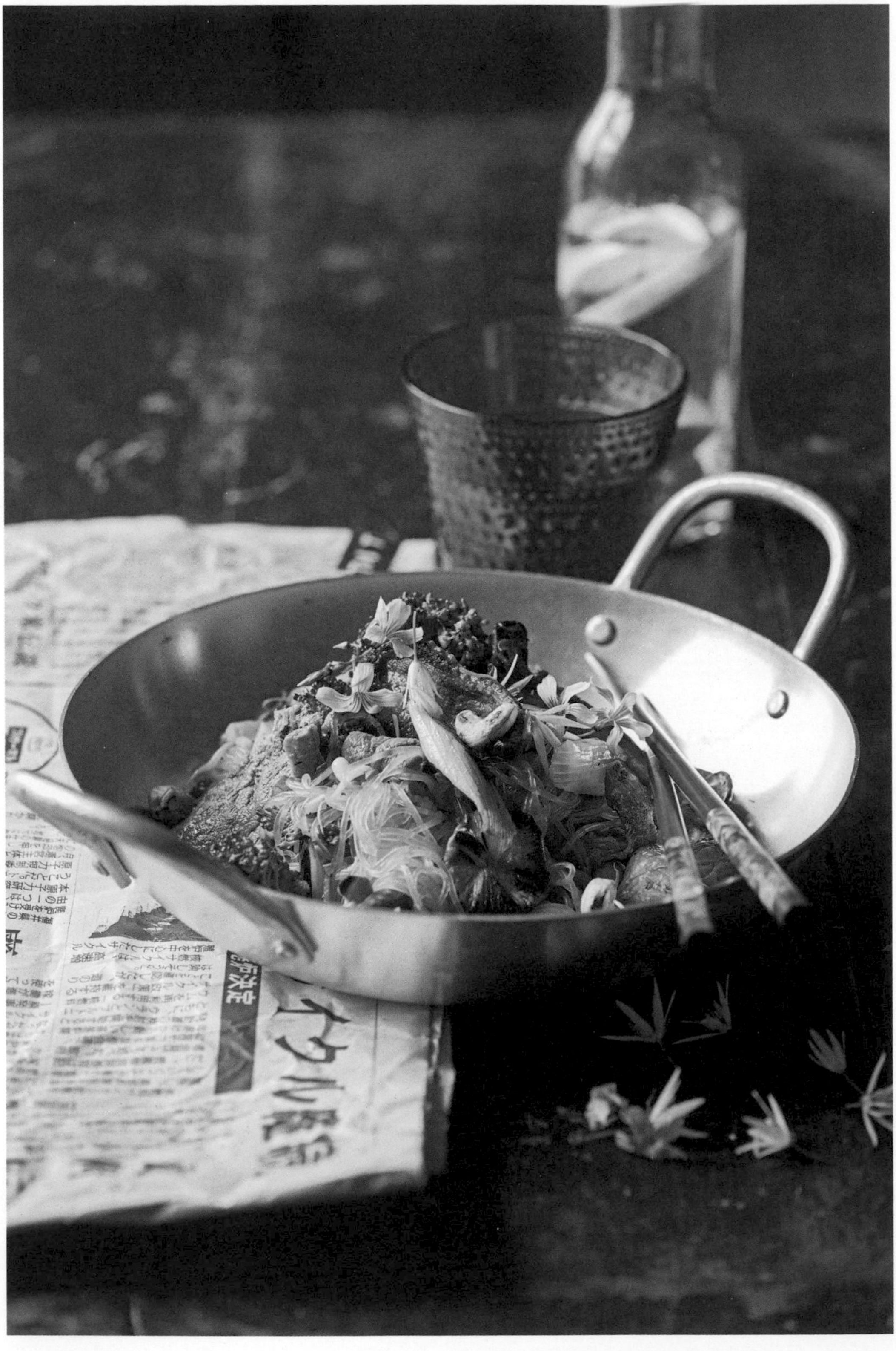

Stir-fried duck breast

PREPARATION TIME: *about 25 minutes*

STIR-FRY:

5 oz duck breast, thinly sliced
$^1/_2$ tablespoon olive oil
$3^1/_2$ oz oyster mushrooms
$3^1/_2$ oz broccoli
2 scallions
$^1/_2$ garlic clove
$^1/_4$ chile
$^1/_2$ inch fresh ginger root
$^1/_2$ cup bean sprouts
1 tablespoon teriyaki sauce
1 teaspoon chicken bouillon powder
Generous $^3/_4$ cup water
1 tablespoon cashews

TO GO WITH IT:

1 oz glass noodles
Sorrel flowers and wild garlic, to garnish

Brown the duck well in the olive oil in a hot wok. Remove from the pan and set aside.

Cut the mushrooms, broccoli, and scallions into small pieces and brown them quickly on all sides.

Thinly slice the garlic, chile, ginger, and bean sprouts. Add them to the wok with the teriyaki sauce, bouillon powder, and water. Return the duck to the wok and heat through thoroughly.

Toast the cashews and sprinkle them over the dish.

Boil the glass noodles in lightly salted water and serve them with the stir-fry. Garnish with sorrel flowers and wild garlic.

WHAT YOU SHOULD HAVE ON YOUR PLATE

Three handfuls of stir-fry and one handful of glass noodles.

HOW IT IS DIVIDED IN THE SCANDI SENSE MEAL-BOX

HANDFUL 1 (+ 2): *Oyster mushrooms, broccoli, scallions, bean sprouts*

HANDFUL 3: *Duck breast*

HANDFUL 4: *Glass noodles*

FAT: *Olive oil, cashews*

FLAVORINGS: *Garlic, chile, ginger, teriyaki sauce, bouillon powder, sorrel flowers, wild garlic*

TIP *Thicken the sauce with a little cornstarch dissolved in cold water.*

TIP *You can use turkey or chicken instead of duck.*

TIP *Combine the glass noodles with the stir-fry while it is still in the wok.*

If men are eating with you

Men can have a little more duck breast, olive oil, cashews, and glass noodles. See page 213.

Energy 545 kcal · Protein 42 g · Carbohydrate 48 g · Dietary fiber 7.5 g · Fat 19 g

REMEMBER!
Twice a day, your plate should contain a combination of the most important elements in the diet: VEGETABLES, PROTEIN, STARCH/ FRUIT, AND FAT

Women's daily diet plan

For those who want to plan

Completed nine-day diet plan—see page 87.

Handful 1 (+2):

Vegetables.

The bracketed (+2) means you can choose to have two handfuls of vegetables, but one is enough.

Handful 3:

Protein from meat, fish, eggs, poultry, low-fat cheese, beans, etc.

Handful 4:

Carbohydrates/starch from bread, pasta, rice, potatoes, etc. as well as fruit.

Fat:

A tablespoon of fat weighs 1/4 to 1 oz, depending on how energy-packed the food item is. A tablespoon of butter weighs about 1/4 oz, and a tablespoon of avocado weighs about 1 oz.

Dairy product:

Milk and cultured milk products with up to 3.5% fat and 5 g sugar per 100 g.

Dairy dressing:

Dairy products with up to 9% fat.

Flavorings:

Spices, seasonings, and herbs, and indulgences used in small quantities to add flavor to the food.

Day 1, woman—total 1,765 kcal

	MEAL-BOX 1: 571 KCAL Breakfast plate with soft-cooked egg	MEAL-BOX 2: 531 KCAL Cottage cheese and mango lunchbox	MEAL-BOX 3: 663 KCAL Spaghetti and meatballs with zucchini
MOST IMPORTANT ELEMENTS IN THE DIET	**Handful 1 (+2):** • ½ yellow bell pepper • 1 lettuce leaf	**Handful 1 (+2):** • 5¼ oz green beans • 1 tomato • ½ red onion • ½ cup peas	**Handful 1 (+2):** • ½ onion • ½ can chopped tomatoes • ½ zucchini
	Handful 3: • 1 egg • 2 slices of air-dried ham	**Handful 3:** • ⅔ cup cottage cheese, max. 4.5% fat	**Handful 3:** • 5½ oz ground pork and veal • 1 small egg
	Handful 4: • Scant ¼ cup Basic Muesli • 1 piece of crispbread • Scant ¼ cup berries	**Handful 4:** • ½ mango	**Handful 4:** • 1 tablespoon bread crumbs • 1 oz spaghetti
	Fat: • 1 slice of cheese, min. 18% fat • Scant ¼ cup almonds	**Fat:** • 1 tablespoon green pesto • Scant ¼ cup almonds • ¼ oz semisweet chocolate	**Fat:** • 2 teaspoons olive oil • ¾ oz Parmesan cheese
OPTIONAL	**Dairy product:** • Generous ¾ cup yogurt	**Dairy product:** –	**Dairy product:** –
	Dairy dressing: –	**Dairy dressing:** –	**Dairy dressing:** –
UNRESTRICTED IN SMALL QUANTITIES	**Flavorings:** • Honey • Salt • Jam or marmalade	**Flavorings:** • Salt • Pepper	**Flavorings:** • Garlic • Chile • Paprika • Salt • Pepper • Parsley • Oregano • Nasturtium flowers

Optional snack between meals: Bouillon drink

Day 2, woman—total 1,655 kcal

	MEAL-BOX 1: 456 KCAL Toast with ricotta, ham, and tomato	MEAL-BOX 2: 579 KCAL Chicken pasta salad	MEAL-BOX 3: 620 KCAL Falafel pita with pesto dressing
MOST IMPORTANT ELEMENTS IN THE DIET	**Handful 1 (+2):** • 1 tomato	**Handful 1 (+2):** • ½ small red onion • ½ red bell pepper • 1 cup mixed salad greens	**Handful 1 (+2):** • ½ onion • ½ cup cherry tomatoes • ⅓ cup peas • 1 cup salad greens
	Handful 3: • ¼ cup ricotta cheese • 1 egg • 2 slices of ham	**Handful 3:** • ½ cup edamame beans • 3 oz cooked chicken	**Handful 3:** • ¾ cup chickpeas • 1 small egg
	Handful 4: • 1 slice of bread	**Handful 4:** • 2¾ oz cooked pasta	**Handful 4:** • 1 to 2 tablespoons flour • 1 tablespoon bread crumbs • ½ pita bread
	Fat: • ⅛ cup pine nuts	**Fat:** • ½ avocado • 1 tablespoon cashews	**Fat:** • 1 tablespoon olive oil • 1 teaspoon pesto
OPTIONAL	**Dairy product:** • 3½ tablespoons milk	**Dairy product:** –	**Dairy product:** –
	Dairy dressing: –	**Dairy dressing:** • 3½ tablespoons plain yogurt	**Dairy dressing:** • 2 tablespoons plain yogurt
UNRESTRICTED IN SMALL QUANTITIES	**Flavorings:** • Salt • Pepper • Chives	**Flavorings:** • Lemon juice • Garlic • Chives • Salt • Pepper	**Flavorings:** • Lemon juice • Garlic • Parsley • Cilantro • Salt • Cayenne pepper • Cumin

Optional snack between meals: Bouillon drink

Day 3, woman—total 1,596 kcal

	MEAL-BOX 1: 506 KCAL Green smoothie	MEAL-BOX 2: 524 KCAL Shrimp noodle salad	MEAL-BOX 3: 566 KCAL Marinated steak with mushrooms and cream
MOST IMPORTANT ELEMENTS IN THE DIET	**Handful 1 (+2):** • $3\frac{3}{4}$ tablespoons spinach • 2 to 3 small carrots • 2 to 3 radishes	**Handful 1 (+2):** • $1\frac{3}{4}$ oz broccoli • 1 small carrot • $\frac{1}{2}$ cup bean sprouts	**Handful 1 (+2):** • 2 mushrooms • $\frac{1}{2}$ leek • $1\frac{2}{3}$ cups mixed salad greens
	Handful 3: • $1\frac{1}{2}$ oz cheese, max. 17% fat • 2 slices of smoked saddle of pork	**Handful 3:** • $4\frac{1}{2}$ oz shrimp	**Handful 3:** • 5 oz skirt steak
	Handful 4: • $1\frac{1}{2}$ cups strawberries	**Handful 4:** • $1\frac{1}{2}$ oz glass noodles	**Handful 4:** • 1 passion fruit
	Fat: • $\frac{1}{4}$ cup cream (38% fat)	**Fat:** • 1 tablespoon peanut butter • $\frac{1}{8}$ cup cashews	**Fat:** • $1\frac{1}{3}$ tablespoons olive oil • $\frac{1}{4}$ cup cream (38% fat) • $\frac{1}{8}$ oz semisweet chocolate
OPTIONAL	**Dairy product:** • Generous $\frac{3}{4}$ cup skim milk	**Dairy product:** –	**Dairy product:** –
	Dairy dressing: –	**Dairy dressing:** –	**Dairy dressing:** • 1 tablespoon crème fraîche, max. 9% fat
UNRESTRICTED IN SMALL QUANTITIES	**Flavorings:** • Vanilla extract • Sweetener	**Flavorings:** • Soy sauce • Honey • Dried red pepper flakes • Lime juice • Cilantro	**Flavorings:** • Soft brown sugar • Soy sauce • Dried red pepper flakes or paprika • Pepper • Vegetable stock • Tarragon • Salt • Vanilla extract • Sweetener

Optional snack between meals: Bouillon drink

Day 4, woman—total 1,503 kcal

	MEAL-BOX 1: 476 KCAL Toast with salmon and avocado cream	MEAL-BOX 2: 514 KCAL Buddha bowl	MEAL-BOX 3: 513 KCAL Curried chicken and rice soup
MOST IMPORTANT ELEMENTS IN THE DIET	**Handful 1 (+2):** • 1 tomato • 2¼ oz cucumber	**Handful 1 (+2):** • 1¾ oz broccoli • 1¾ oz red cabbage • ½ cup peas	**Handful 1 (+2):** • ½ small onion • 1 small leek • 1 small tomato • ½ red bell pepper
	Handful 3: • 3 oz smoked salmon	**Handful 3:** • ½ cup kidney beans • ½ cup chickpeas	**Handful 3:** • 4¼ oz chicken
	Handful 4: • 1 slice of bread	**Handful 4:** • ½ mango	**Handful 4:** • 1½ teaspoons cornstarch • Generous ⅛ cup rice
	Fat: • ½ avocado • 1 tablespoon crème fraîche, min. 18% fat	**Fat:** • ½ tablespoon tahini • ½ tablespoon olive oil • ⅓ cup black olives • 1 tablespoon sesame seeds	**Fat:** • ½ tablespoon olive oil • 1½ tablespoons cream (38% fat)
OPTIONAL	**Dairy product:** –	**Dairy product:** –	**Dairy product:** –
	Dairy dressing: –	**Dairy dressing:** –	**Dairy dressing:** –
UNRESTRICTED IN SMALL QUANTITIES	**Flavorings:** • Lemon juice • Salt • Pepper • Chile • Mint • White wine vinegar • Watercress • Pea shoots • Daisies	**Flavorings:** • Garlic • Lemon juice • Dried red pepper flakes • Cumin • Beet sprouts • Jalapeños	**Flavorings:** • Garlic • Curry powder • Cumin • Chicken stock • Thyme • Salt • Pepper • Parsley • Marigolds
Optional snack between meals: Bouillon drink			

Day 5, woman—total 1,734 kcal

	MEAL-BOX 1: 576 KCAL Oatmeal with stuffed pepper	MEAL-BOX 2: 533 KCAL Roast beef wrap	MEAL-BOX 3: 625 KCAL Cheesy tortilla tart
MOST IMPORTANT ELEMENTS IN THE DIET	**Handful 1 (+2):** • ½ red bell pepper • 2 dill pickles	**Handful 1 (+2):** • 1 carrot • 1 cup mixed salad greens • ½ cup snow peas • ¼ cup dill pickles	**Handful 1 (+2):** • ½ onion • 2 scallions • 3¼ tablespoons spinach
	Handful 3: • ⅓ cup ricotta cheese • 1 egg	**Handful 3:** • 4¼ oz roast beef	**Handful 3:** • 2 bacon slices • 1 egg • ½ cup ricotta cheese
	Handful 4: • ⅓ cup oats	**Handful 4:** • 1 small tortilla (1½ to 1¾ oz)	**Handful 4:** • 1 small tortilla (1½ to 1¾ oz)
	Fat: • 1 teaspoon pine nuts • 2 teaspoons pecans • ¼ oz semisweet chocolate	**Fat:** • 1 tablespoon mayonnaise	**Fat:** • ½ teaspoon olive oil • ¾ oz cheese, min. 18% fat
OPTIONAL	**Dairy product:** –	**Dairy product:** –	**Dairy product:** • 2 tablespoons skim milk
	Dairy dressing: –	**Dairy dressing:** –	**Dairy dressing:** –
UNRESTRICTED IN SMALL QUANTITIES	**Flavorings:** • Salt • Pepper • Cress • Sorrel • Honey	**Flavorings:** • Mango chutney • Curry powder • Salt • Pepper • Wild garlic	**Flavorings:** • Garlic • Nutmeg • Salt • Pepper • Pea shoots • Nasturtiums

Optional snack between meals: Bouillon drink

Day 6, woman—total 1,775 kcal

	MEAL-BOX 1: 576 KCAL Pancakes	MEAL-BOX 2: 586 KCAL Tuna fishcakes with rye	MEAL-BOX 3: 613 KCAL Baked sweet potato with chickpeas
MOST IMPORTANT ELEMENTS IN THE DIET	**Handful 1 (+2):** • 1 cup sugar snap peas	**Handful 1 (+2):** • 2¼ oz sweet potato • 1 scallion • ¼ red onion • ¼ yellow bell pepper • 1 cup baby lettuce greens	**Handful 1 (+2):** • 1 medium sweet potato • ¼ onion • ½ yellow bell pepper
	Handful 3: • 2 eggs • 2 egg whites	**Handful 3:** • 1 can of tuna • 1 egg white	**Handful 3:** • ½ cup chickpeas • 1½ oz cheese, max. 17% fat
	Handful 4: • ½ small banana • ⅛ cup oats • 4 to 6 berries	**Handful 4:** • 2 tablespoons bread crumbs • 1 slice of rye bread	**Handful 4:** –
	Fat: • 1 teaspoon almonds • 2 teaspoons butter • ¼ oz semisweet chocolate	**Fat:** • 1 tablespoon olive oil • 2 teaspoons mayonnaise	**Fat:** • 1 tablespoon olive oil • ½ avocado
OPTIONAL	**Dairy product:** –	**Dairy product:** –	**Dairy product:** –
	Dairy dressing: –	**Dairy dressing:** • 2 tablespoons crème fraîche, max. 9% fat	**Dairy dressing:** • 2 tablespoons crème fraîche, max. 9% fat
UNRESTRICTED IN SMALL QUANTITIES	**Flavorings:** • Salt • Vanilla extract • Cinnamon or cardamom • Honey • Pansy flowers	**Flavorings:** • Garlic • Dried red pepper flakes • Parsley • Dill • Salt • Cilantro or nasturtiums	**Flavorings:** • Garlic • Chile • Cumin • Paprika • Vegetable stock • Lemon juice • Honey • Dill • Salt • Pepper • Wild garlic

Optional snack between meals: Bouillon drink

Day 7, woman—total 1,734 kcal

	MEAL-BOX 1: 557 KCAL **Breakfast plate with cottage cheese**	MEAL-BOX 2: 594 KCAL **Caesar salad with croutons**	MEAL-BOX 3: 598 KCAL **Baked salmon with lemon dressing**
MOST IMPORTANT ELEMENTS IN THE DIET	Handful 1 (+2): • 1³/₄ oz radishes	Handful 1 (+2): • 2 lettuces	Handful 1 (+2): • 1³/₄ oz zucchini • 2³/₄ oz carrot • 1³/₄ oz red bell pepper
	Handful 3: • 1½ oz air-dried ham • ⅓ cup cottage cheese, max. 4.5% fat	Handful 3: • 5 oz roasted chicken breast • 1 anchovy fillet	Handful 3: • 4¼ oz salmon
	Handful 4: • 1³/₄ oz watermelon • 2 pieces of crispbread	Handful 4: • 1 slice of bread	Handful 4: • 3½ oz potatoes
	Fat: • 1 tablespoon sunflower seeds • ½ avocado	Fat: • 1 egg yolk • 1 tablespoon olive oil • ³/₄ oz Parmesan cheese	Fat: • 1 tablespoon mayonnaise • 1 teaspoon olive oil
OPTIONAL	Dairy product: • 7 tablespoons plain yogurt	Dairy product: • 3½ tablespoons plain yogurt	Dairy product: • 3½ tablespoons plain yogurt
	Dairy dressing: -	Dairy dressing: -	Dairy dressing: -
UNRESTRICTED IN SMALL QUANTITIES	Flavorings: • Honey • Raisins • Lemon juice • Red sorrel • Rhubarb curls	Flavorings: • Garlic • Salt • White wine vinegar • Pepper • Pea sprouts • Pansy flowers	Flavorings: • Salt • Garlic • Lemon juice • Pea shoots

Optional snack between meals: Bouillon drink

Day 8, woman—total 1,694 kcal

	MEAL-BOX 1: 528 KCAL Ham on toast	MEAL-BOX 2: 564 KCAL Boston lettuce wraps	MEAL-BOX 3: 602 KCAL Homemade burger
MOST IMPORTANT ELEMENTS IN THE DIET	**Handful 1 (+2):** • 1 tomato • 2 slices of onion	**Handful 1 (+2):** • 1 lettuce • 1 oz carrot • 1 oz yellow bell pepper • 1/4 cup dill pickles • 1/4 cup peas	**Handful 1 (+2):** • 1/4 cucumber • 2 slices of tomato • 2 slices of red onion • 1 3/4 oz red cabbage
	Handful 3: • 1/2 cup edamame beans • 2 1/4 oz ham	**Handful 3:** • 3 slices of roast beef • 2 1/4 oz shrimp • 1 3/4 oz diced chicken • 1/4 cup cottage cheese	**Handful 3:** • 1/2 cup ground beef • 1 bacon slice
	Handful 4: • 1 slice of bread	**Handful 4:** • 3 1/2 oz watermelon	**Handful 4:** • 1 3/4 to 2 1/4 oz burger bun
	Fat: • 1 teaspoon butter • 2 slices of cheese, min. 18% fat • 1 teaspoon olive oil	**Fat:** • 1 1/2 tablespoons mayonnaise	**Fat:** • 1 slice of cheese, min. 18% fat • 1/2 tablespoon mayonnaise
OPTIONAL	**Dairy product:** –	**Dairy product:** –	**Dairy product:** –
	Dairy dressing: –	**Dairy dressing:** –	**Dairy dressing:** • 1 tablespoon crème fraîche, max. 9% fat
UNRESTRICTED IN SMALL QUANTITIES	**Flavorings:** • Mustard • Lemon juice • Salt • Pepper • Watercress	**Flavorings:** • Horseradish or garlic • Salt • Pepper • Chili sauce • Mango chutney • Curry powder • Herbs	**Flavorings:** • White wine vinegar • Sugar • Salt • Pepper • Tomato ketchup • Paprika • Nasturtium flower

Optional snack between meals: Bouillon drink

Day 9, woman—total 1,643 kcal

	MEAL-BOX 1: 573 KCAL Bacon and egg	MEAL-BOX 2: 525 KCAL Spinach, egg, and chicken wrap	MEAL-BOX 3: 545 KCAL Stir-fried duck breast
MOST IMPORTANT ELEMENTS IN THE DIET	**Handful 1 (+2):** • 5¼ oz mushrooms • 1 tomato	**Handful 1 (+2):** • ½ cup spinach • ½ cup cherry tomatoes	**Handful 1 (+2):** • 3½ oz oyster mushrooms • 3½ oz broccoli • 2 scallions • ½ cup bean sprouts
	Handful 3: • 1 bacon slice • 1 egg • ½ can baked beans	**Handful 3:** • 1 egg • 1 egg white • 3 oz cooked chicken	**Handful 3:** • 5 oz duck breast
	Handful 4: • ½ slice of bread • Scant ½ cup raspberries	**Handful 4:** • 1½ to 1¾ oz tortilla	**Handful 4:** • 1 oz glass noodles
	Fat: • 1 teaspoon butter • 1 teaspoon hazelnuts	**Fat:** • 2 tablespoons cream cheese, min. 18% fat • 1 tablespoon pine nuts • 1 tablespoon cream (38% fat)	**Fat:** • ½ tablespoon olive oil • 1 tablespoon cashews
OPTIONAL	**Dairy product:** • 7 tablespoons plain yogurt	**Dairy product:** –	**Dairy product:** –
	Dairy dressing: –	**Dairy dressing:** –	**Dairy dressing:** –
UNRESTRICTED IN SMALL QUANTITIES	**Flavorings:** • Salt • Pepper • Sweet William (petals only) • Pansy flower	**Flavorings:** • Salt • Pepper • Marigolds	**Flavorings:** • Garlic • Chile • Ginger • Teriyaki sauce • Bouillon powder • Sorrel flowers • Wild garlic
	Optional snack between meals: Bouillon drink		

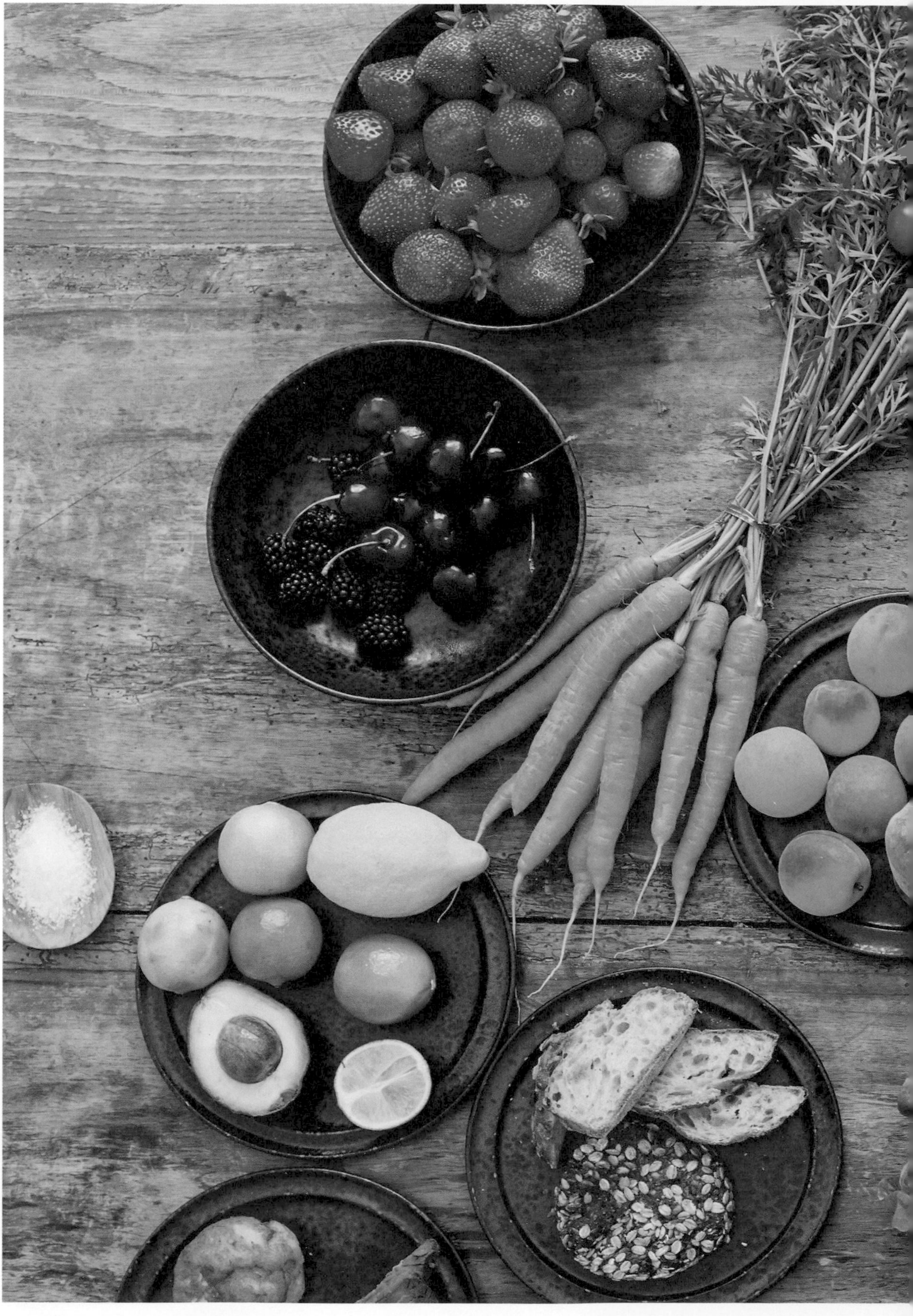

Recipes for men

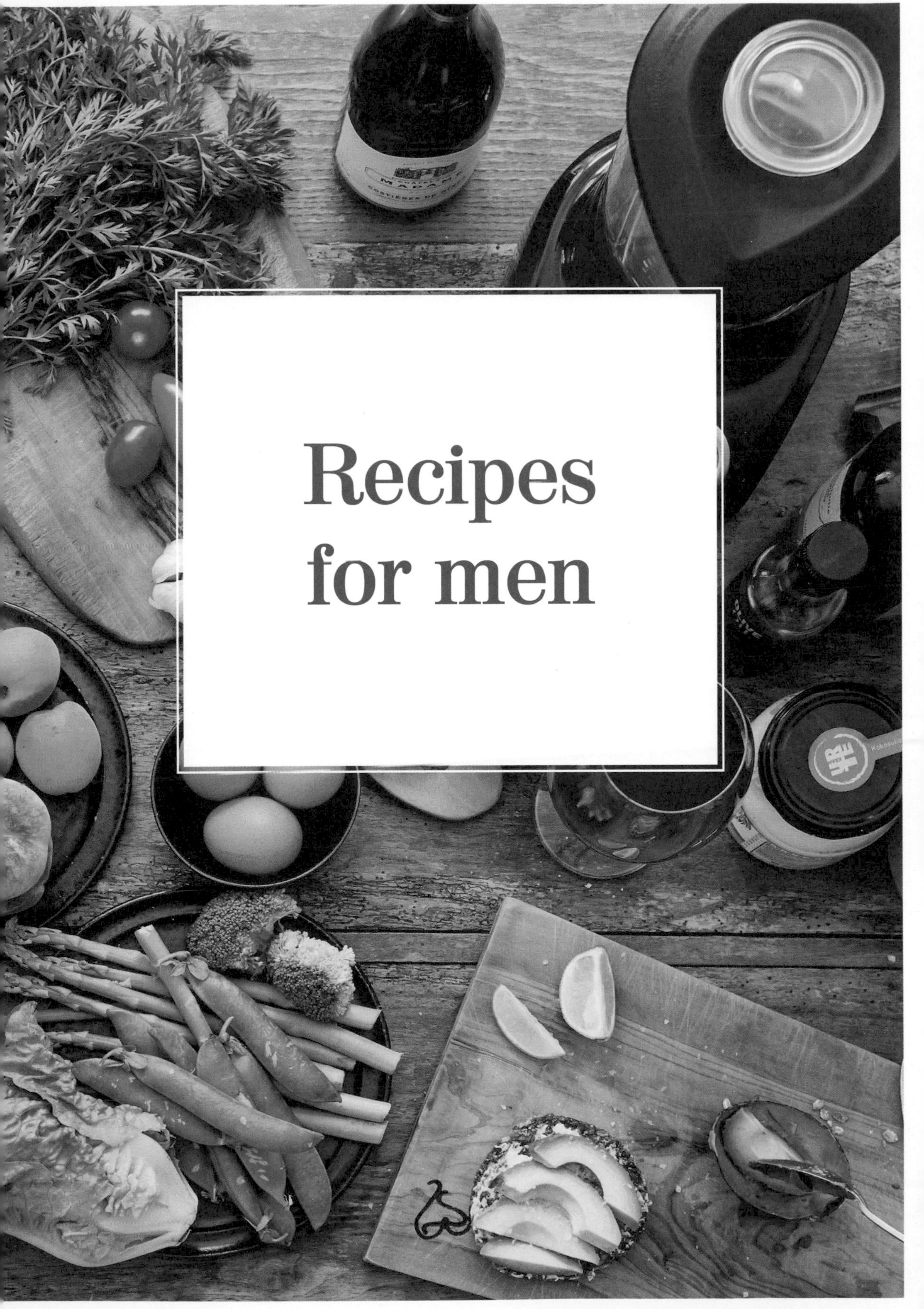

Recipes

ALL RECIPES SERVE 1 MAN

Breakfast

Lunch

Supper

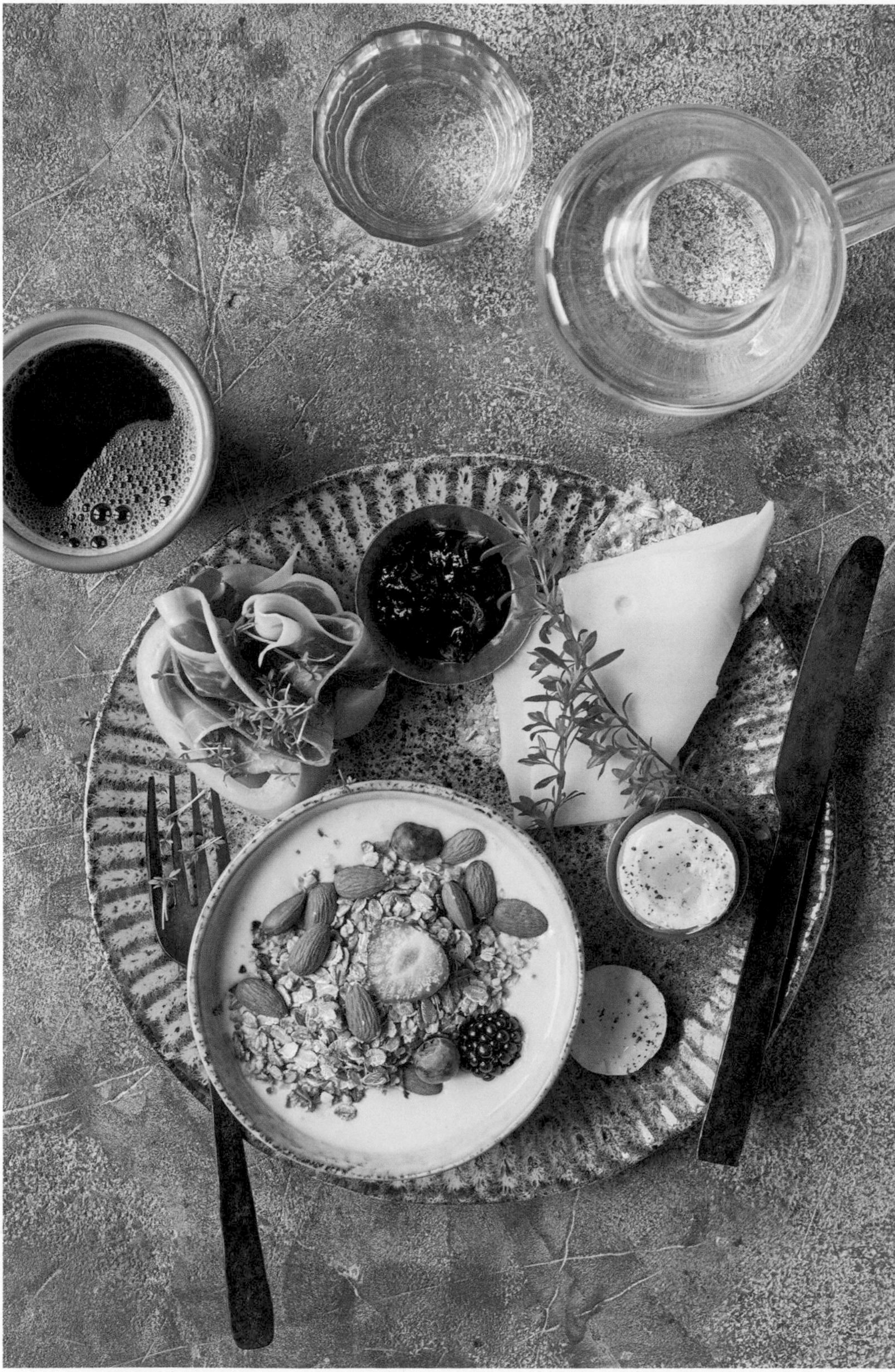

Breakfast plate with soft-cooked egg

PREPARATION TIME: *about 30 minutes*

BASIC MUESLI:

¹/₃ cup rye flakes
²/₃ cup spelt flakes
²/₃ cup oats
2 tablespoons honey
Pinch of salt

PLUS:

1 egg
¹/₂ yellow bell pepper
3 slices of air-dried ham
2 slices of cheese, min. 18% fat
1 piece of crispbread
Thyme, to garnish (optional)
1 tablespoon jam or marmalade
Generous ³/₄ cup plain yogurt
¹/₂ cup Basic Muesli
¹/₄ cup berries
¹/₄ cup almonds

To make the Basic Muesli, toast the rye, spelt, and oats in a skillet over medium heat. When they have browned slightly, stir the honey into the mixture and add the salt. Let cool and store in an airtight container.

Boil the egg for 5 to 6 minutes. Seed the pepper and place the ham inside.

Place the cheese on the crispbread, garnish with thyme, and eat with a little jam or marmalade, if desired.

Pour the yogurt into a glass or bowl. Top with the Basic Muesli, berries, and almonds.

WHAT YOU SHOULD HAVE ON YOUR PLATE

Half a pepper with ham. A piece of crispbread with cheese. Jam or marmalade. A glass or bowl of yogurt with Basic Muesli, berries, and almonds. A soft-cooked egg.

HOW IT IS DIVIDED IN THE SCANDI SENSE MEAL-BOX

HANDFUL 1 (+ 2): *Pepper*

HANDFUL 3: *Egg, ham*

HANDFUL 4: *Muesli, crispbread, berries*

FAT: *Cheese, almonds*

DAIRY PRODUCT: *Yogurt*

FLAVORINGS: *Honey, salt, thyme, jam or marmalade*

TIP *The Basic Muesli will keep for 2 to 3 weeks in an airtight container.*

TIP *You can use store-bought muesli instead of the Basic Muesli, but make sure that the sugar content does not exceed 13 g sugar per 100 g of the product.*

TIP *You can use Skyr yogurt or another cultured milk product instead of plain yogurt, but make sure that the sugar content does not exceed 5 g sugar per 100 g of the product.*

TIP *If you are not full, there is room in the meal-box for another egg.*

Energy 731 kcal · Protein 42 g · Carbohydrate 57 g · Dietary fiber 7.2 g · Fat 36 g

Cottage cheese and mango lunchbox

PREPARATION TIME: *about 10 minutes*

5¹/₄ oz green beans, trimmed
1 tomato
¹/₂ red onion
¹/₂ mango
20 almonds
¹/₂ cup peas
1 tablespoon green pesto
*Generous ³/₄ cup cottage
cheese, max. 4.5% fat*
Salt and pepper
¹/₂ oz semisweet chocolate, min. 70% cocoa

Boil the green beans for 2 to 3 minutes. Drain and set aside.

Halve the cooked green beans. Cut the tomato into small pieces and finely chop the red onion. Remove the mango from its skin and cut the flesh into chunks. Coarsely chop the almonds.

Combine all of the prepared ingredients in a suitable container, along with the peas.

Mix the pesto and cottage cheese together. Season with salt and pepper and serve alongside.

Serve with the chocolate on the side.

WHAT YOU SHOULD HAVE ON YOUR PLATE
The contents of one lunchbox and some semisweet chocolate.

HOW IT IS DIVIDED IN THE SCANDI SENSE MEAL-BOX

HANDFUL 1 (+2): *Green beans, tomato, red onion, peas*

HANDFUL 3: *Cottage cheese*

HANDFUL 4: *Mango*

FAT: *Pesto, almonds, semisweet chocolate*

FLAVORINGS: *Salt, pepper*

TIP *If you are vegan, you can substitute the cottage cheese with beans.*

TIP *You may prefer to use fresh vegetables, but frozen vegetables are fine.*

TIP *You can prepare this lunch the day before and safely store it overnight in the refrigerator.*

TIP *Instead of the almonds, you can use other nuts, grains, or seeds.*

Energy 633 kcal · Protein 38 g · Carbohydrate 44 g · Dietary fiber 13.5 g · Fat 32 g

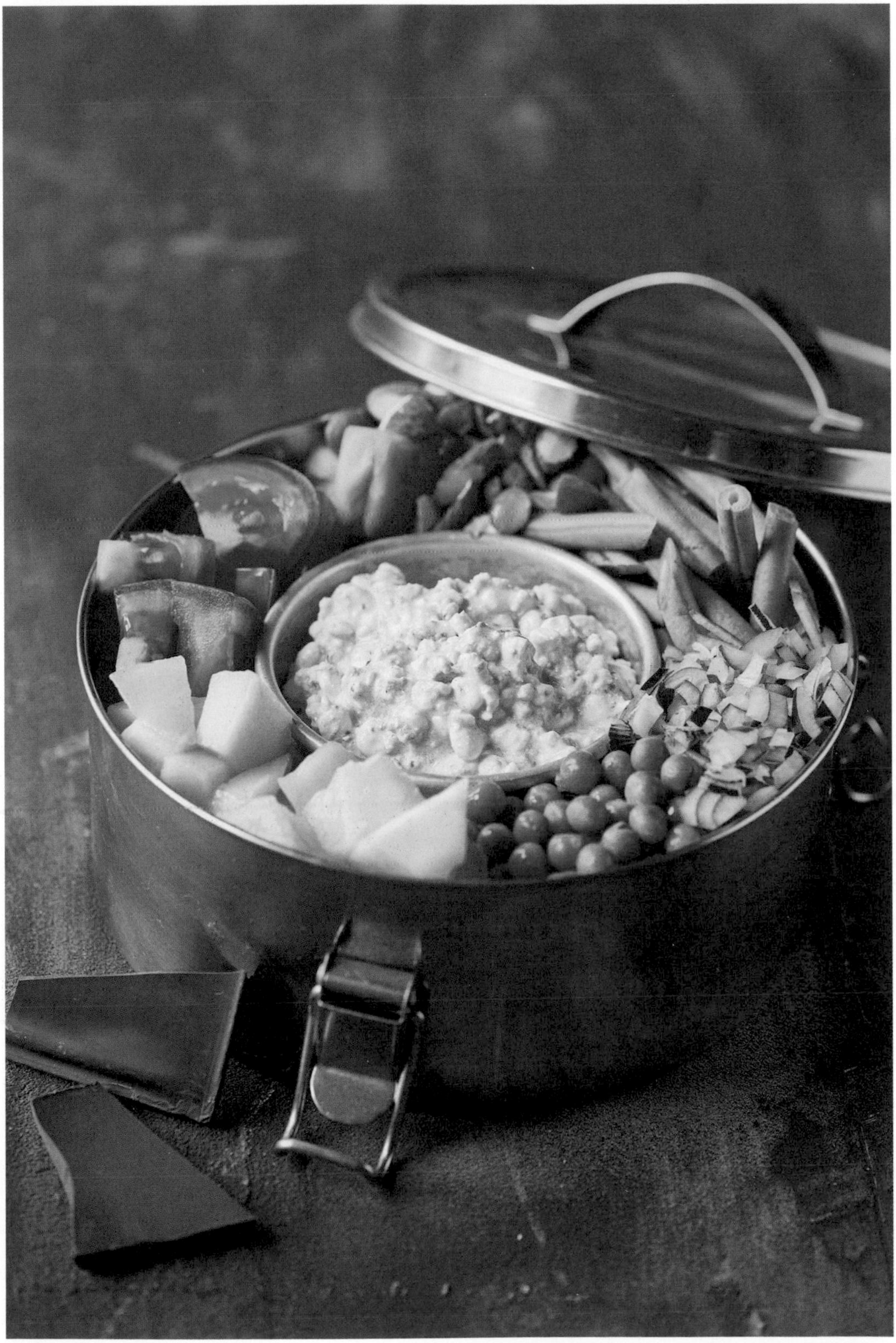

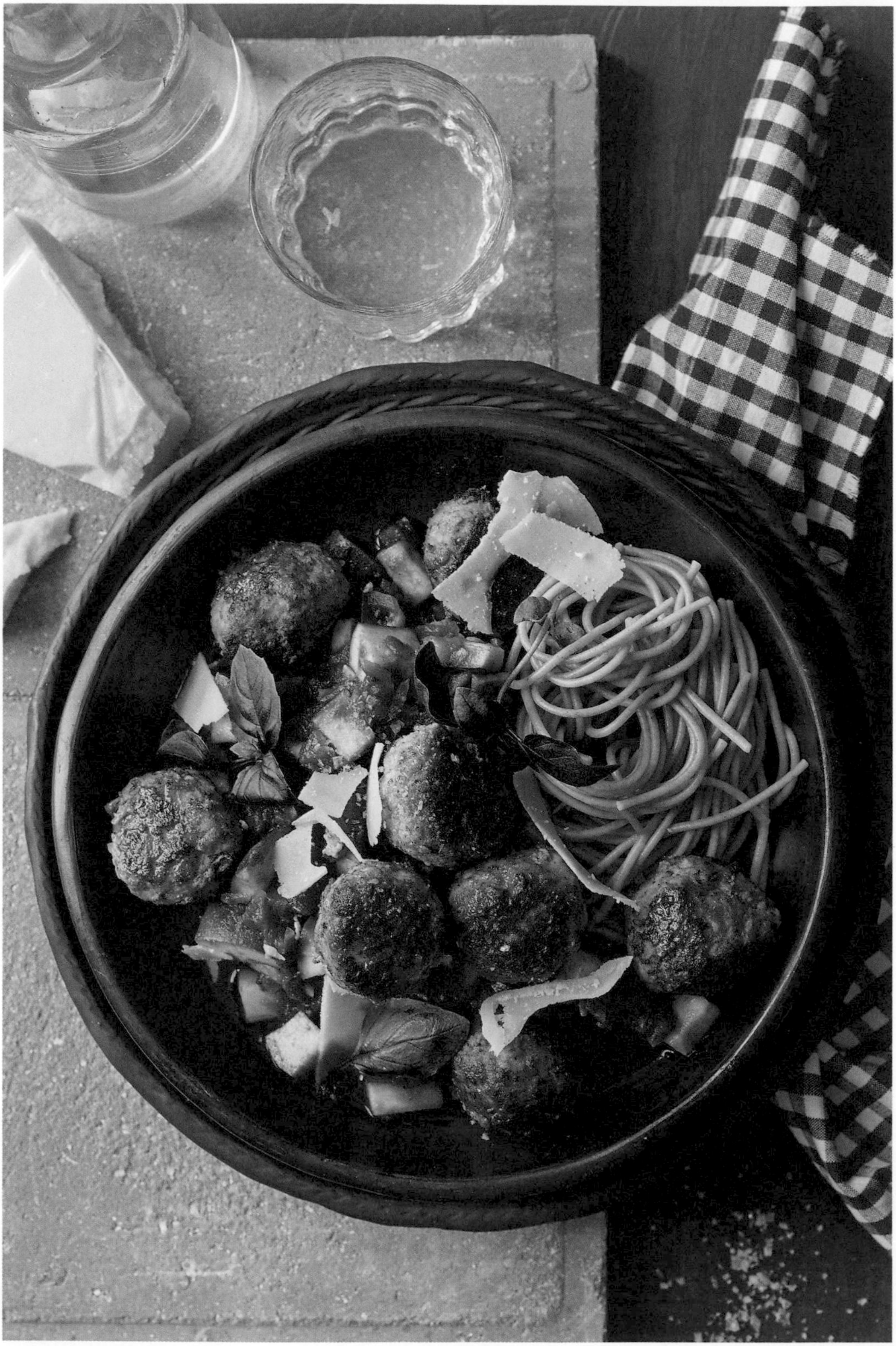

Spaghetti and meatballs with zucchini

PREPARATION TIME: *about 40 minutes*

TOMATO SAUCE:

2 garlic cloves
1/2 onion
1/4 fresh chile (optional)
1 teaspoon olive oil
1/2 teaspoon paprika
1/2 can chopped tomatoes
Salt and pepper, to taste

MEATBALLS:

7 oz ground pork and veal, max. 7% fat
1 tablespoon bread crumbs
1 small egg
1/2 handful parsley, chopped
1 teaspoon dried oregano
1/2 teaspoon salt
1 teaspoon olive oil, for frying

TO GO WITH IT:

1 oz uncooked spaghetti
1/2 zucchini
1 oz Parmesan cheese, shaved
Parsley or red basil, to garnish

Finely chop the garlic, onion, and chile, if using. Heat the olive oil in a skillet and cook them for 2 minutes. Add the paprika and fry for another minute before adding the tomatoes. Season with salt and pepper. Simmer while you make the meatballs.

Mix all the meatball ingredients together and form small balls the size of a walnut. Fry the meatballs in olive oil for 10 minutes, shaking the pan now and then so that they brown evenly.

Cook the spaghetti, following the package directions.

Cut the zucchini into cubes, or shred it, if you'd rather, and add to the tomato sauce 3 minutes before you are ready to serve.

Arrange everything on a dish—first the spaghetti, followed by the tomato sauce and zucchini, and finally the meatballs. Sprinkle with Parmesan and parsley or red basil.

WHAT YOU SHOULD HAVE ON YOUR PLATE

Spaghetti, tomato sauce, and zucchini with meatballs and Parmesan cheese.

HOW IT IS DIVIDED IN THE SCANDI SENSE MEAL-BOX

HANDFUL 1 (+2): *Onions, tomato, zucchini*

HANDFUL 3: *Pork and veal, egg*

HANDFUL 4: *Bread crumbs, spaghetti*

FAT: *Olive oil, Parmesan*

FLAVORINGS: *Garlic, chile, paprika, salt, pepper, parsley, oregano, red basil*

TIP *You can use only pork or only veal instead of mixed pork and veal, or combine meat as desired.*

TIP *You can substitute extra zucchini for the spaghetti if you want to avoid pasta.*

Energy 769 kcal · Protein 68 g · Carbohydrate 46 g · Dietary fiber 11.3 g · Fat 33 g

Toast with ricotta, ham, and tomato

PREPARATION TIME: *about 15 minutes*

RICOTTA MIXTURE:

3¹/₂ tablespoons pine nuts
Scant ¹/₂ cup ricotta cheese
Salt and pepper, to taste

TO GO WITH IT:

2 eggs
1¹/₂ slices of bread, preferably whole-wheat
1 tomato
3 slices of ham
Chives, to garnish
Coffee, tea or water
3¹/₂ tablespoons milk, if required

Toast the pine nuts in a dry pan over medium heat. When they are golden brown, chop them finely and let cool before mixing into the ricotta. Season with salt and pepper.

Boil the eggs for 5 to 6 minutes.

Toast the bread and cut the whole slice in half. Slice the tomato.

Spread the ricotta mixture onto the bread, then add the ham and tomato slices. Season with salt and pepper and garnish with chopped chives.

You can drink a cup of tea or coffee with this meal, and add milk, if desired.

WHAT YOU SHOULD HAVE ON YOUR PLATE

Three half slices of bread with topping, two soft-cooked eggs, and a cup of tea or coffee.

HOW IT IS DIVIDED IN THE SCANDI SENSE MEAL-BOX

HANDFUL 1 (+2): *Tomato*
HANDFUL 3: *Ricotta, egg, ham*
HANDFUL 4: *Bread*
FAT: *Pine nuts*
DAIRY PRODUCT: *Milk, if used*
FLAVORINGS: *Salt, pepper, chives*

TIP *There is room for you to eat 15 to 20 almonds, a piece of semisweet chocolate, or 10 to 15 olives with this meal.*

TIP *You can make do with one egg.*

Energy 686 kcal · Protein 38 g · Carbohydrate 41 g · Dietary fiber 7.9 g · Fat 40 g

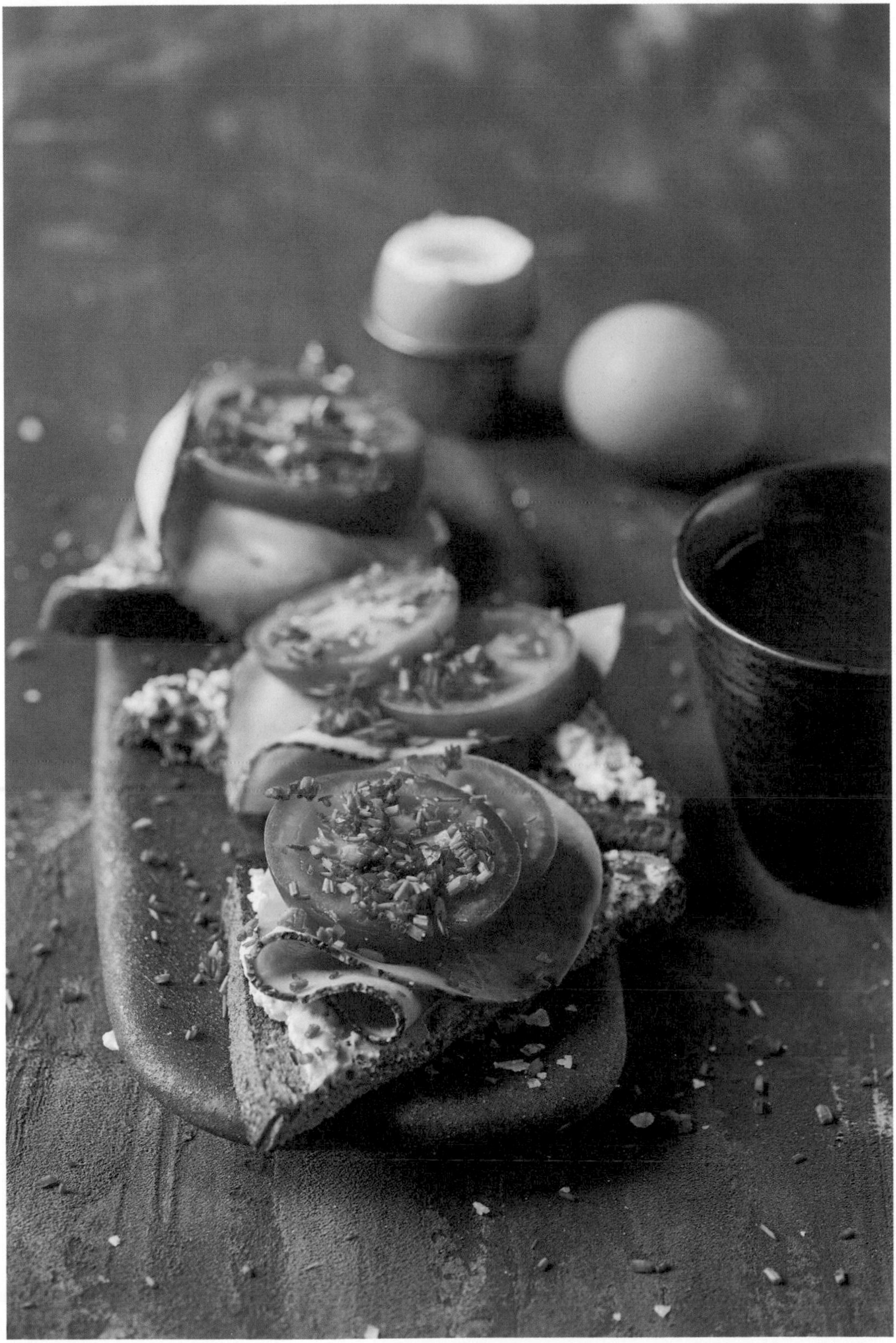

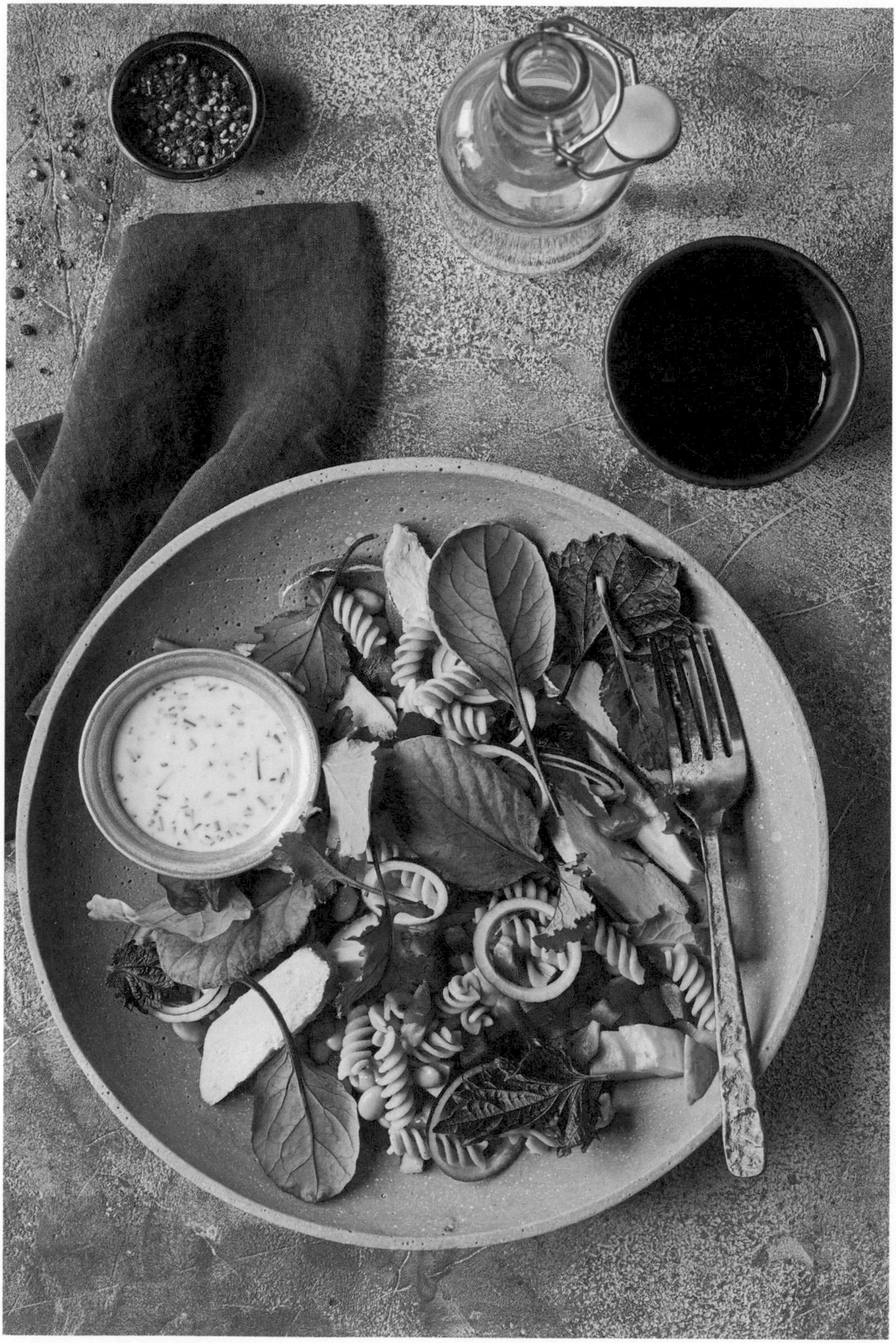

Chicken pasta salad

PREPARATION TIME: *about 10 minutes*
PLEASE NOTE: *The recipe uses cooked pasta.*

³/₄ cup frozen edamame beans
2 tablespoons lemon juice
¹/₂ small red onion
¹/₂ red bell pepper
¹/₂ avocado
¹/₈ cup cashews
1 cup mixed salad greens
4¹/₂ oz cooked chicken, diced or in strips
3 oz cooked pasta, preferably whole-wheat

YOGURT DRESSING:

1 garlic clove
1 tablespoon chives
3¹/₂ tablespoons plain yogurt
¹/₂ teaspoon salt
Sprinkling of pepper
1 tablespoon lemon juice

Place the frozen edamame beans in a bowl and pour over boiling water. Leave for a minute, then drain and toss them in a tablespoon of the lemon juice.

Finely dice the onion and pepper.

Peel and cube the avocado and toss in the remaining lemon juice.

Coarsely chop the cashews.

Finely chop the garlic and mix with the rest of the ingredients for the yogurt dressing.

Arrange all the items, including the chicken and pasta, on a bed of lettuce. Serve the dressing with the salad.

WHAT YOU SHOULD HAVE ON YOUR PLATE

A pasta salad with dressing.

HOW IT IS DIVIDED IN THE SCANDI SENSE MEAL-BOX

HANDFUL 1 (+2): *Red onion, pepper, lettuce*
HANDFUL 3: *Edamame beans, chicken*
HANDFUL 4: *Pasta*
FAT: *Avocado, cashews*
DAIRY PRODUCT: *Yogurt*
FLAVORINGS: *Lemon juice, chives, garlic, salt, pepper*

TIP *You can choose other sources of protein instead of the chicken and edamame beans—you can choose freely between other meat, fish, shellfish, low-fat cheese, or beans. You can easily use up leftovers from supper the day before.*

TIP *Instead of the pasta you can substitute rice, corn, bulgur wheat, couscous, wheat berries, even a piece of baguette—any other carbohydrate item.*

Energy 735 kcal · Protein 50 g · Carbohydrate 60 g · Dietary fiber 12 g · Fat 30 g

Falafel pita with pesto dressing

PREPARATION TIME, INCLUDING BAKING TIME: *about 45 minutes*

PLEASE NOTE: *It is a good idea to let the chickpea dough rest in the refrigerator for 2 hours before you form into balls. However, you can make them straightaway.*

FALAFELS:

1 cup canned chickpeas (drained)
1 tablespoon lemon juice
$^1/_2$ onion
1 garlic clove
2 tablespoons parsley
$^1/_2$ teaspoon ground coriander
$^1/_2$ teaspoon salt
$^1/_2$ teaspoon cayenne pepper
$^1/_2$ teaspoon ground cumin
1 small egg
1 to 2 tablespoons all-purpose flour
1 tablespoon olive oil
1 tablespoon bread crumbs

SALAD:

$^1/_4$ cup cherry tomatoes, sliced
$^1/_3$ cup peas
1 cup corn salad or other salad greens

DRESSING:

2 large tablespoons plain yogurt or
*   other low-fat dairy product*
1 teaspoon red or green pesto

TO GO WITH IT:

1 pita bread, preferably whole-wheat
Lemon wedges

Toss the chickpeas in the lemon juice. Coarsely chop the onion, garlic, and the parsley. Blend in a food processor with the chickpeas. Add the coriander, salt, cayenne pepper, cumin, and egg and blend to a coarse consistency.

Add just enough flour, a tablespoon at a time, so the dough is firm enough to roll into walnut-size balls.

Place the balls on a baking sheet lined with wax paper and brush them with olive oil. Sprinkle with bread crumbs and turn them carefully. Press down lightly on them before you brush them with olive oil again and sprinkle with more bread crumbs. Bake them in the middle of an oven preheated to 400°F for 30 minutes, turning halfway through.

Arrange the salad, falafels, and dressing with the pita. Garnish with lemon wedges.

WHAT YOU SHOULD HAVE ON YOUR PLATE

Two handfuls of salad, one handful of falafels, one pita bread, and two to three tablespoons of dressing.

HOW IT IS DIVIDED IN THE SCANDI SENSE MEAL-BOX

HANDFUL 1 (+ 2): *Onion, tomato, peas, salad*

HANDFUL 3: *Chickpeas, egg*

HANDFUL 4: *Flour, bread crumbs, pita bread*

FAT: *Olive oil, pesto*

DAIRY DRESSING: *Yogurt*

FLAVORINGS: *Lemon juice, garlic, parsley, coriander, salt, cayenne, cumin*

TIP *If you are in a hurry, it is okay to occasionally buy ready-made falafels.*

Energy 754 kcal · Protein 31 g · Carbohydrate 86 g · Dietary fiber 19.4 g · Fat 27 g

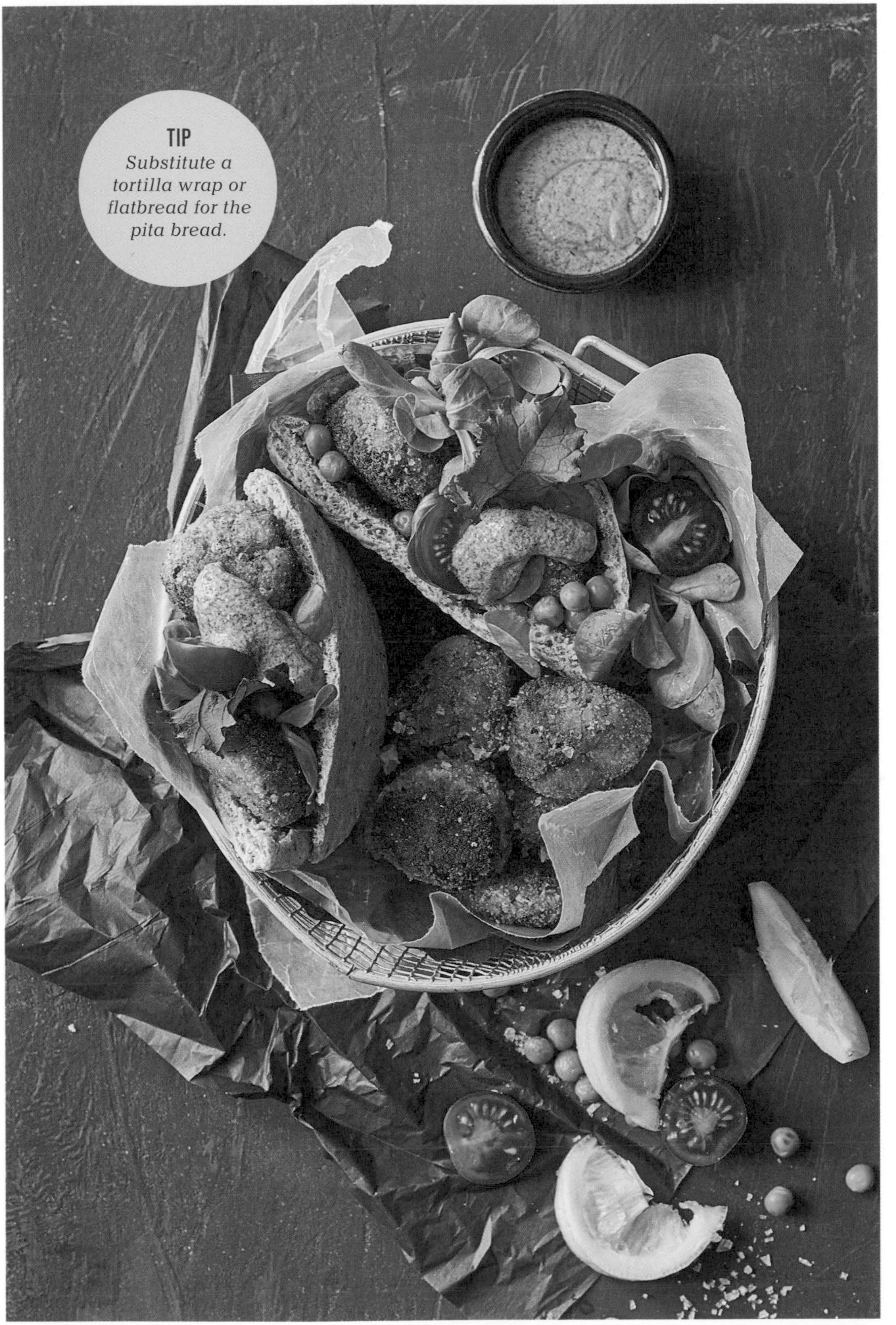
TIP
Substitute a tortilla wrap or flatbread for the pita bread.

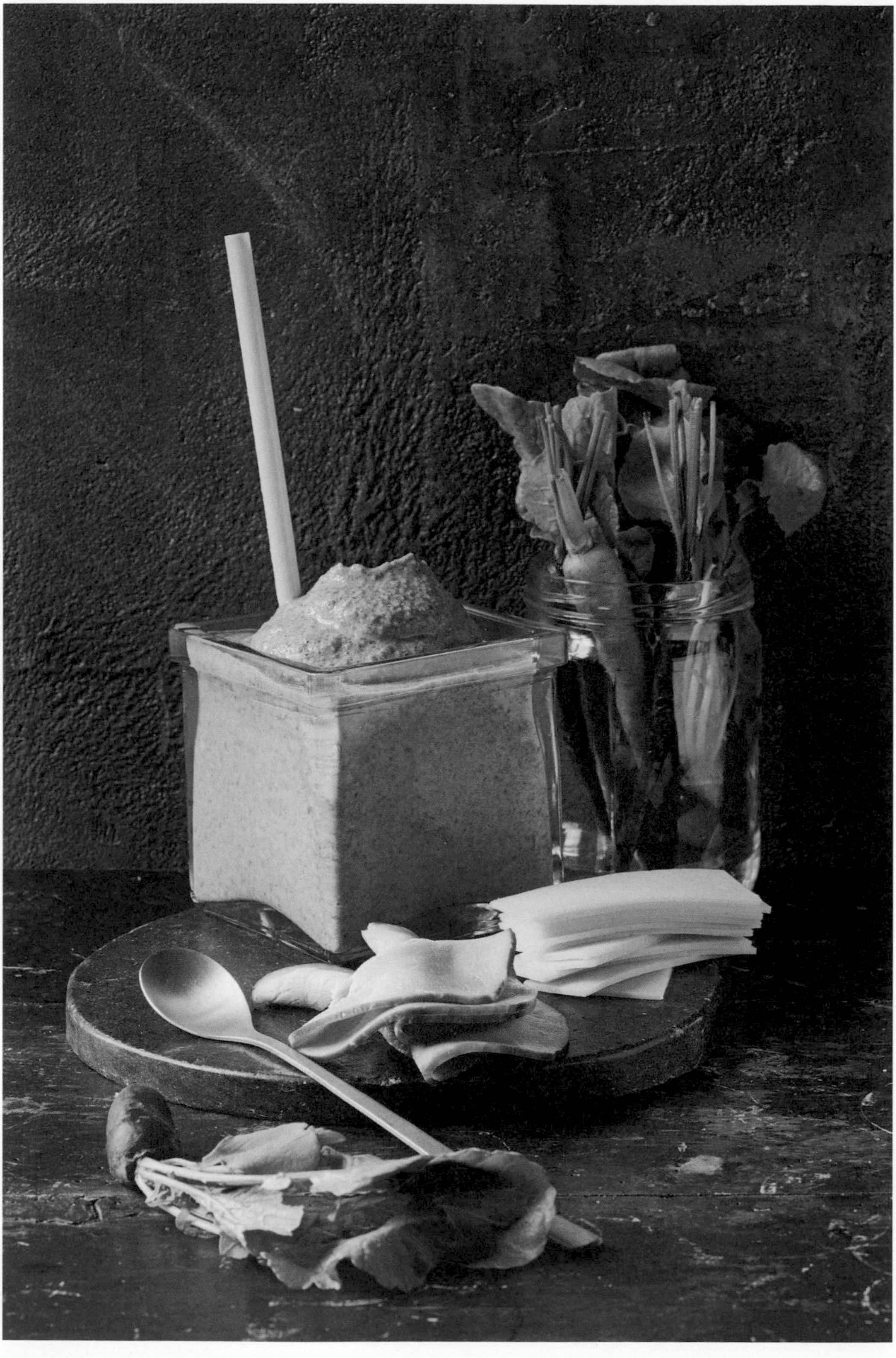

Green smoothie

PREPARATION TIME: *about 10 minutes*

3^1/$_4$ *tablespoons frozen chopped spinach*
1^1/$_2$ *cups strawberries, frozen*
Generous ^{3}/$_4$ *cup skim milk*
^{1}/$_3$ *cup whipping cream (38% fat)*
^{1}/$_2$ *teaspoon vanilla extract*
1 teaspoon liquid sweetener
2^1/$_4$ *oz cheese, max. 17% fat*
4 slices of smoked saddle of pork
2 to 3 small carrots
3 to 4 radishes

Place the spinach, strawberries, skim milk, cream, vanilla extract, and sweetener in a sturdy blender. Blend everything to make a thick smoothie. It may be necessary to stop the blender a few times, stir the ingredients and blend again.

Cut the cheese into sticks or small slices. Serve the cheese, the smoked pork, and the carrots alongside the smoothie.

WHAT YOU SHOULD HAVE ON YOUR PLATE

A smoothie, half a handful of cheese, radishes, sliced meat, and carrots.

HOW IT IS DIVIDED IN
THE SCANDI SENSE MEAL-BOX

HANDFUL 1 (+ 2): *Spinach, carrots, radishes*

HANDFUL 3: *Cheese, smoked pork*

HANDFUL 4: *Strawberries*

FAT: *Cream*

DAIRY PRODUCT: *Skim milk*

FLAVORINGS: *Vanilla extract, sweetener*

TIP *Add a little extra milk if you prefer a more liquid smoothie.*

TIP *Substitute an egg or two for the cheese, if desired.*

TIP *To make a vegan smoothie, use coconut milk, soy milk, almond milk, or other plant-based products instead of cow's milk and cream.*

Energy 629 kcal · Protein 38 g · Carbohydrate 28 g · Dietary fiber 5.9 g · Fat 40 g

Shrimp noodle salad

PREPARATION TIME: *about 15 minutes*

DRESSING:

1 tablespoon soy sauce
1 tablespoon peanut butter
2 teaspoons honey
Pinch of dried red pepper flakes
1 tablespoon lime juice

SALAD:

1³/₄ oz glass noodles
1³/₄ oz broccoli
1 small carrot
¹/₂ cup bean sprouts
6 oz shrimp
1 tablespoon chopped cilantro
¹/₄ cup toasted cashews

PLUS:

Cilantro, to garnish

Combine the soy sauce, peanut butter, honey, red pepper flakes, and lime juice with a whisk to make the dressing.

Cover the glass noodles with boiling water and let them stand for 10 minutes. Drain and rinse the noodles in hot water.

Divide the broccoli into small florets and cut the carrot into matchsticks.

Combine the broccoli, carrot, and bean sprouts in a bowl. Toss the vegetables in the dressing.

Add the shrimp and chopped cilantro.

Arrange the vegetables on top of the glass noodles and sprinkle with the cashews, coarsely chopped. Garnish with sprigs of cilantro.

WHAT YOU SHOULD HAVE ON YOUR PLATE

Two or three handfuls of noodle salad with shrimp, one handful of glass noodles.

HOW IT IS DIVIDED IN THE SCANDI SENSE MEAL-BOX

HANDFUL 1 (+ 2): *Broccoli, carrot, bean sprouts*

HANDFUL 3: *Shrimp*

HANDFUL 4: *Glass noodles*

FAT: *Peanut butter, cashews*

FLAVORINGS: *Soy sauce, honey, dried red pepper flakes, lime juice, cilantro*

Energy 682 kcal · Protein 43 g · Carbohydrate 75 g · Dietary fiber 5.9 g · Fat 23 g

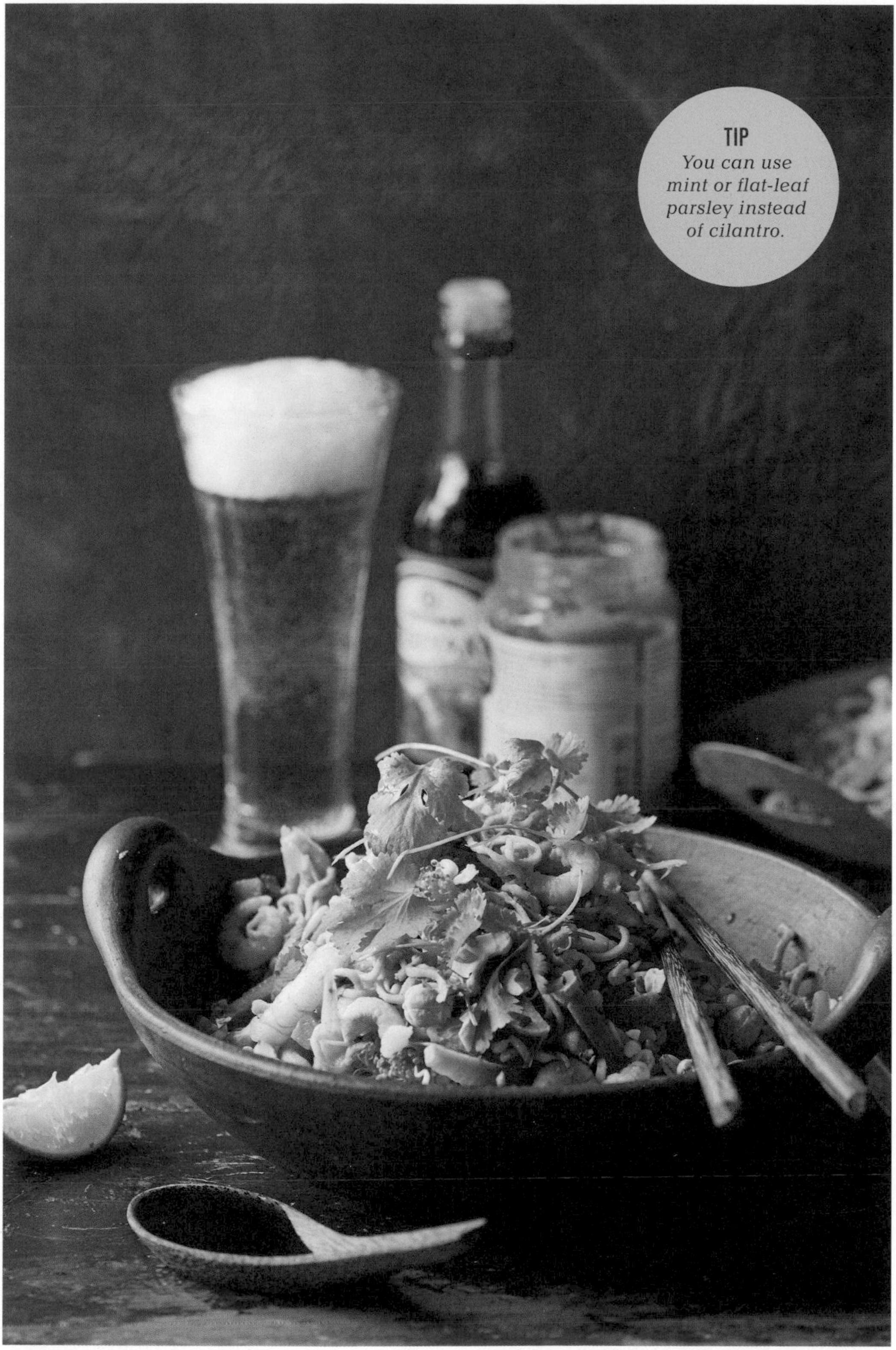

TIP

You can use mint or flat-leaf parsley instead of cilantro.

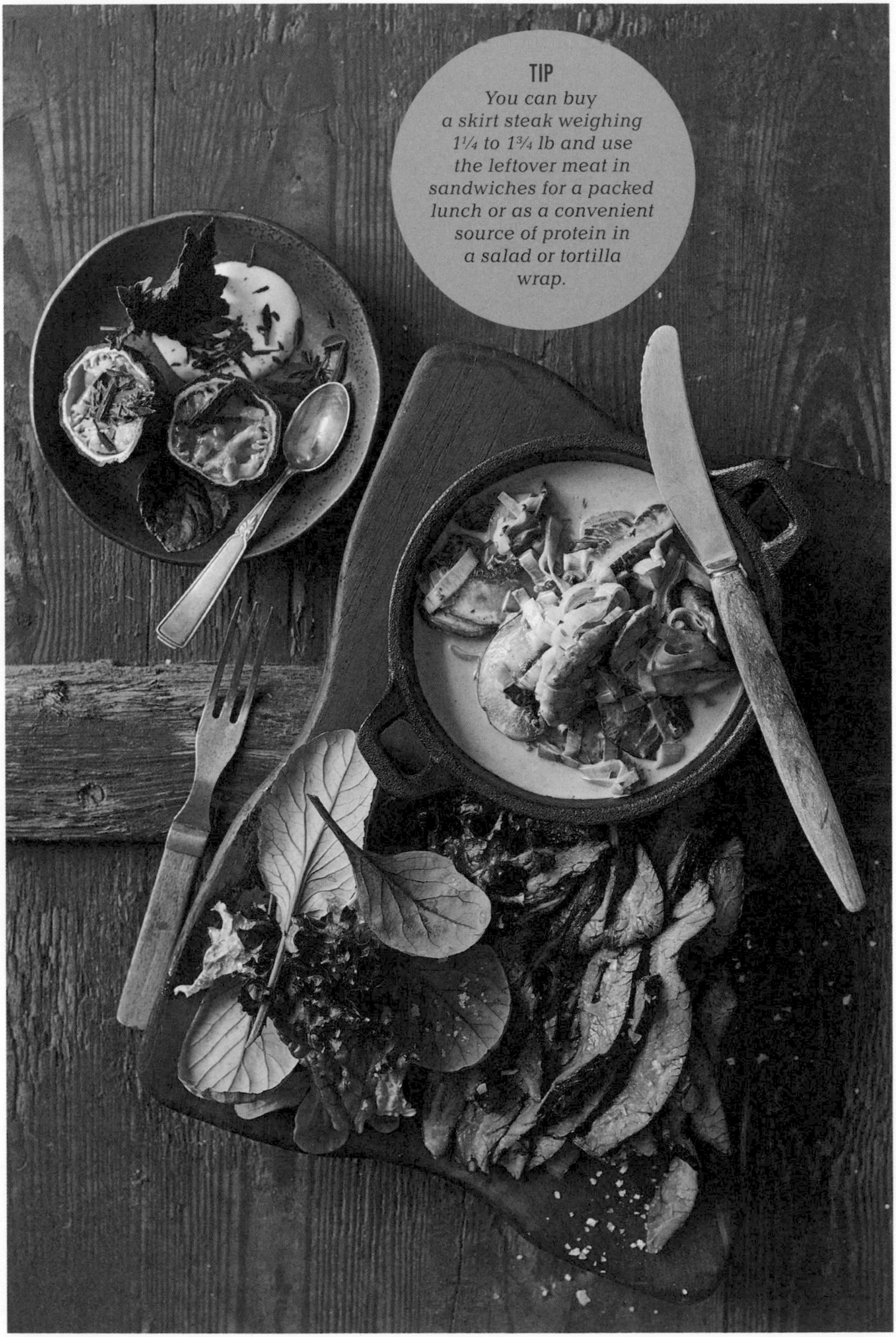
TIP
You can buy a skirt steak weighing 1¼ to 1¾ lb and use the leftover meat in sandwiches for a packed lunch or as a convenient source of protein in a salad or tortilla wrap.

Marinated steak with mushrooms and cream

PREPARATION TIME: *about 25 minutes*

PLEASE NOTE: *Marinate the steak for a couple of hours in the refrigerator, or overnight if possible.*

MARINADE AND MEAT:

1 tablespoon soft brown sugar

2 tablespoons soy sauce

$^1/_2$ tablespoon dried red pepper flakes or paprika

Sprinkling of pepper

1 tablespoon olive oil

1 skirt steak (about 7 oz)

MUSHROOM DISH:

2 portobello mushrooms

$^1/_2$ leek

1 teaspoon olive oil

$^1/_3$ cup whipping cream (38% fat)

$^1/_2$ vegetable bouillon cube dissolved in 7 tablespoons boiling water

$^1/_2$ tablespoon dried tarragon

Salt and pepper, to taste

TO GO WITH IT:

1$^2/_3$ cups mixed salad greens

Fresh tarragon, to garnish

DESSERT:

1 passion fruit

1 tablespoon crème fraîche, max. 9% fat

A drop of vanilla extract

2 drops of liquid sweetener (optional)

$^1/_8$ oz semisweet chocolate, min. 70% cocoa

Mix together the marinade ingredients. Place the steak and marinade in a sandwich bag, close the bag tightly, and marinate in the refrigerator for at least 2 hours.

Slice the mushrooms and leek. Fry the mushrooms in the olive oil for 10 minutes before adding the leek. Add the cream and stock and simmer for 10 to 15 minutes. Season with tarragon, salt, and pepper.

Fry the steak for 6 to 8 minutes on each side. Let rest until the mushroom mix is ready. Arrange slices of steak with the mushroom mix and salad.

Cut the passion fruit in half. Stir the vanilla into the crème fraîche and add sweetener, if using. Serve a spoonful of vanilla dressing with the passion fruit and grate a little chocolate on top.

WHAT YOU SHOULD HAVE ON YOUR PLATE

One handful of salad, one large handful of the mushroom mix, and one handful of steak. One passion fruit with vanilla cream.

HOW IT IS DIVIDED IN THE SCANDI SENSE MEAL-BOX

HANDFUL 1 (+ 2): *Mushroom, leek, salad*

HANDFUL 3: *Skirt steak*

HANDFUL 4: *Passion fruit*

FAT: *Olive oil, cream, semisweet chocolate*

DAIRY DRESSING: *Crème fraîche*

FLAVORINGS: *Sugar, soy sauce, red pepper flakes, pepper, bouillon, tarragon, salt, vanilla extract, sweetener, if using*

Energy 678 kcal · Protein 54 g · Carbohydrate 26 g · Dietary fiber 6.7 g · Fat 39 g

Toast with salmon and avocado cream

PREPARATION TIME: *about 15 minutes*

AVOCADO CREAM:

¹/₂ avocado
1 large tablespoon crème fraîche, min. 18% fat
1 teaspoon lemon juice
Salt and pepper, to taste

DRESSING:

¹/₄ chile
1 tablespoon mint leaves
1 tomato
1 tablespoon lemon juice
1 teaspoon white wine vinegar
Salt, to taste

PLUS:

1¹/₂ slices of bread, preferably whole-wheat
2¹/₄ oz cucumber
4¹/₄ oz smoked salmon
Pepper, to taste
Cress or watercress, to garnish

Mash the avocado with the crème fraîche, lemon juice, salt, and pepper.

Seed the chile. Finely chop the chile and mint. Cut the tomato into small cubes. Toss everything in the lemon juice and white wine vinegar. Season with salt.

Toast the bread and cut it into strips. Slice the cucumber into long strips.

Spread the avocado cream onto the toast, and place the cucumber and salmon on top. Top with the dressing and garnish with cress and pepper.

WHAT YOU SHOULD HAVE ON YOUR PLATE

Strips of bread with avocado cream, cucumber, and salmon with dressing.

HOW IT IS DIVIDED IN THE SCANDI SENSE MEAL-BOX

HANDFUL 1 (+2): *Tomato, cucumber*

HANDFUL 3: *Smoked salmon*

HANDFUL 4: *Bread*

FAT: *Avocado, crème fraîche*

FLAVORINGS: *Lemon juice, salt, pepper, mint, chile, white wine vinegar, watercress*

TIP *If you are in a hurry, just slice the avocado. Arrange it with the salmon and cucumber on top, with crème fraîche instead of the dressing.*

Energy 620 kcal · Protein 32 g · Carbohydrate 45 g · Dietary fiber 8.6 g · Fat 31 g

178

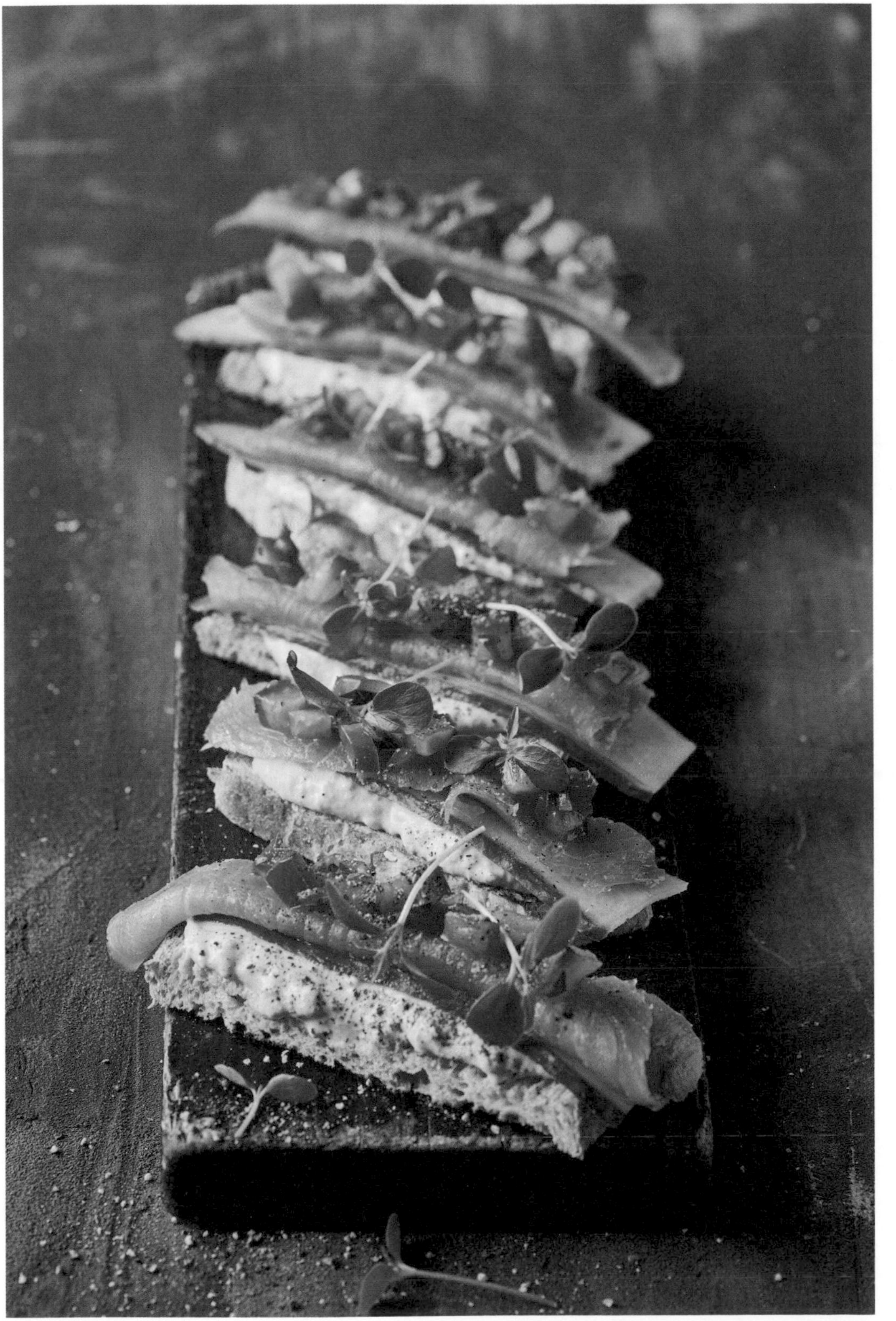

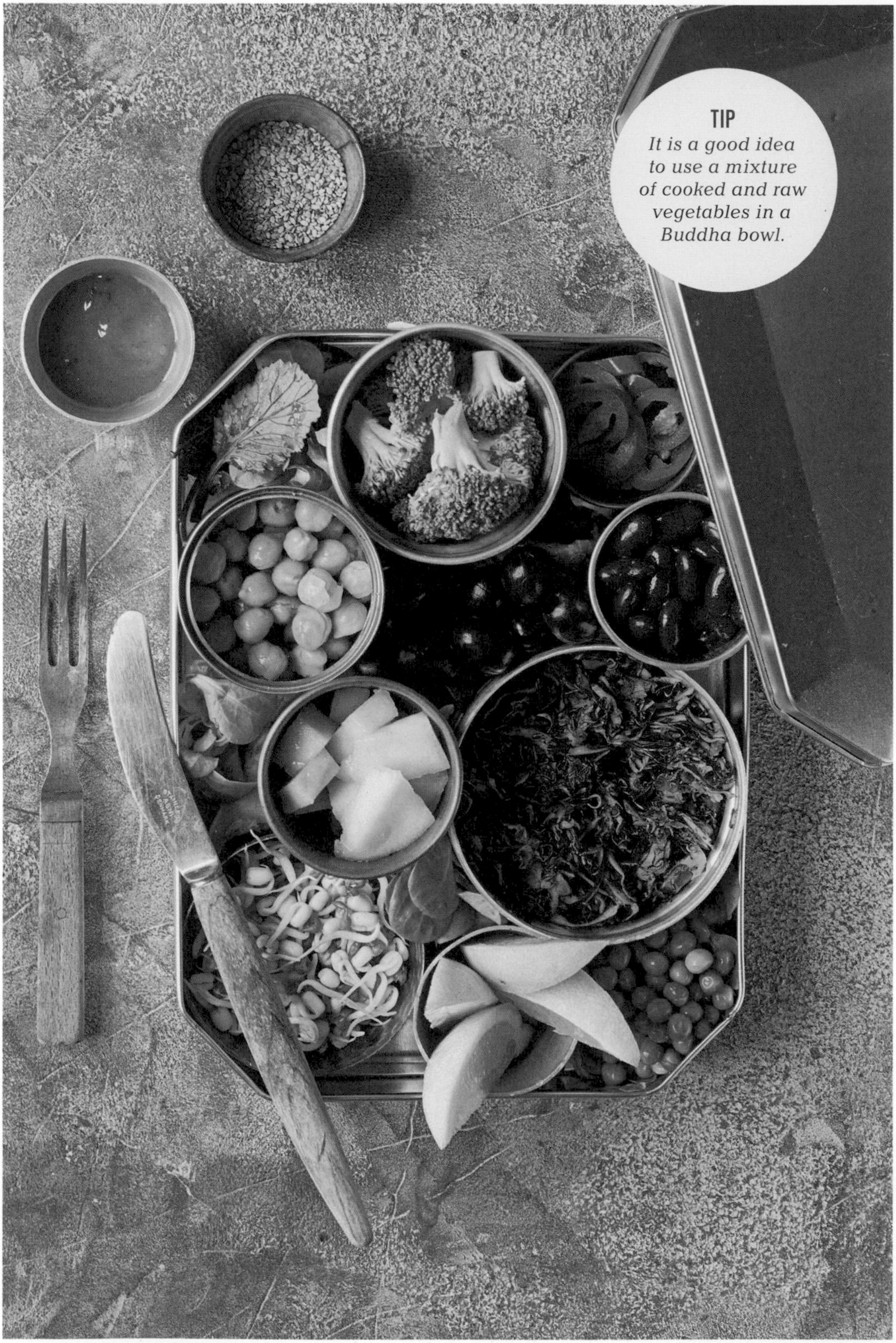

TIP

It is a good idea to use a mixture of cooked and raw vegetables in a Buddha bowl.

Buddha bowl

PREPARATION TIME: *about 15 minutes*

DRESSING:

1 tablespoon tahini
1 tablespoon olive oil
$^1/_2$ garlic clove, crushed
1 tablespoon lemon juice
Pinch of dried red pepper flakes
Pinch of ground cumin

BUDDHA BOWL:

$1^3/_4$ oz broccoli
$^1/_2$ mango
$1^3/_4$ oz red cabbage
$^2/_3$ cup canned kidney beans (drained)
$^2/_3$ cup canned chickpeas (drained)
$^1/_2$ cup peas
$^1/_2$ cup black olives
$^1/_3$ cup bean sprouts
$^1/_4$ oz jalapeños
$^1/_2$ lemon
1 tablespoon sesame seeds

Whisk the tahini, olive oil, garlic, lemon juice, dried red pepper flakes, and cumin together to make the dressing.

Cut the broccoli and mango into bite-size pieces. Finely chop the red cabbage.

Arrange all of the ingredients side by side in bowls.

Serve with the dressing on the side.

WHAT YOU SHOULD HAVE ON YOUR PLATE

Three to four handfuls of Buddha bowl with three tablespoons of dressing.

HOW IT IS DIVIDED IN THE SCANDI SENSE MEAL-BOX

HANDFUL 1 (+ 2): *Broccoli, red cabbage, peas, bean sprouts*

HANDFUL 3: *Kidney beans, chickpeas*

HANDFUL 4: *Mango*

FAT: *Tahini, olive oil, olives, sesame seeds*

FLAVORINGS: *Garlic, lemon juice, dried red pepper flakes, cumin, jalapeños*

Energy 759 kcal · Protein 27 g · Carbohydrate 63 g · Dietary fiber 23.8 g · Fat 38 g

Curried chicken and rice soup

PREPARATION TIME: *about 30 minutes*

¹/₂ small onion
1 small leek
¹/₂ garlic clove
2 teaspoons curry powder
¹/₂ teaspoon ground cumin
1 tablespoon olive oil
5¹/₄ oz chicken
1¹/₄ cups chicken stock
¹/₂ teaspoon dried thyme
1 small tomato
¹/₂ red bell pepper
¹/₂ teaspoon salt
Sprinkling of pepper
2 teaspoons cornstarch dissolved in
* 3¹/₂ tablespoons cold water*
¹/₄ cup rice
2 tablespoons whipping cream (38% fat)
Flat-leaf parsley, to garnish

Dice the onion and slice the leek and garlic.

Heat the curry powder and cumin in a heavy saucepan until fragrant.

Add the olive oil, onion, leek, and garlic, and fry until the onion has softened.

Dice the chicken and add it to the pan. Brown it on all sides, then add the stock and thyme. Cover the soup and let it simmer for about 20 minutes.

Cut the tomato and pepper into cubes then add to the soup. Season with salt and pepper, and thicken the soup with the cornstarch mix.

In a separate saucepan, cook the rice following the package directions.

Heat the soup until it is hot through and add the cream.

Spoon the rice on top. Garnish with sprigs of parsley.

WHAT YOU SHOULD HAVE ON YOUR PLATE

A portion of soup with rice, garnished with parsley.

HOW IT IS DIVIDED IN THE SCANDI SENSE MEAL-BOX

HANDFUL 1 (+2): *Onion, leek, tomato, red bell pepper*

HANDFUL 3: *Chicken*

HANDFUL 4: *Cornstarch, rice*

FAT: *Olive oil, cream*

FLAVORINGS: *Curry powder, cumin, garlic, stock, thyme, salt, pepper, parsley*

Energy 720 kcal · Protein 41 g · Carbohydrate 54 g, Dietary fiber 7.5 g · Fat 36 g

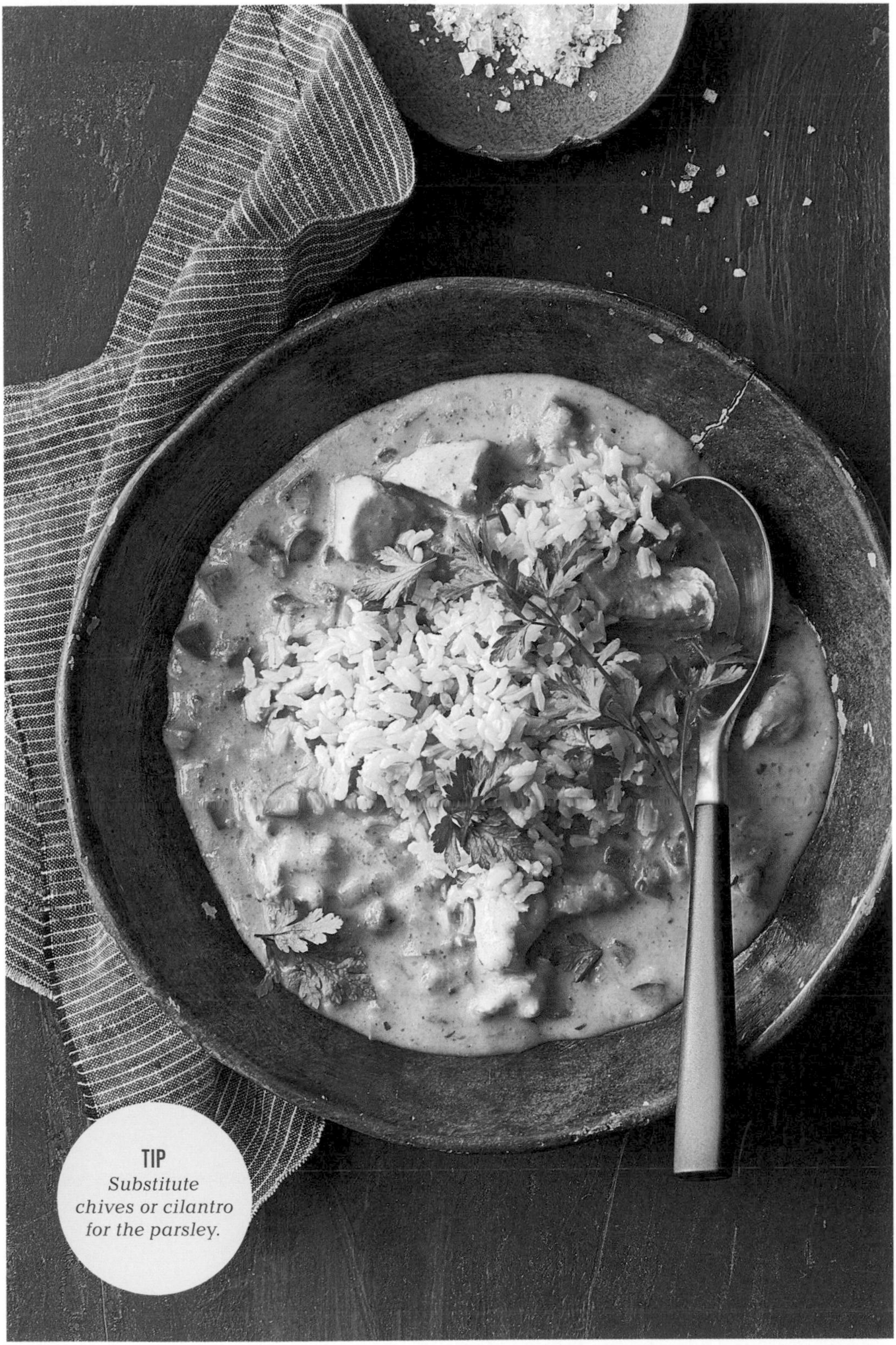

TIP
Substitute chives or cilantro for the parsley.

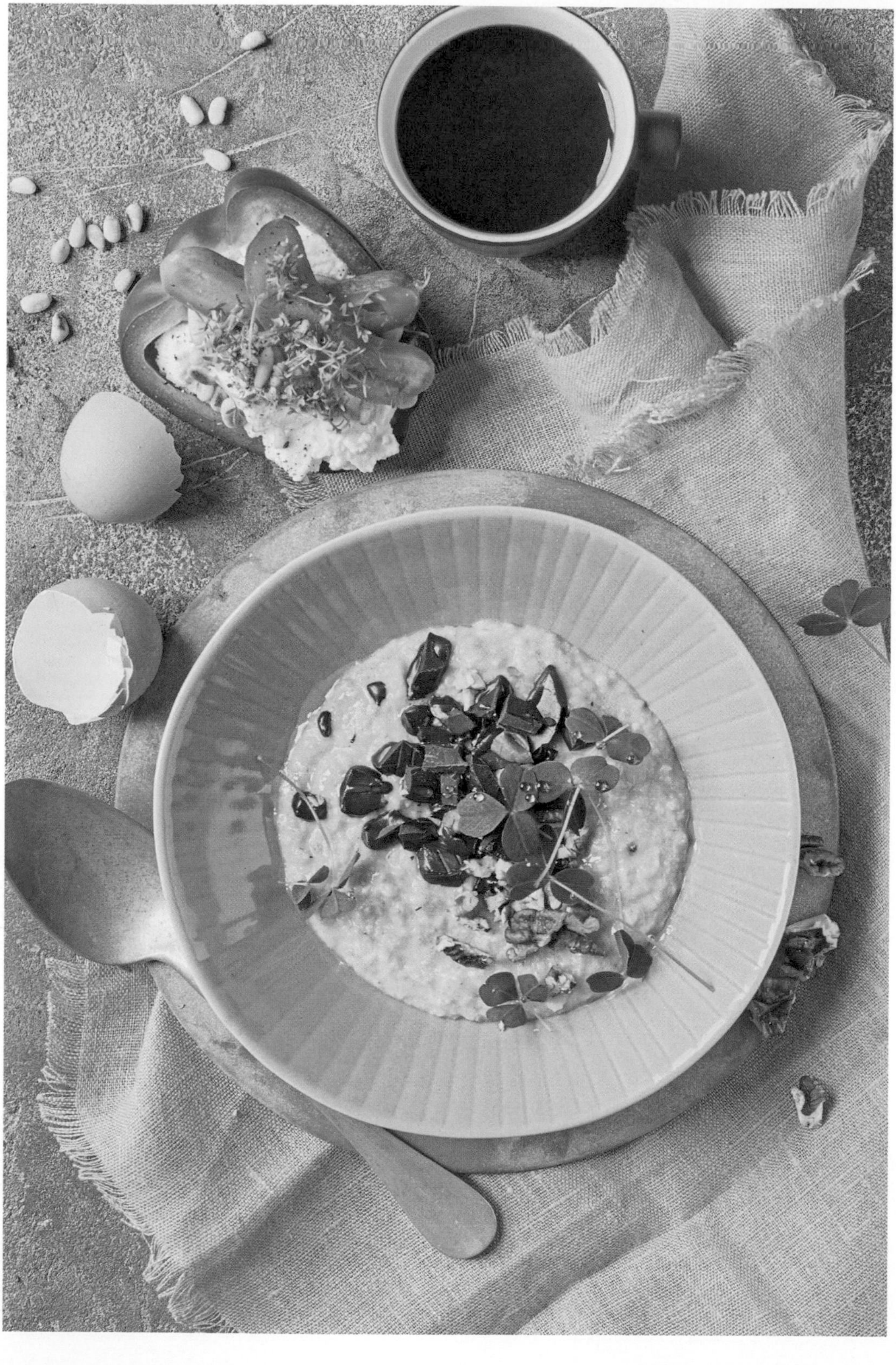

Oatmeal with stuffed pepper

PREPARATION TIME: *about 15 minutes*

STUFFED PEPPER:

2 teaspoons pine nuts
1/2 red bell pepper
1/2 cup ricotta cheese
Salt and pepper, to taste
Cress, to garnish

OATMEAL:

1/3 cup oats
Generous 3/4 cup water
Pinch of salt
1 egg
1/8 cup pecans
1/2 oz semisweet chocolate, min. 70% cocoa
1 teaspoon honey
Red sorrel, to garnish

PLUS:

2 dill pickles or cornichons

Toast the pine nuts in a dry skillet over medium heat. Remove the seeds and white membrane from the pepper. Fill the pepper with ricotta and sprinkle the pine nuts on top. Season with salt and pepper and garnish with cress.

Place the oats, water, and salt in a heavy saucepan. Bring to a boil, stirring the mix continuously for a few minutes, until it has the right consistency. Break the egg into the oatmeal and stir until it is evenly distributed. Coarsely chop the pecans and chocolate.

Garnish the oatmeal with nuts, chocolate, honey, and red sorrel. Serve with the stuffed pepper and dill pickles on the side.

WHAT YOU SHOULD HAVE ON YOUR PLATE

Half a stuffed pepper, two dill pickles or cornichons, and a bowl of oatmeal.

HOW IT IS DIVIDED IN THE SCANDI SENSE MEAL-BOX

HANDFUL 1 (+ 2): *Pepper, dill pickles*

HANDFUL 3: *Ricotta, egg*

HANDFUL 4: *Oats*

FAT: *Pine nuts, pecans, chocolate*

FLAVORINGS: *Salt, pepper, cress, honey, red sorrel*

TIP *You can substitute the ricotta for quark or cottage cheese, if desired.*

TIP *You can substitute the pecans for any other kind of nuts, grains, or seeds.*

Energy 739 kcal · Protein 26 g · Carbohydrate 53 g · Dietary fiber 7.5 g · Fat 46 g

Roast beef wrap

PREPARATION TIME: *about 10 minutes*

MANGO DRESSING:

1 tablespoon mango chutney
2 tablespoons mayonnaise
1/2 teaspoon curry powder
Salt and pepper, to taste

PLUS:

1 carrot
1 large tortilla, preferably whole-
wheat, about 2 1/2 oz
1 cup mixed salad greens
1/2 cup snow peas
1/4 cup dill pickles
5 1/4 oz roast beef, cut into strips

Mix the mango chutney, mayonnaise, and curry powder to make the dressing. Season with salt and pepper.

Cut the carrot into matchsticks.

Lay the tortilla flat on a cutting board and spread half the dressing on it.

Place the salad greens and vegetables loosely on top, then the rest of the dressing and the beef.

Fold in one end to form a base, and then fold in the two sides, so that the wrap forms an envelope.

WHAT YOU SHOULD HAVE ON YOUR PLATE

A wrap filled with one handful of vegetables, one handful of meat, and some mango dressing.

HOW IT IS DIVIDED IN THE SCANDI SENSE MEAL-BOX

HANDFUL 1 (+ 2): *Salad, carrot, snow peas, dill pickle*

HANDFUL 3: *Roast beef*

HANDFUL 4: *Tortilla wrap*

FAT: *Mayonnaise*

FLAVORINGS: *Mango chutney, curry powder, salt, pepper*

TIP *Substitute rye bread for the tortilla.*

Energy 716 kcal · Protein 41 g · Carbohydrate 56 g · Dietary fiber 8.4 g · Fat 34 g

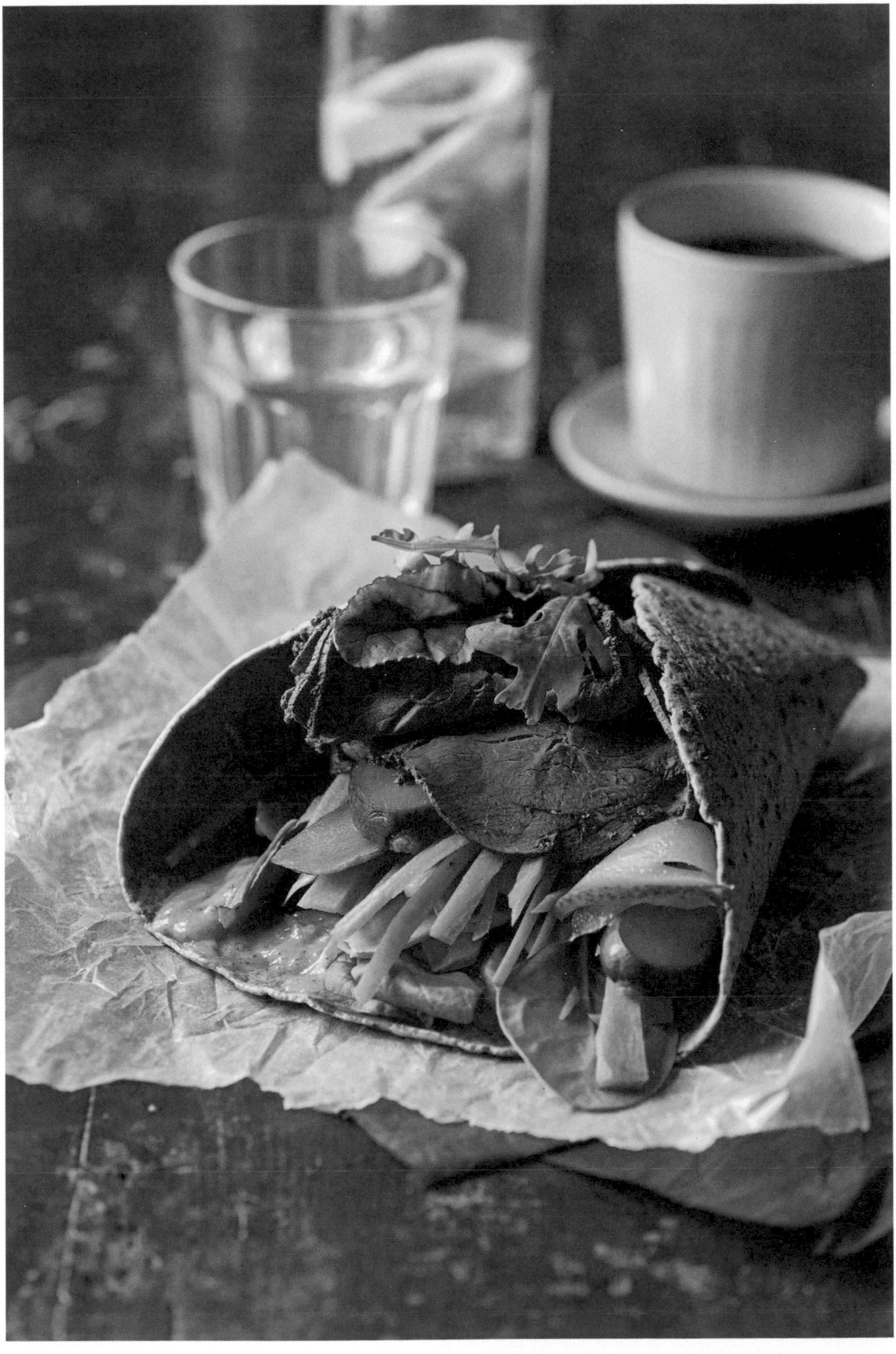

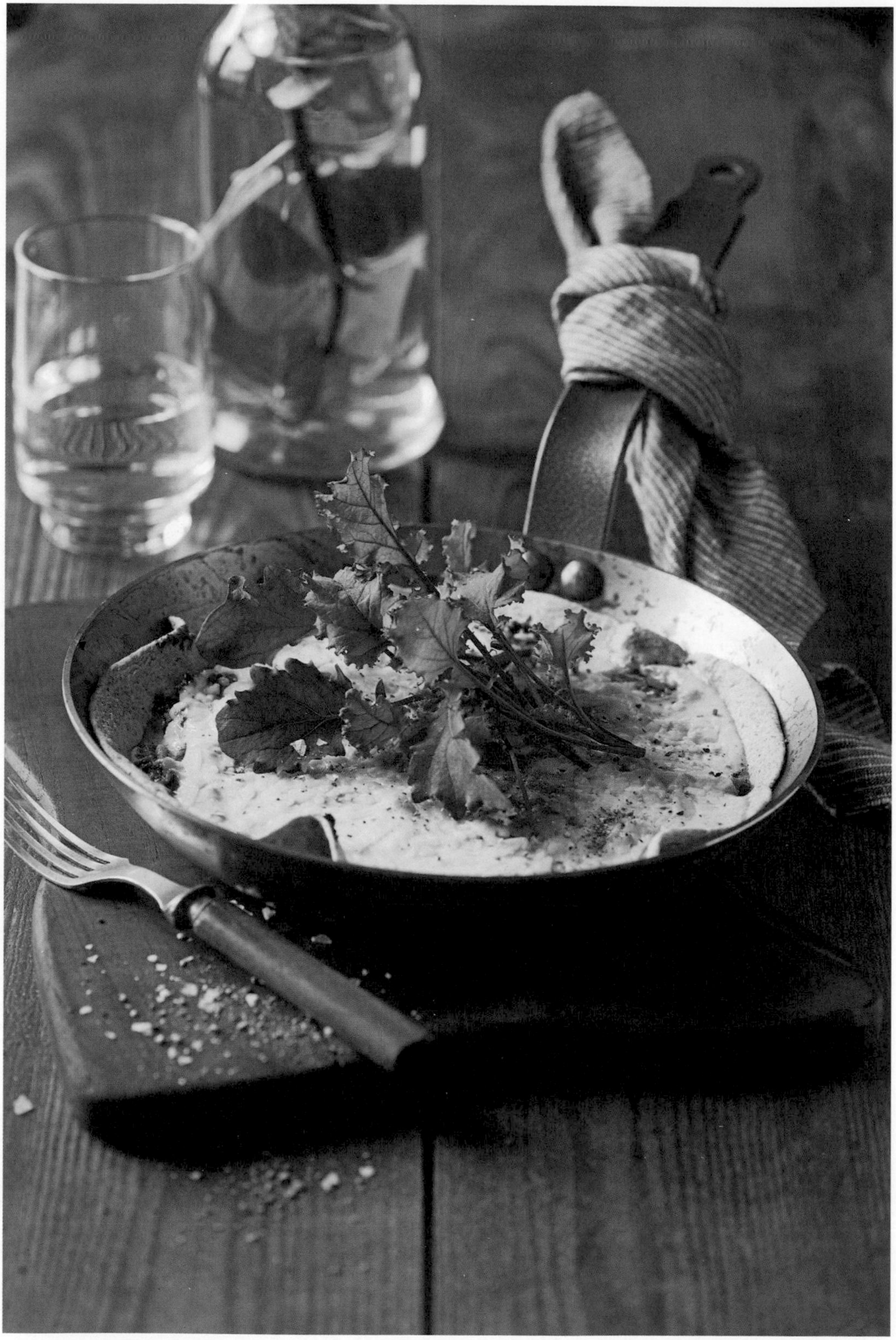

Cheesy tortilla tart

PREPARATION TIME, INCLUDING BAKING TIME: *about 40 minutes*

SPINACH MIXTURE:

¹/2 onion
1 garlic clove
3 scallions
2 bacon slices
3¹/4 tablespoons frozen chopped spinach

CHEESE FILLING:

1 egg
¹/2 cup ricotta cheese
¹/2 teaspoon grated nutmeg
¹/2 teaspoon salt
Sprinkling of pepper
2 tablespoons skim milk
¹/2 teaspoon olive oil

PLUS:

*1 large tortilla, preferably
   whole-wheat, about 2¹/2 oz*
1 oz cup grated cheese, min. 18% fat
Lettuce, to garnish

Finely chop the onion, garlic, and scallions. Chop the bacon into small pieces and fry over medium heat for a few minutes before adding the onion and garlic. Add the spinach and scallions. Continue frying until the spinach has fully defrosted.

Whisk together the egg, ricotta, nutmeg, salt, pepper, and milk to make a smooth custard.

Brush a suitable ovenproof dish with the olive oil and place the tortilla in the dish. Press it into the edges.

Put the filling in the tortilla in the following order: half of the spinach mixture, half of the cheese filling, the rest of the spinach mixture, the rest of the cheese filling. Top with the grated cheese.

Bake in an oven preheated to 400°F for 30 minutes. Garnish with lettuce and serve.

WHAT YOU SHOULD HAVE ON YOUR PLATE

A tortilla tart with a little lettuce on top.

HOW IT IS DIVIDED IN
THE SCANDI SENSE MEAL-BOX

HANDFUL 1 (+ 2): *Onion, scallions, spinach, lettuce*

HANDFUL 3: *Bacon, egg, ricotta*

HANDFUL 4: *Whole-wheat tortilla*

FAT: *Olive oil, cheese*

DAIRY PRODUCT: *Skim milk*

FLAVORINGS: *Garlic, nutmeg, salt, pepper*

TIP *Season with your favorite herb, for example 1 tablespoon dried thyme instead of nutmeg.*

TIP *Why not make an extra as an easy lunch for tomorrow?*

Energy 718 kcal · Protein 38 g · Carbohydrate 46 g · Dietary fiber 9.4 g · Fat 40 g

Pancakes

PREPARATION TIME, INCLUDING RESTING TIME: *about 30 minutes*

PLEASE NOTE: *This makes enough batter for 5 to 7 small pancakes, which constitutes 1 portion.*

PANCAKE BATTER:

³/₄ *small banana*
Scant ¹/₄ *cup oats*
3 eggs
2 egg whites
Pinch of salt
¹/₂ *teaspoon vanilla extract*
¹/₂ *teaspoon ground cinnamon or cardamom*
1 tablespoon honey

PLUS:

2 teaspoons almonds
¹/₂ *oz semisweet chocolate, min. 70% cocoa*
1 tablespoon butter
5 to 7 berries

TO GO WITH IT:

1 cup sugar snap peas

Place all the ingredients for the pancake batter in a blender. Blend until smooth, then let rest for 10 to 15 minutes.

Chop the almonds and chocolate into nibs.

Melt a little butter in a pan and drop the batter on in blobs. When they have begun to set, add a berry to the middle of each one. Turn them over when the batter has set completely to cook the other side.

Arrange the pancakes with a sprinkling of chocolate and almond nibs on top.

Serve the peas in a bowl on the side.

WHAT YOU SHOULD HAVE ON YOUR PLATE

All of the pancakes, with chocolate and almond nibs. One handful of sugar snap peas on the side.

HOW IT IS DIVIDED IN THE SCANDI SENSE MEAL-BOX

HANDFUL 1 (+ 2): *Sugar snap peas*

HANDFUL 3: *Egg, egg whites*

HANDFUL 4: *Banana, oats, berries*

FAT: *Almonds, butter, chocolate*

FLAVORINGS: *Salt, vanilla extract, cinnamon or cardamom, honey*

Energy 799 kcal · Protein 40 g · Carbohydrate 67 g · Dietary fiber 9.1 g · Fat 40 g

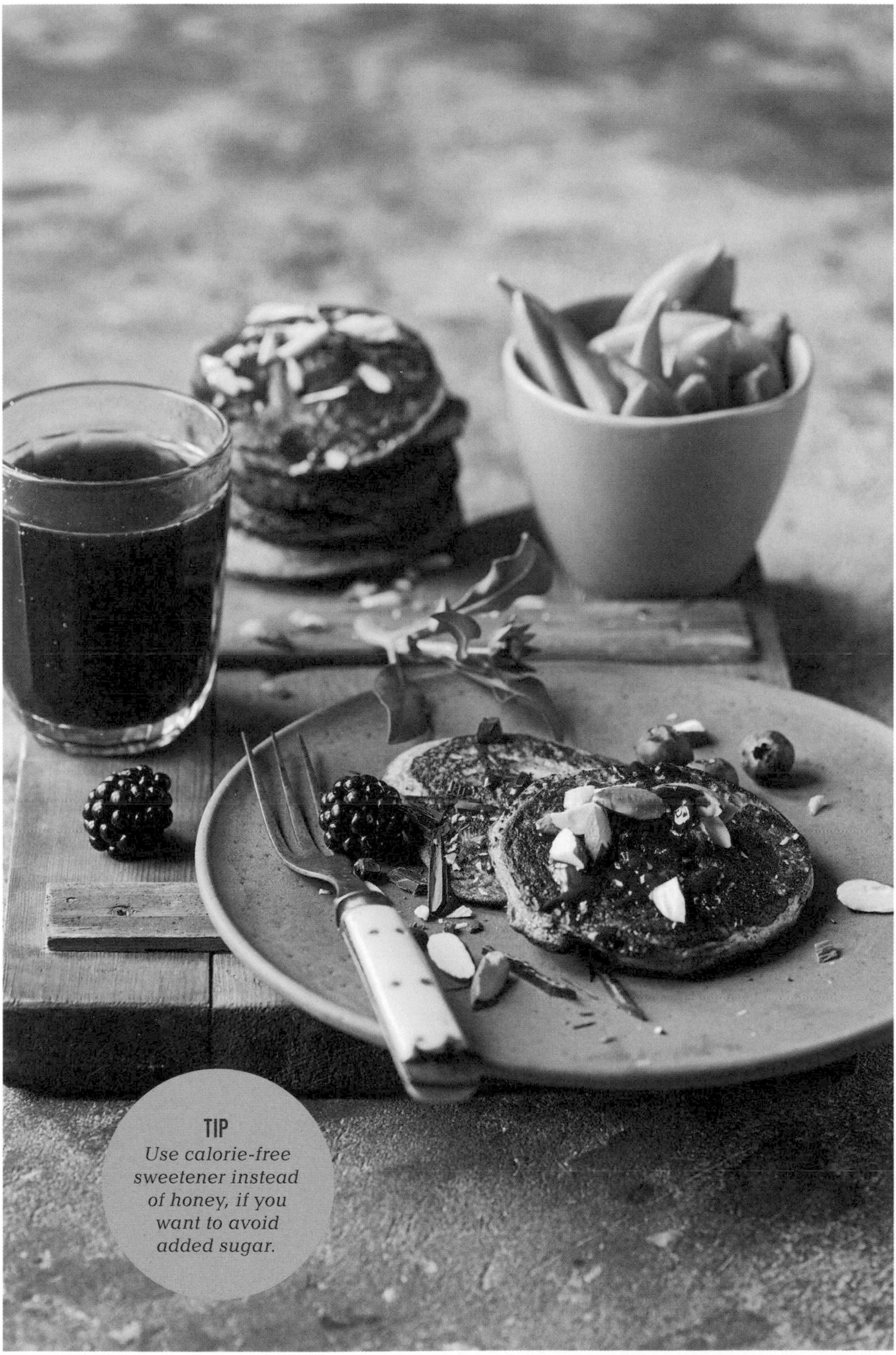

TIP
Use calorie-free sweetener instead of honey, if you want to avoid added sugar.

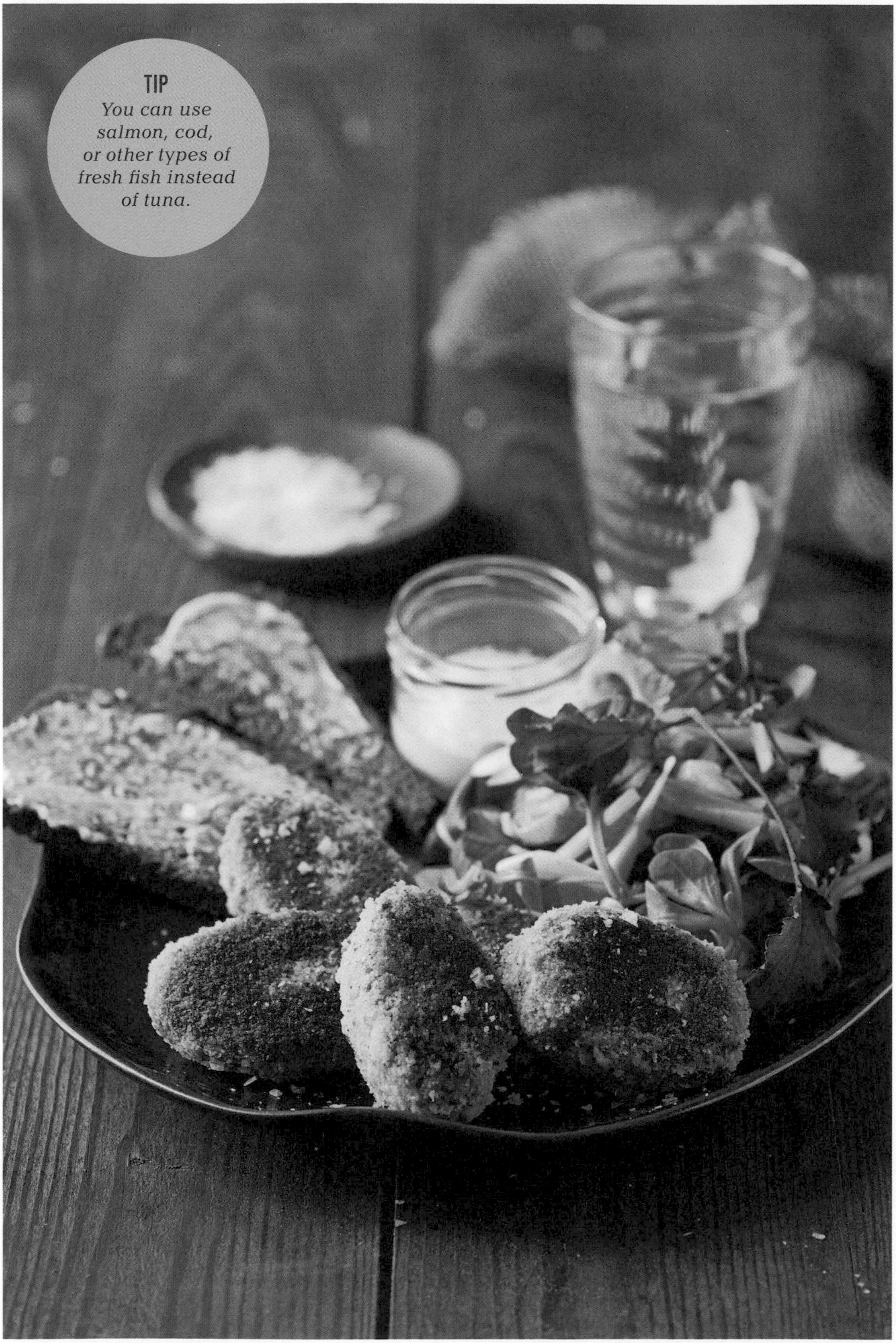

TIP
You can use salmon, cod, or other types of fresh fish instead of tuna.

Tuna fishcakes with rye

PREPARATION TIME: *about 30 minutes*

TUNA FISHCAKES:

$2^1/_4$ oz sweet potato, diced
1 can of tuna (about $4^1/_4$ oz when drained)
1 egg white
1 small garlic clove, crushed
Pinch of dried red pepper flakes
1 tablespoon chopped parsley
1 tablespoon chopped dill
$^1/_2$ teaspoon salt
2 tablespoons bread crumbs
1 tablespoon olive oil

SALAD:

1 scallion, sliced
$^1/_4$ red onion, diced
$^1/_4$ yellow bell pepper, diced
1 cup mixed baby lettuce greens
2 tablespoons crème fraîche, max. 9% fat

PLUS:

$1^1/_2$ slices of rye bread
1 tablespoon mayonnaise

Boil the sweet potato in lightly salted water for about 20 minutes.

Drain and mash the sweet potato. Mix with the tuna, egg white, garlic, dried red pepper flakes, parsley, dill, and salt. Form into patties and press them lightly into the bread crumbs.

Heat the tablespoon of olive oil in a skillet and fry the fishcakes.

Make a salad with the scallion, red onion, pepper, and lettuce and arrange it on a plate.

Serve the crème fraîche in a small bowl on the side.

Spread the mayonnaise on the rye bread. Serve it with the tuna fishcakes and salad.

WHAT YOU SHOULD HAVE ON YOUR PLATE

One large handful of tuna fishcakes, one handful of mixed salad, and two tablespoons of crème fraîche. One handful of rye bread with mayonnaise.

HOW IT IS DIVIDED IN THE SCANDI SENSE MEAL-BOX

HANDFUL 1 (+ 2): *Sweet potato, lettuce, scallion, red onion, pepper*

HANDFUL 3: *Tuna, egg white*

HANDFUL 4: *Bread crumbs, rye bread*

FAT: *Olive oil, mayonnaise*

DAIRY DRESSING: *Crème fraîche*

FLAVORINGS: *Garlic, dried red pepper flakes, parsley, dill, salt*

Energy 668 kcal · Protein 40 g · Carbohydrate 53 g · Dietary fiber 9.9 g · Fat 31 g

Baked sweet potato with chickpeas

PREPARATION TIME, INCLUDING BAKING TIME: *about 1 hour 20 minutes*

1 large sweet potato
¼ onion
1 garlic clove
¼ red chile
½ yellow bell pepper
1 tablespoon olive oil
½ teaspoon ground cumin
½ teaspoon paprika
⅔ cup canned chickpeas (drained)
*½ vegetable bouillon cube dissolved
   in 3½ tablespoons boiling water*
1 tablespoon lemon juice
1 teaspoon honey
½ avocado
*2¼ oz cubed salad cheese, such
   as feta, max. 17% fat*

DILL DRESSING:

2 tablespoons chopped dill
2 tablespoons crème fraîche, max. 9% fat
Salt and pepper, to taste

PLUS:

Dill, to garnish

Wrap the potato in foil and bake for an hour in an oven preheated to 400°F.

Finely chop the onion, garlic, and chile. Dice the pepper.

Heat the olive oil in a hot skillet and fry the cumin, paprika, and chile for 30 seconds, then add the onion, garlic, and pepper. Add the chickpeas after about 3 minutes. Let them fry for another minute, then add the stock. Let simmer for a few minutes and turn off the heat.

Combine the lemon juice and honey. Cut the avocado into slices and toss in the lemon and honey mix.

Stir the dill into the crème fraîche. Season with salt and pepper.

Unwrap the sweet potato and cut a slit in the top lengthwise. Squeeze the potato gently to open it up. Scrape out most of the flesh and mix it with the chickpea mixture. Add the cheese and mix until well combined. Fill the potato generously with the chickpea mixture, then place it under the broiler for 3 to 5 minutes.

Serve with the avocado and dill dressing on top. Garnish with dill.

WHAT YOU SHOULD HAVE ON YOUR PLATE

A filled sweet potato with avocado and dill dressing.

HOW IT IS DIVIDED IN
THE SCANDI SENSE MEAL-BOX

HANDFUL 1 (+2): *Sweet potato, onion, pepper*

HANDFUL 3: *Chickpeas, cheese*

FAT: *Olive oil, avocado*

DAIRY DRESSING: *Crème fraîche*

FLAVORINGS: *Garlic, chile, cumin,
   paprika, vegetable bouillon, lemon
   juice, honey, dill, salt, pepper*

Energy 677 kcal · Protein 19 g · Carbohydrate 57 g · Dietary fiber 14.6 g · Fat 39 g

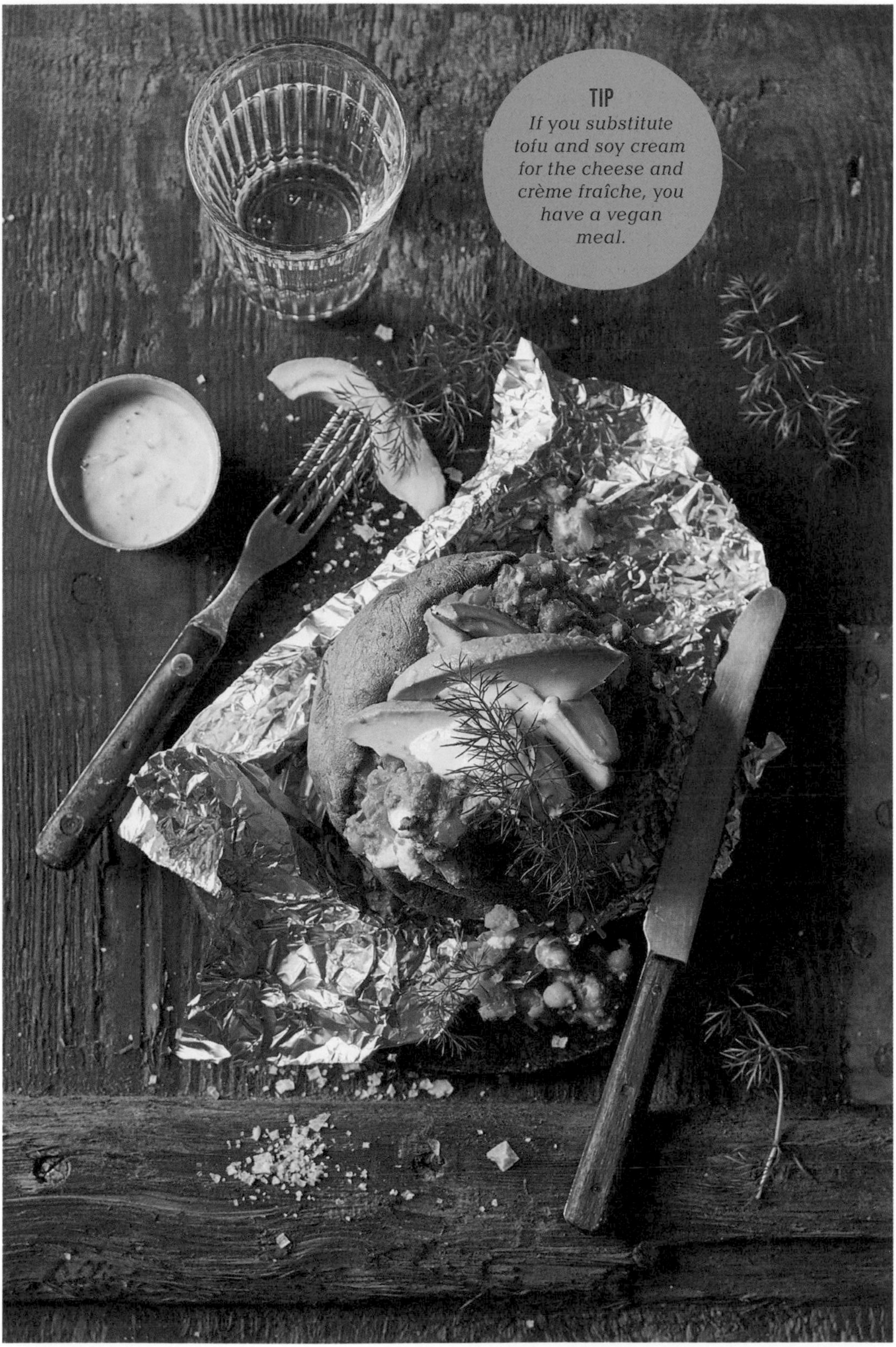
TIP
If you substitute tofu and soy cream for the cheese and crème fraîche, you have a vegan meal.

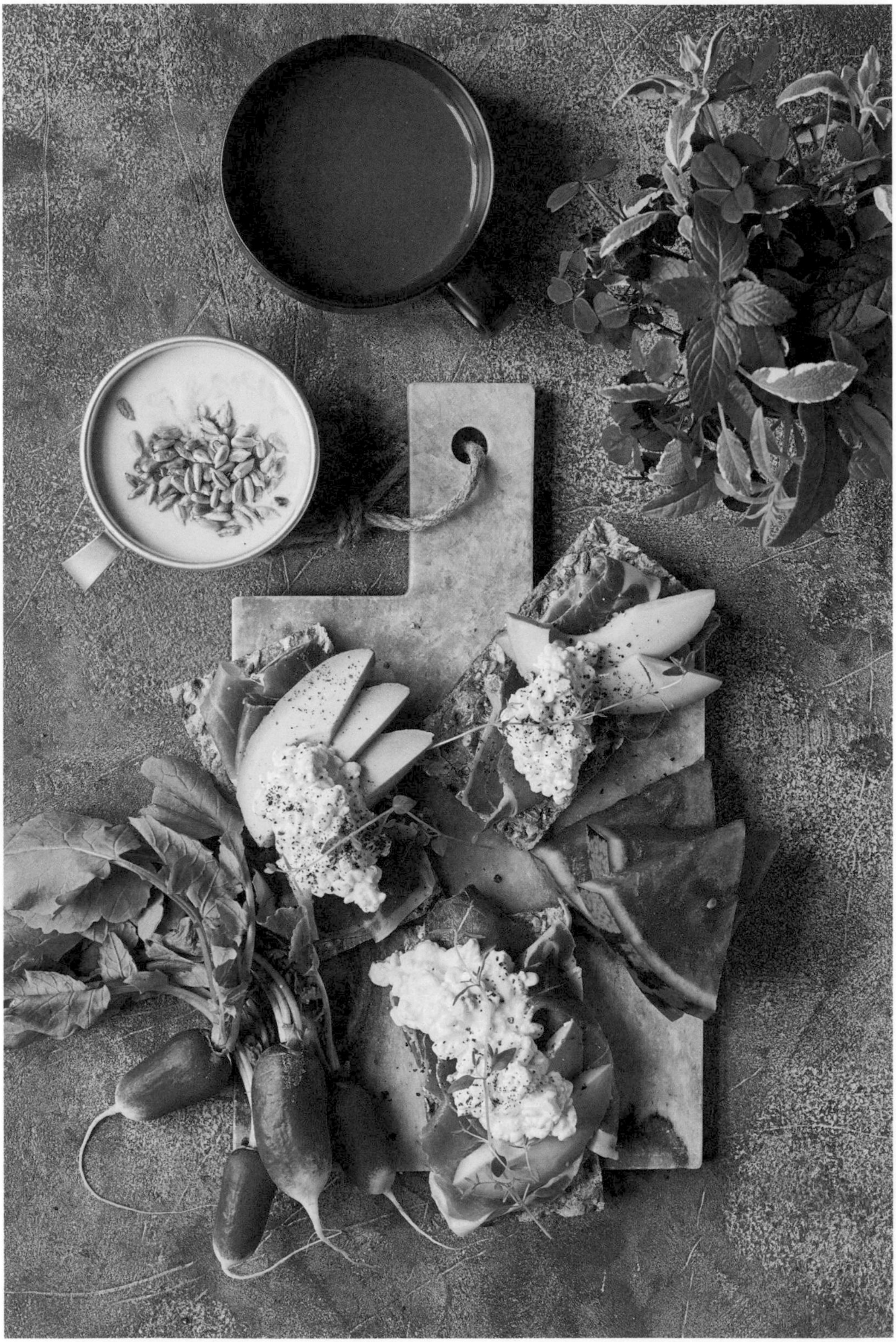

Breakfast plate with cottage cheese

PREPARATION TIME: *about 15 minutes*

$2^1/_2$ *oz radishes*

$2^1/_2$ *oz watermelon*

YOGURT IN A GLASS:

7 tablespoons plain yogurt

2 tablespoons sunflower seeds

1 teaspoon honey

CRISPBREAD WITH TOPPING:

$^1/_2$ *avocado*

1 tablespoon lemon juice

$2^1/_4$ *oz air-dried ham*

Scant $^1/_2$ cup cottage cheese, max. 4.5% fat

3 pieces of crispbread

Fresh thyme and black pepper, to garnish

Clean the radishes but leave the tops on.

Cut the watermelon into slices.

Pour the yogurt into a glass or bowl and top with sunflower seeds and honey.

Slice the avocado and sprinkle with the lemon juice.

Divide the ham, avocado, and cottage cheese between the pieces of crispbread.

WHAT YOU SHOULD HAVE ON YOUR PLATE

Half a handful of radishes and just under half a handful of melon. A portion of yogurt with topping and a crispbread with ham, avocado, and cottage cheese.

HOW IT IS DIVIDED IN THE SCANDI SENSE MEAL-BOX

HANDFUL 1 (+2): *Radishes*

HANDFUL 3: *Ham, cottage cheese*

HANDFUL 4: *Watermelon, crispbread*

FAT: *Sunflower seeds, avocado*

DAIRY PRODUCT: *Yogurt*

FLAVORINGS: *Honey, lemon juice, thyme, black pepper*

TIP *You can use a tablespoon of raisins instead of honey.*

TIP *You can toast the sunflower seeds in a hot pan.*

Energy 703 kcal · Protein 41 g · Carbohydrate 47 g · Dietary fiber 8.9 g · Fat 37 g

Caesar salad with croutons

PREPARATION TIME: *about 20 minutes*

CAESAR DRESSING:

$3^1/_2$ *tablespoons plain yogurt*
1 egg yolk
$^1/_2$ garlic clove, crushed
$^1/_2$ teaspoon salt
2 tablespoons white wine vinegar
1 anchovy fillet (optional)

PLUS:

2 Boston lettuces
1 tablespoon olive oil
$1^1/_2$ slices of bread, preferably whole-wheat
Pinch of salt
1 roasted chicken breast (6 oz), sliced
1 oz Parmesan cheese, shaved
Pepper, to taste

Whisk the yogurt, egg yolk, garlic, salt, and white wine vinegar together to make the dressing. Mash the anchovy fillet, if using, and stir it into the dressing.

Remove and discard the outer leaves of the lettuces and rinse.

Cut one lettuce in half and brush the cut surface with a little olive oil. Fry the cut surfaces for 1 to 2 minutes in a hot skillet.

Brush the bread on both sides with the remaining olive oil, season with a pinch of salt, and sauté in a hot pan until crisp on both sides.

Coarsely tear the leaves from the second lettuce and spread them out on a plate.

Cut the bread into cubes and sprinkle the croutons over the lettuce. Place the fried pieces of lettuce on top. Equally arrange the chicken, Caesar dressing, and Parmesan on top and season with pepper.

WHAT YOU SHOULD HAVE ON YOUR PLATE

Three or four handfuls of fried Caesar salad with dressing and Parmesan.

HOW IT IS DIVIDED IN THE SCANDI SENSE MEAL-BOX

HANDFUL 1 (+2): *Lettuce*

HANDFUL 3: *Chicken breast, anchovy*

HANDFUL 4: *Bread*

FAT: *Egg yolk, olive oil, Parmesan*

DAIRY PRODUCT: *Yogurt*

FLAVORINGS: *Garlic, salt, white wine vinegar, pepper*

Energy 699 kcal · Protein 57 g · Carbohydrate 38 g · Dietary fiber 6.8 g · Fat 33 g

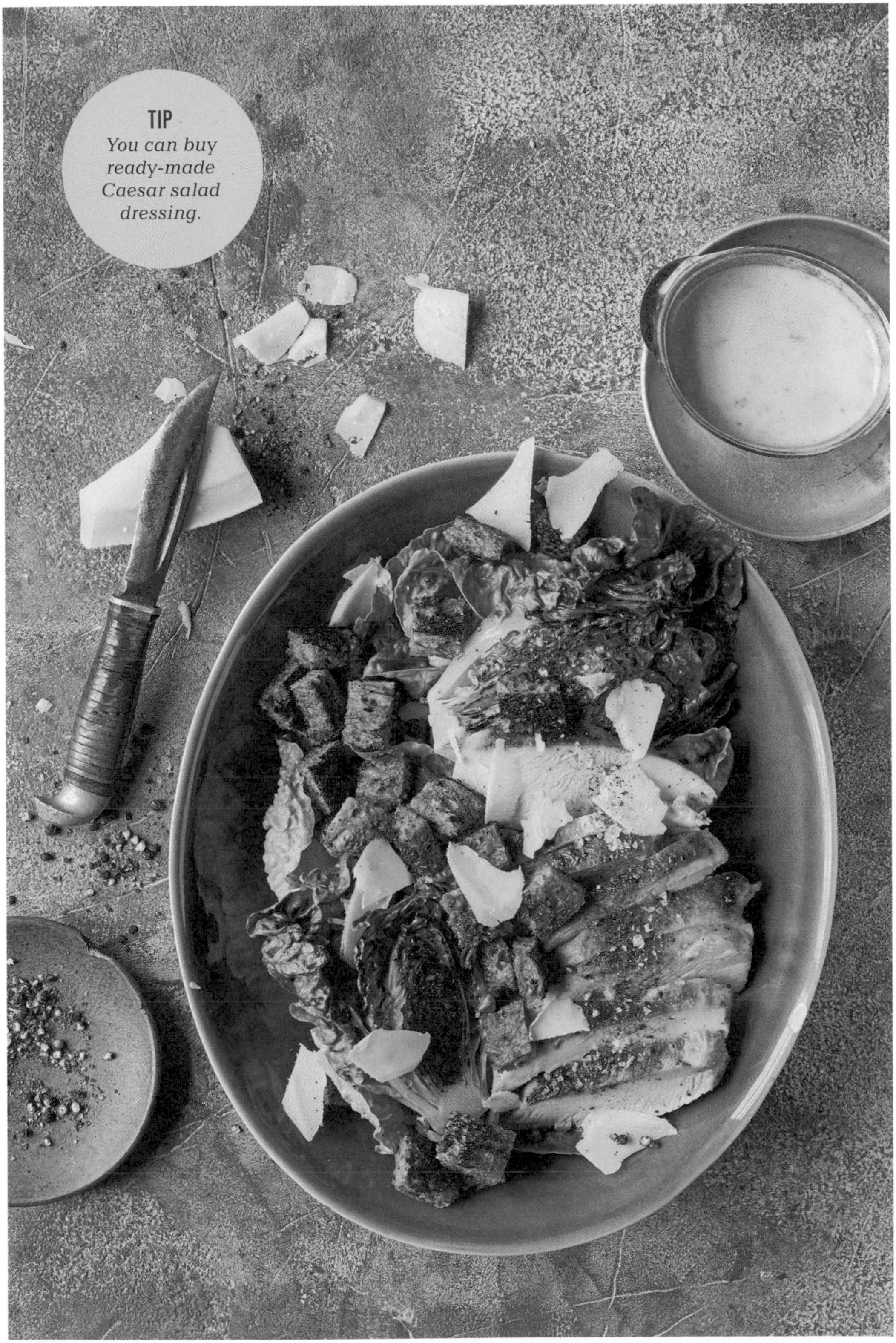
TIP
You can buy ready-made Caesar salad dressing.

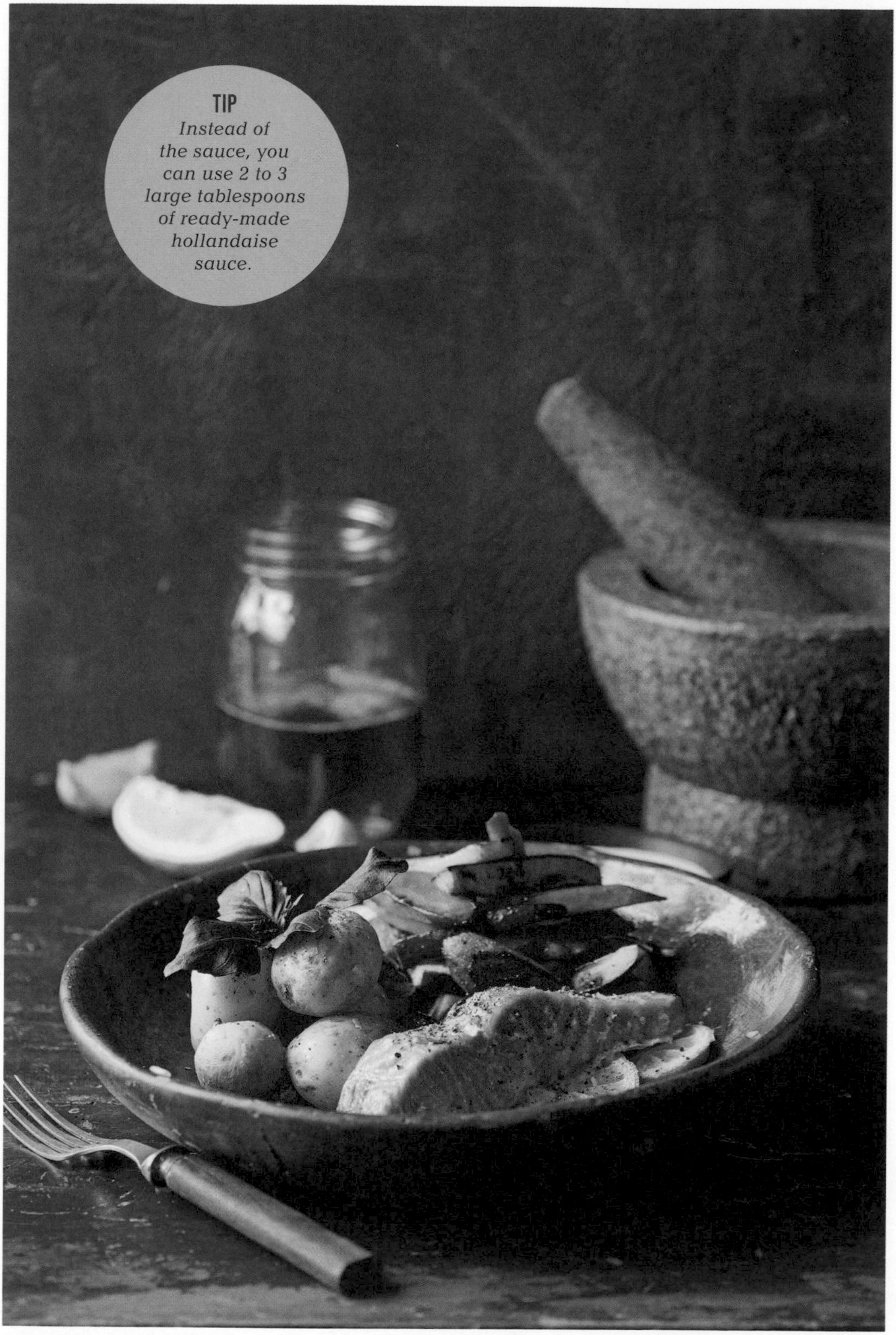

TIP

Instead of the sauce, you can use 2 to 3 large tablespoons of ready-made hollandaise sauce.

Baked salmon with lemon dressing

PREPARATION TIME: *about 20 minutes*

BAKED SALMON:

6 oz salmon
Pinch of coarse salt
¹/₂ garlic clove, crushed
1 lemon, sliced

LEMON DRESSING:

2 tablespoons mayonnaise
¹/₄ cup plain yogurt
2 teaspoons lemon juice
Pinch of salt

TO GO WITH IT:

5¹/₄ oz new potatoes
1³/₄ oz zucchini
2³/₄ oz carrot
1³/₄ oz red bell pepper
1 teaspoon olive oil
Red basil, to garnish

Season the salmon with the salt and garlic. Place the lemon slices in the bottom of an ovenproof dish. Place the salmon on top.

Bake the salmon in an oven preheated to 400°F for about 20 minutes until tender.

Boil the potatoes.

Stir the mayonnaise, yogurt, lemon juice, and salt together to make a dressing.

Cut the zucchini, carrot, and pepper into thin sticks. Stir-fry them in the olive oil.

Serve the salmon with the potatoes, lemon dressing, and stir-fried vegetables. Garnish with red basil.

WHAT YOU SHOULD HAVE ON YOUR PLATE

One handful of salmon, one to two handfuls of vegetables, one handful of potatoes, and about 7 tablespoons of the lemon dressing.

HOW IT IS DIVIDED IN THE SCANDI SENSE MEAL-BOX

HANDFUL 1 (+ 2): *Zucchini, carrot, pepper*

HANDFUL 3: *Salmon*

HANDFUL 4: *Potato*

FAT: *Mayonnaise, olive oil*

DAIRY PRODUCT: *Yogurt*

FLAVORINGS: *Salt, garlic, lemon juice, red basil*

Energy 779 kcal · Protein 41 g · Carbohydrate 37 g · Dietary fiber 6.2 g · Fat 51 g

Ham on toast

PREPARATION TIME: *about 15 minutes*

¹/₂ cup frozen edamame beans
1 tomato
¹/₂ onion
3 oz ham
1 to 2 teaspoons butter
1 slice of bread, preferably whole-wheat
1 teaspoon mustard
2 slices of cheese, min. 18% fat
1 egg
1 tablespoon lemon juice
1 teaspoon olive oil
Salt and pepper, to taste
A few lettuce greens, to garnish

Soak the edamame beans in boiling water for 30 seconds and drain. Cut the tomato and onion into slices. Fry the ham, onion, and edamame beans in butter in a large, nonstick pan.

Toast the bread. Spread with the mustard. Lay the onion and ham on it and place the cheese on top. Place the toast in the pan until the cheese begins to melt. Fry an egg beside the toast in a teaspoon of butter.

Place the edamame beans in a small bowl and toss them in lemon juice and olive oil. Season with salt and pepper.

Arrange the tomato slices on top of the toast. Finish with the fried egg on top. Garnish with a few lettuce greens.

WHAT YOU SHOULD HAVE ON YOUR PLATE

Ham, cheese, and tomato on toast with a fried egg on top and edamame beans on the side.

HOW IT IS DIVIDED IN THE SCANDI SENSE MEAL-BOX

HANDFUL 1 (+2): *Tomato, onion, lettuce*

HANDFUL 3: *Edamame beans, ham, egg*

HANDFUL 4: *Bread*

FAT: *Butter, cheese, olive oil*

FLAVORINGS: *Mustard, lemon juice, salt, pepper*

Energy 672 kcal · Protein 47 g · Carbohydrate 33 g · Dietary fiber 9.3 g · Fat 38 g

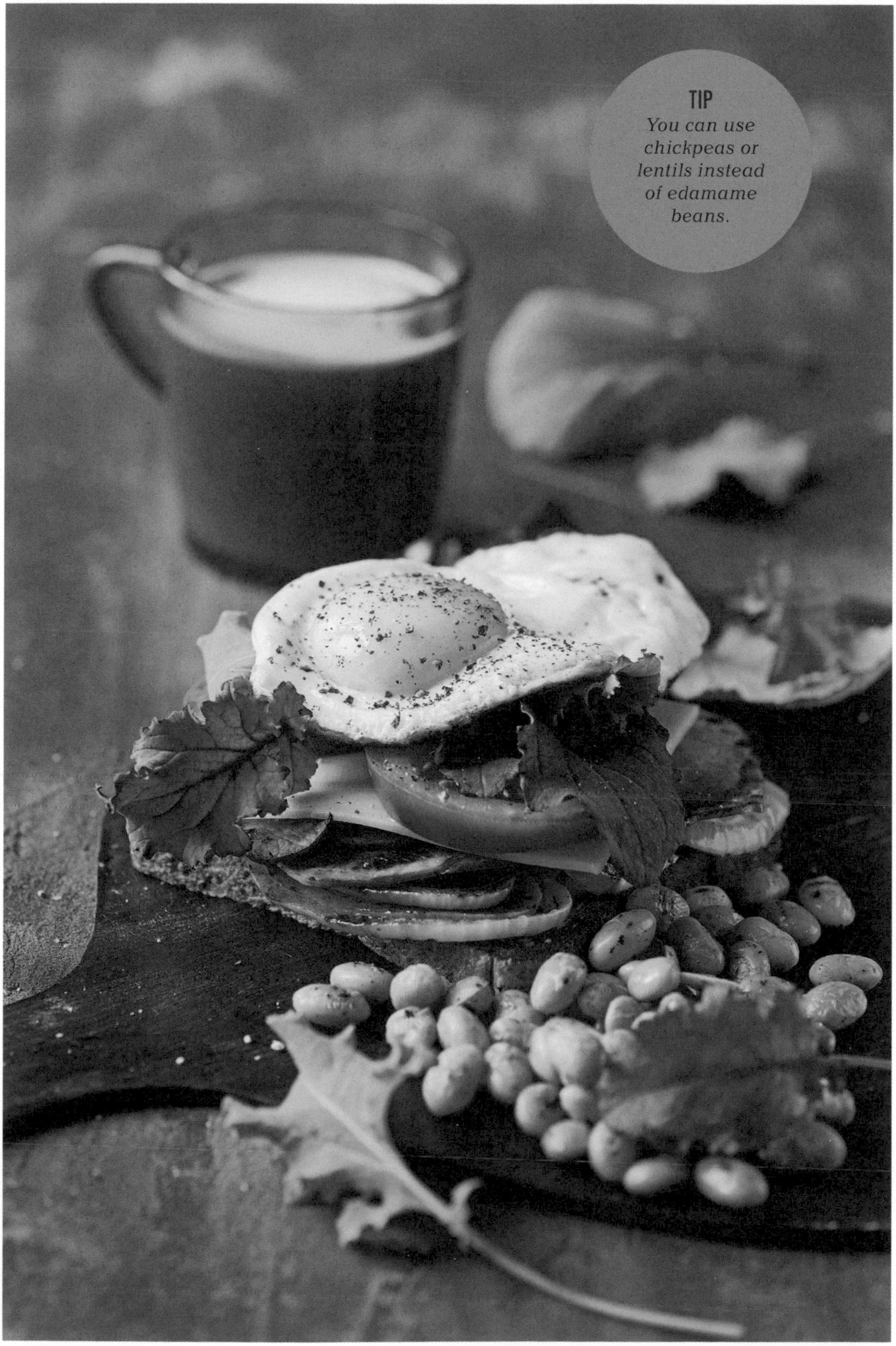
TIP
You can use chickpeas or lentils instead of edamame beans.

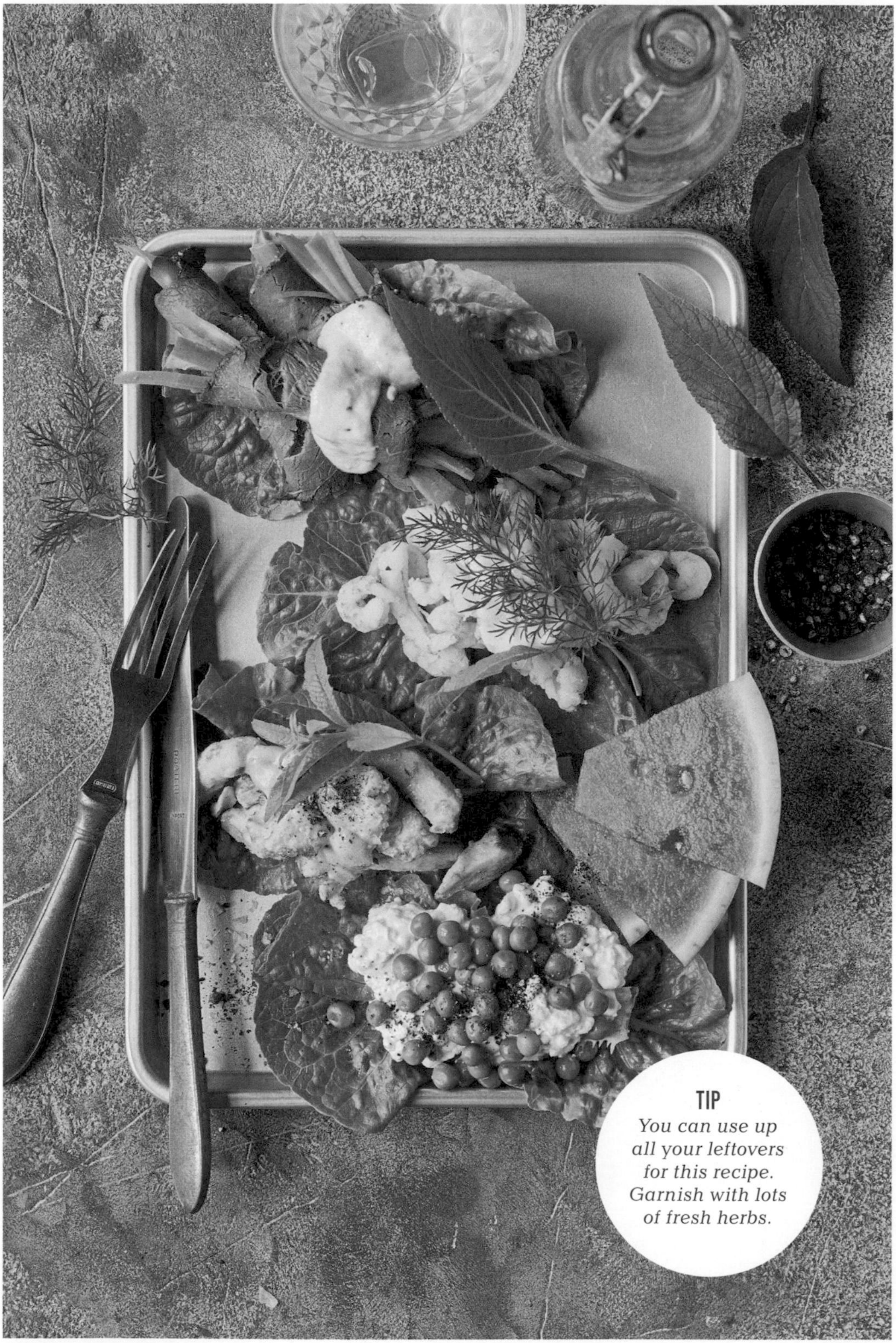
TIP
You can use up all your leftovers for this recipe. Garnish with lots of fresh herbs.

Boston lettuce wraps

PREPARATION TIME: *about 15 minutes*

1 Boston lettuce

ROAST BEEF TOPPING:

1 oz carrot
1 oz yellow bell pepper
¹/₄ cup dill pickles
1 tablespoon mayonnaise
1 teaspoon shredded horseradish
*   or chopped garlic*
Salt and pepper, to taste
4 slices of roast beef

SHRIMP TOPPING:

1 teaspoon sweet chili sauce or paprika
1 tablespoon mayonnaise
Salt and pepper, to taste
2¹/₂ oz shrimp

CHICKEN TOPPING:

1 tablespoon mayonnaise
1 teaspoon mango chutney or curry powder
Salt and pepper, to taste
2¹/₄ oz cooked chicken, diced or in strips

COTTAGE CHEESE TOPPING:

¹/₄ cup cottage cheese, max. 4.5% fat
¹/₄ cup peas
Salt and pepper, to taste

PLUS:

Fresh herbs, to garnish
3¹/₂ oz watermelon

Separate the lettuce leaves and lay them on a plate to form four small "bowls."

Cut the carrot, pepper, and dill pickle into matchsticks. Mix the mayonnaise with the horseradish or garlic and season with salt and pepper. Roll the beef slices around small piles of vegetable matchsticks, adding a little horseradish dressing before rolling. Place onto one lettuce bowl.

Add sweet chili sauce or paprika to the mayonnaise and season with salt and pepper. Place the shrimp with the dressing onto another lettuce bowl.

Mix the mayonnaise with the mango chutney and season with salt and pepper. Place the chicken with the dressing onto a lettuce bowl.

Fill the final bowl with cottage cheese and peas. Season with salt, pepper, and fresh herbs. Serve the watermelon on the side.

WHAT YOU SHOULD HAVE ON YOUR PLATE

Four lettuce bowls with toppings. Watermelon on the side.

HOW IT IS DIVIDED IN THE SCANDI SENSE MEAL-BOX

HANDFUL 1 (+2): *Lettuce, carrot, pepper, dill pickle, peas*

HANDFUL 3: *Roast beef, shrimp, chicken, cottage cheese*

HANDFUL 4: *Watermelon*

FAT: *Mayonnaise*

FLAVORINGS: *Horseradish or garlic, salt, pepper, chili sauce, mango chutney or curry powder, herbs*

Energy 716 kcal · Protein 43 g · Carbohydrate 31 g · Dietary fiber 6.1 g · Fat 46 g

Homemade burger

PREPARATION TIME: *about 25 minutes*

CUCUMBER SALAD:

¹/₄ cucumber or 1 baby cucumber
2 tablespoons white wine vinegar
¹/₂ teaspoon sugar
Salt and pepper, to taste

BURGER FILLING:

2 slices of tomato
2 slices of red onion
1³/₄ oz red cabbage or other type of cabbage
²/₃ cup ground beef, max. 7% fat
1 bacon slice
1 slice of cheese, min. 18% fat
1 small burger bun, about 3 to
   3¹/₄ oz, preferably whole-wheat
1 tablespoon mayonnaise

CREME FRAICHE DRESSING:

1 tablespoon crème fraîche, max. 9% fat
1 tablespoon tomato ketchup
¹/₂ teaspoon paprika

Shred the cucumber into long, thin strips and place them in a bowl of boiling water for about 10 minutes.

Slice the tomato and onion.

Shred the red cabbage very finely—use a mandoline if you have one, but take care not to cut your fingers.

Form the meat into a large, flat patty with your hands. Fry the bacon in a nonstick pan, and when it is cooked, fry the beef patty in the same pan over high heat for a couple of minutes on each side. Drain the bacon on paper towels.

Place the cheese on the beef patty.

Drain the cucumber thoroughly in a strainer. Mix the white wine vinegar, sugar, salt, and pepper, and toss the cucumber in the marinade.

Warm the burger bun. Mix all of the ingredients for the crème fraîche dressing.

Spread crème fraîche dressing on the bottom half of the burger bun and spread mayonnaise on the top half. Place the cabbage on the bottom half, followed by the patty, then tomato and onion slices and finally the cucumber salad and bacon slice.

WHAT YOU SHOULD HAVE ON YOUR PLATE

A burger.

HOW IT IS DIVIDED IN THE SCANDI SENSE MEAL-BOX

HANDFUL 1 (+2): *Cucumber, tomato, red onion, red cabbage*

HANDFUL 3: *Beef, bacon*

HANDFUL 4: *Burger bun*

FAT: *Mayonnaise, cheese*

DAIRY DRESSING: *Crème fraîche*

FLAVORINGS: *White wine vinegar, sugar, salt, pepper, tomato ketchup, paprika*

TIP *This is easy to serve at a party, as you can do everything in advance. Your guests can assemble the burgers themselves.*

TIP *Barbecue enthusiast? Add a little barbecue spice to the patty and give it a few minutes on a hot barbecue.*

Energy 764 kcal · Protein 50 g · Carbohydrate 60 g · Dietary fiber 7.6 g · Fat 33 g

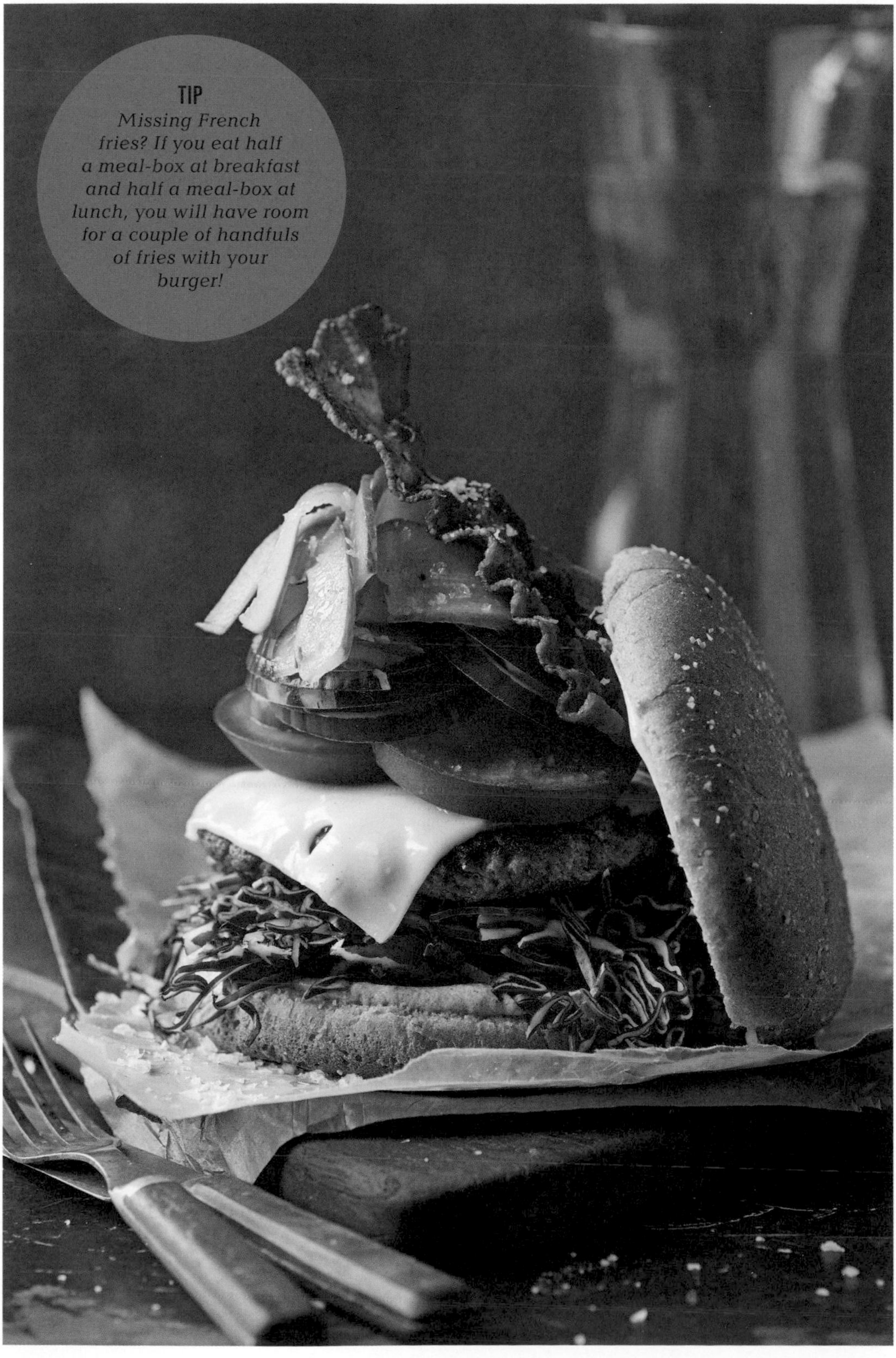

TIP
Missing French fries? If you eat half a meal-box at breakfast and half a meal-box at lunch, you will have room for a couple of handfuls of fries with your burger!

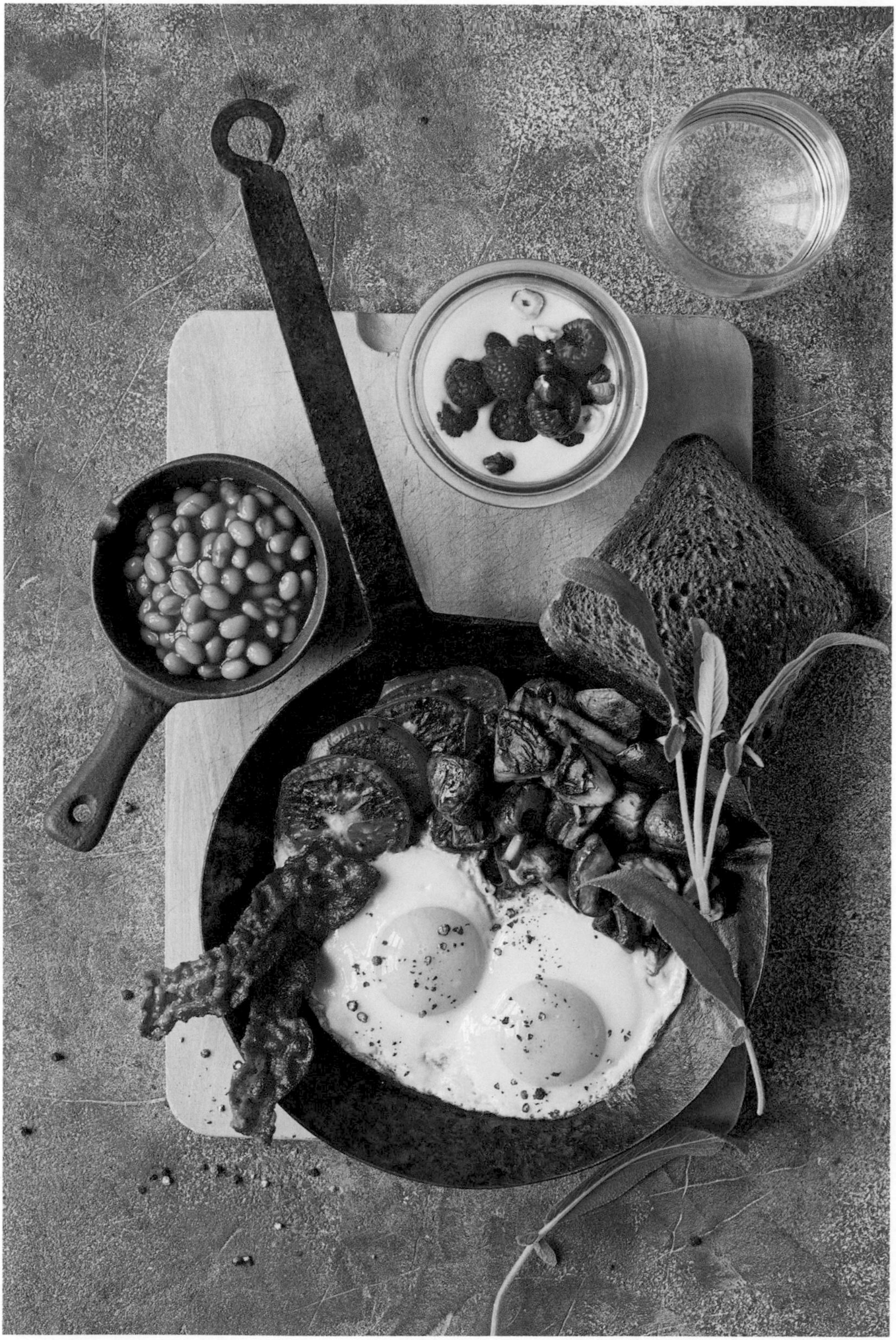

Bacon and egg

PREPARATION TIME: *about 15 minutes*

2 bacon slices
7 oz mushrooms
1 tomato
2 eggs
1 teaspoon butter
Salt and pepper, to taste

BEANS ON TOAST:

¹/₂ can of baked beans (1 cup)
1 slice of bread, preferably whole-wheat

YOGURT IN A GLASS:

7 tablespoons plain yogurt
1 teaspoon hazelnuts
Scant ¹/₂ cup raspberries
Sage or other herbs, to garnish

Fry the bacon until crisp in a nonstick skillet. Place it on paper towels to soak up the excess grease.

Quarter the mushrooms and fry in the same pan, until they darken. Thickly slice the tomato. Let the mushrooms rest at one side of the pan while you fry the tomato and egg in butter on the other side. Season with salt and pepper.

Heat the baked beans in a small saucepan or in the microwave. Toast the bread.

Pour the yogurt into a glass or a bowl. Cut the hazelnuts in half and sprinkle them over the yogurt with the raspberries.

WHAT YOU SHOULD HAVE ON YOUR PLATE

Two handfuls of tomato and mushroom, two bacon slices, two fried eggs, baked beans on toast, and a portion of yogurt with nuts and raspberries.

HOW IT IS DIVIDED IN THE SCANDI SENSE MEAL-BOX

HANDFUL 1 (+2): *Mushrooms, tomato*

HANDFUL 3: *Bacon, eggs, baked beans*

HANDFUL 4: *Bread, raspberries*

FAT: *Butter, hazelnuts*

DAIRY PRODUCT: *Yogurt*

FLAVORINGS: *Salt, pepper, sage or other herbs*

TIP *Not keen on baked beans? Have an extra fried egg or two instead.*

TIP *Try toasting the hazelnuts to get more flavor from them. A little pinch of salt gives the taste an extra edge.*

TIP *You could also add ¹/₄ cup olives to this meal.*

Energy 748 kcal · Protein 43 g · Carbohydrate 67 g · Dietary fiber 23.5 g · Fat 29 g

Spinach, egg, and chicken wrap

PREPARATION TIME: *about 15 minutes*

SCRAMBLED EGG:

2 eggs
1 egg white
1 tablespoon whipping cream (38% fat)
Salt and pepper, to taste

PLUS:

1 large tortilla, about 2¹/₂ oz,
  preferably whole-wheat
Heaping 2¹/₂ tablespoons cream
  cheese, min. 18% fat
¹/₂ cup fresh spinach
¹/₂ cup cherry tomatoes, halved
3¹/₂ oz cooked chicken, cubed
1³/₄ tablespoons pine nuts

Whisk the eggs, egg white, and cream together. Season with salt and pepper.

Pour the egg onto a hot pan and cook, stirring a little every now and then, until it has set. Take the pan off the heat.

Spread the cream cheese onto the tortilla and sprinkle the spinach leaves on top.

Top with the scrambled egg, cherry tomatoes, chicken, and pine nuts. You can toast the pine nuts, if desired.

WHAT YOU SHOULD HAVE ON YOUR PLATE

A tortilla wrap with two tablespoons of cream cheese, one handful of vegetables, a portion of scrambled egg, half a handful of chicken, and a tablespoon of pine nuts.

HOW IT IS DIVIDED IN THE SCANDI SENSE MEAL-BOX

HANDFUL 1 (+2): *Spinach, cherry tomatoes*

HANDFUL 3: *Chicken, egg, egg white*

HANDFUL 4: *Tortilla wrap*

FAT: *Cream cheese, pine nuts, cream*

FLAVORINGS: *Salt, pepper*

Energy 738 kcal · Protein 55 g · Carbohydrate 40 g · Dietary fiber 7.4 g · Fat 38 g

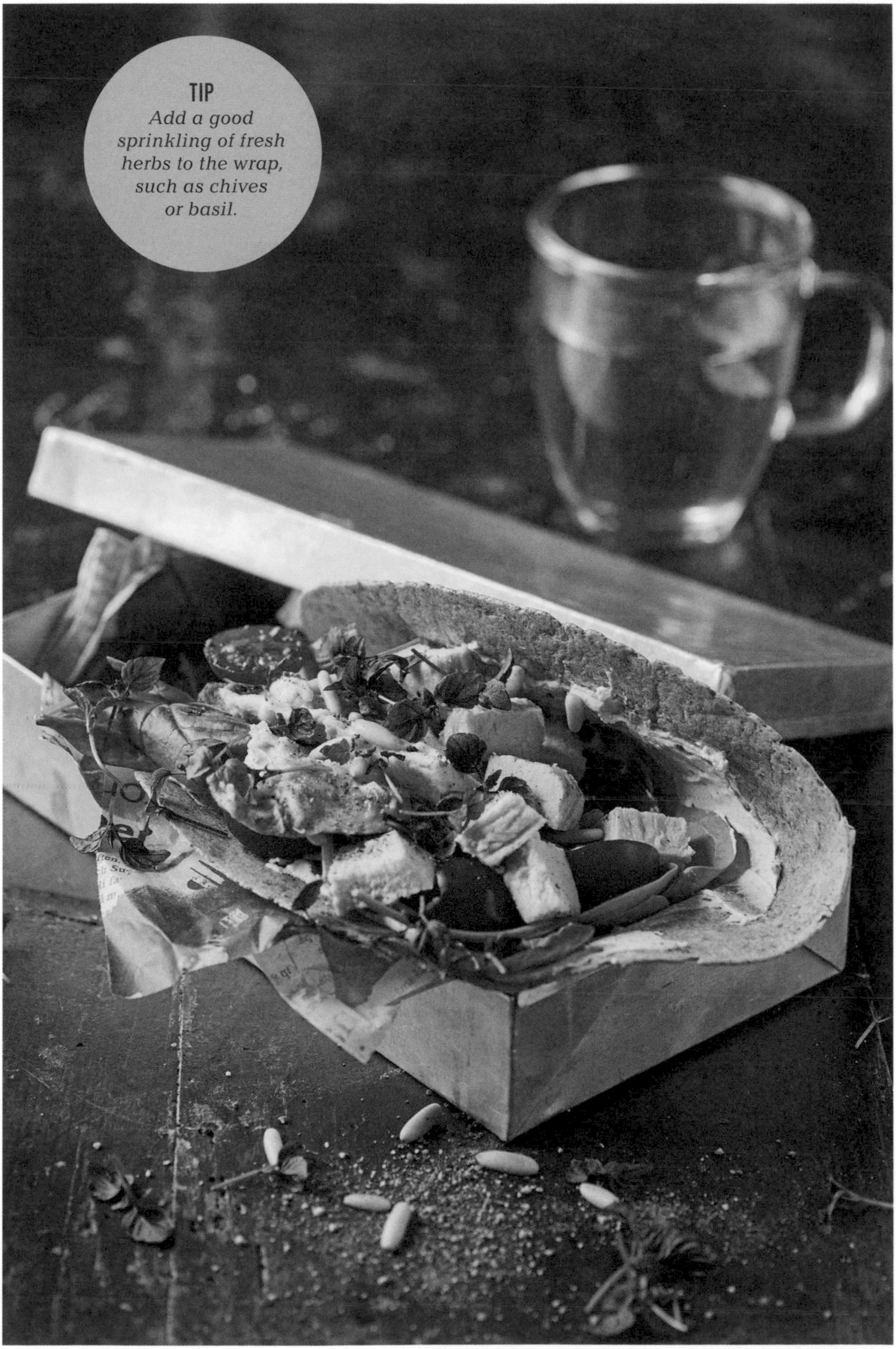

TIP

Add a good sprinkling of fresh herbs to the wrap, such as chives or basil.

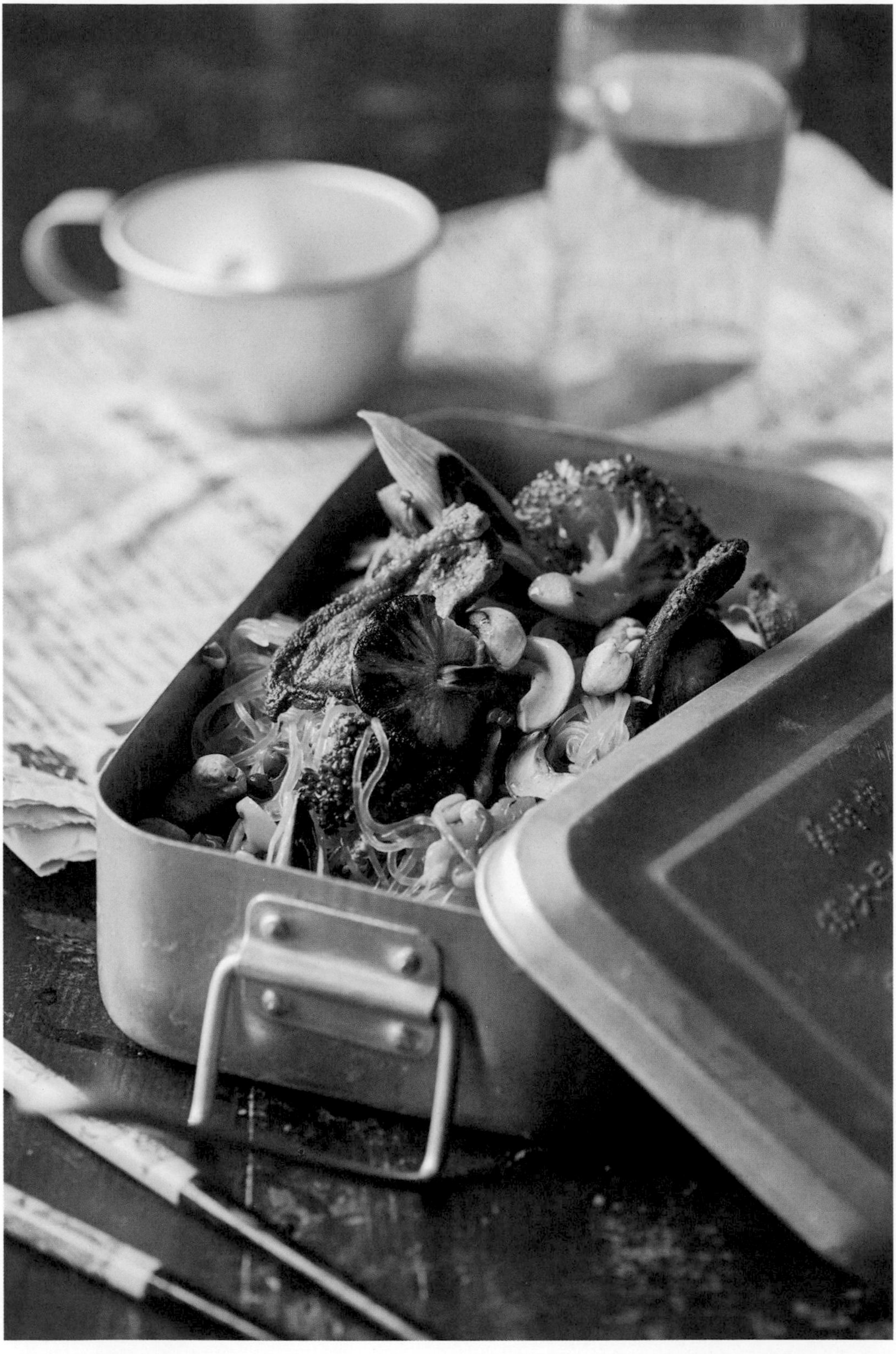

Stir-fried duck breast

PREPARATION TIME: *about 25 minutes*

STIR-FRY:

6$^1/_2$ oz duck breast, thinly sliced
1 tablespoon olive oil
3$^1/_2$ oz oyster mushrooms
3$^1/_2$ oz broccoli
2 scallions
$^1/_2$ garlic clove, thinly sliced
$^1/_4$ chile, thinly sliced
$^1/_2$ inch fresh ginger root, thinly sliced
$^1/_2$ cup bean sprouts
1 tablespoon teriyaki sauce
1 teaspoon chicken bouillon powder
Scant $^1/_3$ to generous $^3/_4$ cup water
$^1/_8$ cup cashews

TO GO WITH IT:

1$^1/_2$ oz glass noodles

Brown the duck well in olive oil in a hot wok. Remove from the pan and set aside.

Cut the mushrooms, broccoli, and scallions into small pieces and brown them quickly on all sides.

Add the garlic, chile, and ginger with the bean sprouts, teriyaki sauce, bouillon powder, and water. Return the duck to the wok and heat through thoroughly.

Toast the cashews and sprinkle them over the dish.

Boil the glass noodles in lightly salted water and serve them with the stir-fry.

WHAT YOU SHOULD HAVE ON YOUR PLATE

Three handfuls of stir-fry and one handful of glass noodles.

HOW IT IS DIVIDED IN THE SCANDI SENSE MEAL-BOX

HANDFUL 1 (+2): *Oyster mushrooms, broccoli, scallions, bean sprouts*

HANDFUL 3: *Duck breast*

HANDFUL 4: *Glass noodles*

FAT: *Olive oil, cashews*

FLAVORINGS: *Garlic, chile, ginger, teriyaki sauce, bouillon powder*

TIP *Thicken the sauce with a little cornstarch dissolved in cold water.*

TIP *You can use turkey or chicken instead of duck.*

TIP *Combine the glass noodles with the stir-fry while it is still in the wok.*

Energy 722 kcal · Protein 52 g · Carbohydrate 58 g · Dietary fiber 7.7 g · Fat 30 g

REMEMBER!

Twice a day, your plate should contain a combination of the most important elements in the diet: VEGETABLES, PROTEIN, STARCH/FRUIT, AND FAT.

Men's daily diet plan

For those who want to plan

Completed nine-day diet plan—see page 87.

Handful 1 (+2):

Vegetables.

The bracketed (+2) means you can choose to have two handfuls of vegetables, but one is enough.

Handful 3:

Protein from meat, fish, eggs, poultry, low-fat cheese, beans, etc.

Handful 4:

Carbohydrates/starch from bread, pasta, rice, potatoes, etc. as well as fruit.

Fat:

A tablespoonful of fat weighs $^1/_4$ to 1 oz, depending on how energy-packed the food item is. A tablespoonful of butter weighs about $^1/_4$ oz, and a tablespoonful of avocado weighs about 1 oz.

Dairy product:

Milk and cultured milk products up to 3.5% fat and 5 g sugar per 100 g.

Dairy dressing:

Dairy products with up to 9% fat.

Flavorings:

Spices, seasonings, herbs, and indulgences used in small amounts to add flavor to the food.

Day 1, man—total 2,133 kcal

	MEAL-BOX 1: 731 KCAL Breakfast plate with soft-cooked egg	MEAL-BOX 2: 633 KCAL Cottage cheese and mango lunchbox	MEAL-BOX 3: 769 KCAL Spaghetti and meatballs with zucchini
MOST IMPORTANT ELEMENTS IN THE DIET	**Handful 1 (+2):** • ½ yellow bell pepper	**Handful 1 (+2):** • 5¼ oz green beans • 1 tomato • ½ red onion • ½ cup peas	**Handful 1 (+2):** • ½ onion • ½ can chopped tomatoes • ½ zucchini
	Handful 3: • 1 egg • 3 slices of air-dried ham	**Handful 3:** • Generous ¾ cup cottage cheese, max. 4.5% fat	**Handful 3:** • 7 oz ground pork and veal • 1 small egg
	Handful 4: • ½ cup Basic Muesli • 1 piece of crispbread • ¼ cup berries	**Handful 4:** • ½ mango	**Handful 4:** • 1 tablespoon bread crumbs • 1 oz spaghetti
	Fat: • 2 slices of cheese, min. 18% fat • ¼ cup almonds	**Fat:** • 1 tablespoon green pesto • ¼ cup almonds • ½ oz semisweet chocolate	**Fat:** • 2 teaspoons olive oil • 1 oz Parmesan cheese
OPTIONAL	**Dairy product:** • Generous ¾ cup yogurt	**Dairy product:** –	**Dairy product:** –
	Dairy dressing: –	**Dairy dressing:** –	**Dairy dressing:** –
UNRESTRICTED IN SMALL QUANTITIES	**Flavorings:** • Honey • Salt • Thyme • Jam or marmalade	**Flavorings:** • Salt • Pepper	**Flavorings:** • Garlic • Chile • Paprika • Salt • Pepper • Parsley • Oregano • Red basil
	Optional snack between meals: Bouillon drink		

Day 2, man—total 2,175 kcal

	MEAL-BOX 1: 686 KCAL Toast with ricotta, ham, and tomato	MEAL-BOX 2: 735 KCAL Chicken pasta salad	MEAL-BOX 3: 754 KCAL Falafel pita with pesto dressing
MOST IMPORTANT ELEMENTS IN THE DIET	**Handful 1 (+2):** · 1 tomato	**Handful 1 (+2):** · ½ small red onion · ½ red bell pepper · 1 cup mixed salad greens	**Handful 1 (+2):** · ½ onion · ¼ cup cherry tomatoes · ⅓ cup peas · 1 cup salad greens
	Handful 3: · Scant ½ cup ricotta cheese · 2 eggs · 3 slices of ham	**Handful 3:** · ¾ cup edamame beans · 4½ oz cooked chicken	**Handful 3:** · 1 cup chickpeas · 1 small egg
	Handful 4: · 1½ slices of bread	**Handful 4:** · 3 oz cooked pasta	**Handful 4:** · 1 to 2 tablespoons flour · 1 tablespoon bread crumbs · 1 pita bread
	Fat: · 3½ tablespoons pine nuts	**Fat:** · ½ avocado · ⅛ cup cashews	**Fat:** · 1 tablespoon olive oil · 1 teaspoon pesto
OPTIONAL	**Dairy product:** · 3½ tablespoons milk	**Dairy product:** –	**Dairy product:** –
	Dairy dressing: –	**Dairy dressing:** · 3½ tablespoons yogurt	**Dairy dressing:** · 2 large tablespoons yogurt
UNRESTRICTED IN SMALL QUANTITIES	**Flavorings:** · Salt · Pepper · Chives	**Flavorings:** · Lemon juice · Garlic · Chives · Salt · Pepper	**Flavorings:** · Lemon juice · Garlic · Parsley · Cilantro · Salt · Cayenne pepper · Cumin

Optional snack between meals: Bouillon drink

Day 3, man—total 1,989 kcal

	MEAL-BOX 1: 629 KCAL Green smoothie	MEAL-BOX 2: 682 KCAL Shrimp noodle salad	MEAL-BOX 3: 678 KCAL Marinated steak with mushrooms and cream
MOST IMPORTANT ELEMENTS IN THE DIET	**Handful 1 (+2):** • 3$\frac{1}{4}$ tablespoons spinach • 2 to 3 small carrots • 3 to 4 radishes	**Handful 1 (+2):** • 1$\frac{3}{4}$ oz broccoli • 1 small carrot • $\frac{1}{2}$ cup bean sprouts	**Handful 1 (+2):** • 2 mushrooms • $\frac{1}{2}$ leek • 1$\frac{2}{3}$ cups mixed salad greens
	Handful 3: • 2$\frac{1}{4}$ oz cheese, max. 17% fat • 4 slices of smoked saddle of pork	**Handful 3:** • 6 oz shrimp	**Handful 3:** • 7 oz skirt steak
	Handful 4: • 1$\frac{1}{2}$ cups strawberries	**Handful 4:** • 1$\frac{3}{4}$ oz glass noodles	**Handful 4:** • 1 passion fruit
	Fat: • $\frac{1}{3}$ cup cream (38% fat)	**Fat:** • 1 tablespoon peanut butter • $\frac{1}{4}$ cup cashews	**Fat:** • 1$\frac{1}{3}$ tablespoons olive oil • $\frac{1}{3}$ cup cream (38% fat) • $\frac{1}{8}$ oz semisweet chocolate
OPTIONAL	**Dairy product:** • Generous $\frac{3}{4}$ cup skim milk	**Dairy product:** –	**Dairy product:** –
	Dairy dressing: –	**Dairy dressing:** –	**Dairy dressing:** • 1 tablespoon crème fraîche, max. 9% fat
UNRESTRICTED IN SMALL QUANTITIES	**Flavorings:** • Vanilla extract • Sweetener	**Flavorings:** • Soy sauce • Honey • Dried red pepper flakes • Lime juice • Cilantro	**Flavorings:** • Soft brown sugar • Soy sauce • Dried red pepper flakes • Paprika • Pepper • Vegetable stock • Tarragon • Salt • Vanilla extract • Sweetener

Optional snack between meals: Bouillon drink

Day 4, man—total 2,099 kcal

	MEAL-BOX 1: 620 KCAL Toast with salmon and avocado cream	MEAL-BOX 2: 759 KCAL Buddha bowl	MEAL-BOX 3: 720 KCAL Curried chicken and rice soup
MOST IMPORTANT ELEMENTS IN THE DIET	**Handful 1 (+2):** • 1 tomato • 2¼ oz cucumber	**Handful 1 (+2):** • 1¾ oz broccoli • 1¾ oz red cabbage • ½ cup peas • ⅓ cup bean sprouts	**Handful 1 (+2):** • ½ small onion • 1 small leek • 1 small tomato • ½ red bell pepper
	Handful 3: • 4¼ oz smoked salmon	**Handful 3:** • ⅔ cup kidney beans • ⅔ cup chickpeas	**Handful 3:** • 5¼ oz chicken
	Handful 4: • 1½ slices of bread	**Handful 4:** • ½ mango	**Handful 4:** • 2 teaspoons cornstarch • ¼ cup rice
	Fat: • ½ avocado • 1 large tablespoon crème fraîche, min. 18% fat	**Fat:** • 1 tablespoon tahini • 1 tablespoon olive oil • ½ cup black olives • 1 tablespoon sesame seeds	**Fat:** • 1 tablespoon olive oil • 2 tablespoons cream (38% fat)
OPTIONAL	**Dairy product:** -	**Dairy product:** -	**Dairy product:** -
	Dairy dressing: -	**Dairy dressing:** -	**Dairy dressing:** -
UNRESTRICTED IN SMALL QUANTITIES	**Flavorings:** • Lemon juice • Salt • Pepper • Mint • Chile • White wine vinegar • Cress • Watercress	**Flavorings:** • Garlic • Lemon juice • Dried red pepper flakes • Cumin • Jalapeños	**Flavorings:** • Garlic • Curry powder • Cumin • Chicken stock • Thyme • Salt • Pepper • Parsley
Optional snack between meals: Bouillon drink			

Day 5, man—total 2,173 kcal

	MEAL-BOX 1: 739 KCAL Oatmeal with stuffed peppers	MEAL-BOX 2: 716 KCAL Roast beef wrap	MEAL-BOX 3: 718 KCAL Cheesy tortilla tart
MOST IMPORTANT ELEMENTS IN THE DIET	**Handful 1 (+2):** • ½ red bell pepper • 2 dill pickles	**Handful 1 (+2):** • 1 carrot • 1 cup mixed salad greens • ½ cup snow peas • ¼ cup dill pickles	**Handful 1 (+2):** • ½ onion • 3 scallions • 3¼ tablespoons spinach
	Handful 3: • ½ cup ricotta cheese • 1 egg	**Handful 3:** • 5¼ oz roast beef	**Handful 3:** • 2 bacon slices • 1 egg • ½ cup ricotta cheese
	Handful 4: • ⅓ cup oats	**Handful 4:** • 1 large tortilla (2½ oz)	**Handful 4:** • 1 large tortilla (2½ oz)
	Fat: • 2 teaspoons pine nuts • ⅛ cup pecans • ½ oz semisweet chocolate	**Fat:** • 2 tablespoons mayonnaise	**Fat:** • ½ teaspoon olive oil • 1 oz cheese, min. 18% fat
OPTIONAL	**Dairy product:** –	**Dairy product:** –	**Dairy product:** • 2 tablespoons skim milk
	Dairy dressing: –	**Dairy dressing:** –	**Dairy dressing:** –
UNRESTRICTED IN SMALL QUANTITIES	**Flavorings:** • Salt • Pepper • Cress • Honey • Red sorrel	**Flavorings:** • Mango chutney • Curry powder • Salt • Pepper	**Flavorings:** • Garlic • Nutmeg • Salt • Pepper
Optional snack between meals: Bouillon drink			

Day 6, man—total 2,144 kcal

	MEAL-BOX 1: 799 KCAL Pancakes	MEAL-BOX 2: 668 KCAL Tuna fishcakes with rye	MEAL-BOX 3: 677 KCAL Baked sweet potato with chickpeas
MOST IMPORTANT ELEMENTS IN THE DIET	**Handful 1 (+2):** • 1 cup sugar snap peas	**Handful 1 (+2):** • 2¼ oz sweet potato • 1 scallion • ¼ red onion • ¼ yellow bell pepper • 1 cup mixed lettuce greens	**Handful 1 (+2):** • 1 large sweet potato • ¼ onion • ½ yellow bell pepper
	Handful 3: • 3 eggs • 2 egg whites	**Handful 3:** • 1 can of tuna • 1 egg white	**Handful 3:** • ⅔ cup chickpeas • 2¼ oz cheese, max. 17% fat
	Handful 4: • ¾ small banana • Scant ¼ cup oats • 5 to 7 berries	**Handful 4:** • 2 tablespoons bread crumbs • 1½ slices of rye bread	**Handful 4:** –
	Fat: • 2 teaspoons almonds • 1 tablespoon butter • ½ oz semisweet chocolate	**Fat:** • 1 tablespoon olive oil • 1 tablespoon mayonnaise	**Fat:** • 1 tablespoon olive oil • ½ avocado
OPTIONAL	**Dairy product:** –	**Dairy product:** –	**Dairy product:** –

	Dairy dressing:
	–
		Dairy dressing:
		• 2 tablespoons crème
		  fraîche, max. 9% fat
			Dairy dressing:
			• 2 tablespoons crème
			  fraîche, max. 9% fat

UNRESTRICTED IN SMALL QUANTITIES	**Flavorings:** • Salt • Vanilla extract • Cinnamon or cardamom • Honey	**Flavorings:** • Garlic • Dried red pepper flakes • Parsley • Dill • Salt	**Flavorings:** • Garlic • Chile • Cumin • Paprika • Vegetable stock • Lemon juice • Honey • Dill • Salt • Pepper

Optional snack between meals: Bouillon drink

Day 7, man—total 2,181 kcal

	MEAL-BOX 1: 703 KCAL **Breakfast plate with cottage cheese**	MEAL-BOX 2: 699 KCAL **Caesar salad with croutons**	MEAL-BOX 3: 779 KCAL **Baked salmon with lemon dressing**
MOST IMPORTANT ELEMENTS IN THE DIET	**Handful 1 (+2):** • 2½ oz radishes	**Handful 1 (+2):** • 2 lettuces	**Handful 1 (+2):** • 1¾ oz zucchini • 2¾ oz carrot • 1¾ oz red bell pepper
	Handful 3: • 2¼ oz air-dried ham • Scant ½ cup cottage cheese, max. 4.5% fat	**Handful 3:** • 6 oz roasted chicken breast • 1 anchovy fillet	**Handful 3:** • 6 oz salmon
	Handful 4: • 2½ oz watermelon • 3 pieces of crispbread	**Handful 4:** • 1½ slices of bread	**Handful 4:** • 5¼ oz potatoes
	Fat: • 2 tablespoons sunflower seeds • ½ avocado	**Fat:** • 1 egg yolk • 1 tablespoon olive oil • 1 oz Parmesan cheese	**Fat:** • 2 tablespoons mayonnaise • 1 teaspoon olive oil
OPTIONAL	**Dairy product:** • 7 tablespoons plain yogurt	**Dairy product:** • 3½ tablespoons yogurt	**Dairy product:** • ¼ cup plain yogurt
	Dairy dressing: –	**Dairy dressing:** –	**Dairy dressing:** –
UNRESTRICTED IN SMALL QUANTITIES	**Flavorings:** • Honey • Raisins • Lemon juice • Thyme • Pepper	**Flavorings:** • Garlic • Salt • White wine vinegar • Pepper	**Flavorings:** • Salt • Garlic • Lemon juice • Red basil
Optional snack between meals: Bouillon drink			

Day 8, man—total 2,152 kcal

	MEAL-BOX 1: 672 KCAL Ham on toast	MEAL-BOX 2: 716 KCAL Boston lettuce wraps	MEAL-BOX 3: 764 KCAL Homemade burger
MOST IMPORTANT ELEMENTS IN THE DIET	**Handful 1 (+2):** • 1 tomato • ½ onion	**Handful 1 (+2):** • 1 lettuce • 1 oz carrot • 1 oz yellow bell pepper • ¼ cup dill pickles • ¼ cup peas	**Handful 1 (+2):** • ¼ cucumber • 2 slices of tomato • 2 slices of red onion • 1¾ oz red cabbage
	Handful 3: • ½ cup edamame beans • 3 oz ham • 1 egg	**Handful 3:** • 4 slices of roast beef • 2½ oz shrimp • 2¼ oz diced chicken • ¼ cup cottage cheese	**Handful 3:** • ⅔ cup ground beef • 1 bacon slice
	Handful 4: • 1 slice of bread	**Handful 4:** • 3½ oz watermelon	**Handful 4:** • 3 to 3¼ oz burger bun
	Fat: • 1 to 2 teaspoons butter • 2 slices of cheese, min. 18% fat • 1 teaspoon olive oil	**Fat:** • 3 tablespoons mayonnaise	**Fat:** • 1 slice of cheese, min. 18% fat • 1 tablespoon mayonnaise
OPTIONAL	**Dairy product:** -	**Dairy product:** -	**Dairy product:** -
	Dairy dressing: -	**Dairy dressing:** -	**Dairy dressing:** • 1 tablespoon crème fraîche, max. 9% fat
UNRESTRICTED IN SMALL QUANTITIES	**Flavorings:** • Mustard • Lemon juice • Salt • Pepper	**Flavorings:** • Horseradish or garlic • Salt • Pepper • Chili sauce • Mango chutney • Curry powder • Herbs	**Flavorings:** • White wine vinegar • Sugar • Salt • Pepper • Tomato ketchup • Paprika
Optional snack between meals: Bouillon drink			

Day 9, man—total 2,208 kcal

	MEAL-BOX 1: 748 KCAL Bacon and egg	MEAL-BOX 2: 738 KCAL Spinach, egg, and chicken wrap	MEAL-BOX 3: 722 KCAL Stir-fried duck breast
MOST IMPORTANT ELEMENTS IN THE DIET	**Handful 1 (+2):** • 7oz mushroom • 1 tomato	**Handful 1 (+2):** • ½ cup spinach • ½ cup cherry tomatoes	**Handful 1 (+2):** • 3½ oz oyster mushrooms • 3½ oz broccoli • 2 scallions • ½ cup bean sprouts
	Handful 3: • 2 bacon slices • 2 eggs • ½ can of baked beans	**Handful 3:** • 2 eggs • 1 egg white • 3½ oz cooked chicken	**Handful 3:** • 6½ oz duck breast
	Handful 4: • 1 slice of bread • Scant ½ cup raspberries	**Handful 4:** • 1 large tortilla (2½ oz)	**Handful 4:** • 1½ oz glass noodles
	Fat: • 1 teaspoon butter • 1 teaspoon hazelnuts	**Fat:** • 1 tablespoon cream (38% fat) • Heaping 2½ tablespoons cream cheese, min. 18% fat • 1¾ tablespoons pine nuts	**Fat:** • 1 tablespoon olive oil • ⅛ cup cashews
OPTIONAL	**Dairy product:** • 7 tablespoons yogurt	**Dairy product:** -	**Dairy product:** -
	Dairy dressing: -	**Dairy dressing:** -	**Dairy dressing:** -
UNRESTRICTED IN SMALL QUANTITIES	**Flavorings:** • Salt • Pepper • Sage or other herbs	**Flavorings:** • Salt • Pepper	**Flavorings:** • Garlic • Chile • Ginger • Teriyaki sauce • Bouillon powder

Optional snack between meals: Bouillon drink

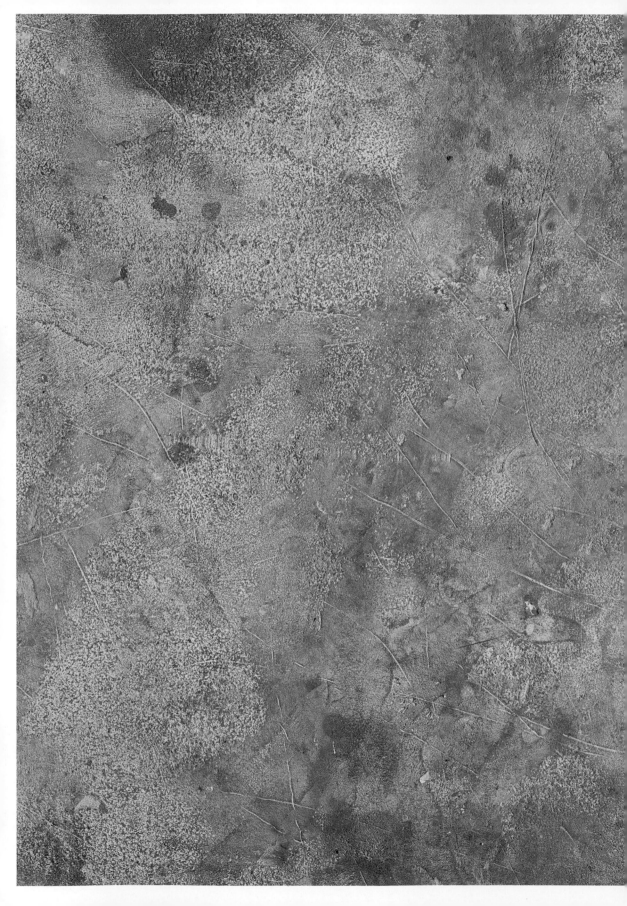

Food
directory

Handful 1 (+2): Vegetables

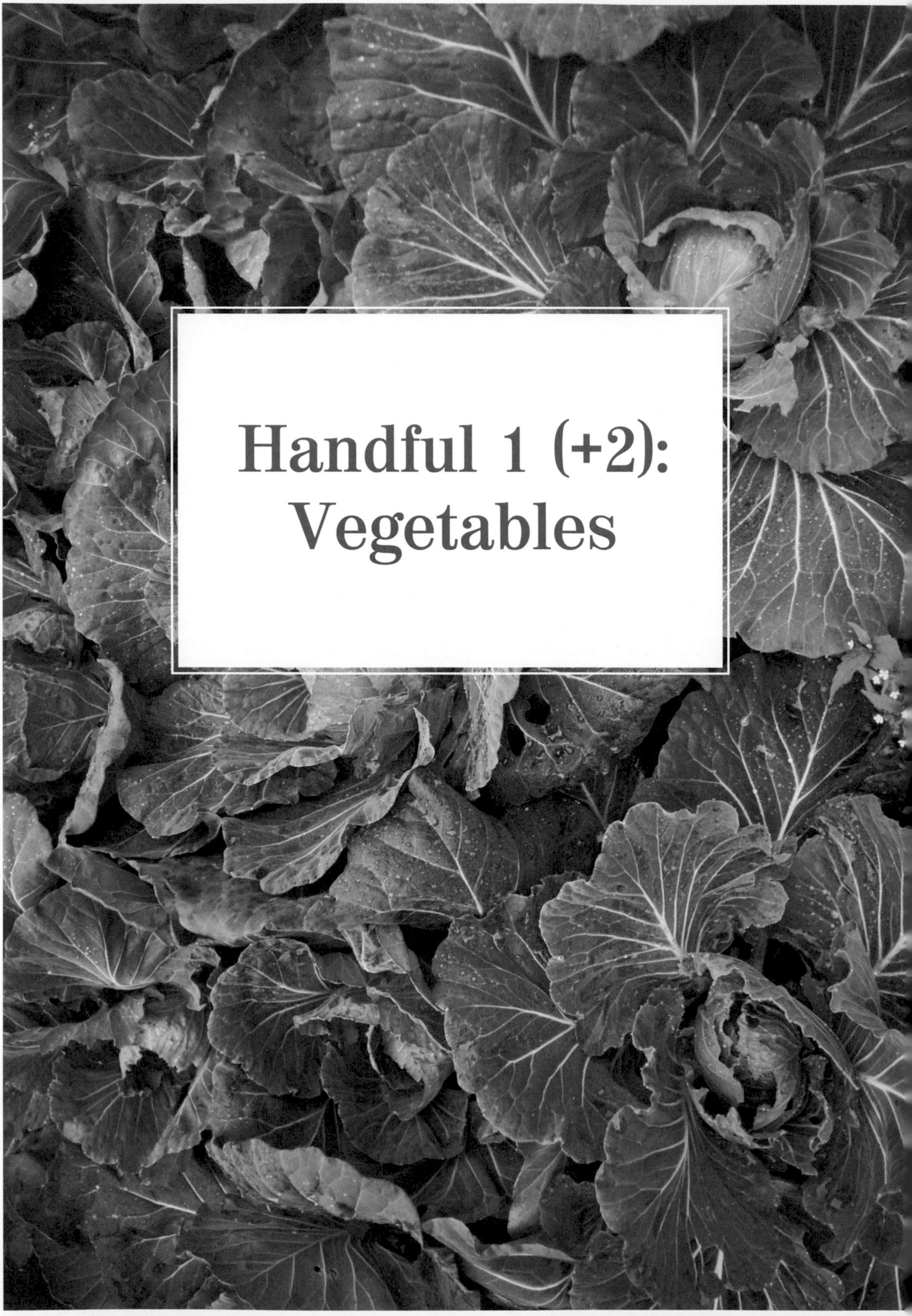

1 (+2)

Vegetables are a fantastic source of filling dietary fiber and important vitamins, minerals, and antioxidants. You should prioritize coarse fibrous vegetables (marked with *) because they contain more dietary fiber than fine vegetables, such as cucumber and tomato. Raw vegetables are tasty, but be careful with quantities if you aren't used to eating them. Too many raw vegetables can cause digestive discomfort and wind whereas cooked vegetables are often slightly easier to digest. Root vegetables can easily be eaten in a weight loss program as part of a varied diet. You can choose whether to settle for just one handful of vegetables per meal or whether to have two.

Quantity

One to two handfuls of vegetables correspond to 3½ to 9 oz.

· Artichoke*
· Arugula
· Asparagus—green/white
· Bamboo shoots, raw
· Bean sprouts
· Beet*
· Broccoli*
· Brussels sprouts*
· Butternut squash
· Cabbage*
· Carrot*
· Cauliflower*
· Celeriac/celery root*
· Celery
· Chanterelle mushrooms*
· Chicory
· Chile—all kinds
· Chinese daikon
· Cucumber
· Eggplant*
· Fennel*
· Garlic*

· Green beans*
· Green peas*
· Hamburg parsley*
· Jalapeños
· Jerusalem artichoke*
· Kale*
· Kohlrabi*
· Leeks*
· Lettuce—all kinds (including iceberg and butterhead)
· Mung beans
· Mushrooms—all kinds
· Napa cabbage
· Onions*—all kinds
· Parsnip*
· Peppers—all kinds
· Pointed cabbage*
· Pumpkin—all kinds of edible pumpkin
· Radishes—all kinds
· Red cabbage*
· Rhubarb*

· Romaine lettuce*
· Savoy cabbage*
· Salsify*
· Scallions*
· Seaweed*
· Spinach*
· Sugar snap peas*
· Sundried tomato
· Sweet potato*
· Tomatoes—all kinds (including canned chopped tomatoes)
· Turnip*
· Zucchini

* Coarse fibrous vegetables

Handful 3: Protein

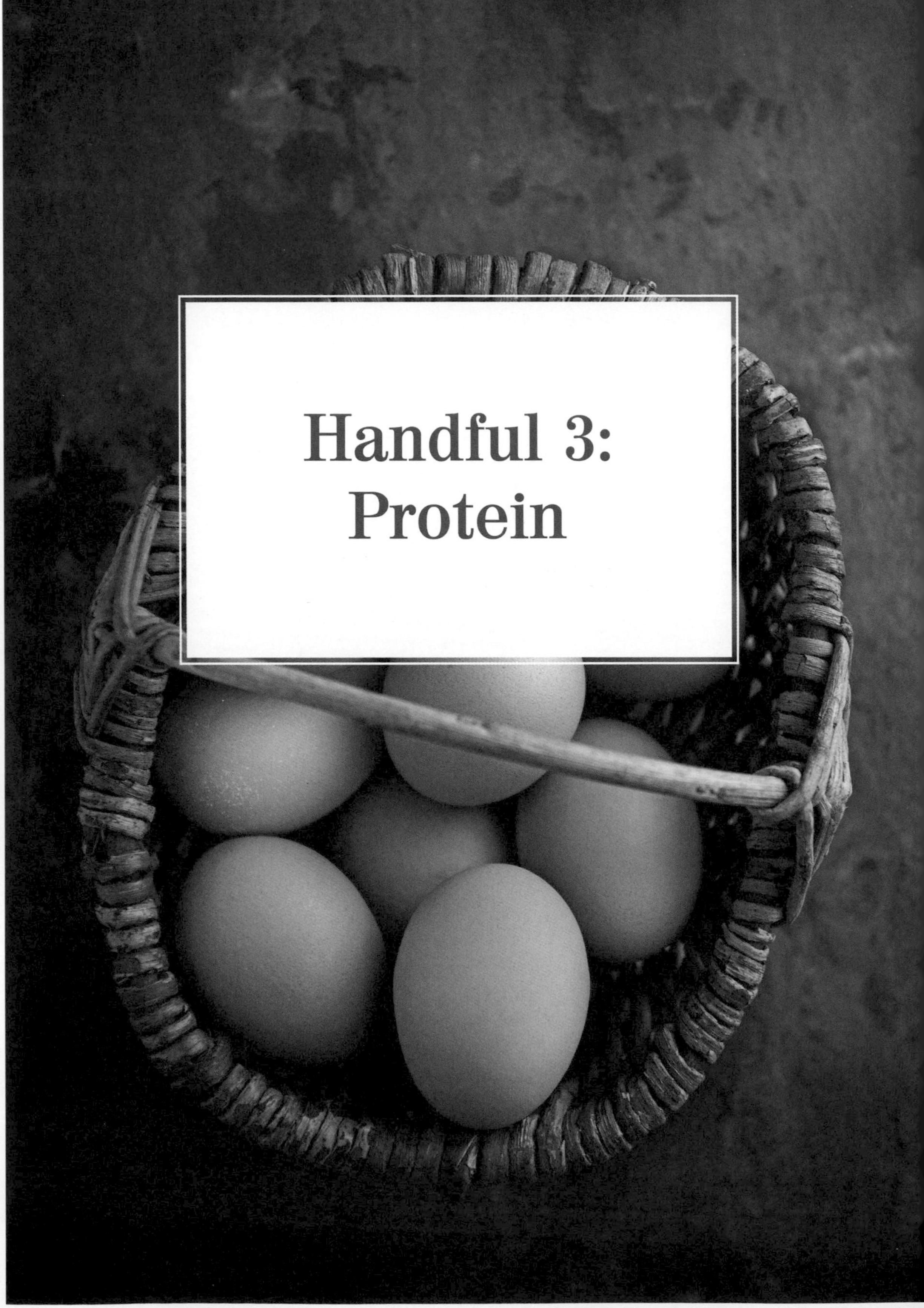

3

Proteins are important building blocks for the body, especially when losing weight, as they make you feel full and help to maintain muscle tissue so that you primarily lose fat.

MEAT FROM FOUR-LEGGED ANIMALS AND POULTRY

Varying your protein is important. Try to get different kinds into your meals over the course of the week. It is a good idea to restrict red meat to two or three times a week.

Quantity

A handful of meat is generally about 3¹/₂ to 7 oz.

· Beef, pork, and lamb
· Chicken, turkey, and other poultry
· Deer, pheasant, rabbit, duck, and similar

PROCESSED MEAT INCLUDING SAUSAGES, PATES, HAM, AND SALAMI

When meat is processed, the risk of accumulating chemical substances increases, which can, for example, become carcinogenic. Processed meat products should therefore only be eaten a few times a week. Choose organic products and go for sausages with a high meat content.

Quantity

Don't eat more processed meat than can cover your palm in a thin layer. For example, 1 to 2 sausages, 1 to 2 tablespoons of pâté, or 2 to 3 slices of ham, salami, or bacon. Use your common sense. Supplement this type of meat with another form of protein, such as half a handful of fish or beans.

· Bacon
· Blood sausage
· Liver sausage
· Meatballs with a long shelf life
· Pâté—all kinds
· Processed ham—all kinds
· Salami
· Sausages—all kinds (including Cumberland)
· Terrine

FISH AND SHELLFISH

All marine animals are a healthy source of protein. Fish, especially the oily ones, are rich in important omega-3 fatty acids and vitamin D.

Quantity

A handful of fish or shellfish corresponds to 3¹/₂ to 7 oz.

· Caviar and other fish eggs (including roe)
· Crab
· Lean fish such as cod, plaice, and flounder
· Lobster
· Mussels
· Oily fish such as halibut, salmon, mackerel, and herring
· Oysters
· Shrimp
· Fishcakes

· Kippers

· Mackerel in tomato sauce

· Peppered mackerel, in water or oil

· Sardines

· Snails (not exactly shellfish, but they do have shells!)

· Tuna, in water or oil

EGGS

Eggs are a fantastic source of nutrition because they contain many of the essential nutrients we need. Egg white is pure protein! You can greatly increase your protein intake by including two egg whites and two whole eggs in a meal. Contrary to popular belief, eggs alone don't raise cholesterol so you can enjoy them with peace of mind. You could combine egg with another source of protein, for example, have an egg and a small handful of shrimp for a main meal. In this way, you distribute your protein allowance across the categories.

Quantity
About 2 to 3 eggs count as a handful.

LOW-FAT CHEESE (MAX 17% FAT)

Use your common sense. The more fat the cheese contains, the smaller the handful you should eat. For example, very few people eat low-fat cream cheese in large quantities, but you can easily pep up a piece of chicken breast with 1 to 2 tablespoons of low-fat cream cheese.

Quantity
A handful of low-fat cheese corresponds to 3 to 3½ oz.

· All kinds of low-fat cheese

· Brie

· Cheese spread

· Cottage cheese (1.5 to 4.5% fat)

· Fromage frais

· Grated cheese

· Quark

· Ricotta

· Salad cheese, such as feta

· Smoked curd cheese (1 to 10% fat)

BEANS

Beans contain vegetable protein and are similar to vegetables in that they also contain carbohydrate in the form of starch. If you are a vegetarian, you should eat a wide selection of vegetables and beans, preferably supplemented by dairy products.

Vegetable proteins aren't as valuable for the body as animal proteins, but they are a good supplement in a varied diet. Choose beans that are frozen, canned, or dried. The dried versions often have to be soaked overnight and then boiled. Edamame beans can be bought frozen and cooked in boiling water in a few minutes. They are available both in their shells and preshelled.

It is fine to brighten up your salad with half a handful of beans to increase the protein content of your meal—on top of a handful of meat or fish.

Quantity

A handful of beans corresponds to 5¹/₄ to 7 oz or about 1 to 1¹/₃ cups.

- Baked beans
- Black beans
- Chickpeas
- Lentils – all kinds
- Lima beans
- Mixed beans
- Red kidney beans
- Soybeans (including edamame)
- Tofu
- White beans

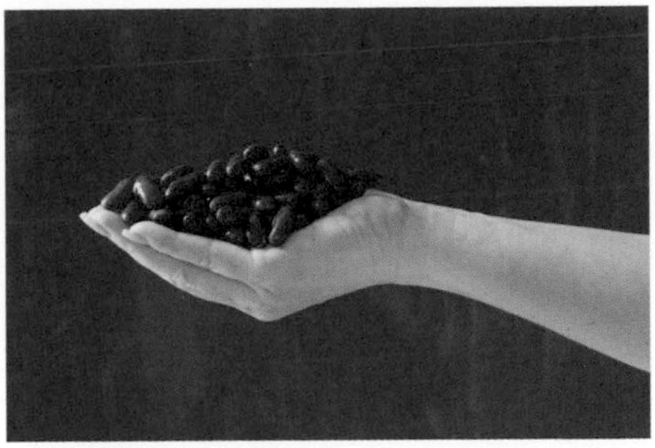

PROTEIN POWDER

For most people, it is entirely unnecessary to eat protein powder. If you eat a varied diet according to the principles of Scandi Sense, you will get all the protein your body needs. However, one of the day's three meals could be replaced by a protein shake or similar.

Quantity

One scoop of protein powder (typically 1 to 1¹/₂ oz) corresponds to about one third to a half of Handful 3.

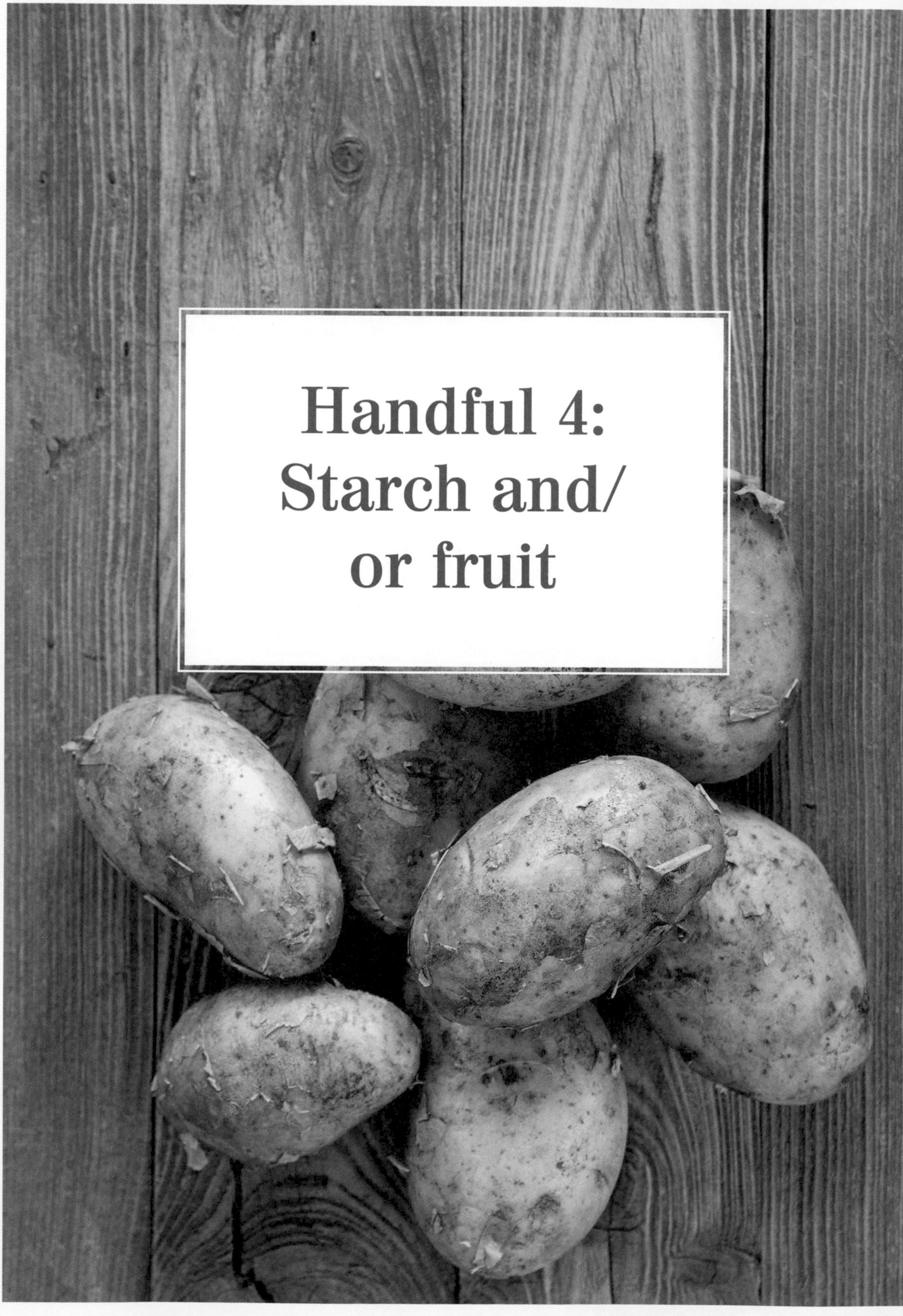

Handful 4: Starch and/ or fruit

4

This handful includes a range of carbohydrate foods.

Handful 4 can include both starch and fruit. You can combine the two groups by, for example, eating half a slice of bread and half a handful of fruit—use your common sense. The only person you cheat by eating more than a handful is yourself.

BREAKFAST CEREALS

Choose products with no more than 13 g of sugar per 100 g. You can easily create a homemade muesli with honey and dried fruit, but don't use so much that the muesli becomes very sweet.

Quantity

A handful of breakfast cereals corresponds to 1^1/$_4$ oz or 1^1/$_2$ cups for a woman and 1^3/$_4$ oz or 2 cups for a man.

· Barley meal or rolled barley flakes
· Cornflakes

LOOK AT THE PRODUCT'S NUTRITIONAL INFORMATION AND GO FOR THE FOLLOWING:

FAT: *No more than 7 g per 100 g*
TOTAL SUGARS: *No more than 13 g per 100 g*
SODIUM: *No more than 0.5 g per 100 g*
DIETARY FIBER: *At least 6 g per 100 g*

· Mixed rolled flakes (for example, three or five grain mixes)
· Oatmeal or rolled oats
· Rolled spelt flakes
· Rolled wheat flakes
· Rye meal or rolled rye flakes
· Weetabix

BREAD PRODUCTS

Bread contains large quantities of starch—and starch is sugar molecules. In other words, when you eat bread, you are also eating sugar! Always choose a whole-wheat option, but be aware that even with whole-wheat, you can't eat as much as you like. All bread affects blood sugar levels, no matter how coarse-grained it is.

Whole-wheat products contain just as many calories as processed bread products, but the fiber in whole-wheat products makes you feel fuller and helps blood sugar levels to stabilize. Look for the whole-wheat logo on packaging. Whole-wheat refers to whole grains, crushed grains, and whole-wheat flour. Whole-wheat flour must contain at least 6 g of dietary fiber per 100 g.

Quantity

One handful corresponds to 1 slice of bread, 1 small roll, half a large roll, or 2 to 3 slices of crispbread (because they are so thin and light).

· Baguette

· Bread rolls

· Crispbread

· Hot dog rolls

· Pastry dough (including phyllo)

· Pita bread

· Pizza dough

· Rolls

· Rye bread

· Sliced bread

· Tacos shells and similar products made from corn flour

· Tortilla wraps

· White loaves

Note: Stone Age bread is a Nordic bread product baked without flour but with seeds, nuts, eggs, and olive oil. The bread therefore contains fewer carbohydrates than bread baked with flour. On the other hand, it contains a lot of fat and protein. A thin slice counts as two tablespoons of fat in the Scandi Sense model, because it consists primarily of fat. A slice of Stone Age bread can be delicious, but in general hold back on the quantity because it contains a lot of calories.

OTHER STARCH PRODUCTS

· Bulgur wheat

· Corn

· Couscous

· Durum wheat

· Farro, kamut, and einkorn wheat

· Flour (preferably whole-wheat)

· Pearl barley, pearl rye, and pearl spelt

· Potatoes

· Quinoa

· Rice—all kinds, including brown, whole grain, and wild

· Whole spelt

· Whole-wheat (including cracked)

· Whole-wheat pasta (penne, lasagna, fusilli, spaghetti, etc.)

TIP: *The size of a handful varies from person to person, but it tends to correspond to energy requirements. For a small woman, 1 oz bread will be enough. 2$^1/_2$ oz will suit a tall woman, and up to 3$^1/_4$ oz bread will satisfy most men.*

FLOUR SUBSTITUTES

A number of flour substitutes appear in sugar-free or gluten-free recipes, as well as low-carb diet recipes. Some of these products also have a high protein content. You are welcome to eat bread and cakes baked with these products instead of products baked with wheat flour, as long as you comply with the Sense Meal-Box Model. There is only one way forward in this, and that is to try them, and use your taste buds to find the ones that you like.

Note that there is a difference in where in the meal-box the different kinds of flour belong.

COUNTS AS HANDFUL 3

· Low-fat almond flour with a high protein content (min. 40%)

· Chickpea flour

· Coconut flour (fine), also known as coconut fibers (contains up to 61% fiber and is very absorbent)

· Pea flour

· Peanut flour

· Sesame flour, has a salty taste and a high protein content (min. 40%)

COUNTS AS HANDFUL 4

· Amaranth flour

· Oat bran

· Quinoa flour

· Tapioca flour

· Wheat bran

COUNTS AS FAT

· Almond flour

· Coconut flour (coarse)—can be ground to a fine flour

FRUIT

Fruit adds color to your plate, as well as lots of beneficial vitamins, minerals, and dietary fiber, but some fruits also contain a lot of sugar. Choose those with low- to medium-sugar content, and eat the fruit instead of drinking it in juice form, so that it doesn't lose its dietary fiber. If you are very fond of fruit juice, you can dilute it with vegetable juice.

Use the very sweet fruits to replace sweeteners. Fruits with a high-sugar content such as mangoes and bananas are good for smoothies. Mix fruit in with your salads, or liven up a cheese sandwich with fruit and vegetables. If you eat dried fruit, be aware that two dates or a small box of raisins are equivalent in energy to one apple. So choose small handfuls of dried fruit.

Quantity

A handful of fruit will be around 3½ to 5¼ oz. Eat up to a handful per meal-box. One handful could be:

· 1 large fruit
· 1 to 2 small fruits such as mandarins, plums, or similar
· ¾ cup berries
· 1 to 2 fresh dates, figs, prunes, or similar

LOW-SUGAR CONTENT

· Lemons
· Limes
· Raspberries
· Blackberries
· Gooseberries
· Cranberries

LOW- TO MEDIUM-SUGAR CONTENT

· Strawberries
· Pomelo
· Papaya
· Melon—all kinds
· Peaches
· Nectarines
· Blueberries
· Apples
· Apricots
· Grapefruit

HIGH-SUGAR CONTENT

· Plums
· Oranges
· Kiwifruit
· Pears
· Pineapple

VERY HIGH-SUGAR CONTENT

· Clementines
· Mandarins
· Cherries
· Grapes
· Pomegranates
· Mangoes
· Fresh figs
· Bananas
· Fresh dates
· Prunes
· Dried fruit such as dates, figs, raisins, cranberries, blueberries, and mulberries

FRUITS ARE LISTED BY SUGAR CONTENT WITH THE LOWEST FIRST

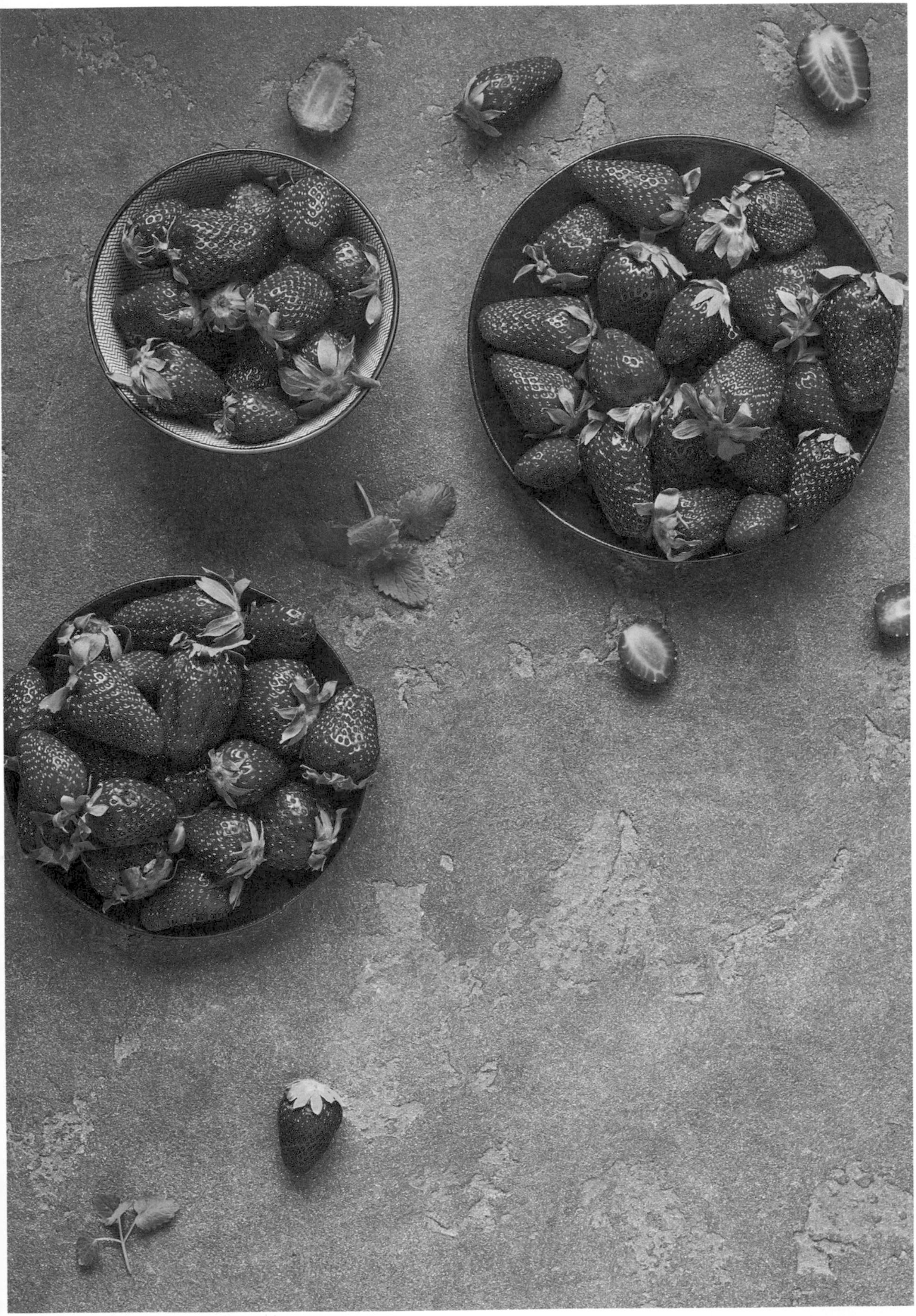

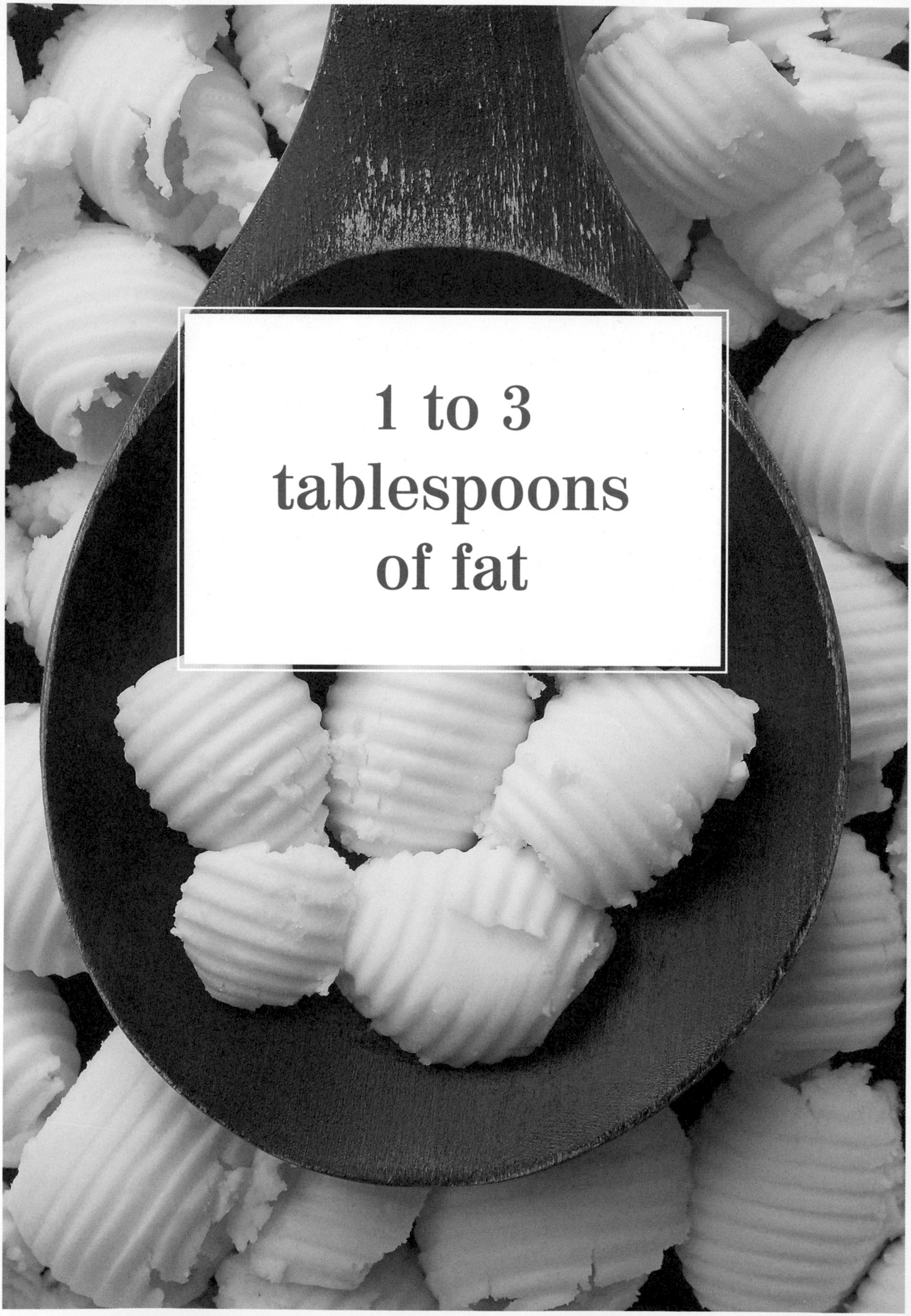

1 to 3 tablespoons of fat

Quantity

If you use concentrated fats such as butter, oil, and mayonnaise, measure with a level tablespoon. When it comes to less concentrated fats such as nuts, avocado, crème fraîche, or cheese, you can use a heaping tablespoon.

A tablespoon of fat varies from 1/4 to 1 oz, depending on how energy-packed the food item is. A tablespoon of butter weighs about 1/4 oz, and a tablespoon of avocado weighs about 1 oz.

BUTTER, COCONUT OIL, AND MIXED OIL PRODUCTS

Ideally use organic butter, and avoid deep-frying, because trans fatty acids can form from intense heating over a long period of time. Trans fatty acids are processed fats that are incredibly bad for your body.

· Aioli
· Butter
· Cocoa butter
· Coconut oil
· Mayonnaise
· Palm kernel oil
· Spreadable butter/plant oil mixes

OILS

A diet with a lot of omega-6 (compared to omega-3) may upset the body's natural processes. So use an oil with a good fatty acid composition.

OILS WITH A GOOD FATTY ACID COMPOSITION

· Almond oil
· Arctic-D Cod Liver Oil and similar fish oils
· Avocado oil
· Canola oil
· Extra virgin olive oil
· Flaxseed oil
· Hazelnut oil
· Walnut oil

OILS WITH A HIGH OMEGA-6 CONTENT

· Corn oil
· Grapeseed oil
· Peanut oil
· Sesame oil
· Soybean oil
· Sunflower oil
· Thistle/safflower oil

FAT FOR FRYING

Fat used for frying still counts as your 1 to 3 tablespoons per meal-box. Assess how much you use for frying and how much extra fat you then have available in your meal-box.

· Butter
· Canola oil
· Coconut oil
· Duck fat
· Ghee (clarified butter)
· Goose fat
· Lard
· Olive oil

SAUCES, DRESSINGS, AND DIPS

Keep in mind that store-bought sauces and dressings often contain sugar and a lot of additives.

· Fatty dressings
· Fatty sauces, such as béarnaise, hollandaise, cream, and butter sauces
· Hummus
· Pesto
· Tapenade
· Tartare sauce

FATTY SALADS

You can find an array of ready-made "salads" comprising different vegetables, meat, fish, or poultry. These salads are often high in fat (generally containing 65 to 90%) fat and should therefore be considered as an energy source under the fat group. They are processed with a long shelf life.

An alternative would be to use natural foods with an added drop of mayonnaise and a sprinkle of spices.

· Chicken salad
· Cucumber and radish salad
· Tuna salad
· Mackerel salad
· Shrimp salad

CREAM, CREME FRAICHE, AND HIGH-FAT CHEESE

The motto here is: good, in moderation! Use cream to add extra flavor to your vegetables or a tasty sauce. Use crème fraîche for soups or as a basis for a delicious dressing. Use high-fat cheese as a flavoring for salads or as topping on meat dishes.

Quantity

A tablespoon of high-fat cheese, cream, or crème fraîche is about ¾ to 1 oz.

· Crème fraîche (18% fat)
· Crème fraîche (38% fat)
· Cream (whipping cream and cooking cream with a fat content of 10% or more)
· Greek yogurt (10% fat)

HIGH-FAT CHEESES (18 TO 45% FAT)

· All kinds of high-fat cheese
· Brie
· Camembert
· Cheddar
· Cheese spread
· Cream cheese
· Danish Blue
· Emmental
· Feta
· Gorgonzola
· Gouda
· Halloumi
· Mascarpone
· Mozzarella
· Parmesan
· Philadelphia
· Roquefort

NUTS AND SEEDS

Nuts and seeds contain a lot of fat.
Nuts are a great food for people who
want to gain weight, as you can quickly
absorb a lot of energy from a small
quantity. Nuts, kernels, and seeds give
flavor and bite to salads.

Quantity

A tablespoon of nuts weights about ¹/₂ oz.

· Almonds
· Blue and white poppy seeds
· Brazil nuts
· Cashews
· Chia seeds
· Fennel seeds
· Flaxseeds
· Hazelnuts
· Macadamia nuts
· Nigella seeds
· Peanuts (and peanut butter)
· Pecans
· Pine nuts
· Pistachios
· Pumpkin seeds
· Sesame seeds
· Sunflower seeds
· Tahini
· Walnuts

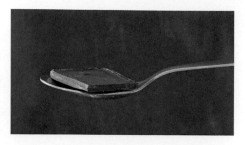

FATTY FRUITS

Avocado is a fruit, but is mostly served as a vegetable because it isn't sweet. It is very nutritious and contains a lot of fat and dietary fiber. Coconuts are fun to crack and a tasty alternative to weekend candies for children, or as a small snack. They also contain lots of dietary fiber.

Quantity

A tablespoon of fatty fruit weighs 1 to 1½ oz. Three heaping tablespoons of avocado works out as about half a large avocado.

· Avocado
· Coconut milk (the high-fat version—for the light version see opposite)
· Fresh coconut
· Olives

SEMISWEET CHOCOLATE PRODUCTS

Chocolate contains a number of substances that can be beneficial to both body and soul. Go for semisweet chocolate with at least 70 percent cocoa content. The higher the cocoa percentage, the less sugar there is. You can get 100 percent chocolate, which is very bitter, but tastes good with a cup of coffee. Cocoa nibs are also bitter, but taste good mixed with muesli or as topping on a fruit salad.

You can use chocolate to satisfy your desire for sugar. But be careful: it should be enjoyed in small quantities.

Quantity

A tablespoon of semisweet chocolate generally weighs about ¼ oz—this will be roughly one square from a large block of chocolate.

· Cocoa nibs
· Cocoa powder (baking cocoa)
· Semisweet chocolate

DAIRY PRODUCTS
Quantity
1¹/₄ cups a day.

· Buttermilk
· Lowfat milk
· Skim milk
· Whole milk
· Fruit yogurt with a sugar content of less than 5 g per 100 g
· Greek yogurt, max. 2% fat
· Natural Skyr yogurt
· Skyr products with a sugar content of less than 5 g per 100 g

ALTERNATIVE "DAIRY" PRODUCTS
Avoid dairy drinks with added sugar. If you would like to use alternative dairy products in your cooking or, for example, soy milk in your coffee, you will have to feel your way forward in terms of quantities. Alternative dairy products typically contain more calories than ordinary milk.

· Oat milk
· Light coconut milk
· Almond milk or other nut milks
· Rice milk
· Soy milk
· Spelt milk

DAIRY DRESSINGS
Quantity
2 tablespoons per meal-box, if desired. Choose a product with a fat content of 9 percent or less.

SOUR DAIRY PRODUCTS SUCH AS:
· Light crème fraîche, max. 5 to 9% fat
· Cooking cream, max. 9% fat
· Natural yogurt, Skyr, etc.

Drinks you can enjoy freely

COLD DRINKS

Be careful, don't be taken in! Many "light" products do have a calorie and sugar content. Check the nutritional information. The product should contain only a few calories per 3½ oz.

· Light sodas
· Light cordial
· Sparkling water
· Water

HOT DRINKS

Too much coffee and tea can cause hormone imbalances and sleep problems. However, you can buy different types of herbal teas, which can have a soothing effect and are therefore good for drinking before bedtime.

· Black tea
· Coffee (including instant)
· Herbal tea and infusions

Indulgences

If you use a little sugar or honey as part of your cooking, it is only counted as a flavoring. If you eat larger quantities from the indulgences, you have to consider how much you need to compensate for them in your meal-boxes. As little as 3½ oz milk chocolate, cake, or potato chips corresponds to approximately one whole meal-box. A Big Mac or a large milkshake fill about one meal-box each.

DIFFERENT VARIETIES OF SUGAR
· Brown sugar
· Cane sugar
· Coconut sugar
· Confectioners' sugar
· Fruit sugar/fructose
· Grape sugar
· Honey—all kinds
· Molasses
· Pearl/nibbed sugar
· Rock/sugary candies
· Soft brown sugar
· Sugar for making jam
· Sweeteners with calories
· Syrup—all kinds (including agave)
· Vanilla sugar
· White sugar

CANDIES AND CAKES
· Cookies—all kinds (including graham crackers)
· Buttercream
· Cake batters
· Cakes—all kinds
· Chewing gum
· Chocolate bars
· Chocolate with less than 70% cocoa content
· Danish pastries
· Desserts such as fromage frais and mousse
· Doughnuts
· Fruit slices and sticks
· Hard candies and lollipops
· Ice cream and ice pops
· Lozenges
· Macaroons
· Marmalade and jam
· Marzipan
· Meringues
· Mixed candies (including licorice, wine gums, marshmallow, foam candies, etc.)
· Muesli bars
· Nougat
· Nut spreads
· Nutella
· Red currant jelly
· Rice cakes
· Snowballs (marshmallow snacks)
· Toffees
· Waffles

BREAKFAST PRODUCTS
· Fruit yogurts containing more than 5 g sugar per 100 g
· Breakfast pastries, such as croissants
· Breakfast cereals containing more than 13 g sugar per 100 g
· Muesli and granola products containing more than 13 g sugar per 100 g

FAST FOOD, TAKEOUT, AND SNACKS

· Burger meals with fries, a dip, and a soda
· Candied nuts (and sweet nut mixes)
· French fries
· Hot dogs
· Pizza (especially deep-pan)
· Popcorn
· Potato chips—all kinds
· Spring rolls

DRINKS WITH SUGAR

· Chocolate milk
· Coffee creamer
· Condensed and sweetened milk
· Cordial
· Elderflower cordial
· Energy drinks—all kinds
· Fruit juice—all kinds
· Fruit smoothies
· Hot chocolate
· Ice tea
· Sodas

ALCOHOLIC DRINKS

If you like to have, for example, a glass of wine with a meal, you don't need to compensate for it in your meal-boxes. But use your common sense and save wine and spirits for special occasions. Bear in mind that you will lose weight more effectively if you don't drink alcohol. You can save on calories by mixing drinks with zero calorie mixers and avoiding very sweet drinks.

· Apple cider
· Beer
· Dessert wine, such as port, sherry, Asti Spumante, Madeira, and Sauternes
· Drinks with syrup, sodas, and juice
· Fizzy alcoholic drinks
· Sweet shots
· Spirits
· Vermouth and liqueurs
· White wine, red wine, and champagne

The Danish Health Authority's recommendations on alcohol:

Women: up to 7 units per week

Men: up to 14 units per week

Flavorings

When food is flavorsome, you often feel full with smaller quantities. With Scandi Sense, you can eat as many herbs and spices as desired. This category also includes products that can be used freely, including raising and thickening agents.

HERBS AND SPICES

Herbs and spices are dried and powdered plants, or parts of a plant, that are added to food to bring out a particular taste or to add flavor. Many herbs and spices help to destroy bacteria, and some of them aid digestion. However, people who have trouble sleeping or suffer from bouts of sweating should minimize consumption of spicy food as this can aggravate restlessness and sweating. The food should taste good and be salted only as needed.

Quantity

Herbs and spices can be used freely.

- Basil
- Bay leaves
- Capers
- Cardamom
- Cayenne
- Chile
- Chives
- Cinnamon
- Cloves
- Coriander and Cilantro
- Cress
- Cumin
- Curry powder
- Dill
- Garam masala
- Garlic (including garlic powder and garlic salt)
- Ginger
- Herbes de Provence
- Honey
- Horseradish
- Juniper berries
- Lemon balm
- Licorice powder
- Marjoram
- Mint
- Mustard powder
- Nutmeg
- Oregano
- Paprika
- Parsley
- Pepper—all kinds
- Piri piri spice
- Rosemary
- Saffron
- Sage
- Salt—all kinds
- Spice mixes, such as barbecue
- Star anise
- Sugar
- Zero-calorie sweeteners
- Tandoori spices
- Tarragon
- Thyme

· Turmeric

· Vanilla extract

· Vanilla beans

· Wasabi

· Watercress

RAISING AND THICKENING AGENTS
Quantity

All raising and thickening agents can be used freely (but use your common sense). Psyllium husk and potato fiber, which are replacements for flour, can be used freely.

· Baking powder

· Cornstarch (in small quantities)

· Gelatin

· Potato fiber (has a neutral taste and is very absorbent)

· Psyllium husk

· Yeast

OTHER MISCELLANEOUS FLAVORINGS
Quantity

To be used in small quantities as needed.

· Brown sauce

· Chili sauce

· Curry paste

· Essences and extracts

· Fish sauce

· Food coloring

· Hot sauce

· Lemon juice

· Mustard

· Sambal oelek

· Soy sauce

· Stock—all kinds

· Teriyaki sauce

· Tomato ketchup (in small quantities)

· Tomato paste

· Vinegar—all kinds (including balsamic)

· Worcestershire sauce

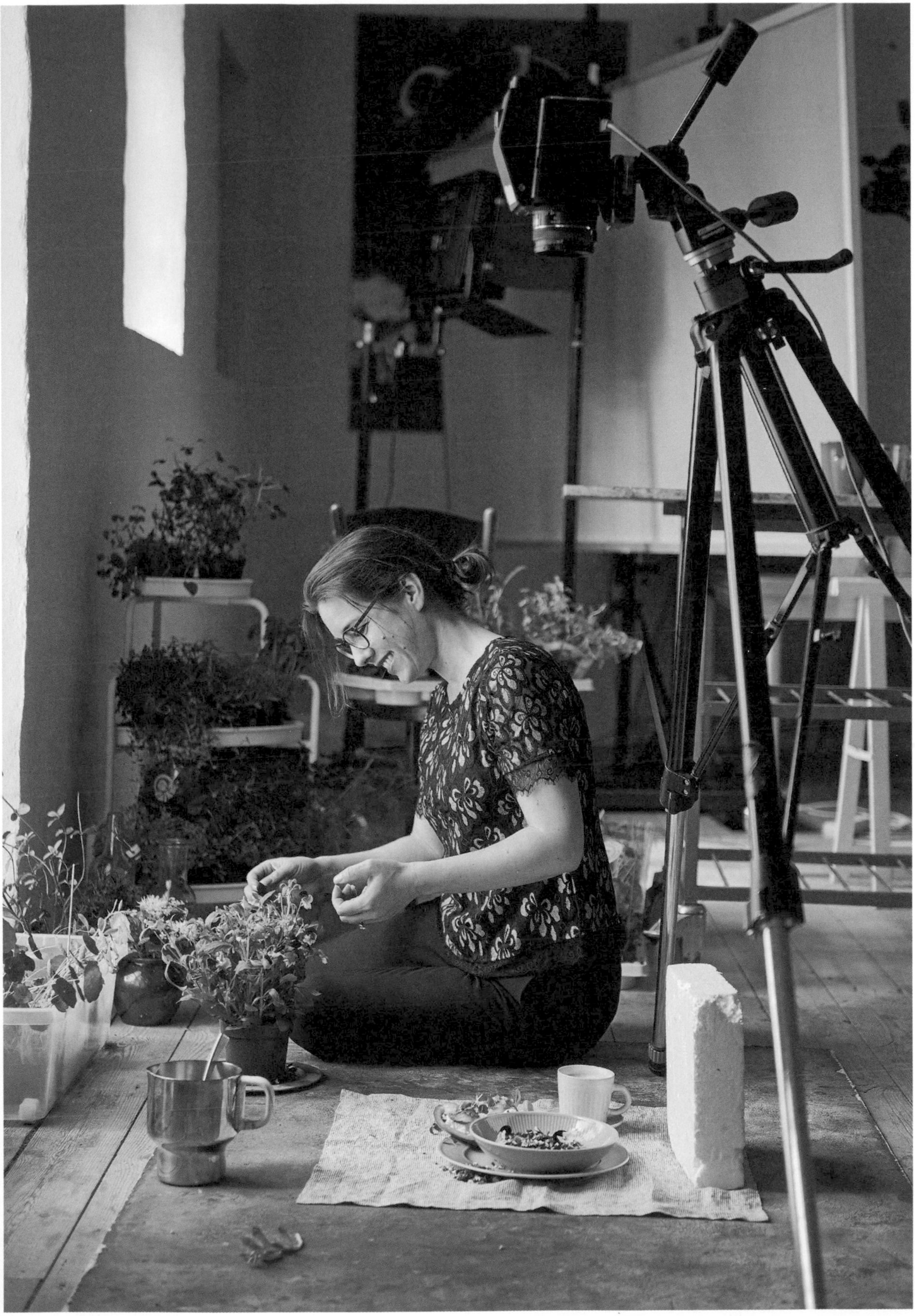

Scandi Sense Measurement Chart

An important part of the journey toward your ideal weight is keeping an eye on your measurements and your weight. It is incredibly motivating to see how many inches and pounds disappear. Tracking the measurements will later help you to maintain your ideal weight.

L = Left   R = Right

TIP
Photocopy this measurement chart and keep it in the bathroom so that it is always to hand.

- Choose a regular weigh-in day, once a week, so that weighing yourself becomes part of your routine. Be sure to only weigh yourself on this day and try to do it at around the same time.
- Measure yourself with a tape measure every fortnight, or as necessary.
- Always measure and weigh yourself naked.
- Make a note of the date, weight, and measurements.

Index

Suzy Wengel is CEO of the Danish biotech company, RiboTask. She is a dietitian, life coach, and entrepreneur married to internationally renowned scientist, Professor Jesper Wengel (who developed artificial DNA).

Suzy is 39 years old and a mother of two boys and step-mother to three children. She lost 88 pounds in 2011 using her own method—and kept it off.

Use of Scandi Sense—including Scandi Sense Diet, Scandi Sense Principles, and the Sense Meal-Box Model—is your own responsibility. Scandi Sense should not replace the advice of a doctor, dietitian, or other healthcare professional. If you are unsure about whether Scandi Sense is suitable for you, we recommend that you consult a doctor. The author and rights holders of this book do not take responsibility for any possible claims that may be made upon or after use of Scandi Sense. Any application of the ideas and information contained in this book is at the reader's sole discretion and risk.

An Hachette UK Company
www.hachette.co.uk

First published in Great Britain
in 2018 by Mitchell Beazley,
a division of Octopus Publishing Group Ltd
Carmelite House
50 Victoria Embankment
London EC4Y 0DZ
www.octopusbooks.co.uk
www.octopusbooksusa.com

Distributed in the US by
Hachette Book Group
1290 Avenue of the Americas
4th and 5th Floors
New York, NY 10104

Distributed in Canada by
Canadian Manda Group
664 Annette St.
Toronto, Ontario, Canada M6S 2C8

First published by as *Sense* by
J/P Politikens Hus A/S, Denmark in 2017

ISBN 978 1 78472 522 8

Printed and bound in China

10 9 8 7 6 5 4 3 2 1

Design and Illustrations: Maria Bramsen/MOM
Food Photography: Skovdal Nordic/
Inge Skovdal
Portrait Photography: Les Kaner

For Mitchell Beazley:
Publisher: Alison Starling
Editorial Assistant: Emily Brickell
Art Director: Yasia Williams
Designer: Abi Read
Senior Production Controller: Allison Gonsalves
Translation: First Edition Translations Ltd